KT-146-483

WON
LIBRARY

RSITY OF
HESTER

KA 0036364 2

DRYDEN

A SELECTION

DRYDEN

A SELECTION

EDITED BY

JOHN CONAGHAN

METHUEN & CO LTD

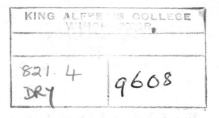

KING ALFRED'S COLLEGE
WINCHESTER.

821.4
DRY   9608

First published in 1978 *by Methuen & Co Ltd*
11 *New Fetter Lane London* EC4P 4EE
© 1978 *John Conaghan*
Phototypeset in V.I.P. Garamond by
Western Printing Services Ltd, Bristol
Printed in Great Britain by
Richard Clay (The Chaucer Press), Ltd
Bungay, Suffolk

ISBN *(hardback)* 0 416 80160 9
ISBN *(paperback)* 0 416 80170 6

This title is available in both hardbound and
paperback editions. The paperback edition is
sold subject to the condition that it shall not, by
way of trade or otherwise, be lent, resold,
hired out or otherwise circulated without the
publisher's prior consent in any form of
binding or cover other than that in which it is
published and without a similar condition
including this condition being imposed on the
subsequent purchaser.

For John and Daniel

CONTENTS

viii   Contents

Contents

PLAYS

PROSE

ACKNOWLEDGEMENTS

In the notes to this selection my path has been eased by the thoroughness of Dryden scholars. W. P. Kerr, Professor James Kinsley, Dr George Watson, and the editors of the California Dryden, oblige all subsequent commentary. My debt to them, and to others listed in the Bibliography, is large indeed.

I am indebted, too, to my colleague Dr Robin Sowerby for his advice on the translated works.

I have relied on the kindness of my family and friends, and would like to thank them, with a special thanks here to my parents.

THE TEXT

All the texts are based on first editions, except for the following: *Mac Flecknoe* (the second edition, in *Miscellany Poems*, 1684); *Absalom and Achitophel* (the second edition, 'augmented and revised', 1681); the *Ode to Anne Killigrew* (*Examen Poeticum, being the Third Part of Miscellany Poems*, 1693); and *To Sir George Etherege* (the manuscript in Etherege's letterbook, British Museum Add. 11, 513). The text for the *Epilogue Spoken to the King at Oxford, 1681* is the copy in the British Museum, printed in London for Richard Royston. They have been modernized, cautiously in respect of the punctuation, and with deference to some of Dryden's spellings, particularly of proper names. The guidance of previous modern-spelling editions, by Ker, Dr Watson, and G. R. Noyes has been helpful on many points. Translations in the notes of Greek and Latin quotations are from the Loeb Classical Library.

INTRODUCTION

The portrait of Dryden by Sir Godfrey Kneller shows its subject with all the composure of an established man of letters; but shows too, in the author's expression, something of his complete seriousness, almost sombreness. We are reminded of his many ambiguities. Whether his personality, his beliefs, or his art is considered, some contrast, inconsistency, or point of reservation is usually found. He was for much of his life a celebrity, 'the poet Dryden'. To be in the same boat with him on the river one day was something for a visitor to the capital to record.[1] But Congreve writes that he was 'something slow, and as it were diffident in his advances to others. He had something in his nature that abhorred intrusion into any society whatsoever . . . he was, of all the men that I ever knew, one of the most modest, and the most easily to be discountenanced in his approaches, either to his superiors or his equals.'[2] He is the author of a poem in praise of Cromwell, and another in praise of the returning Charles II; of one on behalf of Anglicanism, and another upholding the authority of the Catholic church. His achievement is immense, but various, and not consummate in any single work, unless the largest claims are made for one of his great satires.

It is tempting, from the diversity of Dryden's productions, to give his work the character of miscellaneousness. He was always engaged with the world, and he responded readily to its demands and occasions. The times abounded in controversies, literary, religious, and political, in which he was often forward. He had, besides, to earn his living by his writing. His patrimony was modest, and his salary during his twenty years as Laureate irregularly paid. He wrote twenty-nine plays, including those in which he collaborated with others, for a public which of all ages of the theatre was probably the hardest to please. Later in his career he sought an income from translation. But in all this there is a unity. It comes partly from the quality of his work, which is generally distinguishable in his collaborations, and quickly sets aside those which do not bear enough of his stamp; but most from the extraordinary and individual energy of his mind. 'His works abound with knowledge,' says Johnson, 'and sparkle with illustrations.

[1] *The Journal of James Yonge*, ed. F. N. L. Poynter (Longmans, 1963), p. 195.
[2] Dedication to Dryden's *Dramatic Works* (1717).

There is scarcely any science or faculty that does not supply him with occasional images and lucky similitudes; every page discovers a mind very widely acquainted both with art and nature, and in full possession of great stores of intellectual wealth.'[3] This energy informs his prose, in which his use of images is intellectually persuasive, as where he says of rhyme that 'it often makes us swerve from an author's meaning; as, if a mark be set up for an archer at a great distance, let him aim as exactly as he can, the least wind will take his arrow, and divert it from the white'.[4] In his poetry, it turns the occasional into an inspiration, an opportunity for his genius. This can be seen, to take a small example, in the Epilogue spoken to the King at Oxford in 1681,[5] at the time of the crucial meeting of Parliament there. The members are invited to a comparison of their situation with that of the actors:

> Oxford is now the public theatre,
> And you both audience are and actors here:
> The gazing world on the new scene attend,
> Admire the turns, and wish a prosp'rous end.

But the image is governed by another, from contemporary science:

> As from a darkened room some optic glass
> Transmits the distant species as they pass,
> The world's large landscape is from far descried,
> And men contracted on the paper glide . . .

The audience is reduced, neatly disadvantaged not only by the gazing world outside, but as well by the returned appraisal of the real actors, engaged in 'mirth' —

> The King's prerogative, the people's right.

Restoration audiences were not often so effectively enjoined. It typifies Dryden's assertiveness and imaginative resources.

His many quarrels with his contemporaries left him not unscathed by critical and personal attacks. He said, with some truth, 'more libels have been written against me than almost any man now living'.[6] Detraction pursued him to the end. Farquhar, describing his crowded funeral, says: 'And so much for Mr Dryden; whose burial was the same as his life, variety and not of a piece: the quality and mob, farce and heroics; the sublime and ridicule mixed in a piece: great Cleopatra in a hackney coach.'[7] Experience

---

[3] *Life of Dryden*. G. B. Hill, ed., *Lives of the English Poets* (1905), I, 417.
[4] Dedication of the *Aeneis*. Kinsley, ed., *Poems*, III, 1050.
[5] P. 224.   [6] *A Discourse Concerning Satire*, p. 583.
[7] A letter, quoted by J. and H. Kinsley, eds., *Dryden: The Critical Heritage* (1971), p. 242.

and acumen gave him a strong sense of the discordances of his time. It was his constant task, not made easier by the character of Restoration patronage, to try to defend the dignity of the poet's calling, and extricate it from acrimony and incident. Two poems, especially, express his concern with preserving literary standards. In *Mac Flecknoe*, perhaps his greatest poem, he satirizes the confusion of values to which the world of letters was susceptible. Shadwell, by annexing moralizing attitudes to comedy was, in Dryden's view, importing such a confusion. He is identified with dullness, precisely the quality which should be absent from creative writing, as Dryden stresses in his Prologue to *Troilus and Cressida*, written at about the same time:

> Dullness might thrive in any trade but this:
> 'Twould recommend to some fat benefice.
> Dullness, that in a playhouse meets disgrace,
> Might meet with reverence in its proper place . . .
> Dullness is decent in the Church and State.[8]

Flecknoe in the poem is 'king by office' and 'priest by trade':[9] a complete confusion of functions. Possibly (to emphasize the allusiveness of the poem) the character of a monarch choosing an ineffectual son as his successor, with universal acclaim, was suggested by the example of Oliver Cromwell and Richard.[10] The whole, anyway, is a portrayal of muddled aspirations, dissipation of effort, and alienation from the vital realm of letters, the realm of Jonson, Etherege, and Wycherley:

> Success let others teach, learn thou from me
> Pangs without birth, and fruitless industry.[11]

Much later, in the Epistle to Congreve, Dryden writes in similar terms, of defending the kingdom of poetry and preserving the true line — here, from the usurpations of Shadwell and Rymer —

> O that your brows my laurel had sustained;
> Well had I been deposed, if you had reigned! . . .
> But now, not I, but poetry is curst;
> For Tom the Second reigns like Tom the First.[12]

---

[8] Ll. 23–6, 32. Kinsley, I, 172, 173.

[9] L. 119.

[10] Cf. Marvell's poem *The First Anniversary of the Government under Oliver Cromwell*, ll. 7–12, beginning: 'Cromwell alone with greater vigour runs . . .' There is much circumstance and detail to support the parallel.

[11] Ll. 147–8.

[12] Ll. 41–2, 47–8.

To be fair, the preference of Shadwell to this symbolical role was prompted by his abilities. From his beginning in comedy in 1668 he had felt confident enough to oppose the prevailing libertine intrigues, and offer to provide Jonsonian humours instead. He had, too, a talent for satirical writing. *Epsom-Wells*, performed in December 1672, is probably written against Dryden's *Marriage à la Mode*. It takes the anti-matrimonial mode, which Dryden exploits in his play, to inimical lengths, showing the participation of fools in the frolic, and ending with a separation instead of the conventional arrangement of marriage. His approach is interestingly and effectively subversive, and disturbs the serious critical view which Dryden took of libertine comedy, expressed in the Preface to *An Evening's Love* (1671). There, he is aware that libertinism should not be in earnest, but should have the appearance of truancy: 'the faults and vices are but the sallies of youth, and the frailties of human nature, and not premeditated crimes . . . we make not vicious persons happy, but only as Heaven makes sinners so: that is, by reclaiming them first from vice. For so 'tis to be supposed they are, when they resolve to marry . . .'[13] This defence, and *Mac Flecknoe*, should be set against his contrite apologies for his comedies later.[14] Libertine comedy, as best exemplified by *Marriage à la Mode*, Wycherley's *The Country Wife*, and Etherege's *The Man of Mode*, and as revived by Congreve, was discouraged by moral attacks, but not really discredited by them. It suffered more consequentially from exponents like Shadwell who did not share Dryden's critical perception of its form. Dryden's response was to write a comedy of even sharper satirical tendency, and greater sexual fulsomeness, *The Kind Keeper; or, Mr Limberham*, performed in March 1678. As one of the characters puts it: 'Debauchery is on its last legs in England: witty men began the fashion, and now the fops are got into it, 'tis time to leave it.'[15]

1678 is something of a landmark in the literary period. It is the year of the composition of *Mac Flecknoe*, the performance of *Limberham*, and the publication of *All for Love*. It is also the year of Marvell's death, and the eruption of the Popish Plot, of which last the effects were felt immediately by the theatres. By then, the other dramatic form which had been developed after the Restoration, the rhymed heroic play, had virtually expired. A heightened and stylized form of drama, it was, like libertine comedy, vulnerable to satire, and fell victim to Buckingham's *Rehearsal* of 1671. Dryden relinquished it in 1676 with *Aureng-Zebe*, his last heroic play, one which has enjoyed critical partiality, but which as much as any

---

[13] P. 542.
[14] Cf. the *Ode to Anne Killigrew*, St. IV; and *Preface to the Fables*, p. 625.
[15] *Works*, ed. Scott, rev. Saintsbury (1882–3), IV, 33.

gives credence to the view that the audience could not always be obliged to react seriously.[16] It is inclined to preciousness, and arguably has less merit than *The Indian Emperor*, the first rhyming play Dryden wrote by himself, performed in 1665. In two powerful plays which appeared before *The Rehearsal*, *Tyrannic Love* and *The Conquest of Granada*, he still has zest for the form, and confidence in its potentialities beyond the 'happy guess'[17] of *Aureng-Zebe*.

In comedy he followed the taste of his audiences more closely than Etherege or Wycherley, who were not professional dramatists or so productive, had to do; and his popular successes, such as *Sir Martin Mar-All* (1667), are not always among his best plays. However, a selection of his plays which included *The Conquest of Granada*, *Marriage à la Mode*, *All for Love*, *Limberham*, *The Spanish Friar* (1680), *Don Sebastian* (1689), and *Amphitryon* (1690) would yield very little to the best achievements, serious and comic, of his contemporaries.

All for Love is generally regarded as his greatest play, despite a certain amount of critical reservation. Johnson was troubled by the morality of it, that 'by admitting the romantic omnipotence of love, he has recommended, as laudable and worthy of imitation that conduct which, through all ages, the good have censured as vicious, and the bad despised as foolish'.[18] Modern critics sometimes find lack of cohesion between the emotional content of the play and its intellectual design. The love between Antony and Cleopatra does not seem to sustain the grander themes. But perhaps that is the point: the grandeur is seen to be unreal. At the beginning, 'portents and prodigies' are dismissed by Alexas as 'a foolish dream', and as the play progresses Antony's claims to participation in the larger workings of Fate are shown to be delusory. Power and the disposition of conquest are with Octavius, who 'dares not trust his fate for one great action' (II. 132). Fate gradually diminishes in portentousness, almost domesticated by the amorous contexts in which it is invoked. Cleopatra defends herself to Antony after raising his jealousy:

> fate took th' occasion,
> And thus one minute's feigning has destroyed
> My whole life's truth. (IV. 522–4)

But she has already realized, much earlier than Antony, that in the practical world 'we make those fates ourselves' (II. 242). Antony, almost to the end, clings to his belief that he

---

[16] However, the 'comic' elements in Dryden's heroic plays are commended by Bruce King, *Dryden's Major Plays* (1966).
[17] Epilogue, l. 12. Kinsley, I, 157.
[18] *Life of Dryden*, p. 361.

> cannot fall beneath the fate
> Of such a boy as Caesar. (v. 163–4)

But then an aspiring attempt to grasp reality leads to his awakening from his 'golden dream of love and friendship' (v. 205):

> Who knows but we may pierce through all their troops
> And reach my veterans yet. 'Tis worth the 'tempting,
> T' o'erleap this gulf of fate
> And leave our wondering destinies behind. (v. 185–8)

By the end, in Serapion's speech, Fate is nearly 'human chance'. The dead lovers are described ironically:

> See, see how the lovers sit in state together,
> As they were giving laws to half mankind.

All for Love recognizes, in a modern way, the force of evidence over intuition, of circumstance over imagined destiny. It can be seen as part of the criticism of the autonomy of the individual's view of life which gathered impetus in the seventeenth century; that is, near to the heart of important literary and intellectual developments of the time.

If a theme were to be sought in Dryden's writing, it could possibly be identified as the virulence of disorder and the persistence of ties of loyalty. His imagination seizes powerfully on examples of tumult, treachery, and lawlessness. The Great Fire in *Annus Mirabilis* is vigorously personified:

> Now, like some rich or mighty murderer,
>   Too great for prison, which he breaks with gold,
> Who fresher for new mischiefs does appear,
>   And dares the world to tax him with the old;
> So scapes th' insulting fire his narrow jail . . .[19]

Again, his vehemence against the sects in *The Medal*:

> The swelling poison of the sev'ral sects
> Which, wanting vent, the nation's health infects,
> Shall burst its bag; and, fighting out their way,
> The various venoms on each other prey.[20]

In contrast with this, he is drawn to examples of enduring friendships, such as Antony and Ventidius, and Nisus and Euryalus. In his adaptation of Shakespeare's *Troilus and Cressida* he contrives a scene between Hector and Troilus in which their friendship is tried and happily proven. In *Absalom*

[19] Ll. 873–7.
[20] Ll. 294–7. Kinsley, 1, 261.

and Achitophel, the transformation of Charles II from the scapegrace of the opening lines to the 'godlike' monarch of the conclusion is made possible by the example of loyalty provided by the Duke of Ormonde (Barzillai):

> Long since, the rising rebels he withstood
> In regions waste, beyond the Jordan's flood:
> Unfortunately brave to buoy the state,
> But sinking underneath his master's fate.
> In exile with his godlike prince he mourned,
> For him he suffered, and with him returned.[21]

Dryden discovers Charles as a symbol of order, a magnet for loyalties, in *Astraea Redux*. There the sea, disturbed by winds and storms, is an image for the troubles of the nation:

> The rabble now such freedom did enjoy,
> As winds at sea that use it to destroy.[22]

Charles brings control to the turbulence, diffuses calm. The energy of the crowds which 'made a wilder torrent on the shore' is directed towards him, and becomes a source of power:

> Our nation, with united int'rest blest,
> Not now content to poise, shall sway the rest.
> Abroad your empire shall no limits know,
> But, like the sea, in boundless circles flow.[23]

The same calming influence is exercised in *Annus Mirabilis* and *Absalom and Achitophel*. The excruciating tension of *The Hind and the Panther* comes, one feels, from the absence of Charles as a poetic symbol. James, the British Lion, is not an adequate replacement.

His poems to his friends were written in what can be described as his middle style, relaxed and without flourishes. Together they make a distinguished group, reflecting the warmth of his nature and the breadth of his intellectual interests. It is interesting that he employs a similar style for another purpose, in *Religio Laici*, in which he turns to religious argument and the claims of the Anglican church. In this poem, his attentiveness to the proprieties of writing places him under some difficulty. He prefers a plain style, because 'the florid, elevated and figurative way is for the passions; for love and hatred, fear and anger, are begotten in the soul by showing their objects out of their true proportion . . . a man is to be cheated into passion, but reasoned into truth.'[24] But he is also concerned

---

[21] Ll. 819–24.   [22] Ll. 43–4.
[23] Ll. 296–9.   [24] Preface. Kinsley, I, 311.

not to appear too ratiocinative, since the poem declares the limited useful-
ness of reason, that 'Faith is not built on disquisitions vain'.[25] He is
therefore glad, as a help to his 'unpolished, rugged verse', to address his
friend Henry Dickinson, and a passage in praise of Dickinson's translation
of Father Simon's *Critical History* is at the centre of the poem.

Johnson called Dryden 'the father of English criticism', a phrase which,
it has been remarked, suggests somewhat misleadingly a dogged pioneer,
rough-fashioning what later critics were to refine. It is mistaken, too, to
imagine him closely embattled by neo-Aristotelian insistence on the
rules. His method is subtle and strategic, and as a strategist he possesses, or
gives himself, several advantages. He was the foremost practitioner of his
time in prose and verse. His criticism, often prefatory, is directed to
immediate purposes, has in mind the practicalities of writing in his own
time, and not infrequently recommends his own practice. Also, he can look
back securely on the splendid achievements of Elizabethan and Jacobean
drama. Most of all, he has a thorough regard for unprescribed excellences in
individual works, for beauties which 'countervail' faults. He moves easily
from strict examination of plot and structure to those things which appeal
to him, utilizing his marvellous capacity for transitions in prose. The
discussion of *The Silent Woman* in *An Essay of Dramatic Poesy*, ostensibly
dealing with the correctness of the play, dwells on Jonson's skill in
humours. By the end, the reader is persuaded that to consider the 'many and
great beauties' of English plays, and 'wink at some slight and little
imperfections',[26] must be much the superior method. His defence of
Fletcher's *A King and No King* against Rymer in *The Grounds of Criticism in
Tragedy* shows his facility in moving to the positive side of the question:
'The taking of this play, amongst many others, I cannot wholly ascribe to
the excellency of the action; for I find it moving when it is read: 'tis true, the
faults of the plot are so evidently proved that they can no longer be denied.
The beauties of it must therefore lie . . . in the lively touches of the passions
. . .'[27] The essays are strewn with appraisals, brief and extended, of the
works of his fellow authors; an allusive but practical method unembarrassed
by theoretical rigour.

It is in the *Grounds of Criticism in Tragedy* that he comes closest to a
legislative approach. There it is apparent that Thomas Rymer's deter-
mined criticism has impressed him; but also that he prefers quite a
different emphasis, on character and passions rather than on plot. This is
less an evasion or counter than a recognition of the nature of Restoration
drama, which is highly conventional, narrow in its social range, and admits

[25] L. 431.
[26] P. 523.
[27] P. 669.

fewer motives than the drama of the preceding age. Whatever its variety in plotting, it has little in the passions it portrays. Dryden's attack on 'confused passions' and 'undistinguishable characters', on plays in which 'the characters are only distinct in name; but in reality all the men and women in the play are the same person',[28] is therefore the most salutary that could be imagined, and his quotation from Shakespeare, showing the difference between rant and 'natural passions', the most apposite to his purpose.

The later essays, especially the *Discourse Concerning Satire* and the *Preface to the Fables*, disclose the full splendour of his prose style. One a few writers, among whom Keats may be mentioned, are able to rival his easiness in the paragraph, in which, however remote the end from the beginning, digression seems to have no name or place. A comparison between Horace and Juvenal becomes a defence of himself; remarks on Chaucer introduce a critique of Cowley. Everything belongs to the main flow of his thoughts. 'Dryden is always "another and the same",' says Johnson, 'he does not exhibit a second time the same elegances in the same form, nor appears to have any art other than that of expressing with clearness what he thinks with vigour.'[29]

His reputation, hard won in confrontation with opponents of his own time and modern critics fluent on the subject of his 'limitations', might have been helped by attention to his obliquities. But seventeenth-century irony is not very thoroughly appreciated. Irony is present, for example, in his elegy on Oldham, as it is in Milton's poem on Shakespeare, as an intellectual qualification, the intelligent man's anticipation, it may be, of being misunderstood. Much given to praise, he knew that it could turn to satire if applied injudiciously. His irony is not the unremitting irony of Swift, but it *was* sufficient to preserve him easily from the abrasions of that genius. Possibly his constant regard for the epic, and his stated wish to have written an epic poem, have obscured the kind of transcendence he achieved. He overcame the forms of mediocrity to which Restoration literature was liable. Especially, he resisted with humanity and particularity the kind of vehemence which deals in sterile abstractions, and redeemed the typological modes of his day from propaganda. A divided view of him persists, because the perspectives which are sometimes used to diminish his achievement only enlarge it to his admirers. He created his own ethos. No age has been so much the age of a poet, it has been said, as the forty years following the Restoration were the age of Dryden.

[28] P. 563.
[29] *Life of Dryden*, p. 418.

CHRONOLOGY

1631   Dryden born on 9 August (N.S. 19 August), in Aldwinckle, Northamptonshire, the first of fourteen children of Erasmus and Mary Dryden.

1640   November: the Long Parliament sits. December: the 'root and branch' petition against episcopal government in the Church presented to Parliament.

1641   May: Strafford executed. November: Parliament's Grand Remonstrance against the King.

1642   The First Civil War begins.

1645   The Royalists defeated by the New Model Army at Naseby in June.

1646   Dryden enters Westminster School as a King's Scholar about this time.

1649   Charles I executed on 30 January. In August, Cromwell begins his campaign in Ireland. Dryden, still at school, publishes *Upon the Death of the Lord Hastings:*

1650   On 18 May Dryden admitted as pensioner to Trinity College, Cambridge.

1651   Charles II escapes after the battle of Worcester, 3 September.

1652   April: the First Anglo-Dutch War begins.

1653   16 December: Cromwell becomes Protector.

1654   Dryden leaves Cambridge in March with B.A. degree. His father dies in June.

1658   Cromwell dies on 3 September. His son Richard succeeds to the Protectorate.

1659   Dryden's *Heroic Stanzas* on Cromwell.

1660   May: the return of Charles II. Dryden's *Astraea Redux*.

1663   Dryden's first play, *The Wild Gallant*, is acted. On 1 December he marries Lady Elizabeth Howard.

1665   The Second Anglo-Dutch War, lasting until 1667. The Great Plague in London. Dryden retires to Charlton in Wiltshire and begins *An Essay of Dramatic Poesy*.

1666   The Great Fire of London, 2 to 6 September. Charles, the first of Dryden's three sons, born on 6 September.

1667   *Annus Mirabilis*. Milton's *Paradise Lost* published.

1668 Dryden succeeds Davenant as Poet Laureate. Cowley's *Works* published. Dryden's *An Evening's Love*, Etherege's *She Would if She Could*, and Shadwell's *The Sullen Lovers* performed.

1669 On 18 August Dryden succeeds James Howell as Historiographer Royal.

1670 The First Part of Dryden's heroic play *The Conquest of Granada* performed in December; followed by the Second Part in January 1671.

1671 Milton's *Paradise Regained* and *Samson Agonistes*.

1672 *Marriage à la Mode* performed. The Third Anglo-Dutch War (to February 1674).

1676 Etherege, *The Man of Mode*; Shadwell, *The Virtuoso*; Wycherley, *The Plain Dealer*.

1677 *All for Love* performed in December.

1678 *Mac Flecknoe* (not printed until 1682). The Popish Plot breaks out, bringing disturbances which last to 1681.

1681 Parliament meets at Oxford in March, and is dissolved by Charles on the 28th. *Absalom and Achitophel* published in November.

1682 Otway's *Venice Preserved*.

1685 Charles dies on 6 February, and is succeeded by his brother, James II. Monmouth's rebellion is defeated at Sedgemoor in July.

1687 James's first Declaration of Indulgence, for a general religious toleration. Dryden publishes *The Hind and the Panther*.

1688 William of Orange lands at Torbay on 5 November; James II flees to France on 23 December.

1689 William and Mary proclaimed sovereigns on 13 February. England enters into a burdensome war with France, concluded by the Treaty of Ryswick in 1697. Dryden is removed from the Laureateship. His tragedy *Don Sebastian* is performed in December.

1690 Locke's *Essay Concerning Human Understanding*.

1693 The translation of the satires of Juvenal and Persius, with the *Discourse Concerning Satire*, published. Dryden begins work on his translation of Virgil.

1694 *Love Triumphant*, Dryden's last play, performed in January.

1697 *The Works of Virgil* published by subscription.

1700 *Fables Ancient and Modern*. Dryden dies on 1 May, and is buried with great ceremony in Westminster Abbey on the 9th.

POEMS

Henry, Lord Hastings, eldest son of the sixth Earl of Huntingdon, died of smallpox in June 1649 at the age of nineteen. This poem was Dryden's contribution to a commemorative volume entitled *Lachrymae Musarum: The Tears of the Muses*, and is his first published poem.

Must noble Hastings immaturely die,
The honour of his ancient family;
Beauty and learning thus together meet,
To bring a winding for a wedding sheet?
Must virtue prove death's harbinger? must she,
With him expiring, feel mortality?
Is death, sin's wages, grace's now shall ten
Make us more learned, only to depart,
If merit be disease, if virtue death;
To be good, not to be, who'd then bequeath   10
Himself to discipline, who'd not esteem
Labour a crime, study self-murder deem?
Our noble youth now have pretence to be
Dunces securely, ignorant healthfully;
Rare linguist, whose worth speaks itself, whose praise,
Though not his own, all tongues besides do raise:
Than whom great Alexander may seem less,
Who conquer'd men, but not their languages.
In his mouth nations spake; as his tongue might be
Interpreter to Greece, France, Italy.   20
His native soil was the four parts o'th' earth;
All Europe was too narrow for his birth.
A young apostle; and (with rev'rence may
I speak't) inspir'd with gift of tongues, as they.
Nature gave him, a child, what men in vain
Oft strive, by art though further'd, to obtain.
His body was an orb, his sublime soul

27–30 Comparing, somewhat remotely, Hastings' body, with Adam before the
Dryden goes on in ample, painful verses rather than metaphysical conceit.

UPON THE DEATH OF THE LORD HASTINGS

Henry, Lord Hastings, eldest son of the sixth Earl of Huntingdon, died of smallpox in June 1649 at the age of nineteen. The poem is Dryden's contribution to a commemorative volume entitled *Lachrymae Musarum: The Tears of the Muses*, and is his first published poem.

> Must noble Hastings immaturely die,
> The honour of his ancient family?
> Beauty and learning thus together meet,
> To bring a *winding* for a *wedding* sheet?
> Must virtue prove death's harbinger? must she,
> With him expiring, feel mortality?
> Is death, sin's wages, grace's now? shall art
> Make us more learned, only to depart?
> If merit be disease; if virtue death;
> To be good, not to be; who'd then bequeath   10
> Himself to discipline? who'd not esteem
> Labour a crime, study self-murther deem?
> Our noble youth now have pretence to be
> Dunces securely, ign'rant healthfully.
> Rare linguist! whose worth speaks itself, whose praise,
> Though not his own, all tongues besides do raise!
> Than whom great Alexander may seem less,
> Who conquered men, but not their languages.
> In his mouth nations speak; his tongue might be
> Interpreter to Greece, France, Italy.   20
> His native soil was the four parts o'th' earth;
> All Europe was too narrow for his birth.
> A young apostle; and (with rev'rence may
> I speak'it) inspired with gift of tongues, as they.
> Nature gave him, a child, what men in vain
> Oft strive, by art though furthered, to obtain.
> His body was an orb, his sublime soul

27–30 Comparing, somewhat remotely, Hastings' body with Archimedes' sphere of glass. Dryden goes on to imply celestial virtues rather than mortal corruption.

Did move on virtue's and on learning's pole:
Whose reg'lar motions better to our view,
30   Than Archimedes' sphere, the heavens did show.
Graces and virtues, languages and arts,
Beauty and learning, filled up all the parts.
Heav'n's gifts, which do, like falling stars, appear
Scattered in others; all, as in their sphere,
Were fixed and conglobate in's soul; and thence
Shone through his body, with sweet influence;
Letting their glories so on each limb fall,
The whole frame rendered was celestial.
Come, learned Ptolemy, and trial make,
40   If thou this hero's altitude canst take:
But that transcends thy skill; thrice happy all,
Could we but prove thus astronomical.
Lived Tycho now, struck with this ray, which shone
More bright i'th' morn, than others' beam at noon,
He'd take his astrolabe, and seek out here
What new star 'twas did gild our hemisphere.
Replenished then with such rare gifts as these,
Where was room left for such a foul disease?
The nation's sin hath drawn that veil, which shrouds
50   Our day-spring in so sad benighting clouds.
Heaven would no longer trust its pledge; but thus
Recalled it; rapt its Ganymede from us.
Was there no milder way but the smallpox,
The very filth'ness of Pandora's box?
So many spots, like *naeves*, our Venus soil?
One jewel set off with so many a foil?
Blisters with pride swelled, which through's flesh did sprout,
Like rose-buds, stuck i'th' lily skin about.
Each little pimple had a tear in it,
60   To wail the fault its rising did commit:
Who, rebel-like, with their own lord at strife,
Thus made an insurrection 'gainst his life.

35 conglobate] Globular.
39 Ptolemy] Claudius Ptolemaeus, Alexandrian mathematician and astronomer of the
second century.   43 Tycho] Tycho Brahe (1546–1601), Danish astronomer.
49 The nation's sin] The beheading of Charles I in 1649.
52 Ganymede] In mythology, a beautiful boy, son of Tros.
55 *naeves*] From Latin *naevus*, spot or blemish. A remarkable description here of this
wretched disease.

Or were these gems sent to adorn his skin,
The cab'net of a richer soul within?
No comet need foretell his change drew on,
Whose corpse might seem a constellation.
O, had he died of old, how great a strife
Had been, who from his death should draw their life?
Who should, by one rich draught, become whate'er
Seneca, Cato, Numa, Caesar, were: 70
Learned, virtuous, pious, great; and have by this
An universal *metempsuchosis*.
Must all these aged sires in one funeral
Expire? all die in one so young, so small?
Who, had he lived his life out, his great fame
Had swoll'n 'bove any Greek or Roman name.
But hasty winter, with one blast, hath brought
The hopes of autumn, summer, spring, to nought.
Thus fades the oak i'th' sprig, i'th' blade the corn;
Thus, without young, this Phoenix dies, new-born.   80
Must then old three-legged greybeards with their gout,
Catarrhs, rheums, aches, live three ages out?
Time's offal, only fit for th' hospital,
Or t'hang an antiquary's room withal!
Must drunkards, lechers, spent with sinning, live
With such helps as broths, possets, physic give?
None live, but such as should die? shall we meet
With none but ghostly fathers in the street?
Grief makes me rail; sorrow will force its way;
And show'rs of tears tempestuous sighs best lay.   90
The tongue may fail, but overflowing eyes
Will weep out lasting streams of elegies.
    But thou, O virgin-widow, left alone,
Now thy beloved, heaven-ravished spouse is gone,
(Whose skilful sire in vain strove to apply
Med'cines, when thy balm was no remedy,)
With greater than Platonic love, O wed
His soul, though not his body, to thy bed:
Let that make thee a mother; bring thou forth
Th' ideas of his virtue, knowledge, worth;   100
Transcribe th' original in new copies; give

66 constellation] I.e. of gems.
68–72 . . . *metempsuchosis*] Referring to the ancient belief that a man's spirit could be drawn
in from his dying breath.

Hastings o'th' better part: so shall he live
In's nobler half; and the great grandsire be
Of an heroic divine progeny;
An issue, which t'eternity shall last,
Yet but th' irradiations which he cast.
Erect no mausoleums; for his best
Monument is his spouse's marble breast.

HEROIC STANZAS

CONSECRATED TO THE MEMORY OF HIS HIGHNESS
OLIVER
LATE LORD PROTECTOR OF THIS COMMONWEALTH, &C.

WRITTEN AFTER THE CELEBRATING OF HIS FUNERAL

Cromwell died on 3 September 1658. The elaborate funeral celebrations could not be held until 23 November: hence the 'officious haste' (l. 1) of poems to his memory written in the interval. Dryden's poem was published early in 1659, together with panegyrics by William Waller and Thomas Sprat. In later years his enemies made it a reproach to his loyalty. However, there is no trace in the poem of political partisanship beyond a genuine regard for Cromwell's achievements.

1

And now 'tis time; for their officious haste,
    Who would before have borne him to the sky,
Like eager Romans, ere all rites were past,
    Did let too soon the sacred eagle fly.

2

Though our best notes are treason to his fame
    Joined with the loud applause of public voice,
Since Heav'n, what praise we offer to his name,
    Hath rendered too authentic by its choice;

3

Though in his praise no arts can liberal be,
    Since they, whose Muses have the highest flown,   10
Add not to his immortal memory,
    But do an act of friendship to their own;

3–4 Romans . . . fly] When the funeral pyre of a Roman emperor was lit, an eagle was released from the top, supposed to carry his soul to the sky.
8 authentic] Authoritative.
9 liberal] An example of Dryden's fondness for punning.

4

Yet 'tis our duty and our interest too
     Such monuments as we can build to raise,
Lest all the world prevent what we should do
     And claim a title in him by their praise.

5

How shall I then begin, or where conclude,
     To draw a fame so truly circular?
For in a round what order can be shewed,
20   Where all the parts so equal-perfect are?

6

His grandeur he derived from Heav'n alone,
     For he was great ere Fortune made him so;
And wars, like mists that rise against the sun,
     Made him but greater seem, not greater grow.

7

No borrowed bays his temples did adorn,
     But to our crown he did fresh jewels bring;
Nor was his virtue poisoned, soon as born,
     With the too early thoughts of being king.

8

Fortune (that easy mistress of the young,
30   But to her ancient servants coy and hard)
Him at that age her favourites ranked among
     When she her best-loved Pompey did discard.

9

He, private, marked the faults of others' sway,
     And set as sea-marks for himself to shun;
Not like rash monarchs, who their youth betray
     By acts their age too late would wish undone.

10

And yet dominion was not his design;
     We owe that blessing not to him but Heaven,

31–2 Cromwell came to eminence at forty-five, the same age as Pompey when he was at his height. Cromwell's fortunes, however, unlike Pompey's, continued in the ascendant.
34 sea-marks] Objects visible at sea which serve as helps to navigation.

Which to fair acts unsought rewards did join,
    Rewards that less to him than us were given.   40

11

Our former chiefs, like sticklers of the war,
    First sought t'inflame the parties, then to poise;
The quarrel loved, but did the cause abhor,
    And did not strike to hurt, but make a noise.

12

War, our consumption, was their gainful trade;
    We inward bled, whilst they prolonged our pain:
He fought to end our fighting, and assayed
    To staunch the blood by breathing of the vein.

13

Swift and resistless through the land he passed,
    Like that bold Greek who did the East subdue,   50
And made to battles such heroic haste
    As if on wings of victory he flew.

14

He fought, secure of fortune as of fame;
    Till by new maps the Island might be shown,
Of conquests, which he strewed where'er he came,
    Thick as the galaxy with stars is sown.

15

His palms, though under weights they did not stand,
    Still thrived; no winter could his laurels fade:
Heav'n in his portrait showed a workman's hand,
    And drew it perfect, yet without a shade.   60

16

Peace was the prize of all his toils and care,
    Which war had banished and did now restore:
Bologna's walls thus mounted in the air
    To seat themselves more surely than before.

41 sticklers] Moderators or mediators.   50 bold Greek] Alexander the Great.
57–8 palms . . . fade] Palms were supposed to flourish best when weighted down.
63–4 During the siege of Bologna in 1512, according to legend, part of a wall upon which a
chapel was built was blown up and fell back exactly into place.

17

Her safety rescued Ireland to him owes;
　　And treacherous Scotland, to no inter'st true,
Yet blessed that fate which did his arms dispose
　　Her land to civilize as to subdue.

18

Nor was he like those stars which only shine
70　　When to pale mariners they storms portend:
He had his calmer influence, and his mien
　　Did love and majesty together blend.

19

'Tis true, his count'nance did imprint an awe,
　　And naturally all souls to his did bow;
As wands of divination downward draw,
　　And point to beds where sov'reign gold doth grow.

20

When past all offerings to Feretrian Jove,
　　He Mars deposed and arms to gowns made yield,
Successful counsels did him soon approve
80　　As fit for close intrigues, as open field.

21

To suppliant Holland he vouchsafed a peace,
　　Our once bold rival in the British main
Now tamely glad her unjust claim to cease,
　　And buy our friendship with her idol, gain.

22

Fame of th' asserted sea, through Europe blown,
　　Made France and Spain ambitious of his love;
Each knew that side must conquer he would own,
　　And for him fiercely as for empire strove.

23

No sooner was the Frenchman's cause embraced
90　　Than the light Monsieur the grave Don outweighed:

65 Cromwell reconquered Ireland in a campaign from 1649 to 1650.
66–8 Union between Scotland and England was effected in 1654.
77 Feretrian Jove] The god to whom arms taken from opposing commanders were consecrated.　　　　81–4 Cromwell had prevailed over Dutch sea-power by 1654.

His fortune turned the scale where it was cast,
    Though Indian mines were in the other laid.

24

When absent, yet we conquered in his right:
    For, though some meaner artist's skill were shown
In mingling colours, or in placing light,
    Yet still the fair designment was his own.

25

For from all tempers he could service draw;
    The worth of each with its alloy he knew;
And, as the confident of Nature, saw
    How she complexions did divide and brew.   100

26

Or he their single virtues did survey
    By intuition in his own large breast,
Where all the rich ideas of them lay,
    That were the rule and measure to the rest.

27

When such heroic virtue Heav'n sets out,
    The stars, like Commons, sullenly obey,
Because it drains them, when it comes about,
    And therefore is a tax they seldom pay.

28

From this high spring our foreign conquests flow,
    Which yet more glorious triumphs do portend,   110
Since their commencement to his arms they owe,
    If springs as high as fountains may ascend.

29

He made us freemen of the Continent,
    Whom nature did like captives treat before;
To nobler preys the English lion sent,
    And taught him first in Belgian walks to roar.

107 drains them] I.e. of their good influences.

30

That old unquestioned pirate of the land,
    Proud Rome, with dread the fate of Dunkirk heard,
And trembling wished behind more Alps to stand,
    Although an Alexander were her guard.

31

By his command we boldly crossed the Line,
    And bravely fought where southern stars arise;
We traced the far-fetched gold unto the mine,
    And that which bribed our fathers made our prize.

32

Such was our Prince; yet owned a soul above
    The highest acts it could produce to show:
Thus poor mechanic arts in public move,
    Whilst the deep secrets beyond practice go.

33

Nor died he when his ebbing fame went less,
    But when fresh laurels courted him to live;
He seemed but to prevent some new success,
    As if above what triumphs earth could give.

34

His latest victories still thickest came,
    As near the centre motion does increase;
Till he, pressed down by his own weighty name,
    Did, like the Vestal, under spoils decease.

35

But first the Ocean as a tribute sent
    That giant prince of all her watery herd;
And th' Isle, when her protecting Genius went,
    Upon his obsequies loud sighs conferred.

117–18 pirate . . . Rome] I.e. to papal power. Alexander (l. 120) refers to Pope Alexander
VII.   123–4 Referring to Spanish gold, captured near Cadiz in 1656.
134 The old theory of the attraction of the centre.
136 Vestal] The virgin Tarpeia, having betrayed Rome to the Sabines, had their shields
heaped upon her as a 'reward'.
138 giant prince] A great whale was captured in the Thames on 3 June 1658, regarded as a
portent by many.

36

No civil broils have since his death arose,
But faction now by habit does obey;
And wars have that respect for his repose
As winds for halcyons when they breed at sea.

37

His ashes in a peaceful urn shall rest;
His name a great example stands, to show
How strangely high endeavours may be blest,
Where piety and valour jointly go.

144 halcyons] Symbols of peace.

TO MY HONOURED FRIEND SIR ROBERT HOWARD

ON HIS EXCELLENT POEMS

A commendatory poem before Howard's *Poems* of 1660, and as such, in the words of
distinguished editors, not 'tied to the requirements of sober truth' (E. N. Hooker
and H. T. Swedenberg, Jr., Calif., *Works*, 1, 208)

As there is music uninformed by art
In those wild notes, which, with a merry heart,
The birds in unfrequented shades express,
Who, better taught at home, yet please us less:
So in your verse a native sweetness dwells,
Which shames composure, and its art excels.
Singing no more can your soft numbers grace
Than paint adds charms unto a beauteous face.
Yet as when mighty rivers gently creep,
Their even calmness does suppose them deep,
Such is your Muse: no metaphor swelled high
With dangerous boldness lifts her to the sky:
Those mounting fancies, when they fall again,
Show sand and dirt at bottom do remain.
So firm a strength, and yet withal so sweet,
Did never but in Samson's riddle meet.
'Tis strange each line so great a weight should bear,
And yet no sign of toil, no sweat appear.
Either your art hides art, as stoics feign
Then least to feel, when most they suffer pain;
And we, dull souls, admire, but cannot see
What hidden springs within the engine be:
Or 'tis some happiness that still pursues
Each act and motion of your graceful Muse.
Or is it fortune's work, that in your head
The curious net* that is for fancies spread,

* *Rete mirabile*

15–16 For Samson's riddle see Judges 14.
26 The line and Dryden's note refer to a 'marvellous network' supposed to exist in the brain.

Lets through its meshes every meaner thought,
While rich ideas there are only caught?
Sure that's not all; this is a piece too fair
To be the child of chance, and not of care.   30
No atoms casually together hurled
Could e'er produce so beautiful a world.
Nor dare I such a doctrine here admit,
As would destroy the providence of wit.
'Tis your strong genius then which does not feel
Those weights would make a weaker spirit reel.
To carry weight, and run so lightly too,
Is what alone your Pegasus can do.
Great Hercules himself could ne'er do more,
Than not to feel those heav'ns and gods he bore.   40
Your easier odes, which for delight were penned,
Yet our instruction make their second end;
We're both enriched and pleased, like them that woo
At once a beauty and a fortune too.
Of moral knowledge poesy was queen,
And still she might, had wanton wits not been;
Who, like ill guardians, lived themselves at large,
And, not content with that, debauched their charge.
Like some brave captain, your successful pen
Restores the exiled to her crown again;   50
And gives us hope, that having seen the days
When nothing flourished but fanatic bays,
All will at length in this opinion rest:
'A sober prince's government is best.'
This is not all; your art the way has found
To make improvement of the richest ground,
That soil which those immortal laurels bore,
That once the sacred Maro's temples wore.
Elisa's griefs are so expressed by you,
They are too eloquent to have been true.   60
Had she so spoke, Aeneas had obeyed
What Dido, rather than what Jove, had said.
If funeral rites can give a ghost repose,
Your muse so justly has discharged those,
Elisa's shade may now its wand'ring cease,
And claim a title to the fields of peace.

55–66 Howard had translated the fourth book of Virgil's *Aeneid*.

But if Aeneas be obliged, no less
Your kindness great Achilles doth confess;
Who, dressed by Statius in too bold a look,
70   Did ill become those virgin robes he took.
To understand how much we owe to you,
We must your numbers with your author's view:
Then we shall see his work was lamely rough,
Each figure stiff, as if designed on buff;
His colours laid so thick on every place,
As only showed the paint, but hid the face.
But as in perspective we beauties see,
Which in the glass, not in the picture, be;
So here our sight obligingly mistakes
80   That wealth which his your bounty only makes.
Thus vulgar dishes are by cooks disguised,
More for their dressing than their substance prized.
Your curious notes* so search into that age,
When all was fable but the sacred page,
That, since in that dark night we needs must stray,
We are at least misled in pleasant way.
But what we most admire, your verse no less
The prophet than the poet doth confess.
Ere our weak eyes discerned the doubtful streak
90   Of light, you saw great Charles his morning break.
So skilful seamen ken the land from far,
Which shows like mists to the dull passenger.
To Charles your Muse first pays her duteous love,
As still the ancients did begin from Jove.
With Monck you end, whose name preserved shall be,
As Rome recorded Rufus'† memory;
Who thought it greater honour to obey
His country's interest, than the world to sway.

* *Annotations on Statius*
† *Hic situs est Rufus, qui pulso Vindice quondam*
  Imperium asseruit non sibi sed patriae

67–82 Referring to Howard's translation of the *Achilleis* of Statius.
77 perspective] An optical toy, being a device of mirrors arranged to correct a distorted picture.
93–5 Howard's *Poems* begin with a panegyric on Charles and end with one on Monck.
96 Dryden's note: 'Here lies Rufus who once, having routed Vindex, claimed the sovereignty not for himself but for his country.' Verginius Rufus, Roman consul A.D. 63, twice rejected attempts to make him emperor.

But to write worthy things of worthy men,
Is the peculiar talent of your pen: 100
Yet let me take your mantle up, and I
Will venture, in your right, to prophesy.

'This work, by merit first of fame secure,
Is likewise happy in its geniture:
For since 'tis born when Charles ascends the throne,
It shares at once his fortune and its own.'

ASTRÆA REDUX
A POEM ON THE HAPPY RESTORATION AND RETURN OF HIS SACRED MAJESTY
CHARLES THE SECOND

Iam redit et Virgo, redeunt Saturnia regna. Virgil

Astræa Redux ('The Return of Justice') is Dryden's contribution to the flood of poems welcoming the return of Charles II to the throne of England. Charles was proclaimed king on 8 May 1660, landed at Dover on the 25th, and on the 29th entered London, amid great rejoicing. It was a jubilant and hopeful ending to a period of desperate uncertainty. The poem was published in June of the same year.

Now with a general peace the world was blest,
While ours, a world divided from the rest,
A dreadful quiet felt, and worser far
Than arms, a sullen interval of war:
Thus when black clouds draw down the lab'ring skies,
Ere yet abroad the winged thunder flies,
An horrid stillness first invades the ear,
And in that silence we the tempest fear.
Th' ambitious Swede like restless billows tost,
On this hand gaining what on that he lost,
Though in his life he blood and ruin breathed,
To his now guideless kingdom peace bequeathed.
And Heaven, that seemed regardless of our fate,
For France and Spain did miracles create,
Such mortal quarrels to compose in peace

10

Title] Astræa was the daughter of Themis (Justice) and Zeus, and was herself identified as Justice.
9–12 Charles X of Sweden died in February 1660, and recommended in his will that all his wars should be concluded. His son Charles XI was a minor: hence 'guideless'.
13–18 The long war between France and Spain ended in November 1659, with an arrangement of marriage between Louis XIV and the Infanta Maria Theresa.

As nature bred and int'rest did increase.
We sighed to hear the fair Iberian bride
Must grow a lily to the lily's side;
While our cross stars denied us Charles his bed,
Who our first flames and virgin love did wed.   20
For his long absence Church and State did groan; ✝
Madness the pulpit, faction seized the throne:
Experienced age in deep despair was lost
To see the rebel thrive, the loyal crost:
Youth that with joys had unacquainted been
Envied grey hairs that once good days had seen:
We thought our sires, not with their own content,
Had, ere we came to age, our portion spent.
Nor could our nobles hope their bold attempt
Who ruined crowns, would coronets exempt:✗   30
For when by their designing leaders taught
To strike at pow'r which for themselves they sought,
The vulgar, gulled into rebellion, armed;
Their blood to action by the prize was warmed.
The sacred purple then and scarlet gown,✝
Like sanguine dye to elephants, was shown.
Thus when the bold Typhoeus scaled the sky,
And forced great Jove from his own heaven to fly,
(What king, what crown from treason's reach is free,
If Jove and heaven can violated be?)   40
The lesser gods that shared his prosp'rous state
All suffered in the exiled Thund'rer's fate.
The rabble now such freedom did enjoy,
As winds at sea that use it to destroy:
Blind as the Cyclops, and as wild as he,
They owned a lawless savage liberty,
Like that our painted ancestors so prized
Ere empire's arts their breasts had civilized.
How great were then our Charles his woes, who thus
Was forced to suffer for himself and us!   50
He, tossed by fate, and hurried up and down,
Heir to his father's sorrows, with his crown,
Could taste no sweets of youth's desired age,
But found his life too true a pilgrimage.
Unconquered yet in that forlorn estate,

37–42 Typhoeus, or Typhon, was a monstrous giant who frightened the gods from heaven.
45 Cyclops] In mythology, a giant with one eye in his head.

His manly courage overcame his fate.
His wounds he took, like Romans, on his breast,
Which by his virtue were with laurels drest.
As souls reach Heav'n while yet in bodies pent,
60   So did he live above his banishment.
That sun, which we beheld with cozened eyes
Within the water, moved along the skies.
How easy 'tis, when Destiny proves kind,
With full-spread sails to run before the wind!
But those that 'gainst stiff gales laveering go
Must be at once resolved and skilful too.
He would not, like soft Otho, hope prevent,
But stayed and suffered Fortune to repent.
These virtues Galba in a stranger sought,
70   And Piso to adopted empire brought.
How shall I then my doubtful thoughts express
That must his suff'rings both regret and bless?
For when his early valour Heav'n had crost,
And all at Worcester but the honour lost,
Forced into exile from his rightful throne,
He made all countries where he came his own;
And viewing monarchs' secret arts of sway,
A royal factor for their kingdoms lay.
Thus banished David spent abroad his time,
80   When to be God's anointed was his crime,
And, when restored, made his proud neighbours rue
Those choice remarks he from his travels drew.
Nor is he only by afflictions shown
To conquer others' realms, but rule his own:
Recov'ring hardly what he lost before,
His right endears it much, his purchase more.
Inured to suffer ere he came to reign,
No rash procedure will his actions stain.
To bus'ness ripened by digestive thought,

65 laveering] 'to beat to windward; to tack' (OED).
67–70 Marcius Salvius Otho (A.D. 32–69) helped Galba to become emperor of Rome. But subsequently Galba adopted Piso as his successor. Otho revolted, had Galba murdered, was then defeated by Vitellius, and 'prevented' hope of eventual victory by suicide.
74 Worcester] The battle of Worcester, 3 September 1651.
78 factor] Agent or observer.
79 Cf. II Samuel 15–21 and *Absalom and Achitophel*, where Dryden develops the comparison between Charles II and David.
86 purchase] Management.

His future rule is into method brought: 90
As they who first proportion understand
With easy practice reach a master's hand.
Well might the ancient poets then confer
On Night the honoured name of Counsellor;
Since, struck with rays of prosp'rous fortune blind,
We light alone in dark afflictions find.
In such adversities to sceptres trained,
The name of Great his famous grandsire gained;
Who yet a king alone in name and right,
With hunger, cold, and angry Jove did fight;   100
Shocked by a Covenanting League's vast pow'rs,
As holy and as catholic as ours:
Till Fortune's fruitless spite had made it known
Her blows not shook but riveted his throne.   +
    Some lazy ages, lost in sleep and ease,
No action leave to busy chronicles:
Such, whose supine felicity but makes
In story chasms, in epoches mistakes;
O'er whom Time gently shakes his wings of down
Till with his silent sickle they are mown.   110
Such is not Charles his too too active age,
Which, governed by the wild distempered rage
Of some black star infecting all the skies,
Made him at his own cost, like Adam, wise.
Tremble ye nations who, secure before,
Laughed at those arms that 'gainst our selves we bore;
Roused by the lash of his own stubborn tail,
Our Lion now will foreign foes assail.
With alga who the sacred altar strows?
To all the sea-gods Charles an off'ring owes: 120
A bull to thee, Portunus, shall be slain,
A lamb to you, the tempests of the main:
For those loud storms that did against him roar
Have cast his shipwracked vessel on the shore.
Yet, as wise artists mix their colours so
That by degrees they from each other go,
Black steals unheeded from the neighb'ring white
Without offending the well-cozened sight:

98–104 Describing Henry IV of France, maternal grandfather of Charles II, and his troubles
with the Holy League.
121 Portunus] A Roman god of shores and harbours.

So on us stole our blessed change; while we
130   Th' effect did feel but scarce the manner see.
Frosts that constrain the ground, and birth deny
To flow'rs, that in its womb expecting lie,
Do seldom their usurping pow'r withdraw,
But raging floods pursue their hasty thaw:
Our thaw was mild, the cold not chased away,
But lost in kindly heat of lengthened day.
Heav'n would no bargain for its blessings drive,
But what we could not pay for, freely give.
The Prince of Peace would, like himself, confer
140   A gift unhoped without the price of war:
Yet, as He knew His blessing's worth, took care
That we should know it by repeated pray'r;
Which stormed the skies and ravished Charles from thence,
As Heav'n itself is took by violence.
Booth's forward valour only served to show
He durst that duty pay we all did owe:
Th' attempt was fair; but Heav'n's prefixed hour
Not come; so, like the watchful traveller
That by the moon's mistaken light did rise,
150   Lay down again, and closed his weary eyes.
'Twas Monck whom Providence designed to loose
Those real bonds false freedom did impose.
The blessed saints that watched this turning scene
Did from their stars with joyful wonder lean,
To see small clues draw vastest weights along,
Not in their bulk but in their order strong.
Thus pencils can by one slight touch restore
Smiles to that changed face that wept before.
With ease such fond chimeras we pursue
160   As Fancy frames for Fancy to subdue;
But when ourselves to action we betake,
It shuns the mint like gold that chymists make.
How hard was then his task, at once to be
What in the body natural we see.
Man's architect distinctly did ordain
The charge of muscles, nerves, and of the brain,

145 Booth] Sir George Booth was leader of a royalist uprising in the north in August 1659.
He was defeated by Lambert.
151 Monck] General Monck was primarily responsible for the negotiations which led to the
return of Charles.   155 clues] Arrangement of cords, tackle.

Through viewless conduits spirits to dispense,
The springs of motion from the seat of sense.
'Twas not the hasty product of a day,
But the well-ripened fruit of wise delay.   170
He, like a patient angler, ere he struck,
Would let them play a while upon the hook.
Our healthful food the stomach labours thus,
At first embracing what it straight doth crush.
Wise leeches will not vain receipts obtrude,
While growing pains pronounce the humours crude:
Deaf to complaints they wait upon the ill,
Till some safe crisis authorize their skill.
Nor could his acts too close a vizard wear
To scape their eyes whom guilt had taught to fear,   180
And guard with caution that polluted nest
Whence legion twice before was dispossest:
Once sacred House, which when they entered in,
They thought the place could sanctify a sin;
Like those that vainly hoped kind Heav'n would wink,
While to excess on martyrs' tombs they drink.
And as devouter Turks first warn their souls
To part, before they taste forbidden bowls,
So these, when their black crimes they went about,
First timely charmed their useless conscience out.   190
Religion's name against itself was made;
The shadow served the substance to invade:
Like zealous missions, they did care pretend
Of souls in show, but made the gold their end.
Th' incensed pow'rs beheld with scorn from high
An heaven so far distant from the sky,
Which durst, with horses' hoofs that beat the ground,
And martial brass, belie the thunder's sound.
'Twas hence at length just vengeance thought it fit
To speed their ruin by their impious wit.   200
Thus Sforza, cursed with a too fertile brain,
Lost by his wiles the pow'r his wit did gain.
Henceforth their fogue must spend at lesser rate

181 polluted nest] The House of Parliament.
189–200 Puritans called religion to their aid, and held prayer meetings before important
actions.
201–2 Lodovico Sforza (1451–1508) of Milan, famous for his scheming.
203 fogue] 'Fury, passion, ardour, impetuosity' (OED).

Than in its flames to wrap a nation's fate.
Suffered to live, they are like Helots set
A virtuous shame within us to beget.
For by example most we sinned before,
And, glass-like, clearness mixed with frailty bore.
But since, reformed by what we did amiss,
210   We by our suff'rings learn to prize our bliss:
Like early lovers, whose unpractised hearts
Were long the May-game of malicious arts,
When once they find their jealousies were vain,
With double heat renew their fires again.
'Twas this produced the joy that hurried o'er
Such swarms of English to the neighb'ring shore,
To fetch that prize by which Batavia made
So rich amends for our impoverished trade.
Oh, had you seen from Scheveline's barren shore,
220   (Crowded with troops and barren now no more,)
Afflicted Holland to his farewell bring
True sorrow, Holland to regret a king;
While waiting him his royal fleet did ride,
And willing winds to their low'red sails denied,
The wavering streamers, flags, and standards out,
The merry seamen's rude but cheerful shout,
And last the cannons' voice that shook the skies,⎫
And, as it fares in sudden ecstasies,   ⎬
At once bereft us both of ears and eyes.   ⎭
230   The *Naseby*, now no longer England's shame,
But better to be lost in Charles his name,
(Like some unequal bride in nobler sheets)
Receives her lord; the joyful *London* meets
The princely York, himself alone a freight;
The *Swiftsure* groans beneath great Gloucester's weight.
Secure as when the halcyon breeds, with these
He that was born to drown might cross the seas.
Heav'n could not own a Providence, and take
The wealth three nations ventured at a stake.
240   The same indulgence Charles his voyage blessed

205–6 Comparing former republicans with the serf populations of ancient Greece.
215–16 Large numbers of Englishmen hurried to Holland to join Charles just before his
return. He embarked at Scheveningen (l. 219).
230–1 Ships were renamed. *The Naseby* (after the parliamentary victory on 14 June 1645)
became the *Charles*.

Which in his right had miracles confessed.
The winds that never moderation knew,
Afraid to blow too much, too faintly blew;
Or out of breath with joy could not enlarge
Their straitened lungs, or conscious of their charge.
The British Amphitrite, smooth and clear,
In richer azure never did appear;
Proud her returning Prince to entertain
With the submitted fasces of the main.

And welcome now (*great Monarch*) to your own;   250
Behold th' approaching cliffs of Albion:
It is no longer motion cheats your view;
As you meet it, the land approacheth you.
The land returns, and in the white it wears
The marks of penitence and sorrow bears.
But you, whose goodness your descent doth show,
Your heav'nly parentage and earthly too,
By that same mildness which your father's crown
Before did ravish, shall secure your own.
Not tied to rules of policy, you find   260
Revenge less sweet than a forgiving mind.
Thus, when th' Almighty would to Moses give
A sight of all he could behold and live,
A voice before His entry did proclaim
Long-suff'ring, goodness, mercy, in His name.
Your pow'r to justice doth submit your cause,
Your goodness only is above the laws;
Whose rigid letter, while pronounced by you,
Is softer made. So winds that tempests brew,
When through Arabian groves they take their flight,   270
Made wanton with rich odours, lose their spite.
And as those lees that trouble it refine
The agitated soul of generous wine,
So tears of joy, for your returning spilt,
Work out and expiate our former guilt.
Methinks I see those crowds on Dover's strand,
Who in their haste to welcome you to land

249 fasces] Symbols of authority.
261 Charles's intention was to forgive all except those responsible for his father's execution.
Accordingly, the Bill of Indemnity was passed in August 1660.
273 generous] Rich, strong.

Choked up the beach with their still growing store,
And made a wilder torrent on the shore:
280   While, spurred with eager thoughts of past delight,
Those who had seen you, court a second sight;
Preventing still your steps, and making haste
To meet you often wheresoe'er you past.
How shall I speak of that triumphant day,
When you renewed the expiring pomp of May!
(A month that owns an int'rest in your name:
You and the flow'rs are its peculiar claim.)
That star that at your birth shone out so bright
It stained the duller sun's meridian light,
290   Did once again its potent fires renew,
Guiding our eyes to find and worship you.
     And now Time's whiter series is begun,
Which in soft centuries shall smoothly run;
Those clouds that overcast your morn shall fly,
Dispelled to farthest corners of the sky.
Our nation, with united int'rest blest,
Not now content to poise, shall sway the rest.
Abroad your empire shall no limits know,
But, like the sea, in boundless circles flow.
300   Your much-loved fleet shall with a wide command
Besiege the petty monarchs of the land;
And as old Time his offspring swallowed down,
Our ocean in its depths all seas shall drown.
Their wealthy trade from pirates' rapine free,
Our merchants shall no more advent'rers be;
Nor in the farthest East those dangers fear
Which humble Holland must dissemble here.
Spain to your gift alone her Indies owes,
For what the pow'rful takes not he bestows:
310   And France, that did an exile's presence fear,
May justly apprehend you still too near.
At home the hateful names of parties cease,
And factious souls are wearied into peace.
The discontented now are only they
Whose crimes before did your just cause betray:
Of those your edicts some reclaim from sins,
But most your life and blest example wins.

288–91 A star appeared on the day that Charles was born. Cf. *Annus Mirabilis* 69–70.
292 whiter] A Latinism, 'more fortunate'.

Oh happy Prince, whom Heav'n hath taught the way,
By paying vows, to have more vows to pay!
Oh happy age! Oh times like those alone   320
By fate reserved for great Augustus' throne!
When the joint growth of arms and hearts foreshew
The world a monarch, and that monarch *you*.

TO MY HONOURED FRIEND
DR CHARLETON,

ON HIS LEARNED AND USEFUL WORKS, AND MORE PARTICULARLY THIS OF STONEHENGE, BY HIM RESTORED TO THE TRUE FOUNDERS

Prefixed to Charleton's work on Stonehenge, *Chorea Gigantum*, which was published towards the end of 1662. Walter Charleton (1619–1707) was a physician interested in the new science and a learned writer on several subjects.

> The longest tyranny that ever swayed
> Was that wherein our ancestors betrayed
> Their free-born reason to the Stagirite,
> And made his torch their universal light.
> So truth, while only one supplied the state,
> Grew scarce and dear, and yet sophisticate;
> Until 'twas bought, like emp'ric wares or charms,
> Hard words sealed up with Aristotle's arms.
> Columbus was the first that shook his throne.
> And found a temp'rate in a torrid zone:
> The fev'rish air fanned by a cooling breeze,
> The fruitful vales set round with shady trees;
> And guiltless men, who danced away their time,
> Fresh as their groves, and happy as their clime.
> Had we still paid that homage to a name
> Which only God and nature justly claim,
> The western seas had been our utmost bound,
> Where poets still might dream the sun was drowned:
> And all the stars, that shine in southern skies,

10

3 the Stagirite] Aristotle, whose authority was undermined by new scientific and geographical discoveries.
6 sophisticate] Subtle, complicated.
7 emp'ric] Medically unscientific, quack.

Had been admired by none but savage eyes.   20
   Among th' asserters of free reason's claim,
Th' English are not the least in worth or fame.
The world to Bacon does not only owe
Its present knowledge, but its future too.
Gilbert shall live, till loadstones cease to draw,
Or British fleets the boundless ocean awe;
And noble Boyle, not less in nature seen,
Than his great brother, read in states and men.
The circling streams, once thought but pools, of blood
(Whether life's fuel or the body's food),   30
From dark oblivion Harvey's name shall save;
While Ent keeps all the honour that he gave.
Nor are *you*, learned friend, the least renowned;
Whose fame, not circumscribed with English ground,
Flies like the nimble journeys of the light,
And is, like that, unspent too in its flight.
Whatever truths have been, by art or chance,
Redeemed from error, or from ignorance,
Thin in their authors, like rich veins of ore,
Your works unite, and still discover more.   40
Such is the healing virtue of your pen,
To perfect cures on books, as well as men.
Nor is this work the least: you well may give
To men new vigour, who makes stones to live.
Through you, the Danes, their short dominion lost,
A longer conquest than the Saxons boast.
Stonehenge, once thought a temple, you have found
A throne where kings, our earthly gods, were crowned;
Where by their wond'ring subjects they were seen,
Joyed with their stature, and their princely mien.   50
Our Sovereign here above the rest might stand,
And here he chose again to rule the land.
   These ruins sheltered once his sacred head,

25 Gilbert] William Gilbert (1540–1603), physician to Queen Elizabeth and a researcher
into magnetism.
27 Boyle] Robert Boyle (1627–91), natural philosopher and chemist.
28 his great brother] Roger Boyle (1621–79), Earl of Orrery, dramatist and politician.
31 Harvey] William Harvey (1578–1657), discoverer of the circulation of the blood.
32 Ent] Sir George Ent (1604–89), an eminent physician and an associate of Harvey.
45 the Danes] Charleton considered that Stonehenge was the work of the Danes.
53–4 Referring to Charles II's escape after the battle of Worcester in 1651.

Then when from Worcester's fatal field he fled;
Watched by the genius of this royal place,
And mighty visions of the Danish race.
His refuge then was for a temple shown:
But, he restored, 'tis now become a throne.

ANNUS MIRABILIS:

THE YEAR OF WONDERS, 1666

Annus Mirabilis was ready for the press in November 1666, and the first edition is dated 1667. Dryden calls it an 'historical' poem. It describes the extraordinary events of 1666, 'the year of wonders': the second Dutch war, and the Great Fire of London. Dedicated to the City, it celebrates metropolitan activity in commerce and science, and at the same time shows the King in the most favourable light in his concern for the navy and for his people during the Fire. Through the portrayal of Charles as a fatherly monarch a year which many considered ominous is rendered auspicious.

The prefixed 'account' of the poem, to Sir Robert Howard, contains Dryden's well-known definition of wit:

> The composition of all poems is or ought to be of wit; and wit in the poet, or wit-writing (if you will give me leave to use a school-distinction), is no other than the faculty of imagination in the writer, which, like a nimble spaniel, beats over and ranges through the field of memory, till it springs the quarry it hunted after; or, without metaphor, which searches over all the memory for the species or ideas of those things which it designs to represent. Wit written, is that which is well defined, the happy result of thought, or product of that imagination. But to proceed from wit in the general notion of it, to the proper wit of an heroic or historical poem, I judge it chiefly to consist in the delightful imaging of persons, actions, passions, or things. 'Tis not the jerk or sting of an epigram, nor the seeming contradiction of a poor antithesis (the delight of an ill-judging audience in a play of rhyme), nor the jingle of a more poor paronomasia; neither is it so much the morality of a grave sentence, affected by Lucan, but more sparingly used by Virgil; but it is some lively and apt description, dressed in such colours of speech that it sets before your eyes the absent object as perfectly and more delightfully than nature. So then the first happiness of the poet's imagination is properly invention, or finding of the thought; the second is fancy, or the variation, driving, or moulding of that thought, as the judgment represents it proper to the subject; the third is elocution, or the art of clothing and adorning that thought so found and varied, in apt, significant, and sounding words. The quickness of the imagination is seen in the invention, the fertility in the fancy, and the accuracy in the expression.

The account also acknowledges his debt to Virgil, 'my master in this poem', and he evidently wishes to associate Virgil's manner, especially in the *Georgics*, with his own use of technical language (cf. l. 573 nn.).

1

In thriving arts long time had Holland grown,
    Crouching at home, and cruel when abroad;
Scarce leaving us the means to claim our own.
    Our King they courted, and our merchants awed.

2

Trade, which like blood should circularly flow,
    Stopped in their channels, found its freedom lost:
Thither the wealth of all the world did go,
    And seemed but shipwracked on so base a coast.

3

For them alone the heavens had kindly heat,
    [a]In eastern quarries ripening precious dew;
For them the Idumaean balm did sweat,
    And in hot Ceylon spicy forests grew.

4

The sun but seemed the lab'rer of their year;
    [b]Each wexing moon supplied her watery store
To swell those tides, which from the Line did bear
    Their brim-full vessels to the Belgian shore.

5

Thus mighty in her ships stood Carthage long,
    And swept the riches of the world from far;
Yet stooped to Rome, less wealthy, but more strong:
    And this may prove our second Punic war.

[a] *In eastern quarries, etc. Precious stones at first are dew, condensed and hardened by the warmth of the sun, or subterranean fires.*
[b] *Each wexing, etc., according to their opinion, who think that great heap of waters under the line is depressed into tides by the moon, towards the poles.*

---

8 base] A pun, including the meaning 'low-lying'.
11 Idumaean balm] Juice yielded by trees in Idumaea, a region in southern Palestine.
16 Belgian] At this time Belgium was synonymous with the Netherlands.

6

What peace can be, where both to one pretend,
　　But they were diligent, and we more strong?
Or if a peace, it soon must have an end,
　　For they would grow too pow'rful, were it long,

7

Behold two nations then, engaged so far
　　That each sev'n years the fit must shake each land:
Where France will side to weaken us by war,
　　Who only can his vast designs withstand.

8

See how he feeds th' 'Iberian with delays,
　　To render us his timely friendship vain;　　　　　　　30
And while his secret soul on Flanders preys,
　　He rocks the cradle of the babe of Spain.

9

Such deep designs of empire does he lay
　　O'er them whose cause he seems to take in hand;
And, prudently, would make them lords at sea,
　　To whom with ease he can give laws by land.

10

This saw our King; and long within his breast
　　His pensive counsels balanced to and fro;
He grieved the land he freed should be oppressed,
　　And he less for it than usurpers do.　　　　　　　　40

11

His gen'rous mind the fair ideas drew
　　Of fame and honour, which in dangers lay;
Where wealth, like fruit on precipices, grew,
　　Not to be gathered but by birds of prey.

12

The loss and gain each fatally were great;
　　And still his subjects called aloud for war:

(c) *Th' Iberian, the Spaniard.*

---

40 usurpers] Meaning Cromwell, who had defeated the Dutch in the war of 1653–4.

But peaceful kings o'er martial people set,
    Each other's poise and counterbalance are.

13

He, first, surveyed the charge with careful eyes,
    Which none but mighty monarchs could maintain;
50 Yet judged, like vapours that from limbecs rise,
    It would in richer showers descend again.

14

At length resolved t'assert the watery ball,
    He in himself did whole armados bring;
Him aged seamen might their master call,
    And choose for General, were he not their King.

15

It seems as every ship their Sovereign knows,
    His awful summons they so soon obey;
So hear the scaly herd when [d]Proteus blows,
60   And so to pasture follow through the sea.

16

To see this fleet upon the ocean move
    Angels drew wide the curtains of the skies;
And Heav'n, as if there wanted lights above,
    For tapers made two glaring comets rise;

17

Whether they unctuous exhalations are,
    Fired by the sun, or seeming so alone;
Or each some more remote and slippery star,
    Which loses footing when to mortals shown;

[d] *When Proteus blows, or* Caeruleus Proteus immania ponti armenta, et magnas pascit sub gurgite Phocas. *Virg.*

---

49 charge] Cost, expense.
51 limbecs] Instruments used in chemistry for distillation.
53 War was declared on 22 February 1665.
59–60 In Greek mythology Proteus was an 'ancient one of the sea' who herded seals.
64–72 Comets appeared in November and December 1664, creating great interest and speculation.

18

Or one that bright companion of the sun,
    Whose glorious aspect sealed our new-born King;   70
And now, a round of greater years begun,
    New influence from his walks of light did bring.

19

Victorious York did first, with famed success,
    To his known valour make the Dutch give place:
Thus Heav'n our Monarch's fortune did confess,
    Beginning conquest from his royal race.

20

But since it was decreed, auspicious King,
    In Britain's right that thou shouldst wed the main,
Heav'n, as a gage, would cast some precious thing,
    And therefore doomed that Lawson should be slain.   80

21

Lawson amongst the foremost met his fate,
    Whom sea-green Sirens from the rocks lament:
Thus as an offering for the Grecian state,
    He first was killed who first to battle went.

22

°Their chief blown up, in air, not waves, expired,
    To which his pride presumed to give the law:
The Dutch confessed Heav'n present and retired,
    And all was Britain the wide ocean saw.

23

To nearest ports their shattered ships repair,
    Where by our dreadful cannon they lay awed: 90
So reverently men quit the open air
    When thunder speaks the angry gods abroad.

(e) *The admiral of Holland.*

69–70 Charles's birth star. Cf. *Astræa Redux*, 288.

73–6 The Duke of York took command of the fleet on 23 March 1665, and defeated the Dutch in a battle off Harwich on 3 June – the 'memorable day of *An Essay of Dramatic Poesy*.

77–84 Admiral Lawson is seen as the gage or pledge of Charles's marriage to the sea; as, in the Venetian ceremony, it was the custom for the Duke to throw a gold ring into the Adriatic on Ascension Day.

The attempt at Bergen

24

And now approached their fleet from India, fraught
    With all the riches of the rising sun,
And precious sand from ᶠsouthern climates brought,
    (The fatal regions where the war begun.)

25

Like hunted castors conscious of their store,
    Their way-laid wealth to Norway's coasts they bring:
There first the north's cold bosom spices bore,
100   And winter brooded on the eastern spring.

26

By the rich scent we found our perfumed prey,
    Which, flanked with rocks, did close in covert lie;
And round about their murdering cannon lay,
    At once to threaten and invite the eye.

27

Fiercer than cannon, and than rocks more hard,
    The English undertake th' unequal war:
Seven ships alone, by which the port is barred,
    Besiege the Indies and all Denmark dare.

28

These fight like husbands, but like lovers those;
110   These fain would keep, and those more fain enjoy;
And to such height their frantic passion grows,
    That what both love both hazard to destroy.

29

Amidst whole heaps of spices lights a ball,
    And now their odours armed against them fly:
Some preciously by shattered porc'lain fall,
    And some by aromatic splinters die.

(ᶠ) *Southern climates, Guinea.*

93–120 On 2 August 1665 Sir Thomas Tiddeman attacked the Dutch India fleet in Bergen harbour, but was beaten off by the Dutch and the Danes combined.
97 castors] Beavers.

30

And though by tempests of the prize bereft,
    In Heaven's inclemency some ease we find:
Our foes we vanquished by our valour left,
    And only yielded to the seas and wind.   120

31

Nor wholly lost we so deserved a prey,
    For storms, repenting, part of it restored;
Which, as a tribute from the Baltic sea,
    The British ocean sent her mighty lord.

32

Go, mortals, now, and vex yourselves in vain
    For wealth, which so uncertainly must come;
When what was brought so far and with such pain
    Was only kept to lose it nearer home.

33

The son who, twice three months on th' ocean tost,
    Prepared to tell what he had passed before,   130
Now sees in, English ships the Holland coast,
    And parents' arms in vain stretched from the shore.

34

This careful husband had been long away
    Whom his chaste wife and little children mourn,
Who on their fingers learned to tell the day
    On which their father promised to return.

35

[g]Such are the proud designs of human kind,
    And so we suffer shipwrack everywhere!
Alas, what port can such a pilot find
    Who in the night of Fate must blindly steer!   140

36

The undistinguished seeds of good and ill
    Heav'n in His bosom from our knowledge hides,

---

[g] *Such are, etc., from Petronius.* Si, bene calculum ponas ubique fit naufragium.

121–4 On 29 August the Dutch fleet, sailing from Bergen for home, was scattered by a gale, and the English were able to capture a number of ships.

And draws them in contempt of human skill,
        Which oft, for friends, mistaken foes provides.

37

Let Munster's prelate ever be accurst,
        In whom we seek the [h]German faith in vain:
Alas, that he should teach the English first
        That fraud and avarice in the Church could reign!

38

Happy who never trust a stranger's will
150   Whose friendship's in his interest understood!
Since money giv'n but tempts him to be ill,
        When power is too remote to make him good.

War declared by France

39

Till now, alone the mighty nations strove:
        The rest at gaze without the lists did stand;
And threat'ning France, placed like a painted Jove,
        Kept idle thunder in his lifted hand.

40

That eunuch guardian of rich Holland's trade,
        Who envies us what he wants power t' enjoy,
Whose noiseful valour does no foe invade
160   And weak assistance will his friends destroy;

41

Offended that we fought without his leave,
        He takes this time his secret hate to show;
Which Charles does with a mind so calm receive
        As one that neither seeks nor shuns his foe.

42

With France, to aid the Dutch, the Danes unite;
        France as their tyrant, Denmark as their slave;

[h] *The German faith. Tacitus saith of them*, Nullos mortalium fide aut armis ante Germanos
esse.

145–8 Bernhard von Galen, Bishop of Munster, was to support the English by invading
Holland; but the attempt was inadequate, and in April 1666 he made a 'fraudulent' peace.
165 France and Denmark declared war on England in January 1666.

But when with one three nations join to fight,
    They silently confess that one more brave.

43

Lewis had chased the English from his shore,
    But Charles the French as subjects does invite;   170
Would Heav'n for each some Solomon restore,
    Who by their mercy may decide their right!

44

Were subjects so but only by their choice,
    And not from birth did forced dominion take,
Our Prince alone would have the public voice,
    And all his neighbours' realms would deserts make.

45

He without fear a dangerous war pursues,
    Which without rashness he began before:
As honour made him first the danger choose,
    So still he makes it good on virtue's score.   180

46

The doubled charge his subjects' love supplies,
    Who in that bounty to themselves are kind:
So glad Egyptians see their Nilus rise,
    And in his plenty their abundance find.

47

With equal pow'r he does two chiefs create,
    Two such, as each seemed worthiest when alone:
Each able to sustain a nation's fate,
    Since both had found a greater in their own.

48

Both great in courage, conduct, and in fame,
    Yet neither envious of the other's praise;   190
Their duty, faith, and int'rest too the same,
    Like mighty partners, equally they raise.

49

The Prince long time had courted Fortune's love,
    But once possessed did absolutely reign:

Thus with their Amazons the heroes strove,
    And conquered first those beauties they would gain.

50

The Duke beheld, like Scipio, with disdain
    That Carthage which he ruined rise once more,
And shook aloft the fasces of the main
    To fright those slaves with what they felt before.

51

Together to the wat'ry camp they haste,
    Whom matrons passing to their children show;
Infants' first vows for them to Heav'n are cast,
    And ᶦfuture people bless them as they go.

52

With them no riotous pomp nor Asian train
    T' infect a navy with their gaudy fears:
To make slow fights and victories but vain;
    But war severely, like itself, appears.

53

Diffusive of themselves, where'er they pass,
    They make that warmth in others they expect:
Their valour works like bodies on a glass
    And does its image on their men project.

Duke of Albemarle's battle, first day

54

Our fleet divides, and straight the Dutch appear,
    In number and a famed commander bold:
The narrow seas can scarce their navy bear,
    Or crowded vessels can their soldiers hold.

55

The Duke, less numerous, but in courage more,
    On wings of all the winds to combat flies;

[i] *Future people*, Examina infantium futurusque populus. *Plin. Jun. in pan. ad Traj.*

213–20 On 29 May Prince Rupert was detached with 20 ships to intercept the French fleet, mistakenly thought to be entering the Channel. Albemarle, though left with many fewer ships than the Dutch, attacked their fleet on 1 June.

His murdering guns a loud defiance roar
   And bloody crosses on his flag-staffs rise.   220

56

Both furl their sails and strip them for the fight;
   Their folded sheets dismiss the useless air;
ʲTh' Elean plains could boast no nobler sight,
   When struggling champions did their bodies bare.

57

Borne each by others in a distant line,
   The sea-built forts in dreadful order move:
So vast the noise, as if not fleets did join,
   ᵏBut lands unfixed and floating nations strove,

58

Now passed, on either side they nimbly tack;
   Both strive to intercept and guide the wind:
And in its eye more closely they come back   230
   To finish all the deaths they left behind.

59

On high-raised decks the haughty Belgians ride,
   Beneath whose shade our humble frigates go;
Such port the elephant bears, and so defied
   By the rhinoceros, her unequal foe.

60

And as the build, so different is the fight;
   Their mounting shot is on our sails designed:
Deep in their hulls our deadly bullets light
   And through the yielding planks a passage find.   240

61

Our dreaded Admiral from far they threat,
   Whose battered rigging their whole war receives.
All bare, like some old oak which tempests beat,
   He stands, and sees below his scattered leaves.

(ʲ) *Th' Elean, etc. Where the Olympic Games were celebrated.*
(ᵏ) *Lands unfixed, from Virgil*: Credas innare revulsas Cycladas, *etc.*

---

220 bloody crosses] Referring to the cross of St George.

62

Heroes of old when wounded shelter sought;
　　But he, who meets all danger with disdain,
Even in their face his ship to anchor brought
　　And steeple-high stood propped upon the main.

63

At this excess of courage, all amazed,
250　　The foremost of his foes a while withdraw.
With such respect in entered Rome they gazed
　　Who on high chairs the god-like fathers saw.

64

And now, as where Patroclus' body lay,
　　Here Trojan chiefs advanced, and there the Greek,
Ours o'er the Duke their pious wings display,
　　And theirs the noblest spoils of Britain seek.

65

Meantime, his busy mariners he hastes
　　His shattered sails with rigging to restore;
And willing pines ascend his broken masts,
260　　Whose lofty heads rise higher than before.

66

Straight to the Dutch he turns his dreadful prow,
　　More fierce th' important quarrel to decide:
Like swans, in long array his vessels show,
　　Whose crests, advancing, do the waves divide.

67

They charge, recharge, and all along the sea
　　They drive, and squander the huge Belgian fleet.
Berkeley alone, who nearest danger lay,
　　Did a like fate with lost Creusa meet.

68

The night comes on, we eager to pursue
270　　The combat still, and they ashamed to leave:

251–2 When the Gauls invaded Rome in 387 B.C. they were awed by the sight of the chief Roman citizens in their chairs of state.　　255 pious] Dutiful.
268 Creusa] Aeneas' wife, who was cut off from escape after the burning of Troy.

Till the last streaks of dying day withdrew,
　　And doubtful moonlight did our rage deceive.

69

In th' English fleet each ship resounds with joy
　　And loud applause of their great leader's fame:
In fiery dreams the Dutch they still destroy,
　　And, slumb'ring, smile at the imagined flame.

70

Not so the Holland fleet, who, tired and done,
　　Stretched on their decks like weary oxen lie:
Faint sweats all down their mighty members run,
　　(Vast bulks, which little souls but ill supply.)　　　　280

71

In dreams they fearful precipices tread,
　　Or, shipwracked, labour to some distant shore,
Or in dark churches walk among the dead:
　　They wake with horror, and dare sleep no more.

Second day's battle

72

The morn they look on with unwilling eyes,
　　Till from their maintop joyful news they hear
Of ships, which by their mould bring new supplies,
　　And in their colours Belgian lions bear.

73

Our watchful General had discerned from far
　　This mighty succour which made glad the foe.　　　290
He sighed, but, like a father of the war,
　　[1]His face spake hope, while deep his sorrows flow.

74

His wounded men he first sends off to shore,
　　(Never, till now, unwilling to obey:)
They not their wounds but want of strength deplore,
　　And think them happy who with him can stay.

[1] *His face, etc.* Spem vultu simulat premit alto corde dolorem. *Virg.*

---

272 deceive] Thwart.

75

Then to the rest, "Rejoice," said he, "today
    In you the fortune of Great Britain lies:
Among so brave a people you are they
    Whom Heav'n has chose to fight for such a prize.

76

"If number English courages could quell,
    We should at first have shunned, not met our foes,
Whose numerous sails the fearful only tell:
    Courage from hearts and not from numbers grows."

77

He said, nor needed more to say: with haste
    To their known stations cheerfully they go;
And all at once, disdaining to be last,
    Solicit every gale to meet the foe.

78

Nor did th' encouraged Belgians long delay,
    But bold in others, not themselves, they stood:
So thick, our navy scarce could sheer their way,
    But seemed to wander in a moving wood.

79

Our little fleet was now engaged so far
    That like the sword-fish in the whale they fought.
The combat only seemed a civil war,
    Till through their bowels we our passage wrought.

80

Never had valour, no, not ours before,
    Done aught like this upon the land or main;
Where not to be o'ercome was to do more
    Than all the conquests former Kings did gain.

81

The mighty ghosts of our great Harrys rose,
    And armed Edwards looked with anxious eyes,
To see this fleet among unequal foes,
    By which Fate promised them their Charles should rise.

300

310

320

303 tell] Count.

82

Meantime the Belgians tack upon our rear,
    And raking chase-guns through our sterns they send:
Close by, their fire-ships like jackals appear,
    Who on their lions for the prey attend.

83

Silent in smoke of cannons they come on:
    (Such vapours once did fiery Cacus hide:)   330
In these the height of pleased revenge is shown,
    Who burn contented by another's side.

84

Sometimes from fighting squadrons of each fleet,
    (Deceived themselves or to preserve some friend,)
Two grappling Aetnas on the ocean meet,
    And English fires with Belgian flames contend.

85

Now at each tack our little fleet grows less;
    And, like maimed fowl, swim lagging on the main.
Their greater loss their numbers scarce confess
    While they lose cheaper than the English gain.   340

86

Have you not seen when, whistled from the fist,
    Some falcon stoops at what her eye designed,
And, with her eagerness the quarry missed,
    Straight flies at check, and clips it down the wind;

87

The dastard crow, that to the wood made wing
    And sees the groves no shelter can afford,
With her loud caws her craven kind does bring,
    Who, safe in numbers, cuff the noble bird?

---

326 chase-guns] Guns mounted in the bows of the Dutch ships. By the second day the English had few more than 40 ships against about 80 Dutch.

330 Cacus] Son of Vulcan; a fire-breathing monster who tried to hide from Hercules in clouds of smoke. Cf. *Aeneid*, VIII, 225–61.

344 check] A false stoop; pursuit of other than the proper game.

88

Among the Dutch thus Albemarle did fare:
    He could not conquer and disdained to fly:
Past hope of safety, 'twas his latest care,
    Like falling Caesar, decently to die.

89

Yet pity did his manly spirit move,
    To see those perish who so well had fought;
And, generously, with his despair he strove,
    Resolved to live till he their safety wrought.

90

Let other Muses write his prosp'rous fate,
    Of conquered nations tell, and kings restored:
But mine shall sing of his eclipsed estate,
    Which, like the sun's, more wonders does afford.

91

He drew his mighty frigates all before,
    On which the foe his fruitless force employs;
His weak ones deep into the rear he bore,
    Remote from guns as sick men are from noise.

92

His fiery cannon did their passage guide,
    And foll'wing smoke obscured them from the foe.
Thus Israel safe from the Egyptian's pride
    By flaming pillars and by clouds did go.

93

Elsewhere the Belgian force we did defeat,
    But here our courages did theirs subdue:
So Xenophon once led that famed retreat
    Which first the Asian empire overthrew.

94

The foe approached; and one, for his bold sin,
    Was sunk, (as he that touched the Ark was slain;)
The wild waves mastered him and sucked him in,
    And smiling eddies dimpled on the main.

350

360

370

374 he . . . slain] Uzza, in 1 Chronicles 13: 9–10.

95

This seen, the rest at awful distance stood;
　　As if they had been there as servants set,
To stay, or to go on, as he thought good,
　　And not pursue, but wait on his retreat.　　　　　380

96

So Libyan huntsmen on some sandy plain,
　　From shady coverts roused, the lion chase:
The kingly beast roars out with loud disdain,
　　^mAnd slowly moves, unknowing to give place.

97

But if some one approach to dare his force,
　　He swings his tail and swiftly turns him round,
With one paw seizes on his trembling horse,
　　And with the other tears him to the ground.

98

Amidst these toils succeeds the balmy night;
　　Now hissing waters the quenched guns restore;　　390
ⁿAnd weary waves, withdrawing from the fight,
　　Lie lulled and panting on the silent shore.

99

The moon shone clear on the becalmed flood,
　　Where, while her beams like glittering silver play,
Upon the deck our careful General stood,
　　And deeply mused on the ^osucceeding day.

100

"That happy sun," said he, "will rise again,
　　Who twice victorious did our navy see:
And I alone must view him rise in vain,
　　Without one ray of all his star for me.　　　　　400

(m) *The simile is Virgil's*, Vestigia retro improperata refert, *etc.*
(n) *Weary waves, from Statius Sylv.* Nec trucibus fluviis idem sonus, occidit, horror aequoris, ac terris maria acclinata quiescunt.
(o) *The third of June, famous for two former victories.*

---

396 Dryden's note refers to victories in 1653 and 1665.

101

"Yet, like an English gen'ral will I die,
    And all the ocean make my spacious grave.
Women and cowards on the land may lie,
    The sea's a tomb that's proper for the brave."

102

Restless he passed the remnants of the night,
    Till the fresh air proclaimed the morning nigh,
And burning ships, the martyrs of the fight,
    With paler fires beheld the eastern sky.

Third day

103

But now, his stores of ammunition spent,
410   His naked valour is his only guard:
Rare thunders are from his dumb cannon sent,
    And solitary guns are scarcely heard.

104

Thus far had Fortune pow'r, here forced to stay,
    Nor longer durst with virtue be at strife:
This as a ransom Albemarle did pay
    For all the glories of so great a life.

105

For now brave Rupert from afar appears,
    Whose waving streamers the glad General knows;
With full-spread sails his eager navy steers,
420   And every ship in swift proportion grows.

106

The anxious Prince had heard the cannon long,
    And from that length of time dire omens drew
Of English overmatched, and Dutch too strong
    Who never fought three days but to pursue.

107

Then, as an eagle, who with pious care
    Was beating widely on the wing for prey,

To her now silent eyry does repair,
    And finds her callow infants forced away;

108

Stung with her love she stoops upon the plain,
    The broken air loud whistling as she flies;   430
She stops and listens, and shoots forth again,
    And guides her pinions by her young ones' cries:

109

With such kind passion hastes the Prince to fight,
    And spreads his flying canvas to the sound:
Him whom no danger, were he there, could fright,
    Now absent, every little noise can wound.

110

As, in a drought, the thirsty creatures cry,
    And gape upon the gathered clouds for rain,
And first the martlet meets it in the sky,
    And with wet wings joys all the feathered train;   440

111

With such glad hearts did our despairing men
    Salute th' appearance of the Prince's fleet:
And each ambitiously would claim the ken
    That with first eyes did distant safety meet.

112

The Dutch, who came like greedy hinds before
    To reap the harvest their ripe ears did yield,
Now look like those, when rolling thunders roar,
    And sheets of lightning blast the standing field.

113

Full in the Prince's passage, hills of sand
    And dang'rous flats in secret ambush lay,   450
Where the false tides skim o'er the covered land,
    And seamen with dissembled depths betray.

428 callow] 'Of birds: Unfledged, without feathers' (*OED*).
443 ken] Sighting; range of vision.

114

The wily Dutch, who, like fall'n angels, feared
　　This new Messiah's coming, there did wait,
And round the verge their braving vessels steered
　　To tempt his courage with so fair a bait.

115

But he, unmoved, contemns their idle threat,
　　Secure of fame whene'er he please to fight:
His cold experience tempers all his heat,
460　　　And inbred worth does boasting valour slight.

116

Heroic virtue did his actions guide,
　　And he the substance, not th' appearance, chose:
To rescue one such friend he took more pride
　　Than to destroy whole thousands of such foes.

117

But, when approached, in strict embraces bound,
　　Rupert and Albemarle together grow:
He joys to have his friend in safety found,
　　Which he to none but to that friend would owe.

118

The cheerful soldiers, with new stores supplied,
470　　　Now long to execute their spleenful will;
And in revenge for those three days they tried,
　　Wish one like Joshua's, when the sun stood still.

Fourth day's battle

119

Thus reinforced, against the adverse fleet,
　　Still doubling ours, brave Rupert leads the way.
With the first blushes of the morn they meet,
　　And bring night back upon the new-born day.

120

His presence soon blows up the kindling fight,
　　And his loud guns speak thick like angry men:

476 That is, creating darkness by the smoke of the cannon.

It seemed as slaughter had been breathed all night,
    And Death new pointed his dull dart again.   480

121

The Dutch too well his mighty conduct knew,
    And matchless courage, since the former fight:
Whose navy like a stiff stretched cord did show,
    Till he bore in and bent them into flight.

122

The wind he shares, while half their fleet offends
    His open side, and high above him shows;
Upon the rest at pleasure he descends,
    And, doubly harmed, he double harms bestows.

123

Behind, the Gen'ral mends his weary pace,
    And sullenly to his revenge he sails: 490
PSo glides some trodden serpent on the grass,
    And long behind his wounded volume trails.

124

Th' increasing sound is borne to either shore
    And for their stakes the throwing nations fear.
Their passions double with the cannons' roar,
    And with warm wishes each man combats there.

125

Plied thick and close as when the fight begun,
    Their huge unwieldy navy wastes away:
So sicken waning moons too near the sun,
    And blunt their crescents on the edge of day.   500

126

And now, reduced on equal terms to fight,
    Their ships like wasted patrimonies show,
Where the thin scatt'ring trees admit the light
    And shun each other's shadows as they grow.

(P) *So glides, etc. from Virgil*: Quum medii nexus, extremaeque agmina caudae solvuntur;
tardosque trahit sinus ultimus orbes, *etc.*

479 breathed] Rested.   485 offends] Attacks.
492 volume] A Latinism, 'coil'.

127

The warlike Prince had severed from the rest
    Two giant ships, the pride of all the main;
Which, with his one, so vigorously he pressed,
    And flew so home they could not rise again.

128

Already battered, by his lee they lay;
    In vain upon the passing winds they call:
The passing winds through their torn canvas play,
    And flagging sails on heartless sailors fall.

129

Their opened sides receive a gloomy light,
    Dreadful as day let in to shades below;
Without, grim Death rides barefaced in their sight,
    And urges ent'ring billows as they flow.

130

When one dire shot, the last they could supply,
    Close by the board the Prince's main-mast bore:
All three now helpless by each other lie,
    And this offends not and those fear no more.

131

So have I seen some fearful hare maintain
    A course, till tired before the dog she lay;
Who, stretched behind her, pants upon the plain,
    Past power to kill as she to get away.

132

With his lolled tongue he faintly licks his prey,
    His warm breath blows her flix up as she lies;
She, trembling, creeps upon the ground away,
    And looks back to him with beseeching eyes.

133

The Prince unjustly does his stars accuse,
    Which hindered him to push his fortune on;
For what they to his courage did refuse
    By mortal valour never must be done.

510

520

530

526 flix] Fur.

134

This lucky hour the wise Batavian takes
    And warns his tattered fleet to follow home:
Proud to have so got off with equal stakes,
    qWhere 'twas a triumph not to be o'ercome.

135

The General's force, as kept alive by fight,
    Now, not opposed, no longer can pursue:
Lasting till Heaven had done his courage right,
    When he had conquered he his weakness knew.   540

136

He casts a frown on the departing foe,
    And sighs to see him quit the wat'ry field:
His stern fixed eyes no satisfaction show
    For all the glories which the fight did yield.

137

Though, as when fiends did miracles avow,
    He stands confessed ev'n by the boastful Dutch;
He only does his conquest disavow,
    And thinks too little what they found too much.

138

Returned, he with the fleet resolved to stay;
    No tender thoughts of home his heart divide;   550
Domestic joys and cares he puts away,
    For realms are households which the great must guide.

139

As those who unripe veins in mines explore
    On the rich bed again the warm turf lay,
Till time digests the yet imperfect ore,
    And know it will be gold another day;

140

So looks our Monarch on this early fight,
    Th' essay and rudiments of great success,

(q) *From Horace*: Quos opimus fallere et effugere est triumphus.

---

553 unripe veins] Precious metals were supposed to 'grow' or develop.

Which all-maturing time must bring to light,
560   While he, like Heav'n, does each day's labour bless.

141

Heav'n ended not the first or second day,
      Yet each was perfect to the work designed:
God and kings work, when they their work survey,
      And passive aptness in all subjects find.

His Majesty repairs the fleet

142

In burdened vessels, first, with speedy care,
      His plenteous stores do seasoned timber send:
Thither the brawny carpenters repair,
      And as the surgeons of maimed ships attend.

143

With cord and canvas from rich Hamburg sent
570   His navy's moulted wings he imps once more;
Tall Norway fir their masts in battle spent,
      And English oak sprung leaks and planks restore.

144

All hands employed, 'the royal work grows warm:
      Like labouring bees on a long summer's day,
Some sound the trumpet for the rest to swarm,
      And some on bells of tasted lilies play;

145

With glewy wax some new foundation lay
      Of virgin-combs, which from the roof are hung;
Some armed within doors upon duty stay,
580   Or tend the sick, or educate the young.

146

So here, some pick out bullets from the sides,
      Some drive old oakum through each seam and rift:

(r) Fervet opus: *the same similitude in Virgil*.

570 imps] Repairs, provides with feathers.
573 Dryden's note] Cf. *Georgics*, IV, 158–69.
582 oakum] Loose fibre got by untwisting old hemp rope, used in caulking (next line) or sealing.

Their left hand does the caulking-iron guide,
  The rattling mallet with the right they lift.

147

With boiling pitch another near at hand,
  From friendly Sweden brought, the seams instops,
Which well paid o'er, the salt sea waves withstand,
  And shakes them from the rising beak in drops.

148

Some the galled ropes with dauby marling bind,
  Or sear-cloth masts with strong tarpaulin coats: 590
To try new shrouds one mounts into the wind,
  And one, below, their ease or stiffness notes.

149

Our careful Monarch stands in person by,
  His new-cast cannons' firmness to explore:
The strength of big-corned powder loves to try,
  And ball and cartridge sorts for every bore.

150

Each day brings fresh supplies of arms and men,
  And ships which all last winter were abroad;
And such as fitted since the fight had been,
  Or new from stocks were fall'n into the road.   600

"Loyal London" described

151

The goodly London in her gallant trim,
  (The phoenix-daughter of the vanished old,)
Like a rich bride does to the ocean swim,
  And on her shadow rides in floating gold.

152

Her flag aloft, spread ruffling to the wind,
  And sanguine streamers seem the flood to fire:
The weaver, charmed with what his loom designed,
  Goes on to sea and knows not to retire.

589 marling] Marline, 'small line of two strands' (OED).
590 sear-cloth] A verb, 'cover with *cerecloth*'.
601-2 The *Loyal London* replaced the *London*, which had blown up in 1665.

153

With roomy decks, her guns of mighty strength,
          (Whose low-laid mouths each mounting billow laves,)
Deep in her draught, and warlike in her length,
          She seems a sea-wasp flying on the waves.

154

This martial present, piously designed,
          The loyal City give their best-loved King:
And, with a bounty ample as the wind,
          Built, fitted, and maintained to aid him bring.

Digression concerning shipping and navigation

155

By viewing Nature, Nature's handmaid, Art,
          Makes mighty things from small beginnings grow:
Thus fishes first to shipping did impart
          Their tail the rudder, and their head the prow.

156

Some log, perhaps, upon the waters swam,
          An useless drift, which, rudely cut within,
And hollowed, first a floating trough became,
          And cross some riv'let passage did begin.

157

In shipping such as this the Irish kern,
          And untaught Indian, on the stream did glide:
Ere sharp-keeled boats to stem the flood did learn,
          Or fin-like oars did spread from either side.

158

Add but a sail, and Saturn so appeared,
          When from lost empire he to exile went,
And with the golden age to Tiber steered,
          Where coin and first commerce he did invent.

159

Rude as their ships was navigation then,
          No useful compass or meridian known:

625 kern] A poor footsoldier; one of the 'wild Irish'.
629–32 Saturn, dethroned by his son Jove, fled to Latium. Cf. *Aeneid*, VIII, 319ff.

Coasting, they kept the land within their ken,
    And knew no north but when the pole-star shone.

160

Of all who since have used the open sea,
    Than the bold English none more fame have won:
ˢBeyond the year, and out of Heav'n's high way,
    They make discoveries where they see no sun.   640

161

But what so long in vain, and yet unknown,
    By poor mankind's benighted wit is sought,
Shall in this age to Britain first be shown,
    And hence be to admiring nations taught.

162

The ebbs of tides and their mysterious flow
    We as Art's elements shall understand,
And as by line upon the ocean go,
    Whose paths shall be familiar as the land.

163

ᵗInstructed ships shall sail to quick commerce,
    By which remotest regions are allied;   650
Which makes one city of the universe,
    Where some may gain and all may be supplied.

164

Then, we upon our globe's last verge shall go
    And view the ocean leaning on the sky:
From thence our rolling neighbours we shall know,
    And on the lunar world securely pry.

Apostrophe to the Royal Society

165

This I foretell, from your auspicious care,
    Who great in search of God and Nature grow;

⁽ˢ⁾ Extra anni solisque vias. *Virg.*   ⁽ᵗ⁾ *By a more exact measure of longitudes.*

---

649 Dryden's note] Scientists around this time were much exercised over the problem of measuring longitude at sea, to which no satisfactory solution was found until the next century.

657 The Royal Society was founded in 1660. Dryden became a member in November 1662.

Who best your wise Creator's praise declare,
660   Since best to praise His works is best to know.

166

O, truly Royal! who behold the law
      And rule of beings in your Maker's mind,
And thence, like limbecs, rich ideas draw
      To fit the levelled use of human kind.

167

But first the toils of war we must endure
      And from th' injurious Dutch redeem the seas.
War makes the valiant of his right secure,
      And gives up fraud to be chastised with ease.

168

Already were the Belgians on our coast,
670   Whose fleet more mighty every day became
By late success, which they did falsely boast,
      And now by first appearing seemed to claim.

169

Designing, subtle, diligent, and close,
      They know to manage war with wise delay:
Yet all those arts their vanity did cross,
      And by their pride their prudence did betray.

170

Nor stayed the English long; but, well supplied,
      Appear as numerous as th' insulting foe.
The combat now by courage must be tried
680   And the success the braver nation show.

171

There was the Plymouth squadron new come in,
      Which in the Straits last winter was abroad;

669–788 Ships were repaired rapidly, so that towards the end of July the two fleets, nearly equal in numbers, were ready to meet again. They sighted each other off the mouth of the Thames on 24 July, and battle was joined, with Allin leading the van against Everston, and Monck and Rupert the centre against De Ruyter. On the second day (the St James's Day battle) Sir Jeremy Smith fought decisively against Tromp. The outcome was an English victory.

Which twice on Biscay's working bay had been,
    And on the midland sea the French had awed.

172

Old expert Allen, loyal all along,
    Famed for his action on the Smyrna fleet;
And Holmes, whose name shall live in epic song,
    While music numbers, or while verse has feet;

173

Holmes, the Achates of the Gen'rals' fight,
    Who first bewitched our eyes with Guinea gold,   690
As once old Cato in the Romans' sight
    The tempting fruits of Afric did unfold.

174

With him went Spragge, as bountiful as brave,
    Whom his high courage to command had brought;
Harman, who did the twice-fired Harry save
    And in his burning ship undaunted fought;

175

Young Hollis, on a Muse by Mars begot,
    Born, Caesar-like, to write and act great deeds:
Impatient to revenge his fatal shot,
    His right hand doubly to his left succeeds.   700

176

Thousands were there in darker fame that dwell,
    Whose deeds some nobler poem shall adorn;
And though to me unknown, they, sure, fought well
    Whom Rupert led, and who were British born.

685–6 Sir Thomas Allin (1612–85) had attacked the Dutch Smyrna convoy off Cadiz in 1664.

687–92 Sir Robert Holmes (1622–92) attacked the Dutch on the West African coast in 1663–4.

693–4 Sir Edward Spragge (d. 1673).

695–6 Sir John Harman (d. 1673). His exploits in saving the *Henry* were performed in the previous battle.

697–700 Sir Freschville Holles (1641–72). His left arm was shot off in the battle of 2 June.

177

Of every size an hundred fighting sail,
    So vast the navy now at anchor rides,
That underneath it the pressed waters fail,
    And with its weight it shoulders off the tides.

178

Now, anchors weighed, the seamen shout so shrill
710   That heav'n and earth and the wide ocean rings:
A breeze from westward waits their sails to fill
    And rests, in those high beds, his downy wings.

179

The wary Dutch this gathering storm foresaw,
    And durst not bide it on the English coast:
Behind their treach'rous shallows they withdraw,
    And there lay snares to catch the British host.

180

So the false spider, when her nets are spread,
    Deep ambushed in her silent den does lie,
And feels far off the trembling of her thread,
720   Whose filmy cord should bind the struggling fly;

181

Then, if at last she finds him fast beset,
    She issues forth and runs along her loom:
She joys to touch the captive in her net,
    And drags the little wretch in triumph home.

182

The Belgians hoped that with disordered haste
    Our deep-cut keels upon the sands might run;
Or, if with caution leisurely were past,
    Their numerous gross might charge us one by one.

183

But, with a fore-wind pushing them above,
730   And swelling tide that heaved them from below,
O'er the blind flats our warlike squadrons move,
    And with spread sails to welcome battle go.

728 gross] The main body of a fleet or army.   731 blind] Concealed.

184

It seemed as there the British Neptune stood,
    With all his host of waters at command,
Beneath them to submit th' officious flood,
    ᵘAnd with his trident shoved them off the sand.

185

To the pale foes they suddenly draw near
    And summon them to unexpected fight:
They start, like murderers when ghosts appear
    And draw their curtains in the dead of night.   740

Second battle
186

Now van to van the foremost squadrons meet,
    The midmost battles hasting up behind,
Who view, far off, the storm of falling sleet,
    And hear their thunder rattling in the wind.

187

At length the adverse Admirals appear;
    (The two bold champions of each country's right:)
Their eyes describe the lists as they come near,
    And draw the lines of death before they fight.

188

The distance judged for shot of every size,
    The linstocks touch, the pond'rous ball expires: 750
The vigorous seaman every porthole plies,
    And adds his heart to every gun he fires.

189

Fierce was the fight on the proud Belgians' side
    For honour, which they seldom sought before;
But now they by their own vain boasts were tied,
    And forced at least in show to prize it more.

ᵘ Levat ipse tridenti, et vastas aperit Syrtes, *etc. Virg.*

---

735 officious] Helpful, obliging.   743 sleet] Flakes of metal.
750 linstocks] 'A staff about three feet long, having a pointed foot to stick in the deck or ground, and a forked head to hold a lighted match' (*OED*).
expires] Rushes forth.

190

But sharp remembrance on the English part,
　　And shame of being matched by such a foe,
Rouse conscious virtue up in every heart,
760　　ᵛAnd seeming to be stronger makes them so.

191

Nor long the Belgians could that fleet sustain,
　　Which did two Gen'rals' fates, and Caesar's bear:
Each several ship a victory did gain,
　　As Rupert or as Albemarle were there.

192

Their battered Admiral too soon withdrew,
　　Unthanked by ours for his unfinished fight:
But he the minds of his Dutch masters knew,
　　Who called that providence which we called flight.

193

Never did men more joyfully obey,
770　　Or sooner understand the sign to fly:
With such alacrity they bore away,
　　As if to praise them all the States stood by.

194

O famous leader of the Belgian fleet,
　　Thy monument inscribed such praise shall wear
As Varro, timely flying, once did meet,
　　Because he did not of his Rome despair.

195

Behold that navy, which a while before
　　Provoked the tardy English close to fight,
Now draw their beaten vessels close to shore,
780　　As larks lie dared to shun the hobby's flight.

⁽ᵛ⁾ Possunt quia posse videntur. *Virg.*

---

762 Caesar's] Charles II's.
773 famous leader] De Ruyter. Like Varro after the battle of Cannae, he reassembled his shattered forces for defence.
780 dared] Dazed, terrified of the hobby (a small species of falcon).

196

Whoe'er would English monuments survey
    In other records may our courage know:
But let them hide the story of this day,
    Whose fame was blemished by too base a foe.

197

Or if too busily they will enquire
    Into a victory which we disdain,
Then let them know the Belgians did retire
    ᵂBefore the patron saint of injured Spain.

198

Repenting England, this revengeful day,
    ˣTo Philip's manes did an off'ring bring: 790
England, which first, by leading them astray,
    Hatched up rebellion to destroy her King.

199

Our fathers bent their baneful industry
    To check a monarchy that slowly grew;
But did not France or Holland's fate foresee,
    Whose rising pow'r to swift dominion flew.

200

In Fortune's empire blindly thus we go,
    And wander after pathless destiny;
Whose dark resorts since prudence cannot know,
    In vain it would provide for what shall be.   800

201

But whate'er English to the blessed shall go,
    And the fourth Harry or first Orange meet;
Find him disowning of a Bourbon foe,
    And him detesting a Batavian fleet.

(ᵂ) *Patron saint: St James, on whose day this victory was gained.*
(ˣ) *Philip's manes: Philip the Second of Spain, against whom the Hollanders rebelling, were aided by Queen Elizabeth.*

---

803 Bourbon foe] Louis XIV, imagined 'disowned' by his grandfather Henry IV.

202

Now on their coasts our conquering navy rides,
    Waylays their merchants, and their land besets;
Each day new wealth without their care provides;
    They lie asleep with prizes in their nets.

203

So, close behind some promontory lie
810   The huge leviathans t'attend their prey;
And give no chase, but swallow in the fry,
    Which through their gaping jaws mistake the way.

Burning of the fleet in the Vlie by Sir Robert Holmes

204

Nor was this all: in ports and roads remote,
    Destructive fires among whole fleets we send;
Triumphant flames upon the water float,
    And out-bound ships at home their voyage end.

205

Those various squadrons, variously designed,
    Each vessel freighted with a several load,
Each squadron waiting for a several wind,
820   All find but one, to burn them in the road.

206

Some bound for Guinea, golden sand to find,
    Bore all the gauds the simple natives wear;
Some, for the pride of Turkish courts designed,
    For folded turbans finest holland bear.

207

Some English wool, vexed in a Belgian loom,
    And into cloth of spungy softness made,
Did into France or colder Denmark doom,
    To ruin with worse ware our staple trade.

805–32 A small English force under Sir Robert Holmes subsequently attacked and burned stores and merchant ships on the Vlie.
820 road] A sheltered piece of water near the shore.
824 holland] Holland linen.
827 doom] Intend to convey.

208

Our greedy seamen rummage every hold,
 Smile on the booty of each wealthier chest,   830
And, as the priests who with their gods make bold,
 Take what they like and sacrifice the rest.

Transitum to the Fire of London

209

But ah! how unsincere are all our joys!
 Which sent from Heav'n, like lightning make no stay:
Their palling taste the journey's length destroys,
 Or grief, sent post, o'ertakes them on the way.

210

Swelled with our late successes on the foe,
 Which France and Holland wanted power to cross,
We urge an unseen fate to lay us low,
 And feed their envious eyes with English loss.   840

211

Each element His dread command obeys,
 Who makes or ruins with a smile or frown;
Who, as by one He did our nation raise,
 So now He with another pulls us down.

212

Yet, London, empress of the northern clime,
 By an high fate thou greatly didst expire;
ʸGreat as the world's, which at the death of time
 Must fall, and rise a nobler frame by fire.

213

As when some dire usurper Heav'n provides
 To scourge his country with a lawless sway,   850

(ʸ) Quum mare quum tellus correptaque regia Coeli, ardeat, *etc. Ovid.*

---

833 unsincere] Unmixed, incomplete
834ff The Great Fire began in a baker's shop in Pudding Lane early in the morning of
Sunday, 2 September. Fanned by a strong east wind, it soon got out of control, and raged
for four days, at the end of which older London was laid waste to an extent of some 438 acres.
The spectacle, and the distress of the people, are described vividly by Pepys in his *Diary.*

His birth perhaps some petty village hides,
    And sets his cradle out of Fortune's way;

214

Till, fully ripe, his swelling fate breaks out,
    And hurries him to mighty mischiefs on;
His Prince, surprised at first, no ill could doubt,
    And wants the pow'r to meet it when 'tis known:

215

Such was the rise of this prodigious fire,
    Which, in mean buildings first obscurely bred,
From thence did soon to open streets aspire,
860   And straight to palaces and temples spread.

216

The diligence of trades, and noiseful gain,
    And luxury, more late, asleep were laid;
All was the Night's, and in her silent reign
    No sound the rest of Nature did invade.

217

In this deep quiet, from what source unknown,
    Those seeds of fire their fatal birth disclose:
And first few scatt'ring sparks about were blown,
    Big with the flames that to our ruin rose.

218

Then, in some close-pent room it crept along,
870   And, smould'ring as it went, in silence fed:
Till th' infant monster, with devouring strong,
    Walked boldly upright with exalted head.

219

Now, like some rich or mighty murderer,
    Too great for prison, which he breaks with gold,
Who fresher for new mischiefs does appear,
    And dares the world to tax him with the old;

220

So scapes th' insulting fire his narrow jail,
    And makes small outlets into open air:

877 insulting] Exulting.

There the fierce winds his tender force assail,
  And beat him downward to his first repair. 880

221

²The winds, like crafty courtesans, withheld
  His flames from burning but to blow them more;
And, every fresh attempt, he is repelled
  With faint denials, weaker than before.

222

And now, no longer letted of his prey,
  He leaps up at it with enraged desire,
O'erlooks the neighbours with a wide survey,
  And nods at every house his threat'ning fire.

223

The ghosts of traitors from the Bridge descend,
  With bold fanatic spectres to rejoice; 890
About the fire into a dance they bend,
  And sing their sabbath notes with feeble voice.

224

Our guardian angel saw them where he sate
  Above the palace of our slumb'ring King:
He sighed, abandoning his charge to fate,
  And, dropping, oft looked back upon the wing.

225

At length the crackling noise and dreadful blaze
  Called up some waking lover to the sight;
And long it was ere he the rest could raise,
  Whose heavy eyelids yet were full of night. 900

226

The next to danger, hot pursued by fate,
  Half-clothed, half-naked, hastily retire;
And frighted mothers strike their breasts, too late,
  For helpless infants left amidst the fire.

(²) *Like crafty, etc.* Haec arte tractabat cupidum virum, ut illius animum inopia accenderet.

890 fanatic] A term of abuse for Puritan extremists. Their ghosts are imagined taking part in a witches' sabbath.

227

Their cries soon waken all the dwellers near;
    Now murmuring noises rise in every street;
The more remote run stumbling with their fear,
    And in the dark men justle as they meet.

228

So weary bees in little cells repose;
910   But if night-robbers lift the well-stored hive,
An humming through their waxen city grows,
    And out upon each other's wings they drive.

229

Now streets grow thronged and busy as by day;
    Some run for buckets to the hallowed choir;
Some cut the pipes, and some the engines play,
    And some more bold mount ladders to the fire.

230

In vain; for from the east a Belgian wind
    His hostile breath through the dry rafters sent;
The flames impelled soon left their foes behind,
920   And forward with a wanton fury went.

231

A key of fire ran all along the shore,
    [a]And lightened all the river with a blaze;
The wakened tides began again to roar,
    And wond'ring fish in shining waters gaze.

232

Old Father Thames raised up his reverend head,
    But feared the fate of Simois would return;
Deep in his ooze he sought his sedgy bed,
    And shrank his waters back into his urn.

233

The fire meantime walks in a broader gross;
930   To either hand his wings he opens wide;

[a] Sigaea igni freta lata relucent. *Virg.*

914 Fire buckets were kept in churches.
915 cut the pipes] That is, cut the wooden water conduits in order to fill the buckets.

He wades the streets, and straight he reaches cross
    And plays his longing flames on th' other side.

234

At first they warm, then scorch, and then they take;
    Now with long necks from side to side they feed;
At length, grown strong, their mother-fire forsake,
    And a new colony of flames succeed.

235

To every nobler portion of the town
    The curling billows roll their restless tide;
In parties now they straggle up and down,
    As armies, unopposed, for prey divide.   940

236

One mighty squadron, with a side-wind sped,
    Through narrow lanes his cumbered fire does haste,
By pow'rful charms of gold and silver led
    The Lombard bankers and the Change to waste.

237

Another backward to the Tow'r would go,
    And slowly eats his way against the wind;
But the main body of the marching foe
    Against th' imperial palace is designed.

238

Now day appears, and with the day the King,
    Whose early care had robbed him of his rest: 950
Far off the cracks of falling houses ring,
    And shrieks of subjects pierce his tender breast.

239

Near as he draws, thick harbingers of smoke
    With gloomy pillars cover all the place;
Whose little intervals of night are broke
    By sparks that drive against his sacred face.

944 Referring to the bankers of Lombard Street, and the Royal Exchange.
949ff Charles and his brother the Duke of York took control of operations against the fire,
and won great affection and respect in doing so.

240

More than his guards his sorrows made him known,
    And pious tears which down his cheeks did show'r:
The wretched in his grief forgot their own;
    (So much the pity of a king has pow'r.)

241

He wept the flames of what he loved so well,
    And what so well had merited his love;
For never prince in grace did more excel,
    Or royal city more in duty strove.

242

Nor with an idle care did he behold:
    (Subjects may grieve, but monarchs must redress;)
He cheers the fearful, and commends the bold,
    And makes despairers hope for good success.

243

Himself directs what first is to be done,
    And orders all the succours which they bring.
The helpful and the good about him run,
    And form an army worthy such a King.

244

He sees the dire contagion spread so fast
    That, where it seizes, all relief is vain;
And therefore must unwillingly lay waste
    That country which would, else, the foe maintain.

245

The powder blows up all before the fire:
    Th' amazed flames stand gathered on a heap,
And from the precipice's brink retire,
    Afraid to venture on so large a leap.

246

Thus fighting fires a while themselves consume,
    But straight, like Turks, forced on to win or die,

977–80 The use of gunpowder to blow up houses in the path of the fire was effective,
although it was thought that the measure was not taken soon enough.

They first lay tender bridges of their fume,
    And o'er the breach in unctuous vapours fly.

247

Part stays for passage till a gust of wind
    Ships o'er their forces in a shining sheet;
Part, creeping under ground, their journey blind,
    And, climbing from below, their fellows meet.

248

Thus, to some desert plain, or old wood-side,
    Dire night-hags come from far to dance their round;   990
And o'er broad rivers on their fiends they ride,
    Or sweep in clouds above the blasted ground.

249

No help avails: for, hydra-like, the fire
    Lifts up his hundred heads to aim his way;
And scarce the wealthy can one half retire
    Before he rushes in to share the prey.

250

The rich grow suppliant, and the poor grow proud;
    Those offer mighty gain and these ask more:
So void of pity is th' ignoble crowd,
    When others' ruin may increase their store.   1000

251

As those who live by shores with joy behold
    Some wealthy vessel split or stranded nigh;
And, from the rocks, leap down for shipwracked gold,
    And seek the tempest which the others fly:

252

So these but wait the owners' last despair,
    And what's permitted to the flames invade:
Ev'n from their jaws they hungry morsels tear,
    And on their backs the spoils of Vulcan lade.

---

995 retire] Remove (their possessions).
997–1000 Labouring rates, especially for transportation, became extortionate.

253

The days were all in this lost labour spent;
>And when the weary King gave place to night,
His beams he to his royal brother lent,
>And so shone still in his reflective light.

254

Night came, but without darkness or repose,
>A dismal picture of the general doom;
Where souls distracted when the trumpet blows,
>And half unready with their bodies come.

255

Those who have homes, when home they do repair,
>To a last lodging call their wand'ring friends.
Their short uneasy sleeps are broke with care,
>To look how near their own destruction tends.

256

Those who have none sit round where once it was,
>And with full eyes each wonted room require;
Haunting the yet warm ashes of the place,
>As murdered men walk where they did expire.

257

Some stir up coals and watch the vestal fire,
>Others in vain from sight of ruin run;
And, while through burning lab'rinths they retire,
>With loathing eyes repeat what they would shun.

258

The most in fields like herded beasts lie down,
>To dews obnoxious on the grassy floor;
And while their babes in sleep their sorrows drown,
>Sad parents watch the remnants of their store.

259

While by the motion of the flames they guess
>What streets are burning now, and what are near,

1022 require] Search for.
1025 vestal fire] Vesta was the Roman goddess of the household and hearth.
1028 repeat] Experience again.

An infant, waking, to the paps would press
    And meets, instead of milk, a falling tear.

260

No thought can ease them but their Sovereign's care,
    Whose praise th' afflicted as their comfort sing:
Ev'n those whom want might drive to just despair,
    Think life a blessing under such a King.   1040

261

Meantime he sadly suffers in their grief,
    Outweeps an hermit, and outprays a saint:
All the long night he studies their relief,
    How they may be supplied, and he may want.

King's prayer

262

"O God," said he, "Thou patron of my days,
    Guide of my youth in exile and distress!
Who me unfriended broughtst by wondrous ways,
    The kingdom of my fathers to possess:

263

"Be Thou my judge, with what unwearied care
    I since have laboured for my people's good;   1050
To bind the bruises of a civil war,
    And stop the issues of their wasting blood.

264

"Thou, who has taught me to forgive the ill,
    And recompense, as friends, the good misled;
If mercy be a precept of Thy will,
    Return that mercy on Thy servant's head.

265

"Or, if my heedless youth has stepped astray,
    Too soon forgetful of Thy gracious hand;
On me alone Thy just displeasure lay,
    But take Thy judgments from this mourning land.   1060

266

"We all have sinned, and Thou has laid us low,
    As humble earth from whence at first we came:

Like flying shades before the clouds we show,
    And shrink like parchment in consuming flame.

267

"O let it be enough what Thou hast done,
    When spotted deaths ran armed through every street,
With poisoned darts, which not the good could shun,
    The speedy could outfly, or valiant meet.

268

"The living few, and frequent funerals then,
1070   Proclaimed Thy wrath on this forsaken place;
And now those few, who are returned again,
    Thy searching judgments to their dwellings trace.

269

"O pass not, Lord, an absolute decree,
    Or bind Thy sentence unconditional;
But in Thy sentence our remorse foresee,
    And, in that foresight, this Thy doom recall.

270

"Thy threat'nings, Lord, as Thine Thou may'st revoke:
    But if immutable and fixed they stand,
Continue still Thyself to give the stroke,
1080   And let not foreign foes oppress Thy land."

271

Th' Eternal heard, and from the heav'nly choir
    Chose out the cherub with the flaming sword;
And bade him swiftly drive th' approaching fire
    From where our naval magazines were stored.

272

The blessed minister his wings displayed,
    And like a shooting star he cleft the night;
He charged the flames, and those that disobeyed
    He lashed to duty with his sword of light.

1066 spotted deaths] The great plague of the previous year.
1084 The munitions in the Tower were rendered safe by pulling down houses nearby.

273

The fugitive flames, chastised, went forth to prey
  On pious structures, by our fathers reared;   1090
By which to Heav'n they did affect the way,
  Ere faith in churchmen without works was heard.

274

The wanting orphans saw, with wat'ry eyes,
  Their founders' charity in dust laid low;
And sent to God their ever-answered cries,
  (For he protects the poor who made them so.)

275

Nor could thy fabric, Paul's, defend thee long,
  Though thou wert sacred to thy Maker's praise;
Though made immortal by a poet's song,
  And poet's songs the Theban walls could raise.   1100

276

The daring flames peeped in and saw from far
  The awful beauties of the sacred choir;
But, since it was profaned by civil war,
  Heav'n thought it fit to have it purged by fire.

277

Now down the narrow streets it swiftly came,
  And, widely opening, did on both sides prey.
This benefit we sadly owe the flame,
  If only ruin must enlarge our way.

278

And now four days the sun had seen our woes,
  Four nights the moon beheld th' incessant fire: 1110
It seemed as if the stars more sickly rose,
  And farther from the fev'rish north retire.

279

In th' empyrean Heaven (the blessed abode)
  The Thrones and the Dominions prostrate lie,

1090–2 Referring to pre-Reformation churches, built before the doctrine of salvation by
faith alone was promulgated by Calvin and Luther.
1094 founders' charity] Christ's Hospital.
1100 Amphion's magical playing of his lyre drew stones after him to wall the city of Thebes.

Not daring to behold their angry God;
　　And a hushed silence damps the tuneful sky.

280

At length th' Almighty cast a pitying eye,
　　And mercy softly touched His melting breast:
He saw the town's one half in rubbish lie,
　　And eager flames give on to storm the rest.

1120

281

An hollow crystal pyramid he takes,
　　In firmamental waters dipped above;
Of it a broad extinguisher he makes,
　　And hoods the flames that to their quarry strove.

282

The vanquished fires withdraw from every place,
　　Or, full with feeding, sink into a sleep:
Each household Genius shows again his face,
　　And from the hearths the little Lares creep.

283

Our King this more than natural change beholds,
　　With sober joy his heart and eyes abound;
To the All-good his lifted hands he folds,
　　And thanks him low on his redeemed ground.

1130

284

As, when sharp frosts had long constrained the earth,
　　A kindly thaw unlocks it with mild rain,
And first the tender blade peeps up to birth,
　　And straight the green fields laugh with promised grain:

285

By such degrees the spreading gladness grew
　　In every heart, which fear had froze before;
The standing streets with so much joy they view,
　　That with less grief the perished they deplore.

1140

286

The father of the people opened wide
　　His stores, and all the poor with plenty fed:

Thus God's anointed God's own place supplied,
    And filled the empty with his daily bread.

287

This royal bounty brought its own reward,
    And in their minds so deep did print the sense,
That, if their ruins sadly they regard,
    'Tis but with fear the sight might drive him thence.

City's request to the King not to leave them
288

But so may he live long, that town to sway,
    Which by his auspice they will nobler make,   1150
As he will hatch their ashes by his stay,
    And not their humble ruins now forsake.

289

They have not lost their loyalty by fire;
    Nor is their courage or their wealth so low,
That from his wars they poorly would retire,
    Or beg the pity of a vanquished foe.

290

Not with more constancy the Jews of old,
    By Cyrus from rewarded exile sent,
Their royal city did in dust behold,
    Or with more vigour to rebuild it went.   1160

291

The utmost malice of their stars is past,
    And two dire comets which have scourged the town,
In their own plague and fire have breathed their last,
    Or, dimly, in their sinking sockets frown.

292

Now frequent trines the happier lights among,
    And high-raised Jove from his dark prison freed,
(Those weights took off that on his planet hung,)
    Will gloriously the new-laid work succeed.

1150 auspice] Good influence, direction.
1165 trines] Favourable 'aspects'.of planets, being 120° apart.

293

Methinks already, from this chymic flame,
    I see a city of more precious mould;
Rich as the town which gives the [b]Indies name,
    With silver paved, and all divine with gold.

294

Already, labouring with a mighty fate,
    She shakes the rubbish from her mounting brow,
And seems to have renewed her charter's date,
    Which Heav'n will to the death of time allow.

295

More great than human, now, and more [c]August,
    New deified she from her fires does rise:
Her widening streets on new foundations trust,
    And, opening, into larger parts she flies.

296

Before, she like some shepherdess did show,
    Who sate to bathe her by a river's side;
Not answering to her fame, but rude and low,
    Nor taught the beauteous arts of modern pride.

297

Now, like a maiden queen, she will behold,
    From her high turrets, hourly suitors come;
The East with incense, and the West with gold,
    Will stand, like suppliants, to receive her doom.

298

The silver Thames, her own domestic flood,
    Shall bear her vessels, like a sweeping train;
And often wind (as of his mistress proud)
    With longing eyes to meet her face again.

299

The wealthy Tagus, and the wealthier Rhine,
    The glory of their towns no more shall boast;

1170

1180

1190

[b] *Mexico.*
[c] *Augusta, the old name of London.*

And Seine, that would with Belgian rivers join,
    Shall find her lustre stained and traffic lost.

300

The vent'rous merchant, who designed more far,
    And touches on our hospitable shore,
Charmed with the splendour of this northern star,
    Shall here unlade him and depart no more.   1200

301

Our pow'rful navy shall no longer meet,
    The wealth of France or Holland to invade:
The beauty of this town, without a fleet,
    From all the world shall vindicate her trade

302

And, while this famed emporium we prepare,
    The British ocean shall such triumphs boast,
That those who now disdain our trade to share
    Shall rob like pirates on our wealthy coast.

303

Already we have conquered half the war,
    And the less dang'rous part is left behind;   1210
Our trouble now is but to make them dare,
    And not so great to vanquish as to find.

304

Thus to the Eastern wealth through storms we go;
    But now, the Cape once doubled, fear no more:
A constant trade-wind will securely blow,
    And gently lay us on the spicy shore.

1204 vindicate] Defend.
1210 left behind] Still to come.

SONG

From Act IV, Scene ii of *Secret-Love, or the Maiden-Queen*, first performed in March 1667.

> I feed a flame within which so torments me
> That it both pains my heart, and yet contents me:
> 'Tis such a pleasing smart, and I so love it,
> That I had rather die than once remove it.
>
> Yet he for whom I grieve shall never know it;
> My tongue does not betray, nor my eyes show it:
> Not a sigh, nor a tear, my pain discloses,
> But they fall silently, like dew on roses.
>
> Thus to prevent my love from being cruel,
> My heart's the sacrifice, as 'tis the fuel:
> And while I suffer this to give him quiet,
> My faith rewards my love, though he deny it.
>
> On his eyes will I gaze, and there delight me;
> Where I conceal my love, no frown can fright me:
> To be more happy I dare not aspire;
> Nor can I fall more low, mounting no higher.

10

SONG

From Act II, Scene i of *An Evening's Love, or the Mock-Astrologer*, first performed in
June 1668.

After the pangs of a desperate lover,
    When day and night I have sighed all in vain,
Ah what a pleasure it is to discover
    In her eyes pity, who causes my pain!

When with unkindness our love at a stand is,
    And both have punished ourselves with the pain,
Ah what a pleasure the touch of her hand is,
    Ah what a pleasure to press it again!

When the denial comes fainter and fainter,
    And her eyes give what her tongue does deny,
Ah what a trembling I feel when I venture,
    Ah what a trembling does usher my joy!

When, with a sigh, she accords me the blessing,
    And her eyes twinkle 'twixt pleasure and pain,
Ah what a joy 'tis, beyond all expressing,
    Ah what a joy to hear: "Shall we again?"

TO MR LEE,

ON HIS *ALEXANDER*

The poem was printed before Nathaniel Lee's play *The Rival Queens, or the Death of Alexander the Great* (1677). Lee (1649?–92) was a writer of powerful tragedies, undervalued then as now.

> The blast of common censure could I fear,
> Before your play my name should not appear;
> For 'twill be thought, and with some colour too,
> I pay the bribe I first received from you;
> That mutual vouchers for our fame we stand,
> To play the game into each other's hand;
> And as cheap pen'orths to ourselves afford,
> As Bessus and the brothers of the sword.
> Such libels private men may well endure,
> When states and kings themselves are not secure;
> For ill men, conscious of their inward guilt,
> Think the best actions on by-ends are built.
> And yet my silence had not scaped their spite,
> Then envy had not suffered me to write;
> For, since I could not ignorance pretend,
> Such worth I must or envy or commend.
> So many candidates there stand for wit,
> A place in court is scarce so hard to get:
> In vain they crowd each other at the door
> For ev'n reversions are all begged before:
> Desert, how known soe'er, is long delayed;
> And then, too, fools and knaves are better paid.

3–4 The 'bribe' was Lee's flattery in his commendatory poem to Dryden's play *The State of Innocence, and Fall of Man* (1677).
8 Bessus is a cowardly soldier in Beaumont and Fletcher's play *A King and No King*.
20 reversions] 'The right of succession to an office or place of emolument, after the death or retirement of the holder' (*OED*).

Yet, as some actions bear so great a name
That courts themselves are just for fear of shame,
So has the mighty merit of your play
Extorted praise and forced itself a way.
'Tis here as 'tis at sea; who farthest goes,
Or dares the most, makes all the rest his foes.
Yet, when some virtue much outgrows the rest,
It shoots too fast and high to be opprest;   30
As his heroic worth struck envy dumb,
Who took the Dutchman, and who cut the boom:
Such praise is yours, while you the passions move,
That 'tis no longer feigned, 'tis real love,
Where nature triumphs over wretched art;
We only warm the head, but you the heart.
Always you warm! and if the rising year,
As in hot regions, bring the sun too near,
'Tis but to make your fragrant spices blow,
Which in our colder climates will not grow.   40
They only think you animate your theme
With too much fire, who are themselves all phlegm:
Prizes would be for lags of slowest pace,
Were cripples made the judges of the race.
Despise those drones, who praise while they accuse
The too much vigour of your youthful Muse.
That humble style which they their virtue make
Is in your pow'r; you need but stoop and take.
Your beauteous images must be allowed
By all but some vile poets of the crowd.   50
But how should any signpost dauber know
The worth of Titian or of Angelo?
Hard features every bungler can command;
To draw true beauty shows a master's hand.

31–2 Thought to refer to naval actions by Sir Edward Spragge, in the Dutch Wars and at Bugia in the Mediterranean in 1671.

MAC FLECKNOE

Mac Flecknoe, a satire on the dramatist Thomas Shadwell, was first printed in 1682, but is thought to have been written much earlier, in 1678. It is a culmination of some ten years of rivalry with Shadwell in the writing of comedy (see the headnote to the Preface to *An Evening's Love*, p. 536), no doubt aggravated by contentions between coteries of patrons and wits. It is the best example of Dryden's prowess as a bestower of ridicule, from which Shadwell's reputation has scarcely recovered.

All human things are subject to decay,
And when fate summons, monarchs must obey.
This Flecknoe found, who, like Augustus, young
Was called to empire, and had governed long;
In prose and verse was owned, without dispute,
Through all the realms of Nonsense, absolute.
This aged prince, now flourishing in peace,
And blest with issue of a large increase,
Worn out with business, did at length debate
10 To settle the succession of the State;
And, pond'ring which of all his sons was fit
To reign, and wage immortal war with wit,
Cried, "'Tis resolved; for nature pleads that he
Should only rule, who most resembles me.
Sh———— alone my perfect image bears,
Mature in dullness from his tender years:
Sh———— alone, of all my sons, is he
Who stands confirmed in full stupidity.
The rest to some faint meaning make pretence,
20 But Sh———— never deviates into sense.
Some beams of wit on other souls may fall,
Strike through and make a lucid interval;
But Sh————'s genuine night admits no ray,

3 Flecknoe] Richard Flecknoe (d. 1678), an exceedingly bad poet and dramatist.

His rising fogs prevail upon the day.
Besides, his goodly fabric fills the eye,
And seems designed for thoughtless majesty:
Thoughtless as monarch oaks that shade the plain,
And, spread in solemn state, supinely reign.
Heywood and Shirley were but types of thee,
Thou last great prophet of tautology.   30
Even I, a dunce of more renown than they,
Was sent before but to prepare thy way;
And coarsely clad in Norwich druggett came
To teach the nations in thy greater name.
My warbling lute, the lute I whilom strung
When to King John of Portugal I sung,
Was but the prelude to that glorious day,
When thou on silver Thames didst cut thy way,
With well-timed oars before the royal barge,
Swelled with the pride of thy celestial charge;   40
And big with hymn, commander of an host,
The like was ne'er in Epsom blankets tossed.
Methinks I see the new Arion sail,
The lute still trembling underneath thy nail.
At thy well-sharpened thumb from shore to shore
The treble squeaks for fear, the basses roar;
Echoes from Pissing Alley Sh——— call,
And Sh——— they resound from A——— Hall.
About thy boat the little fishes throng,
As at the morning toast that floats along.   50
Sometimes, as prince of thy harmonious band,
Thou wield'st thy papers in thy threshing hand.
St. André's feet ne'er kept more equal time,
Not ev'n the feet of thy own *Psyche*'s rhyme:
Though they in number as in sense excel,
So just, so like tautology, they fell,

---

29 Heywood and Shirley] Thomas Heywood (*c.* 1574–1641) and James Shirley (1596–1666), both prolific dramatists.
33 Norwich druggett] A coarse woollen cloth. Shadwell was from Norfolk.
35 lute] Shadwell claimed proficiency in music.
42 Epsom blankets] Alluding to Shadwell's plays *Epsom Wells* (1672) and *The Virtuoso*, in which Sir Samuel Hearty is tossed in a blanket.
43 Arion was a Greek musician whose playing from a ship enchanted the dolphins.
48 A——— Hall] Aston Hall in the 1682 edition. Not identified.
53 St. André] A French dancing-master, who helped with Shadwell's opera *Psyche* (1675).

That pale with envy, Singleton forswore
The lute and sword which he in triumph bore,
And vowed he ne'er would act Villerius more."
60   Here stopped the good old sire, and wept for joy
In silent raptures of the hopeful boy.
All arguments, but most his plays, persuade,
That for anointed dullness he was made.
    Close to the walls which fair Augusta bind,
(The fair Augusta much to fears inclined,)
An ancient fabric raised t'inform the sight
There stood of yore, and Barbican it hight:
A watchtower once; but now, so fate ordains,
Of all the pile an empty name remains.
70   From its old ruins brothel-houses rise,
Scenes of lewd loves, and of polluted joys,
Where their vast courts the mother-strumpets keep,
And, undisturbed by watch, in silence sleep.
Near these a Nursery erects its head,
Where queens are formed, and future heroes bred;
Where unfledged actors learn to laugh and cry,
Where infant punks their tender voices try,
And little Maximins the gods defy.
Great Fletcher never treads in buskins here,
80   Nor greater Jonson dares in socks appear.
But gentle Simkin just reception finds
Amidst this monument of vanished minds:
Pure clinches the suburbian Muse affords,
And Panton waging harmless war with words.
Here Flecknoe, as a place to fame well known,

57–9 Singleton] John Singleton (d. 1686), one of the King's musicians. Villerius is a character in Davenant's operatic *The Siege of Rhodes* (first performed in 1656).
64 Augusta] London. Inclined to fears about the Popish Plot.
72–3 A parody of ll. 79–80 of the First Book of Cowley's *Davideis*:

> Where their vast court the mother-waters keep,
> And undisturbed by moons in silence sleep.

74 a Nursery] A theatre for training young actors. The one near the Barbican seems to have been particularly disreputable.
78 Maximins] Maximin is a fulsomely ranting character in Dryden's heroic play *Tyrannic Love* (1670).
81 gentle Simkin] A clown in a farce called *The Humours of Simkin*.
83 clinches] Puns.
84 Panton] Perhaps another character of farce.

Ambitiously designed his Sh———'s throne;
For ancient Dekker prophesied long since,
That in this pile should reign a mighty prince,
Born for the scourge of wit and flail of sense:
To whom true dullness should some *Psyches* owe,   90
But worlds of *Misers* from his pen should flow;
Humorists and *Hypocrites* it should produce,
Whole Raymond families, and tribes of Bruce.
    Now Empress Fame had published the renown
Of Sh———'s coronation through the town.
Roused by report of Fame, the nations meet,
From near Bunhill and distant Watling Street.
No Persian carpets spread th' imperial way,
But scattered limbs of mangled poets lay:
From dusty shops neglected authors come,   100
Martyrs of pies, and relics of the bum.
Much Heywood, Shirley, Ogleby there lay,
But loads of Sh——— almost choked the way.
Bilked stationers for yeomen stood prepar'd,
And H——— was captain of the guard.
The hoary prince in majesty appeared,
High on a throne of his own labours reared.
At his right hand our young Ascanius sate,
Rome's other hope, and pillar of the State.
His brows thick fogs, instead of glories, grace,   110
And lambent dullness played around his face.
As Hannibal did to the altars come,
Sworn by his sire a mortal foe to Rome;
So Sh——— swore, nor should his vow be vain,
That he till death true dullness would maintain;
And in his father's right, and realm's defence,
Ne'er to have peace with wit, nor truce with sense.
The king himself the sacred unction made,

87 Dekker] Thomas Dekker (c. 1572–1632), another comparatively undistinguished
dramatist. The list of Shadwell's antecedents in the drama prepares for his dissociation from
Ben Jonson (l. 172), whom Shadwell strove to imitate.
91–3 Three plays of Shadwell's. Raymond and Bruce are characters in *The Humorists* (1671)
and *The Virtuoso* (1676) respectively.
102 Ogleby] John Ogilby (1600–76), translator and printer.
105 H———] Henry Herringman, publisher of some of Shadwell's plays, and of all of
Dryden's up to 1678.
108–11 Ascanius was the younger son of Aeneas. The lines parody Virgil's *Aeneid*, 11, 682–4.

120

As king by office, and as priest by trade.
In his sinister hand, instead of ball,
He placed a mighty mug of potent ale;
Love's Kingdom to his right he did convey,
At once his sceptre and his rule of sway;
Whose righteous lore the prince had practised young,
And from whose loins recorded Psyche sprung.
His temples last with poppies were o'erspread,
That nodding seemed to consecrate his head.
Just at that point of time, if fame not lie,
On his left hand twelve reverend owls did fly.

130

So Romulus, 'tis sung, by Tiber's brook,
Presage of sway from twice six vultures took.
Th' admiring throng loud acclamations make,
And omens of his future empire take.
The sire then shook the honours of his head,
And from his brows damps of oblivion shed
Full on the filial dullness: long he stood,
Repelling from his breast the raging god;
At length burst out in this prophetic mood:)
"Heavens bless my son, from Ireland let him reign

140

To far Barbadoes on the western main;
Of his dominion may no end be known,
And greater than his father's be his throne.
Beyond Love's Kingdom let him stretch his pen!"
He paused, and all the people cried, "Amen."
Then thus continued he, "My son, advance
Still in new impudence, new ignorance.
Success let others teach, learn thou from me
Pangs without birth, and fruitless industry.
Let Virtuosos in five years be writ,

150

Yet not one thought accuse thy toil of wit.
Let gentle George in triumph tread the stage,
Make Dorimant betray, and Loveit rage;
Let Cully, Cockwood, Fopling charm the pit,
And in their folly show the writer's wit.
Yet still thy fools shall stand in thy defence,

122 Love's Kingdom] A play of Flecknoe's (1664).
149 Shadwell prided himself on his speed in writing.
151 gentle George] Sir George Etherege (c. 1635–91), the most polished of Restoration
comic writers. Ll. 152–3 mention characters in his plays.

And justify their author's want of sense.
Let 'em be all by thy own model made
Of dullness, and desire no foreign aid:
That they to future ages may be known,
Not copies drawn, but issue of thy own.   160
Nay, let thy men of wit too be the same,
All full of thee, and differing but in name;
But let no alien S—dl—y interpose
To lard with wit thy hungry *Epsom* prose.
And when false flowers of rhetoric thou wouldst cull,
Trust nature, do not labour to be dull;
But write thy best, and top; and in each line
Sir Formal's oratory will be thine:
Sir Formal, though unsought, attends thy quill,
And does thy northern dedications fill.   170
Nor let false friends seduce thy mind to fame,
By arrogating Jonson's hostile name.
Let father Flecknoe fire thy mind with praise,
And uncle Ogleby thy envy raise.
Thou art my blood, where Jonson has no part;
What share have we in nature or in art?
Where did his wit on learning fix a brand,
And rail at arts he did not understand?
Where made he love in Prince Nicander's vein,
Or swept the dust in *Psyche*'s humble strain?   180
Where sold he bargains, 'whip-stitch, kiss my arse,'
Promised a play and dwindled to a farce?
When did his muse from Fletcher scenes purloin,
As thou whole Eth'rege dost transfuse to thine?
But so transfused as oil on water's flow,
His always floats above, thine sinks below.
This is thy province, this thy wondrous way,
New humours to invent for each new play:

163–4 Sedley wrote a prologue for *Epsom Wells*, and was rumoured to have helped in the writing of the play.
168 Sir Formal] Sir Formal Trifle, in *The Virtuoso*, is full of flowery speech.
170 northern dedications] Shadwell made flattering dedications of his plays to the Duke and Duchess of Newcastle.
177–8 Shadwell ridicules experimental science in *The Virtuoso*.
179 Prince Nicander] A character in *Psyche*.
181 sold he bargains] To sell bargains means to reply mockingly, make a fool of. The coarse phrase is taken from *The Virtuoso*.

This is that boasted bias of thy mind,
190   By which one way, to dullness, 'tis inclined;
Which makes thy writings lean on one side still,
And in all changes that way bends thy will.
Nor let thy mountain-belly make pretence
Of likeness; thine's a tympany of sense.
A tun of man in thy large bulk is writ,
But sure thou'rt but a kilderkin of wit.
Like mine thy gentle numbers fccbly creep,
Thy tragic muse gives smiles, thy comic sleep.
With whate'er gall thou sett'st thyself to write,
200   Thy inoffensive satires never bite.
In thy felonious heart though venom lies,
It does but touch thy Irish pen and dies.
Thy genius calls thee not to purchase fame
In keen iambics, but mild anagram.
Leave writing plays, and choose for thy command
Some peaceful province in acrostic land.
There thou may'st wings display and altars raise,
And torture one poor word ten thousand ways.
Or if thou wouldst thy diff'rent talents suit,
210   Set thy own songs, and sing them to thy lute."
    He said: but his last words were scarcely heard;
For Bruce and Longvil had a trap prepared,
And down they sent the yet declaiming bard.
Sinking he left his drugget robe behind,
Borne upwards by a subterranean wind.
The mantle fell to the young prophet's part,
With double portion of his father's art.

189–92 A parody of the following lines in the Epilogue to *The Humorists*:

> A humour is the bias of the mind,
> By which with violence 'tis one way inclined,
> And makes our actions lean on one side still,
> And in all changes that way bends the will.

194 tympany] An empty swelling.
196 kilderkin] A much smaller cask than a tun.
204 keen iambics] Satiric verse.
206–7 Acrostics were poems shaped to represent their subjects, such as George Herbert's *The Altar*.
212–13 In *The Virtuoso* Bruce and Longvil drop Sir Formal Trifle through a trap door.
215 subterranean wind] A reference to a feature of Shadwell's operatic version of *The Tempest* (1674), Act II: 'Arise, arise ye subterranean winds,' etc.

ABSALOM AND ACHITOPHEL

A POEM

'Si propius stes
Te capiat magis.'

Horace, *Ars Poet*. 361

Absalom and Achitophel was published in November 1681, anonymously, although there was no doubt as to Dryden's authorship. It was an immediate success, for one thing as a well-timed assertion against the tumult and hysteria of the Popish Plot. The misfortunes of Charles's reign; years of anxiety about the succession of his Catholic brother James, Duke of York, to the throne; fomentation of rumour, especially by the infamous Titus Oates in 1678; and finally the murder in mysterious circumstances of the magistrate Sir Edmund Berry Godfrey on 12 October 1678: all produced conditions of fear and panic. Trials and executions of Catholics ensued until the later part of 1679.

In October 1680, still on a tide of this feeling, Parliament met in hopes of excluding James from the succession, with some support for his replacement by the Duke of Monmouth (Absalom of the poem). The move was thwarted by a dissolution, and a brief recall of Parliament in the royalist atmosphere of Oxford in March 1681. There was a great deal of controversy subsequently, but it tended increasingly in the King's favour; and in this Dryden's poem was influential.

TO THE READER

'Tis not my intention to make an apology for my poem: some will think it needs no excuse, and others will receive none. The design, I am sure, is honest; but he who draws his pen for one party must expect to make enemies of the other. For wit and fool are consequents of Whig and Tory;[1] and every man is a knave or an ass to the contrary side. There's a treasury of merits in the Fanatic church as well as in the Papist, and a pennyworth to be had of saintship, honesty, and poetry, for the lewd, the factious, and the block-heads; but the longest chapter in Deuteronomy has not curses enough for an Anti-Bromingham.[2] My comfort is, their manifest prejudice to my cause

---

[1] Whig and Tory] Abusive terms originally, denoting opposite sides in the exclusion controversy. [2] Anti-Bromingham] Anti-Whig.

will render their judgment of less authority against me. Yet if a poem have a genius, it will force its own reception in the world; for there's a sweetness in good verse, which tickles even while it hurts; and no man can be heartily angry with him who pleases him against his will. The commendation of adversaries is the greatest triumph of a writer, because it never comes unless extorted. But I can be satisfied on more easy terms: if I happen to please the more moderate sort, I shall be sure of an honest party and, in all probability, of the best judges; for the least concerned are commonly the least corrupt. And I confess I have laid in for those, by rebating the satire (where justice would allow it) from carrying too sharp an edge. They who can criticize so weakly as to imagine I have done my worst, may be convinced at their own cost that I can write severely with more ease than I can gently. I have but laughed at some men's follies, when I could have declaimed against their vices; and other men's virtues I have commended as freely as I have taxed their crimes. And now, if you are a malicious reader, I expect you should return upon me that I affect to be thought more impartial than I am; but if men are not to be judged by their professions, God forgive you commonwealth's-men[3] for professing so plausibly for the government. You cannot be so unconscionable as to charge me for not subscribing of my name; for that would reflect too grossly upon your own party, who never dare, though they have the advantage of a jury to secure them. If you like not my poem, the fault may possibly be in my writing (though 'tis hard for an author to judge against himself); but more probably 'tis in your morals, which cannot bear the truth of it. The violent on both sides will condemn the character of Absalom, as either too favourably or too hardly drawn; but they are not the violent whom I desire to please. The fault on the right hand is to extenuate, palliate, and indulge; and, to confess freely, I have endeavoured to commit it. Besides the respect which I owe his birth, I have a greater for his heroic virtues; and David himself could not be more tender of the young man's life, than I would be of his reputation. But since the most excellent natures are always the most easy and, as being such, are the soonest perverted by ill counsels, especially when baited with fame and glory, it is no more a wonder that he withstood not the temptations of Achitophel than it was for Adam not to have resisted the two devils, the serpent and the woman. The conclusion of the story I purposely forbore to prosecute, because I could not obtain from myself to show Absalom unfortunate. The frame of it was cut out but for a picture to the waist; and if the draught be so far true, 'tis as much as I designed.

Were I the inventor, who am only the historian, I should certainly

---

[3] commonwealth's-men] Whigs were accused of being anti-monarchist, of favouring a reversion to a commonwealth.

conclude the piece with the reconcilement of Absalom to David. And who knows but this may come to pass? Things were not brought to an extremity where I left the story: there seems yet to be room left for a composure; hereafter there may only be for pity. I have not so much as an uncharitable wish against Achitophel, but am content to be accused of a good-natured error, and to hope with Origen,[4] that the Devil himself may at last be saved. For which reason, in his poem, he is neither brought to set his house in order, nor to dispose of his person afterwards as he in wisdom shall think fit. God is infinitely merciful; and his viceregent is only not so, because he is not infinite.

The true end of satire is the amendment of vices by correction. And he who writes honestly is no more an enemy to the offender than the physician to the patient, when he prescribes harsh remedies to an inveterate disease; for those are only in order to prevent the chirurgeon's work of an *ense rescindendum*,[5] which I wish not to my very enemies. To conclude all: if the body politic have any analogy to the natural, in my weak judgment, an act of oblivion were as necessary in a hot distempered state as an opiate would be in a raging fever.

[4] Origen] C. 185–c. 254. A theologian and scholar of the early Greek Church, whose teachings allowed the possibility that Satan could repent.
[5] *Ense rescinderdum*] Having to be cut away with the knife.

ABSALOM AND ACHITOPHEL

In pious times, ere priestcraft did begin,
Before polygamy was made a sin;
When man on many multiplied his kind,
Ere one to one was cursedly confined;
When nature prompted, and no law denied
Promiscuous use of concubine and bride;
Then Israel's monarch after Heaven's own heart
His vigorous warmth did, variously, impart
To wives and slaves; and, wide as his command,
10   Scattered his Maker's image through the land.
Michal, of royal blood, the crown did wear,
A soil ungrateful to the tiller's care:
Not so the rest; for several mothers bore
To god-like David several sons before.
But since like slaves his bed they did ascend,
No true succession could their seed attend.
Of all this numerous progeny was none
So beautiful, so brave, as Absalon:
Whether, inspired by some diviner lust,
20   His father got him with a greater gust;
Or that his conscious destiny made way
By manly beauty to imperial sway.
Early in foreign fields he won renown,
With kings and states allied to Israel's crown:
In peace the thoughts of war he could remove
And seemed as he were only born for love.

Title] The Biblical story of Absalom's rebellion against David, in conspiracy with David's counsellor Achitophel, is in II Samuel.
11 Michal] Charles's wife, Catherine of Braganza (1638–1705), who bore him no children.
18 Absalon] James, Duke of Monmouth, illegitimate son of Charles and Lucy Walters, born in 1658. He had great personal charm and received much fondness and preference from the King. From 1679, following military successes, he put himself forward boldly for the succession, with great popular support.

Whate'er he did was done with so much ease,
In him alone 'twas natural to please:
His motions all accompanied with grace;
And Paradise was opened in his face.   30
With secret joy indulgent David viewed
His youthful image in his son renewed:
To all his wishes nothing he denied,
And made the charming Annabel his bride.
What faults he had (for who from faults is free?)
His father could not, or he would not see.
Some warm excesses, which the law forbore,
Were construed youth that purged by boiling o'er;
And Amnon's murther, by a specious name,
Was called a just revenge for injured fame.   40
Thus praised and loved, the noble youth remained,
While David, undisturbed, in Sion reigned.
But life can never be sincerely blest:
Heaven punishes the bad, and proves the best.
The Jews, a headstrong, moody, murmuring race,
As ever tried th' extent and stretch of grace;
God's pampered people whom, debauched with ease,
No king could govern, nor no God could please;
(Gods they had tried of every shape and size
That godsmiths could produce or priests devise:)   50
These Adam-wits, too fortunately free,
Began to dream they wanted liberty;
And when no rule, no precedent was found
Of men by laws less circumscribed and bound,
They led their wild desires to woods and caves
And thought that all but savages were slaves.
They who, when Saul was dead, without a blow
Made foolish Ishbosheth the crown forego;
Who banished David did from Hebron bring,

34 Annabel] The Countess of Buccleuth.
39 Amnon's murther] Thought to refer to an attack on Sir John Coventry in December 1670, in which his nose was slit in revenge for a sarcastic remark in Parliament about the King; or possibly to the killing of a watchman by Monmouth in 1671.
42 Sion] London.   43 sincerely] Wholly.   45 The Jews] The English.
51 Adam-wits] Unruly libertarians, impatient of any restraint.
57–8 II Samuel 3–4. The parallel is with Oliver Cromwell and his son Richard who succeeded him briefly in 1658.
59 Hebron] Brussels, whence Charles returned in 1660; or Scotland, where he was crowned in 1651.

60   And with a general shout proclaimed him King:
      Those very Jews who, at their very best,
      Their humour more than loyalty exprest,
      Now wondered why so long they had obeyed
      An idol monarch which their hands had made;
      Thought they might ruin him they could create,
      Or melt him to that golden calf, a State.
      But these were random bolts; no formed design
      Nor interest made the factious crowd to join:
      The sober part of Israel, free from stain,
70   Well knew the value of a peaceful reign;
      And, looking backward with a wise affright,
      Saw seams of wounds, dishonest to the sight:
      In contemplation of whose ugly scars
      They cursed the memory of civil wars.
      The moderate sort of men, thus qualified,
      Inclined the balance to the better side;
      And David's mildness managed it so well,
      The bad found no occasion to rebel.
      But when to sin our biassed nature leans,
80   The careful Devil is still at hand with means,
      And providently pimps for ill desires:
      The Good Old Cause, revived, a plot requires.
      Plots, true or false, are necessary things,
      To raise up commonwealths, and ruin kings.

         Th' inhabitants of old Jerusalem
      Were Jebusites; the town so called from them;
      And theirs the native right——
      But when the chosen people grew more strong,
      The rightful cause at length became the wrong;
90   And every loss the men of Jebus bore,
      They still were thought God's enemies the more.
      Thus worn and weakened, well or ill content,
      Submit they must to David's government:
      Impoverished and deprived of all command,

66 a State] A commonwealth or republic.
72 dishonest] Unseemly, hideous.
82 The Good Old Cause] The Puritan rebellion against the monarchy.
85 Jerusalem] London.
86 Jebusites] The Roman Catholics, in pre-Reformation times.
88 chosen people] Protestants.

Their taxes doubled as they lost their land;
And, what was harder yet to flesh and blood,
Their gods disgraced, and burnt like common wood.
This set the heathen priesthood in a flame,
For priests of all religions are the same:
Of whatsoe'er descent their godhead be,   100
Stock, stone, or other homely pedigree,
In his defence his servants are as bold
As if he had been born of beaten gold.
The Jewish Rabbins, though their enemies,
In this conclude them honest men and wise:
For 'twas their duty, all the learned think,
T'espouse his cause by whom they eat and drink.
From hence began that Plot, the nation's curse,
Bad in itself, but represented worse;
Raised in extremes, and in extremes decried;   110
With oaths affirmed, with dying vows denied;
Not weighed or winnowed by the multitude,
But swallowed in the mass, unchewed and crude.
Some truth there was, but dashed and brewed with lies,
To please the fools and puzzle all the wise.
Succeeding times did equal folly call,
Believing nothing, or believing all.
Th' Egyptian rites the Jebusites embraced,
Where gods were recommended by their taste.
Such savoury deities must needs be good,   120
As served at once for worship and for food.
By force they could not introduce these gods,
For ten to one in former days was odds;
So fraud was used (the sacrificer's trade):
Fools are more hard to conquer than persuade.
Their busy teachers mingled with the Jews,
And raked for converts even the court and stews:
Which Hebrew priests the more unkindly took,
Because the fleece accompanies the flock.

104 Jewish Rabbins] Learned clergymen of the Church of England.
108 that Plot] The Popish Plot.
113 crude] Undigested.
118 Egyptian rites] French Catholic practices. The doctrine of transubstantiation is referred
to in ll. 119–21.
123 ten to one] The proportion of Protestants to Catholics in England.
127 stews] Brothels.

130   Some thought they God's anointed meant to slay
       By guns, invented since full many a day:
       Our author swears it not; but who can know
       How far the Devil and Jebusites may go?
       This plot, which failed for want of common sense,
       Had yet a deep and dangerous consequence;
       For, as when raging fevers boil the blood,
       The standing lake soon floats into a flood,
       And every hostile humour, which before
       Slept quiet in its channels, bubbles o'er;
140   So several factions from this first ferment
       Work up to foam, and threat the government.
       Some by their friends, more by themselves thought wise,
       Opposed the power to which they could not rise.
       Some had in courts been great and, thrown from thence,
       Like fiends were hardened in impenitence.
       Some, by their Monarch's fatal mercy grown
       From pardoned rebels kinsmen to the throne,
       Were raised in power and public office high:
       Strong bands, if bands ungrateful men could tie.
150   Of these the false Achitophel was first;
       A name to all succeeding ages curst:
       For close designs and crooked counsels fit,
       Sagacious, bold, and turbulent of wit,
       Restless, unfixed in principles and place,
       In power unpleased, impatient of disgrace:
       A fiery soul, which, working out its way,
       Fretted the pigmy body to decay,
       And o'er-informed the tenement of clay.
       A daring pilot in extremity;
160   Pleased with the danger, when the waves went high
       He sought the storms; but, for a calm unfit,
       Would steer too nigh the sands, to boast his wit.
       Great wits are sure to madness near allied,
       And thin partitions do their bounds divide:
       Else, why should he, with wealth and honour blest,
       Refuse his age the needful hours of rest?
       Punish a body which he could not please;

150 Achitophel] Anthony Ashley Cooper (1621–83), first Earl of Shaftesbury, an active
politician who became the leader of the opposition to the court and of the movement to
exclude the Duke of York. He was arrested in July 1681 on a charge of treason, which was
dismissed by a grand jury on 24 November, a few days after the publication of this poem.

Bankrupt of life, yet prodigal of ease?
And all to leave what with his toil he won
To that unfeathered two-legged thing, a son;   170
Got, while his soul did huddled notions try;
And born a shapeless lump, like anarchy.
In friendship false, implacable in hate,
Resolved to ruin or to rule the state.
To compass this the triple bond he broke,
The pillars of the public safety shook,
And fitted Israel for a foreign yoke:
Then, seized with fear, yet still affecting fame,
Usurped a patriot's all-atoning name.
So easy still it proves in factious times   180
With public zeal to cancel private crimes.
How safe is treason, and how sacred ill,
Where none can sin against the people's will:
Where crowds can wink, and no offence be known,
Since in another's guilt they find their own.
Yet fame deserved no enemy can grudge;
The statesman we abhor, but praise the judge.
In Israel's courts ne'er sat an Abbethdin
With more discerning eyes, or hands more clean:
Unbribed, unsought, the wretched to redress,   190
Swift of despatch and easy of access.
Oh! had he been content to serve the crown
With virtues only proper to the gown;
Or had the rankness of the soil been freed
From cockle that oppressed the noble seed:
David for him his tuneful harp had strung
And Heaven had wanted one immortal song.
But wild ambition loves to slide, not stand,
And fortune's ice prefers to virtue's land.
Achitophel, grown weary to possess   200
A lawful fame, and lazy happiness,
Disdained the golden fruit to gather free,
And lent the crowd his arm to shake the tree.

170 His son was untalented.
175 the triple bond] The Triple Alliance with Holland and Sweden formed in 1668; which,
however, was subverted by Charles himself by a secret treaty with France in 1670.
179 'Patriot' had acquired the pejorative sense of one who opposed the King. Cf. ll. 965-6.
188 Abbethdin] A presiding officer of the high court of justice of the Jews.
197 wanted] Relinquished.

Now, manifest of crimes contrived long since,
He stood at bold defiance with his Prince;
Held up the buckler of the people's cause
Against the crown, and skulked behind the laws.
The wished occasion of the Plot he takes;
Some circumstances finds, but more he makes;
210   By buzzing emissaries fills the ears
Of listening crowds with jealousies and fears
Of arbitrary counsels brought to light,
And proves the King himself a Jebusite.
Weak arguments! which yet he knew full well
Were strong with people easy to rebel.
For, governed by the moon, the giddy Jews
Tread the same track when she the prime renews:
And once in twenty years, their scribes record,
By natural instinct they change their lord.
220   Achitophel still wants a chief, and none
Was found so fit as warlike Absalon:
Not that he wished his greatness to create,
(For politicians neither love nor hate;)
But, for he knew his title not allowed,
Would keep him still depending on the crowd:
That kingly power, thus ebbing out, might be
Drawn to the dregs of a democracy.
Him he attempts with studied arts to please,
And sheds his venom in such words as these:

230   "Auspicious prince! at whose nativity
Some royal planet ruled the southern sky;
Thy longing country's darling and desire;
Their cloudy pillar and their guardian fire;
Their second Moses, whose extended wand
Divides the seas and shows the promised land,
Whose dawning day in every distant age
Has exercised the sacred prophet's rage:
The people's prayer, the glad diviner's theme,
The young men's vision, and the old men's dream!
240   Thee, Saviour, thee, the nation's vows confess,
And, never satisfied with seeing, bless:

217 prime] 'Confusedly explained as the lunar cycle of 19 years' (*OED*). Dryden would be
thinking of events in England at recent intervals of about twenty years: the beginning of the
Civil War in 1642, and the Restoration in 1660.

Swift unbespoken pomps thy steps proclaim,
And stammering babes are taught to lisp thy name.
How long wilt thou the general joy detain,
Starve and defraud the people of thy reign?
Content ingloriously to pass thy days,
Like one of virtue's fools that feeds on praise;
Till thy fresh glories, which now shine so bright,
Grow stale and tarnish with our daily sight.
Believe me, royal youth, thy fruit must be   250
Or gathered ripe, or rot upon the tree.
Heaven has to all allotted, soon or late,
Some lucky revolution of their fate:
Whose motions if we watch and guide with skill,
(For human good depends on human will,)
Our fortune rolls as from a smooth descent,
And from the first impression takes the bent:
But, if unseized, she glides away like wind,
And leaves repenting folly far behind.
Now, now she meets you with a glorious prize,   260
And spreads her locks before her as she flies.
Had thus old David, from whose loins you spring,
Not dared, when fortune called him, to be King,
At Gath an exile he might still remain,
And Heaven's anointing oil had been in vain.
Let his successful youth your hopes engage,
But shun th' example of declining age:
Behold him setting in his western skies,
The shadows lengthening as the vapours rise.
He is not now, as when on Jordan's sand   270
The joyful people thronged to see him land,
Cov'ring the beach and black'ning all the strand;
But, like the Prince of Angels, from his height
Comes tumbling downward with diminished light:
Betrayed by one poor plot to public scorn,
(Our only blessing since his curst return;)
Those heaps of people, which one sheaf did bind,
Blown off and scattered by a puff of wind.
What strength can he to your designs oppose,
Naked of friends, and round beset with foes?   280
If Pharaoh's doubtful succour he should use,

264 Gath] Brussels.   270 Jordan's sand] Dover.
281 Pharaoh] Louis XIV of France.

A foreign aid would more incense the Jews:
Proud Egypt would dissembled friendship bring,
Foment the war, but not support the King:
Nor would the royal party e'er unite
With Pharaoh's arms, t'assist the Jebusite;
Or, if they should, their interest soon would break,
And with such odious aid make David weak.
All sorts of men by my successful arts
290   Abhorring kings, estrange their altered hearts
From David's rule: and 'tis the general cry,
Religion, commonwealth, and liberty.
If you, as champion of the public good,
Add to their arms a chief of royal blood,
What may not Israel hope, and what applause
Might such a general gain by such a cause?
Not barren praise alone, that gaudy flower
Fair only to the sight, but solid power:
And nobler is a limited command,
300   Giv'n by the love of all your native land,
Than a successive title, long and dark,
Drawn from the mouldy rolls of Noah's ark."

        What cannot praise effect in mighty minds,
When flattery soothes and when ambition blinds!
Desire of power, on earth a vicious weed,
Yet, sprung from high, is of celestial seed:
In God 'tis glory; and when men aspire,
'Tis but a spark too much of heavenly fire.
Th' ambitious youth, too covetous of fame,
310   Too full of angel's metal in his frame,
Unwarily was led from virtue's ways,
Made drunk with honour, and debauched with praise.
Half loth, and half consenting to the ill,
(For loyal blood within him struggled still,)
He thus replied: "And what pretence have I
To take up arms for public liberty?
My father governs with unquestioned right,
The faith's defender, and mankind's delight;
Good, gracious, just, observant of the laws;
320   And Heav'n by wonders has espoused his cause.

310 angel's metal] A pun on 'angel' (a coin) and 'mettle'.

Whom has he wronged in all his peaceful reign?
Who sues for justice to his throne in vain?
What millions has he pardoned of his foes,
Whom just revenge did to his wrath expose?
Mild, easy, humble, studious of our good,
Inclined to mercy and averse from blood.
If mildness ill with stubborn Israel suit,
His crime is God's beloved attribute.
What could he gain his people to betray,
Or change his right for arbitrary sway?   330
Let haughty Pharaoh curse with such a reign
His fruitful Nile, and yoke a servile train.
If David's rule Jerusalem displease,
The dog-star heats their brains to this disease.
Why then should I, encouraging the bad,
Turn rebel, and run popularly mad?
Were he a tyrant who, by lawless might,
Oppressed the Jews and raised the Jebusite,
Well might I mourn; but nature's holy bands
Would curb my spirits and restrain my hands: 340
The people might assert their liberty;
But what was right in them were crime in me.
His favour leaves me nothing to require,
Prevents my wishes, and outruns desire;
What more can I expect while David lives?
All but his kingly diadem he gives;
And that" — But there he paused; then sighing, said —
"Is justly destined for a worthier head.
For when my father from his toils shall rest,
And late augment the number of the blest,   350
His lawful issue shall the throne ascend,
Or the collateral line, where that shall end.
His brother, though oppressed with vulgar spite,
Yet dauntless and secure of native right,
Of every royal virtue stands possest,
Still dear to all the bravest and the best.
His courage foes, his friends his truth proclaim,
His loyalty the King, the world his fame.

334 dog-star] Sirius, anciently supposed to cause great heat on earth.
344 Prevents] Anticipates.
353 brother] James, Duke of York.

His mercy even th' offending crowd will find,
360   For sure he comes of a forgiving kind.
Why should I then repine at Heaven's decree,
Which gives me no pretence to royalty?
Yet O that Fate, propitiously inclined,
Had raised my birth, or had debased my mind;
To my large soul not all her treasure lent,
And then betrayed it to a mean descent!
I find, I find my mounting spirits bold,
And David's part disdains my mother's mould.
Why am I scanted by a niggard birth?
370   My soul disclaims the kindred of her earth,
And, made for empire, whispers me within,
Desire of greatness is a god-like sin."

    Him staggering so when Hell's dire agent found,
While fainting virtue scarce maintained her ground,
He pours fresh forces in, and thus replies:
    "Th' eternal God, supremely good and wise,
Imparts not these prodigious gifts in vain:
What wonders are reserved to bless your reign!
Against your will your arguments have shown,
380   Such virtue's only given to guide a throne.
Not that your father's mildness I condemn;
But manly force becomes the diadem.
'Tis true he grants the people all they crave,
And more perhaps than subjects ought to have:
For lavish grants suppose a monarch tame,
And more his goodness than his wit proclaim.
But when should people strive their bonds to break,
If not when kings are negligent or weak?
Let him give on till he can give no more,
390   The thrifty Sanhedrin shall keep him poor;
And every shekel which he can receive
Shall cost a limb of his prerogative.
To ply him with new plots shall be my care,
Or plunge him deep in some expensive war;
Which when his treasure can no more supply,
He must with the remains of kingship buy.
His faithful friends our jealousies and fears

390 Sanhedrin] The supreme Jewish legislative council: Parliament.

Call Jebusites, and Pharaoh's pensioners;
Whom when our fury from his aid has torn,
He shall be naked left to public scorn.   400
The next successor, whom I fear and hate,
My arts have made obnoxious to the State,
Turned all his virtues to his overthrow,
And gained our elders to pronounce a foe.
His right, for sums of necessary gold,
Shall first be pawned, and afterwards be sold;
Till time shall ever-wanting David draw
To pass your doubtful title into law.
If not, the people have a right supreme
To make their kings; for kings are made for them.   410
All empire is no more than pow'r in trust,
Which, when resumed, can be no longer just.
Succession, for the general good designed,
In its own wrong a nation cannot bind:
If altering that the people can relieve,
Better one suffer than a nation grieve.
The Jews well know their power: ere Saul they chose,
God was their King, and God they durst depose.
Urge now your piety, your filial name,
A father's right, and fear of future fame;   420
The public good, that universal call,
To which even Heav'n submitted, answers all.
Nor let his love enchant your generous mind;
'Tis Nature's trick to propagate her kind.
Our fond begetters, who would never die,
Love but themselves in their posterity.
Or let his kindness by th' effects be tried,
Or let him lay his vain pretence aside.
God said he loved your father; could he bring
A better proof than to anoint him king?   430
It surely showed he loved the shepherd well
Who gave so fair a flock as Israel.
Would David have you thought his darling son?
What means he then to alienate the crown?
The name of godly he may blush to bear:

398 Pharaoh's pensioners] Charles was (rightly) suspected of receiving large sums of money
from the French king.
417–18 Alluding to Cromwell (Saul) and the divine right of the deposed Charles I.
434 alienate] Transfer ownership.

'Tis after God's own heart to cheat his heir.
He to his brother gives supreme command,
To you a legacy of barren land;
Perhaps th' old harp on which he thrums his lays,
440   Or some dull Hebrew ballad in your praise.
Then the next heir, a prince severe and wise,
Already looks on you with jealous eyes;
Sees through the thin disguises of your arts,
And marks your progress in the people's hearts.
Though now his mighty soul its grief contains,
He meditates revenge who least complains;
And like a lion, slumb'ring in the way,
Or sleep dissembling, while he waits his prey,
His fearless foes within his distance draws,
450   Constrains his roaring and contracts his paws;
Till at the last, his time for fury found,
He shoots with sudden vengeance from the ground;
The prostrate vulgar passes o'er and spares,
But with a lordly rage his hunters tears.
Your case no tame expedients will afford;
Resolve on death, or conquest by the sword,
Which for no less a stake than life you draw;
And self-defence is Nature's eldest law.
Leave the warm people no considering time,
460   For then rebellion may be thought a crime.
Prevail yourself of what occasion gives,
But try your title while your father lives;
And, that your arms may have a fair pretence,
Proclaim you take them in the King's defence;
Whose sacred life each minute would expose
To plots, from seeming friends, and secret foes.
And who can sound the depth of David's soul?
Perhaps his fear his kindness may control:
He fears his brother, though he loves his son,
470   For plighted vows too late to be undone.
If so, by force he wishes to be gained,
Like women's lechery, to seem constrained.
Doubt not: but, when he most affects the frown,
Commit a pleasing rape upon the crown.

467–74 Monmouth's 'doubtful title' (l. 408) was being helped into credence by a rumour
that he was legitimate, and the king was obliged in 1679 to declare the contrary: that there
had been no secret marriage with Lucy Walters.

Secure his person to secure your cause:
They who possess the Prince, possess the laws." — *This but what Achit. wants to do to A.B.*

  He said, and this advice above the rest
With Absalom's mild nature suited best:
Unblamed of life (ambition set aside),
Not stained with cruelty, nor puffed with pride,   480
How happy had he been, if Destiny
Had higher placed his birth, or not so high!
His kingly virtues might have claimed a throne,
And blessed all other countries but his own:
But charming greatness since so few refuse,
'Tis juster to lament him than accuse.
Strong were his hopes a rival to remove,
With blandishments to gain the public love;
To head the faction while their zeal was hot,
And popularly prosecute the plot.   490
To farther this, Achitophel unites
The malcontents of all the Israelites;
Whose differing parties he could wisely join,
For several ends, to serve the same design:
The best, (and of the princes some were such,)
Who thought the power of monarchy too much;
Mistaken men, and patriots in their hearts;
Not wicked, but seduced by impious arts.
By these the springs of property were bent,
And wound so high, they cracked the government.   500
The next for interest sought t'embroil the state,
To sell their duty at a dearer rate;
And make their Jewish markets of the throne,
Pretending public good to serve their own.
Others thought kings an useless heavy load,
Who cost too much, and did too little good.
These were for laying honest David by,
On principles of pure good husbandry.
With them joined all th' haranguers of the throng,
That thought to get preferment by the tongue.   510
Who follow next, a double danger bring,
Not only hating David, but the King:
The Solymaean rout, well versed of old
In godly faction and in treason bold;

513 the Solymaean rout] The London mob. Solyma is another name for Jerusalem.

Cowering and quaking at the conqueror's sword,
But lofty to a lawful prince restored;
Saw with disdain an Ethnic plot begun,
And scorned by Jebusites to be outdone.
Hot Levites headed these; who, pulled before
520   From th' ark, which in the Judges' days they bore,
Resumed their cant, and with a zealous cry
Pursued their old beloved theocracy,
Where Sanhedrin and priest enslaved the nation,
And justified their spoils by inspiration:
For who so fit for reign as Aaron's race,
If once dominion they could found in grace?
These led the pack; though not of surest scent,
Yet deepest mouthed against the government.
A numerous host of dreaming saints succeed
530   Of the true old enthusiastic breed:
'Gainst form and order they their power employ,
Nothing to build and all things to destroy.
But far more numerous was the herd of such
Who think too little and who talk too much.
These, out of mere instinct, they knew not why,
Adored their fathers' God and property;
And, by the same blind benefit of Fate,
The Devil and the Jebusite did hate:
Born to be saved, even in their own despite,
540   Because they could not help believing right.
Such were the tools; but a whole Hydra more
Remains, of sprouting heads too long to score.
Some of their chiefs were princes of the land:
In the first rank of these did Zimri stand;
A man so various that he seemed to be
Not one, but all mankind's epitome:
Stiff in opinions, always in the wrong,
Was everything by starts, and nothing long;
But, in the course of one revolving moon,
550   Was chymist, fiddler, statesman, and buffoon;

517 Ethnic] Gentile, i.e. Popish Plot.
519 Levites] Nonconforming clergymen.
530 enthusiastic] Profusely zealous in religion.
544 Zimri] George Villiers (1628–87), second Duke of Buckingham. Dryden's portrait matches other accounts of Buckingham as dissolute, inconsistent, and spendthrift. Like Shaftesbury, he was active in stirring up popular feeling in London.

Then all for women, painting, rhyming, drinking,
Besides ten thousand freaks that died in thinking.
Blest madman, who could every hour employ
With something new to wish or to enjoy!
Railing and praising were his usual themes,
And both (to shew his judgment) in extremes:
So over violent, or over civil,
That every man with him was God or Devil.
In squandering wealth was his peculiar art:
Nothing went unrewarded but desert.   560
Beggared by fools, whom still he found too late,
He had his jest, and they had his estate.
He laughed himself from Court; then sought relief
By forming parties, but could ne'er be chief;
For, spite of him, the weight of business fell
On Absalom and wise Achitophel:
Thus, wicked but in will, of means bereft,
He left not faction, but of that was left.

Titles and names 'twere tedious to rehearse
Of lords below the dignity of verse.   570
Wits, warriors, commonwealth's-men, were the best:
Kind husbands and mere nobles all the rest.
And therefore, in the name of dullness, be
The well-hung Balaam and cold Caleb free;
And canting Nadab let oblivion damn,
Who made new porridge for the paschal lamb.
Let friendship's holy band some names assure;
Some their own worth, and some let scorn secure.
Nor shall the rascal rabble here have place,
Whom kings no titles gave, and God no grace: 580
Not bull-faced Jonas, who could statutes draw
To mean rebellion, and make treason law.
But he, though bad, is followed by a worse,
The wretch who Heaven's anointed dared to curse:
Shimei, whose youth did early promise bring

574 Balaam] Identified as Theopilus Hastings (1650–1701), seventh Earl of Huntingdon.
Caleb] Arthur Capel (1632–83), Earl of Essex.
575 Nadab] William, Lord Howard of Escrick (1626–94).
581 Jonas] Sir William Jones (1631–82).
585 Shimei] Slingsby Bethel (1617–97), a sheriff of London and a republican. He was a successful merchant in leather.

Of zeal to God, and hatred to his King,
Did wisely from expensive sins refrain,
And never broke the Sabbath, but for gain:
Nor ever was he known an oath to vent,
590   Or curse, unless against the government.
Thus heaping wealth, by the most ready way
Among the Jews, which was to cheat and pray,
The city, to reward his pious hate
Against his master, chose him magistrate.
His hand a vare of justice did uphold;
His neck was loaded with a chain of gold.
During his office treason was no crime:
The sons of Belial had a glorious time;
For Shimei, though not prodigal of pelf,
600   Yet loved his wicked neighbour as himself.
When two or three were gathered to declaim
Against the monarch of Jerusalem,
Shimei was always in the midst of them:
And, if they cursed the King when he was by,
Would rather curse than break good company.
If any durst his factious friends accuse,
He packed a jury of dissenting Jews;
Whose fellow-feeling in the godly cause
Would free the suffering saint from human laws:
610   For laws are only made to punish those
Who serve the King, and to protect his foes.
If any leisure time he had from power,
(Because 'tis sin to misemploy an hour,)
His business was by writing to persuade
That kings were useless, and a clog to trade:
And, that his noble style he might refine,
No Rechabite more shunned the fumes of wine.
Chaste were his cellars, and his shrieval board
The grossness of a city feast abhorred:
620   His cooks with long disuse their trade forgot;
Cool was his kitchen, though his brains were hot.
Such frugal virtue malice may accuse;
But sure 'twas necessary to the Jews:

595 vare] A rod or staff carried as a symbol of office.
598 sons of Belial] Depraved and rebellious men.
617 Rechabite] Abstainer from wine: cf. Jeremiah 35: 14.
624 towns once burnt] Referring to the Great Fire of London of 1666.

For towns once burnt such magistrates require
As dare not tempt God's providence by fire.
With spiritual food he fed his servants well,
But free from flesh that made the Jews rebel;
And Moses' laws he held in more account
For forty days of fasting in the mount.
To speak the rest, who better are forgot,   630
Would tire a well-breathed witness of the Plot.
Yet, Corah, thou shalt from oblivion pass;
Erect thyself, thou monumental brass:
High as the serpent of thy metal made,
While nations stand secure beneath thy shade.
What though his birth were base, yet comets rise
From earthy vapours ere they shine in skies.
Prodigious actions may as well be done
By weaver's issue as by prince's son.
This arch-attester for the public good   640
By that one deed ennobles all his blood.
Who ever asked the witnesses' high race,
Whose oath with martyrdom did Stephen grace?
Ours was a Levite, and as times went then,
His tribe were God Almighty's gentlemen.
Sunk were his eyes, his voice was harsh and loud,
Sure signs he neither choleric was nor proud:
His long chin proved his wit; his saint-like grace
A church vermilion, and a Moses' face.
His memory, miraculously great,   650
Could plots, exceeding man's belief, repeat;
Which therefore cannot be accounted lies,
For human wit could never such devise.
Some future truths are mingled in his book;
But where the witness failed, the prophet spoke:
Some things like visionary flights appear;
The spirit caught him up, the Lord knows where;
And gave him his rabbinical degree,

632 Corah] (cf. Korah: Numbers 16) Titus Oates (1649–1705). His education and earlier career, at Cambridge and in orders, comprise transgression and failure. But he drove on the Plot for three years with astonishing contrivance, drawing on some acquaintance he had made with Jesuits in London and on the continent. His persecutions were halted in the summer of 1681; and in 1685 he was sentenced to three years' imprisonment.
633 monumental brass] Comparing Oates with the brazen serpent made by Moses.
658 rabbinical degree] Oates claimed, falsely, a degree from the University of Salamanca.

Unknown to foreign University.
His judgment yet his memory did excel;
Which pieced his wondrous evidence so well,
And suited to the temper of the times,
Then groaning under Jebusitic crimes.
Let Israel's foes suspect his heav'nly call,
And rashly judge his writ apocryphal;
Our laws for such affronts have forfeits made:
He takes his life, who takes away his trade.
Were I myself in witness Corah's place,
The wretch who did me such a dire disgrace
Should whet my memory, though once forgot,
To make him an appendix of my plot.
His zeal to Heav'n made him his Prince despise,
And load his person with indignities:
But zeal peculiar privilege affords,
Indulging latitude to deeds and words;
And Corah might for Agag's murder call,
In terms as coarse as Samuel used to Saul.
What others in his evidence did join,
(The best that could be had for love or coin,)
In Corah's own predicament will fall:
For *witness* is a common name to all.

Surrounded thus with friends of every sort,
Deluded Absalom forsakes the court;
Impatient of high hopes, urged with renown,
And fired with near possession of a crown.
Th' admiring crowd are dazzled with surprise,
And on his goodly person feed their eyes.
His joy concealed, he sets himself to show,
On each side bowing popularly low:
His looks, his gestures, and his words he frames,
And with familiar ease repeats their names.
Thus, formed by nature, furnished out with arts,
He glides unfelt into their secret hearts:
Then with a kind compassionating look,
And sighs, bespeaking pity ere he spoke,

676 Agag] Identified as Sir Edmund Berry Godfrey (see headnote); or Lord Stafford, one of
Oates's victims.
680 predicament] Designation.
695 bespeaking] Requesting.

Few words he said, but easy those and fit,
More slow than Hybla-drops, and far more sweet.
   "I mourn, my countrymen, your lost estate,
Though far unable to prevent your fate:
Behold a banished man, for your dear cause   700
Exposed a prey to arbitrary laws!
Yet Oh! that I alone could be undone,
Cut off from empire, and no more a son!
Now all your liberties a spoil are made;
Egypt and Tyrus intercept your trade,
And Jebusites your sacred rites invade.
My father, whom with reverence yet I name,
Charmed into ease, is careless of his fame;
And, bribed with petty sums of foreign gold,
Is grown in Bathsheba's embraces old;   710
Exalts his enemies, his friends destroys,
And all his pow'r against himself employs.
He gives, and let him give, my right away;
But why should he his own and yours betray?
He only, he can make the nation bleed,
And he alone from my revenge is freed.
Take then my tears (with that he wiped his eyes),
'Tis all the aid my present power supplies:
No court-informer can these arms accuse;
These arms may sons against their fathers use: 720
And 'tis my wish, the next successor's reign
May make no other Israelite complain."

   Youth, beauty, graceful action, seldom fail,
But common interest always will prevail;
And pity never ceases to be shown
To him who makes the people's wrongs his own.
The crowd (that still believe their kings oppress)
With lifted hands their young Messiah bless:
Who now begins his progress to ordain
With chariots, horsemen, and a numerous train;   730

697 Hybla-drops] The fabled honey from Hybla in Sicily.
705 Egypt and Tyrus] France and Holland.
710 Bathsheba] Louise de Kéroualle, Duchess of Portsmouth, one of the king's mistresses,
thought to be an agent of Louis XIV.
729 his progress] Monmouth went on a triumphal progress in the west in the summer of
1680.

From east to west his glories he displays,
And, like the sun, the promised land surveys.
Fame runs before him as the morning star,
And shouts of joy salute him from afar;
Each house receives him as a guardian god,
And consecrates the place of his abode.
But hospitable treats did most commend
Wise Issachar, his wealthy western friend.
This moving court that caught the people's eyes,
740   And seemed but pomp, did other ends disguise:
Achitophel had formed it, with intent
To sound the depths, and fathom, where it went,
The people's hearts, distinguish friends from foes,
And try their strength before they came to blows.
Yet all was coloured with a smooth pretence
Of specious love, and duty to their prince.
Religion, and redress of grievances,
Two names that always cheat and always please,
Are often urged; and good king David's life
750   Endangered by a brother and a wife.
Thus, in a pageant show, a plot is made,
And peace itself is war in masquerade.
Oh foolish Israel! never warned by ill!
Still the same bait, and circumvented still!
Did ever men forsake their present ease,
In midst of health imagine a disease;
Take pains contingent mischiefs to foresee,
Make heirs for monarchs, and for God decree?
What shall we think? Can people give away,
760   Both for themselves and sons, their native sway?
Then they are left defenceless to the sword
Of each unbounded, arbitrary lord;
And laws are vain, by which we right enjoy,
If kings unquestioned can those laws destroy.
Yet, if the crowd be judge of fit and just,
And kings are only officers in trust,
Then this resuming covenant was declared
When kings were made, or is for ever barred.
If those who gave the sceptre could not tie

738 Wise Issachar] Thomas Thynne (1648–82), a supporter of Monmouth. 'Wise' is ironic.
749–50 Oates accused both the Duke of York and the Queen of plots against the king's life.

By their own deed their own posterity,   770
How then could Adam bind his future race?
How could his forfeit on mankind take place?
Or how could heavenly justice damn us all
Who ne'er consented to our father's fall?
Then kings are slaves to those whom they command,
And tenants to their people's pleasure stand.
Add, that the power for property allowed,
Is mischievously seated in the crowd;
For who can be secure of private right,
If sovereign sway may be dissolved by might?   780
Nor is the people's judgment always true:
The most may err as grossly as the few,
And faultless kings run down, by common cry,
For vice, oppression, and for tyranny.
What standard is there in a fickle rout,
Which, flowing to the mark, runs faster out?
Nor only crowds, but Sanhedrins may be
Infected with this public lunacy;
And share the madness of rebellious times,
To murder monarchs for imagined crimes.   790
If they may give and take whene'er they please,
Not kings alone (the Godhead's images),
But government itself at length must fall
To nature's state, where all have right to all.
Yet, grant our lords the people kings can make,
What prudent men a settled throne would shake?
For whatsoe'er their sufferings were before,
That change they covet makes them suffer more.
All other errors but disturb a state,
But innovation is the blow of fate.   800
If ancient fabrics nod, and threat to fall,
To patch the flaws and buttress up the wall,
Thus far 'tis duty: but here fix the mark;
For all beyond it is to touch our ark.
To change foundations, cast the frame anew,
Is work for rebels who base ends pursue,
At once divine and human laws control,
And mend the parts by ruin of the whole.

800 innovation] Revolution.
804 touch our ark] Commit sacrilege.

The tampering world is subject to this curse,
810   To physic their disease into a worse.

        Now what relief can righteous David bring?
        How fatal 'tis to be too good a king!
        Friends he has few, so high the madness grows;
        Who dare be such must be the people's foes.
        Yet some there were, ev'n in the worst of days;
        Some let me name, and naming is to praise.

        In this short file Barzillai first appears;
        Barzillai, crowned with honour and with years.
        Long since, the rising rebels he withstood
820   In regions waste, beyond the Jordan's flood:
        Unfortunately brave to buoy the state,
        But sinking underneath his master's fate.
        In exile with his godlike prince he mourned,
        For him he suffered, and with him returned.
        The court he practised, not the courtier's art:
        Large was his wealth, but larger was his heart,
        Which well the noblest objects knew to choose,
        The fighting warrior, and recording Muse.
        His bed could once a fruitful issue boast;
830   Now more than half a father's name is lost.
        His eldest hope, with every grace adorned,
        By me (so Heav'n will have it) always mourned,
        And always honoured, snatched in manhood's prime
        By'unequal fates, and Providence's crime:
        Yet not before the goal of honour won,   ⎫
        All parts fulfilled of subject and of son;   ⎬
        Swift was the race, but short the time to run.   ⎭
        Oh narrow circle, but of pow'r divine,
        Scanted in space, but perfect in thy line!
840   By sea, by land, thy matchless worth was known,
        Arms thy delight, and war was all thy own:
        Thy force, infused, the fainting Tyrians propped,
        And haughty Pharaoh found his fortune stopped.

817 Barzillai] (II Samuel 19: 31–9) James Butler, Duke of Ormonde (1610–88), an
estimable and devoted royalist throughout Charles's troubles.
819–20 He was Lord Lieutenant of Ireland for Charles I and Charles II.
829–31 He had lost six of his eight sons, among them the eldest, Thomas, Earl of Ossory
(1634–80), a man of exemplary distinction.

Oh ancient honour! oh unconquered hand,
Whom foes unpunished never could withstand!
But Israel was unworthy of thy name:
Short is the date of all immoderate fame.
It looks as Heaven our ruin had designed,
And durst not trust thy fortune and thy mind.
Now, free from earth, thy disencumbered soul   850
Mounts up, and leaves behind the clouds and starry pole:
From thence thy kindred legions mayest thou bring
To aid the guardian angel of thy King.
Here stop, my Muse, here cease thy painful flight;
No pinions can pursue immortal height:
Tell good Barzillai thou canst sing no more,
And tell thy soul she should have fled before:
Or fled she with his life, and left this verse
To hang on her departed patron's hearse?
Now take thy steepy flight from heaven, and see   860
If thou canst find on earth another *he*:
Another he would be too hard to find;
See then whom thou canst see not far behind.
Zadoc the priest, whom, shunning power and place,
His lowly mind advanced to David's grace.
With him the Sagan of Jerusalem,
Of hospitable soul and noble stem;
Him of the western dome, whose weighty sense
Flows in fit words and heavenly eloquence.
The Prophets' sons, by such example led,   870
To learning and to loyalty were bred:
For colleges on bounteous kings depend,
And never rebel was to arts a friend.
To these succeed the pillars of the laws,
Who best could plead, and best can judge a cause.
Next them a train of loyal peers ascend;
Sharp-judging Adriel, the Muses' friend;
Himself a Muse – in Sanhedrin's debate
True to his Prince, but not a slave of state;

864 Zadoc] William Sancroft (1617–93), Archbishop of Canterbury.
866 the Sagan] The Jewish deputy high priest; denoting Henry Compton (1632–1713),
Bishop of London.
868 Him . . . dome] John Dolben, who was Bishop of Westminster from 1662 to 1666,
and gave example (l. 870) to the boys of Westminster School.
877 Adriel] John Sheffield, Earl of Mulgrave (1648–1721).

880   Whom David's love with honours did adorn,
That from his disobedient son were torn.
Jotham of piercing wit and pregnant thought,
Endued by nature, and by learning taught
To move assemblies, who but only tried
The worse a while, then chose the better side;
Nor chose alone, but turned the balance too,
So much the weight of one brave man can do.
Hushai, the friend of David in distress,
In public storms of manly steadfastness;
890   By foreign treaties he informed his youth,
And joined experience to his native truth.
His frugal care supplied the wanting throne,
Frugal for that, but bounteous of his own:
'Tis easy conduct when exchequers flow,
But hard the task to manage well the low;
For sovereign power is too depressed or high,
When kings are forced to sell or crowds to buy.
Indulge one labour more, my weary Muse,
For Amiel: who can Amiel's praise refuse?
900   Of ancient race by birth, but nobler yet
In his own worth, and without title great:
The Sanhedrin long time as chief he ruled,
Their reason guided and their passion cooled:
So dexterous was he in the Crown's defence,
So formed to speak a loyal nation's sense,
That, as their band was Israel's tribes in small,
So fit was he to represent them all.
Now rasher charioteers the seat ascend,
Whose loose careers his steady skill commend:
910   They, like th' unequal ruler of the day,
Misguide the seasons and mistake the way,
While he, withdrawn, at their mad labour smiles
And safe enjoys the sabbath of his toils.

     These were the chief, a small but faithful band

882 Jotham] George Saville (1633–95), Marquis of Halifax, who successfully opposed the Exclusion Bill in the House of Lords in November 1680.
888 Hushai] Laurence Hyde (1641–1711), Earl of Rochester.
899 Amiel] Edward Seymour (1633–1708), Speaker of the House of Commons from 1673 to 1678.
910 th' unequal . . . day] Phaeton, son of Apollo, god of the sun, who made a nearly disastrous attempt to drive his father's chariot.

Of worthies, in the breach who dared to stand
And tempt th' united fury of the land.
With grief they viewed such powerful engines bent
To batter down the lawful government.
A numerous faction, with pretended frights,
In Sanhedrins to plume the regal rights;   920
The true successor from the Court removed;
The plot by hireling witnesses improved.
These ills they saw, and, as their duty bound,
They showed the King the danger of the wound:
That no concessions from the throne would please,
But lenitives fomented the disease;
That Absalom, ambitious of the crown,
Was made the lure to draw the people down;
That false Achitophel's pernicious hate
Had turned the plot to ruin Church and State;   930
The council violent, the rabble worse;
That Shimei taught Jerusalem to curse.

    With all these loads of injuries opprest,
And long revolving in his careful breast
Th' event of things, at last his patience tired,
Thus from his royal throne, by Heaven inspired,
The godlike David spoke: with awful fear
His train their Maker in their master hear.

    "Thus long have I, by native mercy swayed,
My wrongs dissembled, my revenge delayed: 940
So willing to forgive th' offending age,
So much the father did the king assuage.
But now so far my clemency they slight,
Th' offenders question my forgiving right.
That one was made for many, they contend;
But 'tis to rule, for that's a monarch's end.
They call my tenderness of blood my fear,
Though manly tempers can the longest bear.
Yet, since they will divert my native course,
'Tis time to show I am not good by force.   950
Those heaped affronts that haughty subjects bring

920 plume] Pluck.
944 Referring to instances where the King's right to pardon was challenged, as in the case of
the Earl of Danby in 1679.

Are burdens for a camel, not a king.
Kings are the public pillars of the State,
Born to sustain and prop the nation's weight:
If my young Samson will pretend a call
To shake the column, let him share the fall.
But oh that yet he would repent and live!
How easy 'tis for parents to forgive!
With how few tears a pardon might be won
960 From nature, pleading for a darling son!
Poor pitied youth, by my paternal care
Raised up to all the height his frame could bear!
Had God ordained his fate for empire born,
He would have given his soul another turn:
Gulled with a patriot's name, whose modern sense
Is one that would by law supplant his prince;
The people's brave, the politician's tool;
Never was patriot yet but was a fool.
Whence comes it that religion and the laws
970 Should more be Absalom's than David's cause?
His old instructor, ere he lost his place,
Was never thought endued with so much grace.
Good heav'ns, how faction can a patriot paint!
My rebel ever proves my people's saint.
Would they impose an heir upon the throne?
Let Sanhedrins be taught to give their own.
A king's at least a part of government,
And mine as requisite as their consent:
Without my leave a future king to choose
980 Infers a right the present to depose.
True, they petition me t'approve their choice:
But Esau's hands suit ill with Jacob's voice.
My pious subjects for my safety pray,
Which to secure they take my power away.
From plots and treasons Heaven preserve my years,
But save me most from my petitioners.
Unsatiate as the barren womb or grave,
God cannot grant so much as they can crave.
What then is left but with a jealous eye
990 To guard the small remains of royalty?
The law shall still direct my peaceful sway,

971 His old instructor] Shaftesbury.
986 Petitioning the King was a troublesome means of political pressure.

And the same law teach rebels to obey:
Votes shall no more established pow'r control,
Such votes as make a part exceed the whole.
No groundless clamours shall my friends remove,
Nor crowds have power to punish ere they prove;
For gods and godlike kings their care express
Still to defend their servants in distress.
Oh that my power to saving were confined!
Why am I forced, like Heaven, against my mind,   1000
To make examples of another kind?
Must I at length the sword of justice draw?
Oh curst effects of necessary law!
How ill my fear they by my mercy scan!
Beware the fury of a patient man.
Law they require, let Law then show her face:
They could not be content to look on Grace,
Her hinder parts, but with a daring eye
To tempt the terror of her front, and die.
By their own arts, 'tis righteously decreed,   1010
Those dire artificers of death shall bleed.
Against themselves their witnesses will swear
Till, viper-like, their mother-plot they tear,
And suck for nutriment that bloody gore
Which was their principle of life before.
Their Belial with their Beelzebub will fight;
Thus on my foes my foes shall do me right.
Nor doubt th' event; for factious crowds engage
In their first onset all their brutal rage.
Then let 'em take an unresisted course,   1020
Retire and traverse, and delude their force:
But when they stand all breathless, urge the fight,
And rise upon 'em with redoubled might:
For lawful pow'r is still superior found,
When long driven back, at length it stands the ground."

He said. Th' Almighty, nodding, gave consent;
And peals of thunder shook the firmament.
Henceforth a series of new time began,
The mighty years in long procession ran:
Once more the godlike David was restored,   1030
And willing nations knew their lawful lord.

1014 The old belief that vipers at birth devoured the mother.

From

THE SECOND PART OF ABSALOM AND ACHITOPHEL

Ll. 457–509 of *The Second Part of Absalom and Achitophel*, which appeared in November 1682. It was mostly the work of Nahum Tate, with Dryden, according to Tonson (his publisher from 1679 on), contributing ll. 310–509, mainly a satire on Elkanah Settle (Doeg) and Shadwell (Og).

> Now stop your noses, readers, all and some;⎫
> For here's a tun of midnight work to come,⎬
> Og, from a treason-tavern rolling home.⎭
> Round as a globe, and liquored ev'ry chink,
> Goodly and great he sails behind his link.
> With all this bulk there's nothing lost in Og,
> For ev'ry inch that is not fool is rogue:
> A monstrous mass of foul corrupted matter,
> As all the devils had spewed to make the batter.
> When wine has given him courage to blaspheme,
> He curses God, but God before cursed him;
> And if man could have reason, none has more,
> That made his paunch so rich and him so poor.
> With wealth he was not trusted, for Heav'n knew
> What 'twas of old to pamper up a Jew;
> To what would he on quail and pheasant swell,
> That ev'n on tripe and carrion could rebel?
> But though Heav'n made him poor, (with rev'rence speaking,)
> He never was a poet of God's making.
> The midwife laid her hand on his thick skull,
> With this prophetic blessing: *Be thou dull*;
> Drink, swear, and roar, forbear no lewd delight
> Fit for thy bulk, do anything but write:
> Thou art of lasting make, like thoughtless men,
> A strong nativity — but for the pen;
> Eat opium, mingle arsenic in thy drink,
> Still thou mayst live avoiding pen and ink.
> I see, I see 'tis counsel given in vain,

10

20

For treason botched in rhyme will be thy bane;
Rhyme is the rock on which thou art to wreck,   30
'Tis fatal to thy fame and to thy neck:
Why should thy metre good King David blast?
A psalm of his will surely be thy last.
Dar'st thou presume in verse to meet thy foes,
Thou whom the penny pamphlet foiled in prose?
Doeg, whom God for mankind's mirth has made,
O'ertops thy talent in thy very trade;
Doeg to thee, thy paintings are so coarse,
A poet is, though he's the poets' horse.
A double noose thou on thy neck dost pull,   40
For writing treason, and for writing dull;
To die for faction is a common evil,
But to be hanged for nonsense is the devil:
Hadst thou the glories of thy king expressed,
Thy praises had been satire at the best;
But thou in clumsy verse, unlicked, unpointed,
Hast shamefully defied the Lord's anointed:
I will not rake the dunghill of thy crimes,
For who would read thy life that reads thy rhymes?
But of King David's foes, be this the doom,   50
May all be like the young man Absalom;
And for my foes may this their blessing be,
To talk like Doeg, and to write like thee.

RELIGIO LAICI;

OR A LAYMAN'S FAITH

Religio Laici was published in 1682, the ostensible occasion for the poem being the appearance of Dryden's friend Henry Dickinson's translation of Father Simon's *Critical History of the Old Testament*, a learned and controversial work which was printed (and promptly condemned) in Paris in 1678. Dryden pays tribute to it in ll. 234–75.

The receptiveness of Dryden's mind and his responsiveness to movements in contemporary thought have enlarged discussion of his religious views. Students will frequently encounter terms such as Deism (that is, believing in a Supernatural Being independently of Revelation or Christian doctrines: 'natural religion' such as Dryden describes in ll. 42–61 and 168–83); Fideism, or reliance on faith; and Rationalism, or belief in the primacy of reason in religious matters.

Dryden is glad to oppose the use of reason to partisan fervour or religious enthusiasm. However, *Religio Laici* is scrupulous in acknowledging the limitations of reason in matters of faith. In the Preface Dryden says:

They who would prove religion by reason, do but weaken the cause which they endeavour to support: 'tis to take away the pillars from our faith, and to prop it only with a twig; 'tis to design a tower like that of Babel, which if it were possible (as it is not) to reach heaven, would come to nothing by the confusion of the workmen. For every man is building a several way, impotently conceited of his own model, and his own materials. Reason is always striving, and always at a loss, and of necessity it must so come to pass, while 'tis exercised about that which is not its proper object. Let us be content at last, to know God by his own methods; at least so much of him as he is pleased to reveal to us in the sacred scriptures. To apprehend them to be the word of God is all our reason has to do; for all beyond it is the work of faith, which is the seal of Heaven impressed upon our human understanding.

The declension from the grandeur of the opening lines of the poem to the plainness of the ending is consistent: a voluntary subdual of aspiration in the matter of 'reasoning into truth'.

Dim, as the borrowed beams of moon and stars
To lonely, weary, wand'ring travellers,
Is Reason to the soul: and as on high
Those rolling fires discover but the sky,
Not light us here; so Reason's glimmering ray
Was lent, not to assure our doubtful way,
But guide us upward to a better day.
And as those nightly tapers disappear
When day's bright lord ascends our hemisphere,
So pale grows Reason at Religion's sight,   10
So dies, and so dissolves in supernatural light.
Some few, whose lamp shone brighter, have been led
From cause to cause, to Nature's secret head;
And found that one first principle must be:
But what, or who, that UNIVERSAL HE;
Whether some soul encompassing this ball,
Unmade, unmoved, yet making, moving all;
Or various atoms' interfering dance
Leapt into form (the noble work of chance;)
Or this great All was from eternity;   ⎫   20
Not ev'n the Stagirite himself could see, ⎬
And Epicurus guessed as well as he: ⎭
As blindly groped they for a future state;
As rashly judged of Providence and Fate: *Opinions of the*
But least of all could their endeavours find   *several sects*
What most concerned the good of human kind;   *of philosophers*
For Happiness was never to be found,   *concerning the*
But vanished from 'em like enchanted ground.   *summum*
One thought Content the good to be enjoyed;   *bonum.*
This, every little accident destroyed: 30
The wiser madmen did for Virtue toil,
A thorny, or at best a barren soil;
In Pleasure some their glutton souls would steep, ⎫
But found their line too short, the well too deep, ⎬
And leaky vessels which no bliss could keep.   ⎭
Thus, anxious thoughts in endless circles roll,
Without a centre where to fix the soul.
In this wild maze their vain endeavours end:
How can the less the greater comprehend?
Or finite Reason reach Infinity?   40
For what could fathom GOD were more than He.   *System of*
   The Deist thinks he stands on firmer ground;   *Deism.*

Cries: "Εὕρεκα, the mighty secret's found:
God is that spring of good; supreme, and best;
We made to serve, and in that service blest."
If so, some rules of worship must be given,
Distributed alike to all by Heaven;
Else God were partial, and to some denied
The means His justice should for all provide.

50   This general worship is to PRAISE and PRAY,
One part to borrow blessings, one to pay;
And when frail nature slides into offence,
The sacrifice for crimes is penitence.
Yet, since th' effects of Providence, we find,
Are variously dispensed to human kind;
That vice triumphs, and virtue suffers here,
(A brand that sovereign justice cannot bear;)
Our Reason prompts us to a future state,
The last appeal from Fortune and from Fate:

60   Where God's all-righteous ways will be declared,
The bad meet punishment, the good reward.

Of revealed   Thus man by his own strength to Heaven would soar,
religion.   And would not be obliged to God for more.
Vain, wretched creature, how art thou misled
To think thy wit these godlike notions bred!
These truths are not the product of thy mind,
But dropped from Heaven, and of a nobler kind.
Revealed Religion first informed thy sight,
And Reason saw not, till Faith sprung the light.

70   Hence all thy natural worship takes the source:
'Tis revelation what thou thinkst discourse.
Else, how com'st thou to see these truths so clear,
Which so obscure to heathens did appear?
Not Plato these, nor Aristotle found;
Socrates.   Nor he whose wisdom oracles renowned.
Hast thou a wit so deep, or so sublime,
Or canst thou lower dive, or higher climb?
Canst thou, by Reason, more of Godhead know
Than Plutarch, Seneca, or Cicero?

80   Those giant wits, in happier ages born,
(When arms and arts did Greece and Rome adorn,)
Knew no such system; no such piles could raise
Of natural worship, built on pray'r and praise,
To one sole GOD:

Nor did remorse to expiate sin prescribe,
But slew their fellow creatures for a bribe:
The guiltless victim groaned for their offence,
And cruelty and blood was penitence.
If sheep and oxen could atone for men,
Ah! at how cheap a rate the rich might sin!   90
And great oppressors might Heaven's wrath beguile
By offering his own creatures for a spoil!
   Dar'st thou, poor worm, offend Infinity?
And must the terms of peace be given by thee?
Then thou art Justice in the last appeal;
Thy easy God instructs thee to rebel,
And, like a king remote and weak, must take
What satisfaction thou art pleased to make.
   But if there be a pow'r too just and strong
To wink at crimes and bear unpunished wrong,   100
Look humbly upward, see his will disclose
The forfeit first, and then the fine impose:
A mulct thy poverty could never pay,
Had not Eternal Wisdom found the way,
And with celestial wealth supplied thy store:
His justice makes the fine, His mercy quits the score.
See God descending in thy human frame;
Th' offended suffering in th' offender's name:
All thy misdeeds to Him imputed see,
And all His righteousness devolved on thee.   110
   For granting we have sinned, and that th' offence
Of man is made against Omnipotence,
Some price that bears proportion must be paid,
And infinite with infinite be weighed.
See then the Deist lost: remorse for vice
Not paid; or paid, inadequate in price:
What farther means can Reason now direct,
Or what relief from human wit expect?
That shows us sick; and sadly are we sure
Still to be sick, till Heav'n reveal the cure: 120
If then Heaven's will must needs be understood,
(Which must, if we want cure, and Heaven be good,)
Let all records of will revealed be shown, ⎫
With Scripture all in equal balance thrown,⎬
And our one sacred book will be that one. ⎭

102 forfeit] Misdeed, offence.   103 mulct] Fine.

Proof needs not here; for whether we compare
That impious, idle, superstitious ware
Of rites, lustrations, offerings, (which before,
In various ages, various countries bore,)
130   With Christian faith and virtues, we shall find
None answ'ring the great ends of human kind,
But this one rule of life, that shows us best
How God may be appeased, and mortals blest.
Whether from length of time its worth we draw,
The world is scarce more ancient than the law:
Heav'n's early care prescribed for every age,
First, in the soul, and after, in the page.
Or, whether more abstractedly we look,
Or on the writers, or the written book,
140   Whence, but from Heav'n, could men unskilled in arts,
In several ages born, in several parts,
Weave such agreeing truths? or how, or why
Should all conspire to cheat us with a lie?
Unasked their pains, ungrateful their advice,
Starving their gain, and martyrdom their price.
    If on the book itself we cast our view,
Concurrent heathens prove the story true:
The doctrine, miracles; which must convince,
For Heav'n in them appeals to human sense;
150   And though they prove not, they confirm the cause,
When what is taught agrees with Nature's laws.
    Then for the style; majestic and divine,
It speaks no less than God in every line:
Commanding words; whose force is still the same
As the first fiat that produced our frame.
All faiths beside or did by arms ascend,
Or sense indulged has made mankind their friend:
This only doctrine does our lusts oppose,
Unfed by nature's soil, in which it grows;
160   Cross to our interests, curbing sense and sin;
Oppressed without, and undermined within,
It thrives through pain; its own tormentors tires;
And with a stubborn patience still aspires.
To what can Reason such effects assign,
Transcending Nature, but to laws divine?
Which in that sacred volume are contained;
Sufficient, clear, and for that use ordained.

But stay: the Deist here will urge anew,
No supernatural worship can be true;
Because a general law is that alone   170
Which must to all, and everywhere, be known:
A style so large as not this Book can claim,
Nor aught that bears revealed Religion's name.
'Tis said the sound of a Messiah's birth
Is gone through all the habitable earth;
But still that text must be confined alone
To what was then inhabited, and known:
And what provision could from thence accrue
To Indian souls, and worlds discovered new?
In other parts it helps, that, ages past,   180
The Scriptures there were known, and were embraced,
Till Sin spread once again the shades of night:
What's that to these who never saw the light?
    Of all objections this indeed is chief
To startle reason, stagger frail belief:
We grant, 'tis true, that Heav'n from human sense
Has hid the secret paths of Providence;
But boundless wisdom, boundless mercy, may
Find ev'n for those bewildered souls a way:
If from His nature foes may pity claim,   190
Much more may strangers who ne'er heard His name.
And though no name be for salvation known,
But that of His eternal Son's alone;
Who knows how far transcending goodness can
Extend the merits of that Son to man?
Who knows what reasons may His mercy lead,
Or ignorance invincible may plead?
Not only charity bids hope the best,
But more the great Apostle has exprest:
That if the Gentiles (whom no law inspired)   200
By nature did what was by law required,
They, who the written rule had never known,
Were to themselves both rule and law alone:
To Nature's plain indictment they shall plead,
And by their conscience be condemned or freed.
Most righteous doom! because a rule revealed
Is none to those from whom it was concealed.
Then those who followed Reason's dictates right,
Lived up, and lifted high their natural light,

*Objection of
the Deist.*

*The objection
answered.*

210 With Socrates may see their Maker's face;
While thousand rubric-martyrs want a place.
    Nor does it baulk my charity, to find
The Egyptian bishop of another mind:
For though his Creed eternal truth contains,
'Tis hard for man to doom to endless pains
All who believed not all his zeal required,
Unless he first could prove he was inspired.
Then let us either think he meant to say
This faith, where published, was the only way;
220 Or else conclude that, Arius to confute,
The good old man, too eager in dispute,
Flew high; and, as his Christian fury rose,
Damned all for heretics who durst oppose.
    Thus far my charity this path hath tried;

Digression to
the translator
of Father
Simon's Critical
History of the
Old Testament.

(A much unskilful, but well-meaning guide:)
Yet what they are, ev'n these crude thoughts were bred
By reading that which better thou hast read,
Thy matchless author's work; which thou, my friend,
By well translating better dost commend:
230 Those youthful hours which, of thy equals, most
In toys have squandered, or in vice have lost,
Those hours hast thou to nobler use employed,
And the severe delights of truth enjoyed.
Witness this weighty book, in which appears
The crabbed toil of many thoughtful years,
Spent by thy author in the sifting care
Of Rabbins' old sophisticated ware
From gold divine; which he who well can sort
May afterwards make algebra a sport:
240 A treasure, which if country curates buy,
They Junius and Tremellius may defy;
Save pains in various readings, and translations,
And without Hebrew make most learned quotations:
A work so full with various learning fraught,
So nicely pondered, yet so strongly wrought,
As Nature's height and Art's last hand required;
As much as man could compass, uninspired.

213 The Egyptian bishop] Athanasius, Bishop of Alexandria.
228 my friend] Henry Dickinson.
241 Junius and Tremellius] Protestant scholars of the sixteenth century who translated the
Old Testament into Latin.

Where we may see what errors have been made
Both in the copier's and translator's trade:
How Jewish, Popish interests have prevailed,   250
And where infallibility has failed.
    For some, who have his secret meaning guessed,
Have found our author not too much a priest:
For fashion-sake he seems to have recourse
To Pope, and councils, and tradition's force;
But he that old traditions could subdue,
Could not but find the weakness of the new:
If Scripture, though derived from heav'nly birth,
Has been but carelessly preserved on earth;
If God's own people, who of God before   260
Knew what we know, and had been promised more,
In fuller terms, of Heaven's assisting care,
And who did neither time nor study spare
To keep this Book untainted, unperplext,
Let in gross errors to corrupt the text,
Omitted paragraphs, embroiled the sense,
With vain traditions stopped the gaping fence,
Which every common hand pulled up with ease:
What safety from such brushwood-helps as these?
If written words from time are not secured,   270
How can we think have oral sounds endured?
Which thus transmitted, if one mouth has failed,
Immortal lies on ages are entailed;
And that some such have been, is proved too plain;
If we consider interest, Church, and gain.
    "Oh, but," says one, "tradition set aside,   *Of the*
Where can we hope for an unerring guide?   *infallibility*
For since th' original Scripture has been lost   *of tradition*
All copies disagreeing, maimed the most,   *in general.*
Or Christian faith can have no certain ground,
Or truth in Church tradition must be found."   280
    Such an omniscient Church we wish indeed;
'Twere worth both Testaments, and cast in the Creed:
But if this mother be a guide so sure
As can all doubts resolve, all truth secure,
Then her infallibility as well
Where copies are corrupt or lame can tell;

252ff The effect of Simon's book, and the turmoil it produced, are discussed in Harth's
Contexts of Dryden's Thought (1968).

Restore lost canon with as little pains,
As truly explicate what still remains;
290   Which yet no Council dare pretend to do,
Unless, like Esdras, they could write it new;
Strange confidence, still to interpret true,
Yet not be sure that all they have explained
Is in the blest original contained.
More safe, and much more modest 'tis, to say
God would not leave mankind without a way:
And that the Scriptures, though not everywhere
Free from corruption, or entire, or clear,
Are uncorrupt, sufficient, clear, entire,
300   In all things which our needful faith require.
If others in the same glass better see,
'Tis for themselves they look, but not for me;
For MY salvation must its doom receive
Not from what OTHERS, but what I believe.
    Must all tradition then be set aside?

Objection in behalf of tradition, urged by Father Simon.

This to affirm were ignorance or pride.
Are there not many points, some needful sure
To saving faith, that Scripture leaves obscure?
Which every sect will wrest a several way
310   (For what one sect interprets, all sects may):
We hold, and say we prove from Scripture plain,
That Christ is GOD; the bold Socinian
From the same Scripture urges he's but MAN.
Now what appeal can end th' important suit?
Both parts talk loudly, but the rule is mute.
    Shall I speak plain, and in a nation free
Assume an honest layman's liberty?
I think (according to my little skill,
To my own Mother Church submitting still)
320   That many have been saved, and many may,
Who never heard this question brought in play.
Th' unlettered Christian, who believes in gross,
Plods on to Heaven, and ne'er is at a loss;
For the strait gate would be made straiter yet,
Were none admitted there but men of wit.
The few, by nature formed, with learning fraught,
Born to instruct, as others to be taught,

322 in gross] In a general way.

Must study well the sacred page; and see
Which doctrine, this, or that, does best agree
With the whole tenour of the work divine,   330
And plainliest points to Heaven's revealed design;
Which exposition flows from genuine sense,
And which is forced by wit and eloquence.
Not that tradition's parts are useless here,
When general, old, disinteressed, and clear:
That ancient Fathers thus expound the page,
Gives truth the reverend majesty of age;
Confirms its force by biding every test;
For best authorities, next rules, are best;
And still the nearer to the spring we go,   340
More limpid, more unsoiled the waters flow.
Thus, first traditions were a proof alone,
Could we be certain such they were, so known:
But since some flaws in long descent may be,
They make not truth but probability.
Even Arius and Pelagius durst provoke
To what the centuries preceding spoke.
Such difference is there in an oft-told tale:
But truth by its own sinews will prevail.
Tradition written therefore more commends   350
Authority, than what from voice descends:
And this, as perfect as its kind can be,
Rolls down to us the sacred history:
Which, from the Universal Church received,
Is tried, and after for itself believed.
  The partial Papists would infer from hence,   *The second*
Their Church, in last resort, should judge the sense.   *objection.*
But first they would assume, with wondrous art,   *Answer to the*
Themselves to be the whole, who are but part   *objection.*
Of that vast frame, the Church; yet grant they were   360
The handers down, can they from thence infer
A right t'interpret? or would they alone
Who brought the present claim it for their own?
The Book's a common largess to mankind,
Not more for them than every man designed;
The welcome news is in the letter found;
The carrier's not commissioned to expound.

346 Arius and Pelagius] Heretics of the fourth and fifth centuries respectively.

It speaks itself, and what it does contain
In all things needful to be known is plain.
370   In times o'ergrown with rust and ignorance,
A gainful trade their clergy did advance;
When want of learning kept the laymen low,
And none but priests were authorized to know;
When what small knowledge was, in them did dwell,
And he a god who could but read or spell:
Then Mother Church did mightily prevail;
She parcelled out the Bible by retail;
But still expounded what she sold or gave,
To keep it in her power to damn and save.
380 Scripture was scarce, and as the market went,
Poor laymen took salvation on content;
As needy men take money, good or bad:
God's word they had not, but the priest's they had.
Yet, whate'er false conveyances they made,
The lawyer still was certain to be paid.
In those dark times they learned their knack so well,
That by long use they grew infallible.
At last, a knowing age began t'enquire
If they the Book, or that did them inspire;
390 And, making narrower search, they found, though late,
That what they thought the priest's was their estate,
Taught by the will produced (the written word)
How long they had been cheated on record.
Then every man who saw the title fair
Claimed a child's part, and put in for a share;
Consulted soberly his private good,
And saved himself as cheap as e'er he could.
    'Tis true, my friend (and far be flattery hence),
This good had full as bad a consequence:
400 The Book thus put in every vulgar hand,
Which each presumed he best could understand,
The common rule was made the common prey,
And at the mercy of the rabble lay.
The tender page with horny fists was galled,
And he was gifted most that loudest bawled:
The spirit gave the doctoral degree; ⎫
And every member of a Company ⎬
Was of his trade and of the Bible free.⎭
Plain truths enough for needful use they found,

But men would still be itching to expound: 410
Each was amibitious of th' obscurest place,
No measure ta'en from knowledge, all from GRACE.
Study and pains were now no more their care;
Texts were explained by fasting and by prayer:
This was the fruit the private spirit brought,
Occasioned by great zeal, and little thought.
While crowds unlearn'd, with rude devotion warm,
About the sacred viands buzz and swarm,
The fly-blown text creates a crawling brood,
And turns to maggots what was meant for food.   420
A thousand daily sects rise up and die;
A thousand more the perished race supply:
So all we make of Heaven's discovered will
Is, not to have it, or to use it ill.
The danger's much the same; on several shelves
If others wreck us, or we wreck ourselves.
    What then remains, but, waiving each extreme,
The tides of ignorance and pride to stem:
Neither so rich a treasure to forgo;
Nor proudly seek beyond our pow'r to know?   430
Faith is not built on disquisitions vain;
The things we must believe are few and plain:
But since men will believe more than they need,
And every man will make himself a creed,
In doubtful questions 'tis the safest way
To learn what unsuspected ancients say;
For 'tis not likely we should higher soar
In search of Heav'n, than all the Church before;
Nor can we be deceived, unless we see
The Scripture and the Fathers disagree.   440
If, after all, they stand suspected still,
(For no man's faith depends upon his will,)
'Tis some relief, that points not clearly known
Without much hazard may be let alone;
And, after hearing what our Church can say,
If still our reason runs another way,
That private reason 'tis more just to curb
Than by disputes the public peace disturb.

427–50 The topical tendency of the poem is apparent in these lines. Having dealt with the 'extremes' of Catholicism and sectarian zeal, Dryden recommends a conforming 'public peace' and 'common quiet'.

For points obscure are of small use to learn:
450   But common quiet is mankind's concern.
    Thus have I made my own opinions clear;
    Yet neither praise expect, nor censure fear:
    And this unpolished, rugged verse, I chose
    As fittest for discourse, and nearest prose;
    For, while from sacred truth I do not swerve,
    Tom Sternhold's, or Tom Sha——ll's rhymes will serve.

456 Tom Sternhold's] Thomas Sternhold (d. 1549), who with John Hopkins (d. 1570) wrote a metrical version of the psalms still popular in Dryden's time. Dryden uses it on several occasions as an example of bad versifying: cf. the Preface to *All for Love*, p. 398.

TO THE MEMORY OF
MR OLDHAM

John Oldham died in 1683, at the age of twenty-nine. He is remembered most for his *Satires upon the Jesuits*, published in 1681. Dryden's poem first appeared in *Remains of Mr John Oldham in Verse and Prose* (1684).

Farewell, too little, and too lately known,
Whom I began to think and call my own;
For sure our souls were near allied, and thine
Cast in the same poetic mould with mine.
One common note on either lyre did strike,
And knaves and fools we both abhorred alike.
To the same goal did both our studies drive;
The last set out the soonest did arrive.
Thus Nisus fell upon the slippery place,
While his young friend performed and won the race.   10
O early ripe! to thy abundant store
What could advancing age have added more?
It might (what nature never gives the young)
Have taught the numbers of thy native tongue.
But satire needs not those, and wit will shine
Through the harsh cadence of a rugged line:
A noble error, and but seldom made,
When poets are by too much force betrayed.
Thy generous fruits, though gathered ere their prime,
Still shewed a quickness; and maturing time   20
But mellows what we write to the dull sweets of rhyme.
Once more, hail and farewell; farewell, thou young,
But ah too short, Marcellus of our tongue;
Thy brows with ivy, and with laurels bound;
But fate and gloomy night encompass thee around.

9–10 Nisus, competing in a footrace, slipped and fell, but managed to obstruct the next man so that his friend Euryalus could win. *Aeneid*, v, 315–39.
23 Marcellus] Marcellus, nephew of Augustus, was a young man of great promise who died at the age of twenty.

TO THE PIOUS MEMORY OF THE ACCOMPLISHED YOUNG LADY
MRS ANNE KILLIGREW,
EXCELLENT IN THE TWO SISTER-ARTS OF POESY AND PAINTING,
AN ODE

Anne Killigrew died of smallpox in June 1685. Her *Poems* were published soon after, with Dryden's ode at the front. She practised both poetry and painting, and Dryden, in idealizing her, celebrates the artist's function (with a regretful glance, in Stanza IV, at the scandalousness of the Restoration stage).

I

Thou youngest virgin-daughter of the skies,
Made in the last promotion of the blest;
Whose palms, new plucked from paradise,
In spreading branches more sublimely rise,
Rich with immortal green above the rest:
Whether, adopted to some neighbouring star,
Thou roll'st above us, in thy wand'ring race,
    Or, in procession fixed and regular,
    Moved with the heavens' majestic pace;
    Or, called to more superior bliss,
Thou tread'st, with seraphims, the vast abyss:
Whatever happy region is thy place,
Cease thy celestial song a little space;
(Thou wilt have time enough for hymns divine,
    Since heav'n's eternal years is thine.)
Hear then a mortal Muse thy praise rehearse,
    In no ignoble verse;
But such as thy own voice did practise here,
When thy first fruits of poesy were giv'n,

10

2 promotion] That is, to sainthood, from being a religious 'probationer' (l. 21) or novice.
6–9 In Ptolemaic astronomy, planets were erratic ('wand'ring') or fixed.

To make thyself a welcome inmate there;   20
    While yet a young probationer,
    And candidate of heav'n.

II

    If by traduction came thy mind,
    Our wonder is the less to find
A soul so charming from a stock so good;
Thy father was transfused into thy blood:
So wert thou born into the tuneful strain,
(An early, rich, and inexhausted vein.)
    But if thy pre-existing soul
    Was formed, at first, with myriads more,   30
It did through all the mighty poets roll,
    Who Greek or Latin laurels wore,
And was that Sappho last, which once it was before.
    If so, then cease thy flight, O heav'n-born mind!
    Thou hast no dross to purge from thy rich ore;
    Nor can thy soul a fairer mansion find,
    Than was the beauteous frame she left behind:
Return, to fill or mend the choir of thy celestial kind.

III

    May we presume to say, that at thy birth
New joy was sprung in heav'n, as well as here on earth?   40
    For sure the milder planets did combine
    On thy auspicious horoscope to shine,
    And ev'n the most malicious were in trine.
      Thy brother-angels at thy birth
      Strung each his lyre, and tuned it high,
      That all the people of the sky
    Might know a poetess was born on earth.
      And then, if ever, mortal ears
      Had heard the music of the spheres!
      And if no clust'ring swarm of bees   50
      On thy sweet mouth distilled their golden dew,

---

33 Sappho] Greek poetess, born c. 612 B.C.
34–8 In ancient Greek belief, the soul escaped reincarnation when it attained a pure state.
43 in trine] Cf. *Annus Mirabilis*, l. 1165n.
50–1 According to legend this happened to Plato in his cradle, bestowing sweetness of speech.

'Twas that such vulgar miracles
Heav'n had not leisure to renew:
For all the blest fraternity of love
Solemnized there thy birth, and kept thy holiday above.

IV

O gracious God! how far have we
Profaned thy heav'nly gift of poesy!
Made prostitute and profligate the Muse,
Debased to each obscene and impious use,
60   Whose harmony was first ordained above
For tongues of angels, and for hymns of love!
O wretched we! why were we hurried down
      This lubric and adult'rate age
      (Nay, added fat pollutions of our own)
      T'increase the steaming ordures of the stage?
What can we say t'excuse our second fall?
Let this thy vestal, Heav'n, atone for all!
Her Arethusan stream remains unsoiled,
Unmixed with foreign filth, and undefiled;
70   Her wit was more than man, her innocence a child!

V

Art she had none, yet wanted none,
For nature did that want supply:
So rich in treasures of her own,
She might our boasted stores defy:
Such noble vigour did her verse adorn,
That it seemed borrowed, where 'twas only born.
Her morals too were in her bosom bred,
      By great examples daily fed,
What in the best of books, her father's life, she read.
80   And to be read herself she need not fear;
      Each test, and ev'ry light, her Muse will bear,
      Though Epictetus with his lamp were there.
      Ev'n love (for love sometimes her Muse expressed)
Was but a lambent flame which played about her breast,
      Light as the vapours of a morning dream:
      So cold herself, whilst she such warmth expressed,
      'Twas Cupid bathing in Diana's stream.

68 Arethusan] Arethusa was changed into a fountain by Diana, to save her from pursuit by
Alphaeus: 'pure'.   82 Epictetus] Stoic philosopher and moralist.

VI

Born to the spacious empire of the Nine,
One would have thought she should have been content
To manage well that mighty government: 90
But what can young ambitious souls confine?
    To the next realm she stretched her sway,
    For Painture near adjoining lay,
A plenteous province, and alluring prey.
A chamber of dependences was framed,
(As conquerors will never want pretence,
    When armed, to justify the offence,)
And the whole fief in right of Poetry she claimed.
The country open lay without defence;
For poets frequent inroads there had made,   100
    And perfectly could represent
    The shape, the face, with ev'ry lineament;
And all the large demains which the dumb Sister swayed,
    All bowed beneath her government,
    Received in triumph wheresoe'er she went.
Her pencil drew whate'er her soul designed,
And oft the happy draft surpassed the image in her mind.
    The sylvan scenes of herds and flocks
    And fruitful plains and barren rocks,
    Of shallow brooks that flowed so clear   110
    The bottom did the top appear;
    Of deeper too and ampler floods,
    Which, as in mirrors, showed the woods;
    Of lofty trees, with sacred shades,
    And perspectives of pleasant glades,
    Where nymphs of brightest form appear,
    And shaggy satyrs standing near,
    Which them at once admire and fear.
    The ruins too of some majestic piece,
    Boasting the pow'r of ancient Rome or Greece,   120
    Whose statues, friezes, columns broken lie,
    And, though defaced, the wonder of the eye:
    What nature, art, bold fiction, e'er durst frame,
    Her forming hand gave feature to the name.
    So strange a concourse ne'er was seen before,
But when the peopled ark the whole creation bore.

88 the Nine] The nine Muses.   91–8 Dryden has Louis XIV's conquests in mind.

VII

The scene then changed: with bold erected look
Our martial king the sight with reverence strook;
For, not content t'express his outward part,
130 Her hand called out the image of his heart:
His warlike mind, his soul devoid of fear,
His high-designing thoughts were figured there,
As when, by magic, ghosts are made appear.
    Our phoenix queen was portrayed too so bright,
Beauty alone could beauty take so right:
Her dress, her shape, her matchless grace
Were all observed, as well as heav'nly face.
With such a peerless majesty she stands,
As in that day she took the crown from sacred hands;
140 Before a train of heroines was seen,
In beauty foremost, as in rank the queen.
    Thus nothing to her genius was denied,
But like a ball of fire, the further thrown,
    Still with a greater blaze she shone,
And her bright soul broke out on ev'ry side.
What next she had designed, heaven only knows;
To such immod'rate growth her conquest rose,
That fate alone its progress could oppose.

VIII

    Now all those charms, that blooming grace,
150 The well-proportioned shape, and beauteous face,
Shall never more be seen by mortal eyes:
In earth the much-lamented virgin lies!
    Not wit, nor piety could fate prevent;
    Nor was the cruel Destiny content
    To finish all the murder at a blow,
    To sweep at once her life and beauty too;
But, like a hardened felon, took a pride
    To work more mischievously slow,
    And plundered first, and then destroyed.
160 O double sacrilege on things divine,
To rob the relic, and deface the shrine!

127 The scene then changed] From landscape to portrait painting.
154 the cruel Destiny] Smallpox.

But thus Orinda died:
Heav'n, by the same disease, did both translate;
As equal were their souls, so equal was their fate.

IX

Meantime her warlike brother on the seas
His waving streamers to the winds displays,
And vows for his return, with vain devotion, pays.
Ah, generous youth, that wish forbear,
The winds too soon will waft thee here!
Slack all thy sails, and fear to come,   170
Alas, thou know'st not, thou art wrecked at home!
No more shall thou behold thy sister's face;
Thou hast already had her last embrace.
But look aloft, and if thou kenn'st from far
Among the Pleiads a new-kindled star,
If any sparkles than the rest more bright,
'Tis she that shines in that propitious light.

X

When in mid-air the golden trump shall sound,
To raise the nations under ground;
When in the Valley of Jehosaphat   180
The judging God shall close the book of fate,
And there the last assizes keep
For those who wake and those who sleep;
When rattling bones together fly
From the four corners of the sky;
When sinews o'er the skeletons are spread,
Those clothed with flesh, and life inspires the dead;
The sacred poets first shall hear the sound,
And foremost from the tomb shall bound,
For they are covered with the lightest ground;   190
And straight, with inborn vigour, on the wing,
Like mounting larks, to the new morning sing.
There thou, sweet saint, before the choir shalt go,
As harbinger of heav'n, the way to show,
The way which thou so well hast learned below.

162 Orinda] Katherine Philips, 'the Matchless Orinda', also a poet, died of smallpox in
1664.
165 her warlike brother] Henry Killigrew (d. 1712), a captain in the navy.

THE FIRST PART OF
THE HIND AND THE PANTHER

The Hind and the Panther, a poem in three parts, was published in 1687, half-way through the brief and disturbed reign of James II. Dryden had become a convert to Catholicism probably in the previous year, 1686: an act which, as Johnson says, 'at any other time might have passed with little censure'. In the circumstances, his conversion and his poem, a fable in which the authority of the Catholic church is maintained, involved him in the controversies of the time. The first part, with its lively characters of the beasts, is included here.

A milk-white Hind, immortal and unchanged,
Fed on the lawns and in the forest ranged;
Without unspotted, innocent within,
She feared no danger, for she knew no sin.
Yet had she oft been chased with horns and hounds
And Scythian shafts; and many winged wounds
Aimed at her heart; was often forced to fly,
And doomed to death, though fated not to die.
   Not so her young; for their unequal line
10 Was hero's make, half human, half divine.
Their earthly mould obnoxious was to fate,
Th' immortal part assumed immortal state.
Of these a slaughtered army lay in blood,
Extended o'er the Caledonian wood,
Their native walk; whose vocal blood arose,
And cried for pardon on their perjured foes.
Their fate was fruitful, and the sanguine seed,
Endued with souls, increased the sacred breed.
So captive Israel multiplied in chains
20 A numerous exile, and enjoyed her pains.

1 Hind] The Roman Catholic Church.
9 her young] Catholic believers, 'half divine' by their membership of an immortal church.
11 obnoxious] Liable to.
14 the Caledonian wood] Britain.

With grief and gladness mixed, their mother viewed
Her martyred offspring, and their race renewed;
Their crops to perish, but their kind to last,
So much the deathless plant the dying fruit surpassed.
    Panting and pensive now she ranged alone,
And wandered in the kingdoms once her own.
The common hunt, though from their rage restrained
By sov'reign pow'r, her company disdained:
Grinned as they passed, and with a glaring eye
Gave gloomy signs of secret emnity.   30
'Tis true she bounded by and tripped so light,
They had not time to take a steady sight;
For truth has such a face and such a mien
As to be loved needs only to be seen.
    The bloody Bear, an independent beast,
Unlicked to form, in groans her hate expressed.
Among the timorous kind the quaking Hare
Professed neutrality, but would not swear.
Next her the buffoon Ape, as atheists use,
Mimicked all sects, and had his own to chuse;   40
Still when the Lion looked, his knees he bent,
And paid at church a courtier's compliment.
    The bristled Baptist Boar, impure as he,
(But whitened with the foam of sanctity,)
With fat pollutions filled the sacred place, ⎞
And mountains levelled in his furious race; ⎬
So first rebellion founded was in grace. ⎠
But, since the mighty ravage which he made
In German forests had his guilt betrayed,
With broken tusks, and with a borrowed name,   50
He shunned the vengeance and concealed the shame;
So lurked in sects unseen. With greater guile
False Reynard fed on consecrated spoil:
The graceless beast by Athanasius first
Was chased from Nice; then, by Socinus nursed,

28 By sov'reign pow'r] By James II.
35 The bloody Bear] The Independents.
37 the quaking Hare] The Quakers.
39 the buffoon Ape] The Freethinkers.
43–52 Describing the Anabaptists and their excesses during the occupation of Munster
(which they renamed Mount Zion) in 1534.
53 False Reynard] The Fox represents the Arians, opposed by Bishop Athanasius at the
Council of Nicaea in 325.

His impious race their blasphemy renewed,
And nature's King through nature's optics viewed.
Reversed they viewed him lessened to their eye,
Nor in an infant could a God descry.
60　New swarming sects to this obliquely tend,
Hence they began, and here they all will end.
　　What weight of ancient witness can prevail,
If private reason hold the public scale?
But, gracious God, how well dost Thou provide
For erring judgments an unerring guide!
Thy throne is darkness in th' abyss of light,
A blaze of glory that forbids the sight.
O teach me to believe Thee thus concealed,
And search no farther than Thy self revealed;
70　But her alone for my director take,
Whom Thou hast promised never to forsake!
My thoughtless youth was winged with vain desires;
My manhood, long misled by wand'ring fires,
Followed false lights; and when their glimpse was gone,
My pride struck out new sparkles of her own.
Such was I, such by nature still I am;
Be Thine the glory, and be mine the shame.
Good life be now my task: my doubts are done;
(What more could fright my faith than Three in One?)
80　Can I believe eternal God could lie　　⎫
Disguised in mortal mould and infancy?　⎬
That the great Maker of the world could die?⎭
And, after that, trust my imperfect sense
Which calls in question His omnipotence?
Can I my reason to my faith compel,
And shall my sight, and touch, and taste rebel?
Superior faculties are set aside;
Shall their subservient organs be my guide?
Then let the moon usurp the rule of day,
90　And winking tapers show the sun his way;
For what my senses can themselves perceive
I need no revelation to believe.
Can they, who say the Host should be descried
By sense, define a body glorified,

72–149 'The crucial opposition is between Catholic *faith* and Anglican *sense* (and to a lesser extent, *reason*), the bases to which the two sides were sooner or later reduced in arguments over transubstantiation' (Earl Miner, Calif. *Works*, III, 358).

Impassible, and penetrating parts?
Let them declare by what mysterious arts
He shot that body through th' opposing might ⎞
Of bolts and bars impervious to the light, ⎬
And stood before His train confessed in open sight. ⎠

  For since thus wondrously He passed, 'tis plain   100
One single place two bodies did contain,
And sure the same omnipotence as well
Can make one body in more places dwell.
Let Reason then at her own quarry fly,
But how can finite grasp infinity?
  'Tis urged again, that faith did first commence
By miracles, which are appeals to sense,
And thence concluded that our sense must be
The motive still of credibility.
For latter ages must on former wait,   110
And what began belief, must propagate.
  But winnow well this thought, and you shall find
'Tis light as chaff that flies before the wind.
Were all those wonders wrought by pow'r divine
As means or ends of some more deep design?
Most sure as means, whose end was this alone,
To prove the Godhead of th' eternal Son.
God thus asserted: man is to believe
Beyond what sense and reason can conceive,
And for mysterious things of faith rely   120
On the proponent, Heav'n's authority.
If then our faith we for our guide admit,
Vain is the farther search of human wit,
As when the building gains a surer stay,
We take th' unuseful scaffolding away:
Reason by sense no more can understand;
The game is played into another hand.
Why choose we then like bilanders to creep⎞
Along the coast, and land in view to keep, ⎬
When safely we may launch into the deep? ⎠   130
In the same vessel which our Saviour bore, ⎞
Himself the pilot, let us leave the shore, ⎬
And with a better guide a better world explore. ⎠

95 Impassible] 'Incapable of suffering or pain' (OED), with a play on *impassable*, capable of
passing through solid matter. 'Penetrating' means simultaneously occupying the same space
as something else.   128 bilanders] Coastal vessels used in Holland.

Could He his Godhead veil with flesh and blood
And not veil these again to be our food?
His grace in both is equal in extent;
The first affords us life, the second nourishment.
And if He can, why all this frantic pain
To construe what his clearest words contain.
140 And make a riddle what He made so plain?
To take up half on trust, and half to try,
Name it not faith, but bungling bigotry.
Both knave and fool the merchant we may call,
To pay great sums, and to compound the small:
For who would break with Heav'n, and would not break for all?
Rest then, my soul, from endless anguish freed;
Nor sciences thy guide, nor sense thy creed.
Faith is the best ensurer of thy bliss;
The bank above must fail before the venture miss.
150 But heav'n and heav'n-born faith are far from thee,
Thou first apostate to divinity.
Unkennelled range in thy Polonian plains;
A fiercer foe th' insatiate Wolf remains.
    Too boastful Britain, please thyself no more
That beasts of prey are banished from thy shore:
The Bear, the Boar, and every savage name,
Wild in effect, though in appearance tame,
Lay waste thy woods, destroy thy blissful bow'r,
And, muzzled though they seem, the mutes devour.
160 More haughty than the rest, the wolfish race
Appear with belly gaunt and famished face;
Never was so deformed a beast of grace.
His ragged tail betwixt his legs he wears
Close clapped for shame; but his rough crest he rears,
And pricks up his predestinating ears.
His wild disordered walk, his haggered eyes,
Did all the bestial citizens surprise.
Though feared and hated, yet he ruled a while,

139 his clearest words] 'Take, eat; this is my body' (Matthew 26: 26).
150–2 Dryden returns to the Arian and Socinian Fox. Socinus was influential in Poland ('Polonian plains').
153 th' insatiate Wolf] The Presbyterians.
163–4 ragged tail . . . rough crest] The Geneva cloak and black skull-cap of the Presbyterian clergy.
166 haggered] Wild-looking.

As captain or companion of the spoil.
Full many a year his hateful head had been   170
For tribute paid, nor since in Cambria seen:
The last of all the litter scaped by chance,
And from Geneva first infested France.
Some authors thus his pedigree will trace,
But others write him of an upstart race:
Because of Wickliffe's brood no mark he brings
But his innate antipathy to kings.
These last deduce him from th' Helvetian kind,
Who near the Leman lake his consort lined:
That fiery Zuinglius first th' affection bred,   180
And meagre Calvin blessed the nuptial bed.
In Israel some believe him whelped long since,
When the proud Sanhedrim oppressed the Prince,
Or, since he will be Jew, derive him high'r,
When Corah with his brethren did conspire
From Moses' hand the sov'reign sway to wrest,
And Aaron of his ephod to devest;
Till opening earth made way for all to pass,
And could not bear the burden of a class.
The Fox and he came shuffled in the dark,   190
If ever they were stowed in Noah's ark:
Perhaps not made; for all their barking train
The Dog (a common species) will contain;
And some wild curs, who from their masters ran,⎫
Abhorring the supremacy of man,   ⎬
In woods and caves the rebel-race began.   ⎭
    O happy pair, how well have you increased!
What ills in Church and State have you redressed!
With teeth untried and rudiments of claws,
Your first essay was on your native laws: 200

(183) *Vid. Pref. to Heyl, Hist. of Presb.

169 'Captain' during the Civil War; 'companion' during the Commonwealth.
171 Cambria] Wales.
178–81 Zwingli began to preach in Zurich about 1518, Calvin in Geneva in 1636.
183 Dryden's note: Heylyn points out that some Presbyterians claimed the Jewish Sanhedrim as an antecedent (*Aerius Redivivus*, 1670).
185 Corah] Numbers 16.
187 ephod] A Jewish priestly garment.
189 class] In some Presbyterian churches, a judicatory.
197 pair] The Fox and the Wolf.

Those having torn with ease and trampled down,⎞
Your fangs you fastened on the mitred crown,   ⎬
And freed from God and monarchy your town.   ⎠
What though your native kennel still be small,
Bounded betwixt a puddle and a wall;
Yet your victorious colonies are sent
Where the north ocean girds the continent.
Quickened with fire below, your monsters breed
In fenny Holland and in fruitful Tweed;
210   And, like the first, the last affects to be
Drawn to the dregs of democracy.
As, where in fields the fairy rounds are seen,
A rank sour herbage rises on the green;
So, springing where these midnight elves advance,
Rebellion prints the footsteps of the dance.
Such are their doctrines, such contempt they show⎞
To Heav'n above and to their prince below   ⎬
As none but traitors and blasphemers know.   ⎠
God like the tyrant of the skies is placed,
220   And kings like slaves beneath the crowd debased.
So fulsome is their food that flocks refuse
To bite, and only dogs for physic use.
As, where the lightning runs along the ground,
No husbandry can heal the blasting wound,
Nor bladed grass, nor bearded corn succeeds,
But scales of scurf, and putrefaction breeds:
Such wars, such waste, such fiery tracks of dearth
Their zeal has left, and such a teemless earth.
But as the poisons of the deadliest kind
230   Are to their own unhappy coasts confined,
As only Indian shades of sight deprive,
And magic plants will but in Colchos thrive,
So Presbyt'ry and pestilential zeal
Can only flourish in a commonweal.
    From Celtic woods is chased the wolfish crew;
But ah! some pity e'en to brutes is due:
Their native walks, methinks, they might enjoy,
Curbed of their native malice to destroy.
Of all the tyrannies on human kind
240   The worst is that which persecutes the mind.

205 a puddle and a wall] Lake Leman and the Alps.
235 Celtic woods] France, with reference to the flight of Huguenots to England in 1685.

Let us but weigh at what offence we strike;
'Tis but because we cannot think alike.
In punishing of this, we overthrow
The laws of nations and of nature too.
Beasts are the subjects of tyrannic sway,
Where still the stronger on the weaker prey;
Man only of a softer mould is made,
Not for his fellows' ruin, but their aid:
Created kind, beneficent and free,
The noble image of the Deity.   250
  One portion of informing fire was giv'n
To brutes, th' inferior family of heaven:
The smith divine, as with a careless beat,
Struck out the mute creation at a heat;
But when arrived at last to human race,
The Godhead took a deep consid'ring space,
And, to distinguish man from all the rest,
Unlocked the sacred treasures of his breast,
And mercy mixed with reason did impart,
One to his head, the other to his heart: 260
Reason to rule, but mercy to forgive;
The first is law, the last prerogative.
And like his mind his outward form appeared, ⎫
When issuing naked to the wond'ring herd   ⎬
He charmed their eyes, and for they loved they feared. ⎭
Not armed with horns of arbitrary might,   ⎫
Or claws to seize their furry spoils in fight, ⎬
Or with increase of feet t'o'ertake them in their flight: ⎭
Of easy shape, and pliant every way,   ⎫
Confessing still the softness of his clay,   ⎬   270
And kind as kings upon their coronation day: ⎭
With open hands, and with extended space
Of arms to satisfy a large embrace.
Thus kneaded up with milk, the new-made man
His kingdom o'er his kindred world began;
Till knowledge misapplied, misunderstood,
And pride of empire soured his balmy blood.
Then, first rebelling, his own stamp he coins;
The murd'rer Cain was latent in his loins,
And blood began its first and loudest cry   280
For diff'ring worship of the Deity.

251 informing] Animating.

Thus persecution rose, and farther space
Produced the mighty hunter of his race.
Not so the blessed Pan his flock increased,
Content to fold 'em from the famished beast:
Mild were his laws; the Sheep and harmless Hind
Were never of the persecuting kind.
Such pity now the pious pastor shows,
Such mercy from the British Lion flows
290   That both provide protection for their foes.
    Oh happy regions, Italy and Spain,
Which never did those monsters entertain!
The Wolf, the Bear, the Boar, can there advance
No native claim of just inheritance;
And self-preserving laws, severe in show,
May guard their fences from th' invading foe.
Where birth was placed 'em, let 'em safely share
The common benefit of vital air.
Themselves unharmful, let them live unharmed,
300   Their jaws disabled and their claws disarmed:
Here, only in nocturnal howlings bold,
They dare not seize the Hind nor leap the fold.
More pow'rful, and as vigilant as they,
The Lion awfully forbids the prey.
Their rage repressed, though pinched with famine sore,
They stand aloof, and tremble at his roar;
Much is their hunger, but their fear is more.
    These are the chief; to number o'er the rest
And stand, like Adam, naming ev'ry beast,
310   Were weary work; nor will the Muse describe
A slimy-born and sun-begotten tribe,
Who, far from steeples and their sacred sound,
In fields their sullen conventicles found.
These gross, half-animated lumps I leave,
Nor can I think what thoughts they can conceive.
But if they think at all, 'tis sure no higher
Than matter put in motion may aspire;
Souls that can scarce ferment their mass of clay,
So drossy, so divisible are they,
320   As would but serve pure bodies for allay:

284 Pan] Christ.   288 pious pastor] Pope Innocent XI.
289 British Lion] James II.   308 the rest] The lesser sects.
320 allay] Alloy.

Such souls as shards produce, such beetle things
As only buzz to heav'n with ev'ning wings;
Strike in the dark, offending but by chance,
Such are the blindfold blows of ignorance.
They know not beings, and but hate a name;
To them the Hind and Panther are the same.
　　The Panther, sure the noblest, next the Hind,
And fairest creature of the spotted kind;
Oh, could her inborn stains be washed away,
She were too good to be a beast of prey!   330
How can I praise or blame, and not offend,
Or how divide the frailty from the friend?
Her faults and virtues lie so mixed, that she
Nor wholly stands condemned, nor wholly free.
Then, like her injured Lion, let me speak;
He cannot bend her, and he would not break.
Unkind already, and estranged in part,
The Wolf begins to share her wand'ring heart.
Though unpolluted yet with actual ill,
She half commits who sins but in her will.   340
If, as our dreaming Platonists report
There could be spirits of a middle sort,
Too black for heav'n, and yet too white for hell,
Who just dropped half-way down, nor lower fell;
So poised, so gently she descends from high,
It seems a soft dismission from the sky.
Her house not ancient, whatsoe'er pretence
Her clergy heralds make in her defence;
A second century not half-way run,
Since the new honours of her blood begun.   350
A Lion old, obscene, and furious made
By lust, compressed her mother in a shade;
Then by the left-hand marriage weds the dame,
Cov'ring adult'ry with a specious name:
So schism begot; and sacrilege and she,
A well-matched pair, got graceless heresy.
God's and kings' rebels have the same good cause,
To trample down divine and human laws:

321 shards] Patches of cow-dung, thought to breed insects.
327 The Panther] The Church of England.
349 The Act of Supremacy, which made Henry VIII head of the church, was passed in 1534.
351–2 Lion old . . . mother] Henry VIII and Anne Boleyn.

Both would be called reformers, and their hate
360   Alike destructive both to Church and State.
The fruit proclaims the plant; a lawless Prince
By luxury reformed incontinence,
By ruins charity, by riots abstinence;
Confessions, fasts, and penance set aside;
Oh with what ease we follow such a guide,
Where souls are starved and senses gratified!
Where marriage pleasures midnight prayer supply,
And matin bells (a melancholy cry)
Are tuned to merrier notes, *increase and multiply*.
370   Religion shows a rosy-coloured face,
Not hattered out with drudging works of grace:
A down-hill reformation rolls apace.
What flesh and blood would crowd the narrow gate,
Or, till they waste their pampered paunches, wait?
All would be happy at the cheapest rate.
    Though our lean faith these rigid laws has giv'n,
The full-fed Mussulman goes fat to heav'n;
For his Arabian prophet with delights
Of sense allured his Eastern proselytes.
380   The jolly Luther, reading him, began
T'interpret Scriptures by his Alcoran;
To grub the thorns beneath our tender feet,
And make the paths of Paradise more sweet:
Bethought him of a wife, ere halfway gone,
(For 'twas uneasy travailing alone;)
And in this masquerade of mirth and love
Mistook the bless of heav'n for bacchanals above.
Sure he presumed of praise, who came to stock
Th' etherial pastures with so fair a flock,
390   Burnished and batt'ning on their food, to show
The diligence of careful herds below.
    Our Panther, though like these she changed her head,
Yet, as the mistress of a monarch's bed,
Her front erect with majesty she bore,
The crosier wielded and the mitre wore.
Her upper part of decent discipline
Showed affectation of an ancient line;
And Fathers, Councils, Church and Church's head,

371 hattered out] Harassed, worn out.
391 herds] Keepers of herds, pastors.

Were on her reverend phylacteries read.
But what disgraced and disavowed the rest   400
Was Calvin's brand, that stigmatised the beast.
Thus, like a creature of a double kind,
In her own labyrinth she lives confined.
To foreign lands no sound of her is come,
Humbly content to be despised at home.
Such is her faith, where good cannot be had,
At least she leaves the refuse of the bad.
Nice in her choice of ill, though not of best,
And least deformed, because reformed the least.
In doubtful points betwixt her diff'ring friends,   410
Where one for substance, one for sign contends,
Their contradicting terms she strives to join;
Sign shall be substance, substance shall be sign.
A real presence all her sons allow,
And yet 'tis flat idolatry to bow,
Because the Godhead's there they know not how.
Her novices are taught that bread and wine
Are but the visible and outward sign
Received by those who in communion join.
But th' inward grace or the thing signified,   420
His blood and body who to save us died,
The faithful this thing signified receive.
What is't those faithful then partake or leave?
For what is signified and understood
Is, by her own confession, flesh and blood.
Then, by the same acknowledgment, we know
They take the sign and take the substance too.
The lit'ral sense is hard to flesh and blood,
But nonsense never can be understood.

   Her wild belief on ev'ry wave is tost;   430
But sure no Church can better morals boast.
True to her King her principles are found;
Oh that her practice were but half so sound!
Steadfast in various turns of state she stood,
And sealed her vowed affection with her blood:
Nor will I meanly tax her constancy,

399 phylacteries] Small boxes containing texts of scriptures worn by Jews during morning prayer. Figuratively: religious reminders, professions of faith.
410–29 Dryden rejects the compromises in Anglican teaching on the sacrament of the Eucharist.

That int'rest or obligement made the tie,
(Bound to the fate of murdered monarchy.)
Before the sounding axe so falls the vine,
440   Whose tender branches round the poplar twine.
She chose her ruin, and resigned her life,
In death undaunted as an Indian wife:
A rare example! but some souls we see
Grow hard and stiffen with adversity:
Yet these by fortune's favours are undone;
Resolved, into a baser form they run,
And bore the wind, but cannot bear the sun.
Let this be nature's frailty or her fate,
Or *Isgrim's counsel, her new chosen mate;
450   Still she's the fairest of the fallen crew;
No mother more indulgent but the true.
    Fierce to her foes, yet fears her force to try,
Because she wants innate auctority;
For how can she constrain them to obey
Who has herself cast off the lawful sway?
Rebellion equals all, and those who toil
In common theft will share the common spoil.
Let her produce the title and the right
Against her old superiors first to fight;
460   If she reform by text, ev'n that's as plain
For her own rebels to reform again.
As long as words a diff'rent sense will bear,
And each may be his own interpreter,
Our airy faith will no foundation find:
The word's a weathercock for every wind:
The Bear, the Fox, the Wolf by turns prevail;
The most in pow'r supplies the present gale.
The wretched Panther cries aloud for aid
To Church and Councils, whom she first betrayed;
470   No help from Fathers or tradition's train:
Those ancient guides she taught us to disdain,
And by that Scripture which she once abused
To Reformation stands herself accused.
What bills for breach of laws can she prefer,
Expounding which she owns herself may err?

(449) *The Wolf.

---

474 bills] Indictments.

And, after all her winding ways are tried, ⎫
If doubts arise, she slips herself aside, ⎬
And leaves the private conscience for the guide. ⎭
If then that conscience set th' offender free,
It bars her claim to Church auctority.   480
How can she censure, or what crime pretend,
But Scripture may be construed to defend?
Ev'n those whom for rebellion she transmits
To civil pow'r, her doctrine first acquits;
Because no disobedience can ensue,
Where no submission to a judge is due;
Each judging for himself, by her consent,
Whom thus absolved she sends to punishment.
Suppose the magistrate revenge her cause,
'Tis only for transgressing human laws.   490
How answ'ring to its end a Church is made,
Whose pow'r is but to counsel and persuade?
Oh solid rock, on which secure she stands!
Eternal house, not built with mortal hands!
Oh sure defence against th' infernal gate,
A patent during pleasure of the State!
    Thus is the Panther neither loved nor feared,
A mere mock queen of a divided herd;
Whom soon by lawful pow'r she might control,
Herself a part submitted to the whole.   500
Then, as the moon who first receives the light
By which she makes our nether regions bright,
So might she shine, reflecting from afar
The rays she borrowed from a better star;
Big with the beams which from her mother flow,
And reigning o'er the rising tides below:
Now, mixing with a salvage crowd she goes,
And meanly flatters her invet'rate foes;
Ruled while she rules, and losing every hour
Her wretched remnants of precarious pow'r.   510
    One evening, while the cooler shade she sought,
Revolving many a melancholy thought,
Alone she walked, and looked around in vain
With rueful visage for her vanished train:
None of her sylvan subjects made their court;
Levees and couchees passed without resort.

516 Levees and couchees] A levee is a morning reception, a couchee an evening one.

So hardly can usurpers manage well
Those whom they first instructed to rebel:
More liberty begets desire of more;
520   The hunger still increases with the store.
Without respect they brushed along the wood, ⎫
Each in his clan, and filled with loathsome food, ⎬
Asked no permission to the neighb'ring flood. ⎭
The Panther, full of inward discontent,
Since they would go, before 'em wisely went;
Supplying want of pow'r by drinking first,
As if she gave 'em leave to quench their thirst.
Among the rest, the Hind with fearful face
Beheld from far the common wat'ring-place,
530   Nor durst approach; till with an awful roar
The sovereign Lion bade her fear no more.
Encouraged thus, she brought her younglings nigh,
Watching the motions of her patron's eye,
And drank a sober draught; the rest amazed
Stood mutely still and on the stranger gazed;
Surveyed her part by part, and sought to find ⎫
The ten-horned monster in the harmless Hind, ⎬
Such as the Wolf and Panther had designed. ⎭
They thought at first they dreamed; for 'twas offence
540   With them to question certitude of sense,
Their guide in faith: but nearer when they drew, ⎫
And had the faultless object full in view, ⎬
Lord, how they all admired her heav'nly hue! ⎭
Some, who before her fellowship disdained, ⎫
Scarce, and but scarce, from inborn rage restrained, ⎬
Now frisked about her and old kindred feigned. ⎭
Whether for love or int'rest, ev'ry sect
Of all the salvage nation showed respect.
The viceroy Panther could not awe the herd;
550   The more the company, the less they feared.
The surly Wolf with secret envy burst,
Yet could not howl, the Hind had seen him first:
But what he durst not speak, the Panther durst.
    For when the herd suffised did late repair
To ferny heaths, and to their forest lair,
She made a mannerly excuse to stay,

552 In superstition, wolf or man was struck dumb, depending on which saw the other first.

Proffering the Hind to wait her half the way;
That, since the sky was clear, and hour of talk
Might help her to beguile the tedious walk.
With much good-will the motion was embraced, 560
To chat a while on their adventures passed;
Nor had the grateful Hind so soon forgot
Her friend and fellow-suff'rer in the Plot.
Yet wond'ring how of late she grew estranged,
Her forehead cloudy, and her count'nance changed,
She thought this hour th' occasion would present
To learn her secret cause of discontent,
Which well she hoped might be with ease redressed,⎫
Consid'ring her a well-bred civil beast   ⎬
And more a gentlewoman than the rest. ⎭ 570
After some common talk what rumours ran,
The lady of the spotted muff began.

A SONG FOR ST CECILIA'S DAY, 1687

It was customary for poets and composers to combine efforts for 22 November, day of St Cecilia, patroness of music. The composer for Dryden's ode was Giovanni Battista Draghi.

I

From harmony, from heav'nly harmony.
    This universal frame began.
    When Nature underneath a heap
        Of jarring atoms lay,
      And could not heave her head,
The tuneful voice was heard from high:
      'Arise, ye more than dead.'
Then cold, and hot, and moist, and dry,
In order to their stations leap,
      And Music's pow'r obey.
From harmony, from heav'nly harmony
    This universal frame began:
    From harmony to harmony
Through all the compass of the notes it ran,
The diapason closing full in Man.

II

What passion cannot Music raise and quell!
    When Jubal struck the corded shell,
    His list'ning brethren stood around,
    And, wond'ring, on their faces fell
    To worship that celestial sound.
Less than a god they thought there could not dwell
    Within the hollow of that shell
    That spoke so sweetly and so well.
What passion cannot Music raise and quell!

14 compass] The full range of tones which a voice or instrument can produce.
15 diapason] Complete concord or harmony.
17 Jubal] The originator of music (Genesis 4: 21), imagined here with an instrument made of shell and strings.

III

The trumpet's loud clangour
   Excites us to arms,
With shrill notes of anger,
   And mortal alarms.
The double double double beat
   Of the thund'ring Drum   30
Cries: 'Hark! the foes come;
Charge, charge, 'tis too late to retreat.'

IV

The soft complaining Flute
In dying notes discovers
The woes of hopeless lovers,
Whose dirge is whispered by the warbling Lute.

V

Sharp Violins proclaim
Their jealous pangs, and desperation,
Fury, frantic indignation,
Depth of pains, and height of passion,   40
   For the fair, disdainful dame.

VI

But oh! what art can teach,
   What human voice can reach,
The sacred Organ's praise?
   Notes inspiring holy love,
Notes that wing their heav'nly ways
   To mend the choirs above.

VII

Orpheus could lead the savage race;
And trees unrooted left their place,
   Sequacious of the lyre;   50
But bright Cecilia raised the wonder high'r:
When to her Organ vocal breath was giv'n,
An angel heard, and straight appeared,
   Mistaking earth for heaven.

---

47 mend the choirs] Improve their music.

GRAND CHORUS

As from the pow'r of sacred lays
    The spheres began to move,
And sung the great Creator's praise
    To all the blest above;
So, when the last and dreadful hour
This crumbling pageant shall devour,
The Trumpet shall be heard on high,
The dead shall live, the living die,
And Music shall untune the sky.

60

LINES ON MILTON

Printed under Milton's portrait in Tonson's 1688 edition of *Paradise Lost*.

Three poets, in three distant ages born,
Greece, Italy, and England did adorn.
The first in loftiness of thought surpassed;
The next in majesty; in both the last.
The force of Nature could no farther go:
To make a third she joined the former two.

1 Three poets] Homer, Virgil, Milton.

A LETTER TO SIR GEORGE ETHEREGE

A somewhat uncharacteristic but enjoyable poem written in reply to two verse epistles which Etherege had sent from Ratisbon, whither he had gone in 1685 as envoy to the Diet. Etherege, author of three fine comedies and a gentleman of pleasure, was hard put in Ratisbon to make up for the delights of London.

> To you who live in chill degree
> (As map informs) of fifty-three,
> And do not much for cold atone
> By bringing thither fifty-one,
> Methinks all climes should be alike,
> From tropic ev'n to pole artique;
> Since you have such a constitution
> As nowhere suffers diminution.
> You can be old in grave debate,
> And young in love's affairs of state;
> And both to wives and husbands show
> The vigour of a plenipo.
> Like mighty missioner you come
> *Ad partes infidelium.*
> A work of wondrous merit sure
> So far to go, so much endure;
> And all to preach to German dame,
> Where sound of Cupid never came.
> Less had you done, had you been sent
> As far as Drake or Pinto went,
> For cloves and nutmegs to the line-a,
> Or ev'n for oranges to China.

10

20

1–4 Apparently a play on Etherege's age and the (assumed) latitude of Ratisbon.
13 missioner] Missionary.
14 *Ad partes infidelium*] 'To the regions of the infidels'.
20 Sir Francis Drake; and Fernão Mendes Pinto (*c.* 1510–83) who wrote a colourful account of his travels in the Far East.

That had indeed been charity, ⎫
Where lovesick ladies helpless lie, ⎬
Chopped, and for want of liquor dry; ⎭
But you have made your zeal appear
Within the circle of the Bear.
What region of the earth so dull,
That is not of your labours full?
Triptolemus (so sing the Nine)   30
Strewed plenty from his cart divine;
But spite of all those fable-makers,
He never sowed on Almain acres:
No, that was left by fate's decree,
To be performed and sung by thee.
Thou break'st through forms with as much ease
As the French king through articles.
In grand affairs thy days are spent, ⎫
In waging weighty compliment, ⎬
With such as monarchs represent. ⎭   40
They who such vast fatigues attend
Want some soft minutes to unbend,
To show the world that, now and then,
Great ministers are mortal men.
Then Rhenish rummers walk the round;
In bumpers every king is crowned;
Besides three holy mitred Hectors,
And the whole college of Electors.
No health of potentate is sunk
That pays to make his envoy drunk.   50
These Dutch delights I mentioned last
Suit not, I know, your English taste:
For wine to leave a whore or play
Was ne'er your Excellency's way.
Nor need the title give offence,

---

25 Chopped] Chapped.
27 the Bear] 'An eating house in Drury Lane . . . Dryden may also be punning on "the Bear"
as Ursa Major' (Thorpe, ed., *The Poems of Sir George Etherege*, p. 121).
30 Triptolemus flew above the earth in a magic chariot given to him by Ceres, scattering
grain and bringing the knowledge of agriculture to man.
33 Almain] German.
45 rummers] A rummer is 'a kind of large drinking-glass' (*OED*).
47–8 The College of Electors of the German Empire consisted of five temporal rulers and
three archbishops.

For here you were his Excellence,
For gaming, writing, speaking, keeping,
His Excellence for all but sleeping.
Now if you tope in form, and treat,
60   'Tis the sour sauce to your sweet meat,⎫
The fine you pay for being great.   ⎬
Nay, there is a harder imposition,   ⎭
Which is indeed the court's petition,
That setting worldly pomp aside,
(Which poet has at font defied,)
You would be pleased in humble way
To write a trifle called a play.
This truly is a degradation,   ⎫
But would oblige the crown and nation⎬
70   Next to your wise negotiation.   ⎭
If you pretend (as well you may)   ⎫
Your high degree, your friends will say⎬
That Duke St Aignan made a play.   ⎭
If Gallic poet convince you scarce,
His Grace of Bucks has writ a farce,
And you, whose comic wit is terse all,
Can hardly fall below Rehearsal.
Then finish what here you began,
But scribble faster if you can;
80   For yet no George, to our discerning,
Has writ without a ten years' warning.

62–70 The Man of Mode, first performed in 1676 and still popular, was Etherege's final play.
73 Duke St Aignan] François de Beauvillier (1610–87), to whom the tragicomedy
Bradamante (1637) was attributed.
75–81 Referring to George Villiers, Duke of Buckingham, whose satirical play The Rehearsal
(1671) is said to have taken ten years to write.

TO MR SOUTHERNE,

ON HIS COMEDY CALLED *THE WIVES' EXCUSE*

Printed with the play in 1692. This, Southerne's fourth, had not succeeded in the
acting in December 1691. Dryden blames the taste of audiences for farce.

> Sure there's a fate in plays, and 'tis in vain
> To write, while these malignant planets reign:
> Some very foolish influence rules the pit,
> Not always kind to sense, or just to wit;
> And whilst it lasts, let buffoon'ry succeed,
> To make us laugh; for never was more need.
> Farce, in itself, is of a nasty scent;
> But the gain smells not of the excrement.
> The Spanish nymph, a wit and beauty too,
> With all her charms, bore but a single show;   10
> But let a monster Muscovite appear,
> He draws a crowded audience round the year.
> May be thou hast not pleased the box and pit, ⎫
> Yet those who blame thy tale applaud thy wit; ⎬
> So Terence plotted, but so Terence writ.   ⎭
> Like his, thy thoughts are true, thy language clean;
> Ev'n lewdness is made moral in thy scene.
> The hearers may for want of Nokes repine;
> But rest secure, the readers will be thine.
> Nor was thy laboured drama damned or hissed,   20
> But with a kind civility dismissed;
> With such good manners as the Wife* did use,
> Who, not accepting, did but just refuse.
> There was a glance at parting; such a look,

* *The wife in the play, Mrs Friendall.*

9–10 Possibly a reference to the Spanish plot of the play.
18 Nokes] James Nokes (d. 1696), a comic actor.
22–5 Mrs Friendall in the play rejects Lovemore's advances in this fashion.

As bids thee not give o'er, for one rebuke.
But if thou wouldst be seen, as well as read,
Copy one living author, and one dead:
The standard of thy style let Etherege be;
For wit, th' immortal spring of Wycherly.
30   Learn, after both, to draw some just design,
And the next age will learn to copy thine.

27 one dead] Etherege died in 1691; Wycherley lived on to 1716.

ELEONORA

A PANEGYRICAL POEM DEDICATED TO THE MEMORY OF THE LATE COUNTESS OF ABINGDON

Eleonora, wife of the first Earl of Abingdon, died on 31 May 1691. Dryden's poem, delayed by illness, appeared in March of the following year. He describes his purpose in his prefatory letter to the Earl:

> Doctor Donne, the greatest wit, though not the best poet of our nation, acknowledges that he had never seen Mrs Drury, whom he has made immortal in his admirable *Anniversaries*. I have had the same fortune, though I have not succeeded to the same genius. However, I have followed his footsteps in the design of his panegyric, which was to raise an emulation in the living, to copy out the example of the dead. And therefore it was that I once intended to have called this poem *The Pattern*. And though on a second consideration, I changed the title into the name of that illustrious person, yet the design continues, and *Eleonora* is still the pattern of charity, devotion and humility; of the best wife, the best mother, and the best of friends.

Besides the notion of idealizing a woman unknown to the poet, there are reminiscences of Donne in many passages, and two lines are actually borrowed (342–3).

As when some great and gracious monarch dies,
Soft whispers, first, and mournful murmurs rise
Among the sad attendants; then the sound
Soon gathers voice, and spreads the news around
Through town and country, till the dreadful blast
Is blown to distant colonies at last;
Who then, perhaps, were off'ring vows in vain,
For his long life, and for his happy reign:
So slowly, by degrees, unwilling fame ⎫
Did matchless Eleonora's fate proclaim, ⎬
Till public as the loss the news became. ⎭
    The nation felt it in th' extremest parts,
With eyes o'erflowing, and with bleeding hearts;
But most the poor, whom daily she supplied,
Beginning to be such, but when she died.

The introduction.

10

Of her charity.

For, while she lived, they slept in peace by night,
Secure of bread, as of returning light;
And with such firm dependence on the day,
That need grew pampered, and forgot to pray:
20   So sure the dole, so ready at their call,
They stood prepared to see the manna fall.
    Such multitudes she fed, she clothed, she nurst,
That she herself might fear her wanting first.
Of her five talents, other five she made;
Heav'n, that had largely giv'n, was largely paid:
And in few lives, in wondrous few, we find
A fortune better fitted to the mind.
Nor did her alms from ostentation fall,
Or proud desire of praise; the soul gave all:
30   Unbribed it gave; or, if a bribe appear,
No less than heav'n, to heap huge treasures there.
    Want passed for merit at her open door:
Heav'n saw, He safely might increase His poor,
And trust their sustenance with her so well,
As not to be at charge of miracle.
None could be needy, whom she saw or knew;
All in the compass of her sphere she drew:
He, who could teach her garment, was as sure,
As the first Christians of th' apostles' cure.
40   The distant heard, by fame, her pious deeds,
And laid her up for their extremest needs;
A future cordial for a fainting mind;
For, what was ne'er refused, all hoped to find,
Each in his turn: the rich might freely come,
As to a friend; but to the poor, 'twas home.
As to some holy house th' afflicted came, ⎫
The hunger-starved, the naked, and the lame; ⎬
Want and diseases fled before her name. ⎭
For zeal like hers her servants were too slow; ⎫
50   She was the first, where need required, to go; ⎬
Herself the foundress and attendant too. ⎭
    Sure she had guests sometimes to entertain,
Guests in disguise, of her great Master's train:
Her Lord Himself might come, for aught we know,
Since in a servant's form He lived below;
Beneath her roof He might be pleased to stay;

52–5 See Matthew 25: 35–40.

Or some benighted angel, in his way,
Might ease his wings, and, seeing heav'n appear
In its best work of mercy, think it there,
Where all the deeds of charity and love   60
Were in as constant method, as above,
All carried on; all of a piece with theirs; ⎫
As free from alms, as diligent her cares;   ⎬
As loud her praises, and as warm her pray'rs. ⎭

    Yet was she not profuse; but feared to waste,   *Of her prudent*
And wisely managed, that the stock might last;   *management.*
That all might be supplied, and she not grieve,
When crowds appeared, she had not to relieve.
Which to prevent, she still increased her store;
Laid up, and spared, that she might give the more.   70
So Pharaoh, or some greater king than he,
Provided for the sev'nth necessity;
Taught from above his magazines to frame,
That famine was prevented ere it came.
Thus Heav'n, though all-sufficient, shows a thrift
In his economy, and bounds his gift;
Creating for our day one single light,
And his reflection too supplies the night.
Perhaps a thousand other worlds, that lie
Remote from us, and latent in the sky,   80
Are lightened by his beams, and kindly nurst;
Of which our earthly dunghill is the worst.

    Now, as all virtues keep the middle line,
Yet somewhat more to one extreme incline,
Such was her soul; abhorring avarice,
Bounteous, but almost bounteous to a vice:
Had she giv'n more, it had profusion been,
And turned th' excess of goodness into sin.

    These virtues raised her fabric to the sky;   *Of her humility.*
For that which is next heav'n, is charity.   90
But, as high turrets, for their airy steep,
Require foundations in proportion deep;
And lofty cedars as far upward shoot
As to the nether heav'ns they drive the root:
So low did her secure foundation lie,
She was not humble, but Humility.

71–4 See Genesis 41.
90–6 Cf. Donne, II *Anniversary*, ll. 417–24.

Scarcely she knew that she was great, or fair,
Or wise, beyond what other women are,
Or, which is better, knew, but never durst compare.

100 For, to be conscious of what all admire,
And not be vain, advances virtue high'r.
But still she found, or rather thought she found,
Her own worth wanting, others' to abound;
Ascribed above their due to ev'ryone,
Unjust and scanty to herself alone.

Of her piety.   Such her devotion was, as might give rules
Of speculation to disputing schools,
And teach us equally the scales to hold
Betwixt the two extremes of hot and cold;
110 That pious heat may mod'rately prevail,
And we be warmed, but not be scorched with zeal.
Business might shorten, not disturb, her pray'r;
Heav'n had the best, if not the greater share.
An active life long orisons forbids;
Yet still she prayed, for still she prayed by deeds.

Her ev'ry day was Sabbath; only free
From hours of pray'r, for hours of charity:
Such as the Jews from servile toil released,
Where works of mercy were a part of rest;
120 Such as blest angels exercise above,
Varied with sacred hymns and acts of love;
Such Sabbaths as that one she now enjoys,
Ev'n that perpetual one, which she employs
(For such vicissitudes in heav'n there are)
In praise alternate, and alternate pray'r.
All this she practised here, that when she sprung
Amidst the choirs, at the first sight she sung:
Sung, and was sung herself in angels' lays;
For, praising her, they did her Maker praise.

130 All offices of heav'n so well she knew,
Before she came, that nothing there was new;
And she was so familiarly received,
As one returning, not as one arrived.

Of her various   Muse, down again precipitate thy flight;
virtues.   For how can mortal eyes sustain immortal light!
But as the sun in water we can bear,
Yet not the sun, but his reflection there,

126–8 Cf. Donne, 1 *Anniversary*, ll. 9–10.

So let us view her here, in what she was,
And take her image in this wat'ry glass:
Yet look not ev'ry lineament to see;   140
Some will be cast in shades, and some will be
So lamely drawn, you scarcely know 'tis she.
For where such various virtues we recite,
'Tis like the Milky Way, all over bright,
But sown so thick with stars, 'tis undistinguished light.
    Her virtue, not her virtues, let us call;
For one heroic comprehends 'em all:
One, as a constellation is but one,
Though 'tis a train of stars, that, rolling on,
Rise in their turn, and in the zodiac run: 150
Ever in motion; now 'tis faith ascends,
Now hope, now charity, that upward tends,
And downwards with diffusive good descends.
    As in perfumes composed with art and cost,
'Tis hard to say what scent is uppermost;
Nor this part musk or civet can we call,
Or amber, but a rich result of all;
So, she was all a sweet, whose ev'ry part,
In due proportion mixed, proclaimed the Maker's art.
No single virtue we could most commend,   160
Whether the wife, the mother, or the friend;
For she was all, in that supreme degree,
That, as no one prevailed, so all was she.
The sev'ral parts lay hidden in the piece;
Th' occasion but exerted that, or this.
    A wife as tender, and as true withal,   *Of her conjugal*
As the first woman was before her fall: *virtues.*
Made for the man, of whom she was a part;
Made to attract his eyes, and keep his heart.
A second Eve, but by no crime accurst;   170
As beauteous, not as brittle as the first.
Had she been first, still Paradise had bin,
And death had found no entrance by her sin.
So she not only had preserved from ill
Her sex and ours, but lived their pattern still.
    Love and obedience to her lord she bore;
She much obeyed him, but she loved him more:

154–7 Cf. Donne, II *Anniversary*, ll. 127–30.
166–73 Cf. Donne, I *Anniversary*, ll. 179–82.

Not awed to duty by superior sway,
But taught by his indulgence to obey.
180   Thus we love God, as author of our good;
So subjects love just kings, or so they should.
Nor was it with ingratitude returned;
In equal fires the blissful couple burned;
One joy possessed 'em both, and in one grief they mourned.
His passion still improved: he loved so fast,
As if he feared each day would be her last:
Too true a prophet to foresee the fate
That should so soon divide their happy state;
When he to heav'n entirely must restore
190   That love, that heart, where he went halves before.
Yet as the soul is all in ev'ry part,
So God and he, might each have all her heart.

Of her love to   So had her children too; for charity
her children.   Was not more fruitful, or more kind than she:
Each under other by degrees they grew;
A goodly perspective of distant view.
Anchises looked not with so pleased a face,
In numb'ring o'er his future Roman race,
And marshalling the heroes of his name,
200   As, in their order, next to light they came;
Nor Cybele with half so kind an eye
Surveyed her sons and daughters of the sky:
Proud, shall I say, of her immortal fruit?
As far as pride with heav'nly minds may suit.

Her care of their   Her pious love excelled to all she bore;
education.   New objects only multiplied it more.
And as the chosen found the pearly grain
As much as ev'ry vessel could contain;
As in the blissful vision each shall share
210   As much of glory as his soul can bear;
So did she love, and so dispense her care.
Her eldest thus, by consequence, was best,
As longer cultivated than the rest.
The babe had all that infant care beguiles,
And early knew his mother in her smiles:
But when dilated organs let in day

197–200 Cf. Virgil, *Aeneid*, VI, 752–853.
201 Cybele] Mother of Zeus and the greatest Greek gods.
207–8 Exodus 16: 11–18.

To the young soul, and gave it room to play,
At his first aptness, the maternal love
Those rudiments of reason did improve.
The tender age was pliant to command;   220
Like wax it yielded to the forming hand:
True to th' artificer, the laboured mind
With ease was pious, generous, just, and kind;
Soft for impression from the first, prepared,
Till virtue with long exercise grew hard:
With ev'ry act confirmed, and made at last
So durable as not to be effaced,
It turned to habit; and, from vices free,
Goodness resolved into necessity.

    Thus fixed she virtue's image, (that's her own,)   230
Till the whole mother in the children shone;
For that was their perfection: she was such,
They never could express her mind too much.
So unexhausted her perfections were,
That, for more children, she had more to spare;
For souls unborn, whom her untimely death
Deprived of bodies, and of mortal breath;
And (could they take th' impressions of her mind)
Enough still left to sanctify her kind.

    Then wonder not to see this soul extend   240
The bounds, and seek some other self, a friend: *Of her*
As swelling seas to gentle rivers glide,   *friendship*
To seek repose, and empty out the tide;
So this full soul, in narrow limits pent,
Unable to contain her, sought a vent,
To issue out, and in some friendly breast
Discharge her treasures, and securely rest,
T'unbosom all the secrets of her heart,
Take good advice, but better to impart.
For 'tis the bliss of friendship's holy state,   250
To mix their minds, and to communicate;
Though bodies cannot, souls can penetrate.
Fixed to her choice, inviolably true,
And wisely choosing, for she chose but few.
Some she must have; but in no one could find
A tally fitted for so large a mind.
    The souls of friends like kings in progress are;

257–62 Cf. Donne, 1 *Anniversary*, ll. 1–8.

Still in their own, though from the palace far:
Thus her friend's heart her country dwelling was,
260 A sweet retirement to a coarser place;
Where pomp and ceremonies entered not,
Where greatness was shut out, and bus'ness well forgot.
   This is th' imperfect draught; but short as far)
As the true height and bigness of a star }
Exceeds the measures of th' astronomer.)
She shines above, we know; but in what place,
How near the throne, and Heav'n's imperial face,
By our weak optics is but vainly guessed;
Distance and altitude conceal the rest.
270   Though all these rare endowments of the mind

*Reflections on
the shortness of
her life.*

Were in a narrow space of life confined,
The figure was with full perfection crowned;
Though not so large an orb, as truly round.
   As when in glory, through the public place,
The spoils of conquered nations were to pass,
And but one day for triumph was allowed,
The consul was constrained his pomp to crowd;
And so the swift procession hurried on,
That all, though not distinctly, might be shown:
280 So, in the straitened bounds of life confined,
She gave but glimpses of her glorious mind;
And multitudes of virtues passed along,
Each pressing foremost in the mighty throng,
Ambitious to be seen, and then make room
For greater multitudes that were to come.
   Yet unemployed no minute slipped away;
Moments were precious in so short a stay.
The haste of heav'n to have her was so great,)
That some were single acts, though each complete; }
290 But ev'ry act stood ready to repeat.)
   Her fellow saints with busy care will look
For her blessed name in fate's eternal book;
And, pleased to be outdone, with joy will see
Numberless virtues, endless charity:
But more will wonder at so short an age,
To find a blank beyond the thirtieth page;

274–9 Alluding to C. Caninius Rebilus, whom Caesar appointed consul for a few hours in 45
B.C.

And with a pious fear begin to doubt
The piece imperfect, and the rest torn out.
But 'twas her Saviour's time; and, could there be
A copy near th' original, 'twas she.

    As precious gums are not for lasting fire,
They but perfume the temple, and expire:
So was she soon exhaled, and vanished hence;
A short sweet odour, of a vast expense.
She vanished, we can scarcely say she died;
For but a now did heav'n and earth divide:
She passed serenely with a single breath;
This moment perfect health, the next was death.
One sigh did her eternal bliss assure;
So little penance needs, when souls are almost pure.
As gentle dreams our waking thoughts pursue,
Or, one dream passed, we slide into a new;
(So close they follow, such wild order keep,
We think ourselves awake, and are asleep;)
So softly death succeeded life in her;
She did but dream of heav'n, and she was there.
    No pains she suffered, nor expired with noise;
Her soul was whispered out with God's still voice:
As an old friend is beckoned to a feast,
And treated like a long-familiar guest.
He took her as He found, but found her so,
As one in hourly readiness to go;
Ev'n on that day, in all her trim prepared,
As early notice she from heav'n had heard,
And some descending courtier from above
Had giv'n her timely warning to remove;
Or counselled her to dress the nuptial room,
For on that night the bridegroom was to come.
He kept his hour, and found her where she lay,
Clothed all in white, the liv'ry of the day:
Scarce had she sinned, in thought, or word, or act,
Unless omissions were to pass for fact;
That hardly death a consequence could draw,
To make her liable to nature's law.
And, that she died, we only have to show

*She died in her
thirty-third year.*
300

*The manner of
her death.*
310

320

*Her preparedness
to die.*

330
*She died on
Whitsunday
night.*

318–19 Cf. Donne, *A Valediction: Forbidding Mourning*, ll. 1–2.
332 fact] Action, deed.

The mortal part of her she left below:
The rest (so smooth, so suddenly she went)
Looked like translation through the firmament,
Or like the fiery car on the third errand sent.

340
*Apostrophe to
her soul.*

O happy soul! if thou canst view from high,
Where thou art all intelligence, all eye,
If looking up to God, or down to us,
Thou find'st, that any way be pervious,
Survey the ruins of thy house, and see
Thy widowed, and thy orphan family:
Look on thy tender pledges left behind;
And, if thou canst a vacant minute find
From heav'nly joys, that interval afford
To thy sad children, and thy mourning lord.

350
See how they grieve, mistaken in their love,
And shed a beam of comfort from above;
Give 'em as much as mortal eyes can bear,
A transient view of thy full glories there;
That they with mod'rate sorrow may sustain,
And mollify their losses in thy gain.
Or else divide the grief; for such thou wert,
That should not all relations bear a part,
It were enough to break a single heart.

*Epiphonema, or
close of the poem.*

Let this suffice: nor thou, great saint, refuse

360
This humble tribute of no vulgar muse;
Who, not by cares, or wants, or age deprest,
Stems a wild deluge with a dauntless breast;
And dares to sing thy praises in a clime
Where vice triumphs, and virtue is a crime;
Where ev'n to draw the picture of thy mind,
Is satire on the most of humankind:
Take it, while yet 'tis praise; before my rage,
Unsafely just, break loose on this bad age;
So bad, that thou thyself hadst no defence

370
From vice, but barely by departing hence.

Be what, and where thou art: to wish thy place
Were, in the best, presumption more than grace.

338–9 Enoch (Genesis 5: 24) and Elijah were 'translated' into heaven before Eleonora, Elijah in a chariot of fire.
341 Cf. Donne, II *Anniversary*, l. 200.
342–3 Taken directly from Donne's *Obsequies to the Lord Harrington*, ll. 5–6. 'Pervious' means penetrable.

Thy relics (such thy works of mercy are)
Have, in this poem, been my holy care.
As earth thy body keeps, thy soul the sky,
So shall this verse preserve thy memory;
For thou shalt make it live, because it sings of thee.

375–6 Cf. Donne, 1 *Anniversary*, ll. 473–4.

RONDELAY

From *Examen Poeticum: Being the Third Part of Miscellany Poems* (1693).

Chloe found Amyntas lying,
    All in tears, upon the plain;
Sighing to himself, and crying:
    'Wretched I, to love in vain!
Kiss me, dear, before my dying;
    Kiss me once, and ease my pain!'

Sighing to himself, and crying:
    'Wretched I, to love in vain!
Ever scorning, and denying
    To reward your faithful swain;
Kiss me, dear, before my dying;
    Kiss me once, and ease my pain!'

'Ever scorning, and denying
    To reward your faithful swain.'
Chloe, laughing at his crying,
    Told him that he loved in vain.
'Kiss me, dear, before my dying;
    Kiss me once, and ease my pain!'

Chloe, laughing at his crying,
    Told him that he loved in vain;
But repenting, and complying,
    When he kissed, she kissed again:
Kissed him up, before his dying;
    Kissed him up, and eased his pain.

SONG FOR A GIRL

From Act V, Scene i of *Love Triumphant* (1694).

Young I am, and yet unskilled
How to make a lover yield;
How to keep, or how to gain,
When to love, and when to feign:

Take me, take me, some of you,
While I yet am young and true;
Ere I can my soul disguise,
Heave my breasts, and roll my eyes.

Stay not till I learn the way,
How to lie, and to betray: 10
He that has me first, is blest,
For I may deceive the rest.

Could I find a blooming youth,
Full of love, and full of truth,
Brisk, and of a jaunty mien,
I should long to be fifteen.

TO MY DEAR FRIEND MR CONGREVE
ON HIS COMEDY CALLED *THE DOUBLE-DEALER*

Complimentary verses prefixed to the play, Congreve's second, when it was printed in 1694; but written, Dryden says, 'before the play was acted' (Ward, ed., *Letters*, p. 63). The first performance was in late 1693.

Well then, the promised hour is come at last;
The present age of wit obscures the past:
Strong were our sires, and as they fought they writ,
Conqu'ring with force of arms, and dint of wit;
Theirs was the giant race, before the flood;
And thus, when Charles returned, our empire stood.
Like Janus he the stubborn soil manured,
With rules of husbandry the rankness cured;
Tamed us to manners, when the stage was rude;
10 And boist'rous English wit with art indued.
Our age was cultivated thus at length,
But what we gained in skill we lost in strength.
Our builders were with want of genius curst;
The second temple was not like the first:
Till you, the best Vitruvius, come at length;
Our beauties equal, but excel our strength.
Firm Doric pillars found your solid base;   ⎫
The fair Corinthian crowns the higher space: ⎬
Thus all below is strength, and all above is grace. ⎭
20 In easy dialogue is Fletcher's praise;
He moved the mind, but had not power to raise.
Great Jonson did by strength of judgment please;
Yet, doubling Fletcher's force, he wants his ease.
In differing talents both adorned their age;
One for the study, t'other for the stage.

7 Janus] A legendary king of ancient times who came from Thessaly to found a colony on the river Tiber.
15 Vitruvius] A celebrated architect of the reign of Augustus.

But both to Congreve justly shall submit,
One matched in judgment, both o'ermatched in wit.
In him all beauties of this age we see, ⎱
Etherege his courtship, Southerne's purity, ⎰
The satire, wit, and strength of Manly Wycherley. ⎰   30
All this in blooming youth you have achieved,
Nor are your foiled contemporaries grieved.
So much the sweetness of your manners move,
We cannot envy you, because we love.
Fabius might joy in Scipio, when he saw
A beardless consul made against the law;
And join his suffrage to the votes of Rome,
Though he with Hannibal was overcome.
Thus old Romano bowed to Raphael's fame,
And scholar to the youth he taught became.   40
    O that your brows my laurel had sustained;
Well had I been deposed, if you had reigned!
The father had descended for the son;
For only you are lineal to the throne.
Thus, when the state one Edward did depose,
A greater Edward in his room arose.
But now, not I, but poetry is curst;
For Tom the Second reigns like Tom the First.
But let 'em not mistake my patron's part,
Nor call his charity their own desert.   50
Yet this I prophesy: thou shalt be seen
(Though with some short parenthesis between)
High on the throne of wit; and, seated there,
Not mine — that's little — but thy laurel wear.

32 Nor; Now *1694*.

29–30 The three are authors of comparatively few but excellent comedies. Thomas Southerne (1659–1746) published his first play in 1682, some years after the other two had ceased
writing for the stage. Manly is a character in Wycherley's last play, *The Plain Dealer* (1677).
35–8 Scipio was made consul while still below the required age. Fabius, unsuccessful
himself in a long compaign against Hannibal in Italy, was opposed to his plans to carry the
war into Africa.
39–40 This hardly describes Guilio Romano (1499–1546), who was Raphael's junior by
some fourteen years.
45–6 Edward II, deposed in 1327, was succeeded by his son Edward III.
48 Following the accession of William III, Dryden was obliged to give up his posts of Poet
Laureate and Historiographer Royal in 1689. They were given to Thomas Shadwell, who
died in 1692 and was succeeded in the latter post by Thomas Rymer.

Thy first attempt an early promise made;
That early promise this has more than paid.
So bold, yet so judiciously you dare,
That your least praise is to be regular.
Time, place, and action, may with pains be wrought,
60   But genius must be born, and never can be taught.
This is your portion; this your native store;
Heav'n, that but once was prodigal before,
To Shakespeare gave as much; she could not give him more.
     Maintain your post: that's all the fame you need;
For 'tis impossible you should proceed.
Already I am worn with cares and age,
And just abandoning th' ungrateful stage;
Unprofitably kept at Heav'n's expense,
I live a rent-charge on his providence:
70   But you, whom ev'ry Muse and Grace adorn,
Whom I foresee to better fortune born,
Be kind to my remains; and oh defend,
Against your judgment, your departed friend!
Let not the insulting foe my fame pursue,
But shade those laurels which descend to you;
And take for tribute what these lines express:
You merit more; nor could my love do less.

55 Thy first attempt] Congreve's first comedy, *The Old Batchelor*, was performed in March 1693.

ALEXANDER'S FEAST

OR, THE POWER OF MUSIC; AN ODE IN HONOUR OF ST CECILIA'S DAY

On 3 September 1697, Dryden wrote to his sons at Rome: 'I am writing a song for St Celilia's feast, who you know is the patroness of music. This is troublesome, and no way beneficial; but I could not deny the stewards of the feast, who came in a body to me to desire that kindness.' In December, in a letter to Tonson: 'I am glad to hear from all hands that my Ode is esteemed the best of all my poetry by all the town: I thought so myself when I writ it, but being old I mistrusted my own judgment' (Ward, ed., *Letters*, pp. 93 and 98). The poem, which Scott calls an 'unequalled effusion of lyrical poetry', was acclaimed again in 1736 when it was performed with a musical setting by Handel.

'Twas at the royal feast, for Persia won
  By Philip's warlike son:
 Aloft in awful state
 The godlike hero sate
  On his imperial throne:
 His valiant peers were placed around;
Their brows with roses and with myrtles bound:
 (So should desert in arms be crowned).
The lovely Thais, by his side,
Sate like a blooming Eastern bride   10
In flow'r of youth and beauty's pride.
  Happy, happy, happy pair!
 None but the brave,
 None but the brave,
 None but the brave deserves the fair.

CHORUS

Happy, happy, happy pair!
None but the brave,
None but the brave,
None but the brave deserves the fair.

II

20 Timotheus, placed on high
  Amid the tuneful choir,
  With flying fingers touched the lyre:
The trembling notes ascend the sky,
  And heav'nly joys inspire.
The song began from Jove,
Who left his blissful seats above,
(Such is the pow'r of mighty love).
A dragon's fiery form belied the god:
Sublime on radiant spires he rode,
30   When he to fair Olympia pressed;
  And while he sought her snowy breast:
Then, round her slender waist he curled,
And stamped an image of himself, a sov'reign of the world.
The list'ning crowd admire the lofty sound:
'A present deity,' they shout around;
'A present deity,' the vaulted roofs rebound.
  With ravished ears
  The monarch hears,
  Assumes the god,
40   Affects to nod,
And seems to shake the spheres.

CHORUS

With ravished ears
The monarch hears,
Assumes the god,
Affects to nod,
And seems to shake the spheres.

III

The praise of Bacchus then the sweet musician sung,
  Of Bacchus ever fair and ever young:
  The jolly god in triumph comes;
50   Sound the trumpets; beat the drums;
    Flushed with a purple grace
    He shows his honest face:

20 There are many references to the power of Timotheus' playing. Van Doren (p. 205) cites Cowley's thirty-second note to the fourth book of the *Davideis*: 'Timotheus by music inflamed and appeased Alexander to what degrees he pleased.'

Now gives the hautboys breath; he comes, he comes.
  Bacchus, ever fair and young,
    Drinking joys did first ordain;
  Bacchus' blessings are a treasure,
  Drinking is a soldier's pleasure;
        Rich the treasure,
        Sweet the pleasure,
    Sweet is pleasure after pain.   60

CHORUS

Bacchus' blessings are a treasure,
Drinking is the soldier's pleasure;
      Rich the treasure,
      Sweet the pleasure,
  Sweet is pleasure after pain.

IV

  Soothed with the sound, the king grew vain;
    Fought all his battles o'er again;
And thrice he routed all his foes; and thrice he slew the slain.
      The master saw the madness rise;
      His glowing cheeks, his ardent eyes;   70
      And, while he heav'n and earth defied,
      Changed his hand, and checked his pride.
        He chose a mournful Muse,
          Soft pity to infuse:
        He sung Darius great and good,
          By too severe a fate,
      Fallen, fallen, fallen, fallen,
        Fallen from his high estate,
      And welt'ring in his blood;
Deserted at his utmost need,   80
By those his former bounty fed;
On the bare earth exposed he lies,
With not a friend to close his eyes.

With downcast looks the joyless victor sate,
  Revolving in his altered soul
    The various turns of chance below;
  And, now and then, a sigh he stole,
    And tears began to flow.

53 hautboys] Oboes.

CHORUS

Revolving in his altered soul
90   *The various turns of chance below;*
And, now and then, a sigh he stole,
And tears began to flow.

V

The mighty master smiled to see
That love was in the next degree:
'Twas but a kindred sound to move,
For pity melts the mind to love.
          Softly sweet, in Lydian measures,
Soon he soothed his soul to pleasures.
'War,' he sung, 'is toil and trouble;
100   Honour, but an empty bubble.
          Never ending, still beginning,
Fighting still, and still destroying:
          If the world be worth thy winning,
Think, O think it worth enjoying.
          Lovely Thais sits beside thee,
          Take the good the gods provide thee.'

The many rend the skies with loud applause;
So Love was crowned, but Music won the cause.
          The prince, unable to conceal his pain,
110   Gazed on the fair
          Who caused his care,
     And sighed and looked, sighed and looked,
Sighed and looked, and sighed again:
At length, with love and wine at once oppressed,
The vanquished victor sunk upon her breast.

CHORUS

The prince, unable to conceal his pain,
          Gazed on the fair
          Who caused his care,
     And sighed and looked, sighed and looked,
120   *Sighed and looked, and sighed again:*
At length, with love and wine at once oppressed,
The vanquished victor sunk upon her breast.

VI

Now strike the golden lyre again:
A louder yet, and yet a louder strain.
Break his bands of sleep asunder,
And arouse him, like a rattling peal of thunder.
     Hark, hark, the horrid sound
       Has raised up his head:
       As awaked from the dead,
     And amazed, he stares around.   130
'Revenge, revenge!' Timotheus cries,
    'See the Furies arise!
    See the snakes that they rear,
    How they hiss in their hair,
  And the sparkles that flash from their eyes!
    Behold a ghastly band,
    Each a torch in his hand!
Those are Grecian ghosts, that in battle were slain,
      And unburied remain
       Inglorious on the plain: 140
    Give the vengeance due
    To the valiant crew.
Behold how they toss their torches on high,
  How they point to the Persian abodes,
And glitt'ring temples of their hostile gods!'
The princes applaud, with a furious joy;
And the king seized a flambeau with zeal to destroy;
    Thais led the way,
    To light him to his prey,
And, like another Helen, fired another Troy.   150

CHORUS

And the king seized a flambeau with zeal to destroy;
    Thais led the way,
    To light him to his prey,
And, like another Helen, fired another Troy.

VII

    Thus, long ago,
  Ere heaving bellows learned to blow,
    While organs yet were mute;
Timotheus, to his breathing flute,

And sounding lyre,
160   Could swell the soul to rage, or kindle soft desire.
At last, divine Cecilia came,
Inventress of the vocal frame;
The sweet enthusiast, from her sacred store,
Enlarged the former narrow bounds,
And added length to solemn sounds,
With nature's mother wit, and arts unknown before.
Let old Timotheus yield the prize,
Or both divide the crown:
He raised a mortal to the skies;
170   She drew an angel down.

GRAND CHORUS

At last, divine Cecilia came,
Inventress of the vocal frame;
The sweet enthusiast, from her sacred store,
Enlarged the former narrow bounds,
And added length to solemn sounds,
With nature's mother wit, and arts unknown before.
Let old Timotheus yield the prize,
Or both divide the crown:
He raised a mortal to the skies;
180   *She drew an angel down.*

TO MY HONOURED KINSMAN JOHN DRIDEN, OF CHESTERTON, IN THE COUNTY OF HUNTINGDON, ESQUIRE

Published in *Fables, Ancient and Modern* (1700). John Driden (1635–1708) was Dryden's first cousin, being the second son of Sir John Driden, elder brother of the poet's father Erasmus. He was for some time Member of Parliament for the county of Huntingdon. Dryden was pleased with his poem: 'I think I have not only drawn the features of my worthy kinsman, but have also given my own opinion of what an Englishman in Parliament ought to be; and deliver it as a memorial of my own principles to all posterity' (Ward, ed., *Letters*, p. 120).

How blessed is he, who leads a country life,
Unvexed with anxious cares, and void of strife!
Who, studying peace and shunning civil rage,
Enjoyed his youth, and now enjoys his age:
All who deserve his love, he makes his own;
And, to be loved himself, needs only to be known.
    Just, good, and wise, contending neighbours come,⎫
From your award to wait their final doom;   ⎬
And, foes before, return in friendship home.   ⎭
Without their cost, you terminate the cause,   10
And save th' expense of long litigious laws:
Where suits are traversed, and so little won,
That he who conquers is but last undone.
Such are not your decrees; but so designed,   ⎫
The sanction leaves a lasting peace behind;   ⎬
Like your own soul, serene: a pattern of your mind.⎭
    Promoting concord, and composing strife,
Lord of yourself, uncumbered with a wife;
Where, for a year, a month, perhaps a night,
Long penitence succeeds a short delight: 20
Minds are so hardly matched, that ev'n the first,
Though paired by Heav'n, in Paradise were cursed.
For man and woman, though in one they grow,

Yet, first or last, return again to two.
He to God's image, she to his was made;
So, farther from the fount, the stream at random strayed.
  How could he stand, when, put to double pain,
He must a weaker than himself sustain!
Each might have stood perhaps, but each alone;
30 Two wrestlers help to pull each other down.
  Not that my verse would blemish all the fair;   ⎫
But yet if *some* be bad, 'tis wisdom to beware;   ⎬
And better shun the bait, than struggle in the snare. ⎭
Thus have you shunned, and shun the married state,
Trusting as little as you can to fate.
  No porter guards the passage of your door,
T'admit the wealthy, and exclude the poor;
For God, who gave the riches, gave the heart,
To sanctify the whole, by giving part.
40 Heav'n, who foresaw the will, the means has wrought,
And to the second son a blessing brought:
The first-begotten had his father's share;
But you, like Jacob, are Rebecca's heir.
  So may your stores and fruitful fields increase;
And ever be you blessed, who live to bless.
As Ceres sowed, wheree'er her chariot flew;
As Heav'n in deserts rained the bread of dew,
So free to many, to relations most,
You feed with manna your own Israel host.
50   With crowds attended of your ancient race,
You seek the champian sports, or sylvan chase;
With well-breathed beagles you surround the wood,
Ev'n then industrious of the common good;
And often have you brought the wily fox
To suffer for the firstlings of the flocks;
Chased ev'n amid the folds, and made to bleed,
Like felons, where they did the murd'rous deed.
This fiery game your active youth maintained;
Not yet by years extinguished, though restrained:
60 You season still with sports your serious hours;
For age but tastes of pleasures, youth devours.
The hare in pastures or in plains is found,

43 'Sir Robert Driden inherited the paternal estate of Canons-Ashby, while that of Chester-
ton descended to John his second brother, to whom the Epistle is addressed, through his
mother, daughter of Sir Robert Bevile' (Scott).

Emblem of human life, who runs the round;
And after all his wand'ring ways are done,⎫
His circle fills and ends where he begun,   ⎬
Just as the setting meets the rising sun.   ⎭

  Thus princes ease their cares; but happier he
Who seeks not pleasure through necessity,
Than such as once on slipp'ry thrones were placed;
And chasing, sigh to think themselves are chased.   70

  So lived our sires, ere doctors learned to kill,
And multiplied with theirs the weekly bill.
The first physicians by debauch were made;
Excess began, and sloth sustains the trade.
Pity the gen'rous kind their cares bestow
To search forbidden truths, (a sin to know:)
To which if human science could attain,
The doom of death, pronounced by God, were vain.
In vain the leech would interpose delay;
Fate fastens first, and vindicates the prey.   80
What help from art's endeavours can we have?   ⎫
Gibbons but guesses, nor is sure to save;   ⎬
But Maurus sweeps whole parishes, and peoples ev'ry grave;⎭
And no more mercy to mankind will use,
Than when he robbed and murdered Maro's muse.
Would'st thou be soon dispatched, and perish whole?
Trust Maurus with thy life, and M—lb——rne with thy soul.

  By chase our long-lived fathers earned their food;
Toil strung the nerves, and purified the blood:
But we their sons, a pampered race of men,   90
Are dwindled down to threescore years and ten.
Better to hunt in fields, for health unbought,
Than fee the doctor for a nauseous draught.
The wise, for cure, on exercise depend;
God never made his work for man to mend.

  The tree of knowledge, once in Eden placed,
Was easy found, but was forbid the taste:
O had our grandsire walked without his wife,
He first had sought the better plant of life!
Now, both are lost: yet, wand'ring in the dark,   100
Physicians, for the tree, have found the bark.

82 Gibbons] William Gibbons (1649–1728), Dryden's doctor.
83 Maurus] Sir Richard Blackmore, author and physician.
87 Cf. *Preface to the Fables*, p. 624, where Dryden deals with Blackmore and Milbourne.

They, lab'ring for relief of human kind,
With sharpened sight some remedies may find;
Th' apothecary-train is wholly blind.
From files a random recipe they take,
And many deaths of one prescription make.
Garth, gen'rous as his Muse, prescribes and gives;
The shopman sells, and by destruction lives:
Ungrateful tribe! who, like the viper's brood,
110   From med'cine issuing, suck their mother's blood!
Let these obey, and let the learn'd prescribe,
That men may die without a double bribe:
Let them but under their superiors kill,
When doctors first have signed the bloody bill:
He 'scapes the best, who, nature to repair,
Draws physic from the fields, in draughts of vital air.

You hoard not health for your own private use,
But on the public spend the rich produce;
When, often urged, unwilling to be great,
120   Your country calls you from your loved retreat,
And sends to senates, charged with common care,
Which none more shuns, and none can better bear.
Where could they find another formed so fit,
To poise with solid sense a sprightly wit?
Were these both wanting, (as they both abound,)
Where could so firm integrity be found?

Well born, and wealthy, wanting no support,
You steer betwixt the country and the court;
Nor gratify whate'er the great desire,
130   Nor grudging give what public needs require.
Part must be left, a fund when foes invade,
And part employed to roll the wat'ry trade:
Ev'n Canaan's happy land, when worn with toil,
Required a sabbath year to mend the meagre soil.

Good senators (and such are you) so give,
That kings may be supplied, the people thrive:
And he, when want requires, is truly wise,
Who slights not foreign aids, nor overbuys;
But on our native strength, in time of need, relies.
140   Munster was bought, we boast not the success;
Who fights for gain, for greater makes his peace.

107 Garth] Sir Samuel Garth (1661–1719), physician and author of *The Dispensary* (1699),
a humorous poem against mercenary apothecaries.

Our foes, compelled by need, have peace embraced;
The peace both parties want is like to last:
Which if secure, securely we may trade;
Or, not secure, should never have been made.
Safe in ourselves, while on ourselves we stand,
The sea is ours, and that defends the land.
Be, then, the naval stores the nation's care,
New ships to build, and battered to repair.
    Observe the war, in ev'ry annual course;   150
What has been done, was done with British force:
Namur subdued is England's palm alone;
The rest besieged, but we constrained the town:
We saw th' event that followed our success;
France, though pretending arms, pursued the peace,
Obliged, by one sole treaty, to restore
What twenty years of war had won before.
Enough for Europe has our Albion fought;
Let us enjoy the peace our blood has bought.
When once the Persian king was put to flight,   160
The weary Macedons refused to fight;
Themselves their own mortality confessed,
And left the son of Jove to quarrel for the rest.
    Ev'n victors are by victories undone;
Thus Hannibal, with foreign laurels won,
To Carthage was recalled, too late to keep his own.
While sore of battle, while our wounds are green,
Why should we tempt the doubtful die again?
In wars renewed, uncertain of success;
Sure of a share, as umpires of the peace.   170
    A patriot both the king and country serves;
Prerogative and privilege preserves:
Of each our laws the certain limit show;
One must not ebb, nor t'other overflow.
Betwixt the prince and parliament we stand;
The barriers of the state on either hand:
May neither overflow, for then they drown the land.
When both are full, they feed our blessed abode;
Like those that watered once the paradise of God.

142ff The Peace of Ryswick in 1697 had concluded the Nine Years War against France. Parliament, anxious to forestall further military adventures and relieve the financial burden on the country, obliged William III in 1699 to disband the standing army. A stronger navy was advocated.

180   Some overpoise of sway by turns they share;
   In peace the people, and the prince in war:
   Consuls of mod'rate pow'r in calms were made;
   When the Gauls came, one sole dictator swayed.
    Patriots, in peace, assert the people's right,
   With noble stubbornness resisting might:
   No lawless mandates from the court receive,
   Nor lend by force, but in a body give.
   Such was your gen'rous grandsire; free to grant
   In parliaments that weighed their prince's want:
190   But so tenacious of the common cause,
   As not to lend the king against his laws;
   And, in a loathsome dungeon doomed to lie,⎫
   In bonds retained his birthright liberty, ⎬
   And shamed oppression, till it set him free. ⎭
    O true descendant of a patriot line,
   Who, while thou shar'st their lustre, lend'st 'em thine,
   Vouchsafe this picture of thy soul to see;
   'Tis so far good, as it resembles thee.
   The beauties to th' original I owe,
200   Which when I miss, my own defects I show:
   Nor think the kindred Muses thy disgrace;
   A poet is not born in ev'ry race.
   Two of a house few ages can afford;
   One to perform, another to record.
   Praiseworthy actions are by thee embraced,
   And 'tis my praise to make thy praises last.
   For ev'n when death dissolves our human frame,
   The soul returns to heav'n, from whence it came;
   Earth keeps the body, verse preserves the fame.

188 your gen'rous grandsire] Sir Erasmus Dryden, common grandfather of the two cousins, imprisoned in 1628 for opposition to Charles I's illegal loan-raising.

THE SECULAR MASQUE

From *THE PILGRIM*

Dryden wrote to Mrs Steward on 11 April 1700 that 'within this month there will be played for my profit an old play of Fletcher's called *The Pilgrim* corrected by my good friend Mr Vanbrook [Vanbrugh]; to which I have added a new masque, and am to write a new prologue and epilogue' (Ward, ed., *Letters*, p. 136). Tradition has it that he died on the third day of its run.

Enter JANUS

JANUS   Chronos, Chronos, mend thy pace;
             And hundred times the rolling sun
             Around the radiant belt has run
             In his revolving race.
             Behold, behold, the goal in sight;
             Spread thy fans, and wing thy flight.

Enter CHRONOS, *with a scythe in his hand, and a great globe on his back, which he sets down at his entrance.*

CHRONOS   Weary, weary of my weight,
             Let me, let me drop my freight,
               And leave the world behind.
             I could not bear   10
             Another year
             The load of humankind.

Enter MOMUS *laughing*

MOMUS   Ha! ha! ha! ha! ha! ha! well hast thou done
               To lay down thy pack,
               And lighten thy back;
             The world was a fool, e'er since it begun,

Title Secular] From the Latin *saecularis*, of or belonging to a *saeculum*, an age. Here, a masque celebrating the start of a new century.

And since neither Janus, nor Chronos, nor I
          Can hinder the crimes,
          Or mend the bad times,
20   'Tis better to laugh than to cry.

CHORUS OF ALL   'Tis better to laugh than to cry.
THREE

JANUS   Since Momus comes to laugh below,
          Old Time, begin the show,
          That he may see, in every scene,
          What changes in this age have been.

CHRONOS   Then goddess of the silver bow begin.

Horns, or hunting music within.
Enter DIANA

DIANA   With horns and with hounds I waken the day,
          And hie to my woodland walks away;
          I tuck up my robe, and am buskined soon,
30   And tie to my forehead a wexing moon.
          I course the fleet stag, unkennel the fox,
          And chase the wild goats o'er summits of rocks;
          With shouting and hooting we pierce through the sky,
          And Echo turns hunter, and doubles the cry.

CHORUS OF ALL   *With shouting and hooting we pierce through the sky,*
                And Echo turns hunter, and doubles the cry.

JANUS   Then our age was in its prime,

CHRONOS   Free from rage.

DIANA   And free from crime.

MOMUS   A very merry, dancing, drinking,
40   Laughing, quaffing, and unthinking time.

CHORUS OF ALL   *Then our age was in its prime,*
                Free from rage, and free from crime;
                A very merry, dancing, drinking,
                Laughing, quaffing, and unthinking time.

Dance of Diana's attendants.
Enter MARS

25 changes in this age] 'The moral of this emblematical representation is sufficiently

MARS   Inspire the vocal brass, inspire;
       The world is past its infant age:
          Arms and honour,
          Arms and honour,
       Set the martial mind on fire,
       And kindle manly rage.   50
       Mars has looked the sky to red:
       And Peace, the lazy good, is fled.
       Plenty, Peace, and Pleasure fly:
          The sprightly green
       In woodland walks no more is seen;
       The sprightly green has drunk the Tyrian dye.

CHORUS OF ALL   *Plenty, Peace, etc.*

MARS   Sound the trumpet, beat the drum;
       Through all the world around,
       Sound a reveille, sound, sound,   60
       The warrior god is come.

CHORUS OF ALL   *Sound the trumpet, etc.*

MOMUS   Thy sword within the scabbard keep,
          And let mankind agree;
       Better the world were fast asleep,
          Than kept awake by thee.
       The fools are only thinner,
          With all our cost and care;
       But neither side a winner,
          For things are as they were.   70

CHORUS OF ALL   *The fools are only, etc.*

Enter VENUS

VENUS   Calms appear when storms are past;
       Love will have his hour at last:
       Nature is my kindly care;
       Mars destroys, and I repair;
       Take me, take me, while you may;
       Venus comes not ev'ry day.

intelligible. By the introduction of the deities of the chase, of war, and of love, as governing the various changes of the seventeenth century, the poet alludes to the sylvan sports of James the First, the bloody wars of his son, and the licentious gallantry which reigned in the courts of Charles II and James, his successor' (Scott).

CHORUS OF ALL   *Take her, take her, etc.*

CHRONOS   The world was then so light,
                    I scarcely felt the weight;
                    Joy ruled the day, and Love the night.
                    But since the Queen of Pleasure left the ground,
                        I faint, I lag,
                        And feebly drag
                    The pond'rous orb around.

MOMUS   All, all of a piece throughout:

                    Pointing to DIANA

                Thy chase had a beast in view;

                        To MARS

                Thy wars brought nothing about;

                        To VENUS

                Thy lovers were all untrue.

JANUS   'Tis well an old age is out.

CHRONOS   And time to begin a new.

CHORUS OF ALL   *All, all of a piece throughout;*
                    Thy chase had a beast in view;
                    Thy wars brought nothing about;
                    Thy lovers were all untrue.
                    'Tis well an old age is out,
                    And time to begin a new.

                Dance of huntsmen, nymphs, warriors, and lovers.

80

90

82 the Queen of Pleasure] Queen Mary of Modena, then in exile with King James II
(Summers).

PROLOGUES AND
EPILOGUES

Prologues and epilogues are perhaps the best indication of the sensitive and sometimes difficult relationship of the Restoration stage with its public, particularly with one section of it, the high-spirited young men of wit and fashion in the pit whose opinions could decide the fate of the play. A considerable range of address, from flattery to censure, was employed to obtain a settled and contented audience. Dryden's skill made his services much in demand: he wrote over a hundred of these poems, for his own plays and those of others. Besides the behaviour of audiences, there is much else of interest in them: the rivalry and unsteady fortunes of the two theatres; vagaries in taste, for farce or for lavish productions; the effect of important events; and a good deal of critical judgment.

PROLOGUE TO *THE RIVAL LADIES*

The Rival Ladies was first performed around June 1664. Samuel Pepys liked it as 'a very innocent and most pretty witty play' (*Diary*, 4 August).

'Tis much desired, you judges of the town
Would pass a vote to put all prologues down;
For who can show me, since they first were writ,
They e'er converted one hard-hearted wit?
Yet the world's mended well; in former days
Good prologues were as scarce as now good plays.
For the reforming poets of our age,
In this first charge, spend their poetic rage:
Expect no more when once the prologue's done;
The wit is ended ere the play's begun.   10
You now have habits, dances, scenes, and rhymes,
High language often, ay, and sense sometimes.
As for a clear contrivance, doubt it not;
They blow out candles to give light to th' plot.
And for surprise, two bloody-minded men
Fight till they die, then rise and dance again.
Such deep intrigues you're welcome to this day:
But blame yourselves, not him who writ the play.
Though his plot's dull as can be well desired,
Wit stiff as any you have e'er admired,   20
He's bound to please, not to write well; and knows
There is a mode in plays as well as clothes:
Therefore, kind judges—

A Second Prologue enters.

2.   Hold! would you admit
For judges all you see within the pit?
    1. Whom would he then except, or on what score?
    2. All who (like him) have writ ill plays before;

For they, like thieves condemned, are hangmen made,
To execute the members of their trade.
All that are writing now he would disown,
30   But then he must except — ev'n all the town:
All chol'ric losing gamesters, who in spite
Will damn today, because they lost last night;
All servants, whom their mistress' scorn upbraids;
All maudlin lovers, and all slighted maids;
All who are out of humour, or severe;
All that want wit, or hope to find it here.

PROLOGUE TO *THE WILD GALLANT, REVIVED*

Dryden's first play was produced in February 1663. The revival was probably in 1667. It was not printed until 1669.

> As some raw squire, by tender mother bred,
> Till one-and-twenty keeps his maidenhead,
> (Pleased with some sport, which he alone does find,
> And thinks a secret to all humankind,)
> Till mightily in love, yet half afraid,
> He first attempts the gentle dairy-maid.
> Succeeding there, and led by the renown
> Of Whetstone's Park, he comes at length to town;
> Where entered, by some school-fellow or friend,
> He grows to break glass-windows in the end: 10
> His valour too, which with the watch began,
> Proceeds to duel, and he kills his man.
> By such degrees, while knowledge he did want,
> Our unfledged author writ a *Wild Gallant*.
> He thought him monstrous lewd (I'll lay my life)
> Because suspected with his landlord's wife;
> But, since his knowledge of the town began,
> He thinks him now a very civil man;
> And, much ashamed of what he was before,
> Has fairly played him at three wenches more.   20
> 'Tis some amends his frailties to confess;
> Pray pardon him his want of wickedness.
> He's towardly, and will come on apace;
> His frank confession shows he has some grace.
> You baulked him when he was a young beginner,
> And almost spoiled a very hopeful sinner;
> But, if once more you slight his weak endeavour,
> For aught I know, he may turn tail for ever.

8 Whetstone's Park was a lane between Holborn and Lincoln's Inn Fields. It was notorious for debauchery.

PROLOGUE AND EPILOGUE TO *SIR MARTIN MAR-ALL, OR THE FEIGNED INNOCENCE*

Sir Martin Mar-all, one of Dryden's most successful plays, was probably first performed in August 1667.

PROLOGUE

Fools, which each man meets in his dish each day,
Are yet the great regalios of a play;
In which to poets you but just appear,
To prize that highest which costs them so dear.
Fops in the town more easily will pass;
One story makes a statutable ass:
But such in plays must be much thicker sown,
Like yolks of eggs, a dozen beat to one.
Observing poets all their walks invade,
As men watch woodcocks gliding through a glade;
And when they have enough for comedy,
They stow their several bodies in a pie.
The poet's but the cook to fashion it,
For, gallants, you yourselves have found the wit.
To bid you welcome would your bounty wrong;
None welcome those who bring their cheer along.

10

EPILOGUE

As country vicars, when the sermon's done,
Run huddling to the benediction;
Well knowing, though the better sort may stay,
The vulgar rout will run unblest away:
So we, when once our play is done, make haste

2 regalios] Presents of choice food or drink.
6 statutable] One that meets requirements.
10 Woodcocks were notoriously easy to trap: the word came to describe a simpleton.

With a short epilogue to close your taste.
In thus withdrawing we seem mannerly,
But when the curtain's down we peep and see
A jury of the wits who still stay late,
And in their club decree the poor play's fate: 10
Their verdict back is to the boxes brought,
Thence all the town pronounces it their thought.
Thus, gallants, we like Lilly can foresee;
But if you ask us what our doom will be,
We by tomorrow will our fortune cast,
As he tells all things when the year is past.

13 Lilly] William Lilly (1602–81), a famous astrologer.

PROLOGUE TO *THE TEMPEST*

The Tempest; or, The Enchanted Island, a musical adaptation by Dryden and Davenant
of Shakespeare's play, was first performed in November 1667. It was printed in
1670.

As, when a tree's cut down, the secret root
Lives under ground, and thence new branches shoot;
So, from old Shakespeare's honoured dust, this day
Springs up and buds a new reviving play:
Shakespeare, who (taught by none) did first impart
To Fletcher wit, to labouring Jonson art:
He monarch-like gave those his subjects law,
And is that nature which they paint and draw.
Fletcher reached that which on his heights did grow,
Whilst Jonson crept, and gathered all below.
This did his love, and this his mirth digest:
One imitates him most, the other best.
If they have since outwrit all other men,
'Tis with the drops which fell from Shakespeare's pen.
The storm which vanished on the neighb'ring shore
Was taught by Shakespeare's *Tempest* first to roar.
That innocence and beauty which did smile
In Fletcher, grew on this *Enchanted Isle*.
But Shakespeare's magic could not copied be;
Within that circle none durst walk but he.
I must confess 'twas bold, nor would you now
That liberty to vulgar wits allow,
Which works by magic supernatural things;
But Shakespeare's pow'r is sacred as a king's.
Those legends from old priesthood were received,
And he then writ, as people then believed.

10

20

15–16 A reference to Fletcher's *The Sea Voyage*, recently acted by the rival King's Company at
the Theatre Royal ('the neighb'ring shore').

But if for Shakespeare we your grace implore,
We for our theatre shall want it more
Who by our dearth of youths are forced t'employ
One of our women to present a boy;   30
And that's a transformation, you will say,
Exceeding all the magic in the play.
Let none expect in the last act to find
Her sex transformed from man to womankind.
Whate'er she was before the play began,
All you shall see of her is perfect man.
Or if your fancy will be farther led
To find her woman, it must be abed.

30 The role was probably that of Hippolito.

EPILOGUE TO *TYRANNIC LOVE*

SPOKEN BY MRS ELLEN, WHEN SHE WAS TO
BE CARRIED OFF DEAD BY THE BEARERS

Dryden's heroic play about St Catherine was performed in June 1669, and printed in 1670. Eleanor (or Nell) Gwyn played the part of Valeria. She excelled as a comic actress, but appears to have been less happy in serious parts (l. 30).

To the Bearer

Hold! are you mad? you damned, confounded dog!
I am to rise and speak the epilogue.

To the Audience

I come, kind gentlemen, strange news to tell ye,
I am the ghost of poor departed Nelly.
Sweet ladies, be not frighted, I'll be civil;
I'm what I was, a little harmless devil.
For after death, we sprites have just such natures
We had, for all the world, when human creatures;
And therefore I that was an actress here,
10 Play all my tricks in hell, a goblin there.
Gallants, look to't, you say there are no sprites;
But I'll come dance about your beds at nights.
And faith you'll be in a sweet kind of taking,
When I suprise you between sleep and waking.
To tell you true, I walk because I die
Out of my calling in a tragedy.
O poet, damned dull poet, who could prove
So senseless, to make Nelly die for love!
Nay, what's yet worse, to kill me in the prime
20 Of Easter term, in tart and cheese-cake time!

13 taking] Excitement or passion.

I'll fit the fop; for I'll not one word say
T'excuse his godly out-of-fashion play;
A play which if you dare but twice sit out,
You'll all be slandered, and be thought devout.
But farewell, gentlemen, make haste to me,
I'm sure ere long to have your company.
As for my epitaph when I am gone,
I'll trust no poet, but will write my own:—

Here Nelly lies, who, though she lived a slattern,
Yet died a princess, acting in St Cathar'n.   30

PROLOGUE TO THE FIRST PART OF
THE CONQUEST OF GRANADA
SPOKEN BY MRS ELLEN GWYN IN A BROADBRIMMED
HAT AND WAISTBELT

Comic effects such as the 'wheel-broad hat' (l. 42) were frequent in prologues and epilogues.

This jest was first of t'other house's making,
And, five times tried, has never failed of taking;
For 'twere a shame a poet should be killed
Under the shelter of so broad a shield.
This is that hat, whose very sight did win ye
To laugh and clap as though the devil were in ye.
As then, for Nokes, so now I hope you'll be
So dull, to laugh, once more, for love of me.
'I'll write a play,' says one, 'for I have got
10   A broad-brimmed hat, and waist-belt tow'rds a plot.'
Says t'other, 'I have one more large than that.'
Thus they out-write each other with a hat!
The brims still grew with every play they writ;
And grew so large, they covered all the wit.
Hat was the play; 'twas language, wit, and tale:
Like them that find meat, drink, and cloth in ale.
What dullness do these mongrel wits confess,
When all their hope is acting of a dress!
Thus two, the best comedians of the age
20   Must be worn out, with being blocks o'th' stage:
Like a young girl, who better things has known,
Beneath their poet's impotence they groan.
See now what charity it was to save!

1 t'other house] The Duke's Theatre. *The Conquest of Granada*, in two parts, was performed by the King's Company in December 1670 and January 1671.
19 Probably referring to Edward Angel and James Nokes, well-known actors with the Duke's Company.

They thought you liked what only you forgave;
And brought you more dull sense, dull sense much worse
Than brisk gay nonsense, and the heavier curse.
They bring old ir'n and glass upon the stage,
To barter with the Indians of our age.
Still they write on, and like great authors show;⎫
But 'tis as rollers in wet gardens grow   ⎬   30
Heavy with dirt, and gath'ring as they go.   ⎭
May none, who have so little understood,
To like such trash, presume to praise what's good!
And may those drudges of the stage, whose fate
Is damned dull farce more dully to translate,
Fall under that excise the state thinks fit
To set on all French wares, whose worse is wit.
French farce, worn out at home, is sent abroad;
And, patched up here, is made our English mode.
Henceforth, let poets, ere allowed to write,   40
Be searched, like duellists, before they fight,
For wheel-broad hats, dull humour, all that chaff,
Which makes you mourn, and makes the vulgar laugh.
For these, in plays, ere as unlawful arms
As, in a combat, coats of mail and charms.

EPILOGUE TO THE SECOND PART OF
THE CONQUEST OF GRANADA

They who have best succeeded on the stage
Have still conformed their genius to their age.
Thus Jonson did mechanic humour show,
When men were dull, and conversation low.
Then comedy was faultless, but 'twas coarse:
Cobb's tankard was a jest, and Otter's horse.
And, as their comedy, their love was mean;
Except, by chance, in some one laboured scene,
Which must atone for an ill-written play.
They rose, but at their height could seldom stay.   10
Fame then was cheap, and the first comer sped;
And they have kept it since, by being dead.
But were they now to write, when critics weigh
Each line, and ev'ry word, throughout a play,
None of 'em, no not Jonson in his height,
Could pass, without allowing grains for weight.
Think it not envy that these truths are told;
Our poet's not malicious, though he's bold.
'Tis not to brand 'em that their faults are shown,
But, by their errors, to excuse his own.   20
If love and honour now are higher raised,
'Tis not the poet, but the age is praised.
Wit's now arrived to a more high degree;
Our native language more refined and free.
Our ladies and our men now speak more wit

3 mechanic] Vulgar.
6 Cobb is a water-carrier in Ben Jonson's *Every Man in his Humour*. Otter, a captain in the
same author's *Epicoene; or, The Silent Woman*, called one of his tankards 'Horse'.
16 A grain was the smallest unit of weight. Thus, everything would have to pass a finicking
test.
21–6 This is argued at length in Dryden's *Defence of the Epilogue*, an essay appended to the
play when it was published in 1672.

In conversation, than those poets writ.
Then, one of these is, consequently, true;
That what this poet writes comes short of you
And imitates you ill (which most he fears),
Or else his writing is not worse than theirs.   30
Yet, though you judge (as sure the critics will)
That some before him writ with greater skill,
In this one praise he has their fame surpast,
To please an age more gallant than the last.

PROLOGUE SPOKEN AT THE OPENING OF THE NEW HOUSE,

26 MARCH 1674

Two years after the destruction by fire of the Theatre Royal in Bridges Street the King's Company moved into a new theatre in Drury Lane. It could not compare, though, with the grandeur of the Duke's Theatre in Dorset Garden, built in 1671.

A plain-built house, after so long a stay,
Will send you half unsatisfied away;
When, fall'n from your expected pomp, you find
A bare convenience only is designed.
You, who each day can theatres behold,
Like Nero's palace, shining all with gold,
Our mean ungilded stage will scorn, we fear,
And, for the homely room, disdain the cheer.
Yet now cheap druggets to a mode are grown, ⎫
10   And a plain suit, since we can make but one, ⎬
Is better than to be by tarnished gaudry known. ⎭
They who are by your favours wealthy made,
With mighty sums may carry on the trade:
We, broken bankers, half destroyed by fire, ⎫
With our small stock to humble roofs retire: ⎬
Pity our loss, while you their pomp admire. ⎭
For fame and honour we no longer strive,
We yield in both, and only beg to live:
Unable to support their vast expense,
20   Who build and treat with such magnificence;
That, like th' ambitious monarchs of the age,
They give the law to our provincial stage:
Great neighbours enviously promote excess,
While they impose their splendour on the less.

6 shining all with gold] The gilded proscenium arch of the Duke's Theatre.
9 druggets] Coarse cloth. Cf. *Mac Flecknoe*, l. 33.

But only fools, and they of vast estate,
Th' extremity of modes will imitate,
The dangling knee-fringe, and the bib-cravat.
Yet if some pride with want may be allowed,
We in our plainness may be justly proud;
Our royal master willed it should be so;   30
Whate'er he's pleased to own can need no show:
That sacred name gives ornament and grace,
And, like his stamp, makes basest metals pass.
'Twere folly now a stately pile to raise,
To build a playhouse while you throw down plays;
Whilst scenes, machines, and empty operas reign,
And for the pencil you the pen disdain.
While troops of famished Frenchmen hither drive,
And laugh at those upon whose aims they live:
Old English authors vanish, and give place   40
To these new conqu'rors of the Norman race.
More tamely than your fathers you submit;
You're now grown vassals to 'em in your wit.
Mark, when they play, how our fine fops advance
The mighty merits of these men of France,
Keep time, cry *Ben*, and humour the *cadence*.
Well, please yourselves; but sure 'tis understood,
That French machines have ne'er done England good.
I would not prophesy our house's fate:
But while vain shows and scenes you overrate,   50
'Tis to be feared——
That as a fire the former house o'erthrew,
Machines and tempests will destroy the new.

38 Referring to visits by troupes of French comedians to London.
46 'Keeping time' and 'humouring the cadence' probably mean accentuating words in a
French manner, as Melantha does in *Marriage à la Mode. Ben*] *Bien*
53 Referring to the preparations at the Duke's Theatre for a production of an operatic version
of *The Tempest* by Thomas Shadwell.

PROLOGUE TO *AURENG-ZEBE*

Aureng-Zebe, performed in November 1675 by the King's Company, is the last of Dryden's rhymed heroic plays. The Prologue shows complete disillusionment with this form of drama, for which he had had such great enthusiasm at the outset of his career.

Our author by experience finds it true,
'Tis much more hard to please himself than you;
And out of no feigned modesty, this day
Damns his laborious trifle of a play:
Not that it's worse than what before he writ,
But he has now another taste of wit;
And, to confess a truth, (though out of time),
Grows weary of his long-loved mistress, Rhyme.
Passion's too fierce to be in fetters bound,
And Nature flies him like enchanted ground.   10
What verse can do, he has performed in this,
Which he presumes the most correct of his;
But spite of all his pride, a secret shame
Invades his breast at Shakespeare's sacred name:
Awed when he hears his godlike Romans rage,
He, in a just despair, would quit the stage;
And to an age less polished, more unskilled,
Does, with disdain, the foremost honours yield.
As with the greater dead he dares not strive,
He would not match his verse with those who live: 20
Let him retire, betwixt two ages cast,
The first of this, and hindmost of the last.
A losing gamester, let him sneak away;
He bears no ready money from the play.
The fate which governs poets thought it fit
He should not raise his fortunes by his wit.
The clergy thrive, and the litigious bar;
Dull heroes fatten with the spoils of war:

All southern vices, Heav'n be praised, are here;
But wit's a luxury you think too dear.   30
When you to cultivate the plant are loth,
'Tis a shrewd sign 'twas never of your growth:
And wit in northern climates will not blow,
Except, like orange trees, 'tis housed from snow.
There needs no care to put a playhouse down,
'Tis the most desert place of all the town:
We and our neighbours, to speak proudly, are,
Like monarchs, ruined with expensive war;
While, like wise English, unconcerned you sit,
And see us play the tragedy of Wit.   40

38 expensive war] The two theatres had for some years tried to outdo each other in expensive,
elaborate productions.

EPILOGUE TO *THE MAN OF MODE,*
OR SIR FOPLING FLUTTER

Sir George Etherege's third and last play, one of the finest of Restoration comedies, was performed by the Duke's Company at the Dorset Garden theatre in March 1676.

Most modern wits such monstrous fools have shown,
They seemed not of Heav'n's making, but their own.
Those nauseous Harlequins in farce may pass,
But there goes more to a substantial ass!
Something of man must be exposed to view,
That, gallants, they may more resemble you.
Sir Fopling is a fool so nicely writ,
The ladies would mistake him for a wit;
And, when he sings, talks loud, and cocks, would cry,
10   'I vow, methinks, he's pretty company.
So brisk, so gay, so travelled, so refined!'
As he took pains to graff upon his kind.
True fops help nature's work, and go to school,
To file and finish God A'mighty's fool.
Yet none Sir Fopling him, or him can call;
He's knight o'th' shire, and represents ye all.
From each he meets he culls whate'er he can;
Legion's his name, a people in a man.
His bulky folly gathers as it goes,
20   And, rolling o'er you, like a snow-ball grows.
His various modes from various fathers follow;
One taught the toss, and one the new French wallow.
His sword-knot this, his cravat this designed;
And this, the yard-long snake he twirls behind.

16 knight o'th' shire] Member of Parliament for a County.
22 toss] A sudden jerk of the head.
    wallow] A rolling gait.
24 snake] A long curl or tail attached to a wig.

From one the sacred periwig he gained,
Which wind ne'er blew, nor touch of hat profaned.
Another's diving bow he did adore,
Which with a shog casts all the hair before;
Till he with full decorum brings it back,
And rises with a water-spaniel shake.   30
As for his songs (the ladies' dear delight),
Those sure he took from most of you who write.
Yet every man is safe from what he feared;
For no one fool is hunted from the herd.

28 shog] Shake.

PROLOGUE TO
THE UNIVERSITY OF OXFORD

Thought to have been written in 1676 or about 1681. See Gardner's edition, p. 258, and Calif. *Works*, 1, 358.

Though actors cannot much of learning boast,
Of all who want it, we admire it most.
We love the praises of a learned pit,
As we remotely are allied to wit.
We speak our poet's wit, and trade in ore,
Like those who touch upon the golden shore:
Betwixt our judges can distinction make,
Discern how much, and why, our poems take:
Mark if the fools, or men of sense, rejoice;
Whether th' applause be only sound or voice.
When our fop gallants, or our city folly
Clap over-loud, it makes us melancholy:
We doubt that scene which does their wonder raise,
And, for their ignorance, contemn their praise.
Judge then, if we who act, and they who write,
Should not be proud of giving you delight.
London likes grossly; but this nicer pit
Examines, fathoms all the depths of wit;
The ready finger lays on every blot;
Knows what should justly please, and what should not.
Nature herself lies open to your view;
You judge by her what draught of her is true,
Where outlines false, and colours seem too faint,
Where bunglers daub, and where true poets paint.
But, by the sacred genius of this place,
By every muse, by each domestic grace,
Be kind to wit, which but endeavours well,
And, where you judge, presumes not to excel.
Our poets hither for adoption come,

10

20

As nations sued to be made free of Rome: 30
Not in the suffragating tribes to stand,
But in your utmost, last, provincial band.
If his ambition may those hopes pursue,
Who with religion loves your arts and you,
Oxford to him a dearer name shall be,
Than his own mother university.
Thebes did his green, unknowing youth engage;
He chooses Athens in his riper age.

36 mother university] Cambridge.

EPILOGUE SPOKEN TO THE KING AT OXFORD,

19 MARCH 1681

The King's Company moved to Oxford in March 1681, anticipating attendance from members of the Parliament which the King had summoned to meet there during the prevailing troubles. Charles Saunders's *Tamerlane the Great* was the first play performed, and Dryden wrote the Epilogue for the occasion.

> As from a darkened room some optic glass
> Transmits the distant species as they pass,
> The world's large landscape is from far descried
> And men contracted on the paper glide:
> Thus crowded Oxford represents mankind
> And in these walls Great Britain seems confined.
> Oxford is now the public theatre,
> And you both audience are, and actors here:
> The gazing world on the new scene attend,
> Admire the turns, and wish a prosperous end.
> This place, the seat of peace, the quiet cell
> Where arts removed from noisy bus'ness dwell.
> Should calm your wills, unite the jarring parts,
> And with a kind contagion seize your hearts:
> Oh! may its genius, like soft music, move
> And tune you all to concord and to love.
> Our ark that has in tempest long been tossed
> Could never land on so secure a coast.
> From hence you may look back on civil rage
> And view the ruins of the former age:
> Here a new world its glories may unfold,
> And here be saved the remnants of the old.
> But while your days on public thoughts are bent,

10 (line marker)
20 (line marker)

2 species] Images, reflections of things.
10 turns] Movements in the plot of a play.

Past ills to heal, and future to prevent,
Some vacant hours allow to your delight; ⎫
Mirth is the pleasing bus'ness of the night, ⎬
The King's prerogative, the people's right. ⎭
Were all your hours to sullen cares confined,
The body would be jaded by the mind.
'Tis wisdom's part betwixt extremes to steer: 30
Be gods in senates, but be mortals here.

TO THE KING AND QUEEN
AT THE OPENING OF THEIR THEATRE

In May 1682 the failing King's Company was absorbed by the Duke's, to form the United Company. The Duke's Company, with the benefit of Thomas Betterton's management and acting, had had some success; but there is no doubt that the long period of political disturbance had affected the prosperity of the theatres considerably.

PROLOGUE

Since faction ebbs, and rogues grow out of fashion,
Their penny scribes take care t'inform the nation,
How well men thrive in this or that plantation:

How Pennsylvania's air agrees with Quakers,
And Carolina's with Associators:
Both e'en too good for madmen and for traitors.

Truth is, our land with saints is so run o'er,
And every age produces such a store,
That now there's need of two New Englands more.

10 'What's this,' you'll say, 'to us and our vocation?'
Only this much, that we have left our station,
And made this theatre our new plantation.

The factious natives never could agree;
But aiming, as they called it, to be free,
Those playhouse Whigs set up for property.

5 Associators] Shaftesbury and the Whigs proposed an association to defend the King against Papists.
11–12 The United Company occupied the Theatre Royal: the Prologue is spoken by Thomas Betterton, from the Duke's company.
13–21 Dryden is describing dissensions among the actors of the King's Company.

Some say they no obedience paid of late,
But would new fears and jealousies create;
Till topsy-turvy they had turned the State.

Plain sense, without the talent of foretelling,
Might guess 'twould end in downright knocks and quelling: 20
For seldom comes there better of rebelling.

When men will, needlessly, their freedom barter
For lawless pow'r, sometimes they catch a Tartar:
(There's a damned word that rhymes to this called Charter.)

But, since the victory with us remains,
You shall be called to twelve in all our gains:
(If you'll not think us saucy for our pains.)

Old men shall have good old plays to delight 'em;
And you, fair ladies and gallants that slight 'em,
We'll treat with good new plays; if our new wits can write 'em.   30

We'll take no blund'ring verse, no fustian tumour,
No dribbling love, from this or that presumer:
No dull fat fool shammed on the stage for humour.

For, faith, some of 'em such vile stuff have made,
As none but fools or fairies ever played;
But 'twas, as shopmen say, to force a trade.

We've giv'n you tragedies, all sense defying,
And singing men, in woeful metre dying:
This 'tis when heavy lubbers will be flying.

All these disasters we well hope to weather;   40
We bring you none of our old lumber hether:
Whig poets and Whig sheriffs may hang together.

EPILOGUE

New ministers, when first they get in place,
Must have a care to please; and that's our case:

26 called to twelve] Given a share.
33 Apparently a hit at Thomas Shadwell.

Some laws for public welfare we design,
If you, the power supreme, will please to join.
There are a sort of prattlers in the pit,
Who either have, or who pretend to wit:
These noisy sirs so loud their parts rehearse,
That oft the play is silenced by the farce.
Let such be dumb, this penalty to shun,
10   Each to be thought my lady's eldest son,
But stay: methinks some vizard-mask I see
Cast out her lure from the mid gallery:
About her all the flutt'ring sparks are ranged;
The noise continues, though the scene is changed:
Now growling, sputt'ring, wauling, such a clutter,
'Tis just like puss defendant in a gutter.
Fine love no doubt, but e'er two days are o'er ye,
The surgeon will be told a woeful story.
Let vizard-mask her naked face expose,
20   On pain of being thought to want a nose.
Then for your lackeys, and your train beside,
(By whate'er name or title dignified,)
They roar so loud, you'd think behind the stairs
Tom Dove, and all the brotherhood of bears:
They're grown a nuisance, beyond all disasters;
We've none so great but their unpaying masters.
We beg you, sirs, to beg your men, that they
Would please to give you leave to hear the play.
Next, in the playhouse spare your precious lives;
30   Think, like good Christians, on your bearns and wives;
Think on your souls; but by your lugging forth,
It seems you know how little they are worth.
If none of these will move the warlike mind,
Think on the helpless whore you leave behind!
We beg you last, our scene-room to forbear,
And leave our goods and chattels to our care.
Alas, our women are but washy toys,
And wholly taken up in stage employs:
Poor willing tits they are; but yet I doubt

10 my lady's eldest son] Proverbial for a prattler.
11 vizard-mask] By this time worn only by prostitutes in the theatre.
24 Tom Dove] A famous bear, exhibited at the Bear Garden.
31 lugging forth] Drawing swords.
37 washy] Painted.

This double duty soon will wear 'em out.   40
Then you are watched besides, with jealous care:
What if my lady's page should find you there?
My lady knows t'a tittle what there's in ye;
No passing your gilt shilling for a guinea.
Thus, gentlemen, we have summed up in short
Our grievances, from country, town and court:
Which humbly we submit to your good pleasure;
But first vote money, then redress at leisure.

PROLOGUE TO *THE MISTAKES, OR THE FALSE REPORT*

The Mistakes, a tragicomedy by the actor Joseph Harris, was performed in December 1690. The Prologue was written intentionally for the actor Joseph Williams, whose liking for drink was well known.

Enter MR BRIGHT.

Gentlemen, we must beg your pardon, here's no prologue to be had today. Our new play is like to come on without a frontispiece, as bald as one of you young beaux without your periwig. I left our young poet snivelling and sobbing behind the scenes, and cursing somebody that has deceived him.

Enter MR BOWEN.

Hold your prating to the audience: here's honest Mr Williams, just come in, half mellow, from the Rose Tavern. He swears he is inspired with claret, and will come on, and that extempore too, either with a prologue of his own or something like one. O here he comes to his trial, at all adventures; for my part, I wish him a good deliverance.

[*Exeunt* MR BRIGHT *and* MR BOWEN.

Enter MR WILLIAMS.

10   Save ye, sirs, save ye! I am in a hopeful way.
I should speak something, in rhyme, now, for the play:
But the deuce take me, if I know what to say.
I'll stick to my friend the author, that I can tell ye,
To the last drop of claret in my belly.
So far I'm sure 'tis rhyme — that needs no granting:
And, if my verses' feet stumble — you see my own are wanting.
Our young poet has brought a piece of work,
In which though much of art there does not lurk,

3 our young poet] Harris was about forty, but 'young' as a poet.

It may hold out three days — and that's as long as Cork.
But, for this play — (which, till I have done, we show not,)   20
What may be its fortune — by the Lord — I know not.
This I dare swear, no malice here is writ:
'Tis innocent of all things — ev'n of wit.
He's no high-flyer — he makes no sky-rockets,
His squibs are only levelled at your pockets.
And if his crackers light among your pelf,
You are blown up; if not, then he's blown up himself.
By this time, I'm something recovered of my flustered madness:
And now, a word or two in sober sadness.
Ours is a common play; and you pay down   30
A common harlot's price — just half-a-crown.
You'll say, I play the pimp, on my friend's score; ⎫
But since 'tis for a friend, your gibes give o'er ⎬
For many a mother has done that before.   ⎭
How's this, you cry? an actor write — we know it;
But Shakespeare was an actor, and a poet.
Has not great Jonson's learning often failed,
But Shakespeare's greater genius still prevailed?
Have not some writing actors in this age
Deserved and found success upon the stage?   40
To tell the truth, when our old wits are tired,
Not one of us but means to be inspired.
Let your kind presence grace our homely cheer; ⎫
Peace and the butt is all our bus'ness here: ⎬
So much for that — and the devil take small beer. ⎭

19 The proceeds of the third night's acting went to the author. Cork was besieged by English forces for three days in September 1690.

EPILOGUE TO *KING ARTHUR, OR THE BRITISH WORTHY*

King Arthur, an opera by Dryden, was performed in May 1691.

I've had today a dozen *billet-doux*
From fops, and wits, and cits, and Bow-Street *beaux*;
Some from Whitehall, but from the Temple more:
A Covent Garden porter brought me four.
I have not yet read all; but, without feigning,
We maids can make shrewd guesses at your meaning.
What if, to show your styles, I read 'em here? ⎫
Methinks I hear one cry, 'O Lord, forbear! ⎬
No, Madam, no; by Heav'n, that's too severe.' ⎭
10   Well then, be safe——
But swear henceforwards to renounce all writing,
And take this solemn oath of my inditing,
As you love ease, and hate campaigns and fighting.
Yet, faith, 'tis just to make some few examples:
What if I showed you one or two for samples?
   Here one desires my ladyship to meet   *[Pulls one out.*
At the kind couch above in Bridges street.
Oh sharping knave! that would have you know what,
For a poor sneaking treat of chocolate.
20   Now, in the name of luck, I'll break this open,   *[Pulls out*
Because I dreamt last night I had a token;   *another.*
The superscription is exceeding pretty,
'To the desire of all the town and city.'
Now, gallants, you must know, this precious fop
Is foreman of a haberdasher's shop:
One who devoutly cheats, demure in carriage,
And courts me to the holy bands of marriage;
But with a civil innuendo too,
My overplus of love shall be for you.
30   'Madam, I swear your looks are so divine,   *[Reads.*

When I set up, your face shall be my sign:
Though times are hard, to show how I adore you,
Here's my whole heart, and half a guinea for you.
But have a care of *beaux*; they're false, my honey;
And which is worse, have not one rag of money.'
    See how maliciously the rogue would wrong ye!
But I know better things of some among ye.
My wisest way will be to keep the stage,
And trust to the good nature of the age;
And he that likes the music and the play   40
Shall be my favourite gallant today.

PROLOGUE TO *LOVE TRIUMPHANT, OR NATURE WILL PREVAIL*

Love Triumphant, acted in January 1694, was Dryden's last play.

As when some Treasurer lays down the stick,
Warrants are signed for ready money thick,
And many desperate debentures paid,
Which never had been, had his lordship stayed:
So now, this poet, who forsakes the stage,
Intends to gratify the present age.
One warrant shall be signed for every man;
All shall be wits that will, and beaux that can:
Provided still, this warrant be not shown,
10   And you be wits but to yourselves alone;
Provided too, you rail at one another,
For there's no one wit, will allow a brother.
Provided also, that you spare this story,
Damn all the plays that e'er shall come before ye.
If one by chance prove good in half a score,
Let that one pay for all, and damn it more.
For if a good one scape among the crew, ⎫
And you continue judging as you do, ⎬
Every bad play will hope for damning too. ⎭
20   You might damn this, if it were worth your pains; ⎫
Here's nothing you will like; no fustian scenes, ⎬
And nothing too of — you know what he means. ⎭
No *double entendres*, which you sparks allow,
To make the ladies look — they know not how;
Simply as 'twere, and knowing both together,
Seeming to fan their faces in cold weather.
But here's a story which no books relate,
Coined from our own old poet's addle-pate.

21 fustian] Bombastic, ranting.

The fable has a moral too, if sought: ⎞
But let that go; for, upon second thought, ⎬   30
He fears but few come hither to be taught. ⎠
Yet if you will be profited, you may;
And he would bribe you too, to like his play.
He dies, at least to us, and to the stage,
And what he has, he leaves this noble age.
He leaves you, first, all plays of his inditing,
The whole estate which he has got by writing.
The beaux may think this nothing but vain praise; ⎞
They'll find it something, the testator says: ⎬
For half their love is made from scraps of plays. ⎠   40
To his worst foes, he leaves his honesty,
That they may thrive upon't as much as he.
He leaves his manners to the roaring boys,
Who come in drunk, and fill the house with noise.
He leaves to the dire critics of his wit
His silence and contempt of all they writ.
To Shakespeare's critic he bequeaths the curse
To find his faults, and yet himself make worse;
A precious reader in poetic schools,
Who by his own examples damns his rules.   50
Last, for the fair, he wishes you may be
From you dull critics, the lampooners, free.
Though he pretends no legacy to leave you,
An old man may at least good wishes give you.
Your beauty names the play; and may it prove
To each an omen of Triumphant Love.

47 Shakespeare's critic] Thomas Rymer, whose *Short View of Tragedy* (1693) was aggressively critical of Shakespeare.

EPILOGUE TO FLETCHER'S *THE PILGRIM*

Dryden and Vanbrugh adapted Fletcher's comedy for a production for Dryden's benefit in April 1700.

Perhaps the parson stretched a point too far,
When with our theatres he waged a war.
He tells you, that this very moral age
Received the first infection from the stage.
But sure, a banished court, with lewdness fraught,
The seeds of open vice returning brought.
Thus lodged, (as vice by great example thrives,)
It first debauched the daughters and the wives.
London, a fruitful soil, yet never bore
10   So plentiful a crop of horns before.
The poets, who must live by courts or starve,
Were proud, so good a government to serve;
And, mixing with buffoons and pimps profane,
Tainted the stage, for some small snip of gain;
For they, like harlots under bawds professed,
Took all th' ungodly pains, and got the least.
Thus did the thriving malady prevail,
The court its head, the poets but the tail.
The sin was of our native growth, 'tis true;
20   The scandal of the sin was wholly new.
Misses there were, but modestly concealed;
Whitehall the naked Venus first revealed,
Who standing, as at Cyprus, in her shrine,
The strumpet was adored with rites divine.
Ere this, if saints had any secret motion,
'Twas chamber practice all, and close devotion.
I pass the peccadillos of their time;
Nothing but open lewdness was a crime.

1 the parson] Jeremy Collier, author of *A Short View of the Immorality and Profaneness of the English Stage* (1698), which led a reaction against libertinism in the theatre.

A monarch's blood was venial to the nation,
Compared with one foul act of fornication.   30
Now, they would silence us, and shut the door
That let in all the barefaced vice before.
As for reforming us, which some pretend, ⎫
That work in England is without an end; ⎬
Well may we change, but we shall never mend. ⎭
Yet, if you can but bear the present stage,
We hope much better of the coming age.
What would you say, if we should first begin ⎫
To stop the trade of love behind the scene, ⎬
Where actresses make bold with married men? ⎭   40
For while abroad so prodigal the dolt is,
Poor spouse at home as ragged as a colt is.
In short, we'll grow as moral as we can,
Save here and there a woman or a man:
But neither you, nor we, with all our pains, ⎫
Can make clean work; there will be some remains, ⎬
While you have still your Oates, and we our Haines. ⎭

47 Oates . . . Haines] Titus Oates, still living; and John Haynes, comic actor.

TRANSLATIONS

Dryden's first published translations were his contributions to *Ovid's Epistles*, printed in 1680. Thereafter he gave much of his energies to translating, in association with the publisher Jacob Tonson. In this selection, the pieces from Lucretius and Horace are from *Sylvae, or the Second Part of Poetical Miscellanies*, of 1685. Of his renderings of Lucretius, he says in the Preface: 'I was pleased with my own endeavours, which but rarely happens to me, and I am not dissatisfied, upon the review, of anything I have done in this author.' Of the twenty-ninth ode of the Third Book of Horace: 'I have taken some pains to make it my masterpiece in English.' He translated all of Persius, and four of the satires of Juvenal, for a folio publication in 1693, prefaced by the *Discourse Concerning the Original and Progress of Satire*. The Third Satire of Juvenal, with his notes, is included here. *The Last Parting of Hector and Andromache, from the Sixth Book of Homer's Illiads* is from the miscellany *Examen Poeticum* of 1693. The text of *The Episode of Nisus and Euryalus* is taken from the fifth and ninth books of the great 1697 Virgil. They are nearly the same passages as he had translated earlier for publication in *Sylvae*, and which he revised and inserted into his translation of the whole of the *Aeneid*. *Baucis and Philemon* and *Pygmalion and the Statue* from Ovid's *Metamorphoses*, and *The Cock and the Fox*, a rendering of Chaucer's *Nun's Priest's Tale*, were included in *Fables Ancient and Modern* (1700).

LUCRETIUS

THE LATTER PART OF THE THIRD BOOK, AGAINST THE FEAR OF DEATH

What has this bugbear death to frighten man,
If souls can die, as well as bodies can?
For, as before our birth we felt no pain
When Punic arms infested land and main,
When heav'n and earth were in confusion hurled,
For the debated empire of the world,
Which awed with dreadful expectation lay,
Sure to be slaves, uncertain who should sway:
So, when our mortal frame shall be disjoined,
The lifeless lump uncoupled from the mind,   10
From sense of grief and pain we shall be free;
We shall not feel, because we shall not be.
Though earth in seas, and seas in heav'n were lost,
We should not move, we only should be tossed.
Nay, ev'n suppose when we have suffered fate,
The soul could feel in her divided state,
What's that to us? for we are only we
While souls and bodies in one frame agree.
Nay, though our atoms should revolve by chance,
And matter leap into the former dance;   20
Though time our life and motion could restore,
And make our bodies what they were before,
What gain to us would all this bustle bring?
The new-made man would be another thing;
When once an interrupting pause is made,
That individual being is decayed.
We, who are dead and gone, shall bear no part
In all the pleasures, nor shall feel the smart
Which to that other mortal shall accrue,
Whom of our matter time shall mould anew.   30

For backward if you look on that long space
Of ages past, and view the changing face
Of matter, tossed and variously combined
In sundry shapes, 'tis easy for the mind
From thence t'infer, that seeds of things have been
In the same order as they now are seen:
Which yet our dark remembrance cannot trace,
Because a pause of life, a gaping space,
Has come betwixt, where memory lies dead,
And all the wand'ring motions from the sense are fled.
For whosoe'er shall in misfortunes live,
Must be, when those misfortunes shall arrive;
And since the man who is not, feels not woe,
(For death exempts him, and wards off the blow,
Which we, the living, only feel and bear,)
What is there left for us in death to fear?
When once that pause of life has come between,
'Tis just the same as we had never been.
And therefore if a man bemoan his lot,
That after death his mould'ring limbs shall rot,
Or flames, or jaws of beasts devour his mass,
Know, he's an unsincere, unthinking ass.
A secret sting remains within his mind;
The fool is to his own cast offals kind.
He boasts no sense can after death remain, }
Yet makes himself a part of life again,
As if some other *he* could feel the pain.
If, while he live, this thought molest his head,
What wolf, or vulture shall devour me dead?
He wastes his days in idle grief, nor can
Distinguish 'twixt the body and the man;
But thinks himself can still himself survive;
And, what when dead he feels not, feels alive.
Then he repines that he was born to die,
Nor knows in death there is no other *he*,
No living *he* remains his grief to vent,
And o'er his senseless carcass to lament.
If after death 'tis painful to be torn
By birds and beasts, then why not so to burn;
Or, drenched in floods of honey, to be soaked,
Imbalmed, to be at once preserved and choked;
Or on an airy mountain's top to lie,

40

50

60

70

Exposed to cold and heav'n's inclemency;
Or crowded in a tomb to be oppressed
With monumental marble on thy breast?
But to be snatched from all thy household joys,
From thy chaste wife, and thy dear prattling boys,
Whose little arms about thy legs are cast,
And climbing for a kiss prevent their mother's haste,
Inspiring secret pleasure through thy breast,   80
All these shall be no more: thy friends oppressed
Thy care and courage now no more shall free:
'Ah wretch!' thou cry'st, 'ah! miserable me!
One woeful day sweeps children, friends, and wife,
And all the brittle blessings of my life!'
Add one thing more, and all thou say'st is true;
Thy want and wish of them is vanished too;
Which, well considered, were a quick relief
To all thy vain imaginary grief.
For thou shalt sleep, and never wake again,   90
And, quitting life, shalt quit thy living pain.
But we, thy friends, shall all those sorrows find,
Which in forgetful death thou leav'st behind;
No time shall dry our tears, nor drive thee from our mind.
The worst that can befall thee, measured right,
Is a sound slumber, and a long good-night.
Yet thus the fools, that would be thought the wits,
Disturb their mirth with melancholy fits:
When healths go round, and kindly brimmers flow,
Till the fresh garlands on their foreheads glow,   100
They whine, and cry: 'Let us make haste to live.
Short are the joys that human life can give.'
Eternal preachers, that corrupt the draught,
And pall the god, that never thinks, with thought;
Idiots with all that thought, to whom the worst
Of death, is want of drink, and endless thirst,
Or any fond desire as vain as these.
For ev'n in sleep, the body, wrapped in ease,
Supinely lies, as in the peaceful grave;
And wanting nothing, nothing can it crave.   110
Were that sound sleep eternal, it were death;
Yet the first atoms then, the seeds of breath,
Are moving near to sense; we do but shake
And rouse that sense, and straight we are awake.

Then death to us, and death's anxiety,
Is less than nothing, if a less could be.
For then our atoms, which in order lay,
Are scattered from their heap, and puffed away,
And never can return into their place,
120 When once the pause of life has left an empty space.
And last, suppose great Nature's voice should call
To thee, or me, or any of us all:
'What dost thou mean, ungrateful wretch, thou vain,
Thou mortal thing, thus idly to complain,
And sigh and sob that thou shalt be no more?
For if thy life were pleasant heretofore,
If all the bounteous blessings I could give   ⎫
Thou hast enjoyed; if thou hast known to live,   ⎬
And pleasure not leaked through thee like a sieve, ⎭
130 Why dost thou not give thanks as at a plenteous feast,
Crammed to the throat with life, and rise and take thy rest?
But if my blessings thou hast thrown away,
If indigested joys passed through and would not stay,
Why dost thou wish for more to squander still?
If life be grown a load, a real ill,
And I would all thy cares and labours end,
Lay down thy burden, fool, and know thy friend.
To please thee, I have emptied all my store;   ⎫
I can invent and can supply no more,   ⎬
140 But run the round again, the round I ran before.⎭
Suppose thou art not broken yet with years,
Yet still the selfsame scene of things appears,
And would be ever, couldst thou ever live;
For life is still but life, there's nothing new to give.'
What can we plead against so just a bill?
We stand convicted, and our cause goes ill.
But if a wretch, a man oppressed by fate,
Should beg of Nature to prolong his date,
She speaks aloud to him with more disdain:
150 'Be still, thou martyr fool, thou covetous of pain.'
But if an old decrepit sot lament;
'What, thou,' she cries, 'who hast outlived content!
Dost thou complain, who hast enjoyed my store?
But this is still th' effect of wishing more!
Unsatisfied with all that Nature brings;

Loathing the present, liking absent things;
From hence it comes, thy vain desires, at strife
Within themselves, have tantalized thy life;
And ghastly death appeared before thy sight,
Ere thou hadst gorged thy soul and senses with delight.   160
Now leave those joys unsuiting to thy age
To a fresh comer, and resign the stage.'
Is Nature to be blamed if thus she chide?
No, sure; for 'tis her business to provide,
Against this ever-changing frame's decay,
New things to come, and old to pass away.
One being, worn, another being makes;
Changed, but not lost; for Nature gives and takes:
New matter must be found for things to come,
And these must waste like those, and follow Nature's doom.   170
All things, like thee, have time to rise and rot;
And from each other's ruin are begot;
For life is not confined to him or thee;
'Tis giv'n to all for use, to none for property.
Consider former ages past and gone,
Whose circles ended long ere thine begun,
Then tell me, fool, what part in them thou hast.
Thus may'st thou judge the future by the past.
What horror see'st thou in that quiet state?
What bugbear dreams to fright thee after fate?   180
No ghost, no goblins, that still passage keep;
But all is there serene, in that eternal sleep.
For all the dismal tales that poets tell
Are verified on earth, and not in hell.
No Tantalus looks up with fearful eye,
Or dreads th' impending rock to crush him from on high;
But fear of chance on earth disturbs our easy hours,
Or vain imagined wrath of vain imagined pow'rs.
No Tityus torn by vultures lies in hell;
Nor could the lobes of his rank liver swell   190
To that prodigious mass for their eternal meal:
Not though his monstrous bulk has covered o'er
Nine spreading acres, or nine thousand more;
Not though the globe of earth had been the giant's floor:
Nor in eternal torments could he lie,
Nor could his corpse sufficient food supply.

But he's the Tityus, who by love oppressed, ⎫
Or tyrant passion preying on his breast,   ⎬
And ever-anxious thoughts, is robbed of rest.⎭
200 The Sisyphus is he, whom noise and strife
Seduce from all the soft retreats of life,
To vex the government, disturb the laws:
Drunk with the fumes of popular applause,
He courts the giddy crowd to make him great,
And sweats and toils in vain, to mount the sovereign seat.
For still to aim at pow'r, and still to fail,
Ever to strive, and never to prevail,
What is it, but, in reason's true account,
To heave the stone against the rising mount?
210 Which urged, and laboured, and forced up with pain,
Recoils, and rolls impetuous down, and smokes along the plain.
Then still to treat thy ever-craving mind
With ev'ry blessing, and of ev'ry kind,
Yet never fill thy rav'ning appetite;
Though years and seasons vary thy delight,
Yet nothing to be seen of all the store,
But still the wolf within thee barks for more;
This is the fable's moral, which they tell
Of fifty foolish virgins damned in hell
220 To leaky vessels, which the liquor spill;
To vessels of their sex, which none could ever fill.
As for the Dog, the Furies, and their snakes,
The gloomy caverns, and the burning lakes,
And all the vain infernal trumpery,
They neither are, nor were, nor e'er can be.
But here on earth the guilty have in view
The mighty pains to mighty mischiefs due:
Racks, prisons, poisons, the Tarpeian rock,
Stripes, hangmen, pitch, and suffocating smoke;
230 And last, and most, if these were cast behind,
Th' avenging horror of a conscious mind,
Whose deadly fear anticipates the blow,
And sees no end of punishment and woe;
But looks for more, at the last gasp of breath:
This makes a hell on earth, and life a death.
Meantime, when thoughts of death disturb thy head,
Consider, Ancus, great and good, is dead;
Ancus, thy better far, was born to die;

And thou, dost thou bewail mortality?
So many monarchs with their mighty state,   240
Who ruled the world, were overruled by fate.
That haughty king, who lorded o'er the main,
And whose stupendous bridge did the wild waves restrain,
(In vain they foamed, in vain they threatened wreck,
While his proud legions marched upon their back):
Him death, a greater monarch, overcame;
Nor spared his guards the more, for their immortal name.
The Roman chief, the Carthaginian dread,
Scipio, the thunderbolt of war, is dead,
And, like a common slave, by fate in triumph led.   250
The founders of invented arts are lost;
And wits, who made eternity their boast.
Where now is Homer, who possessed the throne?
Th' immortal work remains, the mortal author's gone.
Democritus, perceiving age invade,
His body weakened, and his mind decayed,
Obeyed the summons with a cheerful face;
Made haste to welcome death, and met him half the race.
That stroke ev'n Epicurus could not bar,
Though he in wit surpassed mankind, as far   260
As does the midday sun the midnight star.
And thou, dost thou disdain to yield thy breath,
Whose very life is little more than death?
More than one half by lazy sleep possessed;
And when awake, thy soul but nods at best,
Day-dreams and sickly thoughts revolving in thy breast.
Eternal troubles haunt thy anxious mind,
Whose cause and cure thou never hop'st to find;
But still uncertain, with thyself at strife,
Thou wand'rest in the labyrinth of life.   270
O, if the foolish race of man, who find
A weight of cares still pressing on their mind,
Could find as well the cause of this unrest,
And all this burden lodged within the breast;
Sure they would change their course, nor live as now,
Uncertain what to wish or what to vow.
Uneasy both in country and in town,
They search a place to lay their burden down.
One, restless in his palace, walks abroad,
And vainly thinks to leave behind the load;   280

But straight returns; for he's as restless there,
And finds there's no relief in open air.
Another to his villa would retire,
And spurs as hard as if it were on fire;
No sooner entered at his country door,
But he begins to stretch, and yawn, and snore;
Or seeks the city which he left before.
Thus every man o'erworks his weary will,
To shun himself, and to shake off his ill;
290   The shaking fit returns, and hangs upon him still.
No prospect of repose, nor hope of ease;
The wretch is ignorant of his disease;
Which known would all his fruitless trouble spare,
For he would know the world not worth his care:
Then would he search more deeply for the cause;
And study nature well, and nature's laws:
For in this moment lies not the debate,
But on our future, fixed, eternal state;
That never-changing state, which all must keep,
300   Whom death has doomed to everlasting sleep.
Why are we then so fond of mortal life,
Beset with dangers, and maintained with strife?
A life which all our care can never save;
One fate attends us, and one common grave.
Besides, we tread but a perpetual round;
We ne'er strike out, but beat the former ground,
And the same mawkish joys in the same track are found.
For still we think an absent blessing best,
Which cloys, and is no blessing when possessed;
310   A new arising wish expels it from the breast.
The fev'rish thirst of life increases still;
We call for more and more and never have our fill,
Yet know not what tomorrow we shall try,
What dregs of life in the last draught may lie.
Nor, by the longest life we can attain,
One moment from the length of death we gain;
For all behind belongs to his eternal reign.
When once the Fates have cut the mortal thread,
The man as much to all intents is dead,
320   Who dies today, and will as long be so,
As he who died a thousand years ago.

HORACE

THE TWENTY-NINTH ODE OF THE THIRD BOOK

PARAPHRASED IN PINDARIC VERSE, AND INSCRIBED TO THE
RIGHT HONORABLE LAWRENCE, EARL OF ROCHESTER

I

Descended of an ancient line,
   That long the Tuscan sceptre swayed,
Make haste to meet the generous wine,
   Whose piercing is for thee delayed:
The rosy wreath is ready made;
   And artful hands prepare
The fragrant Syrian oil, that shall perfume thy hair.

II

When the wine sparkles from afar,
   And the well-natured friend cries, 'Come away!'
Make haste, and leave thy business and thy care;   10
   Nor mortal int'rest can be worth thy stay.

III

Leave for a while thy costly country seat;
   And, to be great indeed, forget
The nauseous pleasures of the great:
   Make haste and come;
Come, and forsake thy cloying store;
   Thy turret that surveys, from high,
The smoke, and wealth, and noise of Rome;
   And all the busy pageantry
That wise men scorn, and fools adore: 20
Come, give thy soul a loose, and taste the pleasures of the poor.

IV

Sometimes 'tis grateful to the rich to try
A short vicissitude, and fit of poverty:
    A savoury dish, a homely treat,
    Where all is plain, where all is neat,
    Without the stately spacious room,
The Persian carpet, or the Tyrian loom,
Clear up the cloudy foreheads of the great.

V

    The sun is in the Lion mounted high;
30   The Syrian star
        Barks from afar,
  And with his sultry breath infects the sky;
The ground below is parched, the heav'ns above us fry.
    The shepherd drives his fainting flock
    Beneath the covert of a rock,
    And seeks refreshing rivulets nigh:
    The sylvans to their shades retire,
Those very shades and streams new shades and streams require;
And want a cooling breeze of wind to fan the raging fire.

VI

40   Thou, what befits the new Lord May'r,
    And what the city faction dare,
    And what the Gallic arms will do,
    And what the quiver-bearing foe,
    Art anxiously inquisitive to know;
But God has, wisely, hid from human sight
    The dark decrees of future fate,
    And sown their seeds in depth of night:
He laughs at all the giddy turns of state,
When mortals search too soon, and fear too late.

VII

50   Enjoy the present smiling hour,
    And put it out of Fortune's pow'r:
The tide of bus'ness, like the running stream,
    Is sometimes high, and sometimes low,
  A quiet ebb, or a tempestuous flow,
    And always in extreme.
    Now with a noiseless gentle course

It keeps within the middle bed;
  Anon it lifts aloft the head,
And bears down all before it with impetuous force;
    And trunks of trees come rolling down,   60
    Sheep and their folds together drown:
Both house and homestead into seas are borne,
And rocks are from their old foundations torn,
And woods, made thin with winds, their scattered honours mourn.

VIII

Happy the man, and happy he alone,
  He, who can call today his own;
  He who, secure within, can say:
'Tomorrow do thy worst, for I have lived today.
  Be fair, or foul, or rain, or shine,
The joys I have possessed, in spite of fate, are mine.   70
  Not Heav'n itself upon the past has pow'r;
But what has been, has been, and I have had my hour.'

IX

Fortune, that with malicious joy
  Does man her slave oppress,
Proud of her office to destroy,
  Is seldom pleased to bless:
Still various, and unconstant still,
But with an inclination to be ill,
  Promotes, degrades, delights in strife,
  And makes a lottery of life.   80
I can enjoy her while she's kind;
But when she dances in the wind,
And shakes her wings, and will not stay,
I puff the prostitute away:
The little or the much she gave me is quietly resigned:
  Content with poverty, my soul I arm;
  And virtue, though in rags, will keep me warm.

X

    What is't to me,
Who never sail in her unfaithful sea,
  If storms arise, and clouds grow black;   90
  If the mast split, and threaten wreck?
Then let the greedy merchant fear

For his ill-gotten gain;
And pray to gods that will not hear,
While the debating winds and billows bear
His wealth into the main.
For me, secure from Fortune's blows,
(Secure of what I cannot lose,)
In my small pinnace I can sail,
100   Contemning all the blust'ring roar;
And running with a merry gale,
With friendly stars my safety seek,
Within some little winding creek;
And see the storm ashore.

THE THIRD SATIRE OF JUVENAL

THE ARGUMENT

The story of this satire speaks itself. Umbritius, the supposed friend of Juvenal, and himself a poet, is leaving Rome, and retiring to Cumae. Our author accompanies him out of town. Before they take leave of each other, Umbritius tells his friend the reasons which oblige him to lead a private life, in an obscure place. He complains that an honest man cannot get his bread at Rome; that none but flatterers make their fortunes there; that Grecians and other foreigners raise themselves by those sordid arts which he describes, and against which he bitterly inveighs. He reckons up the several inconveniences which arise from a city life, and the many dangers which attend it; upbraids the noblemen with covetousness, for not rewarding good poets; and arraigns the government for starving them. The great art of this satire is particularly shown in commonplaces, and drawing in as many vices as could naturally fall into the compass of it.

Grieved though I am an ancient friend to lose,⎫
I like the solitary seat he chose,   ⎬
In quiet Cumae¹ fixing his repose: ⎭
Where, far from noisy Rome, secure he lives,
And one more citizen to Sibyl gives;
The road to Bajae,² and that soft recess
Which all the gods with all their bounty bless.
Though I in Prochyta³ with greater ease
Could live, than in a street of palaces.
What scene so desert, or so full of fright,   ⎫   10
As tow'ring houses tumbling in the night,   ⎬
And Rome on fire beheld by its own blazing light?⎭
But worse than all the clatt'ring tiles, and worse
Than thousand padders, is the poet's curse:
Rogues that in dog-days⁴ cannot rhyme forbear,
But without mercy read, and make you hear.
   Now while my friend, just ready to depart,
Was packing all his goods in one poor cart,

He stopped a little at the Conduit-gate,
20 Where Numa[5] modelled once the Roman State,
In mighty councils with his nymph[6] retired:
Though now the sacred shades and founts are hired
By banished Jews, who their whole wealth can lay
In a small basket, on a wisp of hay:
Yet such our avarice is, that every tree
Pays for his head, not sleep itself is free;
Nor place, nor persons, now are sacred held,
From their own grove the Muses are expelled.
Into this lonely vale our steps we bend,
30 I and my sullen discontented friend:
The marble caves, and aqueducts we view;
But how adult'rate now, and different from the true!
How much more beauteous had the fountain been
Embellished with her first created green,
Where crystal streams through living turf had run,
Contented with an urn of native stone!
    Then thus Umbritius (with an angry frown,
And looking back on this degen'rate town):
'Since noble arts in Rome have no support,
40 And ragged virtue not a friend at court,
No profit rises from th' ungrateful stage,
My poverty increasing with my age;
'Tis time to give my just disdain a vent,
And, cursing, leave so base a government.
Where Daedalus[7] his borrowed wings laid by,
To that obscure retreat I choose to fly:
While yet few furrows on my face are seen, ⎫
While I walk upright, and old age is green, ⎬
And Lachesis[8] has somewhat left to spin. ⎭
50 Now, now 'tis time to quit this cursed place,
And hide from villains my too honest face:
Here let Arturius[9] live, and such as he;
Such manners will with such a town agree.
Knaves who in full assemblies have the knack
Of turning truth to lies, and white to black;
Can hire large houses, and oppress the poor
By farmed excise; can cleanse the common-shore,
And rent the fishery; can bear the dead, ⎫
And teach their eyes dissembled tears to shed; ⎬
60 All this for gain; for gain they sell their very head. ⎭

These fellows (see what Fortune's pow'r can do)
Were once the minstrels of a country show;
Followed the prizes through each paltry town,
By trumpet-cheeks and bloated faces known.
But now, grown rich, on drunken holidays,
At their own costs exhibit public plays;
Where, influenced by the rabble's bloody will,
With thumbs bent back,[10] they popularly kill.
From thence returned, their sordid avarice rakes
In excrements again, and hires the jakes.   70
Why hire they not the town, not ev'rything,
Since such as they have Fortune in a string,
Who, for her pleasure, can her fools advance,
And toss 'em topmost on the wheel of chance?
What's Rome to me, what bus'ness have I there?
I who can neither lie, nor falsely swear?
Nor praise my patron's undeserving rhymes,
Nor yet comply with him, nor with his times?
Unskilled in schemes by planets to foreshow,
Like canting rascals, how the wars will go: 80
I neither will, nor can, prognosticate
To the young gaping heir, his father's fate;
Nor in the entrails of a toad have pried,
Nor carried bawdy presents to a bride:
For want of these town-virtues, thus alone
I go, conducted on my way by none;
Like a dead member from the body rent,
Maimed, and unuseful to the government.
   'Who now is loved, but he who loves the times,
Conscious of close intrigues, and dipt in crimes;   90
Lab'ring with secrets which his bosom burn,
Yet never must to public light return?
They get reward alone who can betray:
For keeping honest counsels none will pay.
He who can Verres, when he will, accuse,
The purse of Verres[11] may at pleasure use:
But let not all the gold which Tagus[12] hides,
And pays the sea in tributary tides,
Be bribe sufficient to corrupt thy breast,
Or violate with dreams thy peaceful rest.   100
Great men with jealous eyes the friend behold,
Whose secrecy they purchase with their gold.

'I haste to tell thee, nor shall shame oppose,
What confidents our wealthy Romans chose;
And whom I must abhor: to speak my mind,
I hate, in Rome, a Grecian town to find:
To see the scum of Greece transplanted here,
Received like gods, is what I cannot bear.
Nor Greeks alone, but Syrians here abound;
110   Obscene Orontes,[13] diving under ground,
Conveys his wealth to Tiber's[14] hungry shores,
And fattens Italy with foreign whores:
Hither their crooked harps and customs come;
All find receipt in hospitable Rome.
The barbarous harlots crowd the public place:
Go, fools, and purchase an unclean embrace;
The painted mitre court, and the more painted face.
Old Romulus,[15] and father Mars, look down!
Your herdsman primitive, your homely clown,
120   Is turned a beau in a loose tawdry gown.
His once unkem'd and horrid locks, behold
'Stilling sweet oil; his neck enchained with gold:
Aping the foreigners in ev'ry dress,
Which, bought at greater cost, becomes him less.
Meantime they wisely leave their native land;
From Sicyon, Samos, and from Alaband,
And Amydon, to Rome they swarm in shoals:
So sweet and easy is the gain from fools.
Poor refugees at first, they purchase here;
130   And, soon as denizened, they domineer;
Grow to the great a flatt'ring, servile rout,
Work themselves inward, and their patrons out.
Quick-witted, brazen-faced, with fluent tongues,
Patient of labours, and dissembling wrongs.
Riddle me this, and guess him if you can,
Who bears a nation in a single man?
A cook, a conjurer, a rhetorician,
A painter, pedant, a geometrician,
A dancer on the ropes, and a physician.
140   All things the hungry Greek exactly knows:
And bid him go to heav'n, to heav'n he goes.
In short, no Scythian, Moor, or Thracian born,
But in that town[16] which arms and arts adorn.
Shall he be placed above me at the board,

In purple clothed, and lolling like a lord?
Shall he before me sign, whom t'other day
A small-craft vessel hither did convey;
Where, stowed with prunes, and rotten figs, he lay?
How little is the privilege become
Of being born a citizen of Rome!   150
The Greeks get all by fulsome flatteries;
A most peculiar stroke they have at lies.
They make a wit of their insipid friend;
His blobber-lips and beetle-brows commend;
His long crane-neck and narrow shoulders praise—
You'd think they were describing Hercules.
A creaking voice for a clear treble goes;
Though harsher than a cock that treads and crows.
We can as grossly praise; but, to our grief,
No flatt'ry but from Grecians gains belief.   160
Besides these qualities, we must agree
They mimic better on the stage than we:
The wife, the whore, the shepherdess they play,
In such a free, and such a graceful way,
That we believe a very woman shown,
And fancy something underneath the gown.
But not Antiochus, nor Stratocles,[17]
Our ears and ravished eyes can only please:
The nation is composed of such as these.
All Greece is one comedian: laugh, and they   170
Return it louder than an ass can bray;
Grieve, and they grieve; if you weep silently,
There seems a silent echo in their eye:
They cannot mourn like you; but they can cry.
Call for a fire, their winter clothes they take:
Begin but you to shiver, and they shake:
In frost and snow, if you complain of heat,
They rub th' unsweating brow, and swear they sweat.
We live not on the square with such as these;
Such are our betters who can better please;   180
Who day and night are like a looking-glass,
Still ready to reflect their patron's face;
The panegyric hand, and lifted eye,
Prepared for some new piece of flattery.
Ev'n nastiness occasions will afford;
They praise a belching, or well-pissing lord.

Besides, there's nothing sacred, nothing free
From bold attempts of their rank lechery.
Through the whole family their labours run; ⎫
190   The daughter is debauched, the wife is won; ⎬
Nor 'scapes the bridegroom, or the blooming son.⎭
If none they find for their lewd purpose fit,
They with the walls and very floors commit.
They search the secrets of the house, and so
Are worshipped there, and feared for what they know.
   'And, now we talk of Grecians, cast a view⎫
On what, in schools, their men of morals do: ⎬
A rigid Stoic[18] his own pupil slew; ⎭
A friend, against a friend of his own cloth,
200   Turned evidence, and murdered on his oath.
What room is left for Romans in a town
Where Grecians rule, and cloaks control the gown?
Some Diphilus, or some Protogenes,[19]
Look sharply out, our senators to seize:
Engross 'em wholly, by their native art,
And fear no rivals in their bubbles' heart:
One drop of poison in my patron's ear,
One slight suggestion of a senseless fear,
Infused with cunning, serves to ruin me;
210   Disgraced and banished from the family.
In vain forgotten services I boast;
My long dependance in an hour is lost.
Look round the world, what country will appear,
Where friends are left with greater ease than here?
At Rome (nor think me partial to the poor)
All offices of ours are out of door:
In vain we rise, and to their levees run;
My lord himself is up before, and gone:
The praetor bids his lictors mend their pace,
220   Lest his colleague outstrip him in the race;
The childless matrons are, long since, awake,
And for affronts the tardy visits take.
   ' 'Tis frequent, here, to see a free-born son
On the left hand of a rich hireling run;
Because the wealthy rogue can throw away,
For half a brace of bouts, a tribune's pay:
But you, poor sinner, though you love the vice,
And like the whore, demur upon the price;

And, frighted with the wicked sum, forbear
To lend a hand, and help her from the chair.   230
  'Produce a witness of unblemished life,
Holy as Numa, or as Numa's wife,
Or him who bid[20] th' unhallowed flames retire,
And snatched the trembling goddess from the fire;
The question is not put how far extends
His piety, but what he yearly spends:
Quick, to the bus'ness; how he lives and eats;
How largely gives; how splendidly he treats;
How many thousand acres feed his sheep;
What are his rents; what servants does he keep?   240
Th' account is soon cast up; the judges rate
Our credit in the court by our estate.
Swear by our gods, or those the Greeks adore,
Thou art as sure forsworn, as thou art poor:
The poor must gain their bread by perjury; ⎫
And even the gods, that other means deny, ⎬
In conscience must absolve 'em, when they lie. ⎭
  'Add, that the rich have still a gibe in store,
And will be monstrous witty on the poor;
For the torn surtout and the tattered vest,   250
The wretch and all his wardrobe are a jest;
The greasy gown, sullied with often turning,
Gives a good hint, to say: "The man's in mourning;"
Or if the shoe be ripped, or patches put:
"He's wounded! see the plaister on his foot."
Want is the scorn of ev'ry wealthy fool,
And wit in rags is turned to ridicule.
  '"Pack hence, and from the covered benches rise,"
(The master of the ceremonies cries,)
"This is no place for you, whose small estate   260
Is not the value of the settled rate;
The sons of happy punks, the pander's heir, ⎫
Are privileged to sit in triumph there, ⎬
To clap the first, and rule the theatre. ⎭
Up to the galleries, for shame, retreat;
For, by the Roscian law,[21] the poor can claim no seat."
Who ever brought to his rich daughter's bed
The man that polled but twelvepence for his head?
Who ever named a poor man for his heir,
Or called him to assist the judging chair?   270

The poor were wise, who, by the rich oppressed,
Withdrew, and sought a sacred place of rest.
Once they did well, to free themselves from scorn;
But had done better never to return.
Rarely they rise by virtue's aid, who lie
Plunged in the depth of helpless poverty.
    'At Rome 'tis worse, where house-rent by the year
And servants' bellies cost so dev'lish dear,
And tavern bills run high for hungry cheer.

280   To drink or eat in earthenware we scorn,
Which cheaply country cupboards does adorn;
And coarse blue hoods on holidays are worn.
Some distant parts of Italy are known,
Where none, but only dead men,[22] wear a gown:
On theatres of turf, in homely state,
Old plays they act, old feasts they celebrate;
The same rude song returns upon the crowd,
And, by tradition, is for wit allowed.
The mimic yearly gives the same delights;

290   And in the mother's arms the clownish infant frights.
Their habits (undistinguished by degree)
Are plain, alike; the same simplicity,
Both on the stage, and in the pit, you see.
In his white cloak the magistrate appears;
The country bumpkin the same liv'ry wears.
But here, attired beyond our purse we go,
For useless ornament and flaunting show;
We take on trust, in purple robes to shine,
And poor, are yet ambitious to be fine.

300   This is a common vice, though all things here
Are sold, and sold unconscionably dear.
What will you give that Cossus[23] may but view
Your face, and in the crowd distinguish you;
May take your incense like a gracious god,
And answer only with a civil nod?
To please our patrons, in this vicious age,
We make our entrance by the fav'rite page;
Shave his first down, and when he polls his hair,
The consecrated locks to temples bear;

310   Pay tributary cracknels, which he sells,
And, without our offerings, help to raise his vails.
    'Who fears, in country towns, a house's fall,

Or to be caught betwixt a riven wall?
But we inhabit a weak city, here,
Which buttresses and props but scarcely bear;
And 'tis the village-mason's daily calling,
To keep the world's metropolis from falling,
To cleanse the gutters, and the chinks to close,
And, for one night, secure his lord's repose.
At Cumae we can sleep quite round the year, 320
Nor falls, nor fires, nor nightly dangers fear;
While rolling flames from Roman turrets fly,
And the pale citizens for buckets cry.
Thy neighbour has removed his wretched store,
(Few hands will rid the lumber of the poor;)
Thy own third story smokes, while thou, supine,
Art drenched in fumes of undigested wine.
For if the lowest floors already burn,
Cock-lofts and garrets soon will take the turn,
Where thy tame pigeons[24] next the tiles were bred, 330
Which, in their nests unsafe, are timely fled.
   'Codrus[25] had but one bed, so short to boot,
That his short wife's short legs hung dangling out;
His cupboard's head six earthen pitchers graced,
Beneath 'em was his trusty tankard placed;
And, to support this noble plate, there lay
A bending Chiron cast from honest clay;
His few Greek books a rotten chest contained,
Whose covers much of mouldiness complained;
Where mice and rats devoured poetic bread, 340
And with heroic verse luxuriously were fed.
'Tis true, poor Codrus nothing had to boast,
And yet poor Codrus all that nothing lost;
Begged naked through the streets of wealthy Rome;
And found not one to feed, or take him home.
   'But if the palace of Arturius burn,
The nobles change their clothes, the matrons mourn;
The city praetor will no pleadings hear; ⎫
The very name of fire we hate and fear, ⎬
And look aghast, as if the Gauls were here.⎭ 350
While yet it burns, th' officious nation flies,
Some to condole, and some to bring supplies.
One sends him marble to rebuild; and one
White naked statues of the Parian stone,

The work of Polyclete, that seem to live;
While others images for altars give;
One books and screens, and Pallas to the breast;
Another bags of gold; and he gives best.
Childless Arturius, vastly rich before,
360   Thus by his losses multiplies his store;
Suspected for accomplice to the fire,
That burnt his palace but to build it higher.
    'But, could you be content to bid adieu
To the dear playhouse, and the players too,
Sweet country seats are purchased ev'rywhere,   ⎫
With lands and gardens, at less price than here.⎬
You hire a darksome doghole by the year: ⎭
A small convenience, decently prepared,
A shallow well, that rises in your yard,
370   That spreads his easy crystal streams around,
And waters all the pretty spot of ground.
There, love the fork, thy garden cultivate,
And give thy frugal friends a Pythagorean treat.[26]
'Tis somewhat to be lord of some small ground,
In which a lizard may, at least, turn round.
    ' 'Tis frequent, here, for want of sleep to die;   ⎫
Which fumes of undigested feats deny;   ⎬
And, with imperfect heat, in languid stomachs fry.⎭
What house secure from noise the poor can keep,
380   When ev'n the rich can scarce afford to sleep?
So dear it costs to purchase rest in Rome;
And hence the sources of diseases come.
The drover who his fellow-drover meets
In narrow passages of winding streets;
The wagoners, that curse their standing teams,
Would wake ev'n drowsy Drusus from his dreams.
And yet the wealthy will not brook delay,
But sweep above our heads; and make their way,
In lofty litters borne, and read and write,
390   Or sleep at ease: the shutters make it night.
Yet still he reaches first the public place:
The press before him stops the client's pace.
The crowd that follows crush his panting sides,
And trip his heels; he walks not, but he rides.
One elbows him, one justles in the shoal,
A rafter breaks his head, or chairman's pole:

Stockinged with loads of fat town-dirt he goes; ⎫
And some rogue-soldier, with his hobnailed shoes, ⎬
Indents his legs behind in bloody rows.   ⎭
  'See with what smoke our doles we celebrate: ⎫   400
A hundred guests, invited, walk in state;   ⎬
A hundred hungry slaves, with their Dutch kitchens, wait. ⎭
Huge pans the wretches on their heads must bear,
Which scarce gigantic Corbulo[27] could rear:
Yet they must walk upright beneath the load,
Nay run, and, running, blow the sparkling flames abroad.
Their coats, from botching newly brought, are torn;
Unwieldy timber-trees, in wagons borne,
Stretched at their length, beyond their carriage lie,
That nod, and threaten ruin from on high;   410
For, should their axle break, its overthrow   ⎫
Would crush, and pound to dust, the crowd below: ⎬
Nor friends their friends, nor sires their sons could know; ⎭
Nor limbs, nor bones, nor carcase, would remain,
But a mashed heap, a hotchpotch of the slain;
One vast destruction; not the soul alone,
But bodies, like the soul, invisible are flown.
Meantime, unknowing of their fellows' fate,
The servants wash the platter, scour the plate,
Then blow the fire, with puffing cheeks, and lay ⎫   420
The rubbers, and the bathing-sheets display;   ⎬
And oil them first; and each is handy in his way. ⎭
But he, for whom this busy care they take,
Poor ghost, is wand'ring by the Stygian lake;
Affrighted with the ferryman's[28] grim face,
New to the horrors of that uncouth place,
His passage begs with unregarded pray'r,
And wants two farthings to discharge his fare.
  'Return we to the dangers of the night:
And, first, behold our houses' dreadful height;   430
From whence come broken potsherds tumbling down; ⎫
And leaky ware, from garret-windows thrown: ⎬
Well may they break our heads, that mark the flinty stone. ⎭
'Tis want of sense to sup abroad too late,
Unless thou first hast settled thy estate.
As many fates attend, thy steps to meet,
As there are waking windows in the street.
Bless the good gods, and think thy chance is rare,

To have a piss-pot only for thy share.
'The scouring drunkard, if he does not fight
Before his bed-time, takes no rest that night;
Passing the tedious hours in greater pain
Than stern Achilles,[29] when his friend was slain:
'Tis so ridiculous, but so true withal,
A bully cannot sleep without a brawl.
Yet though his youthful blood he fired with wine,
He wants not wit the danger to decline:
Is cautious to avoid the coach and six,
And on the lackeys will no quarrel fix.
His train of flambeaux, and embroidered coat,
May privilege my lord to walk secure on foot.
But me, who must by moonlight homeward bend,
Or lighted only with a candle's end,
Poor me he fights, if that be fighting, where
He only cudgels, and I only bear.
He stands, and bids me stand: I must abide;
For he's the stronger, and is drunk beside.
    '"Where did you whet your knife tonight?" he cries,
"And shred the leeks that in your stomach rise?
Whose windy beans have stuff'd your guts, and where
Have your black thumbs been dipt in vinegar?
With what companion cobbler have you fed,
On old ox-cheeks, or he-goat's tougher head?
What, are you dumb? Quick with your answer, quick,
Before my foot salutes you with a kick.
Say, in what nasty cellar, under ground,
Or what church-porch, your rogueship may be found?"
Answer, or answer not, 'tis all the same:
He lays me on, and makes me bear the blame.
Before the bar, for beating him, you come;
This is a poor man's liberty in Rome.
You beg his pardon; happy to retreat
With some remaining teeth, to chew your meat.
    'Nor is this all; for when, retired, you think
To sleep securely; when the candles wink,
When every door with iron chains is barred,
And roaring taverns are no longer heard;
The ruffian robbers, by no justice awed,
And unpaid cut-throat soldiers, are abroad.
Those venal souls, who, hardened in each ill,

To save complaints and prosecution, kill.
Chased from their woods and bogs, the padders come ⎫
To this vast city, as their native home; ⎬
To live at ease, and safely skulk in Rome. ⎭
    'The forge in fetters only is employed;
Our iron mines exhausted and destroyed
In shackles; for these villains scarce allow
Goads for the teams, and ploughshares for the plough.
Oh, happy ages of our ancestors,
Beneath the kings[30] and tribunitial pow'rs!   490
One jail did all their criminals restrain,
Which, now, the walls of Rome can scarce contain.
    'More I could say, more causes I could show
For my departure; but the sun is low;
The wagoner grows weary of my stay,
And whips his horses forwards on their way.
    'Farewell; and when, like me, o'erwhelmed with care,
You to your own Aquinum[31] shall repair,
To take a mouthful of sweet country air,
Be mindful of your friend; and send me word,   500
What joys your fountains and cool shades afford:
Then, to assist your satires, I will come;
And add new venom when you write of Rome.'

DRYDEN'S

EXPLANATORY NOTES TO THE THIRD SATIRE

1 Cumae: *a small city in Campania, near Puteoli, or Puzzolo as it is called. The habitation of the Cumaean Sybil.*
2 Bajae: *another little town in Campania, near the sea: a pleasant place.*
3 Prochyta: *a small barren island belonging to the Kingdom of Naples.*
4 in dog-days. *The poets in Juvenal's time used to rehearse their poetry in August.*
5 Numa. *The second king of Rome, who made their laws and instituted their religion.*
6 Nymph. *Ægeria, a nymph or goddess; with whom Numa feigned to converse by night; and to be instructed by her, in modelling his superstitions.*
7 Where Daedalus, etc. *Meaning at Cumae.*
8 Lachesis: *one of three Destinies, whose office was to spin the life of every man; as it was of Clotho to hold the distaff, and Atropos to cut the thread.*
9 Arturius. *Any debauched wicked fellow who gains by the times.*
10 With thumbs bent backward. *In a prize of sword-players, when one of the fencers had the other at his mercy, the vanquished party implored the clemency of the spectators. If they thought he deserved it not, they held up their thumbs and bent them backwards, in sign of death.*
11 Verres: *Praetor in Sicily, contemporary with Cicero; by whom accused of oppressing the province, he was condemned. His name is used here for any rich, vicious man.*
12 Tagus: *a famous river in Spain, which discharges itself into the ocean near Lisbon in Portugal. It was held of old to be full of golden sands.*
13 Orontes: *the greatest river of Syria. The poet here puts the river for the inhabitants of Syria.*
14 Tiber: *the river which runs by Rome.*
15 Romulus: *first king of Rome, son of Mars, as the poets feign. The first Romans were originally herdsmen.*
16 But in that town, etc. *He means Athens, of which Pallas, the goddess of arms and arts was patroness.*
17 Antiochus and Stratocles: *two famous Grecian mimics, or actors, in the poet's time.*
18 A rigid stoic, etc. *Publius Egnatius, a stoic, falsely accused Bareas Soranus, as Tacitus tells us.*
19 Diphilus and Protogenes, etc., *were Grecians living in Rome.*
20 Or him who bid, etc. *Lucius Metellus, the high priest; who when the temple of Vesta was on fire, saved the Palladium.*

21 For by the Roscian law, etc. *Roscius, a tribune, who ordered the distinction of places in public shows betwixt the noblemen of Rome and the plebeians.*

22 Where none but only dead men, etc. *The meaning is that men in some parts of Italy never wore a gown (the usual habit of the Romans) till they were buried in one.*

23 Cossus *is here taken for any great man.*

24 Where the tame pigeons, etc. *The Romans used to breed their tame pigeons in their garrets.*

25 Codrus: *a learned man, very poor; by his books supposed to be a poet. For, in all probability, the heroic verses here mentioned, which rats and mice devoured, were Homer's works.*

26 a Pythagorean treat: *he means herbs, roots, fruits, and salads.*

27 gigantic Corbulo. *Corbulo was a famous general in Nero's time, who conquered Armenia, and was afterwards put to death by that tyrant, when he was in Greece, in reward of his great services. His stature was not only tall, above the ordinary size, but he was also proportionably strong.*

28 ferryman's etc. *Charon, the ferryman of hell, whose fare was a half-penny for every soul.*

29 stern Achilles. *The friend of Achilles was Patroclus, who was slain by Hector.*

30 Beneath the kings, etc. *Rome was originally ruled by kings; till for the rape of Lucretia, Tarquin the proud was expelled. After which it was governed by two consuls, yearly chosen. But they oppressing the people, the commoners mutinied, and procured Tribunes to be created; who defended their privileges, and often opposed the consular authority, and the senate.*

31 Aquinum *was the birth-place of Juvenal.*

THE LAST PARTING OF HECTOR AND ANDROMACHE

FROM THE SIXTH BOOK OF HOMER'S *ILIADS*

ARGUMENT

Hector, returning from the field of battle, to visit Helen his sister-in-law, and his brother Paris, who had fought unsuccessfully hand to hand with Menelaus, from thence goes to his own palace to see his wife Andromache, and his infant son Astyanax. The description of that interview is the subject of this translation.

Thus having said, brave Hector went to see
His virtuous wife, the fair Andromache.
He found her not at home; for she was gone ⎫
(Attended by her maid and infant son),　　　⎬
To climb the steepy tow'r of Ilion:　　　　 ⎭
From whence, with heavy heart, she might survey
The bloody business of the dreadful day.
Her mournful eyes she cast around the plain,
And sought the lord of her desires in vain.
10　　 But he, who thought his peopled palace bare,
When she, his only comfort, was not there,
Stood in the gate, and asked of ev'ry one,
Which way she took, and whither she was gone:
If to the court, or, with his mother's train,
In long procession to Minerva's fane.
The servants answered, neither to the court,
Where Priam's sons and daughters did resort,
Nor to the temple was she gone, to move
With prayers the blue-eyed progeny of Jove;
20　　 But, more solicitous for him alone,
Than all their safety, to the tow'r was gone,
There to survey the labours of the field,
Where the Greeks conquer, and the Trojans yield.

Swiftly she passed, with fear and fury wild;
The nurse went lagging after with the child.
   This heard, the noble Hector made no stay;
Th' admiring throng divide to give him way;
He passed through every street by which he came,
And at the gate he met the mournful dame.
   His wife beheld him, and with eager pace
Flew to his arms, to meet a dear embrace: 30
His wife, who brought in dow'r Cilicia's crown,
And in herself a greater dow'r alone;
Aëtion's heir, who on the woody plain
Of Hippoplacus did in Thebe reign.
Breathless she flew, with joy and passion wild;
The nurse came lagging after with her child.
   The royal babe upon her breast was laid,
Who, like the morning star, his beams displayed.
Scamandrius was his name, which Hector gave,   40
From that fair flood which Ilion's wall did lave;
But him Astyanax the Trojans call,
From his great father who defends the wall.
   Hector beheld him with a silent smile;
His tender wife stood weeping by, the while:
Pressed in her own, his warlike hand she took,
Then sighed, and thus prophetically spoke:
   'Thy dauntless heart, (which I foresee too late,)
Too daring man, will urge thee to thy fate:
Nor dost thou pity, with a parent's mind,   50
This helpless orphan whom thou leav'st behind;
Nor me, th' unhappy partner of thy bed,
Who must in triumph by the Greeks be led:
They seek thy life, and, in unequal fight,
With many will oppress thy single might:
Better it were for miserable me
To die, before the fate which I foresee.
For ah! what comfort can the world bequeath
To Hector's widow, after Hector's death?
   'Eternal sorrow and perpetual tears   60
Began my youth, and will conclude my years:
I have no parents, friends, nor brothers left;
By stern Achilles all of life bereft.
Then when the walls of Thebes he o'er-threw,
His fatal hand my royal father slew;

He slew Aëtion, but despoiled him not,
Nor in his hate the funeral rites forgot;
Armed as he was he sent him whole below,
And reverenced thus the Manes of his foe:
A tomb he raised; the mountain nymphs around
Enclosed with planted elms the holy ground.
   'My sev'n brave brothers in one fatal day
To Death's dark mansions took the mournful way:
Slain by the same Achilles, while they keep
The bellowing oxen and the bleating sheep.
My mother, who the royal sceptre swayed,
Was captive to the cruel victor made,
And hither led; but, hence redeemed with gold,
Her native country did again behold,
And but beheld; for soon Diana's dart
In an unhappy chase transfixed her heart.
   'But thou, my Hector, art thyself alone
My parents, brothers, and my lord in one.
O kill not all my kindred o'er again,⎫
Nor tempt the dangers of the dusty plain;⎬
But in this tow'r, for our defence, remain.⎭
Thy wife and son are in thy ruin lost:
This is a husband's and a father's post.
The Scaean gate commands the plains below;⎫
Here marshal all thy soldiers as they go,⎬
And hence with other hands repel the foe.⎭
By yon wild fig-tree lies their chief ascent,
And thither all their pow'rs are daily bent:
The two Ajaces have I often seen,
And the wronged husband of the Spartan queen:
With him his greater brother; and with these
Fierce Diomede and bold Meriones.
Uncertain if by augury, or chance,
But by this easy rise they all advance:
Guard well that pass, secure of all beside.'
   To whom the noble Hector thus replied:
'That and the rest are in my daily care;
But, should I shun the dangers of the war,
With scorn the Trojans would reward my pains,
And their proud ladies with their sweeping trains.
The Grecian swords and lances I can bear;
But loss of honour is my only fear.

70

80

90

100

Shall Hector, born to war, his birthright yield,
Belie his courage, and forsake the field?
Early in rugged arms I took delight,   110
And still have been the foremost in the fight:
With dangers dearly have I bought renown,
And am the champion of my father's crown.
   'And yet my mind forebodes, with sure presage,
That Troy shall perish by the Grecian rage.
The fatal day draws on, when I must fall,
And universal ruin cover all.
Not Troy itself, though built by hands divine,
Nor Priam, nor his people, nor his line,
My mother, nor my brothers of renown,   120
Whose valour yet defends th' unhappy town;
Not these, nor all their fates which I foresee,
Are half of that concern I have for thee.
I see, I see thee in that fatal hour,
Subjected to the victor's cruel pow'r;
Led hence a slave to some insulting sword,
Forlorn, and trembling at a foreign lord;
A spectacle in Argos, at the loom,
Gracing with Trojan fights a Grecian room;
Or from deep wells the living stream to take,   130
And on thy weary shoulders bring it back:
While, groaning under this laborious life,
They insolently call thee Hector's wife;
Upbraid thy bondage with thy husband's name,
And from my glory propagate thy shame.
This when they say, thy sorrows will increase ⎫
With anxious thoughts of former happiness; ⎬
That he is dead who could thy wrongs redress.⎭
But I, oppressed with iron sleep before,
Shall hear thy unavailing cries no more.'   140
   He said.
Then, holding forth his arms, he took his boy
(The pledge of love and other hope of Troy).
The fearful infant turned his head away,
And on his nurse's neck reclining lay,
His unknown father shunning with affright,
And looking back on so uncouth a sight;
Daunted to see a face with steel o'erspread,
And his high plume that nodded o'er his head.

150   His sire and mother smiled with silent joy,
And Hector hastened to relieve his boy;
Dismissed his burnished helm, that shone afar
(The pride of warriors, and the pomp of war):
Th' illustrious babe, thus reconciled, he took;
Hugged in his arms, and kissed, and thus he spoke:
   'Parent of gods and men, propitious Jove,
And you bright synod of the pow'rs above;
On this my son your gracious gifts bestow;
Grant him to live, and great in arms to grow;

160   To reign in Troy, to govern with renown,
To shield the people, and assert the crown:
That, when hereafter he from war shall come,
And bring his Trojans peace and triumph home,
Some aged man, who lives this act to see,
And who in former times remembered me,
May say the son in fortitude and fame
Outgoes the mark, and drowns his father's name:
That at these words his mother may rejoice,
And add her suffrage to the public voice.'

170   Thus having said,
He first with suppliant hands the gods adored,
Then to the mother's arms the child restored:
With tears and smiles she took her son, and pressed
Th' illustrious infant to her fragrant breast.
He, wiping her fair eyes, indulged her grief,
And eased her sorrows with this last relief:
   'My wife and mistress, drive thy fears away,
Nor give so bad an omen to the day:
Think not it lies in any Grecian's pow'r,

180   To take my life before the fatal hour.
When that arrives, nor good nor bad can fly
Th' irrevocable doom of destiny.
Return, and to divert thy thoughts at home, ⎫
There task thy maids, and exercise the loom, ⎬
Employed in works that womankind become. ⎭
The toils of war and feats of chivalry
Belong to men, and most of all to me.'
At this, for new replies he did not stay,
But laced his crested helm, and strode away.

190   His lovely consort to her house returned,
And looking often back in silence mourned.

Home when she came, her secret woe she vents,
And fills the palace with her loud laments.
Those loud laments her echoing maids restore,
And Hector, yet alive, as dead deplore.

THE EPISODE OF NISUS AND EURYALUS,

FROM THE FIFTH AND NINTH BOOKS OF VIRGIL'S AENEID

FROM THE FIFTH BOOK

From thence his way the Trojan hero bent
Into the neighb'ring plain, with mountains pent,
Whose sides were shaded with surrounding wood.
Full in the midst of this fair valley stood
A native theatre, which, rising slow
By just degrees, o'erlooked the ground below.
High on a sylvan throne the leader sat;
A num'rous train attend in solemn state.
Here those, that in the rapid course delight,
10   Desire of honour, and the prize, invite.
The rival runners without order stand;
The Trojans, mixed with the Sicilian band.
First Nisus, with Euryalus, appears,
Euryalus a boy of blooming years,
With sprightly grace and equal beauty crowned:
Nisus, for friendship to the youth, renowned.
Diores next, of Priam's royal race,
Then Salius, joined with Patron, took their place:
But Patron in Arcadia had his birth,
20   And Salius his, from Acarnanian earth.
Then two Sicilian youths — the names of these
Swift Helymus, and lovely Panopes:
Both jolly huntsmen, both in forests bred,
And owning old Acestes for their head;
With sev'ral others of ignobler name,
Whom Time has not delivered o'er to fame.
To these the hero thus his thoughts explained,
In words which general approbation gained:
'One common largess is for all designed:
30   The vanquished and the victor shall be joined.

Two darts of polished steel and Gnossian wood,
A silver-studded axe, alike bestowed.
The foremost three have olive-wreaths decreed;
The first of these obtains a stately steed
Adorned with trappings; and the next in fame,
The quiver of an Amazonian dame,
With feathered Thracian arrows well supplied: ⎫
A golden belt shall gird his manly side,   ⎬
Which with a sparkling diamond shall be tied;⎭
The third this Grecian helmet shall content.'   40
He said. To their appointed base they went;
With beating hearts th' expected sign receive,
And, starting all at once, the barrier leave.
Spread out, as on the winged winds, they flew,
And seized the distant goal with greedy view.
Shot from the crowd, swift Nisus all o'er-passed;
Nor storms, nor thunder, equal half his haste.
The next, but though the next, yet far disjoined,
Came Salius; and Euryalus behind;
Then Helymus, whom young Diores plied,   50
Step after step, and almost side by side:
His shoulders pressing, and in longer space
Had won, or left at least a dubious race.
   Now spent, the goal they almost reach at last,
When eager Nisus, hapless in his haste,
Slipped first, and slipping, fell upon the plain,
Soaked with the blood of oxen newly slain.
The careless victor had not marked his way;
But, treading where the treach'rous puddle lay,
His heels flew up; and on the grassy floor   60
He fell, besmeared with filth and holy gore.
Not mindless then, Euryalus, of thee,
Nor of the sacred bonds of amity,
He strove th' immediate rival's hope to cross,
And caught the foot of Salius as he rose:
So Salius lay extended on the plain;
Euryalus springs out, the prize to gain,
And leaves the crowd: applauding peals attend
The victor to the goal, who vanquished by his friend.
Next Helymus, and then Diores came,   70
By two misfortunes made the third in fame.
   But Salius enters, and, exclaiming loud

For justice, deafens and disturbs the crowd;
Urges his cause may in the court be heard;
And pleads the prize is wrongfully conferred.
But favour for Euryalus appears;
His blooming beauty, with his tender tears,
Had bribed the judges to protect his claim;
Besides, Diores does as loud exclaim,
80   Who vainly reaches at the last reward,
If the first palm on Salius be conferred.
Then thus the prince: 'Let no disputes arise:
Where Fortune placed it, I award the prize.
But Fortune's errors give me leave to mend,
At least to pity my deserving friend.'
He said, and, from among the spoils, he draws
(Pond'rous with shaggy mane and golden paws)
A lion's hide: to Salius this he gives:
Nisus with envy sees the gift, and grieves.
90   'If such rewards to vanquished men are due,'
He said, 'and falling is to rise by you,
What prize may Nisus from your bounty claim,
Who merited the first rewards and fame?
In falling, both an equal fortune tried;
Would Fortune for my fall so well provide!'
With this he pointed to his face, and showed
His hands and all his habit smeared with blood.
Th' indulgent father of the people smiled,
And caused to be produced an ample shield,
100   Of wondrous art, by Didymaon wrought,
Long since from Neptune's bars in triumph brought.
This giv'n to Nisus, he divides the rest,
And equal justice in his gifts expressed.

FROM THE NINTH BOOK

The post of honour to Messapus falls,
To keep the nightly guard, to watch the walls,
To pitch the fires at distances around,
And close the Trojans in their scanty ground.
Twice seven Rutulian captains ready stand;
And twice seven hundred horse these chiefs command:
All clad in shining arms the works invest,
Each with a radiant helm, and waving crest.

Stretched at their length, they press the grassy ground;
They laugh, they sing, the jolly bowls go round;   10
With lights and cheerful fires renew the day;
And pass the wakeful night in feasts and play.
   The Trojans, from above, their foes beheld,
And with armed legions all the rampires filled.
Seized with affright, their gates they first explore;
Join works to works with bridges, tow'r to tow'r:
Thus all things needful for defence abound;
Mnestheus and brave Serestus walk the round,
Commissioned by their absent prince to share
The common danger, and divide the care.   20
The soldiers draw their lots, and, as they fall,
By turns relieve each other on the wall.
   Nigh where the foes their utmost guards advance,
To watch the gate was warlike Nisus' chance.
His father Hyrtacus, of noble blood;
His mother was a huntress of the wood,
And sent him to the wars. Well could he bear
His lance in fight, and dart the flying spear;
But better skilled unerring shafts to send.
Beside him stood Euryalus, his friend: 30
Euryalus, than whom the Trojan host
No fairer face, or sweeter air, could boast.
Scarce had the down to shade his cheeks begun;
One was their care, and their delight was one.
One common hazard in the war they shared;
And now were both by choice upon the guard.
   Then Nisus thus: 'Or do the gods inspire
This warmth, or make we gods of our desire?
A gen'rous ardour boils within my breast,
Eager of action, enemy to rest: 40
Thus urges me to fight, and fires my mind
To leave a memorable name behind.
Thou seest the foe secure: how faintly shine
Their scattered fires! The most, in sleep supine
Along the ground, an easy conquest lie;
The wakeful few the fuming flagon ply:
All hushed around. Now hear what I revolve,
A thought unripe, and scarcely yet resolve.
Our absent prince both camp and council mourn;
By message both would hasten his return: 50

If they confer what I demand, on thee
(For fame is recompense enough for me),
Methinks, beneath yon hill, I have espied
A way that safely will my passage guide.'
    Euryalus stood list'ning while he spoke;
With love of praise and noble envy struck;
Then to his ardent friend exposed his mind:
'All this alone, and leaving me behind!
Am I unworthy, Nisus, to be joined?
60   Think'st thou I can my share of glory yield,
Or send thee unassisted to the field?
Not so my father taught my childhood arms;
Born in a siege, and bred among alarms.
Nor is my youth unworthy of my friend,
Nor of the heav'n-born hero I attend.
The thing called life with ease I can disclaim,
And think it over-sold to purchase fame.'
    Then Nisus thus: 'Alas! thy tender years
Would minister new matter to my fears.
70   So may the gods who view this friendly strife,
Restore me to thy loved embrace with life,
Condemned to pay my vows (as sure I trust),
This thy request is cruel and unjust.
But if some chance — as many chances are,
And doubtful hazards, in the deeds of war —
If one should reach my head, there let it fall,
And spare thy life; I would not perish all.
Thy blooming youth deserves a longer date:
Live thou to mourn thy love's unhappy fate:
80   To bear my mangled body from the foe,
Or buy it back, and fun'ral rites bestow.
Or, if hard fortune shall those dues deny,
Thou canst at least an empty tomb supply.
O let not me the widow's tears renew;
Nor let a mother's curse my name pursue:
Thy pious parent, who, for love of thee,
Forsook the coasts of friendly Sicily;
Her age committing to the seas and wind,
When ev'ry weary matron stayed behind.'
90   To this, Euryalus: 'You plead in vain,
And but protract the cause you cannot gain.
No more delays, but haste!' With that, he wakes

The nodding watch; each to his office takes.
    The guard relieved, the gen'rous couple went
To find the council at the royal tent.
All creatures else forgot their daily care,
And sleep, the common gift of nature, share;
Except the Trojan peers, who wakeful sat
In nightly council for th' endangered state.
They vote a message to their absent chief,   100
Shew their distress, and beg a swift relief.
Amid the camp a silent seat they chose,
Remote from clamour, and secure from foes.
On their left arms their ample shields they bear,
The right reclined upon the bending spear.
    Now Nisus and his friend approach the guard,⎫
And beg admission, eager to be heard: ⎬
Th' affair important, not to be deferred.   ⎭
Ascanius bids 'em be conducted in,
Ord'ring the more experienced to begin.   110
Then Nisus thus: 'Ye fathers, lend your ears;
Nor judge our bold attempt beyond our years.
The foe, securely drenched in sleep and wine,
Neglect their watch; the fires but thinly shine;
And where the smoke in cloudy vapours flies,
Cov'ring the plain, and curling to the skies,
Betwixt two paths which at the gate divide,⎫
Close by the sea, a passage we have spied,   ⎬
Which will our way to great Æneas guide.   ⎭
Expect each hour to see him safe again,   120
Loaded with spoils of foes in battle slain.
Snatch we the lucky minute while we may:
Nor can we be mistaken in the way;
For, hunting in the vales, we both have seen
The rising turrets, and the stream between;
And know the winding course, with ev'ry ford.'
He ceased; and old Alethes took the word:
'Our country gods, in whom our trust we place,
Will yet from ruin save the Trojan race,
While we behold such dauntless worth appear   130
In dawning youth, and souls so void of fear.'
Then into tears of joy the father broke: ⎫
Each in his longing arms by turns he took;   ⎬
Panted and paused; and thus again he spoke:⎭

'Ye brave young men, what equal gifts can we,
In recompense of such desert, decree?
The greatest, sure, and best you can receive,
The gods and your own conscious worth will give.
The rest our grateful gen'ral will bestow,
140   And young Ascanius, till his manhood, owe.'
'And I, whose welfare in my father lies,'
Ascanius adds, 'by the great deities,
By my dear country, by my household gods,
By hoary Vesta's rites and dark abodes,
Adjure you both (on you my fortune stands:
That and my faith I plight into your hands):
Make me but happy in his safe return,
Whose wanted presence I can only mourn;
Your common gift shall two large goblets be
150   Of silver, wrought with curious imagery,
And high embossed, which, when old Priam reigned,
My conqu'ring sire at sacked Arisba gained;
And, more, two tripods cast in antique mould,
With two great talents of the finest gold;
Beside a costly bowl, engraved with art,
Which Dido gave, when first she gave her heart.
But, if in conquered Italy we reign,
When spoils by lot the victor shall obtain —
Thou saw'st the courser by proud Turnus pressed,
160   That, Nisus! and his arms, and nodding crest,
And shield, from chance exempt, shall be thy share;   ⎫
Twelve lab'ring slaves, twelve handmaids young and fair, ⎬
All clad in rich attire, and trained with care;   ⎭
And, last, a Latian field with fruitful plains,
And a large portion of the king's domains.
But thou, whose years are more to mine allied,
No fate my vowed affection shall divide
From thee, heroic youth! Be wholly mine:
Take full possession; all my soul is thine.
170   One faith, one fame, one fate, shall both attend:
My life's companion, and my bosom friend.
My peace shall be committed to thy care,
And, to thy conduct, my concerns in war.'
    Then thus the young Euryalus replied:
'Whatever fortune, good or bad, betide,
The same shall be my age, as now my youth;

No time shall find me wanting to my truth.
This only from your goodness let me gain
(And, this ungranted, all rewards are vain):
Of Priam's royal race my mother came —   180
And sure the best that ever bore the name —
Whom neither Troy nor Sicily could hold
From me departing, but, o'erspent and old,
My fate she followed. Ignorant of this,
Whatever danger, neither parting kiss
Nor pious blessing taken, her I leave,
And in this only act of all my life deceive.
By this right hand, and conscious night, I swear,
My soul so sad a farewell could not bear.
Be you her comfort; fill my vacant place   190
(Permit me to presume so great a grace);
Support her age, forsaken, and distressed.
That hope alone will fortify my breast
Against the worst of fortunes and of fears.'
He said. The moved assistants melt in tears.
   Then thus Ascanius, wonder-struck to see
That image of his filial piety:
'So great beginnings, in so green an age,
Exact the faith which I again engage.
Thy mother all the dues shall justly claim,   200
Creusa had, and only want the name.
Whate'er event thy bold attempt shall have,
'Tis merit to have borne a son so brave.
Now by my head, a sacred oath, I swear
(My father used it), what, returning here
Crowned with success, I for thyself prepare,
That, if thou fail, shall thy loved mother share.'
   He said, and, weeping while he spoke the word,
From his broad belt he drew a shining sword,
Magnificent with gold. Lycaon made,   210
And in an iv'ry scabbard sheathed the blade.
This was his gift. Great Mnestheus gave his friend
A lion's hide, his body to defend;
And good Alethes furnished him, beside,
With his own trusty helm, of temper tried.
   Thus armed they went. The noble Trojans wait
Their issuing forth, and follow to the gate,
With prayers and vows: above the rest appears

Ascanius, manly far beyond his years:
220 And messages committed to their care,
Which all in winds were lost, and flitting air.
The trenches first they passed; then took their way
Where their proud foes in pitched pavilions lay;
To many fatal, ere themselves were slain.
They found the careless host dispersed upon the plain,
Who, gorged, and drunk with wine, supinely snore.
Unharnessed chariots stand along the shore:
Amidst the wheels and reins, the goblet by,
A medley of debauch and war they lie.
230 Observing Nisus shewed his friend the sight:
'Behold a conquest gained without a fight.
Occasion offers, and I stand prepared;
There lies our way: be thou upon the guard,
And look around, while I securely go,
And hew a passage through the sleeping foe.'
Softly he spoke; then striding took his way,
With his drawn sword, where haughty Rhamnes lay;
His head raised high on tapestry beneath,
And heaving from his breast, he drew his breath:
240 A king and prophet, by king Turnus loved;
But fate by prescience cannot be removed.
Him and his sleeping slaves he slew; then spies
Where Rhemus, with his rich retinue, lies.
His armour-bearer first, and next he kills
His charioteer, intrenched betwixt the wheels
And his loved horses: last invades their lord;
Full on his neck he drives the fatal sword;
The gasping head flies off; a purple flood
Flows from the trunk, that welters in the blood,
250 Which, by the spurning heels dispersed around,
The bed besprinkles, and bedews the ground.
Lamus the bold and Lamyrus the strong,
He slew, and then Sarranus fair and young.
From dice and wine the youth retired to rest,
And puffed the fumy god from out his breast:
Ev'n then he dreamt of drink and lucky play —
More lucky, had it lasted till the day.
    The famished lion thus, with hunger bold,
O'erleaps the fences of the nightly fold,
260 And tears the peaceful flocks: with silent awe

Trembling they lie, and pant beneath his paw.
Nor with less rage Euryalus employs
The wrathful sword, or fewer foes destroys:
But on th' ignoble crowd his fury flew:
He Fadus, Hebesus, and Rhoetus, slew.
Oppressed with heavy sleep the former fall,
But Rhoetus wakeful, and observing all:
Behind a spacious jar he slinked for fear:
The fatal iron found and reached him there;
For, as he rose, it pierced his naked side,   270
And, reeking, thence returned in crimson dyed.
The wound pours out a stream of wine and blood;
The purple soul comes floating in the flood.
   Now where Messapus quartered they arrive:
The fires were fainting there, and just alive;
The warrior-horses, tied in order, fed:
Nisus observed the discipline, and said:
'Our eager thirst of blood may both betray:
And see, the scattered streaks of dawning day,
Foe to nocturnal thefts. No more, my friend: 280
Here let our glutted execution end.
A lane through slaughtered bodies we have made.'
The bold Euryalus, though loth, obeyed.
Of arms, and arras, and of plate, they find
A precious load; but these they leave behind.
Yet fond of gaudy spoils, the boy would stay ⎞
To make the rich caparison his prey,   ⎬
Which on the steed of conquered Rhamnes lay.⎠
Nor did his eyes less longingly behold
The girdle-belt, with nails of burnished gold.   290
This present Caedicus the rich bestowed
On Remulus, when friendship first they vowed,
And, absent, joined in hospitable ties;
He, dying, to his heir bequeathed the prize;
Till, by the conquering Ardean troops oppressed,
He fell; and they the glorious gift possessed.
These glitt'ring spoils (now made the victor's gain)
He to his body suits, but suits in vain.
Messapus' helm he finds among the rest,
And laces on, and wears the waving crest.   300
Proud of their conquest, prouder of their prey,
They leave the camp, and take the ready way.

But far they had not passed, before they spied
Three hundred horse, with Volscens for their guide.
The queen a legion to king Turnus sent;
But the swift horse the slower foot outwent,
And now, advancing, sought the leader's tent.
They saw the pair; for, through the doubtful shade,
His shining helm Euryalus betrayed,
310   On which the moon with full reflection played.
''Tis not for nought,' cried Volscens from the crowd,
'These men go there;' then raised his voice aloud:
'Stand! stand! why thus in arms? and whither bent
From whence, to whom, and on what errand sent?'
Silent they scud away, and haste their flight
To neighb'ring woods, and trust themselves to night.
The speedy horse all passages belay,
And spur their smoking steeds to cross their way,
And watch each entrance of the winding wood.
320   Black was the forest: thick with beech it stood,
Horrid with fern, and intricate with thorn;
Few paths of human feet, or tracks of beasts, were worn.
The darkness of the shades, his heavy prey,
And fear, misled the younger from his way.
But Nisus hit the turns with happier haste,
And thoughtless of his friend, the forest passed,
And Alban plains, from Alba's name so called,
Where king Latinus then his oxen stalled;
Till, turning at the length, he stood his ground,
330   And missed his friend, and cast his eyes around.
'Ah wretch!' he cried, 'where have I left behind
Th' unhappy youth? where shall I hope to find?
Or what way take?' Again he ventures back,
And treads the mazes of his former track.
He winds the wood, and, list'ning, hears the noise
Of trampling coursers, and the riders' voice.
The sound approached; and suddenly he viewed
The foes inclosing, and his friend pursued,
Forelaid and taken, while he strove in vain
340   The shelter of the friendly shades to gain.
What should he next attempt? what arms employ,
What fruitless force, to free the captive boy?
Or desperate should he rush and lose his life,
With odds oppressed, in such unequal strife?

Resolved at length, his pointed spear he shook;
And, casting on the moon a mournful look:
'Guardian of groves, and goddess of the night!
Fair queen!' he said, 'direct my dart aright.
If e'er my pious father, for my sake,
Did grateful off'rings on thy altars make,   350
Or I increased them with my sylvan toils,
And hung thy holy roofs with savage spoils,
Give me to scatter these.' Then from his ear
He poised, and aimed, and launched the trembling spear.
The deadly weapon, hissing from the grove,
Impetuous on the back of Sulmo drove;
Pierced his thin armour, drank his vital blood,
And in his body left the broken wood.
He staggers round; his eyeballs roll in death;
And with short sobs he gasps away his breath.   360
All stand amazed: a second jav'lin flies
With equal strength, and quivers through the skies.
This through thy temples, Tagus, forced the way,
And in the brain-pen warmly buried lay.
Fierce Volscens foams with rage, and gazing round,
Descried not him who gave the deadly wound,
Nor knew to fix revenge: 'But thou,' he cries,
'Shalt pay for both,' and at the pris'ner flies
With his drawn sword. Then, struck with deep despair,
That cruel sight the lover could not bear;   370
But from his covert rushed in open view,
And sent his voice before him as he flew:
'Me! me!' he cried, 'turn all your swords alone
On me: the fact confessed, the fault my own.
He neither could nor durst, the guiltless youth —
Ye moon and stars, bear witness to the truth!
His only crime (if friendship can offend)
Is too much love to his unhappy friend.'
Too late he speaks: the sword, which fury guides,
Driv'n with full force, had pierced his tender sides.   380
Down fell the beauteous youth: the yawning wound
Gushed out a purple stream, and stained the ground.
His snowy neck reclines upon his breast,
Like a fair flower by the keen share oppressed:
Like a white poppy sinking on the plain,
Whose heavy head is overcharged with rain.

Despair, and rage, and vengeance justly vowed,
Drove Nisus headlong on the hostile crowd.
Volscens he seeks; on him alone he bends:
390   Borne back and bored by his surrounding friends,
Onward he pressed, and kept him still in sight,
Then whirled aloft his sword with all his might:
Th' unerring steel descended while he spoke,
Pierced his wide mouth, and through his weazon broke.
Dying, he slew; and stagg'ring on the plain,
With swimming eyes he sought his lover slain;
Then quiet on his bleeding bosom fell,
Content, in death, to be revenged so well.
        O happy friends! for, if my verse can give
400   Immortal life, your fame shall ever live,
Fixed as the Capitol's foundation lies,
And spread, where'er the Roman eagle flies!

BAUCIS AND PHILEMON,

OUT OF THE EIGHTH BOOK OF OVID'S METAMORPHOSES

The Author, pursuing the deeds of Theseus, relates how he with his friend Perithous were invited by Acheloüs, the river god, to stay with him till his waters were abated. Acheloüs entertains them with a relation of his own love to Perimele, who was changed into an island by Neptune at his request. Perithous, being an atheist, derides the legend, and denies the power of the gods to work that miracle. Lelex, another companion of Theseus, to confirm the story of Acheloüs, relates another metamorphosis of Baucis and Philemon into trees; of which he was partly an eye witness.

> Thus Acheloüs ends: his audience hear
> With admiration, and, admiring, fear
> The pow'rs of heav'n; except Ixion's son,
> Who laughed at all the gods, believed in none.
> He shook his impious head, and thus replies:
> 'These legends are no more than pious lies:
> You attribute too much to heavenly sway,
> To think they give us forms, and take away.'
>   The rest, of better minds, their sense declared
> Against this doctrine, and with horror heard.   10
> Then Lelex rose, an old experienced man,
> And thus with sober gravity began:
> 'Heav'n's power is infinite; earth, air, and sea,
> The manufactured mass, the making pow'r obey.
> By proof to clear your doubt: in Phrygian ground
> Two neighb'ring trees, with walls encompassed round,
> Stand on a mod'rate rise, with wonder shown,
> One a hard oak, a softer linden one:
> I saw the place and them, by Pittheus sent
> To Phrygian realms, my grandsire's government.   20
> Not far from thence is seen a lake, the haunt
> Of coots, and of the fishing cormorant:

Here Jove with Hermes came; but in disguise
Of mortal men concealed their deities:
One laid aside his thunder, one his rod;
And many toilsome steps together trod;
For harbour at a thousand doors they knocked —
Not one of all the thousand but was locked.
At last an hospitable house they found,
30   A homely shed; the roof, not far from ground,
Was thatched with reeds and straw together bound.
There Baucis and Philemon lived, and there
Had lived long married, and a happy pair:
Now old in love; though little was their store,
Inured to want, their poverty they bore,
Nor aimed at wealth, professing to be poor.
For master or for servant here to call,
Was all alike, where only two were all.
Command was none, where equal love was paid,
40   Or rather both commanded, both obeyed.
   'From lofty roofs the gods repulsed before,
Now, stooping, entered through the little door:
The man (their hearty welcome first expressed)
A common settle drew for either guest,
Inviting each his weary limbs to rest.
But ere they sat, officious Baucis lays
Two cushions stuffed with straw, the seat to raise;
Coarse, but the best she had; then rakes the load
Of ashes from the hearth, and spreads abroad
50   The living coals, and, lest they should expire,
With leaves and barks she feeds her infant fire:
It smokes, and then with trembling breath she blows,
Till in a cheerful blaze the flames arose.
With brushwood and with chips she strengthens these,
And adds at last the boughs of rotten trees.
The fire thus formed, she sets the kettle on
(Like burnished gold the little seether shone);
Next took the coleworts which her husband got
From his own ground (a small well-watered spot);
60   She stripped the stalks of all their leaves; the best
She culled, and then with handy care she dressed.
High o'er the hearth a chine of bacon hung:
Good old Philemon seized it with a prong,
And from the sooty rafter drew it down;

Then cut a slice, but scarce enough for one;
Yet a large portion of a little store,
Which for their sakes alone he wished were more.
This in the pot he plunged without delay,
To tame the flesh and drain the salt away.
The time between, before the fire they sat,   70
And shortened the delay by pleasing chat.
   'A beam there was, on which a beechen pail
Hung by the handle, on a driven nail:
This filled with water, gently warmed, they set ⎞
Before their guests; in this they bathed their feet, ⎬
And after with clean towels dried their sweat. ⎠
This done, the host produced the genial bed, ⎞
Sallow the feet, the borders, and the stead, ⎬
Which with no costly coverlet they spread, ⎠
But coarse old garments; yet such robes as these   80
They laid alone, at feasts, on holidays.
The good old housewife, tucking up her gown,
The table sets; th' invited gods lie down.
The trivet table of a foot was lame,
A blot which prudent Baucis overcame,
Who thrusts beneath the limping leg a sherd;
So was the mended board exactly reared:
Then rubbed it o'er with newly gathered mint,
A wholesome herb, that breathed a grateful scent.
Pallas began the feast, where first was seen   90
The particoloured olive, black and green;
Autumnal cornels next in order served,
In lees of wine well pickled and preserved;
A garden salad was the third supply,
Of endive, radishes, and succory;
Then curds and cream, the flow'r of country fare, ⎞
And new-laid eggs, which Baucis' busy care ⎬
Turned by a gentle fire, and roasted rear. ⎠
All these in earthenware were served to board; ⎞
And, next in place, an earthen pitcher, stored ⎬   100
With liquor of the best the cottage could afford. ⎠
This was the table's ornament and pride,
With figures wrought: like pages at his side
Stood beechen bowls; and these were shining clean,
Vernished with wax without, and lined within.
By this the boiling kettle had prepared

And to the table sent the smoking lard,
On which with eager appetite they dine,
A sav'ry bit, that served to relish wine:
110　The wine itself was suiting to the rest,
Still working in the must, and lately pressed.
The second course succeeds like that before;
Plums, apples, nuts, and, of their wintry store,
Dry figs, and grapes, and wrinkled dates were set
In canisters, t'enlarge the little treat.
All these a milk-white honeycomb surround,
Which in the midst the country banquet crowned.
But the kind hosts their entertainment grace
With hearty welcome, and an open face:
120　In all they did you might discern with ease
A willing mind, and a desire to please.
　'Meantime the beechen bowls went round, and still,
Though often emptied, were observed to fill;
Filled without hands, and of their own accord
Ran without feet, and danced about the board.
Devotion seized the pair, to see the feast
With wine, and of no common grape, increased;
And up they held their hands, and fell to pray'r,
Excusing, as they could, their country fare.
130　　'One goose they had, ('twas all they could allow,)⎞
A wakeful sentry, and on duty now,　　　　　　⎬
Whom to the gods for sacrifice they vow:　　　⎠
Her, with malicious zeal, the couple viewed;
She ran for life, and, limping, they pursued.
Full well the fowl perceived their bad intent,
And would not make her masters' compliment;
But, persecuted, to the pow'rs she flies,
And close between the legs of Jove she lies.
He with a gracious ear the suppliant heard,
140　And saved her life; then what he was declared,
And owned the god. "The neighbourhood," said he,
"Shall justly perish for impiety:
You stand alone exempted; but obey
With speed, and follow where we lead the way;
Leave these accurst, and to the mountain's height
Ascend, nor once look backward in your flight."
　'They haste, and what their tardy feet denied,
The trusty staff (their better leg) supplied.

An arrow's flight they wanted to the top,
And there secure, but spent with travel, stop;   150
Then turn their now no more forbidden eyes:
Lost in a lake the floated level lies;
A wat'ry desert covers all the plains;
Their cot alone, as in an isle, remains.
Wond'ring with weeping eyes, while they deplore
Their neighbours' fate, and country now no more,
Their little shed, scarce large enough for two,
Seems, from the ground increased, in height and bulk to grow.
A stately temple shoots within the skies;
The crotches of their cot in columns rise;   160
The pavement polished marble they behold,
The gates with sculpture graced, the spires and tiles of gold.
   'Then thus the Sire of Gods, with look serene:
"Speak thy desire, thou only just of men;
And thou, O woman, only worthy found
To be with such a man in marriage bound."
   'A while they whisper; then, to Jove addressed,
Philemon thus prefers their joint request:
"We crave to serve before your sacred shrine,
And offer at your altars rites divine;   170
And since not any action of our life
Has been polluted with domestic strife,
We beg one hour of death; that neither she
With widow's tears may live to bury me,
Nor weeping I, with withered arms, may bear
My breathless Baucis to the sepulchre.
   'The godheads sign their suit. They run their race
In the same tenor all th' appointed space;
Then, when their hour was come, while they relate
These past adventures at the temple gate,   180
Old Baucis is by old Philemon seen
Sprouting with sudden leaves of sprightly green;
Old Baucis looked where old Philemon stood,
And saw his lengthened arms a sprouting wood.
New roots their fastened feet begin to bind,
Their bodies stiffen in a rising rind:
Then, ere the bark above their shoulders grew,
They give and take at once their last adieu:
At once: "Farewell, O faithful spouse," they said;
At once th' incroaching rinds their closing lips invade.   190

Ev'n yet, an ancient Tyanaean shows
A spreading oak, that near a linden grows;
The neighbourhood confirm the prodigy,
Grave men, not vain of tongue, or like to lie.
I saw myself the garlands on their boughs,
And tablets hung for gifts of granted vows;
And off'ring fresher up, with pious pray'r,
"The good," said I, "are God's peculiar care,
And such as honour Heav'n, shall heav'nly honour share." '

PYGMALION AND THE STATUE

OUT OF THE TENTH BOOK OF OVID'S METAMORPHOSES

The Propoetides, for their impudent behaviour, being turned into stone by Venus,
Pygmalion, prince of Cyprus, detested all women for their sake, and resolved never
to marry. He falls in love with a statue of his own making, which is changed into
a maid, whom he marries.

Pygmalion, loathing their lascivious life,
Abhorred all womankind, but a most a wife:
So single chose to live, and shunned to wed,
Well pleased to want a consort of his bed;
Yet fearing idleness, the nurse of ill,
In sculpture exercised his happy skill;
And carved in iv'ry such a maid, so fair,
As Nature could not with his art compare,
Were she to work; but, in her own defence,
Must take her pattern here, and copy hence.   10
Pleased with his idol, he commends, admires,
Adores; and last, the thing adored desires.
A very virgin in her face was seen,
And, had she moved, a living maid had been.
One would have thought she could have stirred, but strove
With modesty, and was ashamed to move.
Art, hid with art, so well performed the cheat,
It caught the carver with his own deceit:
He knows 'tis madness, yet he must adore,
And still the more he knows it, loves the more.   20
The flesh, or what so seems, he touches oft,
Which feels so smooth, that he believes it soft.
Fired with this thought, at once he strained the breast,
And on the lips a burning kiss impressed.
'Tis true, the hardened breast resists the gripe,
And the cold lips return a kiss unripe:

But when, retiring back, he looked again,
To think it iv'ry was a thought too mean;
So would believe she kissed, and courting more,
Again embraced her naked body o'er;
And straining hard the statue, was afraid
His hands had made a dint and hurt his maid;
Explored her, limb by limb, and feared to find
So rude a gripe had left a livid mark behind.
With flatt'ry now he seeks her mind to move,
And now with gifts (the pow'rful bribes of love),
He furnishes her closet first, and fills
The crowded shelves with rarities of shells;
Adds orient pearls, which from the conchs he drew,
And all the sparkling stones of various hue;
And parrots, imitating human tongue,
And singing-birds in silver cages hung;
And ev'ry fragrant flow'r, and od'rous green,
Were sorted well, with lumps of amber laid between.
Rich, fashionable robes her person deck,
Pendants her ears, and pearls adorn her neck:
Her tapered fingers too with rings are graced,
And an embroidered zone surrounds her slender waist.
Thus like a queen arrayed, so richly dressed,
Beauteous she shewed, but naked shewed the best.
Then from the floor he raised a royal bed,
With coverings of Sidonian purple spread;
The solemn rites performed, he calls her bride,
With blandishments invites her to his side;
And as she were with vital sense possessed,
Her head did on a plumy pillow rest.
    The feast of Venus came, a solemn day,
To which the Cypriots due devotion pay;
With gilded horns the milk-white heifers led,
Slaughtered before the sacred altars, bled.
Pygmalion, off'ring, first approached the shrine,
And then with pray'rs implored the pow'rs divine:
'Almighty gods, if all we mortals want,
If all we can require, be yours to grant,
Make this fair statue mine,' he would have said, ⎫
But changed his words for shame, and only prayed: ⎬
'Give me the likeness of my iv'ry maid.' ⎭
    The golden goddess, present at the pray'r,

30

40

50

60

Well knew he meant th' inanimated fair,
And gave the sign of granting his desire;   70
For thrice in cheerful flames ascends the fire.
The youth, returning to his mistress, hies,
And, impudent in hope, with ardent eyes
And beating breast, by the dear statue lies.
He kisses her white lips, renews the bliss,
And looks and thinks they redden at the kiss:
He thought them warm before; nor longer stays,
But next his hand on her hard bosom lays:
Hard as it was, beginning to relent,
It seemed the breast beneath his fingers bent.   80
He felt again, his fingers made a print;
'Twas flesh, but flesh so firm, it rose against the dint.
The pleasing task he fails not to renew:
Soft, and more soft at ev'ry touch it grew;
Like pliant wax, when chafing hands reduce
The former mass to form, and frame for use.
He would believe, but yet is still in pain,
And tries his argument of sense again;
Presses the pulse, and feels the leaping vein.
Convinced, o'erjoyed, his studied thanks and praise   90
To her who made the miracle he pays:
Then lips to lips he joined; now freed from fear,
He found the savour of the kiss sincere:
At this the wakened image oped her eyes,
And viewed at once the light and lover, with surprise.
The goddess, present at the match she made,
So blessed the bed, such fruitfulness conveyed,
That ere ten moons had sharpened either horn,
To crown their bliss, a lovely boy was born;
Paphos his name, who, grown to manhood, walled   100
The city of Paphos, from the founder called.

From THE COCK AND THE FOX, OR THE TALE OF THE NUN'S PRIEST

FROM CHAUCER

There lived, as authors tell, in days of yore,
A widow, somewhat old, and very poor:
Deep in a cell her cottage lonely stood,
Well thatched, and under covert of a wood.
   This dowager, on whom my tale I found,
Since last she laid her husband in the ground,
A simple sober life in patience led,
And had but just enough to buy her bread;
But huswifing the little Heav'n had lent,
She duly paid a groat for quarter-rent;
And pinched her belly, with her daughters two,
To bring the year about with much ado.
   The cattle in her homestead were three sows,
An ewe called Mally, and three brinded cows.
Her parlour window stuck with herbs around,
Of savoury smell; the rushes strewed the ground.
A maple dresser in her hall she had,
On which full many a slender meal she made:
For no delicious morsel passed her throat;
According to her cloth she cut her coat;
No poignant sauce she knew, no costly treat,
Her hunger gave a relish to her meat.
A sparing diet did her health assure;
Or sick, a pepper posset was her cure.
Before the day was done her work she sped,
And never went by candle-light to bed.
With exercise she sweat ill humours out;
Her dancing was not hindered by the gout.
Her poverty was glad, her heart content,
Nor knew she what the spleen or vapours meant.
   Of wine she never tasted through the year,

But white and black was all her homely cheer;
Brown bread, and milk (but first she skimmed her bowls),
And rashers of singed bacon on the coals.
On holy days, an egg or two at most;
But her ambition never reached to roast.
   A yard she had with pales enclosed about,
Some high, some low, and a dry ditch without.
Within this homestead lived, without a peer
For crowing loud, the noble Chanticleer;   40
So hight her cock, whose singing did surpass
The merry notes of organs at the mass.
More certain was the crowing of a cock
To number hours, than is an abbey-clock;
And sooner than the matin-bell was rung,
He clapped his wings upon his roost, and sung:
For when degrees fifteen ascended right,
By sure instinct he knew 'twas one at night.
High was his comb, and coral-red withal,
In dents embattled like a castle wall;   50
His bill was raven-black, and shone like jet;
Blue were his legs, and orient were his feet;
White were his nails, like silver to behold,
His body glitt'ring like the burnished gold.
   This gentle cock, for solace of his life,
Six misses had beside his lawful wife;
Scandal, that spares no king, though ne'er so good,
Says they were all of his own flesh and blood,
His sisters both by sire and mother's side;
And sure their likeness showed them near allied.   60
But make the worst, the monarch did no more
Than all the Ptolemys had done before:
When incest is for int'rest of a nation,
'Tis made no sin by holy dispensation.
Some lines have been maintained by this alone,
Which by their common ugliness are known.
   But passing this as from our tale apart,
Dame Partlet was the sovereign of his heart:
Ardent in love, outrageous in his play,
He feathered her a hundred times a day;   70
And she, that was not only passing fair,
But was withal discreet and debonair,
Resolved the passive doctrine to fulfil,

Though loth, and let him work his wicked will:
At board and bed was affable and kind,
According as their marriage vow did bind,
And as the Church's precept had enjoined.
Ev'n since she was a sennight old, they say,
Was chaste and humble to her dying day,
80   Nor chick nor hen was known to disobey.
   By this her husband's heart she did obtain;
What cannot beauty joined with virtue gain!
She was his only joy, and he her pride;
She, when he walked, went pecking by his side;
If, spurning up the ground, he sprung a corn,
The tribute in his bill to her was borne.
But oh! what joy it was to hear him sing
In summer, when the day began to spring,
Stretching his neck, and warbling in his throat,
90   *Solus cum sola* then was all his note.
For in the days of yore, the birds of parts
Were bred to speak, and sing, and learn the lib'ral arts.
   It happ'ed that perching on the parlour-beam
Amidst his wives, he had a deadly dream,
Just at the dawn; and sighed and groaned so fast,
As ev'ry breath he drew would be his last.
Dame Partlet, ever nearest to his side,
Heard all his piteous moan, and how he cried
For help from gods and men; and sore aghast
100   She pecked and pulled, and wakened him at last.
'Dear heart,' said she, 'for love of Heav'n declare
Your pain, and make me partner of your care.
You groan, Sir, ever since the morning light,
As something had disturbed your noble spright.'
   'And Madam, well I might,' said Chanticleer,
'Never was shrovetide-cock in such a fear.
Even still I run all over in a sweat,
My princely senses not recovered yet.
For such a dream I had of dire portent,
110   That much I fear my body will be shent:
It bodes I shall have wars and woeful strife,
Or in a loathsome dungeon end my life.
Know, dame, I dreamt within my troubled breast,
That in our yard I saw a murd'rous beast,
That on my body would have made arrest.

With waking eyes I ne'er beheld his fellow;
His colour was betwixt a red and yellow:
Tipped was his tail, and both his pricking ears,
With black; and much unlike his other hairs;
The rest, in shape a beagle's whelp throughout,   120
With broader forehead, and a sharper snout:
Deep in his front were sunk his glowing eyes,
That yet, methinks, I see him with surprise.
Reach out your hand, I drop with clammy sweat,
And lay it to my heart, and feel it beat.'
    'Now fie for shame,' quoth she, 'by Heav'n above,
Thou hast for ever lost thy lady's love.
No woman can endure a recreant knight;
He must be bold by day, and free by night:
Our sex desires a husband or a friend   130
Who can our honour and his own defend;
Wise, hardy, secret, liberal of his purse:
A fool is nauseous, but a coward worse:
No bragging coxcomb, yet no baffled knight.
How dar'st thou talk of love, and dar'st not fight?
How dar'st thou tell thy dame thou art affeared?
Hast thou no manly heart, and hast a beard?
    'If aught from fearful dreams may be divined,
They signify a cock of dunghill kind.
All dreams, as in old Galen I have read,   140
Are from repletion and complexion bred;
From rising fumes of indigested food,
And noxious humours that infest the blood:
And sure, my lord, if I can read aright,
These foolish fancies you have had tonight
Are certain symptoms (in the canting style)
Of boiling choler, and abounding bile;
This yellow gall that in your stomach floats
Engenders all these visionary thoughts.
When choler overflows, then dreams are bred   150
Of flames, and all the family of red;
Red dragons and red beasts in sleep we view,
For humours are distinguished by their hue.
From hence we dream of wars and warlike things,
And wasps and hornets with their double wings.
    'Choler adust congeals our blood with fear;
Then black bulls toss us, and black devils tear.

In sanguine airy dreams aloft we bound;
With rheums oppressed, we sink in rivers drowned.
'More I could say, but thus conclude my theme,
The dominating humour makes the dream.
Cato was in his time accounted wise,
And he condemns them all for empty lies.
Take my advice, and when we fly to ground, ⎞
With laxatives preserve your body sound,   ⎬
And purge the peccant humours that abound. ⎠
I should be loth to lay you on a bier;
And though there lives no 'pothecary near,
I dare for once prescribe for your disease,
And save long bills, and a damned doctor's fees.
    'Two sovereign herbs, which I by practice know,
Are both at hand (for in our yard they grow),
On peril of my soul shall rid you wholly
Of yellow choler, and of melancholy:
You must both purge and vomit; but obey,
And for the love of Heav'n make no delay.
Since hot and dry in your complexion join,
Beware the Sun when in a vernal sign;
For when he mounts exalted in the Ram,
If then he finds your body in a flame,
Replete with choler, I dare lay a groat,
A tertian ague is at least your lot.
Perhaps a fever (which the gods forfend)
May bring your youth to some untimely end:
And therefore, Sir, as you desire to live,
A day or two before your laxative,
Take just three worms, nor over nor above,
Because the gods unequal numbers love.
These digestives prepare you for your purge;
Of fumetery, centaury, and spurge,
And of ground-ivy add a leaf or two,
All which within our yard or garden grow.
Eat these, and be, my lord, of better cheer;
Your father's son was never born to fear.'
    'Madam,' quoth he, 'grammercy for your care,
But Cato, whom you quoted, you may spare;
'Tis true, a wise and worthy man he seems,
And, as you say, gave no belief to dreams;

160

170

180

190

But other men of more authority,
And by th' immortal pow'rs as wise as he,   200
Maintain, with sounder sense, that dreams forebode;
For Homer plainly says they come from God.
Nor Cato said it; but some modern fool
Imposed in Cato's name on boys at school.
  'Believe me, Madam, morning dreams foreshow
Th' events of things, and future weal or woe:
Some truths are not by reason to be tried,
But we have sure experience for our guide.
An ancient author, equal with the best,
Relates this tale of dreams among the rest: 210
  'Two friends, or brothers, with devout intent,
On some far pilgrimage together went.
It happened so, that, when the sun was down,
They just arrived by twilight at a town:
That day had been the baiting of a bull,
'Twas at a feast, and every inn so full,
That no void room in chamber or on ground,
And but one sorry bed was to be found,
And that so little it would hold but one,
Though till this hour they never lay alone.   220
  'So were they forced to part; one stayed behind,
His fellow sought what lodging he could find;
At last he found a stall where oxen stood,
And that he rather chose than lie abroad.
'Twas in a farther yard without a door;
But, for his ease, well littered was the floor.
  'His fellow, who the narrow bed had kept,
Was weary, and without a rocker slept:
Supine he snored; but in the dead of night
He dreamt his friend appeared before his sight,   230
Who, with a ghastly look and doleful cry,
Said, "Help me, brother, or this night I die:
Arise and help, before all help be vain,
Or in an ox's stall I shall be slain."
  'Roused from his rest, he wakened in a start,
Shiv'ring with horror, and with aching heart:
At length to cure himself by reason tries;   ⎫
'Tis but a dream, and what are dreams but lies? ⎬
So thinking changed his side, and closed his eyes. ⎭

240   His dream returns; his friend appears again:
     "The murd'rers come, now help, or I am slain:"
     'Twas but a vision still, and visions are but vain.
       'He dreamt the third: but now his friend appeared
     Pale, naked, pierced with wounds, with blood besmeared:
     "Thrice warned, awake," said he; "relief is late,
     The deed is done, but thou revenge my fate:
     Tardy of aid, unseal thy heavy eyes,
     Awake, and with the dawning day arise:
     Take to the western gate thy ready way,
250   For by that passage they my corpse convey:
     My corpse is in a tumbril laid, among
     The filth and ordure, and enclosed with dung.
     That cart arrest, and raise a common cry;
     For sacred hunger of my gold I die;"
     Then showed his grisly wounds; and last he drew
     A piteous sigh, and took a long adieu.
       'The frighted friend arose by break of day,
     And found the stall where late his fellow lay.
     Then of his impious host inquiring more,
260   Was answered that his guest was gone before:
     "Mutt'ring he went," said he, "by morning light,
     And much complained of his ill rest by night."
     This raised suspicion in the pilgrim's mind;
     Because all hosts are of an evil kind,
     And oft, to share the spoil, with robbers joined.
       'His dream confirmed his thought: with troubled look
     Straight to the western gate his way he took;
     There, as his dream foretold, a cart he found,
     That carried composs forth to dung the ground.
270   This when the pilgrim saw, he stretched his throat,
     And cried out "Murder" with a yelling note.
     "My murdered fellow in this cart lies dead;
     Vengeance and justice on the villain's head!
     You, magistrates, who sacred laws dispense,
     On you I call to punish this offence."
       'The word thus giv'n, within a little space
     The mob came roaring out, and thronged the place.
     All in a trice they cast the cart to ground,
     And in the dung the murdered body found;
280   Though breathless, warm and reeking from the wound.

   279 found] bound *1700*.

Good Heav'n, whose darling attribute we find
Is boundless grace and mercy to mankind,
Abhors the cruel; and the deeds of night
By wondrous ways reveals in open light:
Murder may pass unpunished for a time,
But tardy justice will o'ertake the crime.
And oft a speedier pain the guilty feels;
The hue and cry of Heav'n pursues him at the heels,
Fresh from the fact; as in the present case,
The criminals are seized upon the place: 290
Carter and host confronted face to face.
Stiff in denial, as the law appoints,
On engines they distend their tortured joints:
So was confession forced, th' offence was known,
And public justice on th' offenders done.
  'Here may you see that visions are to dread;
And in the page that follows this, I read
Of two young merchants, whom the hope of gain
Induced in partnership to cross the main:
Waiting till willing winds their sails supplied,   300
Within a trading town they long abide,
Full fairly situate on a haven's side.
  'One evening it befel, that looking out,
The wind they long had wished was come about:
Well pleased they went to rest; and if the gale
Till morn continued, both resolved to sail.
But as together in a bed they lay,
The younger had a dream at break of day.
A man, he thought, stood frowning at his side,
Who warned him for his safety to provide,   310
Not put to sea, but safe on shore abide.
"I come, thy genius, to command thy stay;
Trust not the winds, for fatal is the day,
And death unhoped attends the wat'ry way."
  'The vision said, and vanished from his sight;
The dreamer wakened in a mortal fright;
Then pulled his drowsy neighbour, and declared
What in his slumber he had seen and heard.
His friend smiled scornful, and, with proud contempt,
Rejects as idle what his fellow dreamt.   320
"Stay who will stay; for me no fears restrain,
Who follow Mercury, the God of gain:

Let each man do as to his fancy seems,
I wait not, I, till you have better dreams.
Dreams are but interludes, which fancy makes;
When monarch reason sleeps, this mimic wakes;
Compounds a medley of disjointed things,
A mob of cobblers and a court of kings:
Light fumes are merry, grosser fumes are sad;
330   Both are the reasonable soul run mad;
And many monstrous forms in sleep we see,
That neither were, nor are, nor e'er can be.
Sometimes, forgotten things long cast behind
Rush forward in the brain, and come to mind.
The nurse's legends are for truths received,
And the man dreams but what the boy believed.
  '"Sometimes we but rehearse a former play,⎫
The night restores our actions done by day, ⎬
As hounds in sleep will open for their prey. ⎭
340   In short, the farce of dreams is of a piece,
Chimeras all; and more absurd, or less.
You, who believe in tales, abide alone;
Whate'er I get, this voyage is my own."
  'Thus while he spoke he heard the shouting crew
That called aboard, and took his last adieu.
The vessel went before a merry gale,
And for quick passage put on ev'ry sail:
But when least feared, and ev'n in open day,
The mischief overtook her in the way:
350   Whether she sprung a leak, I cannot find,
Or whether she was overset with wind,
Or that some rock below her bottom rent;
But down at once with all her crew she went.
Her fellow ships from far her loss descried;
But only she was sunk, and all were safe beside.
  'By this example you are taught again,
That dreams and visions are not always vain:
But if, dear Partlet, you are yet in doubt,
Another tale shall make the former out.
360   'Kenelm, the son of Kenulph, Mercia's king,
Whose holy life the legends loudly sing,
Warned in a dream, his murder did foretel
From point to point as after it befel:
All circumstances to his nurse he told,

(A wonder from a child of sev'n years old):
The dream with horror heard, the good old wife
From treason counselled him to guard his life;
But close to keep the secret in his mind,
For a boy's vision small belief would find.
The pious child, by promise bound, obeyed,   370
Nor was the fatal murder long delayed:
By Quenda slain, he fell before his time,
Made a young martyr by his sister's crime.
The tale is told by venerable Bede,
Which, at your better leisure, you may read.
   'Macrobius too relates the vision sent
To the great Scipio, with the famed event;
Objections makes, but after makes replies,
And adds, that dreams are often prophecies.
   'Of Daniel you may read in holy writ,   ⎫   380
Who, when the King his vision did forget,   ⎬
Could word for word the wondrous dream repeat.⎭
Nor less of patriarch Joseph understand,
Who by a dream enslaved th' Egyptian land,
The years of plenty and of dearth foretold,
When for their bread their liberty they sold.
Nor must th' exalted butler be forgot,
Nor he whose dream presaged his hanging lot.
   'And did not Croesus the same death foresee,
Raised in his vision on a lofty tree?   390
The wife of Hector, in his utmost pride,
Dreamt of his death the night before he died:
Well was he warned from battle to refrain,   ⎫
But men to death decreed are warned in vain: ⎬
He dared the dream, and by his fatal foe was slain.⎭
   'Much more I know, which I forbear to speak,
For see, the ruddy day begins to break:
Let this suffice, that plainly I foresee
My dream was bad, and bodes adversity;
But neither pills nor laxatives I like,   400
They only serve to make a well-man sick:
Of these his gain the sharp physician makes,
And often gives a purge, but seldom takes:
They not correct, but poison all the blood,
And ne'er did any but the doctors good.
Their tribe, trade, trinkets, I defy them all,

With ev'ry work of 'Pothecaries' Hall.
   'These melancholy matters I forbear:
But let me tell thee, Partlet mine, and swear,
That when I view the beauties of thy face,
I fear not death nor dangers nor disgrace;
So may my soul have bliss, as when I spy
The scarlet red about thy partridge eye,
While thou art constant to thy own true knight,⎫
While thou are mine, and I am thy delight,   ⎬
All sorrows at thy presence take their flight. ⎭
For true it is, as *in principio,*
Mulier est hominis confusio.
Madam, the meaning of this Latin is,
That woman is to man his sovereign bliss.
For when by night I feel your tender side,
Though for the narrow perch I cannot ride,
Yet I have such a solace in my mind,
That all my boding cares are cast behind,
And ev'n already I forget my dream.'
He said, and downward flew from off the beam,
For daylight now began apace to spring,
The thrush to whistle, and the lark to sing.
Then crowing clapped his wings, th' appointed call,
To chuck his wives together in the hall.

MARRIAGE À LA MODE
A COMEDY

The first performance of *Marriage à la Mode* is not certainly known, but was probably in April 1672. The play was printed in the following year. It has two plots, a serious and a comic, with, as Dryden admits, very little interdependence, complying with what he considered to be an English preference for variety. However, the complications of marriage are a common theme to both parts. As a comedy, it belongs to that surprisingly limited category known as the Comedy of Manners, showing, in the words of the Dedication to Rochester, the influence of courtly society in its 'gallantries' and 'delicacy of expression'. The alteration in tone from the Dedication here to the attack on Rochester in the Preface to *All for Love* reflects the deterioration of relations between the two men, and perhaps also some disillusionment in Dryden, and an increased awareness of his critics.

TO THE RIGHT HONOURABLE
THE EARL OF ROCHESTER[1]

My Lord,

I humbly dedicate to your Lordship that poem of which you were pleased to appear an early patron before it was acted on the stage. I may yet go farther, with your permission, and say that it received amendment from your noble hands ere it was fit to be presented. You may please likewise to remember, with how much favour to the author, and indulgence to the play, you commended it to the view of his Majesty, then at Windsor, and, by his approbation of it in writing, made way for its kind reception on the theatre. In this dedication, therefore, I may seem to imitate a custom of the ancients, who offered to their gods the firstlings of the flock (which, I think, they called Ver sacrum), because they helped 'em to increase. I am sure if there be anything in this play wherein I have raised myself beyond the ordinary lowness of my comedies, I ought wholly to acknowledge it to the favour of being admitted into your Lordship's conversation. And not only I, who pretend not to this way, but the best comic writers of our age, will join with me to acknowledge, that they have copied the gallantries of courts, the delicacy of expression, and the decencies of behaviour, from your Lordship, with more success, than if they had taken their models from the court of France. But this, my Lord, will be no wonder to the world, which knows the excellency of your natural parts, and those you have acquired in a noble education. That which with more reason I admire is, that being so absolute a courtier, you have not forgot either the ties of friendship, or the practice of generosity. In my little experience of a court (which, I confess, I desire not to improve), I have found in it much of interest, and more of detraction: few men there have that assurance of a friend as not to be made ridiculous by him when they are absent. There are a middling sort of courtiers who become happy by their want of wit; but they supply that want by an excess of malice to those who have it. And there is no such persecution as that of fools: they can never be considerable enough to be talked of themselves; so that they are safe only in their obscurity, and grow

---

[1] John Wilmot (1647–80), second Earl of Rochester, an abundantly gifted and notoriously dissolute courtier.

mischievous to witty men, by the great diligence of their envy, and by being always present to represent and aggravate their faults. In the meantime, they are forced, when they endeavour to be pleasant, to live on the offals of their wit whom they decry; and either to quote it (which they do unwillingly), or to pass it upon others for their own. These are the men who make it their business to chase wit from the knowledge of princes, lest it should disgrace their ignorance. And this kind of malice your Lordship has not so much avoided, as surmounted. But if by the excellent temper of a royal master, always more ready to hear good than ill; if by his inclination to love you; if by your own merit and address; if by the charms of your conversation, the grace of your behaviour, your knowledge of greatness and habitude in courts, you have been able to preserve yourself with honour in the midst of so dangerous a course; yet at least the remembrance of those hazards has inspired you with pity for other men, who, being of an inferior wit and quality to you, are yet persecuted, for being that in little which your lordship is in great. For the quarrel of those people extends itself to anything of sense; and if I may be so vain to own it amongst the rest of the poets, has sometimes reached to the very borders of it, even to me. So that if our general good fortune had not raised up your Lordship to defend us, I know not whether anything had been more ridiculous in court than writers. 'Tis to your Lordship's favour we generally owe our protection and patronage; and to the nobleness of your nature, which will not suffer the least shadow of your wit to be contemned in other men. You have been often pleased not only to excuse my imperfections, but to vindicate what was tolerable in my writings from their censures; and, what I never can forget, you have not only been careful of my reputation, but of my fortune. You have been solicitous to supply my neglect of myself; and to overcome the fatal modesty of poets, which submits them to perpetual wants, rather than to become importunate with those people who have the liberality of kings in their disposing, and who, dishonouring the bounty of their master, suffer such to be in necessity who endeavour at least to please him; and for whose entertainment he has generously provided, if the fruits of his royal favour were not often stopped in other hands. But your Lordship has given me occasion not to complain of courts whilst you are there. I have found the effects of your mediation in all my concernments; and they were so much the more noble in you, because they were wholly voluntary. I became your Lordship's (if I may venture on the similitude) as the world was made, without knowing him who made it; and brought only a passive obedience to be your creature. This nobleness of yours I think myself the rather obliged to own because otherwise it must have been lost to all remembrance: for you are endued with that excellent quality of frank nature, to forget the good which you have done.

But, my Lord, I ought to have considered that you are as great a judge as you are a patron; and that, in praising you ill, I should incur a higher note of ingratitude than that I thought to have avoided. I stand in need of all your accustomed goodness for the dedication of this play; which, though perhaps it be the best of my comedies, is yet so faulty, that I should have feared you for my critic, if I had not, with some policy, given you the trouble of being my protector. Wit seems to have lodged itself more nobly in this age than in any of the former; and people of my mean condition are only writers because some of the nobility, and your Lordship in the first place, are above the narrow praises which poesy could give you. But, let those who love to see themselves exceeded encourage your Lordship in so dangerous a quality: for my own part, I must confess that I have so much of self-interest as to be content with reading some papers of your verses, without desiring you should proceed to a scene or play; with the common prudence of those who are worsted in a duel, and declare they are satisfied when they are first wounded. Your Lordship has but another step to make, and from the patron of wit you may become its tyrant, and oppress our little reputations with more ease than you now protect them. But these, my Lord, are designs which I am sure you harbour not, any more than the French king is contriving the conquest of the Swissers. 'Tis a barren triumph, which is not worthy your pains, and would only rank him amongst your slaves, who is already,

My Lord,
Your Lordship's most obedient
and most faithful servant,
JOHN DRYDEN.

PROLOGUE

Lord, how reformed and quiet are we grown,
Since all our braves and all our wits are gone!
Fop-corner now is free from civil war,
White-wig and vizard make no longer jar.

5   France, and the fleet, have swept the town so clear
That we can act in peace, and you can hear.
'Twas a sad sight, before they marched from home,
To see our warriors in red waistcoats come,
With hair tucked up, into our tiring-room.

10   But 'twas more sad to hear their last adieu:
The women sobbed, and swore they would be true;
And so they were, as long as e'er they could,
But powerful guinea cannot be withstood,
And they were made of playhouse flesh and blood.

15   Fate did their friends for double use ordain;
In wars abroad they grinning honour gain,
And mistresses, for all that stay, maintain.
Now they are gone, 'tis dead vacation here,
For neither friends nor enemies appear.

20   Poor pensive punk now peeps ere plays begin,
Sees the bare bench, and dares not venture in;
But manages her last half-crown with care,
And trudges to the Mall, on foot, for air.
Our city friends so far will hardly come,

25   They can take up with pleasures nearer home;
And see gay shows and gaudy scenes elsewhere:

3 Fop-corner] Where the gallants congregated.
5–10 Probably referring to preparations for the Third Dutch War, which was declared on
17 March.
22 punk] prostitute.
24 half-crown] The price of admission to the pit.
25 the Mall] A fashionable walk by St James's Park.

For we presume they seldom come to hear.
But they have now ta'en up a glorious trade, 30
And cutting Moorcraft struts in masquerade.
There's all our hope, for we shall show today
A masking ball, to recommend our play;
Nay, to endear 'em more, and let 'em see
We scorn to come behind in courtesy, 35
We'll follow the new mode which they begin,
And treat 'em with a room, and couch within:
For that's one way, howe'er the play fall short,
T'oblige the town, the city, and the court.

31 cutting Moorcraft] Morecraft is a character in Beaumont and Fletcher's *The Scornful Lady*. 'Cutting' means swaggering.

DRAMATIS PERSONAE

POLYDAMAS, usurper of Sicily
LEONIDAS, the rightful prince, unknown
ARGALEON, favourite to Polydamas
HERMOGENES, foster-father to Leonidas
EUBULUS, his friend and companion
RHODOPHIL, captain of the guards
PALAMEDE, a courtier
STRATON, servant to Palamede

PALMYRA, daughter to the usurper
AMALTHEA, sister to Argaleon
DORALICE, wife to Rhodophil
MELANTHA, an affected lady
PHILOTIS, woman to Melantha
BELIZA, woman to Doralice
ARTEMIS, a court-lady

Scene – Sicily

ACT I

SCENE I

Walks near the court

Enter DORALICE *and* BELIZA.

DORALICE Beliza, bring the lute into this arbour, the walks are empty:
I would try the song the princess Amalthea bade me learn.

[*They go in, and sing.*

1.

Why should a foolish marriage vow
  Which long ago was made,
Oblige us to each other now   5
  When passion is decayed?
We loved, and we loved, as long as we could,
  'Till our love was loved out in us both;
But our marriage is dead, when the pleasure is fled:
  'Twas pleasure first made it an oath.   10

2.

If I have pleasures for a friend,
  And further love in store,
What wrong has he whose joys did end,
  And who could give no more?
'Tis a madness that he should be jealous of me,   15
  Or that I should bar him of another:
For all we can gain, is to give ourselves pain,
  When neither can hinder the other.

Enter PALAMEDE, *in riding habit, and hears the song.*
Re-enter DORALICE *and* BELIZA.

BELIZA Madam, a stranger.
DORALICE I did not think to have had witnesses of my bad singing.   20
PALAMEDE If I have erred, madam, I hope you'll pardon the curiosity of

a stranger; for I may well call myself so, after five years' absence from the court: but you have freed me from one error.

DORALICE   What's that, I beseech you?

25   PALAMEDE   I thought good voices, and ill faces, had been inseparable; and that to be fair, and sing well, had been only the privilege of angels.

DORALICE   And how many more of these fine things can you say to me?

PALAMEDE   Very few, madam; for if I should continue to see you some hours longer, you look so killingly, that I should be mute with wonder.

30   DORALICE   This will not give you the reputation of a wit with me. You travelling monsieurs live upon the stock you have got abroad, for the first day or two: to repeat with a good memory, and apply with a good grace, is all your wit. And, commonly your gullets are sewed up like cormorants: when you have regorged what you have taken in, you are the leanest

35   things in nature.

PALAMEDE   Then, madam, I think you had best make that use of me; let me wait on you for two or three days together, and you shall hear all I have learnt of extraordinary in other countries; and one thing which I never saw 'till I came home, that is, a lady of a better voice, better face,

40   and better wit, than any I have seen abroad. And, after this, if I should not declare myself most passionately in love with you, I should have less wit than yet you think I have.

DORALICE   A very plain and pithy declaration. I see, sir, you have been travelling in Spain or Italy, or some of the hot countries, where men

45   come to the point immediately. But are you sure these are not words of course? For I would not give my poor heart an occasion of complaint against me, that I engaged it too rashly, and then could not bring it off.

PALAMEDE   Your heart may trust itself with me safely; I shall use it very civilly while it stays, and never turn it away, without fair warning to

50   provide for itself.

DORALICE   First, then, I do receive your passion with as little consideration, on my part, as ever you gave it me, on yours. And now see what a miserable wretch you have made yourself!

PALAMEDE   Who, I miserable? Thank you for that. Give me love

55   enough, and life enough, and I defy fortune.

DORALICE   Know, then, thou man of vain imagination, know, to thy utter confusion, that I am virtuous.

PALAMEDE   Such another word, and I give up the ghost.

DORALICE   Then, to strike you quite dead, know that I am married too.

33–4 gullets . . . cormorants] Cormorants, voracious sea-birds, could be used to catch fish. Cf. *His Majesty's Declaration Defended* (1681) where Dryden describes the King being 'used as fishers do their cormorant, have his mouth left open, to swallow the prey for them, but his throat gagged that nothing may go down'. Calif. *Works*, XVII, 204.

PALAMEDE   Art thou married? O thou damnable virtuous woman!   60
DORALICE   Yes, married to a gentleman; young, handsome, rich, valiant, and with all the good qualities that will make you despair and hang
yourself.
PALAMEDE   Well, in spite of all that, I'll love you: Fortune has cut us
out for one another; for I am to be married within these three days.   65
Married past redemption, to a young, fair, rich, and virtuous lady; and it
shall go hard, but I will love my wife as little as I perceive you do your
husband.
DORALICE   Remember I invade no propriety: my servant you are only
'till you are married.   70
PALAMEDE   In the meantime, you are to forget you have a husband.
DORALICE   And you, that you are to have a wife.
BELIZA [aside to her Lady]   O madam, my lord's just at the end of the
walks; and, if you make not haste, will discover you.
DORALICE   Some other time, new servant, we'll talk further of the   75
premises; in the meanwhile, break not my first commandment, that is
not to follow me.
PALAMEDE   But where, then, shall I find you again?
DORALICE   At court. Yours for two days, sir.
PALAMEDE   And nights, I beseech you, madam.   80

[Exeunt DORALICE and BELIZA.

Well, I'll say that for thee, thou art a very dext'rous executioner; thou
has done my business at one stroke: yet I must marry another . . . and yet
I must love this; and if it lead me into some little inconveniencies, as
jealousies, and duels, and death, and so forth, yet, while sweet love is in
the case, fortune, do thy worst, and avaunt mortality!   85

Enter RHODOPHIL, who seems speaking to one within.

RHODOPHIL   Leave 'em with my lieutenant, while I fetch new orders
from the king. How? Palamede!   [Sees PALAMEDE.
PALAMEDE   Rhodophil!
RHODOPHIL   Who thought to have seen you in Sicily?
PALAMEDE   Who thought to have found the court so far from Syracuse?   90
RHODOPHIL   The king best knows the reason of the progress. But
answer me, I beseech you, what brought you home from travel?
PALAMEDE   The commands of an old rich father.
RHODOPHIL   And the hopes of burying him?

69 propriety] Property, ownership.
76 premisses] What has been mentioned: the aforesaid.

95 PALAMEDE   Both together, as you see, have prevailed on my good-
nature. In few words, my old man has already married me; for he has
agreed with another old man, as rich and as covetous as himself; the
articles are drawn, and I have given my consent, for fear of being
disinherited; and yet know not what kind of woman I am to marry.

100 RHODOPHIL   Sure your father intends you some very ugly wife, and has
a mind to keep you in ignorance till you have shot the gulf.

PALAMEDE   I know not that; but obey I will, and must.

RHODOPHIL   Then I cannot choose but grieve for all the good girls and
courtesans of France and Italy. They have lost the most kind-hearted,
105   doting, prodigal, humble servant in Europe.

PALAMEDE   All I could do, in these three years I stayed behind you, was
to comfort the poor creatures for the loss of you. But what's the reason
that in all this time, a friend could never hear from you?

RHODOPHIL   Alas, dear Palamede, I have had no joy to write, nor
110   indeed to do anything in the world to please me. The greatest misfortune
imaginable is fall'n upon me.

PALAMEDE   Pr'ythee, what's the matter?

RHODOPHIL   In one word, I am married: wretchedly married; and have
been above these two years. Yes, faith, the devil has had power over me,
115   in spite of my vows and resolutions to the contrary.

PALAMEDE   I find you have sold yourself for filthy lucre; she's old, or
ill-conditioned.

RHODOPHIL   No, none of these: I'm sure she's young; and, for her
humour, she laughs, sings, and dances eternally; and, which is more, we
120   never quarrel about it, for I do the same.

PALAMEDE   You're very unfortunate indeed: then the case is plain, she is
not handsome.

RHODOPHIL   A great beauty too, as people say.

PALAMEDE   As people say? Why, you should know that best yourself.

125 RHODOPHIL   Ask those who have smelt to a strong perfume two years
together, what's the scent.

PALAMEDE   But here are good qualities enough for one woman.

RHODOPHIL   Ay, too many, Palamede. If I could put 'em into three or
four women, I should be content.

130 PALAMEDE   O, now I have found it, you dislike her for no other reason
but because she's your wife.

RHODOPHIL   And is not that enough? All that I know of her perfections
now, is only by memory. I remember, indeed, that about two years ago I
loved her passionately; but those golden days are gone, Palamede. Yet I

101 shot the gulf] Here, perhaps 'committed yourself', or 'got over the difficulties'.

loved her a whole half year, double the natural term of any mistress; and I   135
think in my conscience I could have held out another quarter; but then
the world began to laugh at me, and a certain shame of being out of
fashion seized me. At last, we arrived at that point, that there was
nothing left in us to make us new to one another. Yet still I set a good face
upon the matter, and am infinite fond of her before company; but when   140
we are alone, we walk like lions in a room, she one way, and I another.
And we lie with our backs to each other, so far distant as if the fashion of
great beds was only invented to keep husband and wife sufficiently
asunder.

PALAMEDE   The truth is, your disease is very desperate; but, though you   145
cannot be cured, you may be patched up a little: you must get you a
mistress, Rhodophil. That, indeed, is living upon cordials; but, as fast as
one fails, you must supply it with another. You're like a gamester who
has lost his estate; yet, in doing that, you have learned the advantages of
play, and can arrive to live upon't.   150

RHODOPHIL   Truth is, I have been thinking on't, and have just resolved
to take your counsel; and, faith, considering the damned disadvantages
of a married man, I have provided well enough, for a poor humble sinner,
that is not ambitious of great matters.

PALAMEDE   What is she, for a woman?   155

RHODOPHIL   One of the stars of Syracuse, I assure you: young enough,
fair enough, and but for one quality just such a woman as I could wish.

PALAMEDE   O friend, this is not an age to be critical in beauty. When
we had good store of handsome women, and but few chapmen, you
might have been more curious in your choice; but now the price is   160
enhanced upon us, and all mankind set up for mistresses, so that poor
little creatures, without beauty, birth, or breeding, but only impudence, go off at unreasonable rates; and a man, in these hard times, snaps
at 'em, as he does at broad gold; never examines the weight, but takes
light or heavy, as he can get it.   165

RHODOPHIL   But my mistress has one fault that's almost unpardonable;
for being a town-lady, without any relation to the court, yet she thinks
herself undone if she be not seen there three or four times a day with the
princess Amalthea. And, for the king, she haunts and watches him so
narrowly in a morning, that she prevents even the chemists who beset his   170
chamber to turn their mercury into his gold.

147 cordials] Stimulating drinks.
159 chapmen] Buyers.
164 broad gold] Twenty-shilling pieces from the time of James I and Charles I, broader and
thinner than the Restoration guinea.
170 chemists] Alchemists.

PALAMEDE   Yet hitherto, methinks, you are no very unhappy man.

RHODOPHIL   With all this, she's the greatest gossip in nature; for,
besides the court, she's the most eternal visitor of the town: and yet
175   manages her time so well, that she seems ubiquitary. For my part, I can
compare her to nothing but the sun; for, like him, she takes no rest, nor
ever sets in one place but to rise in another.

PALAMEDE   I confess, she had need be handsome, with these qualities.

RHODOPHIL   No lady can be so curious of a new fashion as she is of a new
180   French word: she's the very mint of the nation; and as fast as any bullion
comes out of France, coins it immediately into our language.

PALAMEDE   And her name is——

RHODOPHIL   No naming; that's not like a cavalier. Find her, if you can,
by my description; and I am not so ill a painter that I need write the name
185   beneath the picture.

PALAMEDE   Well, then, how far have you proceeded in your love?

RHODOPHIL   'Tis yet in the bud, and what fruit it may bear I cannot
tell; for this insufferable humour of haunting the court is so predominant, that she has hitherto broken all her assignations with me for fear of
190   missing her visits there.

PALAMEDE   That's the hardest part of your adventure. But, for aught I
see, fortune has used us both alike: I have a strange kind of mistress too in
court, besides her I am to marry.

RHODOPHIL   You have made haste to be in love then; for if I am not
195   mistaken, you are but this day arrived.

PALAMEDE   That's all one: I have seen the lady already who has charmed
me; seen her in these walks, courted her, and received, for the first time,
an answer that does not put me into despair.

To them ARGALEON, AMALTHEA, and ARTEMIS.

I'll tell you at more leisure my adventures. The walks fill apace I see.
200   Stay, is not that the young lord Argaleon, the king's favourite?

RHODOPHIL   Yes, and as proud as ever, as ambitious and as revengeful.

PALAMEDE   How keeps he the king's favour with these qualities?

RHODOPHIL   Argaleon's father helped him to the crown: besides, he
gilds over all his vices to the king, and, standing in the dark to him, sees
205   all his inclinations, interests, and humours, which he so times and
soothes that, in effect, he reigns.

PALAMEDE   His sister Amalthea, who, I guess, stands by him, seems
not to be of his temper.

RHODOPHIL   O, she's all goodness and generosity.

210 ARGALEON   Rhodophil, the king expects you earnestly.

15

RHODOPHIL   'Tis done, my lord, what he commanded: I only waited
his return from hunting. Shall I attend your lordship to him?
ARGALEON   No; I go first another way.   ·   [*Exit hastily.*
PALAMEDE   He seems in haste, and discomposed.
AMALTHEA [*to* RHODOPHIL *after a short whisper*] Your friend? then   215
he must needs be of much merit.
RHODOPHIL   When he has kissed the king's hand, I know he'll beg the
honour to kiss yours. Come, Palamede.

[*Exeunt* RHODOPHIL *and* PALAMEDE *bowing to* AMALTHEA.

ARTEMIS   Madam, you tell me most surprising news.
AMALTHEA   The fear of it, you see,   220
Has discomposed my brother; but to me
All that can bring my country good is welcome.
ARTEMIS   It seems incredible that this old king,
Whom all the world thought childless,
Should come to search the farthest parts of Sicily   225
In hope to find an heir.
AMALTHEA   To lessen your astonishment, I will
Unfold some private passages of state,
Of which you are yet ignorant: know, first,
That this Polydamas, who reigns, unjustly   230
Gained the crown.
ARTEMIS   Somewhat of this I have confus'dly heard.
AMALTHEA   I'll tell you all in brief: Theagenes,
Our last great king,
Had, by his queen, one only son, an infant   235
Of three years old, called, after him, Theagenes.
The general, this Polydamas, then married;
The public feasts for which were scarcely past,
When a rebellion in the heart of Sicily
Called out the king to arms.
ARTEMIS   Polydamas   240
Had then a just excuse to stay behind.
AMALTHEA   His temper was too warlike to accept it.
He left his bride, and the new joys of marriage,
And followed to the field. In short, they fought,
The rebels were o'ercome; but in the fight   245
The too bold king received a mortal wound.
When he perceived his end approaching near,
He called the general, to whose care he left
His widow queen, and orphan son; then died.

250 ARTEMIS   Then false Polydamas betrayed his trust?
    AMALTHEA   He did; and with my father's help — for which
        Heav'n pardon him! — so gained the soldier's hearts,
        That in few days he was saluted king:
        And when his crimes had impudence enough
255   To bear the eye of day,
        He marched his army back to Syracuse.
        But see how heav'n can punish wicked men.
        In granting their desires: the news was brought him
        That day he was to enter it, that Eubulus,
260   Whom his dead master had left governor,
        Was fled, and with him bore away the queen,
        And royal orphan; but, what more amazed him,
        His wife, now big with child, and much detesting
        Her husband's practices, had willingly
265   Accompanied their flight.
    ARTEMIS   How I admire her virtue!
    AMALTHEA   What became
        Of her and them since that, was never known;
        Only, some few days since, a famous robber
        Was taken with some jewels of vast price,
270   Which, when they were delivered to the king,
        He knew had been his wife's; with these, a letter,
        Much torn and sullied, but which yet he knew
        To be her writing.
    ARTEMIS   Sure from hence he learned
        He had a son?
    AMALTHEA   It was not left so plain:
275   The paper only said she died in childbed;
        But when it should have mentioned son or daughter,
        Just there it was torn off.
    ARTEMIS   Madam, the king.

        To them POLYDAMAS, ARGALEON, Guard *and* Attendants.

    ARGALEON   The robber, though thrice racked, confessed no more,
        But that he took those jewels near this place.
280 POLYDAMAS   But yet the circumstances strongly argue
        That those for whom I search are not far off.
    ARGALEON   I cannot easily believe it.
    ARTEMIS   No,
        You would not have it so.   [*Aside*.
    POLYDAMAS   Those I employed have in the neighbouring hamlet,

Amongst the fishers' cabins, made discovery   285
Of some young persons, whose uncommon beauty
And graceful carriage make it seem suspicious
They are not what they seem: I therefore sent
The captain of my guards this morning early,
With orders to secure and bring 'em to me.   290

Enter RHODOPHIL *and* PALAMEDE.

O, here he is. Have you performed my will?
RHODOPHIL   Sir, those whom you commanded me to bring
Are waiting in the walks.
POLYDAMAS   Conduct 'em hither.
RHODOPHIL   First, give me leave
To beg your notice of this gentleman.   295
POLYDAMAS   He seems to merit it. His name and quality?
RHODOPHIL   Palamede, son to lord Cleodemus of Palermo,
And new returned from travel.

[PALAMEDE *approaches, and kneels to kiss the* King's *hand.*

POLYDAMAS   You're welcome.
I knew your father well, he was both brave
And honest; we two once were fellow-soldiers   300
In the last civil wars.
PALAMEDE   I bring the same unquestioned honesty
And zeal to serve your majesty; the courage
You were pleased to praise in him,
Your royal prudence, and your people's love,   305
Will never give me leave to try like him
In civil wars; I hope it may in foreign.
POLYDAMAS   Attend the court, and it shall be my care
To find out some employment worthy you.
Go, Rhodophil, and bring in those without.   310

[*Exeunt* RHODOPHIL *and* PALAMEDE.

RHODOPHIL *returns again immediately, and with him enter*
HERMOGENES, LEONIDAS, *and* PALMYRA.

Behold two miracles! [*Looking earnestly on* LEONIDAS *and* PALMYRA.
Of different sexes, but of equal form:
So matchless both, that my divided soul
Can scarcely ask the gods a son or daughter,
For fear of losing one. If from your hands,   315

You powers, I shall this day receive a daughter,
Argaleon, she is yours; but if a son,
Then Amalthea's love shall make him happy.

ARGALEON   Grant, heav'n, this admirable nymph may prove
320   That issue, which he seeks!

AMALTHEA   Venus Urania, if thou art a goddess,
Grant that sweet youth may prove the prince of Sicily.

POLYDAMAS   Tell me, old man, and tell me true, from whence

[*To* HERMOGENES.

Had you that youth and maid?

HERMOGENES   From whence you had
325   Your sceptre, sir: I had 'em from the gods.

POLYDAMAS   The gods then have not such another gift.
Say who their parents were.

HERMOGENES   My wife, and I.

ARGALEON   It is not likely a virgin of so excellent a beauty.
Should come from such a stock.

330   AMALTHEA   Much less that such a youth, so sweet, so graceful,
Should be produced from peasants.

HERMOGENES   Why, nature is the same in villages,
And much more fit to form a noble issue
Where it is least corrupted.

335   POLYDAMAS   He talks too like a man that knew the world
To have been long a peasant. But the rack
Will teach him other language. Hence with him!

[*As the* Guards *are carrying him away, his peruke falls off.*

Sure I have seen that face before. Hermogenes!
'Tis he, 'tis he who fled away with Eubulus,
340   And with my dear Eudoxia?

HERMOGENES   Yes, sir, I am Hermogenes!
And if to have been loyal be a crime,
I stand prepared to suffer.

POLYDAMAS   If thou wouldst live, speak quickly,
345   What is become of my Eudoxia?
Where is the queen and young Theagenes?
Where Eubulus? and which of these is mine?

[*Pointing to* LEONIDAS *and* PALMYRA.

321 Venus Urania] Goddess of beauty and generation.

HERMOGENES   Eudoxia is dead, so is the queen,
  The infant king her son, and Eubulus.
POLYDAMAS   Traitor, 'tis false: produce 'em, or——
HERMOGENES   Once more   350
  I tell you, they are dead; but leave to threaten,
  For you shall know no further.
POLYDAMAS   Then prove indulgent to my hopes, and be
  My friend for ever. Tell me, good Hermogenes,
  Whose son is that brave youth?
HERMOGENES   Sir, he is yours.   355
POLYDAMAS   Fool that I am, thou see'st that so I wish it,
  And so thou flatter'st me.
HERMOGENES   By all that's holy!
POLYDAMAS   Again. Thou canst not swear too deeply.
  Yet hold, I will believe thee . . . yet I doubt.
HERMOGENES   You need not, sir.   360
ARGALEON   Believe him not; he sees you credulous,
  And would impose his own base issue on you,
  And fix it to your crown.
AMALTHEA   Behold his goodly shape and feature, sir;
  Methinks he much resembles you.   365
ARGALEON   I say, if you have any issue here,
  It must be that fair creature;
  By all my hopes I think so.
AMALTHEA [aside]   Yes, brother, I believe you by your hopes,
  For they are all for her.
POLYDAMAS   Call the youth nearer.   370
HERMOGENES   Leonidas, the king would speak with you.
POLYDAMAS   Come near, and be not dazzled with the splendour
  And greatness of a court.
LEONIDAS   I need not this encouragement;
  I can fear nothing but the gods.   375
  And for this glory, after I have seen
  The canopy of state spread wide above
  In the abyss of heaven, the court of stars,
  The blushing morning, and the rising sun,
  What greater can I see?   380
POLYDAMAS   This speaks thee born a prince; thou art thyself

                                       [*Embracing him.*

That rising sun, and shalt not see on earth
A brighter than thyself. All of you witness

That for my son I here receive this youth,
385   This brave, this—— but I must not praise him further,
Because he now is mine.
LEONIDAS I wonnot, sir, believe
That I am made your sport;
For I find nothing in myself, but what
390   Is much above a scorn. I dare give credit
To whatsoe'er a king, like you, can tell me.
Either I am, or will deserve to be your son.
ARGALEON I yet maintain it is impossible.
This young man should be yours; for, if he were,
395   Why should Hermogenes so long conceal him,
When he might gain so much by his discovery?
HERMOGENES I stayed a while to make him worthy, sir, of you.

[*To the* King.

But in that time I found
Somewhat within him, which so moved my love,
400   I never could resolve to part with him.
LEONIDAS You ask too many questions, and are [*To* ARGALEON.
Too saucy for a subject.
ARGALEON You rather over-act your part, and are
Too soon a prince.
LEONIDAS Too soon you'll find me one.
405 POLYDAMAS Enough, Argaleon;
I have declared him mine; and you, Leonidas,
Live well with him I love.
ARGALEON Sir, if he be your son, I may have leave
To think your queen had twins. Look on this virgin;
410   Hermogenes would enviously deprive you
Of half your treasure.
HERMOGENES Sir, she is my daughter.
I could, perhaps, thus aided by this lord,
Prefer her to be yours; but truth forbid
I should procure her greatness by a lie!
415 POLYDAMAS Come hither, beauteous maid: are you not sorry
Your father will not let you pass for mine?
PALMYRA I am content to be what heav'n has made me.
POLYDAMAS Could you not wish yourself a princess then?
PALMYRA Not to be sister to Leonidas.
POLYDAMAS Why, my sweet maid?

PALMYRA   Indeed I cannot tell;   420
  But I could be content to be his handmaid.
ARGALEON   I wish I had not seen her.   [*Aside.*
PALMYRA   I must weep for your good fortune;   [*To* LEONIDAS.
  Pray, pardon me, indeed I cannot help it.
  Leonidas (alas, I had forgot,   425
  Now I must call you prince) but must I leave you?
LEONIDAS   I dare not speak to her; for if I should,
  I must weep too.   [*Aside.*
POLYDAMAS   No, you shall live at court, sweet innocence,
  And see him there. Hermogenes,   430
  Though you intended not to make me happy,
  Yet you shall be rewarded for th' event.
  Come, my Leonidas, let's thank the gods;
  Thou for a father, I for such a son.

           [*Exeunt all but* LEONIDAS *and* PALMYRA.

LEONIDAS   My dear Palmyra, many eyes observe me,   435
  And I have thoughts so tender, that I cannot
  In public speak 'em to you: some hours hence
  I shall shake off these crowds of fawning courtiers,
  And then——   [*Exit* LEONIDAS.
PALMYRA   Fly swift, you hours, you measure time for me in vain,   440
  Till you bring back Leonidas again.
  Be shorter now; and to redeem that wrong,
  When he and I are met, be twice as long.   [*Exit.*

ACT II

SCENE I

Enter MELANTHA *and* PHILOTIS.

PHILOTIS   Count Rhodophil's a fine gentleman indeed, madam; and I
  think deserves your affection.
MELANTHA   Let me die but he's a fine man; he sings and dances *en
  français*, and writes the *billets-doux* to a miracle.
PHILOTIS   And those are no small talents, to a lady that understands and   5
  values the French air, as your ladyship does.

MELANTHA   How charming is the French air! and what an *étourdi bête* is
one of our untravelled islanders! When he would make his court to me,
let me die but he is just Aesop's ass, that would imitate the courtly French
in his addresses; but, instead of those, comes pawing upon me, and doing
all things so *maladroitly*.

PHILOTIS   'Tis great pity Rhodophil's a married man, that you may not
have an honourable intrigue with him.

MELANTHA   Intrigue, Philotis! that's an old phrase; I have laid that
word by: *amour* sounds better. But thou art heir to all my cast words, as
thou art to my old wardrobe. Oh, Count Rhodophil! Ah *mon cher!* I could
live and die with him.

Enter PALAMEDE *and a* Servant.

SERVANT   Sir, this is my lady.

PALAMEDE   Then this is she that is to be divine, and nymph, and
goddess, and with whom I am to be desperately in love. [*Bows to her,
delivering a letter.*] This letter, madam, which I present you from your
father, has given me both the happy opportunity, and the boldness, to
kiss the fairest hands in Sicily.

MELANTHA   Came you lately from Palermo, sir?

PALAMEDE   But yesterday, madam.

MELANTHA [*reading the letter*]   *Daughter, receive the bearer of this letter, as a
gentleman whom I have chosen to make you happy.* (O Venus, a new servant
sent me! and let me die but he has the air of a *galant homme!*) *His father is
the rich lord Cleodemus, our neighbour: I suppose you'll find nothing disagreeable
in his person or his converse; both which he has improved by travel. The treaty is
already concluded, and I shall be in town within these three days; so that you have
nothing to do but to obey your careful father.*
[*To* PALAMEDE] Sir, my father, for whom I have a blind obedience, has
commanded me to receive your passionate addresses; but you must also
give me leave to avow that I cannot merit 'em from so accomplished a
cavalier.

PALAMEDE   I want many things, madam, to render me accomplished;
and the first and greatest of 'em is your favour.

MELANTHA   Let me die, Philotis, but this is extremely French; but yet
Count Rhodophil . . . A gentleman, sir, that understands the *grand
monde* so well, who has haunted the best conversations, and who, in
short, has voyaged, may pretend to the good graces of a lady.

---

7 *étourdi bête*] Thoughtless creature.
9 Aesop's ass] The ass who foolishly tried to imitate the farmer's lap-dog with clumsy pawing
and frolicking.
41 haunted] Frequented.

PALAMEDE [*aside*] Hey-day! *Grand monde! conversation! voyaged!* and *good graces!* I find my mistress is one of those that run mad in new French words. 45

MELANTHA I suppose, sir, you have made the *tour* of France; and having seen all that's fine there, will make a considerable reformation in the rudeness of our court: for let me die, but an unfashioned, untravelled, mere Sicilian, is a *bête*; and has nothing in the world of an *honnête homme*.

PALAMEDE I must confess, madam, that— 50

MELANTHA And what new minuets have you brought over with you? Their minuets are to a miracle! and our Sicilian jigs are so dull and sad to 'em!

PALAMEDE For minuets, madam—

MELANTHA And what new plays are there in vogue? and who danced 55
best in the last grand ballet? Come, sweet servant, you shall tell me all.

PALAMEDE [*aside*] Tell her all? Why she asks all, and will hear nothing.
. . . To answer in order, madam, to your demands—

MELANTHA I am thinking what a happy couple we shall be! for you shall keep up your correspondence abroad, and everything that's new 60
writ, in France, and fine, I mean all that's delicate, and *bien tourné*, we will have first.

PALAMEDE But, madam, our fortune—

MELANTHA I understand you, sir; you'll leave that to me: for the *ménage* of a family, I know it better than any lady in Sicily. 65

PALAMEDE Alas, madam, we—

MELANTHA Then, we will never make visits together, nor see a play, but always apart; you shall be every day at the king's *levée*, and I at the queen's; and we will never meet, but in the drawing-room.

PHILOTIS Madam, the new prince is just passed by the end of the walk. 70

MELANTHA The new prince, say'st thou? Adieu, dear servant; I have not made my court to him these two long hours. O, 'tis the sweetest prince! so *obligeant, charmant, ravissant*, that — Well, I'll make haste to kiss his hands, and then make half a score visits more, and be with you again in a twinkling. 75

[*Exit running with* PHILOTIS.

PALAMEDE [*solus*] Now heaven, of thy mercy, bless me from this tongue! it may keep the field against a whole army of lawyers, and that in their own language, French gibberish. It is true, in the daytime, 'tis tolerable, when a man has field-room to run from it; but to be shut up in a bed with her, like two cocks in a pit, humanity cannot support it: I 80

68–9 the queen's] Apparently forgetting that Polydamas is a widower.

must kiss all night in my own defence, and hold her down, like a boy at
cuffs, and give her the rising blow every time she begins to speak.

Enter RHODOPHIL.

But here comes Rhodophil. 'Tis pretty odd that my mistress should so
much resemble his: the same newsmonger, the same passionate lover of a

85   court, the same – But *Basta*, since I must marry her, I'll say nothing,
because he shall not laugh at my misfortune.

RHODOPHIL   Well, Palamede, how go the affairs of love? You've seen
your mistress?

PALAMEDE   I have so.

90   RHODOPHIL   And how, and how? Has the old Cupid, your father,
chosen well for you? Is he a good woodman?

PALAMEDE   She's much handsomer than I could have imagined. In
short, I love her, and will marry her.

RHODOPHIL   Then you are quite off from your other mistress?

95   PALAMEDE   You are mistaken; I intend to love 'em both, as a reasonable
man ought to do. For, since all women have their faults and imperfections, 'tis fit that one of 'em should help out t'other.

RHODOPHIL   This were a blessed doctrine, indeed, if our wives would
hear it; but they're their own enemies. If they would suffer us but now

100   and then to make excursions, the benefit of our variety would be theirs;
instead of one continued, lazy, tired love, they would, in their turns,
have twenty vigorous, fresh, and active loves.

PALAMEDE   And I would ask any of 'em whether a poor narrow brook,
half dry the best part of the year, and running ever one way, be to be

105   compared to a lusty stream, that has ebbs and flows?

RHODOPHIL   Ay, or is half so profitable for navigation?

Enter DORALICE, *walking by, and reading.*

PALAMEDE   Ods my life, Rhodophil, will you keep my counsel?

RHODOPHIL   Yes: where's the secret?

PALAMEDE   There 'tis – [*showing* DORALICE] – I may tell you, as my

110   friend, *sub sigillo*, etc., this is that very numerical lady with whom I am
in love.

RHODOPHIL   By all that's virtuous, my wife!   [*Aside*.

PALAMEDE   You look strangely: how do you like her? Is she not very
handsome?

85   *Basta*] Enough!
91   woodman] Huntsman: that is, a good chooser of 'game'.
110 *sub sigillo*] Under a seal, in confidence.
        numerical] Particular, the very same.

RHODOPHIL   Sure he abuses me [*Aside*]. Why the devil do you ask my   115
judgment?

PALAMEDE   You are so dogged now, you think no man's mistress
handsome but your own. Come, you shall hear her talk too; she has wit, I
assure you.

RHODOPHIL   This is too much, Palamede.   [*Going back.*   120

PALAMEDE   Pr'ythee do not hang back so: of an old tried lover, thou are
the most bashful fellow!   [*Pulling him forward.*

DORALICE   Were you so near, and would not speak, dear husband?

[*Looking up.*

PALAMEDE   Husband, quoth a! I have cut out a fine piece of work for
myself.   [*Aside.*   125

RHODOPHIL   Pray, spouse, how long have you been acquainted with
this gentleman?

DORALICE   Who? I acquainted with this stranger? To my best knowledge, I never saw him before.

Enter MELANTHA *at the other end.*

PALAMEDE   Thanks, fortune, thou hast helped me   [*Aside.*   130

RHODOPHIL   Palamede, this must not pass so. I must know your
mistress a little better.

PALAMEDE   It shall be your own fault else. Come, I'll introduce you.

RHODOPHIL   Introduce me! where?

PALAMEDE   There. To my mistress.   135

[*Pointing to* MELANTHA, *who swiftly passes over the stage.*

RHODOPHIL   Who? Melantha! O heavens, I did not see her.

PALAMEDE   But I did: I am an eagle where I love; I have seen her this
half hour.

DORALICE [*aside*]   I find he has wit, he has got off so readily; but it
would anger me if he should love Melantha.   140

RHODOPHIL [*aside*]   Now I could e'en wish it were my wife he loved: I
find he's to be married to my mistress.

PALAMEDE   Shall I run after, and fetch her back again, to present you to
her?

RHODOPHIL   No, you need not; I have the honour to have some small   145
acquaintance with her.

PALAMEDE [*aside*]   O Jupiter! what a blockhead was I not to find it out!
my wife that must be, is his mistress. I did a little suspect it before.

117 dogged] Obstinate, awkward.

150   Well, I must marry her, because she's handsome, and because I hate to be
disinherited for a younger brother, which I am sure I shall be if I disobey;
and yet I must keep in with Rhodophil, because I love his wife.
[*To* RHODOPHIL] I must desire you to make my excuse to your lady, if
I have been so unfortunate to cause any mistake; and, withal, to beg the
honour of being known to her.

155 RHODOPHIL   O, that's but reason. Hark you, spouse, pray look upon
this gentleman as my friend; whom, to my knowledge, you have never
seen before this hour.

DORALICE   I'm so obedient a wife, sir, that my husband's commands
shall ever be a law to me.

Enter MELANTHA *again, hastily, and runs to embrace* DORALICE.

160 MELANTHA   O, my dear, I was just going to pay my devoirs to you; I
had not time this morning, for making my court to the king, and our
new prince. Well, never nation was so happy, and all that, in a young
prince; and he's the kindest person in the world to me, let me die if he is
not.

165 DORALICE   He has been bred up far from court, and therefore—

MELANTHA   That imports not: though he has not seen the *grand monde*,
and all that, let me die but he has the air of the court most absolutely.

PALAMEDE   But yet, madam, he—

MELANTHA   O, servant, you can testify that I am in his good graces.

170 Well, I cannot stay long with you, because I have promised him this
afternoon to [*Whispers to* DORALICE]. But hark you, my dear, I'll tell
you a secret.

RHODOPHIL   The devil's in me, that I must love this woman. [*Aside.*

PALAMEDE   The devil's in me, that I must marry this woman. [*Aside.*

175 MELANTHA[*raising her voice*]   So the prince and I – But you must make a
secret of this, my dear; for I would not for the world your husband should
hear it, or my tyrant, there, that must be.

PALAMEDE   Well, fair impertinent, your whisper is not lost, we hear
you.   [*Aside.*

180 DORALICE   I understand then that—

MELANTHA   I'll tell you, my dear, the prince took me by the hand, and
pressed it *à la dérobée* because the king was near, made the *doux yeux* to
me, and *en suite*, said a thousand gallantries, or let me die, my dear.

DORALICE   Then I am sure you—

185 MELANTHA   You are mistaken, my dear.

182 *à la dérobée*] Secretly, on concealment.
    doux yeux] Tender glance.
183 *en suite*] Then, afterwards.

DORALICE   What, before I speak?

MELANTHA   But I know your meaning. You think, my dear, that I
assumed something of *fierté* into my countenance, to *rebute* him; but,
quite contrary, I regarded him, I know not how to express it in our dull,
Sicilian language, *d'un air enjoué*; and said nothing but *à d'autres, à*   190
d'autres, and that it was all *grimace*, and would not pass upon me.

Enter ARTEMIS: MELANTHA *sees her, and runs away from* DORALICE.

[*To* ARTEMIS] My dear, I must beg your pardon, I was just making a
loose from Doralice, to pay my respects to you. Let me die, if I ever pass
time so agreeably as in your company, and if I would leave it for any
lady's in Sicily.   195

ARTEMIS   The princess Amalthea is coming this way.

Enter AMALTHEA: MELANTHA *runs to her.*

MELANTHA   O, dear madam! I have been at your lodgings, in my new
calèche, so often, to tell you of a new *amour*, betwixt two persons whom
you would little suspect for it, that, let me die if one of my coach-horses
be not dead, and another quite tired, and sunk under the *fatigue*.   200

AMALTHEA   O, Melantha, I can tell you news, the prince is coming this
way.

MELANTHA   The prince? O sweet prince! He and I are to — and I forgot
it. — Your pardon, sweet madam, for my abruptness. Adieu, my dears.
Servant, Rhodophil; servant, servant, servant all.   205

[*Exit running.*

AMALTHEA   Rhodophil, a word with you.   [*Whispers.*

DORALICE [*to* PALAMEDE]   Why do you not follow your mistress, sir?

PALAMEDE   Follow her? Why, at this rate she'll be at the Indies within
this half hour.

DORALICE   However, if you can't follow her all day, you'll meet her at   210
night, I hope?

PALAMEDE   But can you, in charity, suffer me to be so mortified,
without affording me some relief? If it be but to punish that sign of a
husband there, that lazy matrimony, that dull insipid taste, who leaves
such delicious fare at home, to dine abroad on worse meat, and pay dear   215
for't into the bargain.

188 *fierté*] Haughtiness, superciliousness.
190 *d'un air enjoué*] Playfully.
    à d'autres] Nonsense; tell it to someone else.
191 *grimace*] Affectation.
192–3 making a loose] Getting away from.
198 *calèche*] A kind of light carriage.

DORALICE   All this is in vain. Assure yourself, I will never admit of any
visit from you in private.

PALAMEDE   That is to tell me, in other words, my condition is desper-
220   ate.

DORALICE   I think you in so ill a condition, that I am resolved to pray
for you, this very evening, in the close walk behind the terrace; for that's
a private place, and there I am sure nobody will disturb my devotions.
And so, good-night, sir.

[*Exit*.

225   PALAMEDE   This is the newest way of making an appointment I ever
heard of. Let women alone to contrive the means; I find we are but dunces
to 'em. Well, I will not be so profane a wretch as to interrupt her
devotions; but to make 'em more effectual, I'll down upon my knees, and
endeavour to join my own with 'em.

[*Exit*.

230   AMALTHEA [*to* RHODOPHIL]   I know already they do not love each
other; and that my brother acts but a forced obedience to the king's
commands; so that if a quarrel should arise betwixt the prince and him, I
were most miserable on both sides.

RHODOPHIL   There shall be nothing wanting in me, madam, to prevent
235   so sad a consequence.

Enter the King *and* LEONIDAS; *the* King *whispers to* AMALTHEA.

[*To himself*] I begin to hate this Palamede, because he is to marry my
mistress: yet break with him I dare not, for fear of being quite excluded
from her company. 'Tis a hard case, when a man must go by his rival to
his mistress: but 'tis at worst but using him like a pair of heavy boots in a
240   dirty journey; after I have fouled him all day, I'll throw him off at night.

[*Exit*.

AMALTHEA [*to the* King]   This honour is too great for me to hope.

POLYDAMAS   You shall this hour have the assurance of it.
Leonidas, come hither; you have heard,
I doubt not, that the father of this princess
245   Was my most faithful friend, while I was yet
A private man; and when I did assume
This crown, he served me in the high attempt.
You see, then, to what gratitude obliges me;
Make your addresses to her.

250   LEONIDAS   Sir, I am yet too young to be a courtier;

I should too much betray my ignorance
And want of breeding to so fair a lady.
AMALTHEA   Your language speaks you not bred up in deserts,
But in the softness of some Asian court,
Where luxury and ease invent kind words,   255
To cozen tender virgins of their hearts.
POLYDAMAS   You need not doubt,
But in what words soe'er a prince can offer
His crown and person, they will be received.
You know my pleasure, and you know your duty.   260
LEONIDAS   Yes, sir, I shall obey, in what I can.
POLYDAMAS   In what you can, Leonidas? Consider,
He's both your king, and father, who commands you.
Besides, what is there hard in my injunction?
LEONIDAS   'Tis hard to have my inclination forced.   265
I would not marry, sir; and, when I do,
I hope you'll give me freedom in my choice.
POLYDAMAS   View well this lady,
Whose mind as much transcends her beauteous face,
As that excels all others.   270
AMALTHEA   My beauty, as it ne'er could merit love,
So neither can it beg: and, sir, you may
Believe that what the king has offered you
I should refuse, did I not value more
Your person than your crown.
LEONIDAS   Think it not pride   275
Or my new fortunes swell me to contemn you;
Think less, that I want eyes to see your beauty;
And, least of all, think duty wanting in me
T'obey a father's will: but—
POLYDAMAS   But what, Leonidas?   280
For I must know your reason; and be sure
It be convincing too.
LEONIDAS   Sir, ask the stars,
Which have imposed love on us, like a fate,
Why minds are bent to one, and fly another?
Ask why all beauties cannot move all hearts?   285
For though there may
Be made a rule for colour, or for feature,
There can be none for liking.
POLYDAMAS   Leonidas, you owe me more
Than to oppose your liking to my pleasure.   290

LEONIDAS   I owe you all things, sir; but something too I owe myself.
POLYDAMAS   You shall dispute no more; I am a king,
   And I will be obeyed.
LEONIDAS   You are a king, sir, but you are no god;
295   Or if you were, you could not force my will.
POLYDAMAS [aside]   But you are just, you gods; O, you are just,
   In punishing the crimes of my rebellion
   With a rebellious son!
   Yet I can punish him, as you do me.
300   Leonidas, there is no jesting with   [To him.
   My will: I ne'er had done so much to gain
   A crown, but to be absolute in all things.
AMALTHEA   O, sir, be not so much a king, as to
   Forget you are a father: soft indulgence
305   Becomes that name. Though nature gives you power
   To bind his duty, 'tis with silken bonds:
   Command him, then, as you command yourself;
   He is as much a part of you, as are
   Your appetite and will, and those you force not,
310   But gently bend, and make 'em pliant to your reason.
POLYDAMAS   It may be I have used too rough a way:
   Forgive me, my Leonidas; I know
   I lie as open to the gusts of passion,
   As the bare shore to every beating surge:
315   I will not force thee now; but I entreat thee,
   Absolve a father's vow to this fair virgin:
   A vow, which hopes of having such a son
   First caused.
LEONIDAS   Show not my disobedience by your prayers;
320   For I must still deny you, though I now
   Appear more guilty to myself, than you:
   I have some reasons, which I cannot utter,
   That force my disobedience; yet I mourn
   To death, that the first thing you e'er enjoined me,
325   Should be that only one command in nature
   Which I could not obey.
POLYDAMAS   I did descend too much below myself,
   When I entreated him – Hence, to thy desert!
   Thou'rt not my son, or art not fit to be.
330 AMALTHEA   Great sir, I humbly beg you, make not me   [Kneeling.
   The cause of your displeasure. I absolve
   Your vow; far, far from me be such designs;

So wretched a desire of being great,
By making him unhappy. You may see
Something so noble in the prince's nature,   335
As grieves him more not to obey, than you
That you are not obeyed.
POLYDAMAS   Then, for your sake,
I'll give him one day longer to consider,
Not to deny; for my resolves are firm
As fate, that cannot change   [*Exeunt* King *and* AMALTHEA.
LEONIDAS   And so are mine.   340
This beauteous princess, charming as she is,
Could never make me happy: I must first
Be false to my Palmyra, and then wretched.
But, then, a father's anger!
Suppose he should recede from his own vow,   345
He never would permit me to keep mine.

        Enter PALMYRA; ARGALEON *following her a little after.*

See, she appears!
I'll think no more of anything, but her.
Yet I have one good hour ere I am wretched.
But, oh! Argaleon follows her! so night   350
Treads on the footsteps of a winter's sun,
And stalks all black behind him.
PALMYRA   O, Leonidas,
(For I must call you still by that dear name)
Free me from this bad man.   355
LEONIDAS   I hope he dares not be injurious to you.
ARGALEON   I rather was injurious to myself
Than her.
LEONIDAS   That must be judged when I hear what you said.
ARGALEON   I think you need not give yourself that trouble: 360
It concerned us alone.
LEONIDAS   You answer saucily, and indirectly:
What interest can you pretend in her?
ARGALEON   It may be, sir, I made her some expressions
Which I would not repeat, because they were   365
Below my rank, to one of hers.
LEONIDAS   What did he say, Palmyra?
PALMYRA   I'll tell all. First, he began to look,
And then he sighed, and then he looked again;
At last, he said my eyes wounded his heart: 370

And, after that, he talked of flames and fires,
And such strange words, that I believed he conjured.
LEONIDAS   O my heart! Leave me, Argaleon.
ARGALEON   Come, sweet Palmyra,
375   I will instruct you better in my meaning:
You see he would be private.
LEONIDAS   Go yourself,
And leave her here.
ARGALEON   Alas, she's ignorant,
And is not fit to entertain a prince.
LEONIDAS   First learn what's fit for you; that's to obey.
380   ARGALEON   I know my duty is to wait on you.
A great king's son, like you, ought to forget
Such mean converse.
LEONIDAS   What? a disputing subject?
Hence, or my sword shall do me justice on thee.
ARGALEON   Yet I may find a time—   [*Going.*
LEONIDAS   What's that you mutter,   [*Going after him.*
385   To find a time?
ARGALEON   To wait on you again—
In the meanwhile I'll watch you.   [*Softly.*

[*Exit, and watches during the scene.*

LEONIDAS   How precious are the hours of love in courts!
In cottages, where love has all the day,
Full, and at ease, he throws it half away.
390   Time gives himself, and is not valued, there;
But sells at mighty rates each minute, here:
There, he is lazy, unemployed, and slow;
Here, he's more swift; and yet has more to do.
So many of his hours in public move,
395   That few are left for privacy and love.
PALMYRA   The sun, methinks, shines faint and dimly, here;
Light is not half so long, nor half so clear:
But, oh! when every day was yours and mine,
How early up! what haste he made to shine!
400   LEONIDAS   Such golden days no prince must hope to see,
Whose every subject is more blessed than he.
PALMYRA   Do you remember, when their tasks were done,
How all the youth did to our cottage run?
While winter-winds were whistling loud without,
405   Our cheerful hearth was circled round about:

With strokes in ashes maids their lovers drew;
And still you fell to me, and I to you.
LEONIDAS When love did of my heart possession take,
   I was so young, my soul was scarce awake:
   I cannot tell when first I thought you fair;   410
   But sucked in love, insensibly as air.
PALMYRA I know too well when first my love began,
   When at our wake you for the chaplet ran:
   Then I was made the lady of the May,
   And, with the garland, at the goal did stay: 415
   Still, as you ran, I kept you full in view;
   I hoped, and wished, and ran, methought, for you.
   As you came near, I hastily did rise,
   And stretched my arm outright, that held the prize.
   The custom was to kiss whom I should crown: 420
   You kneeled, and in my lap your head laid down.
   I blushed, and blushed, and did the kiss delay:
   At last my subjects forced me to obey;
   But, when I gave the crown, and then the kiss,
   I scarce had breath to say, Take that — and this.   425
LEONIDAS I felt, the while, a pleasing kind of smart;
   That kiss went, tingling, to my very heart.
   When it was gone, the sense of it did stay;
   The sweetness clinged upon my lips all day,
   Like drops of honey, loth to fall away.   430
PALMYRA Life, like a prodigal, gave all his store
   To my first youth, and now can give no more.
   You are a prince; and, in that high degree,
   No longer must converse with humble me.
LEONIDAS 'Twas to my loss the gods that title gave;   435
   A tyrant's son is doubly born a slave:
   He gives a crown; but, to prevent my life
   From being happy, loads it with a wife.
PALMYRA Speak quickly; what have you resolved to do?
LEONIDAS To keep my faith inviolate to you.   440
   He threatens me with exile, and with shame,
   To lose my birthright, and a prince's name;
   But there's a blessing which he did not mean,
   To send me back to love and you again.

413 wake] Rural festival.
   chaplet] A wreath for the head.

445 PALMYRA   Why was not I a princess for your sake?
       But heaven no more such miracles can make:
       And, since that cannot, this must never be;
       You shall not lose a crown for love of me.
       Live happy, and a nobler choice pursue;
450   I shall complain of fate, but not of you.
     LEONIDAS   Can you so easily without me live?
       Or could you take the counsel which you give?
       Were you a princess would you not be true?
     PALMYRA   I would; but cannot merit it from you.
455 LEONIDAS   Did you not merit, as you do, my heart;
       Love gives esteem, and then it gives desert.
       But if I basely could forget my vow,
       Poor helpless innocence, what would you do?
     PALMYRA   In woods, and plains, where first my love began,
460   There would I live, retired from faithless man:
       I'd sit all day within some lonely shade,
       Or that close arbour which your hands have made:
       I'd search the groves, and every tree, to find
       Where you had carved our names upon the rind:
465   Your hook, your scrip, all that was yours I'd keep,
       And lay 'em by me when I went to sleep.
       Thus would I live: and maidens, when I die,
       Upon my hearse white true-love-knots should tie:
       And thus my tomb should be inscribed above,
470   *Here the forsaken Virgin rests from love.*
     LEONIDAS   Think not that time or fate shall e'er divide
       Those hearts, which love and mutual vows have tied.
       But we must part; farewell, my love.
     PALMYRA   Till when?
     LEONIDAS   Till the next age of hours we meet again.
475   Meantime — we may
       When near each other we in public stand,
       Contrive to catch a look, or steal a hand:
       Fancy will every touch and glance improve;
       And draw the most spirituous parts of love.
480   Our souls sit close and silently within,
       And their own web from their own entrails spin;
       And when eyes meet far off, our sense is such,
       That, spider-like, we feel the tend'rest touch.   [*Exeunt*.

       465 hook . . . scrip] Shepherd's crook and bag.

ACT III

SCENE I

Enter RHODOPHIL, *meeting* DORALICE *and* ARTEMIS.
RHODOPHIL *and* DORALICE *embrace.*

RHODOPHIL   My own dear heart!

DORALICE   My own true love! [*She starts back*] I had forgot myself to be
so kind; indeed, I am very angry with you, dear; you are come home an
hour after you appointed: if you had stayed a minute longer, I was just   5
considering whether I should stab, hang, or drown myself.

[*Embracing him.*

RHODOPHIL   Nothing but the king's business could have hindered me;
and I was so vexed, that I was just laying down my commission, rather
than have failed my dear.   [*Kisses her hand.*

ARTEMIS   Why, this is love as it should be betwixt man and wife: such
another couple would bring marriage into fashion again. But is it always   10
thus betwixt you?

RHODOPHIL   Always thus! This is nothing. I tell you, there is not such
a pair of turtles in Sicily; there is such an eternal cooing and kissing
betwixt us, that indeed it is scandalous before civil company.

DORALICE   Well, if I had imagined I should have been this fond fool, I   15
would never have married the man I loved: I married to be happy, and
have made myself miserable by over-loving. Nay, and now my case is
desperate; for I have been married above these two years, and find myself
every day worse and worse in love: nothing but madness can be the end
on't.   20

ARTEMIS   Dote on, to the extremity, and you are happy.

DORALICE   He deserves so infinitely much, that, the truth is, there can
be no doting in the matter; but to love well, I confess, is a work that
pays itself: 'tis telling gold, and after taking it for one's pains.

RHODOPHIL   By that I should be a very covetous person; for I am ever   25
pulling out my money, and putting it into my pocket again.

DORALICE   O dear Rhodophil!

RHODOPHIL   O sweet Doralice!   [*Embracing each other.*

ARTEMIS [*aside*]   Nay, I am resolved, I'll never interrupt lovers: I'll leave
'em as happy as I found 'em.   [*Steals away.*   30

RHODOPHIL   What, is she gone?   [*Looking up.*

DORALICE   Yes; and without taking leave.

RHODOPHIL Then there's enough for this time. [*Parting from her.*

DORALICE Yes sure, the scene is done, I take it.

[*They walk contrary ways on the stage; he with his hands in his pockets, whistling; she singing a dull melancholy tune.*]

35 RHODOPHIL Pox o' your dull tune, a man can't think for you.

DORALICE Pox o' your damned whistling; you can neither be company to me yourself, nor leave me to the freedom of my own fancy.

RHODOPHIL Well, thou art the most provoking wife!

DORALICE Well, thou art the dullest husband, thou art never to be
40 provoked.

RHODOPHIL I was never thought dull till I married thee; and now thou hast made an old knife of me, thou hast whetted me so long, till I have no edge left.

DORALICE I see you are in the husband's fashion; you reserve all your
45 good humours for your mistresses, and keep your ill for your wives.

RHODOPHIL Pr'ythee leave me to my own cogitations; I am thinking over all my sins, to find for which of them it was I married thee.

DORALICE Whatever your sin was, mine's the punishment.

RHODOPHIL My comfort is, thou art not immortal; and, when that
50 blessed, that divine day comes of thy departure, I'm resolved I'll make one holiday more in the almanac for thy sake.

DORALICE Ay, you had need make a holiday for me, for I am sure you have made me a martyr.

RHODOPHIL Then, setting my victorious foot upon thy head, in the
55 first hour of thy silence (that is, the first hour thou art dead, for I despair of it before), I will swear by the ghost — an oath as terrible to me as Styx is to the gods — never more to be in danger of the banes of matrimony.

DORALICE And I am resolved to marry the very same day thou diest, if it be but to show how little I'm concerned for thee.

60 RHODOPHIL Pr'ythee, Doralice, why do we quarrel thus a-days? ha? This is but a kind of heathenish life, and does not answer the ends of marriage. If I have erred, propound what reasonable atonement may be made before we sleep, and I will not be refractory: but withal consider, I have been married these three years, and be not too tyrannical.

65 DORALICE What should you talk of a peace abed, when you can give no security for performance of articles?

RHODOPHIL Then, since we must live together, and both of us stand upon our terms, as to matter of dying first, let us make ourselves as merry as we can with our misfortunes.

57 banes] Marriage banns, with a pun on 'bane'.
66 articles] The formal agreement.

Why, there's the devil on't! If thou couldst make my enjoying thee but   70
a little less easy, or a little more unlawful, thou shouldst see what a
termagant lover I would prove. I have taken such pains to enjoy thee,
Doralice, that I have fancied thee all the fine women in the town, to help
me out. But now there's none left for me to think on, my imagination is
quite jaded. Thou art a wife, and thou wilt be a wife, and I can make thee   75
another no longer.

> [*Exit* RHODOPHIL.

DORALICE   Well, since thou art a husband, and wilt be a husband, I'll
try if I can find out another! 'Tis a pretty time we women have on't, to be
made widows while we are married. Our husbands think it reasonable to
complain that we are the same and the same to them, when we have more   80
reason to complain that they are not the same to us. Because they cannot
feed on one dish, therefore we must be starved. 'Tis enough that they
have a sufficient ordinary provided, and a table ready spread for 'em: if
they cannot fall to and eat heartily, the fault is theirs; and 'tis pity,
methinks, that the good creature should be lost, when many a poor   85
sinner would be glad on't.

Enter MELANTHA *and* ARTEMIS *to her.*

MELANTHA   Dear, my dear, pity me, I am so *chagrin* today, and have
had the most signal affront at court! I went this afternoon to do my devoir
to princess Amalthea, found her, conversed with her, and helped to make
her court some half an hour; after which, she went to take the air, chose   90
out two ladies to go with her that came in after me, and left me most
barbarously behind her.
ARTEMIS   You are the less to be pitied, Melantha, because you subject
yourself to these affronts by coming perpetually to court, where you have
no business nor employment.   95
MELANTHA   I declare, I had rather of the two be *rallied*, nay, *mal traitée*
at court, than be deified in the town; for, assuredly, nothing can be so
ridicule as a mere town lady.
DORALICE   Especially at court. How I have seen 'em crowd and sweat
in the drawing-room on a holiday-night! for that's their time to swarm   100
and invade the presence. O, how they catch at a bow, or any little salute
from a courtier, to make show of their acquaintance! And, rather than be
thought to be quite unknown they court'sy to one another; but they take
true pains to come near the circle, and press and peep upon the princess,

72 termagant] Quarrelsome, overbearing.
83 ordinary] Regular daily meal.
104 circle] An assembly of courtiers surrounding the principal person.

105 to write letters into the country how she was dressed, while the ladies that stand about make their court to her with abusing them.

ARTEMIS   These are sad truths, Melantha; and therefore I would e'en advise you to quit the court, and live either wholly in the town, or, if you like not that, in the country.

110 DORALICE   In the country! nay, that's to fall beneath the town, for they live upon our offals here. Their entertainment of wit is only the remembrance of what they had when they were last in town; they live this year upon the last year's knowledge, as their cattle do all night, by chewing the cud of what they eat in the afternoon.

115 MELANTHA   And they tell, for news, such unlikely stories! A letter from one of us is such a present to them, that the poor souls wait for the carrier's-day with such devotion that they cannot sleep the night before.

ARTEMIS   No more than I can, the night before I am to go a journey.

DORALICE   Or I, before I am to try on a new gown.

120 MELANTHA   A song that's stale here, will be new there a twelvemonth hence; and if a man of the town by chance come amongst 'em, he's reverenced for teaching them the tune.

DORALICE   A friend of mine, who makes songs sometimes, came lately out of the west, and vowed he was so put out of countenance with a song 125 of his; for at the first country gentleman's he visited, he saw three tailors crossed-legged upon the table in the hall, who were tearing out as loud as ever they could sing,

After the pangs of a desperate lover, etc.

And that all day he heard nothing else but the daughters of the house and 130 the maids humming it over in every corner, and the father whistling it.

ARTEMIS   Indeed, I have observed of myself that when I am out of town but a fortnight, I am so humble that I would receive a letter from my tailor or mercer for a favour.

MELANTHA   When I have been at grass in the summer, and am new 135 come up again, methinks I'm to be turned into *ridicule* by all that see me; but when I have been once or twice at court, I begin to value myself again, and to despise my country acquaintance.

ARTEMIS   There are places where all people may be adored, and we ought to know ourselves so well as to choose 'em.

140 DORALICE   That's very true; your little courtier's wife, who speaks to the king but once a month, need but go to a town lady, and there she may vapour and cry 'The king and I' at every word. Your town lady, who is

117, carrier's-day] That is, the day when letters were brought by the carrier.
128 *After . . . lover, etc.*] The song is from Act II of Dryden's comedy *An Evening's Love*, performed in 1668. See p. 80.

laughed at in the circle, takes her coach into the city, and there's she's
called Your Honour, and has a banquet from the merchant's wife, whom
she laughs at for her kindness. And as for my finical cit, she removes but   145
to her country house, and there insults over the country gentlewoman
that never comes up, who treats her with frumity and custard, and opens
her dear bottle of *mirabilis* beside, for a gill-glass of it at parting.

ARTEMIS   At last, I see, we shall leave Melantha where we found her;
for, by your description of the town and country, they are become more   150
dreadful to her than the court, where she was affronted. But you forget
we are to wait on the princess Amalthea. Come, Doralice.

DORALICE   Farewell, Melantha.

MELANTHA   Adieu, my dear.

ARTEMIS   You are out of charity with her, and therefore I shall not give   155
your service.

MELANTHA   Do not omit it, I beseech you; for I have such a tender for
the court that I love it even from the drawing-room to the lobby, and can
never be *rebutée* by any usage. But hark you, my dears, one thing I had
forgot of great concernment.   160

DORALICE   Quickly then, we are in haste.

MELANTHA   Do not call it my service, that's too vulgar; but do my
baise-mains to the princess Amalthea; that is *spirituelle*!

DORALICE   To do you service then, we will *prendre* the *carosse* to court,
and do your *baise-mains* to the princess Amalthea, in your phrase   165
spirituelle.

[*Exeunt* ARTEMIS *and* DORALICE.

Enter PHILOTIS, *with a paper in her hand*.

MELANTHA   O, are you there, minion? And, well, are not you a most
precious damsel, to retard all my visits for want of language, when you
know you are paid so well for furnishing me with new words for my daily
conversation? Let me die, if I have not run the risk already to speak like   170
one of the vulgar, and if I have one phrase left in all my store that is not
threadbare *et usé*, and fit for nothing but to be thrown to peasants.

PHILOTIS   Indeed, madam, I have been very diligent in my vocation;
but you have so drained all the French plays and romances, that they are
not able to supply you with words for your daily expenses.   175

147 frumity] 'A dish made of small, hulled wheat boiled in milk, and seasoned with cinna-
mon, sugar, etc.' (*OED*).
148 *mirabilis*] Aqua mirabilis, a drink made of wine and spices.
163 *baise-mains*] Compliments.
163 *spirituelle*] Witty.
164 *prendre* the *carosse*] Take the coach.

MELANTHA   Drained? What a word's there! *Epuisée*, you sot you. Come
produce your morning's work.
PHILOTIS   'Tis here, madam.   [*Shows the paper.*
MELANTHA   O, my Venus! fourteen or fifteen words to serve me a whole
180   day! Let me die, at this rate I cannot last till night. Come, read your
works: twenty to one, half of 'em will not pass muster neither.
PHILOTIS   *Sottises.*   [*Reads.*
MELANTHA   *Sottises: bon.* That's an excellent word to begin withal; as,
for example, he or she said a thousand *sottises* to me. Proceed.
185   PHILOTIS   *Figure*: as, what a figure of a man is there! *Naïve* and *naïveté.*
MELANTHA   *Naïve*! as how?
PHILOTIS   Speaking of a thing that was naturally said — it was so *naïve*; or
such an innocent piece of simplicity — 'twas such a *naïveté.*
MELANTHA   Truce with your interpretations: make haste.
190   PHILOTIS   *Foible, chagrin, grimace, embarrassé, double entendre, équivoque,
éclaircissement, suite, bévue, façon, penchant, coup d'étourdi,* and *ridicule.*
MELANTHA   Hold, hold; how did they begin?
PHILOTIS   They began at *sottises*, and ended *en ridicule.*
MELANTHA   Now, give me your paper in my hand, and hold you my
195   glass, while I practise my postures for the day. [MELANTHA *laughs in
the glass.*] How does that laugh become my face?
PHILOTIS   Sovereignly well, madam.
MELANTHA   *Sovereignly*? Let me die, that's not amiss. That word shall
not be yours; I'll invent it, and bring it up myself. My new point gorget
200   shall by yours upon't: not a word of the word, I charge you.
PHILOTIS   I am dumb, madam.
MELANTHA   That glance, how suits it with my face?

                                            [*Looking in the glass again.*

PHILOTIS   'Tis so *languissant.*
MELANTHA   *Languissant*! that word shall be mine too, and my last
205   Indian gown thine for't.
That sigh?   [*Looks again.*
PHILOTIS   'Twill make many a man sigh, madam. 'Tis a mere *incendiary.*
MELANTHA   Take my gimp petticoat for that truth. If thou hast more of
these phrases, let me die but I could give away all my wardrobe, and go
210   naked for 'em.

182 *Sottises*] Foolishnesses.
190–1 *Foible . . . ridicule*] Weakness, heart-ache, affected look, embarrassed, double meaning, ambiguity, clarification, retinue, a blunder, appearance, inclination, a foolish act,
ridicule.
199 point gorget] Needlework neck-garment.
208 gimp] 'Silk, worsted or cotton twist with a cord or wire running through it' (*OED*).

PHILOTIS   Go naked? Then you would be a Venus, madam. O Jupiter!
what had I forgot? This paper was given me by Rhodophil's page.
MELANTHA [*reading the letter*]   Beg the favour from you.—Gratify my
passion—so   far—assignation—in   the   grotto—behind   the   terrace—clock this evening———Well, for the *billets-doux* there is no man in   215
Sicily must dispute with Rhodophil; they are so French, so *gallant*, and
so *tendre*, that I cannot resist the temptation of the assignation. Now go
you away, Philotis; it imports me to practise what I shall say to my
servant when I meet him.

[*Exit* PHILOTIS.

Rhodophil, you'll wonder at my assurance to meet you here; let me die, I   220
am so out of breath with coming, that I can render you no reason of it.
Then he will make this *repartee*; Madam, I have no reason to accuse you for
that which is so great a favour to me. Then I reply, But why have you
drawn me to this solitary place? Let me die, but I am apprehensive of
some violence from you. Then says he, Solitude, madam, is most fit for   225
lovers; but by this fair hand—Nay, now I vow you're rude, sir. O fie, fie,
fie; I hope you'll be honourable?—You'd laugh at me if I should,
madam——What do you mean to throw me down thus? Ah me! ah! ah! ah!

Enter POLYDAMAS, LEONIDAS, *and* Guards.

O Venus! the king and court. Let me die, but I fear they have found my
foible, and will turn me into *ridicule*.   [*Exit, running.*   230
LEONIDAS   Sir, I beseech you.
POLYDAMAS   Do not urge my patience.
LEONIDAS   I'll not deny,
But what your spies informed you of is true:
I love the fair Palmyra; but I loved her
Before I knew your title to my blood.   235

Enter PALMYRA, *guarded.*

See, here she comes, and looks, amidst her guards,
Like a weak dove under the falcon's gripe.
O heav'n, I cannot bear it.
POLYDAMAS   Maid, come hither.
Have you presumed so far, as to receive
My son's affection?   .   240
PALMYRA   Alas, what shall I answer? To confess it
Will raise a blush upon a virgin's face;
Yet I was ever taught 'twas base to lie.
POLYDAMAS   You've been too bold, and you must love no more.

245 PALMYRA   Indeed I must; I cannot help my love;
          I was so tender when I took the bent,
          That now I grow that way.
     POLYDAMAS   He is a prince, and you are meanly born.
     LEONIDAS   Love either finds equality, or makes it;
250   Like death, he knows no difference in degrees,
          But plains, and levels all.
     PALMYRA   Alas! I had not rendered up my heart,
          Had he not loved me first; but he preferred me
          Above the maidens of my age and rank;
255   Still shunned their company, and still sought mine.
          I was not won by gifts, yet still he gave;
          And all his gifts, though small, yet spoke his love.
          He picked the earliest strawberries in woods,
          The clustered filberts, and the purple grapes;
260   He taught a prating stare to speak my name,
          And when he found a nest of nightingales
          Or callow linnets, he would show 'em me,
          And let me take 'em out.
     POLYDAMAS   This is a little mistress, meanly born,
265   Fit only for a prince's vacant hours,
          And then, to laugh at her simplicity,
          Not fix a passion there. Now hear my sentence.
     LEONIDAS   Remember, ere you give it, 'tis pronounced
          Against us both.
270 POLYDAMAS   First, in her hand
          There shall be placed a player's painted sceptre,
          And, on her head, a gilded pageant crown:
          Thus shall she go,
          With all the boys attending on her triumph;
275   That done, be put alone into a boat,
          With bread and water only for three days;
          So on the sea she shall be set adrift,
          And who relieves her dies.
     PALMYRA   I only beg that you would execute
280   The last part first: let me be put to sea;
          The bread and water for my three days' life
          I give you back, I would not live so long;
          But let me 'scape the shame.
     LEONIDAS   Look to me, piety; and you, O gods, look to my piety:

261 stare] Starling.

Keep me from saying that which misbecomes a son;   285
But let me die before I see this done.
POLYDAMAS   If you for ever will abjure her sight,
I can be yet a father; she shall live.
LEONIDAS   Hear, O you pow'rs, is this to be a father?
I see 'tis all my happiness and quiet   290
You aim at, sir; and take 'em:
I will not save even my Palmyra's life
At that ignoble price; but I'll die with her.
PALMYRA   So had I done by you,
Had fate made me a princess. Death, methinks,   295
Is not a terror now:
He is not fierce, or grim, but fawns, and soothes me,
And slides along, like Cleopatra's aspick,
Offering his service to my troubled breast.
LEONIDAS   Begin what you have purposed when you please;   300
Lead her to scorn, your triumph shall be doubled.
As holy priests
In pity go with dying malefactors,
So I will share her shame.
POLYDAMAS   You shall not have your will so much; first part 'em,   305
Then execute your office.
LEONIDAS   No; I'll die
In her defence.

[Draws his sword.

PALMYRA   Ah, hold, and pull not on
A curse, to make me worthy of my death:
Do not by lawless force oppose your father,
Whom you have too much disobeyed for me.   310
LEONIDAS   Here, take it, sir, and with it pierce my heart:

[*Presenting his sword to his* Father *upon his knees.*

You have done more in taking my Palmyra.
You are my father, therefore I submit.
POLYDAMAS   Keep him from anything he may design
Against his life, while the first fury lasts;   315
And now perform what I commanded you.
LEONIDAS   In vain; if sword and poison be denied me,
I'll hold my breath and die.
PALMYRA   Farewell, my last, Leonidas; yet live,
I charge you live, 'till you believe me dead.   320
I cannot die in peace, if you die first.

If life's a blessing, you shall have it last.
POLYDAMAS   Go on with her, and lead him after me.

Enter ARGALEON *hastily, with* HERMOGENES.

ARGALEON   I bring you, sir, such news as must amaze you,
325   And such as will prevent you from an action
Which would have rendered all your life unhappy.

[HERMOGENES *kneels.*

POLYDAMAS   Hermogenes, you bend your knees in vain,
My doom's already past.
HERMOGENES   I kneel not for Palmyra, for I know
330   She will not need my pray'rs; but for myself:
With a feigned tale I have abused your ears,
And therefore merit death; but since, unforced,
I first accuse myself, I hope your mercy.
POLYDAMAS   Haste to explain your meaning.
335   HERMOGENES   Then, in few words, Palmyra is your daughter.
POLYDAMAS   How can I give belief to this impostor?
He who has once abused me, often may.
I'll hear no more.
ARGALEON   For your own sake, you must.
HERMOGENES   A parent's love (for I confess my crime)
340   Moved me to say Leonidas was yours;
But when I heard Palmyra was to die,
The fear of guiltless blood so stung my conscience,
That I resolved, ev'n with my shame, to save
Your daughter's life.
345   POLYDAMAS   But how can I be certain, but that interest,
Which moved you first to say your son was mine,
Does not now move you too, to save your daughter?
HERMOGENES   You had but then my word; I bring you now
Authentic testimonies. Sir, in short,

[*Delivers on his knees a jewel, and a letter.*

350   If this will not convince you, let me suffer.
POLYDAMAS   I know this jewel well; 'twas once my mother's,

[*Looking first on the jewel.*

Which, marrying, I presented to my wife.
And this, O this, is my Eudoxia's hand.   [*Reads.*
This was the pledge of love given to Eudoxia,

Who, dying, to her young Palmyra leaves it;   355
And this, when you, my dearest lord, receive,
Own her, and think on me, dying Eudoxia.
Take it; 'tis well there is no more to read,   [*To* ARGALEON.
My eyes grow full, and swim in their own light.

[He embraces PALMYRA.

PALMYRA   I fear, sir, this is your intended pageant.   360
   You sport yourself at poor Palmyra's cost;
   But if you think to make me proud,
   Indeed I cannot be so: I was born
   With humble thoughts, and lowly, like my birth.
   A real fortune could not make me haughty,   365
   Much less a feigned.
POLYDAMAS   This was her mother's temper.
   I have too much deserved thou shouldst suspect
   That I am not thy father; but my love
   Shall henceforth show I am. Behold my eyes,
   And see a father there begin to flow: 370
   This is not feigned, Palmyra.
PALMYRA   I doubt no longer, sir; you are a king,
   And cannot lie: falsehood's a vice too base
   To find a room in any royal breast.
   I know, in spite of my unworthiness,   375
   I am your child; for when you would have killed me,
   Methought I loved you then.
ARGALEON   Sir, we forget the prince Leonidas,
   His greatness should not stand neglected thus.
POLYDAMAS   Guards, you may now retire: give him his sword,   380
   And leave him free.
LEONIDAS   Then the first use I make of liberty
   Shall be, with your permission, mighty sir,
   To pay that reverence to which nature binds me.

[Kneels to HERMOGENES.

ARGALEON   Sure you forget your birth, thus to misplace   385
   This act of your obedience; you should kneel
   To nothing but to heav'n, and to a king.
LEONIDAS   I never shall forget what nature owes,
   Nor be ashamed to pay it; though my father
   Be not a king, I know him brave and honest,   390
   And well deserving of a worthier son.

POLYDAMAS   He bears it gallantly.
LEONIDAS   Why would you not instruct me, sir, before.

[*To* HERMOGENES.

Where I should place my duty?
395   From which, if ignorance have made me swerve,
I beg your pardon for an erring son.
PALMYRA   I almost grieve I am a princess, since
It makes him lose a crown.
LEONIDAS   And next, to you, my king, thus low I kneel,
400   T'implore your mercy; if in that small time
I had the honour to be thought your son,
I paid not strict obedience to your will.
I thought, indeed, I should not be compelled,
But thought it as your son; so what I took
405   In duty from you, I restored in courage,
Because your son should not be forced.
POLYDAMAS   You have my pardon for it.
LEONIDAS   To you, fair princess, I congratulate
Your birth; of which I ever thought you worthy:
410   And give me leave to add, that I am proud
The gods have picked me out to be the man
By whose dejected fate yours is to rise;
Because no man could more desire your fortune,
Or franklier part with his to make you great.
415   PALMYRA   I know the king, though you are not his son,
Will still regard you as my foster-brother,
And so conduct you downward from a throne,
By slow degrees, so unperceived and soft,
That it may seem no fall: or if it be,
420   My fortune lay a bed of down beneath you.
POLYDAMAS   He shall be ranked with my nobility,
And kept from scorn by a large pension given him.
LEONIDAS   You are all great and royal in your gifts;   [*Bowing.*
But at the donor's feet I lay 'em down:
425   Should I take riches from you, it would seem
As I did want a soul to bear that poverty
To which the gods designed my humble birth:
And should I take your honours without merit,
It would appear, I wanted manly courage
430   To hope 'em, in your service, from my sword.
POLYDAMAS   Still brave, and like yourself.

The court shall shine this night in its full splendour,
And celebrate this new discovery.
Argaleon, lead my daughter: as we go,
I shall have time to give her my commands,   435
In which you are concerned.   [*Exeunt all but* LEONIDAS.
LEONIDAS Methinks I do not want
That huge long train of fawning followers,
That swept a furlong after me.
'Tis true I am alone;   440
So was the Godhead ere he made the world,
And better served Himself, than served by nature.
And yet I have a soul
Above this humble fate. I could command,
Love to do good, give largely to true merit,   445
All that a king should do. But though these are not
My province, I have scene enough within,
To exercise my virtue.
All that a heart, so fixed as mine, can move,
Is, that my niggard fortune starves my love.   [*Exit.*   450

SCENE II

PALAMEDE *and* DORALICE *meet: she, with a book in her hand, seems to start at sight of him.*

DORALICE 'Tis a strange thing that no warning will serve your turn; and that no retirement will secure me from your impertinent addresses! Did I not tell you that I was to be private here at my devotions?

PALAMEDE Yes; and you see I have observed my cue exactly: I am come to relieve you from them. Come, shut up, shut up your book; the man's   5
come who is to supply all your necessities.

DORALICE Then, it seems, you are so impudent to think it was an assignation? This, I warrant, was your lewd interpretation of my innocent meaning.

PALAMEDE Venus forbid that I should harbour so unreasonable a   10
thought of a fair young lady, that you should lead me hither into temptation. I confess I might think indeed it was a kind of honourable challenge to meet privately without seconds, and decide the difference betwixt the two sexes; but heaven forgive me if I thought amiss.

DORALICE You thought too, I'll lay my life on't, that you might as well   15
make love to me, as my husband does to your mistress.

PALAMEDE I was so unreasonable to think so too.

DORALICE And then you wickedly inferred that there was some justice

20   in the revenge of it; or at least but little injury for a man to endeavour
to enjoy that which he counts a blessing, and which is not valued as it
ought by the dull possessor. Confess your wickedness, did you not think
so?

PALAMEDE   I confess I was thinking so as fast as I could; but you think so
much before me, that you will let me think nothing.

25 DORALICE   'Tis the very thing that I designed: I have forestalled all your
arguments, and left you without a word more to plead for mercy. If you
have anything farther to offer, ere sentence pass — Poor animal, I brought
you hither only for my diversion.

PALAMEDE   That you may have, if you'll make use of me the right way;
30   but I tell thee, woman, I am now past talking.

DORALICE   But it may be I came hither to hear what fine things you
could say for yourself.

PALAMEDE   You would be very angry, to my knowledge, if I should lose
so much time to say many of 'em. — By this hand you would!

35 DORALICE   Fie, Palamede, I am a woman of honour.

PALAMEDE   I see you are; you have kept touch with your assignation:
and before we part, you shall find that I am a man of honour . . . yet I
have one scruple of conscience—

DORALICE   I warrant you will not want some naughty argument or
40   other to satisfy yourself. — I hope you are afraid of betraying your friend?

PALAMEDE   Of betraying my friend! I am more afraid of being betrayed
by you to my friend. You women now are got into the way of telling first
yourselves: a man, who has any care of his reputation, will be loth to trust
it with you.

45 DORALICE   O, you charge your faults upon our sex! You men are like
cocks; you never make love, but you clap your wings, and crow when you
have done.

PALAMEDE   Nay, rather you women are like hens; you never lay, but
you cackle an hour after, to discover your nest. — But I'll venture it for
50   once.

DORALICE   To convince you that you are in the wrong, I'll retire into the
dark grotto to my devotion, and make so little noise, that it shall be
impossible for you to find me.

PALAMEDE   But if I find you—

55 DORALICE   Ay, if you find me — But I'll put you to search in more
corners than you imagine.   [*She runs in, and he after her.*

Enter RHODOPHIL *and* MELANTHA.

MELANTHA   Let me die, but this solitude, and that grotto are scandalous; I'll go no further; besides, you have a sweet lady of your own.

RHODOPHIL   But a sweet mistress, now and then, makes my sweet lady
so much more sweet.   60
MELANTHA   I hope you will not force me?
RHODOPHIL   But I will, if you desire it.
PALAMEDE [*within*]   Where the devil are you, madam? 'Sdeath, I begin
to be weary of this hide and seek: if you stay a little longer, till the fit's
over, I'll hide in my turn, and put you to the finding me.   65

He enters and sees RHODOPHIL *and* MELANTHA.

How! Rhodophil and my mistress!
MELANTHA   My servant to apprehend me! This is *surprenant au dernier*.
RHODOPHIL   I must on; there's nothing but impudence can help me
out.
PALAMEDE   Rhodophil, how came you hither in so good company.   70
RHODOPHIL   As you see, Palamede; an effect of pure friendship; I was
not able to live without you.
PALAMEDE   But what makes my mistress with you?
RHODOPHIL   Why, I heard you were here alone, and could not in
civility but bring her to you.   75
MELANTHA   You'll pardon the effects of a passion which I may now
avow for you, if it transported me beyond the rules of *bienséance*.
PALAMEDE   But who told you I was here? they that told you that may
tell you more, for aught I know.
RHODOPHIL   O, for that matter, we had intelligence.   80
PALAMEDE   But let me tell you, we came hither so very privately, that
you could not trace us.
RHODOPHIL   Us? What us? You are alone.
PALAMEDE   Us! The devil's in me for mistaking: me, I meant. Or us,
that is, you are me, or I you, as we are friends: that's us.   85
DORALICE   Palamede, Palamede!   [*Within.*
RHODOPHIL   I should know that voice; who's within there, that calls
you?
PALAMEDE   Faith, I can't imagine; I believe the place is haunted.
DORALICE   Palamede, Palamede, all cocks hidden.   [*Within.*   90
PALAMEDE   Lord, lord, what shall I do? Well, dear friend, to let you see
I scorn to be jealous, and that I dare trust my mistress with you, take her
back, for I would not willingly have her frighted, and I am resolved to see
who's there; I'll not be daunted with a bugbear, that's certain: prithee

67   *surprenant au dernier*] Extremely surprising.
77   *bienséance*] Propriety, decorum.
90   all cocks hidden] This is perhaps a cry in a sport or game.

95   dispute it not, it shall be so; nay, do not put me to swear, but go quickly:
     there's an effort of pure friendship for you now.

Enter DORALICE, *and looks amazed, seeing them.*

RHODOPHIL   Doralice! I am thunder-struck to see you here.

PALAMEDE   So am I! Quite thunder-struck. Was it you that called me
     within? (I must be impudent.)

100 RHODOPHIL   How came you hither, spouse?

PALAMEDE   Ay, how came you hither? And which is more, how could
     you be here without my knowledge?

DORALICE [*to her husband*]   O, gentleman, have I caught you i'faith!
     Have I broke forth in an ambush upon you! I thought my suspicions

105 would prove true.

RHODOPHIL   Suspicions? This is very fine, spouse! Prithee, what suspi-
     cions?

DORALICE   O, you feign ignorance: why, of you and Melantha; here
     have I stayed these two hours, waiting with all the rage of a passionate,

110 loving wife, but infinitely jealous, to take you two in the manner; for
     hither I was certain you would come.

RHODOPHIL   But you are mistaken, spouse, in the occasion; for we
     came hither on purpose to find Palamede, on intelligence he was gone
     before.

115 PALAMEDE   I'll be hanged then if the same party who gave you intellig-
     ence I was here, did not tell your wife you would come hither. Now I
     smell the malice on't on both sides.

DORALICE   Was it so, think you? nay, then I'll confess my part of the
     malice too. As soon as ever I spied my husband and Melantha come

120 together, I had a strange temptation to make him jealous in revenge; and
     that made me call Palamede, Palamede, as though there had been an
     intrigue between us.

MELANTHA   Nay, I avow, there was an apparence of an intrigue be-
     tween us too.

125 PALAMEDE   To see how things will come about!

RHODOPHIL   And was it only thus, my dear Doralice?   [*Embrace.*

DORALICE   And did I wrong none, Rhodophil, with a false suspicion?

                                                    [*Embracing him.*

PALAMEDE [*aside*]   Now I am confident we had all four the same design:
     'tis a pretty odd kind of game this, where each of us plays for double

130 stakes. This is just thrust and parry with the same motion; I am to get his
     wife, and yet to guard my own mistress. But I am vilely suspicious that,
     while I conquer in the right wing, I shall be routed in the left; for both

our women will certainly betray their party, because they are each of
them for gaining of two, as well as we; and I much fear,   135
    If their necessities and ours were known,
    They have more need of two, than we of one.

                                   [Exeunt, embracing one another.

ACT IV

SCENE I

Enter LEONIDAS, *musing*; AMALTHEA, *following him*.

AMALTHEA   Yonder he is, and I must speak or die;
    And yet 'tis death to speak; yet he must know
    I have a passion for him, and may know it
    With a less blush; because to offer it
    To his low fortunes, shows I loved before   5
    His person, not his greatness.
LEONIDAS   First scorned, and now commanded from the court!
    The king is good; but he is wrought to this
    By proud Argaleon's malice.
    What more disgrace can love and fortune join   10
    T'inflict upon one man? I cannot now
    Behold my dear Palmyra: she, perhaps, too,
    Is grown ashamed of a mean ill-placed love.
AMALTHEA   Assist me, Venus, for I tremble when
    I am to speak, but I must force myself.   *[Aside.* 15
    Sir, I would crave but one short minute with you,
    And some few words.
LEONIDAS   The proud Argaleon's sister!   *[Aside.*
AMALTHEA   Alas, it will not out; shame stops my mouth. *[Aside.*
    Pardon my error, sir; I was mistaken,
    And took you for another.   20
LEONIDAS   In spite of all his guards, I'll see Palmyra; *[Aside.*
    Though meanly born, I have a kingly soul.
AMALTHEA   I stand upon a precipice, where fain
    I would retire, but love still thrusts me on:
    Now I grow bolder, and will speak to him.   *[Aside.* 25
    Sir, 'tis indeed to you that I would speak,
    And if—
LEONIDAS   O, you are sent to scorn my fortunes;

Your sex and beauty are your privilege;
But should your brother—
30   AMALTHEA   Now he looks angry, and I dare not speak.
I had some business with you, sir,
But 'tis not worth your knowledge.
LEONIDAS   Then 'twill be charity to let me mourn
My griefs alone, for I am much disordered.
35   AMALTHEA   'Twill be more charity to mourn 'em with you:
Heav'n knows I pity you.
LEONIDAS   Your pity, madam,
Is generous, but 'tis unavailable.
AMALTHEA   You know not till 'tis tried.
Your sorrows are no secret; you have lost
40   A crown, and mistress.
LEONIDAS   Are not these enough?
Hang two such weights on any other soul,
And see if it can bear 'em.
AMALTHEA   More; you are banished, by my brother's means,
And ne'er must hope again to see your princess;
45   Except as prisoners view fair walks and streets,
And careless passengers going by their grates,
To make 'em feel the want of liberty.
But worse than all,
The king this morning has enjoined his daughter
50   T'accept my brother's love.
LEONIDAS   Is this your pity?
You aggravate my griefs, and print 'em deeper,
In new and heavier stamps.
AMALTHEA   'Tis as physicians show the desperate ill,
T'endear their art, by mitigating pains
55   They cannot wholly cure: when you despair
Of all you wish, some part of it, because
Unhoped for, may be grateful; and some other—
LEONIDAS   What other?
AMALTHEA   Some other may—
60   My shame again has seized me, and I can go
No farther.   [Aside.
LEONIDAS   These often failing sighs and interruptions
Make me imagine you have grief like mine:
Have you ne'er loved.

37 unavailable] Of no avail.
46 passengers] Passers-by.

AMALTHEA   I? never! — 'Tis in vain;
  I must despair in silence.   [*Aside.*   65
LEONIDAS   You come as I suspected then, to mock,
  At least observe, my griefs: take it not ill
  That I must leave you.   [*Is going.*
AMALTHEA   You must not go with these unjust opinions.
  Command my life and fortunes: you are unwise;   70
  Think, and think well, what I can do to serve you.
LEONIDAS   I have but one thing in my thoughts and wishes:
  If by your means I can obtain the sight
  Of my adored Palmyra; or, what's harder,
  One minute's time, to tell her I die hers.   [*She starts back.*   75
  I see I am not to expect it from you;
  Nor could, indeed, with reason.
AMALTHEA   Name any other thing; is Amalthea
  So despicable, she can serve your wishes
  In this alone?
LEONIDAS   If I should ask of heav'n,   80
  I have no other suit.
AMALTHEA   To show you, then, I can deny you nothing,
  Though 'tis more hard to me than any other,
  Yet I will do it for you.
LEONIDAS   Name quickly, name the means! Speak, my good angel!   85
AMALTHEA   Be not so much o'erjoyed; for, if you are,
  I'll rather die than do't. This night the court
  Will be in masquerade;
  You shall attend on me; in that disguise
  You may both see and speak to her, if you   90
  Dare venture it.
LEONIDAS   Yes, were a god her guardian,
  And bore in each hand thunder, I would venture.
AMALTHEA   Farewell then; two hours hence I will expect you:
  My heart's so full, that I can stay no longer.   [*Exit.*
LEONIDAS   Already it grows dusky; I'll prepare   95
  With haste for my disguise. But who are these?

Enter HERMOGENES *and* EUBULUS.

HERMOGENES   'Tis he; we need not fear to speak to him.
EUBULUS   Leonidas.
LEONIDAS   Sure I have known that voice.
HERMOGENES   You have some reason, sir: 'tis Eubulus,
  Who bred you with the princess: and, departing,   100

Bequeathed you to my care.

LEONIDAS   My foster-father! Let my knees express
My joys for your return!   [*Kneeling.*

EUBULUS   Rise, sir, you must not kneel.

LEONIDAS   E'er since you left me,
105   I have been wand'ring in a maze of fate,
Led by false fires of a fantastic glory,
And the vain lustre of imagined crowns.
But, ah! why would you leave me? or how could you
Absent yourself so long?

110   EUBULUS   I'll give you a most just account of both:
And something more I have to tell you, which
I know must cause your wonder; but this place,
Though almost hid in darkness, is not safe.
Already I discern some coming towards us   [*Torches appear.*
115   With lights, who may discover me. Hermogenes,
Your lodgings are hard by, and much more private.

HERMOGENES   There you may freely speak.

LEONIDAS   Let us make haste;
For some affairs, and of no small importance.
Call me another way.   [*Exeunt.*

Enter PALAMEDE *and* RHODOPHIL, *with vizor-masks in their hands,
and torches before 'em*

120   PALAMEDE   We shall have noble sport tonight, Rhodophil; this mas-
querading is a most glorious invention.

RHODOPHIL   I believe it was invented first by some jealous lover, to
discover the haunts of his jilting mistress; or perhaps, by some distressed
servant, to gain an opportunity with a jealous man's wife.

125   PALAMEDE   No, it must be the invention of a woman, it has so much of
subtlety and love in it.

RHODOPHIL   I am sure 'tis extremely pleasant; for to go unknown is the
next degree to going invisible.

PALAMEDE   What with our antic habits and feigned voices, *Do you know*
130   *me? and I know you?* methinks we move and talk just like so many
overgrown puppets.

RHODOPHIL   Masquerade is only vizor-mask improved; a heightening
of the same fashion.

PALAMEDE   No, masquerade is vizor-mask in debauch, and I like it the
135   better for't: for, with a vizor-mask, we fool ourselves into courtship, for
the sake of an eye that glanced, or a hand that stole itself out of the glove,
sometimes, to give us a sample of the skin; but in masquerade there is

nothing to be known, she's all *terra incognita*, and the bold discoverer leaps ashore, and takes his lot among the wild Indians and savages without the vile consideration of safety to his person, or of beauty or   140
wholesomeness in his mistress.

Enter BELIZA.

RHODOPHIL   Beliza, what make you here?

BELIZA   Sir, my lady sent me after you, to let you know she finds herself a little indisposed; so that she cannot be at court, but is retired to rest in her own apartment, where she shall want the happiness of your dear   145
embraces tonight.

RHODOPHIL   A very fine phrase, Beliza, to let me know my wife desires to lie alone.

PALAMEDE   I doubt, Rhodophil, you take the pains sometimes to instruct your wife's woman in these elegancies.   150

RHODOPHIL   Tell my dear lady, that since I must be so unhappy as not to wait on her tonight, I will lament bitterly for her absence. 'Tis true I shall be at court, but I will take no divertisement there; and when I return to my solitary bed, if I am so forgetful of my passion as to sleep, I will dream of her; and betwixt sleep and waking, put out my foot   155
towards her side for midnight consolation; and not finding her, I will sigh and imagine myself a most desolate widower.

BELIZA   I shall do your commands, sir.   [*Exit*.

RHODOPHIL [*aside*]   She's sick as aptly for my purpose as if she had contrived it so. Well, if ever woman was a help-mate for man, my spouse   160
is so; for within this hour I received a note from Melantha that she would meet this evening in masquerade in boy's habit, to rejoice with me before she entered into fetters: for I find she loves me better than Palamede, only because he's to be her husband. There's something of antipathy in the word *marriage* to the nature of love; marriage is the mere ladle of   165
affection, that cools it when 'tis never so fiercely boiling over.

PALAMEDE   Dear Rhodophil, I must needs beg your pardon; there is an occasion fall'n out which I had forgot: I cannot be at court tonight.

RHODOPHIL   Dear Palamede, I am sorry we shall not have one course together at the herd; but I find your game lies single: good fortune to you   170
with your mistress.   [*Exit*.

PALAMEDE   He has wished me good fortune with his wife: there's no sin in this then, there's fair leave given. Well, I must go visit the sick; I cannot resist the temptations of my charity. O what a difference will she find betwixt a dull resty husband and a quick vigorous lover! He sets out   175

175 resty] Indolent, lazy.

like a carrier's horse, plodding on, because he knows he must, with the
bells of matrimony chiming so melancholy about his neck, in pain till
he's at his journey's end; and, despairing to get thither, he is fain to
fortify imagination with the thoughts of another woman: I take heat after
180   heat, like a well-breathed courser, and – But hark, what noise is that?
Swords! [*Clashing of swords within*] Nay, then have with you.

[*Exit* PALAMEDE.

Re-enter PALAMEDE, *with* RHODOPHIL; *and* DORALICE *in man's
habit*.

RHODOPHIL   Friend, your relief was very timely, otherwise I had been
oppressed.
PALAMEDE   What was the quarrel?
185   RHODOPHIL   What I did was in rescue of this youth.
PALAMEDE   What cause could he give 'em?
DORALICE   The cause was nothing but only the common cause of
fighting in masquerades: they were drunk, and I was sober.
RHODOPHIL   Have they not hurt you?
190   DORALICE   No; but I am exceeding ill with the fright on't.
PALAMEDE   Let's lead him to some place where he may refresh himself.
RHODOPHIL   Do you conduct him then.
PALAMEDE [*aside*]   How cross this happens to my design of going to
Doralice! for I am confident she was sick on purpose that I should visit
195   her. Hark you, Rhodophil, could not you take care of the stripling? I am
partly engaged tonight.
RHODOPHIL   You know I have business; but come, youth, if it must be
so.
DORALICE [*to* RHODOPHIL]   No, good sir, do not give yourself that
200   trouble; I shall be safer, and better pleased with your friend here.
RHODOPHIL   Farewell then; once more I wish you a good adventure.
PALAMEDE   Damn this kindness! Now must I be troubled with this
young rogue, and miss my opportunity with Doralice.

[*Exit* RHODOPHIL *alone*; PALAMEDE *with* DORALICE.

SCENE II

Enter POLYDAMAS.

POLYDAMAS   Argaleon counselled well to banish him;
He has, I know not what,
Of greatness in his looks, and of high fate,

That almost awes me; but I fear my daughter,
Who hourly moves me for him; and I marked   5
She sighed when I but named Argaleon to her.
But see, the maskers. Hence my cares, this night
At least take truce, and find me on my pillow.

Enter the Princess *in masquerade, with* Ladies. *At the other end,*
ARGALEON *and* Gentlemen *in masquerade; then* LEONIDAS *leading*
AMALTHEA. *The king sits. A Dance. After the Dance,*

AMALTHEA [*to* LEONIDAS]   That's the princess;
I saw the habit ere she put it on.   10
LEONIDAS   I know her by a thousand other signs,
She cannot hide so much divinity.
Disguised, and silent, yet some graceful motion
Breaks from her, and shines round her like a glory.

[*Goes to* PALMYRA.

AMALTHEA   Thus she reveals herself, and knows it not: 15
Like love's dark lantern I direct his steps,
And yet he sees not that which gives him light.
PALMYRA   I know you; but, alas, Leonidas,
Why should you tempt this danger on yourself?
LEONIDAS   Madam, you know me not, if you believe   20
I would not hazard greater for your sake.
But you, I fear, are changed.
PALMYRA   No, I am still the same;
But there are many things became Palmyra,
Which ill become the princess.
LEONIDAS   I ask nothing   25
Which honour will not give you leave to grant:
One hour's short audience at my father's house
You cannot sure refuse me.
PALMYRA   Perhaps I should, did I consult strict virtue;
But something must be given to love and you.   30
When would you I should come?
LEONIDAS   This evening, with the speediest opportunity.
I have a secret to discover to you,
Which will surprise and please you.
PALMYRA   'Tis enough.
Go now, for we may be observed and known.   35
I trust your honour; give me not occasion
To blame myself or you.

LEONIDAS   You never shall repent your good opinion.

[*Kisses her hand, and exit.*

ARGALEON   I cannot be deceived; that is the princess:
40   One of her maids betrayed the habit to me.
       But who was he with whom she held discourse?
       'Tis one she favours, for he kissed her hand.
       Our shapes are like, our habits near the same,
       She may mistake and speak to me for him.
45   I am resolved, I'll satisfy my doubts,
       Though to be more tormented.

SONG

1.

Whilst Alexis lay prest
   In her arms he loved best,
With his hands round her neck,
50   *And his head on her breast,*
He found the fierce pleasure too hasty to stay,
And his soul in the tempest just flying away.

2.

When Caelia saw this,
With a sigh and a kiss,
55   *She cried, Oh my dear, I am robbed of my bliss!*
'Tis unkind to your love, and unfaithfully done,
To leave me behind you, and die all alone.

3.

The youth, though in haste,
And breathing his last,
60   *In pity died slowly, while she died more fast;*
Till at length she cried, — Now, my dear, now let us go,
Now die, my Alexis, and I will die too.

4.

Thus entranced they did lie,
Till Alexis did try
65   *To recover new breath, that again he might die:*
Then often they died; but the more they did so,
The nymph died more quick, and the shepherd more slow.

57 die] With a sexual meaning.

Another Dance. After it, ARGALEON *re-enters, and stands by the* Princess.

PALMYRA   Leonidas, what means this quick return? [*To* ARGALEON.
ARGALEON   O heav'n! 'tis what I feared.
PALMYRA   Is aught of moment happened since you went?   70
ARGALEON   No, madam, but I understood not fully
    Your last commands.
PALMYRA   And yet you answered to 'em.
    Retire; you are too indiscreet a lover:
    I'll meet you where I promised.   [*Exit.*
ARGALEON   O my curst fortune! what have I discovered!   75
    But I will be revenged.   [*Whispers to the* King.
POLYDAMAS   But are you certain you are not deceived?
ARGALEON   Upon my life.
POLYDAMAS   Her honour is concerned.
    Somewhat I'll do; but I am yet distracted,
    And know not where to fix. I wished a child,   80
    And heav'n, in anger, granted my request.
    So blind we are, our wishes are so vain,
    That what we most desire, proves most our pain.   [*Exeunt omnes.*

SCENE III

An Eating-house. Bottles of wine on the table.
PALAMEDE, *and* DORALICE *in man's habit.*

DORALICE [*aside*]   Now cannot I find in my heart to discover myself,
    though I long he should know me.
PALAMEDE   I tell thee, boy, now I have seen thee safe, I must be gone: I
    have no leisure to throw away on thy raw conversation; I am a person that
    understands better things, I.   5
DORALICE   Were I a woman, oh how you would admire me! cry up every
    word I said, and screw your face into a submissive smile; as I have seen a
    dull gallant act wit, and counterfeit pleasantness, when he whispers to a
    great person in a play-house; smile and look briskly when the other
    answers, as if something of extraordinary had past betwixt 'em, when,   10
    heaven knows, there was nothing else but, What a clock does your
    lordship think it is? And my lord's *repartee* is, It is almost park-time: or,
    at most, Shall we out of the pit, and go behind the scenes for an act or
    two? And yet such fine things as these would be wit in a mistress's
    mouth.   15
PALAMEDE   Ay, boy; there's Dame Nature in the case: he who cannot
    find wit in a mistress, deserves to find nothing else, boy. But these are

riddles to thee, child, and I have not leisure to instruct thee; I have affairs
to dispatch, great affairs; I am a man of business.

20 DORALICE   Come, you shall not go: you have no affairs but what you
may dispatch here, to my knowledge.

PALAMEDE   I find now, thou art a boy of more understanding than I
thought thee; a very lewd wicked boy: o' my conscience, thou wouldst
debauch me, and hast some evil designs upon my person.

25 DORALICE   You are mistaken, sir; I would only have you show me a
more lawful reason why you would leave me, than I can why you should
not, and I'll not stay you; for I am not so young, but I understand the
necessities of flesh and blood, and the pressing occasions of mankind, as
well as you.

30 PALAMEDE   A very forward and understanding boy! Thou art in great
danger of a page's wit, to be brisk at fourteen, and dull at twenty. But I'll
give thee no further account; I must, and will go.

DORALICE   My life on't, your mistress is not at home.

PALAMEDE   This imp will make me very angry. — I tell thee, young sir,
35 she is at home, and at home for me; and which is more, she is abed for me,
and sick for me.

DORALICE   For you only?

PALAMEDE   Ay, for me only.

DORALICE   But how do you know she's sick abed?

40 PALAMEDE   She sent her husband word so.

DORALICE   And are you such a novice in love, to believe a wife's message
to her husband?

PALAMEDE   Why, what the devil should be her meaning else?

DORALICE   It may be, to go in masquerade as well as you; to observe
45 your haunts, and keep you company without your knowledge.

PALAMEDE   Nay, I'll trust her for that: she loves me too well to disguise
herself from me.

DORALICE   If I were she, I would disguise on purpose to try
your wit; and come to my servant like a riddle — Read me, and
50 take me.

PALAMEDE   I could know her in any shape: my good genius would
prompt me to find out a handsome woman: there's something in her that
would attract me to her without my knowledge.

DORALICE   Then you make a loadstone of your mistress?

55 PALAMEDE   Yes, and I carry steel about me which has been so often
touched that it never fails to point to the north pole.

DORALICE   Yet still my mind gives me, that you have met her disguised
tonight, and have not known her.

PALAMEDE   This is the most pragmatical conceited little fellow, he will

needs understand my business better than myself. I tell thee once more,   60
thou dost not know my mistress.

DORALICE   And I tell you once more, that I know her better than you do.

PALAMEDE   The boy's resolved to have the last word. I find I must go
without reply.   [Exit.

DORALICE   Ah mischief, I have lost him with my fooling. Palamede,   65
Palamede!

He returns. She plucks off her peruke, and puts it on again when he knows her.

PALAMEDE   O heavens! is it you, madam?

DORALICE   Now, where was your good genius, that would prompt you
to find me out?

PALAMEDE   Why, you see I was not deceived; you yourself were my   70
good genius.

DORALICE   But where the steel, that knew the loadstone? Ha?

PALAMEDE   The truth is, madam, the steel has lost its virtue; and
therefore, if you please, we'll new touch it.

Enter RHODOPHIL; *and* MELANTHA *in boy's habit*
RHODOPHIL *sees* PALAMEDE *kissing* DORALICE's *hand.*

RHODOPHIL   Palamede again! Am I fall'n into your quarters? What?   75
Engaging with a boy? Is all honourable?

PALAMEDE   Oh, very honourable in my side. I was just chastising this
young villain; he was running away, without paying his share of the
reckoning,

RHODOPHIL   Then I find I was deceived in him.   80

PALAMEDE   Yes, you are deceived in him: 'tis the archest rogue, if you
did but know him.

MELANTHA   Good Rhodophil, let us get off *à la dérobée*, for fear I should
be discovered.

RHODOPHIL   There's no retiring now; I warrant you for discovery. Now   85
have I the oddest thought, to entertain you before your servant's face, and
he never the wiser; 'twill be the prettiest juggling trick to cheat him
when he looks upon us.

MELANTHA   This is the strangest *caprice* in you.

PALAMEDE [*to* DORALICE]   This Rhodophil's the unluckiest fellow to   90
me! This is now the second time he has barred the dice when we were just
ready to have nicked him; but if ever I get the box again—

DORALICE   Do you think he will not know me? Am I like myself?

85 warrant you for] Give assurance (that we will not be discovered).
91 barred the dice] Declared the throw void.
92 nicked] In the game of hazard, a nick is a winning throw.

PALAMEDE   No more than a picture in the hangings.

95   DORALICE   Nay, then he can never discover me, now the wrong side of
the arras is turned towards him.

PALAMEDE   At least, it will be some pleasure to me to enjoy what
freedom I can while he looks on; I will storm the outworks of matrimony
even before his face.

100 RHODOPHIL   What wine have you there, Palamede?

PALAMEDE   Old Chios, or the rogue's damn'd that drew it.

RHODOPHIL   Come, to the most constant of mistresses, that I believe is
yours, Palamede.

DORALICE   Pray spare your seconds; for my part I am but a weak
105 brother.

PALAMEDE   Now, to the truest of turtles; that is your wife Rhodophil,
that lies sick at home in the bed of honour.

RHODOPHIL   Now let's have one common health, and so have done.

DORALICE   Then, for once, I'll begin it. Here's to him that has the
110 fairest lady of Sicily in masquerade tonight.

PALAMEDE   This is such an obliging health, I'll kiss thee, dear rogue,
for thy invention.   [Kisses her.

RHODOPHIL   He who has this lady is a happy man, without dispute. —
I'm most concerned in this, I am sure.   [Aside.

115 PALAMEDE   Was it not well found out, Rhodophil?

MELANTHA   Ay, this was *bien trouvée* indeed.

DORALICE [*to* MELANTHA] I suppose I shall do you a kindness to
inquire if you have not been in France, sir?

MELANTHA   To do you service, sir.

120 DORALICE   O, monsieur, *votre valet bien humble*.   [Saluting her.

MELANTHA   *Votre esclave, monsieur, de tout mon cœur.*

[Returning the salute.

DORALICE   I suppose, sweet sir, you are the hope and joy of some
thriving citizen, who has pinched himself at home, to breed you abroad,
where you have learned your exercises, as it appears, most awkwardly,
125 and are returned with the addition of a new-laced bosom and a clap, to
your good old father, who looks at you with his mouth, while you spout
French with your *mon monsieur*.

PALAMEDE   Let me kiss thee again for that, dear rogue.

MELANTHA   And you, I imagine, are my young master, whom your
130 mother durst not trust upon salt-water, but left you to be your own tutor

94 hangings] Tapestries.
101 Chios] From the island of Chios in the Aegean.
104 seconds] Second drinks.

at fourteen, to be very brisk and *entreprenant*, to endeavour to be debauched ere you have learned the knack on't, to value yourself upon a clap before you can get it, and to make it the height of your ambition to get a player for your mistress.

RHODOPHIL [*embracing* MELANTHA] O dear young bully, thou hast 135
tickled him with a *repartee*, i'faith.

MELANTHA You are one of those that applaud our country plays, where drums, and trumpets, and blood, and wounds, are wit.

RHODOPHIL Again, my boy? Let me kiss thee most abundantly.

DORALICE You are an admirer of the dull French poetry, which is so 140
thin that it is the very leaf-gold of wit, the very wafers and whipped cream of sense, for which a man opens his mouth, and gapes, to swallow nothing: and to be an admirer of such profound dullness, one must be endowed with a great perfection of impudence and ignorance.

PALAMEDE Let me embrace thee most vehemently. 145

MELANTHA I'll sacrifice my life for French poetry.   [*Advancing.*

DORALICE I'll die upon the spot for our country wit.

RHODOPHIL [*to* MELANTHA] Hold, hold, young Mars! Palamede, draw back your hero.

PALAMEDE 'Tis time; I shall be drawn in for a second else at the wrong 150
weapon.

MELANTHA O that I were a man for thy sake!

DORALICE You'll be a man as soon as I shall.

Enter a Messenger to RHODOPHIL.

MESSENGER Sir, the king has instant business with you.
I saw the guard drawn up by your lieutenant, 155
Before the palace gate, ready to march.

RHODOPHIL 'Tis somewhat sudden; say that I am coming.

[Exit Messenger.

Now, Palamede, what think you of this sport?
This is some sudden tumult: will you along?

PALAMEDE Yes, yes, I will go; but the devil take me if ever I was less in humour. Why the pox could they not have stayed their tumult till tomorrow? Then I had done my business, and been ready for them. Truth is, I had a little transitory crime to have committed first; and I am the worst man in the world at repenting, till a sin be thoroughly done: but what shall we do with the two boys? 165

RHODOPHIL Let them take a lodging in the house 'till the business be over.

DORALICE What, lie with a boy? For my part, I own it, I cannot endure to lie with a boy.

170 PALAMEDE   The more's my sorrow, I cannot accommodate you with a
 better bedfellow.

 MELANTHA   Let me die, if I enter into a pair of sheets with him that
 hates the French.

 DORALICE   Pish, take no care for us, but leave us in the streets; I warrant
175 you, as late as it is, I'll find my lodging as well as any drunken bully of
 'em all.

 RHODOPHIL   I'll fight in mere revenge, and wreak my passion
 On all that spoil this hopeful assignation.   [*Aside.*

 PALAMEDE   I'm sure we fight in a good quarrel:
180 Rogues may pretend religion, and the laws;
 But a kind mistress is the Good Old Cause.   [*Exeunt.*

SCENE IV

Enter PALMYRA, EUBULUS, *and* HERMOGENES.

PALMYRA   You tell me wonders; that Leonidas
 Is prince Theagenes, the late king's son.

EUBULUS   It seemed as strange to him, as now to you,
 Before I had convinced him; but, besides
5 His great resemblance to the king his father,
 The queen his mother lives, secured by me
 In a religious house, to whom each year
 I brought the news of his increasing virtues.
 My last long absence from you both was caused
10 By wounds, which in my journey I received,
 When set upon by thieves; I lost those jewels
 And letters, which your dying mother left.

HERMOGENES   The same he means, which since, brought to the king,
 Made him first know he had a child alive:
15 'Twas then my care of prince Leonidas
 Caused me to say he was th' usurper's son;
 Till after, forced by your apparent danger,
 I made the true discovery of your birth,
 And once more hid my prince's.

Enter LEONIDAS.

20 LEONIDAS   Hermogenes, and Eubulus, retire;
 Those of our party whom I left without
 Expect your aid and counsel.

      [*Exeunt* HERMOGENES *and* EUBULUS.

PALMYRA   I should, Leonidas, congratulate
   This happy change of your exalted fate;
   But, as my joy, so you my wonder move.   25
   Your looks have more of business than of love;
   And your last words some great design did show.
LEONIDAS   I frame not any to be hid from you;
   You, in my love, all my designs may see.
   But what have love and you designed for me?   30
   Fortune, once more, has set the balance right:
   First, equalled us in lowness; then, in height.
   Both of us have so long, like gamesters, thrown,
   Till fate comes round, and gives to each his own.
   As fate is equal, so may love appear: 35
   Tell me, at least, what I must hope, or fear.
PALMYRA   After so many proofs, how can you call
   My love in doubt? Fear nothing, and hope all.
   Think what a prince, with honour, may receive,
   Or I may give, without a parent's leave.   40
LEONIDAS   You give, and then restrain the grace you show;
   As ostentatious priests, when souls they woo,
   Promise their heav'n to all, but grant to few.
   But do for me, what I have dared for you.
   I did no argument from duty bring: 45
   Duty's a name, and love's a real thing.
PALMYRA   Man's love may, like wild torrents, overflow;
   Woman's as deep, but in its banks must go.
   My love is mine, and that I can impart;
   But cannot give my person, with my heart.   50
LEONIDAS   Your love is then no gift:
   For, when the person it does not convey,
   'Tis to give gold, and not to give the key.
PALMYRA   Then ask my father.
LEONIDAS   He detains my throne;
   Who holds back mine, will hardly give his own.   55
PALMYRA   What then remains?
LEONIDAS   That I must have recourse
   To arms, and take my love and crown by force.
   Hermogenes is forming the design;
   And with him all the brave and loyal join.
PALMYRA   And is it thus you court Palmyra's bed?   60
   Can she the murd'rer of her parent wed?
   Desist from force: so much you well may give

To love, and me, to let my father live.

LEONIDAS   Each act of mine my love to you has shown;
65   But you, who tax my want of it, have none.
You bid me part with you, and let him live;
But they should nothing ask, who nothing give.

PALMYRA   I give what virtue and what duty can,
In vowing ne'er to wed another man.

70   LEONIDAS   You will be forced to be Argaleon's wife.

PALMYRA   I'll keep my promise, though I lose my life.

LEONIDAS   Then you lose love, for which we both contend;
For life is but the means, but love's the end.

PALMYRA   Our souls shall love hereafter.

LEONIDAS   I much fear,
75   That soul, which could deny the body here
To taste of love, would be a niggard there.

PALMYRA   Then 'tis past hope: our cruel fate, I see,
Will make a sad divorce 'twixt you and me.
For, if you force employ, by heav'n I swear,
80   And all blessed beings—

LEONIDAS   Your rash oath forbear.

PALMYRA   I never—

LEONIDAS   Hold once more. But yet, as he
Who 'scapes a dang'rous leap, looks back to see;
So I desire, now I am past my fear,
To know what was that oath you meant to swear.

85   PALMYRA   I meant that if you hazarded your life,
Or sought my father's, ne'er to be your wife.

LEONIDAS   See now, Palmyra, how unkind you prove!
Could you, with so much ease, forswear my love?

PALMYRA   You force me with your ruinous design.

90   LEONIDAS   Your father's life is more your care, than mine.

PALMYRA   You wrong me: 'tis not, though it ought to be;
You are my care, heav'n knows, as well as he.

LEONIDAS   If now the execution I delay,
My honour, and my subjects, I betray.
95   All is prepared for the just enterprise;
And the whole city will tomorrow rise.
The leaders of the party are within,
And Eubulus has sworn that he will bring,
To head their arms, the person of their king.

100   PALMYRA   In telling this, you make me guilty too;
I therefore must discover what I know;

What honour bids you do, nature bids me prevent;
But kill me first, and then pursue your black intent.
LEONIDAS   Palmyra, no; you shall not need to die;
Yet I'll not trust so strict a piety.   105
Within there!

Enter EUBULUS.

Eubulus, a guard prepare;
Here, I commit this pris'ner to your care.

[*Kisses* PALMYRA's *hand, then gives it to* EUBULUS.

PALMYRA   Leonidas, I never thought these bands
Could e'er be giv'n me by a lover's hands.
LEONIDAS   Palmyra, thus your judge himself arraigns;   [*Kneeling.* 110
He, who imposed these bands, still wears your chains:
When you to love or duty false must be,
Or to your father guilty, or to me,
These chains, alone, remain to set you free.

[*Noise of swords clashing.*

POLYDAMAS [*within*]   Secure these, first; then search the inner room.   115
LEONIDAS   From whence do these tumultuous clamours come?

Enter HERMOGENES, *hastily.*

HERMOGENES   We are betrayed; and there remains alone
This comfort, that your person is not known.

Enter the King, ARGALEON, RHODOPHIL, PALAMEDE, Guards;
some like citizens, as prisoners.

POLYDAMAS   What mean these midnight consultations here,
Where I like an unsummoned guest appear?   120
LEONIDAS   Sir—
ARGALEON   There needs no excuse; 'tis understood;
You were all watching for your prince's good.
POLYDAMAS   My reverend city friends, you are well met!
On what great work were your grave wisdoms set?
Which of my actions were you scanning here?   125
What French invasion have you found to fear?
LEONIDAS   They are my friends; and come, sir, with intent
To take their leaves before my banishment.
POLYDAMAS   Your exile in both sexes friends can find:
I see the ladies, like the men, are kind.   [*Seeing* PALMYRA.   130

PALMYRA   Alas, I came but—   [*Kneeling.*
POLYDAMAS   Add not to your crime
  A lie: I'll hear you speak some other time.
  How? Eubulus! Nor time, nor thy disguise,
  Can keep thee undiscovered from my eyes.
135   A guard there! Seize 'em all.
RHODOPHIL   Yield, sir; what use of valour can be shown?
PALAMEDE   One, and unarmed, against a multitude!
LEONIDAS   O for a sword!

      [*He reaches at one of the* Guards' *halberds, and is seized behind.*

  I w'not lose my breath
  In fruitless prayers; but beg a speedy death.
140 PALMYRA   O spare Leonidas, and punish me.
POLYDAMAS   Mean girl, thou want'st an advocate for thee.
  Now the mysterious knot will be untied;
  Whether the young king lives, or where he died:
  Tomorrow's dawn shall the dark riddle clear,
145   Crown all my joys, and dissipate my fear.   [*Exeunt.*

ACT V

SCENE I

PALAMEDE, STRATON. PALAMEDE *with a letter in his hand.*

PALAMEDE   This evening, say'st thou? Will they both be here?
STRATON   Yes, sir, both my old master and your mistress's father. The
  old gentlemen ride hard this journey; they say it shall be the last time
  they will see the town; and both of 'em are so pleased with this marriage,
5   which they have concluded for you, that I am afraid they will live some
  years longer to trouble you with the joy of it.
PALAMEDE   But this is such an unreasonable thing, to impose upon me
  to be married tomorrow; 'tis hurrying a man to execution, without
  giving him time to say his prayers.
10 STRATON   Yet, if I might advise you, sir, you should not delay it; for
  your younger brother comes up with 'em, and is got already into their
  favours. He has gained much upon my old master, by finding fault with
  innkeepers' bills, and by starving us and our horses to show his frugality;
  and he is very well with your mistress's father, by giving him recipes for
15   the spleen, gout and scurvy, and other infirmities of old age.

PALAMEDE   I'll rout him and his country education. Pox on him, I
remember him before I travelled, he had nothing in him but mere
jockey; used to talk loud, and make matches, and was all for the crack of
the field: sense and wit were as much banished from his discourse as they
are when the court goes out of town to a horse race. Go now and provide   20
your master's lodgings.
STRATON   I go, sir.   [*Exit.*

PALAMEDE   It vexes me to the heart to leave all my designs with
Doralice unfinished; to have flown her so often to a mark, and still to be
bobbed at retrieve. If I had once enjoyed her, though I could not have   25
satisfied my stomach with the feast, at least I should have relished my
mouth a little; but now—

Enter PHILOTIS.

PHILOTIS   Oh, sir, you are happily met; I was coming to find you.
PALAMEDE   From your lady, I hope.
PHILOTIS   Partly from her, but more especially from myself: she has just   30
now received a letter from her father, with an absolute command to
dispose herself to marry you tomorrow.
PALAMEDE   And she takes it to the death?
PHILOTIS   Quite contrary: the letter could never have come in a more
lucky minute; for it found her in an ill humour with a rival of yours, that   35
shall be nameless, about the pronunciation of a French word.
PALAMEDE   Count Rhodophil? never disguise it, I know the amour: but
I hope you took the occasion to strike in for me?
PHILOTIS   It was my good fortune to do you some small service in it: for
your sake I discommended him all over: clothes, person, humour,   40
behaviour, everything; and to sum up all, told her it was impossible to
find a married man that was otherwise; for they were all so mortified at
home with their wives' ill humours, that they could never recover
themselves to be company abroad.
PALAMEDE   Most divinely urged!   45
PHILOTIS   Then I took occasion to commend your good qualities: as, the
sweetness of your humour, the comeliness of your person, your good
mien, your valour; but, above all, your liberality.
PALAMEDE   I vow to God I had like to have forgot that good quality in
myself, if thou hadst not remembered me on't: here are five pieces for   50
thee.
PHILOTIS   Lord, you have the softest hand, sir! it would do a woman

18–19 crack of the field] The best horses.
24 mark] The quarry of a hawk.
25 bobbed at retrieve] Cheated, at the second discovery and flight of the game.

good to touch it: Count Rhodophil's is not half so soft; for I remember I
felt it once, when he gave me ten pieces for my new-year's gift.

55 PALAMEDE   O, I understand you, madam; you shall find my hand as soft
as Count Rhodophil's: there are twenty pieces for you. The former was
but a retaining fee; now I hope you'll plead for me.

PHILOTIS   Your own merits speak enough. Be sure only to ply her with
French words, and I'll warrant you'll do your business. Here are a list of
60   her phrases for this day: use 'em to her upon all occasions, and foil her at
her own weapon; for she's like one of the old Amazons, she'll never
marry, except it be the man who has first conquered her.

PALAMEDE   I'll be sure to follow your advice: but you'll forget to further
my design.

65 PHILOTIS   What, do you think I'll be ungrateful? – But, however, if you
distrust my memory, put some token on my finger to remember it by:
that diamond there would do admirably.

PALAMEDE   There 'tis; and I ask your pardon heartily for calling your
memory into question: I assure you I'll trust it another time, without
70   putting you to the trouble of another token.

Enter PALMYRA *and* ARTEMIS.

ARTEMIS   Madam, this way the prisoners are to pass;
Here you may see Leonidas.
PALMYRA   Then here I'll stay, and follow him to death.

Enter MELANTHA *hastily*.

MELANTHA   O, here's her highness. Now is my time to introduce
75   myself, and to make my court to her, in my new French phrases. Stay, let
me read my catalogue – *suite, figure, chagrin, naïveté*, and *let me die*, for the
parenthis of all.

PALAMEDE [*aside*]   Do, persecute her; and I'll persecute thee as fast in
thy own dialect.

80 MELANTHA   Madam, the princess! Let me die, but this is a most horrid
spectacle, to see a person who makes so grand a figure in the court,
without the *suite* of a princess, and entertaining your *chagrin* all alone –
Naïveté should have been there, but the disobedient word would not
come in.   [*Aside.*

85 PALMYRA   What is she, Artemis?
ARTEMIS   An impertinent lady, madam; very ambitious of being known
to your highness.
PALAMEDE [*to* MELANTHA]   Let me die, madam, if I have not waited

you here these two long hours, without so much as the *suite* of a single
servant to attend me; entertaining myself with my own *chagrin*, till I had   90
the honour of seeing your ladyship, who are a person that makes so
considerable a figure in the court.

MELANTHA   Truce with your *douceurs*, good servant; you see I am
addressing to the princess; pray do not *embarrass* me – *Embarrass* me! what
a delicious French word do you make me lose upon you too!   95
[*To the* Princess] Your highness, madam, will please to pardon the *bévue*
which I made, in not sooner finding you out to be a princess: but let me
die if this *éclaircissement* which is made this day of your quality does not
ravish me; and give me leave to tell you—

PALAMEDE   But first give me leave to tell you, madam, that I have so   100
great a *tendre* for your person, and such a *penchant* to do you service,
that—

MELANTHA   What, must I still be troubled with your *sottises*?
(There's another word lost that I meant for the princess, with a mischief
to you.) But your highness, madam—   105

PALAMEDE   But your ladyship, madam—

Enter LEONIDAS *guarded, and led over the stage.*

MELANTHA   Out upon him, how he looks, madam! now he's found no
prince, he is the strangest figure of a man; how could I make that *coup
d'étourdi* to think him one?

PALMYRA   Away, impertinent. – my dear Leonidas!   110

LEONIDAS   My dear Palmyra!

PALMYRA   Death shall never part us; my destiny is yours.

[*He is led off; she follows.*

MELANTHA   Impertinent! Oh I am the most unfortunate person this day
breathing: that the princess should thus *rompre en visière*, without occasion. Let me die but I'll follow her to death, till I make my peace.   115

PALAMEDE [*holding her*]   And let me die, but I'll follow you to the
infernals till you pity me.

MELANTHA [*turning towards him angrily*]   Ay, 'tis long of you that this
malheur is fallen upon me; your impertinence has put me out of the good
graces of the princess, and all that, which has ruined me and all that, and   120
therefore let me die but I'll be revenged, and all that.

PALAMEDE   *Façon, façon*, you must and shall love me, and all that; for
my old man is coming up, and all that; and I am *désespéré au dernier*, and
will not be disinherited, and all that.

114 *rompre en visière*] Be openly hostile.
122 *Façon*] Mere affectation.

125 MELANTHA   How durst you interrupt me so *mal à propos*, when you
knew I was addressing to the princess?

PALAMEDE   But why would you address yourself so much *à contretemps*
then?

MELANTHA   Ah *mal peste!*

130 PALAMEDE   Ah *l'enragée.*

PHILOTIS   *Radoucissez vous, de grâce, madame; vous êtes bien en colère pour peu
de chose. Vous n'entendez pas la raillerie galante.*

MELANTHA   *A d'autres, à d'autres*: he mocks himself of me, he abuses
me: ah me unfortunate!   [*Cries.*

135 PHILOTIS   You mistake him, madam, he does but accommodate his
phrase to your refined language. *Ah qu'il est un cavalier accompli!* Pursue
your point, sir—   [*To him.*

PALAMEDE   *Ah qu'il fait beau dans ces bocages;*   [*Singing.*
Ah que le ciel donne un beau jour!

140 There I was with you, with a *minuet.*

MELANTHA   Let me die now, but this singing is fine, and extremely
French in him. [*Laughs*] But then, that he should use my own words, as it
were in contempt of me, I cannot bear it.   [*Crying.*

PALAMEDE   *Ces beaux séjours, ces doux ramages*—   [*Singing.*

145 MELANTHA   *Ces beaux séjours, ces doux ramages.*   [*Singing after him.*
Ces beaux séjours nous invitent à l'amour!

Let me die, but he sings *en cavalier*, and so humours the cadence!

[*Laughing.*

PALAMEDE   *Vois, ma Climène, vois sous ce chêne,*   [*Singing again.*
S'entrebaiser ces oiseaux amoureux!

150 Let me die now, but that was fine. Ah, now, for three or four brisk
Frenchmen, to be put into masking habits, and to sing it on a theatre,
how witty it would be! And then to dance helterskelter to a *chanson à
boire*: *toute la terre, toute la terre est à moi!* What's matter though it were
made and sung two or three years ago in *cabarets*, how it would attract

155 the admiration, especially of everyone that's an *éveilleé!*

127 *à contretemps*] Inopportunely.

131–2 *Radoucissez . . . galante*] 'Calm yourself, for mercy's sake, Madam, you are angry for
nothing. You don't understand fashionable raillery.'

138–9 *Ah . . . jour!*] 'Ah, how fine it is in the woods; what a lovely day heaven grants!'

144–6 *Ces . . . amour*] 'These beautiful places, these sweet songs of the birds, summon us to
love.'

148–9 *Vois . . . amoureaux*] 'See, my Climène, see, under this oak, the amorous birds kiss
one another.'

152–3 *chanson . . . moi*] 'A drinking song: all the world, all the world is mine.'

155 an *éveillé*] One who is lively, animated.

MELANTHA   Well, I begin to have a *tendre* for you; but yet, upon condition that – when we are married, you—

[PALAMEDE *sings, while she speaks.*

PHILOTIS   You must drown her voice: if she makes her French conditions you are a slave for ever.

MELANTHA   First, you will engage – that—   160

PALAMEDE   Fa, la, la, la, etc.   [*Louder.*

MELANTHA   Will you hear the conditions?

PALAMEDE   No! I will hear no conditions! I am resolved to win you *en français*: to be very airy, with abundance of noise, and no sense: Fa, la, la, la, etc.   165

MELANTHA   Hold, hold: I am vanquished with your *gaité d'esprit*. I am yours, and will be yours, *sans nulle réserve, ni condition*: and let me die, if I do not think myself the happiest nymph in Sicily. – My dear French dear, stay but a *minuit*, till I *raccommode* myself with the princess; and then I am yours, *jusqu'à la mort. Allons donc*—   170

[*Exeunt* MELANTHA, PHILOTIS.

PALAMEDE [*solus, fanning himself with his hat*]   I never thought before that wooing was so laborious an exercise. If she were worth a million, I have deserved her; and now methinks too, with taking all this pains for her, I begin to like her. 'Tis so; I have known many who never cared for hare nor partridge, but those they caught themselves would eat heartily: 175 the pains, and the story a man tells of the taking of 'em, makes the meat go down more pleasantly. Besides, last night I had a sweet dream of her, and, gad, she I have once dreamed of, I am stark mad till I enjoy her, let her be never so ugly.

Enter DORALICE.

DORALICE   Who's that you are so mad to enjoy, Palamede?   180

PALAMEDE   You may easily imagine that, sweet Doralice.

DORALICE   More easily than you think I can: I met just now with a certain man, who came to you with letters from a certain old gentleman, y-cleped your father; whereby I am given to understand, that tomorrow you are to take an oath in the church to be grave henceforward, to go   185 ill-dressed and slovenly, to get heirs for your estate, and to dandle 'em for your diversion; and, in short, that love and courtship are to be no more.

PALAMEDE   Now have I so much shame to be thus apprehended in the manner, that I can neither speak nor look upon you; I have abundance of grace in me, that I find. But if you have any spark of true friendship in   190 you, retire with me a little into the next room, that has a couch or bed in't, and bestow your charity upon a poor dying man: a little comfort from a mistress before a man is going to give himself in marriage, is as good as a lusty dose of strong-water to a dying malefactor: it takes away

195   the sense of hell and hanging from him.

DORALICE   No, good Palamede, I must not be so injurious to your bride: 'tis ill drawing from the bank today, when all your ready money is payable tomorrow.

PALAMEDE   A wife is only to have the ripe fruit that falls of itself; but a

200   wise man will always preserve a shaking for a mistress.

DORALICE   But a wife for the first quarter is a mistress.

PALAMEDE   But when the second comes. . . .

DORALICE   When it does come, you are so given to variety, that you would make a wife of me in another quarter.

205   PALAMEDE   No, never, except I were married to you: married people can never oblige one another; for all they do is duty, and consequently there can be no thanks: but love is more frank and generous than he is honest; he's a liberal giver, but a cursed pay-master.

DORALICE   I declare I will have no gallant; but, if I would, he should

210   never be a married man; a married man is but a mistress's half-servant, as a clergyman is but the king's half-subject. For a man to come to me that smells of the wife! 'Slife, I would as soon wear her old gown after her as her husband.

PALAMEDE   Yet 'tis a kind of fashion to wear a princess's cast shoes; you

215   see the country ladies buy 'em to be fine in them.

DORALICE   Yes, a princess's shoes may be worn after her, because they keep their fashion by being so very little used. But generally a married man is the creature of the world the most out of fashion; his behaviour is dumpish; his discourse, his wife and family; his habit so much neglected,

220   it looks as if that were married too; his hat is married, his peruke is married, his breeches are married, and if we could look within his breeches we should find him married there too.

PALAMEDE   Am I then to be discarded for ever? Pray do but mark how terrible that word sounds; for ever! It has a very damn'd sound, Doralice.

225   DORALICE   Ay, for ever! It sounds as hellishly to me as it can do to you, but there's no help for't.

PALAMEDE   Yet if we had but once enjoyed one another! But then once only is worse than not at all: it leaves a man with such a ling'ring after it.

DORALICE   For ought I know 'tis better that we have not; we might

230   upon trial have liked each other less, as many a man and woman that have loved as desperately as we, and yet when they came to possession have sighed and cried to themselves, Is this all?

194 strong-water] Spirits.

PALAMEDE   That is only if the servant were not found a man of this
world; but if, upon trial, we had not liked each other, we had certainly
left loving; and faith, that's the greater happiness of the two.   235

DORALICE   'Tis better as 'tis; we have drawn off already as much of our
love as would run clear; after possessing, the rest is but jealousies, and
disquiets, and quarrelling, and piecing.

PALAMEDE   Nay, after one great quarrel there's never any sound piecing; the love is apt to break in the same place again.   240

DORALICE   I declare I would never renew a love; that's like him who
trims an old coach for ten years together, he might buy a new one better
cheap.

PALAMEDE   Well, madam, I am convinced that 'tis best for us not to
have enjoyed; but, gad, the strongest reason is because I can't help it.   245

DORALICE   The only way to keep us new to one another is never to
enjoy, as they keep grapes by hanging 'em upon a line, they must touch
nothing if you would preserve 'em fresh.

PALAMEDE   But then they wither, and grow dry in the very keeping.
However, I shall have a warmth for you, and an eagerness every time I see   250
you; and if I chance to outlive Melantha—

DORALICE   And if I chance to outlive Rhodophil—

PALAMEDE   Well, I'll cherish my body as much as I can upon that hope.
'Tis true, I would not directly murder the wife of my bosom; but to kill
her civilly, by the way of kindness, I'll put as fair as another man: I'll   255
begin tomorrow night, and be very wrathful with her, that's resolved
on.

DORALICE   Well, Palamede, here's my hand, I'll venture to be your
second wife, for all your threat'nings.

PALAMEDE   In the meantime I'll watch you hourly, as I would the   260
ripeness of a melon, and I hope you'll give me leave now and then to look
on you, and to see if you are not ready to be cut yet.

DORALICE   No, no, that must not be, Palamede, for fear the gardener
should come and catch you taking up the glass.

Enter RHODOPHIL.

RHODOPHIL [*aside*]   Billing so sweetly! now I am confirmed in my   265
suspicions; I must put an end to this ere it go further.
[*To* DORALICE] Cry you mercy, spouse, I fear I have interrupted your
recreations.

DORALICE   What recreations?

RHODOPHIL   Nay, no excuses, good spouse: I saw fair hand conveyed,   270
to lip, and pressed, as though you had been squeezing soft wax together

for an indenture. Palamede, you and I must clear this reckoning: why would you have seduced my wife?

PALAMEDE   Why would you have debauched my mistress?

275 RHODOPHIL   What do you think of that civil couple that played at a game called Hide and Seek last evening, in the grotto?

PALAMEDE   What do you think of that innocent pair who made it their pretence to seek for others, but came, indeed, to hide themselves there?

RHODOPHIL   All things considered, I begin vehemently to suspect that

280 the young gentleman I found in your company last night was a certain youth of my acquaintance.

PALAMEDE   And I have an odd imagination that you could never have suspected my small gallant, if your little villainous Frenchman had not been a false brother.

285 RHODOPHIL   Further arguments are needless; draw off; I shall speak to you now by the way of *bilbo*.   [*Claps his hands to his sword.*

PALAMEDE   And I shall answer you by the way of Dangerfield.

[*Claps his hands on his.*

DORALICE   Hold, hold; are not you two a couple of mad fighting fools, to cut one another's throats for nothing?

290 PALAMEDE   How for nothing? He courts the woman I must marry.

RHODOPHIL   And he courts you whom I have married.

DORALICE   But you can neither of you be jealous of what you love not.

RHODOPHIL   Faith I am jealous, and that makes me partly suspect that I love you better than I thought.

295 DORALICE   Pish! A mere jealousy of honour.

RHODOPHIL   Gad, I am afraid there's something else in't; for Palamede has wit, and, if he loves you, there's something more in ye than I have found: some rich mine, for aught I know, that I have not yet discovered.

PALAMEDE   'S life, what's this? Here's an argument for me to love

300 Melantha; for he has loved her, and he has wit too, and, for aught I know, there may be a mine; but if there be, I am resolved I'll dig for't.

DORALICE [*to* RHODOPHIL]   Then I have found my account in raising your jealousy. O! 'tis the most delicate sharp sauce to a cloyed stomach; it will give you a new edge, Rhodophil.

305 RHODOPHIL   And a new point too, Doralice, if I could be sure thou art honest.

DORALICE   If you are wise, believe me for your own sake: love and religion have but one thing to trust to; that's a good sound faith. Consider, if I have played false, you can never find it out by any

310 experiment you can make upon me.

272 indenture] A deed or sealed agreement.

RHODOPHIL   No? Why, suppose I had a delicate screwed gun; if I left
her clean, and found her foul, I should discover, to my cost, she had been
shot in.

DORALICE   But if you left her clean, and found her only rusty, you
would discover, to your shame, she was only so for want of shooting.   315

PALAMEDE   Rhodophil, you know me too well to imagine I speak for
fear; and therefore in consideration of our past friendship I will tell you,
and bind it by all things holy, that Doralice is innocent.

RHODOPHIL   Friend, I will believe you, and vow the same for your
Melantha; but the devil on't is, how shall we keep 'em so?   320

PALAMEDE   What dost think of a blessed community betwixt us four,
for the solace of the women, and relief of the men? Methinks it would be a
pleasant kind of life: wife and husband for the standing dish, and
mistress and gallant for the dessert.

RHODOPHIL   But suppose the wife and mistress should both long for   325
the standing dish, how should they be satisfied together?

PALAMEDE   In such a case they must draw lots; and yet that would not
do neither, for they would both be wishing for the longest cut!

RHODOPHIL   Then I think, Palamede, we had as good make a firm
league not to invade each other's propriety.   330

PALAMEDE   Content, say I. From henceforth let all acts of hostility cease
betwixt us; and that in the usual form of treaties, as well by sea as land,
and in all fresh waters.

DORALICE   I will add but one *proviso*, that whoever breaks the league,
either by war abroad, or neglect at home, both the women shall revenge   335
themselves by the help of the other party.

RHODOPHIL   That's but reasonable. Come away, Doralice; I have a
great temptation to be sealing articles in private.

PALAMEDE   Hast thou so?   [*Claps him on the shoulder.*
'Fall on, Macduff,   340
And cursed be he that first cries, Hold, enough.'

Enter POLYDAMAS, PALMYRA, ARTEMIS, ARGALEON; *after them*
EUBULUS *and* HERMOGENES, *guarded*.

PALMYRA   Sir, on my knees I beg you.
POLYDAMAS   Away, I'll hear no more.
PALMYRA   For my dead mother's sake; you say you loved her,
And tell me I resemble her.   345
Thus she had begged.
POLYDAMAS   And thus I had denied her.

340–1 Fall . . . enough] A misquotation of *Macbeth*, v. viii. 32–3.

PALMYRA   You must be merciful.

ARGALEON   You must be constant.

350 POLYDAMAS   Go, bear 'em to the torture; you have boasted
 You have a king to head you: I would know
 To whom I must resign.

EUBULUS   This is our recompense
 For serving thy dead queen.

HERMOGENES   And education
355 Of thy daughter.

ARGALEON   You are too modest, in not naming all
 His obligations to you: why did you
 Omit his son, the prince Leonidas?

POLYDAMAS   That imposture
360 I had forgot; their tortures shall be doubled.

HERMOGENES   You please me, I shall die the sooner.

EUBULUS   No; could I live an age, and still be racked,
 I still would keep the secret.   [As they are going off,

Enter LEONIDAS, *guarded.*

LEONIDAS   Oh whither do you hurry innocence!
365 If you have any justice, spare their lives;
 Or if I cannot make you just, at least
 I'll teach you to more purpose to be cruel.

PALMYRA   Alas, what does he seek!

LEONIDAS   Make me the object of your hate and vengeance!
370 Are those decrepid bodies worn to ruin,
 Just ready of themselves to fall asunder,
 And to let drop the soul,
 Are these fit subjects for a rack and tortures?
 Where would you fasten any hold upon 'em?
375 Place pains on me; united fix 'em here;
 I have both youth, and strength, and soul to bear 'em;
 And if they merit death, then I much more,
 Since 'tis for me they suffer.

HERMOGENES   Heav'n forbid
 We should redeem our pains, or worthless lives,
380 By our exposing yours.

EUBULUS   Away with us. Farewell, sir:
 I only suffer in my fears for you.

ARGALEON   So much concerned for him?   [Aside.
 Then my suspicion's true.   [Whispers *the* King.

385 PALMYRA   Hear yet my last request for poor Leonidas,

Or take my life with his.

ARGALEON   Rest satisfied, Leonidas is he.   [*To the* King.

POLYDAMAS   I am amazed: what must be done?

ARGALEON   Command his execution instantly:
Give him not leisure to discover it;   390
He may corrupt the soldiers.

POLYDAMAS   Hence with that traitor, bear him to his death:
Haste there, and see my will performed.

LEONIDAS   Nay, then I'll die like him the gods have made me.
Hold, gentlemen, I am—   395

[ARGALEON *stops his mouth.*

ARGALEON   Thou art a traitor; 'tis not fit to hear thee.

LEONIDAS   I say, I am the—   [*Getting loose a little.*

ARGALEON   So; gag him, and lead him off.

[*Again stopping his mouth.*

[LEONIDAS, HERMOGENES, EUBULUS, *led off.* POLYDAMAS *and*
ARGALEON *follow.*

PALMYRA   Duty and love by turns possess my soul,
And struggle for a fatal victory.   400
I will discover he's the king; Ah, no:
That will perhaps save him;
But then I am guilty of a father's ruin.
What shall I do, nor not do? Either way
I must destroy a parent, or a lover.   405
Break heart; for that's the least of ills to me,
And death the only cure.   [*Swoons.*

ARTEMIS   Help, help the princess.

RHODOPHIL   Bear her gently hence, where she may
Have more succour.

[*She is borne off;* ARTEMIS *follows her.*

[*Shouts within, and clashing of swords.*

PALAMEDE   What noise is that?   410

Enter AMALTHEA, *running.*

AMALTHEA   Oh, gentlemen, if you have loyalty
Or courage, show it now! Leonidas
Broke on the sudden from his guards, and snatching
A sword from one, his back against the scaffold,

415   Bravely defends himself, and owns aloud
       He is our long-lost king; found for this moment,
       But, if your valours help not, lost for ever.
       Two of his guards, moved by the sense of virtue,
       Are turned for him, and there they stand at bay
420   Against a host of foes.
RHODOPHIL   Madam, no more;
       We lose time: my command, or my example,
       May move the soldiers to the better cause.
       You'll second me?   [*To* PALAMEDE.
PALAMEDE   Or die with you: no subject e'er can meet
425   A nobler fate, than at his sovereign's feet.   [*Exeunt*.

                        [*Clashing of swords within, and shouts.*

       Enter LEONIDAS, RHODOPHIL, PALAMEDE, EUBULUS, HER-
       MOGENES, *and their party, victorious*; POLYDAMAS *and* ARGALEON,
                              disarmed.

LEONIDAS   That I survive the dangers of this day,
       Next to the gods, brave friends, be yours the honour.
       And let heaven witness for me, that my joy
       Is not more great for this my right restored,
430   Than 'tis that I have power to recompense
       Your loyalty and valour. Let mean princes,
       Of abject souls, fear to reward great actions;
       I mean to show
       That whatso'er subjects like you dare merit,
435   A king like me dares give.
RHODOPHIL   You make us blush, we have deserved so little.
PALAMEDE   And yet instruct us how to merit more.
LEONIDAS   And as I would be just in my rewards,
       So should I in my punishments; these two,
440   This the usurper of my crown, the other
       Of my Palmyra's love, deserve that death
       Which both designed for me.
POLYDAMAS   And we expect it.
ARGALEON   I have too long been happy to live wretched.
POLYDAMAS   And I too long have governed, to desire
445   A life without an empire.
LEONIDAS   You are Palmyra's father; and as such,
       Though not a king, shall have obedience paid
       From him who is one. Father, in that name
       All injuries forgot, and duty owned.   [*Embraces him.*

POLYDAMAS O, had I known you could have been this king,   450
Thus god-like, great and good, I should have wished
To have been dethroned before. 'Tis now I live,
And more than reign; now all my joys flow pure,
Unmixed with cares, and undisturbed by conscience.

Enter PALMYRA, AMALTHEA, ARTEMIS, DORALICE, *and*
MELANTHA.

LEONIDAS See, my Palmyra comes! the frighted blood   455
Scarce yet recalled to her pale cheeks,
Like the first streaks of light broke loose from darkness,
And dawning into blushes. – Sir, you said   [*To* POLYDAMAS.
Your joys were full; oh, would you make mine so!
I am but half restored without this blessing.   460
POLYDAMAS The gods, and my Palmyra, make you happy,
As you make me!   [*Gives her hand to* LEONIDAS.
PALMYRA Now all my prayers are heard:
I may be dutiful, and yet may love.
Virtue and patience have at length unravelled   465
The knots which fortune tied.
MELANTHA Let me die, but I'll congratulate his majesty: how admir-
ably well his royalty becomes him! Becomes! that is *lui sied*, but our
damned language expresses nothing.
PALAMEDE How? Does it become him already? 'Twas but just now you   470
said he was such a figure of a man.
MELANTHA True, my dear, when he was a private man he was a figure;
but since he is a king, methinks he has assumed another figure: he looks
so grand, and so august!   [*Going to the* King.
PALAMEDE Stay, stay; I'll present you when it is more convenient. I   475
find I must get her a place at court; and when she is once there, she can be
no longer ridiculous; for she is young enough, and pretty enough, and
fool enough, and French enough to bring up a fashion there to be
affected.
LEONIDAS [*to* RHODOPHIL] Did she then lead you to this brave
attempt?   480
[*To* AMALTHEA] To you, fair Amalthea, what I am,
And what all these, from me, we jointly owe:
First, therefore, to your great desert we give
Your brother's life; but keep him under guard
Till our power be settled. What more grace   485
He may receive, shall from his future carriage
Be given as he deserves.

ARGALEON   I neither now desire, nor will deserve it;
My loss is such as cannot be repaired,
490   And, to the wretched, life can be no mercy.
LEONIDAS   Then be a prisoner always: thy ill fate
And pride will have it so: but since in this I cannot,
Instruct me, generous Amalthea, how
A king may serve you.
AMALTHEA   I have all I hope,
495   And all I now must wish; I see you happy.
Those hours I have to live, which heav'n in pity
Will make but few, I vow to spend with vestals:
The greatest part in pray'rs for you; the rest
In mourning my unworthiness.
500   Press me not further to explain myself;
'Twill not become me, and may cause your trouble.
LEONIDAS   Too well I understand her secret grief,   [*Aside.*
But dare not seem to know it. – Come, my fairest;   [*To* PALMYRA.
Beyond my crown I have one joy in store,
505   To give that crown to her whom I adore.   [*Exeunt omnes.*

EPILOGUE

Thus have my spouse and I informed the nation,
And led you all the way to reformation.
Not with dull morals, gravely writ, like those
Which men of easy phlegm with care compose—
Your poets, of stiff words and limber sense,   5
Born on the confines of indifference—
But by examples drawn, I dare to say,
From most of you who hear and see the play.
There are more Rhodophils in this theatre,
More Palamedes, and some few wives, I fear.   10
But yet too far our poet would not run:
Though 'twas well offered, there was nothing done,
He would not quite the women's frailty bare,
But stript 'em to the waist, and left 'em there;
And the men's faults are less severely shown,   15
For he considers that himself is one.
Some stabbing wits, to bloody satire bent,
Would treat both sexes with less compliment:
Would lay the scene at home, of husbands tell,
For wenches taking up their wives i'th' Mell;   20
And a brisk bout which each of them did want,
Made by mistake of mistress and gallant.
Our modest author thought it was enough
To cut you off a sample of the stuff:
He spared my shame, which you, I'm sure, would not,   25
For you were all for driving on the plot:
You sighed when I came in to break the sport,
And set your teeth when each design fell short.
To wives and servants all good wishes lend,
But the poor cuckold seldom finds a friend.   30
Since, therefore, court and town will take no pity,
I humbly cast myself upon the city.

20 Mell] Mall.

ALL FOR LOVE
OR
THE WORLD WELL LOST

A TRAGEDY

The earliest known performance of *All For Love*, Dryden's 'imitation' of Shakespeare's *Antony and Cleopatra*, was in December 1677. Its success on the stage appears to have been moderate, but long-lasting, for it was performed in preference to Shakespeare's play into the latter half of the next century. It was printed in 1678 with a dedication to Thomas Osborne, first Earl of Danby. The Preface contains an extended censure of Rochester (chief among those 'witty men' who could 'decide sovereignly concerning poetry'), who had attacked Dryden in his poem 'An Allusion to Horace'.

With *All For Love* Dryden takes an opportunity of liberating himself from rhyme and writing a blank verse tragedy. His critical intentions in the play are apparent. Unities of time and place are obtained by concentrating on the later part of Antony's story and by confining the scene to Alexandria. The geographical expansiveness and the action of Shakespeare's play are forgone, and attention is reserved for the love of Antony and Cleopatra, a subject much to Dryden's purpose. In *Heads of an Answer to Rhymer* (q.v.), written in the same year, he argues against the Aristotelian view of the primacy of the plot, conducing to the passions of pity and terror. Love, he says, 'being an heroic passion, is fit for tragedy'; and 'words and discourse' are the means to produce it. His success in this, and in dealing with the 'excellency of the moral', are considered uncertain by many critics, notwithstanding his own satisfaction with his play.

PREFACE

The death of Antony and Cleopatra is a subject which has been treated by the greatest wits of our nation, after Shakespeare;[1] and by all so variously, that their example has given me the confidence to try myself in this bow of Ulysses amongst the crowd of suitors; and, withal, to take my own measures in aiming at the mark. I doubt not but the same motive has prevailed with all of us in this attempt; I mean the excellency of the moral: for the chief persons represented were famous patterns of unlawful love; and their end accordingly was unfortunate. All reasonable men have long since concluded, that the hero of the poem ought not to be a character of perfect virtue, for then he could not, without injustice, be made unhappy; nor yet altogether wicked, because he could not then be pitied. I have therefore steered the middle course; and have drawn the character of Antony as favourably as Plutarch, Appian, and Dion Cassius would give me leave: the like I have observed in Cleopatra. That which is wanting to work up the pity to a greater height, was not afforded me by the story; for the crimes of love which they both committed were not occasioned by any necessity, or fatal ignorance, but were wholly voluntary; since our passions are, or ought to be, within our power. The fabric of the play is regular enough, as to the inferior parts of it; and the unities of time, place, and action more exactly observed than, perhaps, the English theatre requires. Particularly, the action is so much one, that it is the only of the kind without episode, or underplot; every scene in the tragedy conducing to the main design, and every act concluding with a turn of it. The greatest error in the contrivance seems to be in the person of Octavia: for though I might use the privilege of a poet to introduce her into Alexandria, yet I had not enough considered that the compassion she moved to herself and children was destructive to that which I reserved for Antony and Cleopatra; whose mutual love, being founded upon vice, must lessen the favour of the audience to them when virtue and innocence were oppressed by it. And though I justified Antony in some measure by making Octavia's departure to proceed wholly from

---

[1] Besides Shakespeare's play there had been, among others, Samuel Daniel's *Tragedy of Cleopatra* (1594), Thomas May's *Cleopatra, Queen of Egypt* (1626), and, recently, Sir Charles Sedley's *Antony and Cleopatra* (1677).

herself; yet the force of the first machine still remained; and the dividing of
pity, like the cutting of a river into many channels, abated the strength of
the natural stream. But this is an objection which none of my critics have
urged against me; and therefore I might have let it pass, if I could have
resolved to have been partial to myself. The faults my enemies have found
are rather cavils concerning little and not essential decencies; which a
master of the ceremonies may decide betwixt us. The French poets, I
confess, are strict observers of these punctilios: they would not, for
example, have suffered Cleopatra and Octavia to have met; or, if they had
met, there must only have passed betwixt them some cold civilities, but no
eagerness of repartee, for fear of offending against the greatness of their
characters, and the modesty of their sex. This objection I foresaw, and at the
same time contemned; for I judged it both natural and probable that
Octavia, proud of her new-gained conquest, would search out Cleopatra to
triumph over her; and that Cleopatra, thus attacked, was not of a spirit to
shun the encounter: and 'tis not unlikely that two exasperated rivals should
use such satire as I have put into their mouths; for after all, though the one
were a Roman, and the other a queen, they were both women. 'Tis true,
some actions, though natural, are not fit to be represented; and broad
obscenities in words ought in good manners to be avoided: expressions
therefore are a modest clothing of our thoughts, as breeches and petticoats
are of our bodies. If I have kept myself within the bounds of modesty, all
beyond it is but nicety and affectation; which is no more but modesty
depraved into a vice: they betray themselves who are too quick of apprehension in such cases, and leave all reasonable men to imagine worse of them,
than of the poet.

Honest Montaigne goes yet further: *Nous ne sommes que cérémonie; la
cérémonie nous emporte, et laissons la substance des choses. Nous nous tenons aux
branches, et abandonnons le tronc and le corps. Nous avons appris aux dames de
rougir, oyant seulement nommer ce qu'elles ne craignent aucunement à faire. Nous
n'osons appeller à droit nos membres, et ne craignons pas de les employer à toute sorte de
débauche. La cérémonie nous défend d'exprimer par paroles les choses licites et
naturelles, et nous l'en croyons; la raison nous défend de n'en faire point d'illicites et
mauvaises, et personne ne l'en croit.*[2] My comfort is that by this opinion my
enemies are but sucking critics, who would fain be nibbling ere their teeth
are come.

[2] Montaigne's essay 'De la présomption', *Essais* (1580), II, 17: 'We are nothing but
ceremony: ceremony carries us away, and we leave the substance of things. We hold on to
the branches, and leave the trunk and body. We have taught the ladies to blush at merely
hearing named what they are not at all afraid to do. We dare not call our members by their
proper names, and are yet not afraid to employ them in all kinds of debauchery. Ceremony
forbids us to express in words lawful and natural things, and we believe in it; reason forbids
us to do unlawful and bad things, and no-one believes in it.'

Yet in this nicety of manners does the excellency of French poetry consist: their heroes are the most civil people breathing; but their good breeding seldom extends to a word of sense. All their wit is in their ceremony; they want the genius which animates our stage; and therefore 'tis but necessary, when they cannot please, that they should take care not to offend. But as the civillest man in the company is commonly the dullest, so these authors, while they are afraid to make you laugh or cry, out of pure good manners make you sleep. They are so careful not to exasperate a critic that they never leave him any work; so busy with the broom, and make so clean a riddance, that there is little left either for censure or for praise: for no part of a poem is worth our discommending where the whole is insipid; as when we have once tasted of palled wine, we stay not to examine it glass by glass. But while they affect to shine in trifles, they are often careless in essentials. Thus their Hippolytus[3] is so scrupulous in point of decency that he will rather expose himself to death than accuse his stepmother to his father; and my critics, I am sure, will commend him for it: but we of grosser apprehensions are apt to think that this excess of generosity is not practicable but with fools and madmen. This was good manners with a vengeance; and the audience is like to be much concerned at the misfortunes of this admirable hero: but take Hippolytus out of his poetic fit, and I suppose he would think it a wiser part to set the saddle on the right horse, and choose rather to live with the reputation of a plain-spoken, honest man, than to die with the infamy of an incestuous villain. In the meantime we may take notice that where the poet ought to have preserved the character as it was delivered to us by antiquity, when he should have given us the picture of a rough young man, of the Amazonian strain, a jolly huntsman, and both by his profession and his early rising a mortal enemy to love, he has chosen to give him the turn of gallantry, sent him to travel from Athens to Paris, taught him to make love, and transformed the Hippolytus of Euripides into Monsieur Hippolyte. I should not have troubled myself thus far with French poets, but that I find our Chedreux[4] critics wholly form their judgments by them. But for my part, I desire to be tried by the laws of my own country; for it seems unjust to me that the French should prescribe here till they have conquered. Our little sonneteers who follow them have too narrow souls to judge of poetry. Poets themselves are the most proper, though I conclude not the only critics. But till some genius as universal as Aristotle shall arise, one who can penetrate into all arts and sciences without the practice of them, I shall think it reasonable that the judgment of an artificer in his own art should be preferable to the opinion of another man; at least where he is not bribed by interest, or prejudiced by malice: and this, I suppose, is manifest

[3] A character in Racine's *Phèdre* (1677).
[4] Chedreux wigs were fashionable: modish, Frenchified critics.

by plain induction. For, first, the crowd cannot be presumed to have more than a gross instinct of what pleases or displeases them: every man will grant me this; but then, by a particular kindness to himself, he draws[5] his own stake first, and will be distinguished from the multitude, of which other men may think him one. But, if I come closer to those who are allowed for witty men, either by the advantage of their quality, or by common fame, and affirm that neither are they qualified to decide sovereignly concerning poetry, I shall yet have a strong party of my opinion; for most of them severally will exclude the rest, either from the number of witty men, or at least of able judges. But here again they are all indulgent to themselves; and every one who believes himself a wit, that is, every man, will pretend at the same time to a right of judging. But to press it yet farther, there are many witty men, but few poets; neither have all poets a taste of tragedy. And this is the rock on which they are daily splitting. Poetry, which is a picture of nature, must generally please; but it is not to be understood that all parts of it must please every man; therefore is not tragedy to be judged by a witty man, whose taste is only confined to comedy. Nor is every man who loves tragedy a sufficient judge of it: he must understand the excellencies of it too, or he will only prove a blind admirer, not a critic. From hence it comes that so many satires on poets, and censures of their writings, fly abroad. Men of pleasant conversation (at least esteemed so), and endued with a trifling kind of fancy, perhaps helped out with some smattering of Latin, are ambitious to distinguish themselves from the herd of gentlemen by their poetry:

> rarus enim ferme sensus communis in illa
> fortuna.[6]

And is not this a wretched affectation, not to be contented with what fortune has done for them, and sit down quietly with their estates, but they must call their wits in question, and needlessly expose their nakedness to public view? Not considering that they are not to expect the same approbation from sober men which they have found from their flatterers after the third bottle. If a little glittering in discourse has passed them on us for witty men, where was the necessity of undeceiving the world? Would a man who has an ill title to an estate, but yet is in possession of it, would he bring it of his own accord, to be tried at Westminster? We who write, if we want the talent, yet have the excuse that we do it for a poor subsistence; but what can be urged in their defence, who, not having the vocation of poverty to scribble, out of mere wantonness take pains to make themselves ridiculous? Horace was certainly in the right where he said that *no man is satisfied with*

---

[5] Withdraws.

[6] Juvenal, *Satires*, VIII, 73–4: 'for in those high places regard for others is rarely to be found'.

his own condition. A poet is not pleased, because hĕ is not rich; and the rich are discontented, because the poets will not admit them of their number. Thus the case is hard with writers: if they succeed not, they must starve; and if they do, some malicious satire is prepared to level them for daring to please without their leave. But while they are so eager to destroy the fame of others, their ambition is manifest in their concernment; some poem of their own is to be produced, and the slaves are to be laid flat with their faces on the ground, that the monarch may appear in the greater majesty.

Dionysius and Nero had the same longings, but with all their power they could never bring their business well about. 'Tis true, they proclaimed themselves poets by sound of trumpet; and poets they were upon pain of death to any man who durst call them otherwise. The audience had a fine time on't, you may imagine; they sat in a bodily fear, and looked as demurely as they could: for 'twas a hanging matter to laugh unseasonably; and the tyrants were suspicious, as they had reason, that their subjects had 'em in the wind; so, every man in his own defence set as good a face upon the business as he could. 'Twas known beforehand that the monarchs were to be crowned laureates; but when the show was over, and an honest man was suffered to depart quietly, he took out his laughter which he had stifled, with a firm resolution never more to see an emperor's play, though he had been ten years a-making it. In the meantime the true poets were they who made the best markets, for they had wit enough to yield the prize with a good grace, and not contend with him who had thirty legions:[7] they were sure to be rewarded if they confessed themselves bad writers, and that was somewhat better than to be martyrs for their reputation. Lucan's example was enough to teach them manners; and after he was put to death, for overcoming Nero, the emperor carried it without dispute for the best poet in his dominions. No man was ambitious of that grinning honour;[8] for if he heard the malicious trumpeter proclaiming his name before his betters, he knew there was but one way with him. Maecenas took another course, and we know he was more than a great man, for he was witty too: but finding himself far gone in poetry, which Seneca assures us was not his talent, he thought it his best way to be well with Virgil and with Horace; that at least he might be a poet at the second hand; and we see how happily it has succeeded with him; for his own bad poetry is forgotten, and their panegyrics of him still remain. But they who should be our patrons are for no such expensive ways to fame; they have much of the poetry of Maecenas, but little of his liberality. They are for persecuting Horace and Virgil, in the persons of their successors (for such is every man who has any part of their

---

[7] The philosopher Favorinus gave the Emperor Hadrian's thirty legions as grounds for yielding to him on a point of argument.
[8] From Falstaff's remark about Sir Walter Blunt in *Henry IV*, v. iii.

soul and fire, though in a less degree). Some of their little zanies yet go further; for they are persecutors even of Horace himself, as far as they are able, by their ignorant and vile imitations of him;[9] by making an unjust use of his authority, and turning his artillery against his friends. But how would he disdain to be copied by such hands! I dare answer for him, he would be more uneasy in their company than he was with Crispinus, their forefather, in the Holy Way;[10] and would no more have allowed them a place amongst the critics than he would Demetrius the mimic, and Tigellius the Buffoon:

> Demetri, teque, Tigelli
> discipulorum inter jubeo plorare cathedras.[11]

With what scorn would he look down on such miserable translators, who make doggerel of his Latin, mistake his meaning, misapply his censures, and often contradict their own? He is fixed as a landmark to set out the bounds of poetry:

> saxum antiquum, ingens, . . .
> limes agro positus, litum ut discerneret arvis.[12]

But other arms than theirs, and other sinews are required, to raise the weight of such an author; and when they would toss him against enemies,

> genua labant, gelidus concrevit frigor sanguis.
> tum lapis ipse, viri vacuum per inane volutus,
> nec spatium evasit totum, nec pertulit ictum.[13]

For my part, I would wish no other revenge, either for myself or the rest of the poets, from this rhyming judge of the twelvepenny gallery,[14] this legitimate son of Sternhold, than that he would subscribe his name to his censure, or (not to tax him beyond his learning) set his mark: for should he own himself publicly, and come from behind the lion's skin, they whom he

---

[9] Probably with Rochester's poem 'An Allusion to Horace' in mind.

[10] The prattler whom Horace meets in the Via Sacra in *Satires*, I, ix, is identified as the Crispinus of I, iv.

[11] *Satires*, I, x, 90–1: 'But you, Demetrius, and you, Tigellius, I bid you go whine amidst the easy chairs of your pupils.'

[12] Virgil, *Aeneid*, XII, 897–8: 'a giant stone and ancient, set for a landmark, to ward dispute from the fields'.

[13] *Aeneid*, XII, 905–7: 'His knees totter, his blood is frozen cold. Yea, the hero's stone itself, whirled through the empty void, traversed not all the space, nor carried home its blow.'

[14] The attack on Rochester continues somewhat obliquely. Rochester had censured the taste of middle-class citizens in theatre audiences (they tended to occupy the twelvepenny gallery, rather than the fashionable pit and boxes) in the Epilogue to Sir Francis Fane's comedy *Love in the Dark* (1675).
Sternhold: cf. *Religio Laici*, l. 456n.

condemns would be thankful to him, they whom he praises would choose to be condemned; and the magistrates whom he has elected would modestly withdraw from their employment, to avoid the scandal of his nomination.[15] The sharpness of his satire, next to himself, falls most heavily on his friends, and they ought never to forgive him for commending them perpetually the wrong way, and sometimes by contraries. If he have a friend whose hastiness in writing is his greatest fault, Horace would have taught him to have minced the matter, and to have called it readiness of thought, and a flowing fancy; for friendship will allow a man to christen an imperfection by the name of some neighbour virtue:

> vellem in amicitia sic erraremus: et isti
> errori nomen virtus posuisset honestum.[16]

But he would never have allowed him to have called a slow man hasty, or a hasty writer a slow drudge,[17] as Juvenal explains it:

> canibus pigris, scabieque vetusta
> laevibus, et siccae lambentibus ora lucernae,
> nomen erit, Pardus, Tigris, Leo; si quid adhuc est
> quod fremit in terris violentius.[18]

Yet Lucretius laughs at a foolish lover, even for excusing the imperfections of his mistress:

> nigra μελίχροος est, immunda et foetida ἄκοσμος
> balba loqui non quit, τραυλίζει; muta pudens est, etc.[19]

But to drive it *ad Aethiopem cygnum*[20] is not to be endured. I leave him to interpret this by the benefit of his French version on the other side, and without further considering him than I have the rest of my illiterate

---

[15] Rochester's 'Allusion to Horace' ends:

> I loathe the rabble: 'tis enough for me
> If Sedley, Shadwell, Sheppard, Wycherley,
> Godolphin, Butler, Buckhurst, Buckingham,
> And some few more, whom I omit to name,
> Approve my sense. I count their censure fame.

[16] *Satires*, I, iii, 41–2: 'I could wish that we made the like mistake in friendship and that to such an error our ethics had given an honourable name.'
[17] In the 'Allusion' Rochester refers to 'Hasty Shadwell and slow Wycherley' (l. 123).
[18] *Satires*, VIII, 34–7: 'Lazy hounds that are bald with chronic mange, and who lick the edges of a dry lamp, will bear the names of "Pard", "Tiger", "Lion", or of any other animal in the world that roars more fiercely.'
[19] *De rerum natura*, IV, 1160, 1164: 'The black girl is a nut-brown maid, the dirty and rank is a sweet disorder. If she stutters and cannot speak, she lisps; the dumb is modest, etc.'
[20] Juvenal, *Satires*, VIII, 33: 'a black "swan"'.

censors, whom I have disdained to answer, because they are not qualified for judges. It remains that I acquaint the reader that I have endeavoured in this play to follow the practice of the Ancients, who, as Mr Rymer has judiciously observed, are and ought to be our masters. Horace likewise gives it for a rule in his art of poetry:

> vos exemplaria Graeca
> nocturna versate manu, versate diurna.[21]

Yet, though their models are regular, they are too little for English tragedy, which requires to be built in a larger compass. I could give an instance in the *Oedipus Tyrannus*, which was the masterpiece of Sophocles; but I reserve it for a more fit occasion, which I hope to have hereafter.[22] In my style I have professed to imitate the divine Shakespeare; which that I might perform more freely, I have disencumbered myself from rhyme. Not that I condemn my former way, but that this is more proper to my present purpose. I hope I need not to explain myself that I have not copied my author servilely: words and phrases must of necessity receive a change in succeeding ages; but 'tis almost a miracle that much of his language remains so pure; and that he who began dramatic poetry amongst us, untaught by any, and as Ben Jonson tells us, without learning, should by the force of his own genius perform so much, that in a manner he has left no praise for any who come after him. The occasion is fair, and the subject would be pleasant, to handle the differences of styles betwixt him and Fletcher, and wherein, and how far they are both to be imitated. But since I must not be over-confident of my own performance after him, it will be prudence in me to be silent. Yet I hope I may affirm, and without vanity, that by imitating him, I have excelled myself throughout the play; and particularly, that I prefer the scene betwixt Antony and Ventidius in the first act to anything which I have written in this kind.

---

[21] *Ars Poetica*, ll. 268–9: 'For yourselves, handle Greek models by night, handle them by day.'

[22] Dryden was soon to do an adaptation of this play, in collaboration with Nathaniel Lee. It was acted in September 1678.

PROLOGUE

What flocks of critics hover here today, }
As vultures wait on armies for their prey, }
All gaping for the carcase of a play! }
With croaking notes they bode some dire event,
And follow dying poets by the scent.   5
Ours gives himself for gone; y'have watched your time!
He fights this day unarmed — without his rhyme;
And brings a tale which often has been told;
As sad as Dido's; and almost as old.
His hero, whom you wits his bully call,   10
Bates of his mettle, and scarce rants at all:
He's somewhat lewd, but a well-meaning mind;
Weeps much, fights little, but is wond'rous kind.
In short, a pattern, and companion fit,
For all the keeping Tonies of the pit.   15
I could name more: a wife, and mistress too;
Both (to be plain) too good for most of you:
The wife well-natured, and the mistress true.
    Now poets, if your fame has been his care,
Allow him all the candour you can spare.   20
A brave man scorns to quarrel once a day;
Like Hectors, in at every petty fray.
Let those find fault whose wit's so very small,
They've need to show that they can think at all;
Errors, like straws, upon the surface flow;   25
He who would search for pearls must dive below.
Fops may have leave to level all they can,
As pigmies would be glad to lop a man.
Half-wits are fleas; so little and so light,

15 Tonies] Simpletons.
22 Hectors] Bullies.

30   We scarce could know they live, but that they bite.
               But, as the rich, when tired with daily feasts,
               For change, become their next poor tenant's guests,
               Drink hearty draughts of ale from plain brown bowls,
               And snatch the homely rasher from the coals:
35   So you, retiring from much better cheer,
               For once, may venture to do penance here.
               And since that plenteous autumn now is past,
               Whose grapes and peaches have indulged your taste,
               Take in good part, from our poor poet's board,
40   Such rivelled fruits as winter can afford.

DRAMATIS PERSONAE

MARK ANTONY
VENTIDIUS, his general
DOLABELLA, his friend
ALEXAS, the Queen's eunuch
SERAPION, priest of Isis
[MYRIS,] another priest
SERVANTS TO ANTONY

CLEOPATRA, Queen of Egypt
OCTAVIA, Antony's wife
CHARMION
IRAS } Cleopatra's maids
ANTONY'S TWO LITTLE DAUGHTERS

Scene – Alexandria

ACT I

Scene: *The Temple of Isis*

Enter SERAPION, MYRIS, Priests of Isis.

SERAPION   Portents and prodigies are grown so frequent,
That they have lost their name. Our fruitful Nile
Flowed ere the wonted season, with a torrent
So unexpected, and so wondrous fierce,

5   That the wild deluge overtook the haste
Ev'n of the hinds that watched it: men and beasts
Were borne above the tops of trees, that grew
On th' utmost margin of the water-mark.
Then, with so swift an ebb the flood drove backward,

10   It slipped from underneath the scaly herd:
Here monstrous phocae panted on the shore;
Forsaken dolphins there with their broad tails,
Lay lashing the departing waves: hard by 'em,
Sea-horses flound'ring in the slimy mud,

15   Tossed up their heads, and dashed the ooze about 'em.

Enter ALEXAS *behind them.*

MYRIS   Avert these omens, Heaven!
SERAPION   Last night, between the hours of twelve and one,
In a lone aisle o'th' temple while I walked,
A whirlwind rose, that, with a violent blast,

20   Shook all the dome: the doors around me clapped;
The iron wicket, that defends the vault,
Where the long race of Ptolemies is laid,
Burst open, and disclosed the mighty dead.
From out each monument, in order placed,

25   An armed ghost starts up: the boy-king last
Reared his inglorious head. A peal of groans

11 phocae] Seals.
14 Sea-horses] Hippopotami.
25 boy-king] Ptolemy XIV, whom Julius Caesar made joint ruler and Cleopatra's husband in 47 B.C., when he was only eleven. He was murdered in 44 B.C. by Cleopatra's orders.

Then followed, and a lamentable voice
Cried, Egypt is no more! My blood ran back,
My shaking knees against each other knocked;
On the cold pavement down I fell entranced,   30
And so unfinished left the horrid scene.

ALEXAS   And dreamed you this? or did invent the story,

[*Showing himself.*

To frighten our Egyptian boys withal,
And train 'em up betimes in fear of priesthood?

SERAPION   My lord, I saw you not,   35
Nor meant my words should reach your ears; but what
I uttered was most true.

ALEXAS   A foolish dream,
Bred from the fumes of indigested feasts,
And holy luxury.

SERAPION   I know my duty:
This goes no further.

ALEXAS   'Tis not fit it should;   40
Nor would the times now bear it, were it true.
All southern, from yon hills, the Roman camp
Hangs o'er us black and threat'ning, like a storm
Just breaking on our heads.

SERAPION   Our faint Egyptians pray for Antony;   45
But in their servile hearts they own Octavius.

MYRIS   Why then does Antony dream out his hours,
And tempts not fortune for a noble day,
Which might redeem what Actium lost?

ALEXAS   He thinks 'tis past recovery.

SERAPION   Yet the foe   50
Seems not to press the siege.

ALEXAS   Oh, there's the wonder.
Maecenas and Agrippa, who can most
With Caesar, are his foes. His wife Octavia,
Driv'n from his house, solicits her revenge;
And Dolabella, who was once his friend,   55
Upon some private grudge, now seeks his ruin:
Yet still war seems on either side to sleep.

49 Actium] The naval battle of 31 B.C., in which Antony was defeated by Octavius. This
and the surrounding events, background to Dryden's play, occupy Act III in Shakespeare's.
53 Octavia] Octavius' sister, whom Antony married in 40 B.C., after the death of Fulvia in
41 B.C. Her virtuousness was widely admired.

SERAPION   'Tis strange that Antony, for some days past,
          Has not beheld the face of Cleopatra;
60   But here, in Isis' temple, lives retired,
          And makes his heart a prey to black despair.
ALEXAS   'Tis true; and we much fear he hopes by absence
          To cure his mind of love.
SERAPION   If he be vanquished,
          Or make his peace, Egypt is doomed to be
65   A Roman province; and our plenteous harvests
          Must then redeem the scarceness of their soil.
          While Antony stood firm, our Alexandria
          Rivalled proud Rome (dominion's other seat),
          And Fortune striding, like a vast Colossus,
70   Could fix an equal foot of empire here.
ALEXAS   Had I my wish, these tyrants of all nature
          Who lord it o'er mankind, should perish, – perish,
          Each by the other's sword; but, since our will
          Is lamely followed by our power, we must
75   Depend on one, with him to rise or fall.
SERAPION   How stands the queen affected?
ALEXAS   Oh, she dotes,
          She dotes, Serapion, on this vanquished man,
          And winds herself about his mighty ruins;
          Whom would she yet forsake, yet yield him up,
80   This hunted prey, to his pursuer's hands,
          She might preserve us all: but 'tis in vain –
          This changes my designs, this blasts my counsels,
          And makes me use all means to keep him here,
          Whom I could wish divided from her arms
85   Far as the earth's deep centre. Well, you know
          The state of things; no more of your ill omens
          And black prognostics; labour to confirm
          The people's hearts.

          Enter VENTIDIUS, *talking aside with a* GENTLEMAN *of* Antony's.

SERAPION   These Romans will o'erhear us.
          But, who's that stranger? By his warlike port,
90   His fierce demeanour, and erected look,
          He's of no vulgar note.
ALEXAS   Oh 'tis Ventidius,
          Our emperor's great lieutenant in the East,
          Who first showed Rome that Parthia could be conquered.

When Antony returned from Syria last,
  He left this man to guard the Roman frontiers.   95
SERAPION   You seem to know him well.
ALEXAS   Too well. I saw him in Cilicia first,
  When Cleopatra there met Antony:
  A mortal foe he was to us, and Egypt.
  But, let me witness to the worth I hate,   100
  A braver Roman never drew a sword;
  Firm to his prince, but as a friend, not slave.
  He ne'er was of his pleasures; but presides
  O'er all his cooler hours, and morning counsels:
  In short the plainness, fierceness, rugged virtue,   105
  Of an old true-stampt Roman lives in him.
  His coming bodes I know not what of ill
  To our affairs. Withdraw to mark him better;
  And I'll acquaint you why I sought you here,
  And what's our present work.

They withdraw to a corner of the stage; and VENTIDIUS, *with the other,*
comes forward to the front.

VENTIDIUS   Not see him, say you?   110
  I say, I must, and will.
GENTLEMAN   He has commanded,
  On pain of death, none should approach his presence.
VENTIDIUS   I bring him news will raise his drooping spirits,
  Give him new life.
GENTLEMAN   He sees not Cleopatra.
VENTIDIUS   Would he had never seen her!   115
GENTLEMAN   He eats not, drinks not, sleeps not, has no use
  Of anything, but thought; or if he talks,
  'Tis to himself, and then 'tis perfect raving:
  Then he defies the world, and bids it pass;
  Sometimes he gnaws his lip, and curses loud   120
  The boy Octavius; then he draws his mouth
  Into a scornful smile, and cries, 'Take all,
  The world's not worth my care.'
VENTIDIUS   Just, just his nature.
  Virtue's his path; but sometimes 'tis too narrow
  For his vast soul; and then he starts out wide,   125
  And bounds into a vice that bears him far

121 The boy Octavius] He was thirty-three, some twenty years younger than Antony.

From his first course, and plunges him in ills:
But, when his danger makes him find his fault,
Quick to observe, and full of sharp remorse,
130   He censures eagerly his own misdeeds,
Judging himself with malice to himself,
And not forgiving what as man he did,
Because his other parts are more than man.
         He must not thus be lost. [ALEXAS *and the* Priests *come forward.*
135   ALEXAS   You have your full instructions, now advance;
Proclaim your orders loudly.
SERAPION   Romans, Egyptians, hear the queen's command.
Thus Cleopatra bids: Let labour cease;
To pomp and triumphs give this happy day,
140   That gave the world a lord: 'tis Antony's.
Live, Antony; and Cleopatra live!
Be this the general voice sent up to heav'n,
And every public place repeat this echo.
VENTIDIUS   Fine pageantry!   [*Aside.*
SERAPION   Set out before your doors
145   The images of all your sleeping fathers,
With laurels crowned; with laurels wreathe your posts,
And strew with flowers the pavement; let the priests
Do present sacrifice; pour out the wine,
And call the gods to join with you in gladness.
150   VENTIDIUS   Curse on the tongue that bids this general joy!
Can they be friends of Antony, who revel
When Antony's in danger? Hide, for shame,
You Romans, your great grandsires' images,
For fear their souls should animate their marbles,
155   To blush at their degenerate progeny.
ALEXAS   A love, which knows no bounds, to Antony,
Would mark the day with honours, when all heaven
Laboured for him, when each propitious star
Stood wakeful in his orb, to watch that hour,
160   And shed his better influence. Her own birthday
Our queen neglected, like a vulgar fate
That passed obscurely by.
VENTIDIUS   Would it had slept,
Divided far from his; till some remote

145 images . . . fathers] The *imagines*, or wax masks of ancestors kept in the homes of noble
Roman families.
148 present] Immediate.

And future age had called it out to ruin
Some other prince, not him!
ALEXAS Your emperor,   165
Though grown unkind, would be more gentle than
T' upbraid my queen for loving him too well.
VENTIDIUS Does the mute sacrifice upbraid the priest?
He knows him not his executioner.
Oh, she has decked his ruin with her love,   170
Led him in golden bands to gaudy slaughter,
And made perdition pleasing: she has left him
The blank of what he was.
I tell thee, eunuch, she has quite unmanned him.
Can any Roman see, and know him now,   175
Thus altered from the lord of half mankind,
Unbent, unsinewed, made a woman's toy,
Shrunk from the vast extent of all his honours,
And crampt within a corner of the world?
O Antony!   180
Thou bravest soldier, and thou best of friends!
Bounteous as nature; next to nature's god!
Couldst thou but make new worlds, so wouldst thou give 'em,
As bounty were thy being! rough in battle
As the first Romans when they went to war;   185
Yet after victory more pitiful
Than all their praying virgins left at home!
ALEXAS Would you could add to those more shining virtues
His truth to her who loves him.
VENTIDIUS Would I could not!
But wherefore waste I precious hours with thee?   190
Thou art her darling mischief, her chief engine,
Antony's other fate. Go, tell thy queen
Ventidius is arrived to end her charms.
Let your Egyptian timbrels play alone,
Nor mix effeminate sounds with Roman trumpets.   195
You dare not fight for Antony; go pray,
And keep your cowards' holiday in temples.
                                       [*Exeunt* ALEXAS, SERAPION.
                Enter another GENTLEMAN *of* M. Antony.
2 GENTLEMAN The emperor approaches, and commands,
On pain of death, that none presume to stay.

197 S.D. *Enter another; Re-enter the* 1678.

200   1 GENTLEMAN   I dare not disobey him.   [*Going out with the other.*
       VENTIDIUS   Well, I dare.
          But I'll observe him first unseen, and find
          Which way his humour drives: the rest I'll venture.   [*Withdraws.*

       Enter ANTONY, *walking with a disturbed motion before he speaks.*

       ANTONY   They tell me 'tis my birthday, and I'll keep it
          With double pomp of sadness.
205   'Tis what the day deserves which gave me breath.
          Why was I raised the meteor of the world,
          Hung in the skies, and blazing as I travelled,
          Till all my fires were spent; and then cast downward,
          To be trod out by Caesar?
       VENTIDIUS   On my soul,   [*Aside.*
210   'Tis mournful, wondrous mournful!
       ANTONY   Count thy gains.
          Now, Antony, wouldst thou be born for this?
          Glutton of fortune, thy devouring youth
          Has starved thy wanting age.
       VENTIDIUS   How sorrow shakes him!   [*Aside.*
          So, now the tempest tears him up by th' roots,
215   And on the ground extends the noble ruin.
       ANTONY Lie there, thou shadow of an emperor;

                                        [*Having thrown himself down.*

          The place thou pressest on thy mother earth
          Is all thy empire now: now it contains thee;
          Some few days hence, and then 'twill be too large,
220   When thou'rt contracted in thy narrow urn,
          Shrunk to a few cold ashes; then Octavia
          (For Cleopatra will not live to see it),
          Octavia then will have thee all her own,
          And bear thee in her widowed hand to Caesar;
225   Caesar will weep, the crocodile will weep,
          To see his rival of the universe
          Lie still and peaceful there. I'll think no more on't.
          Give me some music: look that it be sad:
          I'll soothe my melancholy, till I swell
230   And burst myself with sighing —   [*Soft music.*
          'Tis somewhat to my humour. Stay, I fancy
          I'm now turned wild, a commoner of nature;
          Of all forsaken, and forsaking all;

Live in a shady forest's sylvan scene,
Stretched at my length beneath some blasted oak,   235
I lean my head upon the mossy bark,
And look just of a piece as I grew from it;
My uncombed locks, matted like mistletoe,
Hang o'er my hoary face; a murm'ring brook
Runs at my foot.
VENTIDIUS   Methinks I fancy   240
Myself there too.
ANTONY   The herd come jumping by me,
And, fearless, quench their thirst, while I look on,
And take me for their fellow-citizen.
More of this image, more; it lulls my thoughts.   [*Soft music again.*
VENTIDIUS   I must disturb him; I can hold no longer.   245

[*Stands before him.*

ANTONY [*starting up*]   Art thou Ventidius?
VENTIDIUS   Are you Antony?
I'm liker what I was than you to him
I left you last.
ANTONY   I'm angry.
VENTIDIUS   So am I.
ANTONY   I would be private: leave me.
VENTIDIUS   Sir, I love you,
And therefore will not leave you.
ANTONY   Will not leave me?   250
Where have you learnt that answer? Who am I?
VENTIDIUS   My emperor; the man I love next Heaven:
If I said more, I think 'twere scarce a sin;
Y'are all that's good, and god-like.
ANTONY   All that's wretched.
You will not leave me then?
VENTIDIUS   'Twas too presuming   255
To say I would not; but I dare not leave you:
And 'tis unkind in you to chide me hence
So soon, when I so far have come to see you.
ANTONY   Now thou hast seen me, art thou satisfied?
For, if a friend, thou hast beheld enough;   260
And, if a foe, too much.
VENTIDIUS   Look, emperor, this is no common dew.   [*Weeping.*
I have not wept this forty year; but now

254 god-like; good-like *1678.*

My mother comes afresh into my eyes;
265   I cannot help her softness.
ANTONY   By heav'n, he weeps, poor good old man, he weeps!
The big round drops course one another down
The furrows of his cheeks. Stop 'em, Ventidius,
Or I shall blush to death: they set my shame
270   That caused 'em full before me.
VENTIDIUS   I'll do my best.
ANTONY   Sure there's contagion in the tears of friends:
See, I have caught it too. Believe me, 'tis not
For my own griefs, but thine. — Nay, father!
VENTIDIUS   Emperor.
ANTONY   Emperor! Why, that's the style of victory;
275   The conqu'ring soldier, red with unfelt wounds,
Salutes his general so: but never more
Shall that sound reach my ears.
VENTIDIUS   I warrant you.
ANTONY   Actium, Actium! Oh! —
VENTIDIUS   It sits too near you.
ANTONY   Here, here it lies; a lump of lead by day,
280   And, in my short distracted nightly slumbers,
The hag that rides my dreams —
VENTIDIUS   Out with it; give it vent.
ANTONY   Urge not my shame.
I lost a battle.
VENTIDIUS   So has Julius done.
ANTONY   Thou favour'st me, and speak'st not half thou think'st;
285   For Julius fought it out, and lost it fairly:
But Antony —
VENTIDIUS   Nay, stop not.
ANTONY   Antony,
(Well, thou wilt have it) like a coward, fled,
Fled while his soldiers fought; fled first, Ventidius.
Thou long'st to curse me, and I give thee leave.
290   I know thou cam'st prepared to rail.
VENTIDIUS   I did.
ANTONY   I'll help thee — I have been a man, Ventidius.
VENTIDIUS   Yes, and a brave one; but —
ANTONY   I know thy meaning.
But I have lost my reason, have disgraced

281 hag] A spirit or 'nightmare' which oppresses the victim during sleep.

The name of soldier with inglorious ease.
In the full vintage of my flowing honours   295
Sat still, and saw it prest by other hands.
Fortune came smiling to my youth, and wooed it,
And purple greatness met my ripened years.
When first I came to empire, I was borne
On tides of people crowding to my triumphs;   300
The wish of nations, and the willing world
Received me as its pledge of future peace;
I was so great, so happy, so beloved,
Fate could not ruin me; till I took pains,
And worked against my fortune, chid her from me,   305
And turned her loose; yet still she came again.
My careless days, and my luxurious nights,
At length have wearied her, and now she's gone,
Gone, gone, divorced for ever. Help me, soldier,
To curse this madman, this industrious fool,   310
Who laboured to be wretched: pr'ythee, curse me.
VENTIDIUS No.
ANTONY Why?
VENTIDIUS You are too sensible already
  Of what y'have done, too conscious of your failings,
  And like a scorpion, whipt by others first
  To fury, sting yourself in mad revenge.   315
  I would bring balm and pour it in your wounds,
  Cure your distempered mind, and heal your fortunes.
ANTONY I know thou would'st.
VENTIDIUS I will.
ANTONY Ha, ha, ha, ha!
VENTIDIUS You laugh.
ANTONY I do, to see officious love
  Give cordials to the dead.
VENTIDIUS You would be lost, then?   320
ANTONY I am.
VENTIDIUS I say you are not. Try your fortune.
ANTONY I have, to th' utmost. Dost thou think me desperate,
  Without just cause? No, when I found all lost
  Beyond repair, I hid me from the world,
  And learnt to scorn it here; which now I do   325
  So heartily, I think it is not worth
  The cost of keeping.
VENTIDIUS Caesar thinks not so:

He'll thank you for the gift he could not take.
You would be killed like Tully, would you? do,
330   Hold out your throat to Caesar, and die tamely.
ANTONY   No, I can kill myself; and so resolve.
VENTIDIUS   I can die with you too, when time shall serve;
        But fortune calls upon us now to live,
        To fight, to conquer.
ANTONY   Sure thou dream'st, Ventidius.
335 VENTIDIUS   No; 'tis you dream; you sleep away your hours
        In desperate sloth, miscalled philosophy.
        Up, up, for honour's sake; twelve legions wait you,
        And long to call you chief: by painful journeys
        I led 'em, patient both of heat and hunger,
340   Down from the Parthian marches to the Nile.
        'Twill do you good to see their sunburnt faces,
        Their scarred cheeks, and chopped hands: there's virtue in 'em,
        They'll sell those mangled limbs at dearer rates
        Than yon trim bands can buy.
ANTONY   Where left you them?
345 VENTIDIUS   I said in lower Syria.
ANTONY.   Bring 'em hither;
        There may be life in these.
VENTIDIUS   They will not come.
ANTONY   Why didst thou mock my hopes with promised aids,
        To double my despair? They're mutinous.
VENTIDIUS   Most firm and loyal.
ANTONY   Yet they will not march
350   To succour me. O trifler!
VENTIDIUS   They petition
        You would make haste to head 'em.
ANTONY   I'm besieged.
VENTIDIUS   There's but one way shut up: how came I hither?
ANTONY   I will not stir.
VENTIDIUS   They would perhaps desire
        A better reason.
ANTONY   I have never used
355   My soldiers to demand a reason of

329 Tully] Cicero, proscribed by the triumvirate in 43 B.C., fled, and when overtaken by
Antony's soldiers gave himself up bravely to be killed. Cf. II. 394n.
340 marches] Borders.
342 chopped] Chapped, cracked.
354 used] Accustomed.

My actions. Why did they refuse to march?
VENTIDIUS   They said they would not fight for Cleopatra.
ANTONY   What was't they said?
VENTIDIUS   They said, they would not fight for Cleopatra.
  Why should they fight indeed, to make her conquer,   360
  And make you more a slave? to gain you kingdoms,
  Which, for a kiss, at your next midnight feast,
  You'll sell to her? Then she new-names her jewels,
  And calls this diamond such or such a tax;
  Each pendant in her ear shall be a province.   365
ANTONY   Ventidius, I allow your tongue free licence
  On all my other faults; but, on your life,
  No word of Cleopatra: she deserves
  More worlds than I can lose.
VENTIDIUS   Behold, you Pow'rs,
  To whom you have intrusted humankind!   370
  See Europe, Afric, Asia, put in balance,
  And all weighed down by one light worthless woman!
  I think the gods are Antonies, and give,
  Like prodigals, this nether world away
  To none but wasteful hands.
ANTONY   You grow presumptuous.   375
VENTIDIUS   I take the privilege of plain love to speak.
ANTONY   Plain love! plain arrogance, plain insolence!
  Thy men are cowards, thou an envious traitor
  Who, under seeming honesty, has vented
  The burden of thy rank o'erflowing gall.   380
  O that thou wert my equal, great in arms
  As the first Caesar was, that I might kill thee
  Without a stain to honour!
VENTIDIUS   You may kill me;
  You have done more already, called me traitor.
ANTONY   Art thou not one?
VENTIDIUS   For showing you yourself,   385
  Which none else durst have done? but had I been
  That name, which I disdain to speak again,
  I needed not have sought your abject fortunes,
  Come to partake your fate, to die with you.
  What hindered me t'have led my conqu'ring eagles   390
  To fill Octavius' bands? I could have been
  A traitor then, a glorious, happy traitor,
  And not have been so called.

ANTONY   Forgive me, soldier;
I've been too passionate.
VENTIDIUS   You thought me false;
395   Thought my old age betrayed you: kill me, sir,
Pray, kill me; yet you need not, your unkindness
Has left your sword no work.
ANTONY   I did not think so;
I said it in my rage: pr'ythee, forgive me.
Why didst thou tempt my anger, by discovery
400   Of what I would not hear?
VENTIDIUS   No prince but you
Could merit that sincerity I used,
Nor durst another man have ventured it;
But you, ere love misled your wand'ring eyes,
Were sure the chief and best of human race,
405   Framed in the very pride and boast of nature,
So perfect, that the gods, who formed you, wondered
At their own skill, and cried — A lucky hit
Has mended our design. Their envy hindered,
Else you had been immortal, and a pattern,
410   When heav'n would work for ostentation sake
To copy out again.
ANTONY   But Cleopatra —
Go on, for I can bear it now.
VENTIDIUS   No more.
ANTONY   Thou dar'st not trust my passion, but thou may'st;
Thou only lov'st, the rest have flattered me.
415   VENTIDIUS   Heav'n's blessing on your heart for that kind word!
May I believe you love me? Speak again.
ANTONY   Indeed I do. Speak this, and this, and this.
                                          [Hugging him.

Thy praises were unjust, but I'll deserve 'em,
And yet mend all. Do with me what thou wilt;
420   Lead me to victory, thou know'st the way.
VENTIDIUS   And, will you leave this —
ANTONY   Pr'ythee, do not curse her,
And I will leave her; though, heav'n knows, I love
Beyond life, conquest, empire, all, but honour;
But I will leave her.
VENTIDIUS   That's my royal master.
425   And, shall we fight?
ANTONY   I warrant thee, old soldier.

Thou shalt behold me once again in iron,
And at the head of our old troops, that beat
The Parthians, cry aloud, Come follow me!

VENTIDIUS   Oh, now I hear my emperor! in that word
Octavius fell. Gods, let me see that day,   430
And, if I have ten years behind, take all:
I'll thank you for th' exchange.

ANTONY   O Cleopatra!

VENTIDIUS   Again?

ANTONY   I've done: in that last sigh she went.
Caesar shall know what 'tis to force a lover
From all he holds most dear.

VENTIDIUS   Methinks you breathe   435
Another soul: your looks are more divine;
You speak a hero, and you move a god.

ANTONY   Oh, thou hast fired me; my soul's up in arms,
And mans each part about me: once again,
That noble eagerness of fight has seized me;   440
That eagerness with which I darted upward
To Cassius' camp: in vain the steepy hill
Opposed my way, in vain a war of spears
Sung round my head, and planted all my shield:
I won the trenches, while my foremost men   445
Lagged on the plain below.

VENTIDIUS   Ye gods, ye gods,
For such another hour!

ANTONY   Come on, my soldier!
Our hearts and arms are still the same: I long
Once more to meet our foes; that thou and I,
Like Time and Death, marching before our troops,   450
May taste fate to 'em; mow 'em out a passage,
And, ent'ring where the foremost squadrons yield,
Begin the noble harvest of the field.   [*Exeunt.*

ACT II

Enter CLEOPATRA, IRAS, *and* ALEXAS.

CLEOPATRA   What shall I do, or whither shall I turn?
Ventidius has o'ercome, and he will go.

442 Cassius' camp] At Philippi in 42 B.C. Cf. Shakespeare's *Julius Caesar*, Act V.
451 taste . . . 'em] As food and drink is tasted beforehand for a monarch.

ALEXAS   He goes to fight for you.

CLEOPATRA   Then he would see me, ere he went to fight:

5   Flatter me not: if once he goes, he's lost,
       And all my hopes destroyed.

ALEXAS   Does this weak passion
       Become a mighty queen?

CLEOPATRA   I am no queen:
       Is this to be a queen, to be besieged
       By yon insulting Roman, and to wait

10   Each hour the victor's chain? These ills are small,
       For Antony is lost, and I can mourn
       For nothing else but him. Now come, Octavius,
       I have no more to lose; prepare thy bands;
       I'm fit to be a captive: Antony

15   Has taught my mind the fortune of a slave.

IRAS   Call reason to assist you.

CLEOPATRA   I have none,
       And none would have: my love's a noble madness,
       Which shows the cause deserved it. Moderate sorrow
       Fits vulgar love, and for a vulgar man:

20   But I have loved with such transcendent passion,
       I soared, at first, quite out of reason's view,
       And now am lost above it. No, I'm proud
       'Tis thus: would Antony could see me now
       Think you he would not sigh, though he must leave me?

25   Sure he would sigh; for he is noble-natured,
       And bears a tender heart: I know him well.
       Ah, no, I know him not; I knew him once,
       But now 'tis past.

IRAS   Let it be past with you:
       Forget him, madam.

CLEOPATRA   Never, never, Iras.

30   He once was mine; and once, though now 'tis gone,
       Leaves a faint image of possession still.

ALEXAS   Think him inconstant, cruel, and ungrateful.

CLEOPATRA   I cannot: if I could, those thoughts were vain.
       Faithless, ungrateful, cruel, though he be,

35   I still must love him.

                    Enter CHARMION.

Now, what news my Charmion?

13 bands] Bonds.

Will he be kind? and will he not forsake me?
Am I to live, or die? – nay, do I live?
Or am I dead? for when he gave his answer,
Fate took the word, and then I lived or died.
CHARMION   I found him, madam –
CLEOPATRA   A long speech preparing?   40
If thou bring'st comfort, haste, and give it me,
For never was more need.
IRAS   I know he loves you.
CLEOPATRA   Had he been kind, her eyes had told me so,
Before her tongue could speak it: now she studies,
To soften what he said; but give me death,   45
Just as he sent it, Charmion, undisguised,
And in the words he spoke.
CHARMION   I found him, then,
Encompassed round, I think, with iron statues,
So mute, so motionless his soldiers stood,
While awfully he cast his eyes about,   50
And ev'ry leader's hopes or fears surveyed:
Methought he looked resolved, and yet not pleased.
When he beheld me struggling in the crowd,
He blushed, and bade make way.
ALEXAS   There's comfort yet.
CHARMION   Ventidius fixed his eyes upon my passage   55
Severely, as he meant to frown me back,
And sullenly gave place: I told my message,
Just as you gave it, broken and disordered;
I numbered in it all your sighs and tears,
And while I moved your pitiful request,   60
That you but only begged a last farewell,
He fetched an inward groan, and ev'ry time
I named you, sighed, as if his heart were breaking,
But shunned my eyes, and guiltily looked down:
He seemed not now that awful Antony   65
Who shook an armed assembly with his nod,
But making show as he would rub his eyes,
Disguised and blotted out a falling tear.
CLEOPATRA   Did he then weep? and was I worth a tear?
If what thou hast to say be not as pleasing,   70
Tell me no more, but let me die contented.
CHARMION   He bid me say, – he knew himself so well,
He could deny you nothing, if he saw you;

And therefore. . . . .

CLEOPATRA   Thou wouldst say, he would not see me?

75   CHARMION   And therefore begged you not to use a power
Which he could ill resist; yet he should ever
Respect you as he ought.

CLEOPATRA   Is that a word
For Antony to use to Cleopatra?
O that faint word 'Respect'! how I disdain it!

80   Disdain myself, for loving after it!
He should have kept that word for cold Octavia.
Respect is for a wife. Am I that thing,
That dull, insipid lump, without desires,
And without pow'r to give 'em?

ALEXAS   You misjudge;

85   You see through love, and that deludes your sight;
As, what is straight, seems crooked through the water:
But I, who bear my reason undisturbed,
Can see this Antony, this dreaded man,
A fearful slave, who fain would run away,

90   And shuns his master's eyes: if you pursue him,
My life on't, he still drags a chain along,
That needs must clog his flight.

CLEOPATRA   Could I believe thee! –

ALEXAS   By every circumstance I know he loves.
True, he's hard prest, by int'rest and by honour;

95   Yet he but doubts, and parleys, and casts out
Many a long look for succour.

CLEOPATRA   He sends word
He fears to see my face.

ALEXAS   And would you more?
He shows his weakness who declines the combat,
And you must urge your fortune. Could he speak

100   More plainly? To my ears, the message sounds –
Come to my rescue, Cleopatra, come;
Come, free me from Ventidius, from my tyrant:
See me, and give me a pretence to leave him!
I hear his trumpets. This way he must pass.

105   Please you, retire a while; I'll work him first,
That he may bend more easy.

CLEOPATRA   You shall rule me;
But all, I fear, in vain.   [Exit with CHARMION and IRAS.

ALEXAS   I fear so too;

Though I concealed my thoughts, to make her bold;
But 'tis our utmost means, and fate befriend it!   [*Withdraws.*

Enter Lictors *with Fasces; one bearing the Eagle; then enter* ANTONY *with*
VENTIDIUS, *followed by other* Commanders.

ANTONY   Octavius is the minion of blind chance,   110
  But holds from virtue nothing.
VENTIDIUS   Has he courage?
ANTONY   But just enough to season him from coward.
  Oh, 'tis the coldest youth upon a charge,
  The most deliberate fighter! if he ventures
  (As in Illyria once they say he did   115
  To storm a town) 'tis when he cannot choose,
  When all the world have fixt their eyes upon him;
  And then he lives on that for seven years after;
  But, at a close revenge he never fails.
VENTIDIUS   I heard you challenged him.
ANTONY   I did, Ventidius.   120
  What think'st thou was his answer? 'Twas so tame! –
  He said he had more ways than one to die;
  I had not.
VENTIDIUS   Poor!
ANTONY   He has more ways than one,
  But he would choose 'em all before that one.
VENTIDIUS   He first would choose an ague, or a fever.   125
ANTONY   No: it must be an ague, not a fever;
  He has not warmth enough to die by that.
VENTIDIUS   Or old age, and a bed.
ANTONY   Ay, there's his choice.
  He would live, like a lamp, to the last wink,
  And crawl upon the utmost verge of life.   130
  O Hercules! Why should a man like this,
  Who dares not trust his fate for one great action,
  Be all the care of heav'n? Why should he lord it
  O'er fourscore thousand men, of whom each one
  Is braver than himself?
VENTIDIUS   You conquered for him: 135
  Philippi knows it; there you shared with him
  That empire which your sword made all your own.

119 close] Secret.

ANTONY   Fool that I was, upon my eagle's wings
    I bore this wren, till I was tired with soaring,
140   And now he mounts above me.
    Good heav'ns, is this, is this the man who braves me?
    Who bids my age make way? Drives me before him,
    To the world's ridge, and sweeps me off like rubbish?
VENTIDIUS   Sir, we lose time; the troops are mounted all.
145 ANTONY   Then give the word to march:
    I long to leave this prison of a town,
    To join thy legions, and in open field
    Once more to show my face. Lead, my deliverer.

Enter ALEXAS.

ALEXAS   Great emperor,
150   In mighty arms renowned above mankind,
    But, in soft pity to th' oppressed, a god;
    This message sends the mournful Cleopatra
    To her departing lord.
VENTIDIUS   Smooth sycophant!
ALEXAS   A thousand wishes, and ten thousand prayers,
155   Millions of blessings wait you to the wars;
    Millions of sighs and tears she sends you too,
    And would have sent
    As many dear embraces to your arms,
    As many parting kisses to your lips;
160   But those, she fears, have wearied you already.
VENTIDIUS [*aside*] False crocodile!
ALEXAS   And yet she begs not now, you would not leave her;
    That were a wish too mighty for her hopes,
    Too presuming
165   For her low fortune, and your ebbing love;
    That were a wish for her more prosp'rous days,
    Her blooming beauty, and your growing kindness.
ANTONY [*aside*] Well, I must man it out. What would the queen?
ALEXAS   First, to these noble warriors who attend
170   Your daring courage in the chase of fame
    (Too daring and too dangerous for her quiet)
    She humbly recommends all she holds dear,
    All her own cares and fears, the care of you.

138–40 Alluding to the fable of the wren who claimed to fly higher than the eagle after
ascending on the other's back.

VENTIDIUS   Yes, witness Actium.
ANTONY   Let him speak, Ventidius.
ALEXAS   You, when his matchless valour bears him forward,   175
   With ardour too heroic, on his foes,
   Fall down, as she would do, before his feet;
   Lie in his way, and stop the paths of death:
   Tell him, this god is not invulnerable;
   That absent Cleopatra bleeds in him;   180
   And, that you may remember her petition,
   She begs you wear these trifles, as a pawn,
   Which at your wished return she will redeem

                  [*Gives jewels to the* Commanders.

   With all the wealth of Egypt:
   This to the great Ventidius she presents,   185
   Whom she can never count her enemy,
   Because he loves her lord.
VENTIDIUS   Tell her, I'll none on't;
   I'm not ashamed of honest poverty;
   Not all the diamonds of the east can bribe
   Ventidius from his faith. I hope to see   190
   These and the rest of all her sparkling store,
   Where they shall more deservingly be placed.
ANTONY   And who must wear 'em then?
VENTIDIUS   The wronged Octavia.
ANTONY   You might have spared that word.
VENTIDIUS   And he that bribe.
ANTONY   But have I no remembrance?
ALEXAS   Yes, a dear one: 195
   Your slave the queen –
ANTONY   My mistress.
ALEXAS   Then your mistress;
   Your mistress would, she says, have sent her soul,
   But that you had long since; she humbly begs
   This ruby bracelet, set with bleeding hearts,
   (The emblems of her own) may bind your arm.   200

                  [*Presenting a bracelet.*

VENTIDIUS   Now, my best lord, in honour's name, I ask you,
   For manhood's sake, and for your own dear safety,
   Touch not these poisoned gifts,
   Infected by the sender, touch 'em not;

205   Myriads of bluest plagues lie underneath 'em,
           And more than aconite has dipt the silk.
ANTONY   Nay, now you grow too cynical, Ventidius.
           A lady's favours may be worn with honour.
           What, to refuse her bracelet! On my soul,
210   When I lie pensive in my tent alone,
           'Twill pass the wakeful hours of winter nights,
           To tell these pretty beads upon my arm,
           To count for every one a soft embrace,
           A melting kiss at such and such a time:
215   And now and then the fury of her love,
           When . . . And what harm's in this?
ALEXAS   None, none, my lord,
           But what's to her, that now 'tis past for ever.
ANTONY [*going to tie it*] We soldiers are so awkward – help me tie it.
ALEXAS   In faith, my lord, we courtiers too are awkward
220   In these affairs: so are all men indeed,
           Ev'n I, who am not one. But shall I speak?
ANTONY   Yes, freely.
ALEXAS   Then, my lord, fair hands alone
           Are fit to tie it; she who sent it can.
VENTIDIUS   Hell, death! this eunuch pander ruins you.
225   You will not see her?

                           [ALEXAS *whispers an* Attendant, *who goes out*.

ANTONY   But to take my leave.
VENTIDIUS   Then I have washed an Aethiop. Y'are undone;
           Y'are in the toils; y'are taken; y'are destroyed:
           Her eyes do Caesar's work.
ANTONY   You fear too soon.
           I'm constant to myself: I know my strength;
230   And yet she shall not think me barbarous neither,
           Born in the depths of Afric: I am a Roman,
           Bred to the rules of soft humanity.
           A guest, and kindly used, should bid farewell.
VENTIDIUS   You do not know
235   How weak you are to her, how much an infant:
           You are not proof against a smile, or glance;
           A sigh will quite disarm you.
ANTONY   See, she comes!

206 aconite] A deadly poison.
226 washed an Aethiop] Proverbial for a hopeless task.

Now you shall find your error. Gods, I thank you:
I formed the danger greater than it was,
And now 'tis near, 'tis lessened.
VENTIDIUS   Mark the end yet.   240

Enter CLEOPATRA, CHARMION, *and* IRAS.

ANTONY   Well, madam, we are met.
CLEOPATRA   Is this a meeting?
  Then, we must part?
ANTONY   We must.
CLEOPATRA   Who says we must?
ANTONY   Our own hard fates.
CLEOPATRA   We make those fates ourselves.
ANTONY   Yes, we have made 'em; we have loved each other
  Into our mutual ruin.   245
CLEOPATRA   The gods have seen my joys with envious eyes;
  I have no friends in heav'n; and all the world
  (As 'twere the bus'ness of mankind to part us)
  Is armed against my love: ev'n you yourself
  Join with the rest; you, you are armed against me.   250
ANTONY   I will be justified in all I do
  To late posterity, and therefore hear me.
  If I mix a lie
  With any truth, reproach me freely with it;
  Else, favour me with silence.
CLEOPATRA   You command me,   255
  And I am dumb.
VENTIDIUS   I like this well: he shows authority.
ANTONY   That I derive my ruin
  From you alone —
CLEOPATRA   O heav'ns! I ruin you!
ANTONY   You promised me your silence, and you break it   260
  Ere I have scarce begun.
CLEOPATRA   Well, I obey you.
ANTONY   When I beheld you first, it was in Egypt
  Ere Caesar saw your eyes; you gave me love,
  And were too young to know it; that I settled
  Your father in his throne, was for your sake;   265
  I left th' acknowledgment for time to ripen.
  Caesar stepped in, and, with a greedy hand
  Plucked the green fruit ere the first blush of red,
  Yet cleaving to the bough. He was my lord,

270   And was, beside, too great for me to rival;
        But I deserved you first, though he enjoyed you.
        When, after, I beheld you in Cilicia,
        An enemy to Rome, I pardoned you.
CLEOPATRA   I cleared myself —
ANTONY   Again you break your promise.
275   I loved you still, and took your weak excuses,
        Took you into my bosom, stained by Caesar,
        And not half mine: I went to Egypt with you
        And hid me from the bus'ness of the world,
        Shut out inquiring nations from my sight,
280   To give whole years to you.
VENTIDIUS   Yes, to your shame be't spoken.   [Aside.
ANTONY.   How I loved
        Witness, ye days and nights, and all ye hours,
        That danced away with down upon your feet,
        As all your bus'ness were to count my passion!
285   One day passed by, and nothing saw but love;
        Another came, and still 'twas only love:
        The suns were wearied out with looking on,
        And I untired with loving.
        I saw you every day, and all the day;
290   And every day was still but as the first,
        So eager was I still to see you more.
VENTIDIUS   'Tis all too true.
ANTONY   Fulvia, my wife, grew jealous,
        As she indeed had reason; raised a war
        In Italy, to call me back.
VENTIDIUS   But yet
295   You went not.
ANTONY   While within your arms I lay,
        The world fell mould'ring from my hands each hour,
        And left me scarce a grasp — I thank you love for't.
VENTIDIUS   Well pushed: that last was home.
CLEOPATRA   Yet may I speak?
ANTONY   If I have urged a falsehood, yes; else, not.
300   Your silence says I have not. Fulvia died,
        (Pardon, you gods, with my unkindness died).
        To set the world at peace, I took Octavia,
        This Caesar's sister; in her pride of youth
        And flow'r of beauty, did I wed that lady,
305   Whom blushing I must praise, because I left her.

You called; my love obeyed the fatal summons:
This raised the Roman arms; the cause was yours.
I would have fought by land, where I was stronger;
You hindered it: yet, when I fought at sea,
Forsook me fighting; (O stain to honour!   310
O lasting shame!) I knew not that I fled;
But fled to follow you.
VENTIDIUS   What haste she made to hoist her purple sails!
  And, to appear magnificent in flight,
  Drew half our strength away.
ANTONY   All this you caused.   315
  And would you multiply more ruins on me?
  This honest man, my best, my only friend,
  Has gathered up the shipwreck of my fortunes;
  Twelve legions I have left, my last recruits,
  And you have watched the news, and bring your eyes   320
  To seize them too. If you have aught to answer,
  Now speak, you have free leave.
ALEXAS [aside]   She stands confounded:
  Despair is in her eyes.
VENTIDIUS   Now lay a sigh i'th' way to stop his passage:
  Prepare a tear, and bid it for his legions;   325
  'Tis like they shall be sold.
CLEOPATRA   How shall I plead my cause, when you, my judge,
  Already have condemned me? Shall I bring
  The love you bore me for my advocate?
  That now is turned against me, that destroys me;   330
  For love, once past, is, at the best, forgotten;
  But oftener sours to hate: 'twill please my lord
  To ruin me, and therefore I'll be guilty.
  But, could I once have thought it would have pleased you,
  That you would pry, with narrow searching eyes,   335
  Into my faults, severe to my destruction,
  And watching all advantages with care,
  That serve to make me wretched? Speak, my lord,
  For I end here. Though I deserve this usage,
  Was it like you to give it?
ANTONY   Oh, you wrong me   340
  To think I sought this parting, or desired
  To accuse you more than what will clear myself,
  And justify this breach.
CLEOPATRA   Thus low I thank you.

And, since my innocence will not offend,
345   I shall not blush to own it.
VENTIDIUS   After this
   I think she'll blush at nothing.
CLEOPATRA   You seemed grieved
   (And therein you are kind) that Caesar first
   Enjoyed my love, though you deserved it better:
   I grieve for that, my lord, much more than you;
350   For, had I first been yours, it would have saved
   My second choice: I never had been his,
   And ne'er had been but yours. But Caesar first,
   You say, possessed my love. Not so, my lord:
   He first possessed my person, you my love:
355   Caesar loved me, but I loved Antony.
   If I endured him after, 'twas because
   I judged it due to the first name of men;
   And, half constrained, I gave, as to a tyrant,
   What he would take by force.
VENTIDIUS   O Syren! Syren!
360   Yet grant that all the love she boasts were true,
   Has she not ruined you? I still urge that,
   The fatal consequence.
CLEOPATRA   The consequence indeed,
   For I dare challenge him, my greatest foe,
   To say it was designed: 'tis true, I loved you,
365   And kept you far from an uneasy wife,
   (Such Fulvia was).
   Yes, but he'll say, you left Octavia for me; —
   And, can you blame me to receive that love,
   Which quitted such desert for worthless me?
370   How often have I wished some other Caesar,
   Great as the first, and as the second young,
   Would court my love to be refused for you!
VENTIDIUS   Words, words; but Actium, sir; remember Actium.
CLEOPATRA   Ev'n there I dare his malice. True, I counselled
375   To fight at sea; but I betrayed you not.
   I fled, but not to the enemy. 'Twas fear:
   Would I had been a man, not to have feared,
   For none would then have envied me your friendship,
   Who envy me your love.
ANTONY   We're both unhappy:
380   If nothing else, yet our ill fortune parts us.

Speak, would you have me perish by my stay?
CLEOPATRA If as a friend you ask my judgment, go;
  If as a lover stay. If you must perish —
  'Tis a hard word — but stay.
VENTIDIUS See now th' effects of her so boasted love!   385
  She strives to drag you down to ruin with her:
  But, could she 'scape without you, oh, how soon
  Would she let go her hold, and haste to shore,
  And never look behind!
CLEOPATRA Then judge my love by this.

                            [Giving ANTONY *a writing.*

  Could I have borne   390
  A life or death, a happiness or woe
  From yours divided, this had giv'n me means.
ANTONY By Hercules, the writing of Octavius!
  I know it well: 'tis that proscribing hand,
  Young as it was, that led the way to mine,   395
  And left me but the second place in murder. —
  See, see, Ventidius! here he offers Egypt,
  And joins all Syria to it, as a present,
  So, in requital, she forsake my fortunes,
  And joins her arms with his.
CLEOPATRA And yet you leave me!   400
  You leave me, Antony; and yet I love you,
  Indeed I do: I have refused a kingdom,
  That's a trifle:
  For I could part with life, with anything,
  But only you. Oh, let me die but with you!   405
  Is that a hard request?
ANTONY Next living with you,
  'Tis all that heav'n can give.
ALEXAS He melts; we conquer.   *[Aside.*
CLEOPATRA No, you shall go: your int'rest calls you hence;
  Yes, your dear interest pulls too strong for these
  Weak arms to hold you here.   *[Takes his hand.*
  Go, leave me, soldier   410
  (For you're no more a lover), leave me dying:
  Push me, all pale and panting, from your bosom,

394 proscribing] In 43 B.C. the triumvirate of Octavius, Antony, and Lepidus drew up a list
of enemies to be put to death.

                  And, when your march begins, let one run after
                  Breathless almost for joy, and cry, she's dead.
415   The soldiers shout; you then perhaps may sigh,
                  And muster all your Roman gravity:
                  Ventidius chides; and straight your brow clears up,
                  As I had never been.
        ANTONY   Gods, 'tis too much; too much for man to bear!
420   CLEOPATRA   What is't for me then,
                  A weak forsaken woman, and a lover? —
                  Here let me breathe my last: envy me not
                  This minute in your arms: I'll die apace,
                  As fast as e'er I can, and end your trouble.
425   ANTONY   Die! rather let me perish: loosened nature
                  Leap from its hinges, sink the props of heav'n,
                  And fall the skies to crush the nether world.
                  My eyes, my soul, my all!   [Embraces her.
        VENTIDIUS   And what's this toy
                  In balance with your fortune, honour, fame?
430   ANTONY   What is't, Ventidius? it outweighs 'em all;
                  Why, we have more than conquered Caesar now:
                  My queen's not only innocent, but loves me.
                  This, this is she who drags me down to ruin!
                  'But, could she 'scape without me, with what haste
435   Would she let slip her hold, and make to shore,
                  And never look behind!'
                  Down on thy knees, blasphemer as thou art,
                  And ask forgiveness of wronged innocence.
        VENTIDIUS   I'll rather die than take it. Will you go?
440   ANTONY   Go! whither? Go from all that's excellent.
                  Faith, honour, virtue, all good things forbid
                  That I should go from her who sets my love
                  Above the price of kingdoms. Give, you gods,
                  Give to your boy, your Caesar,
445   This rattle of a globe to play withal,
                  This gewgaw world, and put him cheaply off:
                  I'll not be pleased with less than Cleopatra.
        CLEOPATRA   She wholly yours. My heart's so full of joy,
                  That I shall do some wild extravagance
450   Of love, in public; and the foolish world,
                  Which knows not tenderness, will think me mad.
        VENTIDIUS   O women! women! women! all the gods
                  Have not such pow'r of doing good to man,

As you of doing harm.   [*Exit.*

ANTONY   Our men are armed.
    Unbar the gate that looks to Caesar's camp: 455
    I would revenge the treachery he meant me,
    And long security makes conquest easy.
    I'm eager to return before I go;
    For, all the pleasures I have known beat thick
    On my remembrance: how I long for night!   460
      That both the sweets of mutual love may try,
      And once triumph o'er Caesar ere we die.   [*Exeunt.*

ACT III

At one door enter CLEOPATRA, CHARMION, IRAS, *and* ALEXAS,
   a Train of Egyptians: *at the other* ANTONY *and* Romans. *The*
entrance on both sides is prepared by music; the trumpets first sounding on
ANTONY'S *part: then answered by timbrels, etc., on* CLEOPATRA'S.
CHARMION *and* IRAS *hold a laurel wreath betwixt them. A Dance of*
   Egyptians. *After the ceremony,* CLEOPATRA *crowns* ANTONY.

ANTONY   I thought how those white arms would fold me in,
    And strain me close, and melt me into love;
    So pleased with that sweet image, I sprung forwards,
    And added all my strength to every blow.
CLEOPATRA   Come to me, come, my soldier, to my arms!   5
    You've been too long away from my embraces;
    But, when I have you fast, and all my own,
    With broken murmurs, and with amorous sighs,
    I'll say, you were unkind, and punish you,
    And mark you red with many an eager kiss.   10
ANTONY   My brighter Venus!
CLEOPATRA   O my greater Mars!
ANTONY   Thou join'st us well, my love!
    Suppose me come from the Phlegraean plains,
    Where gasping giants lay, cleft by my sword,
    And mountain-tops pared off each other blow,   15

462 *1678* omits ere.

---

13 Phlegraean plains] Where Hercules assisted the gods to overwhelm the giants. The giants
were believed to be each buried under a volcano.

To bury those I slew. Receive me, goddess!
Let Caesar spread his subtle nets; like Vulcan,
In thy embraces I would be beheld
By heav'n and earth at once

20   And make their envy what they meant their sport.
Let those who took us blush; I would love on
With awful state, regardless of their frowns,
As their superior god.
There's no satiety of love in thee:

25   Enjoyed, thou still art new; perpetual spring
Is in thy arms; the ripened fruit but falls,
And blossoms rise to fill its empty place;
And I grow rich by giving.

Enter VENTIDIUS, *and stands apart.*

ALEXAS   Oh, now the danger's past, your general comes.
30   He joins not in your joys nor minds your triumphs,
But with contracted brows looks frowning on,
As envying your success.
ANTONY   Now, on my soul, he loves me, truly loves me:
He never flattered me in any vice,
35   But awes me with his virtue: even this minute
Methinks he has a right of chiding me.
Lead to the temple: I'll avoid his presence;
It checks too strong upon me.   [*Exeunt the rest.*

[*As* ANTONY *is going,* VENTIDIUS *pulls him by the robe.*

VENTIDIUS   Emperor!
ANTONY   'Tis the old argument; I pr'ythee, spare me.

[*Looking back.*

40   VENTIDIUS   But this one hearing, emperor.
ANTONY   Let go
My robe; or, by my father Hercules –
VENTIDIUS   By Hercules his father, that's yet greater,
I bring you somewhat you would wish to know.
ANTONY   Thou see'st we are observed; attend me here,

17–23 Vulcan trapped his wife, Venus, and her lover, Mars, in bed with a net, and called the
other gods to witness their shame. Mercury, however, said that he would gladly change
places with Mars (*Odyssey*, VIII, 266–366).
41 my father Hercules] Antony claimed descent from Hercules.
42 Hercules his father] Jupiter.

And I'll return. [*Exit.* 45
VENTIDIUS I'm waning in his favour, yet I love him;
  I love this man, who runs to meet his ruin;
  And sure the gods, like me, are fond of him:
  His virtues lie so mingled with his crimes,
  As would confound their choice to punish one, 50
  And not reward the other.

Enter ANTONY.

ANTONY We can conquer,
  You see, without your aid.
  We have dislodged their troops;
  They look on us at distance, and, like curs
  Scaped from the lion's paws, they bay far off, 55
  And lick their wounds, and faintly threaten war.
  Five thousand Romans, with their faces upward,
  Lie breathless on the plain.
VENTIDIUS 'Tis well: and he
  Who lost 'em could have spared ten thousand more.
  Yet if by this advantage you could gain 60
  An easier peace, while Caesar doubts the chance
  Of arms! —
ANTONY Oh think not on't, Ventidius!
  The boy pursues my ruin, he'll no peace;
  His malice is considerate in advantage.
  Oh, he's the coolest murderer, so staunch, 65
  He kills, and keeps his temper.
VENTIDIUS Have you no friend
  In all his army who has power to move him?
  Maecenas or Agrippa might do much.
ANTONY They're both too deep in Caesar's interests.
  We'll work it out by dint of sword, or perish. 70
VENTIDIUS Fain I would find some other.
ANTONY Thank thy love.
  Some four or five such victories as this
  Will save thy farther pains.
VENTIDIUS Expect no more; Caesar is on his guard:
  I know, sir, you have conquered against odds; 75
  But still you draw supplies from one poor town,
  And of Egyptians: he has all the world,
  And at his back nations come pouring in
  To fill the gaps you make. Pray think again.

80 ANTONY Why dost thou drive me from myself, to search
      For foreign aids? to hunt my memory,
      And range all o'er a waste and barren place
      To find a friend? The wretched have no friends. . . .
      Yet I had one, the bravest youth of Rome,
85   Whom Caesar loves beyond the love of women:
      He could resolve his mind, as fire does wax,
      From that hard rugged image melt him down,
      And mould him in what softer form he pleased.
    VENTIDIUS Him would I see; that man, of all the world:
90   Just such a one we want.
    ANTONY He loved me too;
      I was his soul, he lived not but in me:
      We were so closed within each other's breasts
      The rivets were not found that joined us first.
      That does not reach us yet: we were so mixt
95   As meeting streams, both to ourselves were lost;
      As were one mass, we could not give or take
      But from the same; for he was I, I he.
    VENTIDIUS He moves as I would wish him.   [Aside.
    ANTONY After this,
      I need not tell his name: 'twas Dolabella.
100 VENTIDIUS He's now in Caesar's camp.
    ANTONY No matter where,
      Since he's no longer mine. He took unkindly
      That I forbade him Cleopatra's sight,
      Because I feared he loved her: he confessed
      He had a warmth, which, for my sake, he stifled;
105   For 'twere impossible that two, so one,
      Should not have loved the same. When he departed,
      He took no leave; and that confirmed my thoughts.
    VENTIDIUS It argues that he loved you more than her,
      Else he had stayed; but he perceived you jealous,
110   And would not grieve his friend: I know he loves you.
    ANTONY I should have seen him, then, ere now.
    VENTIDIUS Perhaps
      He has thus long been lab'ring for your peace.
    ANTONY Would he were here!
    VENTIDIUS Would you believe he loved you?
      I read your answer in your eyes, you would.
115   Not to conceal it longer, he has sent
      A messenger from Caesar's camp, with letters.

ANTONY   Let him appear.
VENTIDIUS   I'll bring him instantly.

[*Exit* VENTIDIUS, *and re-enters immediately with* DOLABELLA.

ANTONY   'Tis he himself! himself, by holy friendship!

[*Runs to embrace him.*

Art thou returned at last, my better half?
Come, give me all myself!   120
Let me not live,
If the young bridegroom, longing for his night,
Was ever half so fond.
DOLABELLA   I must be silent, for my soul is busy
About a nobler work: she's new come home,   125
Like a long-absent man, and wanders o'er
Each room, a stranger to her own, to look
If all be safe.
ANTONY   Thou hast what's left of me;
For I am now so sunk from what I was
Thou find'st me at my lowest water-mark.   130
The rivers that ran in and raised my fortunes
Are all dried up, or take another course:
What I have left is from my native spring;
I've still a heart that swells in scorn of fate
And lifts me to my banks.   135
DOLABELLA   Still you are lord of all the world to me.
ANTONY   Why, then I yet am so; for thou art all.
If I had any joy when thou wert absent,
I grudged it to myself; methought I robbed
Thee of thy part. But, O my Dolabella!   140
Thou hast beheld me other than I am.
Hast thou not seen my morning chambers filled
With sceptred slaves, who waited to salute me?
With eastern monarchs, who forgot the sun
To worship my uprising? Menial kings   145
Ran coursing up and down my palace-yard,
Stood silent in my presence, watched my eyes,
And, at my least command, all started out
Like racers to the goal.
DOLABELLA   Slaves to your fortune.
ANTONY   Fortune is Caesar's now; and what am I?   150
VENTIDIUS   What you have made yourself; I will not flatter.

ANTONY   Is this friendly done?
DOLABELLA   Yes; when his end is so, I must join with him;
    Indeed I must, and yet you must not chide:
155   Why am I else your friend?
ANTONY   Take heed, young man,
    How thou upbraid'st my love: the queen has eyes,
    And thou too hast a soul. Canst thou remember
    When, swelled with hatred, thou beheld'st her first
    As accessary to thy brother's death?
160 DOLABELLA   Spare my remembrance; 'twas a guilty day,
    And still the blush hangs here.
ANTONY   To clear herself
    For sending him no aid she came from Egypt.
    Her galley down the silver Cydnus rowed,
    The tackling silk, the streamers waved with gold,
165   The gentle winds were lodged in purple sails:
    Her nymphs, like Nereids, round her couch were placed,
    Where she, another sea-born Venus, lay.
DOLABELLA   No more; I would not hear it.
ANTONY   Oh, you must!
    She lay, and leant her cheek upon her hand,
170   And cast a look so languishingly sweet,
    As if, secure of all beholders' hearts,
    Neglecting she could take 'em: boys like Cupids
    Stood fanning, with their painted wings, the winds
    That played about her face: but if she smiled
175   A darting glory seemed to blaze abroad,
    That men's desiring eyes were never wearied,
    But hung upon the object. To soft flutes
    The silver oars kept time; and while they played
    The hearing gave new pleasure to the sight,
180   And both to thought. 'Twas heav'n, or somewhat more;
    For she so charmed all hearts, that gazing crowds
    Stood panting on the shore, and wanted breath
    To give their welcome voice.
    Then, Dolabella, where was then thy soul?
185   Was not thy fury quite disarmed with wonder?
    Didst thou not shrink behind me from those eyes
    And whisper in my ear, Oh tell her not
    That I accused her of my brother's death?

163–83 Dryden's adaptation of Shakespeare's famous description in *Antony and Cleopatra*, II.
ii. 191–218.

DOLABELLA   And should my weakness be a plea for yours?
  Mine was an age when love might be excused, 190
  When kindly warmth, and when my springing youth
  Made it a debt to nature. Yours—
VENTIDIUS   Speak boldly.
  Yours, he would say, in your declining age,
  When no more heat was left but what you forced,
  When all the sap was needful for the trunk, 195
  When it went down, then you constrained the course,
  And robbed from nature, to supply desire;
  In you (I would not use so harsh a word)
  But 'tis plain dotage.
ANTONY   Ha!
DOLABELLA   'Twas urged too home.
  But yet the loss was private that I made; 200
  'Twas but myself I lost: I lost no legions;
  I had no world to lose, no people's love.
ANTONY   This from a friend?
DOLABELLA   Yes, Antony, a true one;
  A friend so tender, that each word I speak
  Stabs my own heart, before it reach your ear. 205
  Oh, judge me not less kind because I chide:
  To Caesar I excuse you.
ANTONY   O ye gods!
  Have I then lived to be excused to Caesar?
DOLABELLA   As to your equal.
ANTONY   Well, he's but my equal:
  While I wear this he never shall be more. 210
DOLABELLA   I bring conditions from him.
ANTONY   Are they noble?
  Methinks thou shouldst not bring them else; yet he
  Is full of deep dissembling; knows no honour
  Divided from his int'rest. Fate mistook him
  For nature meant him for an usurer: 215
  He's fit indeed to buy, not conquer kingdoms.
VENTIDIUS   Then, granting this,
  What pow'r was theirs who wrought so hard a temper
  To honourable terms?
ANTONY   It was my Dolabella, or some god. 220
DOLABELLA   Nor I, nor yet Maecenas, nor Agrippa:

210 this] Presumably his sword.

They were your enemies, and I a friend
Too weak alone; yet 'twas a Roman's deed.
ANTONY   'Twas like a Roman done: show me that man
225   Who has preserved my life, my love, my honour;
Let me but see his face.
VENTIDIUS   That task is mine,
And, Heaven, thou know'st how pleasing.

[*Exit* VENTIDIUS.

DOLABELLA   You'll remember
To whom you stand obliged?
ANTONY   When I forget it,
Be thou unkind, and that's my greatest curse.
230   My queen shall thank him too.
DOLABELLA   I fear she will not.
ANTONY   But she shall do't: the queen, my Dolabella!
Hast thou not still some grudgings of thy fever?
DOLABELLA   I would not see her lost.
ANTONY   When I forsake her,
Leave me, my better stars; for she has truth
235   Beyond her beauty. Caesar tempted her,
At no less price than kingdoms, to betray me;
But she resisted all; and yet thou chid'st me
For loving her too well. Could I do so?
DOLABELLA   Yes; there's my reason.

Re-enter VENTIDIUS, *with* OCTAVIA, *leading* ANTONY'S *two little*
Daughters.

ANTONY   Where? – Octavia there!   [*Starting back.*
240 VENTIDIUS   What, is she poison to you? a disease?
Look on her, view her well, and those she brings:
Are they all strangers to your eyes? has nature
No secret call, no whisper they are yours?
DOLABELLA   For shame, my lord, if not for love, receive 'em
245   With kinder eyes. If you confess a man,
Meet 'em, embrace 'em, bid 'em welcome to you.
Your arms should open ev'n without your knowledge
To clasp them in, your feet should turn to wings
To bear you to them, and your eyes dart out
250   And aim a kiss ere you could reach the lips.

232 grudgings] Traces.
245 confess] Admit to being.

ANTONY   I stood amazed to think how they came hither.
VENTIDIUS   I sent for 'em; I brought 'em in unknown
  To Cleopatra's guards.
DOLABELLA   Yet are you cold?
OCTAVIA   Thus long I have attended for my welcome,
  Which, as a stranger, sure I might expect.   255
  Who am I?
ANTONY   Caesar's sister.
OCTAVIA   That's unkind!
  Had I been nothing more than Caesar's sister,
  Know, I had still remained in Caesar's camp:
  But your Octavia, your much injured wife,
  Though banished from your bed, driv'n from your house,   260
  In spite of Caesar's sister, still is yours.
  'Tis true, I have a heart disdains your coldness,
  And prompts me not to seek what you should offer;
  But a wife's virtue still surmounts that pride:
  I come to claim you as my own; to show   265
  My duty first; to ask, nay beg, your kindness:
  Your hand, my lord; 'tis mine, and I will have it.

                                [Taking his hand.

VENTIDIUS   Do, take it; thou deserv'st it.
DOLABELLA   On my soul,
  And so she does: she's neither too submissive,
  Nor yet too haughty; but so just a mean   270
  Shows, as it ought, a wife and Roman too.
ANTONY   I fear, Octavia, you have begged my life.
OCTAVIA   Begged it, my lord?
ANTONY   Yes, begged it, my ambassadress;
  Poorly and basely begged it of your brother.
OCTAVIA   Poorly and basely I could never beg: 275
  Nor could my brother grant.
ANTONY   Shall I, who to my kneeling slave could say,
  Rise up, and be a king; shall I fall down
  And cry, Forgive me, Caesar! Shall I set
  A man, my equal, in the place of Jove,   280
  As he could give me being? No; that word
  'Forgive' would choke me up,
  And die upon my tongue.
DOLABELLA   You shall not need it.
ANTONY   I will not need it. Come, you've all betrayed me —

285   My friend too! — to receive some vile conditions.
          My wife has bought me with her prayers and tears,
          And now I must become her branded slave.
          In every peevish mood, she will upbraid
          The life she gave: if I but look awry,
290   She cries, I'll tell my brother.
     OCTAVIA My hard fortune
          Subjects me still to your unkind mistakes.
          But the conditions I have brought are such
          You need not blush to take: I love your honour
          Because 'tis mine; it never shall be said
295   Octavia's husband was her brother's slave.
          Sir, you are free; free, ev'n from her you loathe;
          For though my brother bargains for your love,
          Makes me the price and cement of your peace,
          I have a soul like yours; I cannot take
300   Your love as alms, nor beg what I deserve.
          I'll tell my brother we are reconciled;
          He shall draw back his troops, and you shall march
          To rule the East: I may be dropped at Athens;
          No matter where, I never will complain,
305   But only keep the barren name of wife,
          And rid you of the trouble.
     VENTIDIUS Was ever such a strife of sullen honour!   [*Aside.*
          Both scorn to be obliged.
     DOLABELLA Oh, she has touched him in the tend'rest part;
310   See how he reddens with despite and shame
          To be outdone in generosity!
     VENTIDIUS See how he winks! how he dries up a tear,
          That fain would fall!
     ANTONY Octavia, I have heard you, and must praise
315   The greatness of your soul;
          But cannot yield to what you have proposed:
          For I can ne'er be conquered but by love,
          And you do all for duty. You would free me,
          And would be dropped at Athens; was't not so?
320 OCTAVIA It was, my lord.
     ANTONY Then I must be obliged
          To one who loves me not, who to herself,
          May call me thankless and ungrateful man:
          I'll not endure it, no.
     VENTIDIUS I'm glad it pinches there.   [*Aside.*

OCTAVIA   Would you triumph o'er poor Octavia's virtue?   325
  That pride was all I had to bear me up,
  That you might think you owed me for your life,
  And owed it to my duty, not my love.
  I have been injured, and my haughty soul
  Could brook but ill the man who slights my bed.   330
ANTONY   Therefore you love me not.
OCTAVIA   Therefore, my lord,
  I should not love you.
ANTONY   Therefore you would leave me?
OCTAVIA   And therefore I should leave you – if I could.
DOLABELLA   Her soul's too great, after such injuries,
  To say she loves; and yet she lets you see it.   335
  Her modesty and silence plead her cause.
ANTONY   O Dolabella, which way shall I turn?
  I find a secret yielding in my soul;
  But Cleopatra, who would die with me,
  Must she be left? Pity pleads for Octavia,   340
  But does it not plead more for Cleopatra?
VENTIDIUS   Justice and pity both plead for Octavia;
  For Cleopatra, neither.
  One would be ruined with you, but she first
  Had ruined you; the other you have ruined,   345
  And yet she would preserve you.
  In everything their merits are unequal.
ANTONY   O my distracted soul!
OCTAVIA   Sweet heav'n compose it!
  Come, come, my lord, if I can pardon you,
  Methinks you should accept it. Look on these,   350
  Are they not yours? or stand they thus neglected
  As they are mine? Go to him, children, go;
  Kneel to him, take him by the hand, speak to him;
  For you may speak, and he may own you too,
  Without a blush; and so he cannot all   355
  His children: go, I say, and pull him to me,
  And pull him to yourselves, from that bad woman.
  You, Agrippina, hang upon his arms,
  And you, Antonia, clasp about his waist:
  If he will shake you off, if he will dash you   360
  Against the pavement, you must bear it, children,

355–6 all/His children] Antony had three children by Cleopatra.

For you are mine, and I was born to suffer.

[*Here the* Children *go to him, etc.*

VENTIDIUS   Was ever sight so moving? Emperor!
DOLABELLA   Friend!
OCTAVIA   Husband!
BOTH CHILDREN   Father!
ANTONY   I am vanquished: take me,
365   Octavia; take me, children; share me all.   [*Embracing them.*
        I've been a thriftless debtor to your loves,
        And run out much, in riot, from your stock;
        But all shall be amended.
OCTAVIA   O blest hour!
DOLABELLA   O happy change!
VENTIDIUS   My joy stops at my tongue,
370   But it has found two channels here for one,
        And bubbles out above.
ANTONY [*to* OCTAVIA]   This is thy triumph, lead me where thou
            wilt,
        Ev'n to thy brother's camp.
OCTAVIA   All there are yours.

Enter ALEXAS *hastily.*

ALEXAS   The queen, my mistress, sir, and yours —
ANTONY   'Tis past.
375   Octavia, you shall stay this night. Tomorrow,
        Caesar and we are one.

[*Exit leading* OCTAVIA; DOLABELLA *and the* Children *follow.*

VENTIDIUS   There's news for you; run, my officious eunuch,
        Be sure to be the first; haste forward:
        Haste, my dear eunuch, haste.   [*Exit.*
380 ALEXAS   This downright fighting fool, this thick-skulled hero,
        This blunt unthinking instrument of death,
        With plain dull virtue has outgone my wit.
        Pleasure forsook my earliest infancy,
        The luxury of others robbed my cradle,
385   And ravished thence the promise of a man:
        Cast out from nature, disinherited
        Of what her meanest children claim by kind;
        Yet greatness kept me from contempt: that's gone.
        Had Cleopatra followed my advice,

Then he had been betrayed who now forsakes.   390
She dies for love; but she has known its joys:
Gods, is this just, that I, who know no joys,
Must die, because she loves?

Enter CLEOPATRA, CHARMION, IRAS, *and Train.*

Oh madam, I have seen what blasts my eyes!
Octavia's here.
CLEOPATRA   Peace with that raven's note.   395
I know it too, and now am in
The pangs of death.
ALEXAS   You are no more a queen;
Egypt is lost.
CLEOPATRA   What tell'st thou me of Egypt?
My life, my soul is lost! Octavia has him!
O fatal name to Cleopatra's love!   400
My kisses, my embraces now are hers,
While I . . . . But thou hast seen my rival, speak,
Does she deserve this blessing? Is she fair?
Bright as a goddess? and is all perfection
Confined to her? It is. Poor I was made   405
Of that coarse matter which, when she was finished,
The gods threw by for rubbish.
ALEXAS   She is indeed a very miracle.
CLEOPATRA   Death to my hopes, a miracle!
ALEXAS   A miracle,   [*Bowing.*
I mean of goodness; for in beauty, madam,   410
You make all wonders cease.
CLEOPATRA   I was too rash:
Take this in part of recompense. But, oh!   [*Giving a ring.*
I fear thou flatt'rest me.
CHARMION   She comes! she's here!
IRAS   Fly, madam, Caesar's sister!
CLEOPATRA   Were she the sister of the thund'rer Jove, 415
And bore her brother's lightning in her eyes,
Thus would I face my rival.

Meets OCTAVIA *with* VENTIDIUS. OCTAVIA *bears up to her. Their
Trains come up on either side.*

OCTAVIA   I need not ask if you are Cleopatra,

415 sister . . . Jove] Juno, Jupiter's sister and jealous wife.

      Your haughty carriage —
CLEOPATRA   Shows I am a queen:
420   Nor need I ask you who you are.
OCTAVIA   A Roman:
    A name that makes and can unmake a queen.
CLEOPATRA   Your lord, the man who serves me, is a Roman.
OCTAVIA   He was a Roman, till he lost that name
    To be a slave in Egypt; but I come
425   To free him thence.
CLEOPATRA   Peace, peace, my lover's Juno.
    When he grew weary of that household clog,
    He chose my easier bonds.
OCTAVIA   I wonder not
    Your bonds are easy: you have long been practised
    In that lascivious art: he's not the first
430   For whom you spread your snares: let Caesar witness.
CLEOPATRA   I loved not Caesar; 'twas but gratitude
    I paid his love. The worst your malice can,
    Is but to say the greatest of mankind
    Has been my slave. The next, but far above him
435   In my esteem, is he whom law calls yours,
    But whom his love made mine.
OCTAVIA   I would view nearer   [*Coming up close to her.*
    That face which has so long usurped my right,
    To find th' inevitable charms, that catch
    Mankind so sure, that ruined my dear lord.
440 CLEOPATRA   Oh, you do well to search; for had you known
    But half these charms, you had not lost his heart.
OCTAVIA   Far be their knowledge from a Roman lady,
    Far from a modest wife. Shame of our sex,
    Dost thou not blush to own those black endearments
445   That make sin pleasing?
CLEOPATRA.   You may blush who want 'em.
    If bounteous nature, if indulgent heav'n
    Have giv'n me charms to please the bravest man,
    Should I not thank 'em? Should I be ashamed
    And not be proud? I am, that he has loved me;
450   And, when I love not him, heav'n change this face
    For one like that.
OCTAVIA   Thou lov'st him not so well.
CLEOPATRA   I love him better, and deserve him more.
OCTAVIA   You do not; cannot; you have been his ruin.

Who made him cheap at Rome, but Cleopatra?
Who made him scorned abroad, but Cleopatra?   455
At Actium, who betrayed him? Cleopatra.
Who made his children orphans, and poor me
A wretched widow? only Cleopatra.

CLEOPATRA   Yet she who loves him best is Cleopatra.
If you have suffered, I have suffered more.   460
You bear the specious title of a wife,
To gild your cause, and draw the pitying world
To favour it: the world contemns poor me.
For I have lost my honour, lost my fame,
And stained the glory of my royal house,   465
And all to bear the branded name of mistress.
There wants but life, and that too I would lose
For him I love.

OCTAVIA   Be't so, then; take thy wish.   [*Exit with her Train.*

CLEOPATRA   And 'tis my wish,
Now he is lost for whom alone I lived.   470
My sight grows dim, and every object dances
And swims before me, in the maze of death.
My spirits, while they were opposed, kept up;
They could not sink beneath a rival's scorn:
But now she's gone they faint.

ALEXAS   Mine have had leisure   475
To recollect their strength and furnish counsel
To ruin her, who else must ruin you.

CLEOPATRA   Vain promiser!
Lead me, my Charmion; nay, your hand too, Iras.
My grief has weight enough to sink you both.
Conduct me to some solitary chamber,   480
And draw the curtains round;
Then leave me to myself, to take alone
My fill of grief:
There I till death will his unkindness weep;
As harmless infants moan themselves asleep.   [*Exeunt.*   485

ACT IV

Enter ANTONY *and* DOLABELLA.

DOLABELLA   Why would you shift it from yourself on me?

Can you not tell her you must part?
ANTONY   I cannot.
    I could pull out an eye and bid it go
    And t'other should not weep. Oh Dolabella,
5   How many deaths are in this word 'Depart'!
    I dare not trust my tongue to tell her so:
    One look of hers would thaw me into tears,
    And I should melt till I were lost again.
DOLABELLA   Then let Ventidius;
10   He's rough by nature.
ANTONY   Oh, he'll speak too harshly;
    He'll kill her with the news: thou, only thou.
DOLABELLA   Nature has cast me in so soft a mould
    That but to hear a story feigned for pleasure
    Of some sad lover's death, moistens my eyes,
15   And robs me of my manhood. I should speak
    So faintly, with such fear to grieve her heart,
    She'd not believe it earnest.
ANTONY   Therefore, therefore
    Thou only, thou art fit: think thyself me,
    And when thou speak'st (but let it first be long)
20   Take off the edge from every sharper sound,
    And let our parting be as gently made
    As other loves begin. Wilt thou do this?
DOLABELLA   What you have said so sinks into my soul
    That, if I must speak, I shall speak just so.
25 ANTONY   I leave you then to your sad task. Farewell.
    I sent her word to meet you.   [Goes to the door, and comes back.
    I forgot;
    Let her be told I'll make her peace with mine:
    Her crown and dignity shall be preserved
    If I have pow'r with Caesar. – Oh be sure
30   To think on that.
DOLABELLA   Fear not, I will remember.

            [ANTONY goes again to the door, and comes back.

ANTONY   And tell her, too, how much I was constrained;
    I did not this, but with extremest force:
    Desire her not to hate my memory,
    For I still cherish hers; . . . insist on that.
35 DOLABELLA   Trust me, I'll not forget it.
    ANTONY   Then that's all.   [Goes out, and returns again.

Wilt thou forgive my fondness this once more?
Tell her, though we shall never meet again,
If I should hear she took another love,
The news would break my heart. — Now I must go,
For every time I have returned, I feel   40
My soul more tender; and my next command
Would be, to bid her stay, and ruin both.   [*Exit.*

DOLABELLA   Men are but children of a larger growth,
Our appetites as apt to change as theirs,
And full as craving too, and full as vain;   45
And yet the soul, shut up in her dark room,
Viewing so clear abroad, at home sees nothing;
But, like a mole in earth, busy and blind,
Works all her folly up, and casts it outward
To the world's open view: thus I discovered,   50
And blamed the love of ruined Antony;
Yet wish that I were he, to be so ruined.

Enter VENTIDIUS *above.*

VENTIDIUS   Alone? and talking to himself? concerned too?
Perhaps my guess is right; he loved her once,
And may pursue it still.
DOLABELLA   O friendship! friendship!   55
Ill canst thou answer this; and reason, worse:
Unfaithful in th' attempt; hopeless to win;
And if I win, undone: mere madness all.
And yet th' occasion's fair. What injury
To him, to wear the robe which he throws by!   60
VENTIDIUS   None, none at all. This happens as I wish,
To ruin her yet more with Antony.

Enter CLEOPATRA, *talking with* ALEXAS; CHARMION, IRAS *on the
other side.*

DOLABELLA   She comes! What charms have sorrow on that face!
Sorrow seems pleased to dwell with so much sweetness;
Yet, now and then, a melancholy smile   65
Breaks loose, like lightning in a winter's night,
And shows a moment's day.
VENTIDIUS   If she should love him too! her eunuch there?
That porc'pisce bodes ill weather. Draw, draw nearer,

69 porc'pisce] Porpoise, thought to be a sign of storms.

70   Sweet devil, that I may hear.
     ALEXAS   Believe me; try

          [DOLABELLA *goes over to* CHARMION *and* IRAS; *seems to talk*
          with them.

          To make him jealous; jealousy is like
          A polished glass held to the lips when life's in doubt:
          If there be breath, 'twill catch the damp and show it.
     CLEOPATRA   I grant you jealousy's a proof of love,
75   But 'tis a weak and unavailing medicine;
          It puts out the disease, and makes it show,
          But has no pow'r to cure.
     ALEXAS   'Tis your last remedy, and strongest too:
          And then this Dolabella, who so fit
80   To practise on? He's handsome, valiant, young,
          And looks as he were laid for nature's bait
          To catch weak women's eyes.
          He stands already more than half suspected
          Of loving you: the least kind word or glance
85   You give this youth, will kindle him with love:
          Then, like a burning vessel set adrift,
          You'll send him down amain before the wind,
          To fire the heart of jealous Antony.
     CLEOPATRA   Can I do this? Ah no; my love's so true
90   That I can neither hide it where it is
          Nor show it where it is not. Nature meant me
          A wife, a silly, harmless, household dove,
          Fond without art and kind without deceit;
          But Fortune, that has made a mistress of me,
95   Has thrust me out to the wide world, unfurnished
          Of falsehood to be happy.
     ALEXAS   Force yourself.
          Th' event will be your lover will return,
          Doubly desirous to possess the good
          Which once he feared to lose.
     CLEOPATRA   I must attempt it,
100   But oh, with what regret!

                    [*Exit* ALEXAS. *She comes up to* DOLABELLA.

     VENTIDIUS   So, now the scene draws near; they're in my reach.

     76 puts out] Brings out.

CLEOPATRA [*to* DOLABELLA]   Discoursing with my women!
   might not I
  Share in your entertainment?
CHARMION   You have been
  The subject of it, madam.
CLEOPATRA   How! and how?
IRAS   Such praises of your beauty!
CLEOPATRA   Mere poetry.   105
  Your Roman wits, your Gallus and Tibullus,
  Have taught you this from Cytheris and Delia.
DOLABELLA   Those Roman wits have never been in Egypt,
  Cytheris and Delia else had been unsung:
  I, who have seen — had I been born a poet,   110
  Should choose a nobler name.
CLEOPATRA   You flatter me.
  But 'tis your nation's vice: all of your country
  Are flatterers, and all false. Your friend's like you.
  I'm sure he sent you not to speak these words.
DOLABELLA   No, madam; yet he sent me —
CLEOPATRA   Well, he sent you —   115
DOLABELLA   Of a less pleasing errand.
CLEOPATRA   How less pleasing?
  Less to yourself, or me?
DOLABELLA   Madam, to both;
  For you must mourn, and I must grieve to cause it.
CLEOPATRA   You, Charmion, and your fellow, stand at distance.
  Hold up, my spirits. [*Aside*] — Well, now your mournful matter,   120
  For I'm prepared, perhaps can guess it too.
DOLABELLA   I wish you would, for 'tis a thankless office
  To tell ill news: and I, of all your sex,
  Most fear displeasing you.
CLEOPATRA   Of all your sex
  I soonest could forgive you, if you should.   125
VENTIDIUS   Most delicate advances! Woman! woman!
  Dear, damned, inconstant sex!
CLEOPATRA   In the first place,
  I am to be forsaken; is't not so?
DOLABELLA   I wish I could not answer to that question.
CLEOPATRA   Then pass it o'er, because it troubles you: 130
  I should have been more grieved another time.

106 Gallus and Tibullus] Poets of the time. Their love poems were addressed to Cytheris and
Delia, respectively.

Next, I'm to lose my kingdom . . . . . Farewell, Egypt!
Yet, is there any more?
DOLABELLA   Madam, I fear
Your too deep sense of grief has turned your reason.
135 CLEOPATRA   No, no, I'm not run mad; I can bear fortune:
And love may be expelled by other love,
As poisons are by poisons.
DOLABELLA   You o'erjoy me, madam,
To find your griefs so moderately borne.
140   You've heard the worst; all are not false like him.
CLEOPATRA   No; heav'n forbid they should.
DOLABELLA   Some men are constant.
CLEOPATRA   And constancy deserves reward, that's certain.
DOLABELLA   Deserves it not; but give it leave to hope.
VENTIDIUS   I'll swear thou hast my leave. I have enough:
145   But how to manage this! Well, I'll consider.   [*Exit.*
DOLABELLA   I came prepared
To tell you heavy news; news, which I thought
Would fright the blood from your pale cheeks to hear:
But you have met it with a cheerfulness
150   That makes my task more easy; and my tongue,
Which on another's message was employed,
Would gladly speak its own.
CLEOPATRA   Hold, Dolabella.
First tell me, were you chosen by my lord?
Or sought you this employment?
155 DOLABELLA   He picked me out; and, as his bosom friend,
He charged me with his words.
CLEOPATRA   The message then
I know was tender, and each accent smooth,
To mollify that rugged word 'Depart'.
DOLABELLA   Oh, you mistake: he chose the harshest words,
160   With fiery eyes and with contracted brows
He coined his face in the severest stamp,
And fury shook his fabric like an earthquake;
He heaved for vent, and burst like bellowing Aetna,
In sounds scarce human: 'Hence away for ever,
165   Let her begone, the blot of my renown,
And bane of all my hopes;

[*All the time of this speech,* CLEOPATRA *seems more and more
concerned, till she sinks quite down.*]

Let her be driv'n as far as men can think
From man's commerce: she'll poison to the centre.'
CLEOPATRA Oh, I can bear no more!
DOLABELLA Help, help! − O wretch! O cursed, cursed wretch!   170
    What have I done!
CHARMION Help, chafe her temples, Iras.
IRAS Bend, bend her forward quickly.
CHARMION Heaven be praised,
    She comes again.
CLEOPATRA Oh, let him not approach me.
    Why have you brought me back to this loath'd being,
    Th' abode of falsehood, violated vows,   175
    And injured love? For pity, let me go;
    For, if there be a place of long repose,
    I'm sure I want it, My disdainful lord
    Can never break that quiet; nor awake
    The sleeping soul, with hollowing in my tomb   180
    Such words as fright her hence. Unkind, unkind!
DOLABELLA Believe me, 'tis against myself I speak;   [*Kneeling.*
    That sure deserves belief; I injured him:
    My friend ne'er spoke those words. Oh, had you seen
    How often he came back, and every time   185
    With something more obliging and more kind,
    To add to what he said; what dear farewells;
    How almost vanquished by his love he parted,
    And leaned to what unwillingly he left.
    I, traitor as I was, for love of you   190
    (But what can you not do, who made me false?)
    I forged that lie; for whose forgiveness kneels
    This self-accused, self-punished criminal.
CLEOPATRA With how much ease believe we what we wish!
    Rise, Dolabella; if you have been guilty,   195
    I have contributed, and too much love
    Has made me guilty too.
    Th' advance of kindness which I made was feigned,
    To call back fleeting love by jealousy,
    But 'twould not last. Oh, rather let me lose   200
    Than so ignobly trifle with his heart.
DOLABELLA I find your breast fenced round from human reach,
    Transparent as a rock of solid crystal,
    Seen through, but never pierced, My friend, my friend!
    What endless treasure hast thou thrown away,   205

And scattered like an infant, in the ocean,
Vain sums of wealth which none can gather thence!
CLEOPATRA   Could you not beg
An hour's admittance to his private ear?
210   Like one who wanders through long barren wilds
And yet foreknows no hospitable inn
Is near to succour hunger,
Eats his fill before his painful march:
So would I feed a while my famished eycs
215   Before we part; for I have far to go,
If death be far, and never must return.

VENTIDIUS *with* OCTAVIA, *behind.*

VENTIDIUS   From hence you may discover – oh, sweet, sweet!
Would you indeed? The pretty hand in earnest?
DOLABELLA   I will, for this reward –   [*Takes her hand.*
220   Draw it not back,
'Tis all I e'er will beg.
VENTIDIUS   They turn upon us.
OCTAVIA   What quick eyes has guilt!
VENTIDIUS   Seem not to have observed 'em, and go on.

They enter.

DOLABELLA   Saw you the emperor, Ventidius?
VENTIDIUS   No.
225   I sought him; but I heard that he was private,
None with him but Hipparchus, his freedman.
DOLABELLA   Know you his bus'ness?
VENTIDIUS   Giving him instructions,
And letters to his brother Caesar.
DOLABELLA   Well,
He must be found.   [*Exeunt* DOLABELLA *and* CLEOPATRA.
OCTAVIA   Most glorious impudence!
230   VENTIDIUS   She looked methought
As she would say – Take your old man, Octavia;
Thank you, I'm better here.
Well, but what use
Make we of this discovery?
OCTAVIA   Let it die.
235   VENTIDIUS   I pity Dolabella; but she's dangerous:
Her eyes have pow'r beyond Thessalian charms
To draw the moon from heav'n; for eloquence,

The sea-green Syrens taught her voice their flatt'ry,
And while she speaks night steals upon the day,
Unmarked of those that hear. Then she's so charming,   240
Age buds at sight of her and swells to youth:
The holy priests gaze on her when she smiles,
And with heaved hands, forgetting gravity,
They bless her wanton eyes. Even I, who hate her,
With a malignant joy behold such beauty,   245
And, while I curse, desire it. Antony
Must needs have some remains of passion still,
Which may ferment into a worse relapse
If now not fully cured. I know this minute
With Caesar he's endeavouring her peace.   250
OCTAVIA   You have prevailed: . . . . . but for a farther purpose

                                                        [*Walks off.*

I'll prove how he will relish this discovery.
What, make a strumpet's peace! it swells my heart:
It must not, sha'not be.
VENTIDIUS   His guards appear.
Let me begin, and you shall second me.   255

                    Enter ANTONY.

ANTONY   Octavia, I was looking you, my love:
What, are your letters ready? I have giv'n
My last instructions.
OCTAVIA   Mine, my lord, are written.
ANTONY   Ventidius!   [*Drawing him aside.*
VENTIDIUS   My lord?
ANTONY   A word in private.
When saw you Dolabella?
VENTIDIUS   Now, my lord,   260
He parted hence; and Cleopatra with him.
ANTONY   Speak softly. 'Twas by my command he went,
To bear my last farewell.
VENTIDIUS   It looked indeed   [*Aloud.*
Like your farewell.
ANTONY   More softly. — My farewell?
What secret meaning have you in those words   265
Of my farewell? He did it by my order.
VENTIDIUS   Then he obeyed your order. I suppose   [*Aloud.*
You bid him do it with all gentleness,

All kindness, and all . . . . . . love.

ANTONY   How she mourned,

270   The poor forsaken creature!

VENTIDIUS   She took it as she ought; she bore your parting
As she did Caesar's, as she would another's,
Were a new love to come.

ANTONY   Thou dost belie her;   [*Aloud.*
Most basely, and maliciously belie her.

275   VENTIDIUS   I thought not to displease you; I have done.

OCTAVIA   You seemed disturbed, my lord.   [*Coming up.*

ANTONY   A very trifle.
Retire, my love.

VENTIDIUS   It was indeed a trifle.
He sent —

ANTONY   No more. Look how thou disobey'st me;   [*Angrily.*
Thy life shall answer it.

OCTAVIA   Then 'tis no trifle.

280   VENTIDIUS [*to* OCTAVIA]   'Tis less, a very nothing: you too saw it
As well as I, and therefore 'tis no secret.

ANTONY   She saw it!

VENTIDIUS   Yes: she saw young Dolabella —

ANTONY   Young Dolabella!

VENTIDIUS   Young, I think him young,
And handsome too; and so do others think him.

285   But what of that? He went by your command,
Indeed 'tis probable, with some kind message;
For she received it graciously; she smiled;
And then he grew familiar with her hand,
Squeezed it, and worried it with ravenous kisses;

290   She blushed, and sighed, and smiled, and blushed again;
At last she took occasion to talk softly,
And brought her cheek up close, and leaned on his;
At which, he whispered kisses back on hers;
And then she cried aloud, that constancy

295   Should be rewarded.

OCTAVIA   This I saw and heard.

ANTONY   What woman was it, whom you heard and saw
So playful with my friend?
Not Cleopatra?

VENTIDIUS   Ev'n she, my lord.

ANTONY   My Cleopatra?

300   VENTIDIUS   Your Cleopatra;

Dolabella's Cleopatra; every man's Cleopatra.
ANTONY Thou liest.
VENTIDIUS I do not lie, my lord.
  Is this so strange? Should mistresses be left,
  And not provide against a time of change?
  You know she's not much used to lonely nights.   305
ANTONY I'll think no more on't.
  I know 'tis false, and see the plot betwixt you.
  You needed not have gone this way, Octavia.
  What harms it you that Cleopatra's just?
  She's mine no more. I see, and I forgive: 310
  Urge it no farther, love.
OCTAVIA Are you concerned
  That she's found false?
ANTONY I should be, were it so;
  For, though 'tis past, I would not that the world
  Should tax my former choice, that I loved one
  Of so light note; but I forgive you both.   315
VENTIDIUS What has my age deserved, that you should think
  I would abuse your ears with perjury?
  If heav'n be true, she's false.
ANTONY Though heav'n and earth
  Should witness it, I'll not believe her tainted.
VENTIDIUS I'll bring you then a witness   320
  From hell to prove her so. Nay, go not back;

[*Seeing* ALEXAS *just entering, and starting back.*

For stay you must and shall.
ALEXAS What means my lord?
VENTIDIUS To make you do what most you hate: speak truth.
  You are of Cleopatra's private counsel,
  Of her bed-counsel, her lascivious hours;   325
  Are conscious of each nightly change she makes,
  And watch her as Chaldeans do the moon,
  Can tell what signs she passes through, what day.
ALEXAS My noble lord!
VENTIDIUS My most illustrious pander,
  No fine set speech, no cadence, no turned periods,   330
  But a plain homespun truth, is what I ask:
  I did, myself, o'erhear your queen make love

327 Chaldeans] Babylonian astronomers and astrologers.

To Dolabella. Speak; for I will know,
By your confession, what more passed betwixt 'em;
335 How near the bus'ness draws to your employment;
And when the happy hour.
ANTONY   Speak truth, Alexas, whether it offend
Or please Ventidius, care not: justify
Thy injured queen from malice; dare his worst.
340 OCTAVIA [aside]   See how he gives him courage! how he fears
To find her false! and shuts his eyes to truth,
Willing to be misled!
ALEXAS   As far as love may plead for woman's frailty,
Urged by desert and greatness of the lover,
345 So far, divine Octavia, may my queen
Stand ev'n excused to you for loving him
Who is your lord: so far, from brave Ventidius,
May her past actions hope a fair report.
ANTONY   'Tis well, and truly spoken: mark, Ventidius.
350 ALEXAS   To you, most noble emperor, her strong passion
Stands not excused, but wholly justified.
Her beauty's charms alone, without her crown,
From Ind and Meroe drew the distant vows
Of sighing kings; and at her feet were laid
355 The sceptres of the earth, exposed on heaps,
To choose where she would reign:
She thought a Roman only could deserve her,
And, of all Romans, only Antony;
And, to be less than wife to you, disdained
360 Their lawful passion.
ANTONY   'Tis but truth.
ALEXAS   And yet, though love and your unmatched desert
Have drawn her from the due regard of honour,
At last heav'n opened her unwilling eyes
To see the wrongs she offered fair Octavia,
365 Whose holy bed she lawlessly usurped.
The sad effects of this improsperous war
Confirmed those pious thoughts.
VENTIDIUS [aside]   Oh, wheel you there?
Observe him now; the man begins to mend,
And talk substantial reason. — Fear not, eunuch,
370 Th' emperor has given thee leave to speak.

353 Meroe] A region of the upper Nile.

ALEXAS   Else had I never dared t' offend his ears
   With what the last necessity has urged
   On my forsaken mistress; yet I must not
   Presume to say her heart is wholly altered.
ANTONY   No, dare not for thy life, I charge thee dare not   375
   Pronounce that fatal word!
OCTAVIA   Must I bear this? Good heav'n, afford me patience.

                                     [*Aside.*

VENTIDIUS   On, sweet eunuch; my dear half-man, proceed.
ALEXAS   Yet Dolabella
   Has loved her long; he, next my god-like lord,   380
   Deserves her best; and should she meet his passion,
   Rejected, as she is, by him she loved —
ANTONY   Hence from my sight! for I can bear no more:
   Let furies drag thee quick to hell; let all
   The longer damned have rest; each torturing hand   385
   Do thou employ, till Cleopatra comes;
   Then join thou too, and help to torture her!

                   [*Exit* ALEXAS, *thrust out by* ANTONY.

OCTAVIA   'Tis not well,
   Indeed, my lord, 'tis much unkind to me,
   To show this passion, this extreme concernment,   390
   For an abandoned, faithless prostitute.
ANTONY   Octavia, leave me; I am much disordered.
   Leave me, I say.
OCTAVIA   My lord?
ANTONY   I bid you leave me.
VENTIDIUS   Obey him, madam: best withdraw a while,
   And see how this will work.   395
OCTAVIA   Wherein have I offended you, my lord,
   That I am bid to leave you? Am I false,
   Or infamous? Am I a Cleopatra?
   Were I she,
   Base as she is, you would not bid me leave you,   400
   But hang upon my neck, take slight excuses,
   And fawn upon my falsehood.
ANTONY   'Tis too much,
   Too much, Octavia; I am pressed with sorrows
   Too heavy to be borne; and you add more:
   I would retire, and recollect what's left   405

Of man within, to aid me.

OCTAVIA   You would mourn
In private for your love who has betrayed you.
You did but half return to me: your kindness
Lingered behind with her. I hear, my lord,
410   You make conditions for her,
And would include her treaty. Wondrous proofs
Of love to me!

ANTONY   Are you my friend, Ventidius?
Or are you turned a Dolabella too,
And let this fury loose?

VENTIDIUS   Oh, be advised,
415   Sweet madam, and retire.

OCTAVIA   Yes, I will go; but never to return.
You shall no more be haunted with this Fury.
My lord, my lord, love will not always last
When urged with long unkindness and disdain:
420   Take her again whom you prefer to me,
She stays but to be called. Poor cozened man!
Let a feigned parting give her back your heart,
Which a feigned love first got; for injured me,
Tho' my just sense of wrongs forbid my stay,
425   My duty shall be yours.
To the dear pledges of our former love
My tenderness and care shall be transferred,
And they shall cheer, by turns, my widowed nights:
So, take my last farewell; for I despair
430   To have you whole, and scorn to take you half.   [Exit.

VENTIDIUS   I combat heav'n, which blasts my best designs:
My last attempt must be to win her back;
But oh! I fear in vain.   [Exit.

ANTONY   Why was I framed with this plain honest heart,
435   Which knows not to disguise its griefs and weakness,
But bears its workings outward to the world?
I should have kept the mighty anguish in,
And forced a smile at Cleopatra's falsehood:
Octavia had believed it, and had stayed.
440   But I am made a shallow-forded stream,
Seen to the bottom: all my clearness scorned,
And all my faults exposed! — See where he comes

Enter DOLABELLA.

Who has profaned the sacred name of friend
And worn it into vileness!
With how secure a brow, and specious form,   445
He gilds the secret villain! Sure that face
Was meant for honesty; but heav'n mismatched it,
And furnished treason out with nature's pomp,
To make it's work more easy.
DOLABELLA   O my friend!
ANTONY   Well, Dolabella, you performed my message?   450
DOLABELLA   I did, unwillingly.
ANTONY   Unwillingly?
   Was it so hard for you to bear our parting?
   You should have wished it.
DOLABELLA   Why?
ANTONY   Because you love me.
   And she received my message with as true,
   With as unfeigned a sorrow as you brought it?   455
DOLABELLA   She loves you, ev'n to madness.
ANTONY   Oh, I know it.
   You, Dolabella, do not better know
   How much she loves me. And should I
   Forsake this beauty? This all-perfect creature?
DOLABELLA   I could not, were she mine.
ANTONY   And yet you first   460
   Persuaded me: how come you altered since?
DOLABELLA   I said at first I was not fit to go.
   I could not hear her sighs and see her tears
   But pity must prevail: and so, perhaps,
   It may again with you, for I have promised   465
   That she should take her last farewell: and, see,
   She comes to claim my word.

                    Enter CLEOPATRA.

ANTONY   False Dolabella!
DOLABELLA   What's false, my lord?
ANTONY   Why, Dolabella's false,
   And Cleopatra's false; both false and faithless.
   Draw near, you well-joined wickedness, you serpents,   470
   Whom I have in my kindly bosom warmed
   Till I am stung to death.
DOLABELLA   My lord, have I
   Deserved to be thus used?

CLEOPATRA   Can heav'n prepare
A newer torment? Can it find a curse
475   Beyond our separation?
ANTONY   Yes, if fate
Be just, much greater: Heaven should be ingenious
In punishing such crimes. The rolling stone
And gnawing vulture were slight pains, invented
When Jove was young, and no examples known
480   Of mighty ills; but you have ripened sin
To such a monstrous growth, 'twill pose the gods
To find an equal torture. Two, two such,
Oh there's no further name, two such! – to me,
To me, who locked my soul within your breasts,
485   Had no desires, no joys, no life, but you;
When half the globe was mine, I gave it you
In dowry with my heart; I had no use,
No fruit of all, but you: a friend and mistress
Was what the world could give. O Cleopatra!
490   O Dolabella! how could you betray
This tender heart, which with an infant fondness
Lay lulled betwixt your bosoms, and there slept
Secure of injured faith?
DOLABELLA   If she has wronged you,
Heav'n, hell, and you revenge it.
ANTONY   If she wronged me!
495   Thou wouldst evade thy part of guilt; but swear
Thou lov'st not her.
DOLABELLA   Not so as I love you.
ANTONY   Not so! Swear, swear, I say, thou dost not love her.
DOLABELLA   No more than friendship will allow.
ANTONY   No more?
Friendship allows thee nothing: thou art perjured –
500   And yet thou didst not swear thou lov'st her not;
But not so much, no more. O trifling hypocrite,
Who dar'st not own to her thou dost not love,
Nor own to me thou dost! Ventidius heard it,
Octavia saw it.
CLEOPATRA   They are enemies.

477–8 rolling stone . . . vulture] The torments of Sisyphus and Tityus in Hades. Sisyphus
was doomed to roll a heavy stone up a hill, which always rolled down again; Tityus to have
vultures gnawing at his liver.
493 Secure of] Safe from.

ANTONY   Alexas is not so: he, he confessed it;   505
   He, who, next hell, best knew it, he avowed it.
   Why do I seek a proof beyond yourself?
   You, whom I sent to bear my last farewell,   [*To* DOLABELLA.
   Returned to plead her stay.
DOLABELLA   What shall I answer?
   If to have loved be guilt, then I have sinned;   510
   But if to have repented of that love
   Can wash away my crime, I have repented.
   Yet, if I have offended past forgiveness,
   Let not her suffer: she is innocent.
CLEOPATRA   Ah, what will not a woman do who loves?   515
   What means will she refuse to keep that heart
   Where all her joys are placed? 'Twas I encouraged,
   'Twas I blew up the fire that scorched his soul,
   To make you jealous, and by that regain you.
   But all in vain; I could not counterfeit: 520
   In spite of all the dams my love broke o'er
   And drowned my heart again: fate took th' occasion,
   And thus one minute's feigning has destroyed
   My whole life's truth.
ANTONY   Thin cobweb arts of falsehood,
   Seen and broke through at first.
DOLABELLA   Forgive your mistress.   525
CLEOPATRA   Forgive your friend.
ANTONY   You have convinced yourselves,
   You plead each other's cause. What witness have you
   That you but meant to raise my jealousy?
CLEOPATRA   Ourselves, and heav'n.
ANTONY   Guilt witnesses for guilt. Hence, love and friendship!   530
   You have no longer place in human breasts,
   These two have driv'n you out. Avoid my sight!
   I would not kill the man whom I loved,
   And cannot hurt the woman; but avoid me:
   I do not know how long I can be tame;   535
   For, if I stay one minute more to think
   How I am wronged, my justice and revenge
   Will cry so loud within me that my pity
   Will not be heard for either.
DOLABELLA   Heav'n has but
   Our sorrow for our sins, and then delights   540
526 convinced] Confuted.

To pardon erring man: sweet mercy seems
Its darling attribute, which limits justice,
As if there were degrees in infinite,
And infinite would rather want perfection
545   Than punish to extent.
ANTONY I can forgive
A foe, but not a mistress and a friend.
Treason is there in its most horrid shape,
Where trust is greatest; and the soul resigned
Is stabbed by its own guards: I'll hear no more;
550   Hence from my sight for ever!
CLEOPATRA How? for ever!
I cannot go one moment from your sight,
And must I go for ever?
My joys, my only joys are centred here:
What place have I to go to? My own kingdom?
555   That I have lost for you: or to the Romans?
They hate me for your sake: or must I wander
The wide world o'er, a helpless, banished woman,
Banished for love of you; banished from you?
Ay, there's the banishment! Oh, hear me; hear me,
560   With strictest justice, for I beg no favour,
And if I have offended you, then kill me,
But do not banish me.
ANTONY I must not hear you.
I have a fool within me takes your part,
But honour stops my ears.
CLEOPATRA For pity hear me!
565   Would you cast off a slave who followed you,
Who crouched beneath your spurn? – He has no pity!
See, if he gives one tear to my departure,
One look, one kind farewell: O iron heart!
Let all the gods look down and judge betwixt us
570   If he did ever love!
ANTONY No more: Alexas!
DOLABELLA A perjured villain!
ANTONY [to CLEOPATRA] Your Alexas; yours.
CLEOPATRA Oh, 'twas his plot: his ruinous design
T'engage you in my love by jealousy.
Hear him; confront him with me; let him speak.
575   ANTONY I have, I have.
CLEOPATRA And if he clear me not –

ANTONY Your creature! one who hangs upon your smiles!
  Watches your eye, to say or to unsay
  Whate'er you please! I am not to be moved.
CLEOPATRA Then must we part? Farewell, my cruel lord!
  Th' appearance is against me, and I go   580
  Unjustified, for ever from your sight.
  How I have loved, you know; how yet I love,
  My only comfort is, I know myself:
  I love you more, even now you are unkind,
  Than when you loved me most; so well, so truly,   585
  I'll never strive against it; but die pleased
  To think you once were mine.
ANTONY Good heav'n, they weep at parting.
  Must I weep too? that calls them innocent.
  I must not weep; and yet I must, to think   590
  That I must not forgive. —
  Live; but live wretched, 'tis but just you should
  Who made me so. Live from each other's sight:
  Let me not hear you meet. Set all the earth
  And all the seas betwixt your sundered loves: 595
  View nothing common but the sun and skies.
  Now, all take several ways;
    And each your own sad fate with mine deplore;
    That you were false, and I could trust no more.

                                              [*Exeunt severally.*

ACT V

Enter CLEOPATRA, CHARMION, *and* IRAS.

CHARMION Be juster, heav'n; such virtue punished thus
  Will make us think that chance rules all above,
  And shuffles with a random hand the lots
  Which man is forced to draw.
CLEOPATRA I could tear out these eyes that gained his heart   5
  And had not power to keep it. O the curse
  Of doting on, ev'n when I find it dotage!
  Bear witness, gods, you heard him bid me go,
  You, whom he mocked with imprecating vows
  Of promised faith! — I'll die, I will not bear it.   10

You may hold me —

[*She pulls out her dagger, and they hold her.*

But I can keep my breath; I can die inward,
And choke this love.

Enter ALEXAS.

IRAS   Help, O Alexas, help!
    The queen grows desperate; her soul struggles in her
15   With all the agonies of love and rage,
    And strives to force its passage.
CLEOPATRA   Let me go.
    Art thou there, traitor! — O,
    O for a little breath to vent my rage!
    Give, give me way, and let me loose upon him.
20 ALEXAS   Yes, I deserve it, for my ill-timed truth.
    Was it for me to prop
    The ruins of a falling majesty?
    To place myself beneath the mighty flaw,
    Thus to be crushed and pounded into atoms
25   By its o'erwhelming weight? 'Tis too presuming
    For subjects to preserve that wilful power
    Which courts its own destruction.
CLEOPATRA   I would reason
    More calmly with you. Did not you o'errule,
    And force my plain, direct, and open love
30   Into these crooked paths of jealousy?
    Now, what's th' event? Octavia is removed,
    But Cleopatra's banished. Thou, thou, villain,
    Has pushed my boat to open sea, to prove
    At my sad cost if thou canst steer it back.
35   It cannot be; I'm lost too far; I'm ruined:
    Hence, thou impostor, traitor, monster, devil! —
    I can no more: thou and my griefs have sunk
    Me down so low that I want voice to curse thee.
ALEXAS   Suppose some shipwrecked seaman near the shore,
40   Dropping and faint, with climbing up the cliff,
    If, from above, some charitable hand
    Pull him to safety, hazarding himself
    To draw the other's weight; would he look back
    And curse him for his pains? The case is yours;
45   But one step more and you have gained the height.

CLEOPATRA Sunk, never more to rise.
ALEXAS Octavia's gone, and Dolabella banished.
  Believe me, madam, Antony is yours.
  His heart was never lost, but started off
  To jealousy, love's last retreat and covert,   50
  Where it lies hid in shades, watchful in silence,
  And list'ning for the sound that calls it back.
  Some other, any man ('tis so advanced),
  May perfect this unfinished work, which I
  (Unhappy only to myself) have left   55
  So easy to his hand.
CLEOPATRA Look well thou do't, else —
ALEXAS Else what your silence threatens. — Antony
  Is mounted up the Pharos, from whose turret
  He stands surveying our Egyptian galleys
  Engaged with Caesar's fleet. Now death or conquest!   60
  If the first happen, fate acquits my promise:
  If we o'ercome, the conqueror is yours.   [A distant shout within.
CHARMION Have comfort, madam: did you mark that shout?

                                        [Second shout nearer.

IRAS Hark! they redouble it.
ALEXAS 'Tis from the port.
  The loudness shows it near: good news, kind heavens!   65
CLEOPATRA Osiris make it so!

                    Enter SERAPION.

SERAPION Where, where's the queen?
ALEXAS How frightfully the holy coward stares
  As if not yet recovered of th' assault,
  When all his gods, and, what's more dear to him,
  His offerings were at stake.
SERAPION O horror, horror!   70
  Egypt has been; our latest hour has come:
  The queen of nations from her ancient seat
  Is sunk for ever in the dark abyss:
  Time has unrolled her glories to the last,
  And now closed up the volume.
CLEOPATRA Be more plain: 75
  Say whence thou com'st (though fate is in thy face,

58 Pharos] The lighthouse in the harbour of Alexandria.

Which from thy haggard eyes looks wildly out,
And threatens ere thou speak'st).
SERAPION   I came from Pharos,
From viewing (spare me, and imagine it)
80   Our land's last hope, your navy —
CLEOPATRA   Vanquished?
SERAPION   No.
They fought not.
CLEOPATRA   Then they fled.
SERAPION   Nor that. I saw,
With Antony, your well-appointed fleet
Row out; and thrice he waved his hand on high,
And thrice with cheerful cries they shouted back:
85   'Twas then false Fortune, like a fawning strumpet
About to leave the bankrupt prodigal,
With a dissembled smile would kiss at parting,
And flatter to the last; the well-timed oars,
Now dipped from every bank, now smoothly run
90   To meet the foe; and soon indeed they met,
But not as foes. In few, we saw their caps
On either side thrown up; th' Egyptian galleys,
Received like friends, passed through, and fell behind
The Roman rear: and now, they all come forward,
95   And ride within the port.
CLEOPATRA   Enough, Serapion:
I've heard my doom. This needed not, you gods:
When I lost Antony, your work was done;
'Tis but superfluous malice. Where's my lord?
How bears he this last blow?
100   SERAPION   His fury cannot be expressed by words:
Thrice he attempted headlong to have fall'n
Full on his foes, and aimed at Caesar's galley:
Withheld, he raves on you; cries, he's betrayed.
Should he now find you —
ALEXAS   Shun him, seek your safety
105   Till you can clear your innocence.
CLEOPATRA   I'll stay.
ALEXAS   You must not, haste you to your monument,
While I make speed to Caesar.
CLEOPATRA   Caesar! No,
I have no business with him.
ALEXAS   I can work him

To spare your life and let this madman perish.
CLEOPATRA Base fawning wretch! wouldst thou betray him too? 110
  Hence from my sight, I will not hear a traitor;
  'Twas thy design brought all this ruin on us.
  Serapion, thou art honest, counsel me:
  But haste, each moment's precious.
SERAPION Retire, you must not yet see Antony. 115
  He who began this mischief,
  'Tis just he tempt the danger: let him clear you;
  And since he offered you his servile tongue
  To gain a poor precarious life from Caesar,
  Let him expose that fawning eloquence 120
  And speak to Antony.
ALEXAS O heavens! I dare not,
  I meet my certain death.
CLEOPATRA Slave, thou deserv'st it.
  Not that I fear my lord will I avoid him;
  I know him noble: when he banished me,
  And thought me false, he scorned to take my life; 125
  But I'll be justified, and then die with him.
ALEXAS O pity me and let me follow you.
CLEOPATRA To death, if thou stir hence. Speak, if thou canst,
  Now for thy life, which basely thou wouldst save;
  While mine I prize at – this! Come, good Serapion. 130

    [*Exeunt* CLEOPATRA, SERAPION, CHARMION, *and* IRAS.

ALEXAS O that I less could fear to lose this being,
  Which, like a snowball in my coward hand,
  The more 'tis grasped, the faster melts away.
  Poor reason! what a wretched aid art thou!
  For still, in spite of thee, 135
  These two long lovers, soul and body, dread
  Their final separation. Let me think:
  What can I say to save myself from death?
  No matter what becomes of Cleopatra.
ANTONY Which way? where? [*Within.*
VENTIDIUS This leads to the monument. [*Within.* 140
ALEXAS Ah me! I hear him, yet I'm unprepared:
  My gift of lying's gone,
  And this court-devil which I so oft have raised
  Forsakes me at my need. I dare not stay,
  Yet cannot far go hence. [*Exit.* 145

Enter ANTONY *and* VENTIDIUS.

ANTONY O happy Caesar! thou hast men to lead:
    Think not 'tis thou hast conquered Antony,
    But Rome has conquered Egypt. I'm betrayed.
VENTIDIUS Curse on this treach'rous train!
150   Their soil and heav'n infect 'em all with baseness,
    And their young souls come tainted to the world
    With the first breath they draw.
ANTONY Th' original villain sure no god created;
    He was a bastard of the sun by Nile,
155   Aped into man with all his mother's mud
    Crusted about his soul.
VENTIDIUS The nation is
    One universal traitor, and their queen
    The very spirit and extract of 'em all.
ANTONY Is there yet left
160   A possibility of aid from valour?
    Is there one god unsworn to my destruction?
    The least unmortgaged hope? for, if there be,
    Methinks I cannot fall beneath the fate
    Of such a boy as Caesar.
165   The world's one half is yet in Antony,
    And from each limb of it, that's hewed away,
    The soul comes back to me.
VENTIDIUS There yet remain
    Three legions in the town. The last assault
    Lopped off the rest: if death be your design —
170   As I must wish it now — these are sufficient
    To make a heap about us of dead foes,
    An honest pile for burial.
ANTONY They're enough.
    We'll not divide our stars, but side by side
    Fight emulous, and with malicious eyes
175   Survey each other's acts: so every death
    Thou giv'st I'll take on me as a just debt,
    And pay thee back a soul.
VENTIDIUS Now you shall see I love you. Not a word
    Of chiding more. By my few hours of life,
180   I am so pleased with this brave Roman fate,
    That I would not be Caesar, to outlive you.
    When we put off this flesh, and mount together,

I shall be shown to all th' ethereal crowd —
Lo, this is he who died with Antony!
ANTONY   Who knows but we may pierce through all their troops   185
And reach my veterans yet? 'Tis worth the 'tempting,
T' o'erleap this gulf of fate
And leave our wondering destinies behind.

Enter ALEXAS, *trembling.*

VENTIDIUS   See, see, that villain!
See Cleopatra stamped upon that face,   190
With all her cunning, all her arts of falsehood!
How she looks out through those dissembling eyes!
How he sets his countenance for deceit,
And promises a lie before he speaks!
Let me despatch him first.   [*Drawing.*
ALEXAS   O spare me, spare me!   195
ANTONY   Hold, he's not worth your killing. On thy life
(Which thou may'st keep, because I scorn to take it)
No syllable to justify thy queen;
Save thy base tongue its office.
ALEXAS   Sir, she's gone
Where she shall never be molested more   200
By love, or you.
ANTONY   Fled to her Dolabella!
Die, traitor, I revoke my promise, die!   [*Going to kill him.*
ALEXAS   O hold! she is not fled.
ANTONY   She is: my eyes
Are open to her falsehood; my whole life
Has been a golden dream of love and friendship;   205
But, now I wake, I'm like a merchant roused
From soft repose to see his vessel sinking
And all his wealth cast o'er. Ungrateful woman!
Who followed me but as the swallow summer,
Hatching her young ones in my kindly beams,   210
Singing her flatt'ries to my morning wake:
But now my winter comes she spreads her wings
And seeks the spring of Caesar.
ALEXAS   Think not so:
Her fortunes have in all things mixed with yours.
Had she betrayed her naval force to Rome,   215
How easily might she have gone to Caesar,

Secure by such a bribe!
VENTIDIUS   She sent it first,
To be more welcome after.
ANTONY   'Tis too plain;
Else would she have appeared, to clear herself.

220   ALEXAS   Too fatally she has: she could not bear
To be accused by you, but shut herself
Within her monument; looked down and sighed;
While, from her unchanged face, the silent tears
Dropt, as they had not leave, but stole their parting.

225   Some undistinguished words she inly murmured;
At last she raised her eyes, and with such looks
As dying Lucrece cast —
ANTONY   My heart forebodes —
VENTIDIUS   All for the best: go on.
ALEXAS   She snatched her poniard,
And ere we could prevent the fatal blow,

230   Plunged it within her breast; then turned to me:
Go, bear my lord, said she, my last farewell,
And ask him, if he yet suspect my faith.
More she was saying, but death rushed betwixt.
She half pronounced your name with her last breath,

235   And buried half within her.
VENTIDIUS   Heav'n be praised!
ANTONY   Then art thou innocent, my poor dear love,
And art thou dead?
O these two words! their sound should be divided:
Hadst thou been false and died, or hadst thou lived

240   And hadst been true. . . . But innocence and death!
This shows not well above. Then what am I,
The murderer of this truth, this innocence!
Thoughts cannot form themselves in words so horrid
As can express my guilt!

245   VENTIDIUS   Is't come to this? The gods have been too gracious;
And thus you thank 'em for't!
ANTONY [to ALEXAS]   Why stay'st thou here?
Is it for thee to spy upon my soul
And see its inward mourning? Get thee hence,
Thou art not worthy to behold what now

250   Becomes a Roman emperor to perform.
ALEXAS   He loves her still: [Aside.
His grief betrays it. Good! the joy to find

She's yet alive completes the reconcilement.
I've saved myself, and her. But, oh! the Romans!
Fate comes too fast upon my wit,   255
Hunts me too hard, and meets me at each double.   [*Exit.*
VENTIDIUS Would she had died a little sooner, though,
  Before Octavia went; you might have treated:
  Now 'twill look tame, and would not be received.
  Come, rouse yourself, and let's die warm together.   260
ANTONY I will not fight: there's no more work for war.
  The bus'ness of my angry hours is done.
VENTIDIUS Caesar is at your gates.
ANTONY Why, let him enter;
  He's welcome now.
VENTIDIUS What lethargy has crept into your soul?   265
ANTONY 'Tis but a scorn of life, and just desire
  To free myself from bondage.
VENTIDIUS Do it bravely.
ANTONY I will, but not by fighting. O Ventidius!
  What should I fight for now? My queen is dead.
  I was but great for her; my power, my empire,   270
  Were but my merchandise to buy her love,
  And conquered kings my factors. Now she's dead,
  Let Caesar take the world —
  An empty circle, since the jewel's gone
  Which made it worth my strife: my being's nauseous,   275
  For all the bribes of life are gone away.
VENTIDIUS Would you be taken?
ANTONY Yes, I would be taken;
  But as a Roman ought, dead, my Ventidius:
  For I'll convey my soul from Caesar's reach,
  And lay down life myself. 'Tis time the world   280
  Should have a lord, and know whom to obey.
  We two have kept its homage in suspense,
  And bent the globe, on whose each side we trod,
  Till it was dented inwards. Let him walk
  Alone upon't: I'm weary of my part.   285
  My torch is out, and the world stands before me
  Like a black desert at th' approach of night:
  I'll lay me down, and stray no farther on.
VENTIDIUS I could be grieved,

256 double] I.e. doubling back.

290   But that I'll not outlive you: choose your death,
        For I have seen him in such various shapes
        I care not which I take: I'm only troubled
        The life I bear is worn to such a rag,
        'Tis scarce worth giving. I could wish indeed
295   We threw it from us with a better grace;
        That, like two lions taken in the toils,
        We might at last thrust out our paws, and wound
        The hunters that inclose us.
        ANTONY   I have thought on't.
        Ventidius, you must live.
        VENTIDIUS   I must not, sir.
300   ANTONY   Wilt thou not live, to speak some good of me?
        To stand by my fair fame, and guard th' approaches
        From the ill tongues of men?
        VENTIDIUS   Who shall guard mine
        For living after you?
        ANTONY   Say, I command it.
        VENTIDIUS   If we die well, our deaths will speak themselves,
305   And need no living witness.
        ANTONY   Thou hast loved me,
        And fain I would reward thee. I must die;
        Kill me, and take the merit of my death,
        To make thee friends with Caesar.
        VENTIDIUS   Thank your kindness.
        You said I loved you, and in recompense
310   You bid me turn a traitor: did I think
        You would have used me thus? that I should die
        With a hard thought of you?
        ANTONY   Forgive me, Roman.
        Since I have heard of Cleopatra's death
        My reason bears no rule upon my tongue,
315   But lets my thoughts break all at random out.
        I've thought better; do not deny me twice.
        VENTIDIUS   By heav'n, I will not.
        Let it not be t'outlive you.
        ANTONY   Kill me first,
        And then die thou; for 'tis but just thou serve
320   Thy friend before thyself.
        VENTIDIUS   Give me your hand.
        We soon shall meet again. Now, farewell, emperor!   [Embrace.
        Methinks that word's too cold to be my last:

Since death sweeps all distinctions, farewell, friend!
That's all —
I will not make a bus'ness of a trifle: 325
And yet I cannot look on you, and kill you;
Pray turn your face.
ANTONY   I do: strike home, be sure.
VENTIDIUS   Home, as my sword will reach.   [*Kills himself.*
ANTONY   Oh, thou mistak'st;
That wound was not of thine; give it me back:
Thou robb'st me of my death.
VENTIDIUS   I do indeed;   330
But think 'tis the first time I e'er deceived you,
If that may plead my pardon. And you, gods,
Forgive me, if you will; for I die perjured,
Rather than kill my friend.   [*Dies.*
ANTONY   Farewell. Ever my leader, ev'n in death!   335
My queen and thou have got the start of me,
And I'm the lag of honour. . . . Gone so soon?
Is Death no more? He used him carelessly,
With a familiar kindness: ere he knocked,
Ran to the door, and took him in his arms,   340
As who should say, Y'are welcome at all hours,
A friend need give no warning. Books had spoiled him,
For all the learn'd are cowards by profession.
'Tis not worth
My farther thought; for death, for aught I know,   345
Is but to think no more. Here's to be satisfied.

[*Falls on his sword.*

I've missed my heart. O unperforming hand!
Thou never couldst have erred in a worse time.
My fortune jades me to the last; and death,
Like a great man, takes state, and makes me wait   350
For my admittance. —   [*Trampling within.*
Some perhaps from Caesar:
If he should find me living, and suspect
That I played booty with my life! I'll mend
My work ere they can reach me.   [*Rises upon his knees.*

Enter CLEOPATRA, CHARMION, *and* IRAS.

353 played booty] Played falsely, cheated.

355   CLEOPATRA   Where is my lord? where is he?
　　　CHARMION   There he lies,
　　　　And dead Ventidius by him.
　　　CLEOPATRA   My fears were prophets; I am come too late.
　　　　O that accursed Alexas!　　　　　　　　　　[*Runs to him.*
　　　ANTONY   Art thou living?
　　　　Or am I dead before I knew, and thou
360　　　The first kind ghost that meets me?
　　　CLEOPATRA   Help me seat him.
　　　　Send quickly, send for help!　　　　[*They place him in a chair.*
　　　ANTONY   I am answered.
　　　　We live both. Sit thee down, my Cleopatra:
　　　　I'll make the most I can of life, to stay
　　　　A moment more with thee.
　　　CLEOPATRA   How is it with you?
365　　ANTONY   'Tis as with a man
　　　　Removing in a hurry; all packed up,
　　　　But one dear jewel that his haste forgot;
　　　　And he, for that, returns upon the spur:
　　　　So I come back for thee.
370　　CLEOPATRA   Too long, you heavens, you have been cruel to me:
　　　　Now show your mended faith, and give me back
　　　　His fleeting life.
　　　ANTONY   It will not be, my love.
　　　　I keep my soul by force.
　　　　Say but thou art not false.
　　　CLEOPATRA   'Tis now too late
375　　　To say I'm true: I'll prove it, and die with you.
　　　　Unknown to me, Alexas feigned my death:
　　　　Which, when I knew, I hasted to prevent
　　　　This fatal consequence. My fleet betrayed
　　　　Both you and me.
　　　ANTONY   And Dolabella . . .
380　　CLEOPATRA   Scarce esteemed before he loved; but hated now.
　　　ANTONY   Enough: my life's not long enough for more.
　　　　Thou say'st thou will come after: I believe thee;
　　　　For I can now believe whate'er thou sayest,
　　　　That we may part more kindly.
　　　CLEOPATRA   I will come:
　　　　Doubt not, my life, I'll come, and quickly too:
　　　　Caesar shall triumph o'er no part of thee.
　　　ANTONY   But grieve not, while thou stay'st

My last disastrous times:
Think we have had a clear and glorious day,
And heav'n did kindly to delay the storm   390
Just till our close of evening. Ten years' love,
And not a moment lost, but all improved
To th' utmost joys: what ages have we lived!
And now to die each other's; and so dying,
While hand in hand we walk in groves below   395
Whole troops of lovers' ghosts shall flock about us,
And all the train be ours.
CLEOPATRA   Your words are like the notes of dying swans,
Too sweet to last. Were there so many hours
For your unkindness, and not one for love?   400
ANTONY   No, not a minute. . . . This one kiss . . . more worth
Than all I leave to Caesar.   [*Dies.*
CLEOPATRA   O tell me so again,
And take ten thousand kisses for that word.
My lord, my lord: speak, if you yet have being;   405
Sigh to me if you cannot speak; or cast
One look! Do anything that shows you live.
IRAS   He's gone too far to hear you;
And this you see, a lump of senseless clay,
The leavings of a soul.
CHARMION   Remember, madam,   410
He charged you not to grieve.
CLEOPATRA   And I'll obey him.
I have not loved a Roman not to know
What should become his wife; his wife, my Charmion!
For 'tis to that high title I aspire,
And now I'll not die less. Let dull Octavia   415
Survive, to mourn him dead: my nobler fate
Shall knit our spousals with a tic too strong
For Roman laws to break.
IRAS   Will you then die?
CLEOPATRA   Why shouldst thou make that question?
IRAS   Caesar is merciful.
CLEOPATRA   Let him be so   420
To those that want his mercy: my poor lord
Made no such cov'nant with him, to spare me
When he was dead. Yield me to Caesar's pride?
What! to be led in triumph through the streets,
A spectacle to base plebeian eyes;   425

While some dejected friend of Antony's
Close in a corner, shakes his head, and mutters
A secret curse on her who ruined him?
I'll none of that.
CHARMION   Whatever you resolve,
430   I'll follow ev'n to death.
IRAS   I only feared
For you, but more should fear to live without you.
CLEOPATRA   Why, now 'tis as it should be. Quick, my friends,
Despatch; ere this, the town's in Caesar's hands:
My lord looks down concerned, and fears my stay,
435   Lest I should be surprised;
Keep him not waiting for his love too long.
You, Charmion, bring my crown and richest jewels;
With 'em, the wreath of victory I made
(Vain augury!) for him who now lies dead;
440   You, Iras, bring the cure of all our ills.
IRAS   The aspics, madam?
CLEOPATRA   Must I bid you twice?

                              [*Exeunt* CHARMION *and* IRAS.

'Tis sweet to die when they would force life on me,
To rush into the dark abode of death,
And seize him first; if he be like my love,
445   He is not frightful sure.
We're now alone, in secrecy and silence;
And is not this like lovers? I may kiss
These pale, cold lips; Octavia does not see me;
And, oh! 'tis better far to have him thus,
450   Than see him in her arms. — Oh, welcome, welcome!

                    Enter CHARMION *and* IRAS.

CHARMION   What must be done?
CLEOPATRA   Short ceremony, friends;
But yet it must be decent. First, this laurel
Shall crown my hero's head: he fell not basely,
Nor left his shield behind him. Only thou
455   Couldst triumph o'er thyself; and thou alone
Wert worthy so to triumph.
CHARMION   To what end
These ensigns of your pomp and royalty?
CLEOPATRA   Dull that thou art! why 'tis to meet my love;

As when I saw him first, on Cydnus' bank,
All sparkling, like a goddess; so adorned,   460
I'll find him once again; my second spousals
Shall match my first in glory. Haste, haste, both,
And dress the bride of Antony.
CHARMION   'Tis done.
CLEOPATRA   Now seat me by my lord. I claim this place;
For I must conquer Caesar too, like him,   465
And win my share o'th' world. Hail, you dear relics
Of my immortal love!
O let no impious hand remove you hence,
But rest for ever here! Let Egypt give
His death that peace which it denied his life.   470
Reach me the casket.
IRAS   Underneath the fruit the aspic lies.
CLEOPATRA   Welcome, thou kind deceiver!   [*Putting aside the leaves.*
Thou best of thieves; who, with an easy key,
Dost open life, and, unperceived by us,   475
Ev'n steal us from ourselves; discharging so
Death's dreadful office, better than himself;
Touching our limbs so gently into slumber,
That Death stands by, deceived by his own image,
And thinks himself but sleep.
SERAPION   The queen, where is she?   [*Within.*   480
The town is yielded, Caesar's at the gates.
CLEOPATRA   He comes too late t'invade the rights of death.
Haste, bare my arm, and rouse the serpent's fury.

[*Holds out her arm, and draws it back.*

Coward flesh —
Wouldst thou conspire with Caesar to betray me,   485
As thou wert none of mine? I'll force thee to 't,
And not be sent by him,
But bring, myself, my soul to Antony.

[*Turns aside, and then shows her arm bloody.*

Take hence; the work is done.
SERAPION   Break ope the door,   [*Within.*
And guard the traitor well.
CHARMION   The next is ours.   490
IRAS   Now, Charmion, to be worthy
Of our great queen and mistress.   [*They apply the aspics.*

CLEOPATRA   Already, death, I feel thee in my veins;
   I go with such a will to find my lord
495   That we shall quickly meet.
   A heavy numbness creeps through every limb,
   And now 'tis at my head: My eyelids fall,
   And my dear love is vanquished in a mist.
   Where shall I find him, where? O turn me to him,
500   And lay me on his breast. . . . Caesar, thy worst;
   Now part us, if thou canst.   [*Dies.*

[IRAS *sinks down at her feet, and dies*; CHARMION *stands behind her
chair, as dressing her head.*]

Enter SERAPION, *two* Priests, ALEXAS *bound*, Egyptians.

PRIESTS   Behold, Serapion, what havoc death has made!
SERAPION   'Twas what I feared.
   Charmion, is this well done?
505 CHARMION   Yes, 'tis well done, and like a queen, the last
   Of her great race: I follow her.   [*Sinks down: dies.*
   ALEXAS   'Tis true,
   She has done well: much better thus to die,
   Than live to make a holiday in Rome.
   SERAPION   See, see how the lovers sit in state together,
510   As they were giving laws to half mankind.
   Th' impression of a smile left in her face
   Shows she died pleased with him for whom she lived,
   And went to charm him in another world.
   Caesar's just ent'ring; grief has now no leisure.
515   Secure that villain as our pledge of safety
   To grace th' imperial triumph. Sleep, blest pair,
   Secure from human chance, long ages out,
   While all the storms of fate fly o'er your tomb;
     And fame to late posterity shall tell,
520   No lovers lived so great, or died so well.   [*Exeunt.*

EPILOGUE

Poets, like disputants, when reasons fail,
Have one sure refuge left, and that's to rail.
Fop, coxcomb, fool, are thundered through the pit;
And this is all their equipage of wit.
We wonder how the devil this diff'rence grows   5
Betwixt our fools in verse and yours in prose:
For, 'faith the quarrel rightly understood,
'Tis civil war with their own flesh and blood.
The threadbare author hates the gaudy coat;
And swears at the gilt coach, but swears afoot: 10
For 'tis observed of every scribbling man,
He grows a fop as fast as e'er he can;
Pruncs up, and asks his oracle the glass,
If pink or purple best become his face.
For our poor wretch, he neither rails nor prays; ⎫   15
Nor likes your wit just as you like his plays;   ⎬
He has not yet so much of Mr Bayes.   ⎭
He does his best; and if he cannot please,
Would quietly sue out his writ of ease.
Yet, if he might his own grand jury call,   20
By the fair sex he begs to stand or fall.
Let Caesar's pow'r the men's ambition move,
But grace you him who lost the world for love.
Yet if some antiquated lady say,
The last age is not copied in his play,   25
Heav'n help the man who for that face must drudge,
Which only has the wrinkles of a judge.
Let not the young and beauteous join with those;
For should you raise such numerous hosts of foes,
Young wits and sparks he to his aid must call;   30
'Tis more than one man's work to please you all.

17 Mr Bayes] The character representing Dryden in the Duke of Buckingham's satirical play
The Rehearsal (1671).
19 writ of ease] A certificate of discharge from employment.

PROSE

AN ESSAY OF DRAMATIC POESY

According to Dryden's statement in the Dedication to Buckhurst, the *Essay* was written in a period of retirement in the country, while the theatres were closed by the plague of mid-1665. It was registered for publication in August 1667, but the first edition is dated 1668. The second edition of 1684 is revised, mainly in point of style, and might be preferred. But the work has such historical importance that attention is bound, I think, to the first printing.

It takes the form of a dialogue, after the platonic manner, between four characters, Lisideius, Eugenius, Crites, and Neander; identifiable as Sedley, Buckhurst ('well-born'), Robert Howard (a captious opponent of Dryden's, much in character in the *Essay*), and Dryden, a somewhat diffident 'new man', in Samuel Johnson's phrase 'yet a timorous candidate for reputation'. The dialogue method, besides being self-effacing, has advantages for comparison of views, digression, and persuasion.

The imagined occasion, the day of a naval victory, is linked with the nationalistic purpose of the *Essay*. The intention is to clear the way for a new generation of English drama, by establishing the superiority of the English tradition, and by holding at a distance classical precedents and stricter French regularities. The possibilities of rhyming drama, obviously exciting to Dryden at this time, are explored towards the end. This part of Dryden's programme was to be relinquished before many years (see the prologue to *Aureng-Zebe*, p. 218) but it was for some time an issue for literary quarrels, here, and in previous and subsequent exchanges between Dryden and Howard (see the note on p. 528).

In the lively and copious discussions of the Ancients, the three Unities, and the claims of French drama over the English, it is perhaps as well to remember two things. First, that Dryden is on much safer ground than he pretends for much of the *Essay* with respect to the achievements of English literature, especially of the Elizabethan and Jacobean age. Second, that his chief concern is with comedy, which is less susceptible to regulation and prescription than tragedy; and that his discussion of serious drama is extensively bound up with the question of rhyme. It is as unassuming a procedure as could be imagined; but always refreshing, and always rewarding.

It was that memorable day,[1] in the first summer of the late war, when our

---

[1] 3 June 1665, when a naval battle of the second Dutch war took place off Harwich.

navy engaged the Dutch: a day wherein the two most mighty and best appointed fleets which any age had ever seen disputed the command of the greater half of the globe, the commerce of nations, and the riches of the universe. While these vast floating bodies, on either side, moved against each other in parallel lines, and our countrymen, under the happy conduct of his Royal Highness,[2] went breaking, by little and little, into the line of the enemies, the noise of the cannon from both navies reached our ears about the City;[3] so that all men being alarmed with it, and in a dreadful suspense of the event which we knew was then deciding, every one went following the sound as his fancy led him; and leaving the town almost empty, some took towards the park, some cross the river, others down it; all seeking the noise in the depth of silence.

Among the rest, it was the fortune of Eugenius, Crites, Lisideius, and Neander[4] to be in company together: three of them persons whom their wit and quality have made known to all the town; and whom I have chose to hide under these borrowed names that they may not suffer by so ill a relation as I am going to make of their discourse.

Taking then a barge which a servant of Lisideius had provided for them, they made haste to shoot the bridge, and left behind them that great fall of waters which hindered them from hearing what they desired: after which, having disengaged themselves from many vessels which rode at anchor in the Thames, and almost blocked up the passage towards Greenwich, they ordered the watermen to let fall their oars more gently; and then, every one favouring his own curiosity with a strict silence, it was not long ere they perceived the air break about them like the noise of distant thunder, or of swallows in a chimney: those little undulations of sound, though almost vanishing before they reached them, yet still seeming to retain somewhat of their first horror which they had betwixt the fleets. After they had attentively listened till such time as the sound by little and little went from them, Eugenius, lifting up his head, and taking notice of it, was the first who congratulated to the rest that happy omen of our nation's victory: adding, we had but this to desire in confirmation of it, that we might hear no more of that noise which was now leaving the English coast. When the rest had concurred in the same opinion, Crites, a person of a sharp judgment, and somewhat too delicate a taste in wit, which the world have mistaken in him for ill nature, said, smiling to us, that if the concernment of this battle had not been so exceeding great, he could scarce have wished the victory at the price he knew he must pay for it, in being subject to the

[2] James, Duke of York, the King's brother.

[3] noise . . . City] Pepys has a similar description of the atmosphere in London in his diary for that day.

[4] Eugenius . . . Neander] For their identities, see the headnote above.

reading and hearing of so many ill verses as he was sure would be made upon it; adding that no argument could scape some of those eternal rhymers, who watch a battle with more diligence than the ravens and birds of prey; and the worst of them surest to be first in upon the quarry, while the better able, either out of modesty writ not at all, or set that due value upon their poems as to let them be often called for and long expected. 'There are some of those impertinent people you speak of,' answered Lisideius, 'who to my know-ledge are already so provided, either way, that they can produce not only a panegyric upon the victory but, if need be, a funeral elegy upon the Duke; and after they have crowned his valour with many laurels, at last deplore the odds under which he fell, concluding that his courage deserved a better destiny.' All the company smiled at the conceit of Lisideius; but Crites, more eager than before, began to make particular exceptions against some writers, and said the public magistrate ought to send betimes to forbid them; and that it concerned the peace and quiet of all honest people that ill poets should be as well silenced as seditious preachers. 'In my opinion,' replied Eugenius, 'you pursue your point too far; for as to my own particular, I am so great a lover of poesy that I could wish them all rewarded who attempt but to do well; at least, I would not have them worse used than Sylla the Dictator did one of their brethren heretofore: *quem in concione vidimus* (says Tully speaking of him) *cum ei libellum malus poeta de populo subjecisset, quod epigramma in eum fecisset tantummodo alternis versibus longius-culis, statim ex iis rebus quas tunc vendebat jubere ei praemium tribui, sub ea conditione ne quid postea scriberet.*[5] 'I could wish with all my heart,' replied Crites, 'that many whom we know were as bountifully thanked upon the same condition, that they would never trouble us again. For amongst others, I have a mortal apprehension of two poets[6] whom this victory with the help of both her wings will never be able to escape.' ''Tis easy to guess whom you intend,' said Lisideius; 'and without naming them, I ask you if one of them does not perpetually pay us with clenches[7] upon words, and a certain clownish kind of raillery? If now and then he does not offer at a catachresis[8] or Clevelandism,[9] wresting and torturing a word into another meaning: in fine, if he be not one of those whom the French would call *un mauvais buffon*; one that is so much a well-willer to the satire that he spares

---

[5] Cicero, *Pro Archia*, x, 25: 'It will be remembered that once at a public meeting some poetaster from the crowd handed up to the great man a paper containing an epigram upon him, improvised in somewhat unmetrical elegiacs. Sulla immediately offered a reward to be paid out of the proceeds of the sale which he was then holding, but added the stipulation that he should never write again.'

[6] Robert Wild (1609–79) and Richard Flecknoe (d. 1678) have been suggested.

[7] Puns.

[8] An unapt use of a word.

[9] The poet John Cleveland (1613–58) was notoriously extravagant in his use of language.

no man; and though he cannot strike a blow to hurt any, yet ought to be punished for the malice of the action, as our witches are justly hanged because they think themselves so; and suffer deservedly for believing they did mischief, because they meant it.' 'You have described him,' said Crites, 'so exactly, that I am afraid to come after you with my other extremity of poetry. He is one of those who, having had some advantage of education and converse, knows better than the other what a poet should be, but puts it into practice more unluckily than any man; his style and matter are everywhere alike; he is the most calm, peaceable writer you ever read; he never disquiets your passions with the least concernment, but still leaves you in as even a temper as he found you; he is a very Leveller in poetry, he creeps along with ten little words in every line[10] and helps out his numbers with *for to* and *unto*, and all the pretty expletives he can find, till he drags them to the end of another line; while the sense is left tired halfway behind it; he doubly starves all his verses, first for want of thought, and then of expression; his poetry neither has wit in it, nor seems to have it; like him in Martial:

> Pauper videri Cinna vult, et est pauper.[11]

'He affects plainness, to cover his want of imagination: when he writes the serious way, the highest flight of his fancy is some miserable antithesis, or seeming contradiction; and in the comic he is still reaching at some thin conceit, the ghost of a jest, and that too flies before him, never to be caught; these swallows which we see before us on the Thames are the just resemblance of his wit: you may observe how near the water they stoop, how many proffers they make to dip, and yet how seldom they touch it; and when they do, 'tis but the surface: they skim over it but to catch a gnat, and then mount into the air and leave it.'

'Well, gentlemen,' said Eugenius, 'you may speak your pleasure of these authors; but though I and some few more about the town may give you a peaceable hearing, yet, assure yourselves, there are multitudes who would think you malicious and them injured: especially him whom you first described; he is the very Withers[12] of the city: they have bought more editions of his works than would serve to lay under all their pies at the Lord Mayor's Christmas. When his famous poem first came out in the year 1660,

---

[10] creeps . . . line] Cf. Pope's *Essay on Criticism*, ll. 346–7:
  While expletives their feeble aid to join,
  And ten low words oft creep in one dull line.
[11] *Epigrams*, VIII, xix, 17: 'Cinna wishes to appear poor, and he is poor.'
[12] George Wither (1588–1667), a prolific, undistinguished poet who was opposed to the Court.

I have seen them reading it in the midst of 'Change time;[13] nay, so vehement they were at it, that they lost their bargain by the candles' ends;[14] but what will you say if he has been received amongst the great ones? I can assure you he is, this day, the envy of a great person who is lord in the art of quibbling; and who does not take it well that any man should intrude so far into his province.' 'All I would wish,' replied Crites, 'is that they who love his writings may still admire him, and his fellow poet: *qui Bavium non odit, &c.*,[15] is curse sufficient.' 'And farther,' added Lisideius, 'I believe there is no man who writes well, but would think himself very hardly dealt with, if their admirers should praise anything of his: *nam quos contemnimus, eorum quoque laudes contemnimus.*'[16] 'There are so few who write well in this age,' says Crites, 'that methinks any praises should be welcome; they neither rise to the dignity of the last age, nor to any of the Ancients; and we may cry out of the writers of this time, with more reason than Petronius of his, *pace vestra liceat dixisse, primi omnium eloquentiam perdidistis*:[17] you have debauched the true old poetry so far, that nature, which is the soul of it, is not in any of your writings.'

'If your quarrel,' said Eugenius, 'to those who now write, be grounded only on your reverence to antiquity, there is no man more ready to adore those great Greeks and Romans than I am: but on the other side, I cannot think so contemptibly of the age I live in, or so dishonourably of my own country, as not to judge we equal the Ancients in most kinds of poesy, and in some surpass them; neither know I any reason why I may not be as zealous for the reputation of our age, as we find the Ancients themselves in reference to those who lived before them. For you hear your Horace saying,

> indignor quicquam reprehendi, non quia crasse
> compositum, illepideve putetur, sed quia nuper.[18]

And after:

> si meliora dies, ut vina, poemata reddit,
> scire velim, pretium chartis quotus arroget annus?[19]

---

[13] The time when merchants met at the Exchange.

[14] At auctions, a piece of candle was lit, and bidding closed when it burned itself out.

[15] Virgil, *Eclogues*, III, 90: 'Let him who hates not Bavius [love your songs, Mavius].'

[16] 'For we despise the praises of those whom we despise.' The source of the quotation has not been identified.

[17] *Satyricon*, 2: 'With your permission I must tell you the truth, that you [teachers of rhetoric] more than anyone have been the ruin of true eloquence.'

[18] *Epistles*, II, i, 76–7: 'I am impatient that my work is censured, not because it is thought to be coarse or inelegant in style, but because it is modern.'

[19] Ibid., ll. 43–5: 'If poems are like wine which time improves, I should like to know what is the year that gives to writings fresh value.'

'But I see I am engaging in a wide dispute, where the arguments are not like to reach close on either side; for poesy is of so large an extent, and so many both of the Ancients and Moderns have done well in all kinds of it, that in citing one against the other we shall take up more time this evening than each man's occasions will allow him: therefore I would ask Crites to what parts of poesy he would confine his arguments, and whether he would defend the general cause of the Ancients against the Moderns, or oppose any age of the Moderns against this of ours?'

Crites, a little while considering upon this demand, told Eugenius he approved his propositions and, if he pleased, he would limit their dispute to dramatic poesy; in which he thought it not difficult to prove either that the Ancients were superior to the Moderns, or the last age to this of ours.

Eugenius was somewhat surprised when he heard Crites make choice of that subject. 'For aught I see,' said he, 'I have undertaken a harder province than I imagined; for though I never judged the plays of the Greek or Roman poets comparable to ours; yet on the other side those we now see acted come short of many which were written in the last age: but my comfort is, if we are o'ercome, it will be only by our own countrymen; and if we yield to them in this one part of poesy, we more surpass them in all the other; for in the epic or lyric way it will be hard for them to show us one such amongst them, as we have many now living, or who lately were so. They can produce nothing so courtly writ, or which expresses so much the conversation of a gentleman, as Sir John Suckling; nothing so even, sweet, and flowing, as Mr Waller; nothing so majestic, so correct as Sir John Denham; nothing so elevated, so copious, and full of spirit, as Mr Cowley; as for the Italian, French, and Spanish plays, I can make it evident that those who now write surpass them; and that the drama is wholly ours.'

All of them were thus far of Eugenius his opinion that the sweetness of English verse was never understood or practised by our fathers; even Crites himself did not much oppose it: and every one was willing to acknowledge how much our poesy is improved by the happiness of some writers yet living, who first taught us to mould our thoughts into easy and significant words, to retrench the superfluities of expression, and to make our rhyme so properly a part of the verse that it should never mislead the sense, but itself be led and governed by it.[20]

Eugenius was going to continue this discourse, when Lisideius told him it was necessary, before they proceeded further, to take a standing measure of their controversy; for how was it possible to be decided who writ the best plays, before we know what a play should be? But, this once agreed on by

---

[20] This paragraph and the preceding one describe a taste for qualities of smoothness and polish in verse which of course prevailed well into the next century

both parties, each might have recourse to it, either to prove his own advantages, or to discover the failings of his adversary.

He had no sooner said this, but all desired the favour of him to give the definition of a play; and they were the more importunate, because neither Aristotle, nor Horace, nor any other who writ of that subject, had ever done it.

Lisideius, after some modest denials, at last confessed he had a rude notion of it; indeed rather a description than a definition; but which served to guide him in his private thoughts, when he was to make a judgment of what others writ: that he conceived a play ought to be *A just and lively image of human nature, representing its passions and humours, and the changes of fortune to which it is subject, for the delight and instruction of mankind.*

This definition, though Crites raised a logical objection against it, that it was only *a genere et fine*,[21] and so not altogether perfect, was yet well received by the rest: and after they had given order to the watermen to turn their barge, and row softly, that they might take the cool of the evening in their return, Crites, being desired by the company to begin, spoke on behalf of the Ancients, in this manner:

'If confidence presage a victory, Eugenius, in his own opinion, has already triumphed over the Ancients: nothing seems more easy to him than to overcome those whom it is our greatest praise to have imitated well; for we do not only build upon their foundation, but by their models. Dramatic poesy had time enough, reckoning from Thespis (who first invented it) to Aristophanes, to be born, to grow up, and to flourish in maturity. It has been observed of arts and sciences, that in one and the same century they have arrived to a great perfection; and no wonder, since every age has a kind of universal genius which inclines those that live in it to some particular studies: the work then being pushed on by many hands, must of necessity go forward.

'Is it not evident in these last hundred years (when the study of philosophy[22] has been the business of all the virtuosi in Christendom), that almost a new nature has been revealed to us? that more errors of the school[23] have been detected, more useful experiments in philosophy have been made, more noble secrets in optics, medicine, anatomy, astronomy discovered, than in all those credulous and doting ages from Aristotle to us? so true it is, that nothing spreads more fast than science, when rightly and generally cultivated.

'Add to this the more than common emulation that was in those times of

---

[21] 'Of class and end'; not comprehensive.

[22] philosophy] Natural science, in which Dryden, as a member of the Royal Society, was keenly interested.

[23] the school] Philosophers of the scholastic tradition.

writing well; which though it be found in all ages and all persons that
pretend to the same reputation, yet poesy, being then in more esteem than
now it is, had greater honours decreed to the professors of it, and consequently the rivalship was more high between them; they had judges
ordained to decide their merit, and prizes to reward it; and historians have
been diligent to record of Aeschylus, Euripides, Sophocles, Lycophron, and
the rest of them, both who they were that vanquished in these wars of the
theatre, and how often they were crowned: while the Asian kings and
Grecian commonwealths scarce afforded them a nobler subject than the
unmanly luxuries of a debauched court, or giddy intrigues of a factious city.
Alit aemulatio ingenia (says Paterculus), *et nunc invidia, nunc admiratio
incitationem accendit*:[24] emulation is the spur of wit; and sometimes envy,
sometimes admiration, quickens our endeavours.

'But now, since the rewards of honour are taken away, that virtuous
emulation is turned into direct malice; yet so slothful, that it contents itself
to condemn and cry down others, without attempting to do better: 'tis a
reputation too unprofitable to take the necessary pains for it; yet wishing
they had it is incitement enough to hinder others from it. And this, in
short, Eugenius, is the reason why you have now so few good poets, and so
many severe judges. Certainly, to imitate the Ancients well, much labour
and long study is required; which pains, I have already shown, our poets
would want encouragement to take, if yet they had ability to go through
with it. Those Ancients have been faithful imitators and wise observers of
that nature which is so torn and ill represented in our plays; they have
handed down to us a perfect resemblance of her; which we, like ill copiers,
neglecting to look on, have rendered monstrous and disfigured. But, that
you may know how much you are indebted to those your masters, and be
ashamed to have so ill requited them, I must remember you that all the
rules by which we practise the drama at this day, either such as relate to the
justness and symmetry of the plot, or the episodical ornaments, such as
descriptions, narrations, and other beauties, which are not essential to the
play, were delivered to us from the observations which Aristotle made of
those poets, which either lived before him, or were his contemporaries: we
have added nothing of our own, except we have the confidence to say our wit
is better; which none boast of in this our age, but such as understand not
theirs. Of that book which Aristotle has left us, περὶ τῆς Ποιητικῆς,
Horace his *Art of Poetry* is an excellent comment and, I believe, restores to us
that second book of his concerning comedy, which is wanting in him.[25]

'Out of these two has been extracted the famous rules which the French

---

[24] Velleius Paterculus, *History of Rome*, I, 17.
[25] The part of Aristotle's *Poetics* which deals with comedy has been lost.

call *des trois unités*, or the Three Unities, which ought to be observed in every regular play: namely, of time, place, and action.[26]

'The unity of time they comprehend in twenty-four hours, the compass of a natural day, or as near as it can be contrived; and the reason of it is obvious to every one, that the time of the feigned action, or fable of the play, should be proportioned as near as can be to the duration of that time in which it is represented; since, therefore, all plays are acted on the theatre in a space of time much within the compass of twenty-four hours, that play is to be thought the nearest imitation of nature whose plot or action is confined within that time; and, by the same rule which concludes this general proportion of time, it follows that all the parts of it are to be equally subdivided; as namely, that one act take not up the supposed time of half a day, which is out of proportion to the rest; since the other four are then to be straitened within the compass of the remaining half: for it is unnatural that one act, which being spoke or written is not longer than the rest, should be supposed longer by the audience; 'tis therefore the poet's duty to take care that no act should be imagined to exceed the time in which it is represented on the stage; and that the intervals and inequalities of time be supposed to fall out between the acts.

'This rule of time, how well it has been observed by the Ancients, most of their plays will witness; you see them in their tragedies (wherein to follow this rule is certainly most difficult) from the very beginning of their plays, falling close into that part of the story which they intend for the action or principal object of it, leaving the former part to be delivered by narration: so that they set the audience, as it were, at the post where the race is to be concluded; and, saving them the tedious expectation of seeing the poet set out and ride the beginning of the course, you behold him not till he is in sight of the goal, and just upon you.

'For the second unity, which is that of place, the Ancients meant by it that the scene ought to be continued through the play, in the same place where it was laid in the beginning: for the stage on which it is represented being but one and the same place, it is unnatural to conceive it many, and those far distant from one another. I will not deny but, by the variation of painted scenes, the fancy (which in these cases will contribute to its own deceit) may sometimes imagine it several places, with some appearance of probability; yet it still carries the greater likelihood of truth if those places be supposed so near each other, as in the same town or city; which may all be comprehended under the larger denomination of one place; for a greater distance will bear no proportion to the shortness of time which is allotted in

---

[26] Aristotle deals with unity of action and time, but it was Castelvetro in 1570 who 'extracted' the three unities into principles.

the acting, to pass from one of them to another; for the observation of this, next to the Ancients, the French are to be most commended. They tie themselves so strictly to the unity of place that you never see in any of their plays a scene changed in the middle of an act: if the act begins in a garden, a street, or chamber, 'tis ended in the same place; and that you may know it to be the same, the stage is so supplied with persons that it is never empty all the time: he that enters the second has business with him who was on before; and before the second quits the stage, a third appears who has business with him.

'This Corneille calls *la liaison des scènes*,[27] the continuity or joining of the scenes; and 'tis a good mark of a well contrived play when all the persons are known to each other, and every one of them has some affairs with all the rest.

'As for the third unity, which is that of action, the Ancients meant no other by it than what the logicians do by their *finis*, the end or scope of any action; that which is the first in intention, and last in execution: now the poet is to aim at one great and complete action, to the carrying on of which all things in his play, even the very obstacles, are to be subservient; and the reason of this is as evident as any of the former.

'For two actions, equally laboured and driven on by the writer, would destroy the unity of the poem; it would be no longer one play, but two: not but that there may be many actions in a play, as Ben Jonson has observed in his *Discoveries*;[28] but they must be all subservient to the great one, which our language happily expresses in the name of *under-plots*: such as in Terence's *Eunuch* is the difference and reconcilement of Thais and Phaedria, which is not the chief business of the play, but promotes the marriage of Chaerea and Chremes's sister, principally intended by the poet. There ought to be but one action, says Corneille,[29] that is, one complete action which leaves the mind of the audience in a full repose; but this cannot be brought to pass but by many other imperfect ones which conduce to it, and hold the audience in a delightful suspense of what will be.

'If by these rules (to omit many other drawn from the precepts and practice of the Ancients) we should judge our modern plays, 'tis probable that few of them would endure the trial: that which should be the business of a day, takes up in some of them an age; instead of one action, they are the epitomes of a man's life; and for one spot of ground (which the stage should

---

[27] *la liaison des scènes*] Keeping a continuity in the action from scene to scene is recommended by Corneille in the *Discours des trois unités* (1660). Corneille, though, regards it as an added beauty, not as a rule.

[28] Jonson, in *Timber, or Discoveries* (1640), points out that if there is more than one plot in a play they should be 'wrought together'.

[29] *Discours des trois unités*. See *Œuvres* (1862), I, 99.

represent) we are sometimes in more countries than the map can show us.

'But if we will allow the Ancients to have contrived well, we must acknowledge them to have writ better; questionless we are deprived of a great stock of wit in the loss of Menander among the Greek poets, and of Caecilius, Afranus, and Varius among the Romans: we may guess of Menander's excellency by the plays of Terence, who translated some of his, and yet wanted so much of him that he was called by C. Caesar the half-Menander; and of Varius, by the testimonies of Horace, Martial, and Velleius Paterculus. 'Tis probable that these, could they be recovered, would decide the controversy; but so long as Aristophanes in the old comedy and Plautus in the new are extant, while the tragedies of Euripides, Sophocles, and Seneca are to be had, I can never see one of these plays which are now written but it increased my admiration of the Ancients. And yet I must acknowledge further that, to admire them as we ought, we should understand them better than we do. Doubtless many things appear flat to us, whose wit depended on some custom or story which never came to our knowledge; or perhaps upon some criticism in their language, which being so long dead, and only remaining in their books, 'tis not possible they should make us know it perfectly. To read Macrobius explaining the propriety and elegancy of many words in Virgil which I had before passed over without consideration as common things, is enough to assure me that I ought to think the same of Terence; and that in the purity of his style (which Tully so much valued that he ever carried his works about him) there is yet left in him great room for admiration, if I knew but where to place it. In the mean time I must desire you to take notice that the greatest man of the last age (Ben Jonson) was willing to give place to them in all things: he was not only a professed imitator of Horace, but a learned plagiary of all the others; you track him everywhere in their snow. If Horace, Lucan, Petronius Arbiter, Seneca, and Juvenal had their own from him, there are few serious thoughts which are new in him: you will pardon me, therefore, if I presume he loved their fashion when he wore their clothes. But since I have otherwise a great veneration for him, and you, Eugenius, prefer him above all other poets, I will use no farther argument to you than his example: I will produce Father Ben to you, dressed in all the ornaments and colours of the Ancients; you will need no other guide to our party if you follow him; and whether you consider the bad plays of our age, or regard the good ones of the last, both the best and worst of the modern poets will equally instruct you to esteem the Ancients.'

Crites had no sooner left speaking, but Eugenius, who waited with some impatience for it, thus began:

'I have observed in your speech that the former part of it is convincing as to what the Moderns have profited by the rules of the Ancients; but in the latter you are careful to conceal how much they have excelled them. We own all the helps we have from them, and want neither veneration nor gratitude while we acknowledge that to overcome them we must make use of the advantages we have received from them; but to these assistances we have joined our own industry; for (had we sat down with a dull imitation of them) we might then have lost somewhat of the old perfection, but never acquired any that was new. We draw not therefore after their lines, but those of nature; and having the life before us, besides the experience of all they knew, it is no wonder if we hit some airs and features which they have missed. I deny not what you urge of arts and sciences, that they have flourished in some ages more than others; but your instance in philosophy makes for me: for if natural causes be more known now than in the time of Aristotle, because more studied, it follows that poesy and other arts may, with the same pains, arrive still nearer to perfection; and, that granted, it will rest for you to prove that they wrought more perfect images of human life than we; which, seeing in your discourse you have avoided to make good, it shall now be my task to show you some part of their defects, and some few excellencies of the Moderns. And I think there is none among us can imagine I do it enviously, or with purpose to detract from them; for what interest of fame or profit can the living lose by the reputation of the dead? On the other side, it is a great truth which Velleius Paterculus affirms: *audita visis libentius laudamus; et praesentia invidia, praeterita admiratione prosequimur; et his nos obrui, illis instrui credimus*,[30] that praise or censure is certainly the most sincere which unbribed posterity shall give us.

'Be pleased then in the first place to take notice that the Greek poesy, which Crites has affirmed to have arrived to perfection in the reign of the Old Comedy, was so far from it that the distinction of it into acts was not known to them; or if it were, it is yet so darkly delivered to us that we cannot make it out.

'All we know of it is from the singing of their Chorus, and that too is so uncertain that in some of their plays we have reason to conjecture they sung more than five times. Aristotle indeed divides the integral parts of a play into four.[31] First, the *protasis*, or entrance, which gives light only to the characters of the persons, and proceeds very little into any part of the action. Secondly, the *epitasis*, or working up of the plot, where the play grows warmer, the design or action of it is drawing on, and you see something

---

[30] *History of Rome*, II, 92: 'We are naturally more inclined to praise what we have heard than what has occurred before our eyes; we regard the present with envy, the past with veneration, and believe that we are eclipsed by the former, but derive instruction from the latter.'

[31] Ker points out that the division is not from Aristotle, but from Scaliger, *Poetices* (1561).

promising that it will come to pass. Thirdly, the *catastasis*, or counterturn, which destroys that expectation, imbroils the action in new difficulties, and leaves you far distant from that hope in which it found you; as you may have observed in a violent stream resisted by a narrow passage: it runs round to an eddy, and carries back the waters with more swiftness than it brought them on. Lastly, the *catastrophe*, which the Grecians called λύσις, the French *le dénouement*, and we the discovery or unravelling of the plot: there you see all things settling again upon their first foundations, and the obstacles which hindered the design or action of the play once removed, it ends with that resemblance of truth and nature that the audience are satisfied with the conduct of it. Thus this great man delivered to us the image of a play, and I must confess it is so lively that from thence much light has been derived to the forming it more perfectly into acts and scenes; but what poet first limited to five the number of the acts I know not, only we see it so firmly established in the time of Horace that he gives it for a rule in comedy: *neu brevior quinto, neu sit productior actu*.[32] So that you see the Grecians cannot be said to have consummated this art; writing rather by entrances than by acts, and having rather a general indigested notion of a play, than knowing how and where to bestow the particular graces of it.

'But since the Spaniards at this day allow but three acts, which they call *jornadas*,[33] to a play, and the Italians in many of theirs follow them, when I condemn the Ancients, I declare it is not altogether because they have not five acts to every play, but because they have not confined themselves to one certain number: 'tis building an house without a model; and when they succeeded in such undertakings, they ought to have sacrificed to Fortune, not to the Muses.

'Next, for the plot, which Aristotle called 'ο μῦθος and often τῶν πραγμάτων σύνθεσις,[34] and from him the romans *fabula*, it has already been observed by a late writer that in their tragedies it was only some tale derived from Thebes or Troy, or at least something that happened in those two ages, which was worn so threadbare by the pens of all the epic poets, and even by tradition itself of the talkative Greeklings (as Ben Jonson calls them) that before it came upon the stage it was already known to all the audience: and the people, so soon as ever they heard the name of Oedipus, knew as well as the poet that he had killed his father by a mistake, and committed incest with his mother, before the play; that they were now to hear of a great plague, an oracle, and the ghost of Laius: so that they sat with

---

[32] *Ars Poetica*, l. 189: 'Let no play be shorter or longer than five acts.' Not an exact quotation from Horace, but Dryden is inclined to unpedantic departures from textual accuracy.

[33] Lope de Vega (1562–1635) favoured the three-act structure. *Jornadas*, though, is not his, but a word of later currency.

[34] The ordering of events.

a yawning kind of expectation, till he was to come with his eyes pulled out, and speak a hundred or two of verses in a tragic tone, in complaint of his misfortunes. But one Oedipus, Hercules, or Medea had been tolerable: poor people, they scaped not so good cheap; they had still the *chapon bouillé* set before them, till their appetites were cloyed with the same dish, and the novelty being gone, the pleasure vanished; so that one main end of dramatic poesy in its definition, which was to cause delight, was of consequence destroyed.

'In their comedies, the Romans generally borrowed their plots from the Greek poets; and theirs was commonly a little girl stolen or wandered from her parents, brought back unknown to the same city, there got with child by some lewd young fellow who, by the help of his servant, cheats his father; and when her time comes to cry *Juno Lucina, fer opem*,[35] one or other sees a little box or cabinet which was carried away with her, and so discovers her to her friends, if some god do not prevent it by coming down in a machine, and take the thanks of it to himself.

'By the plot you may guess much of the characters of the persons. An old father who would willingly, before he dies, see his son well married; his debauched son, kind in his nature to his wench, but miserably in want of money; a servant or slave, who has so much wit to strike in with him, and help to dupe his father; a braggadochio captain, a parasite, and a lady of pleasure.

'As for the poor honest maid, whom all the story is built upon, and who ought to be one of the principal actors in the play, she is commonly a mute in it: she has the breeding of the old Elizabeth way, for maids to be seen and not to be heard; and it is enough you know she is willing to be married when the fifth act requires it.

'These are plots built after the Italian mode of houses: you see through them all at once. The characters are indeed the imitations of nature, but so narrow as if they had imitated only an eye or an hand, and did not dare to venture on the lines of a face, or the proportion of a body.

'But in how strait a compass soever they have bounded their plots and characters, we will pass it by if they have regularly pursued them, and perfectly observed those three unities of time, place, and action; the knowledge of which you say is derived to us from them. But in the first place give me leave to tell you that the unity of place, however it might be practised by them, was never any of their rules: we neither find it in Aristotle, Horace, or any who have written of it, till in our age the French poets first made it a precept of the stage. The unity of time even Terence himself (who was the best and most regular of them) has neglected: his

---

[35] Terence, *Andria*, III. i. 15: 'Our Lady of childbirth, help me.'

Heautontimoroumenos, or *Self-Punisher*, takes up visibly two days; therefore, says Scaliger,[36] the two first acts concluding the first day were acted overnight, the three last on the ensuing day; and Euripides, in tying himself to one day, has committed an absurdity never to be forgiven him; for in one of his tragedies he has made Theseus go from Athens to Thebes, which was about forty English miles, under the walls of it to give battle, and appear victorious in the next act; and yet from the time of his departure to the return of the Nuntius, who gives the relation of his victory, Aethra and the Chorus have but thirty-six verses; that is not for every mile a verse.

'The like error is as evident in Terence his *Eunuch*, when Laches, the old man, enters in a mistake the house of Thais; where, betwixt his exit and the entrance of Pythias, who comes to give an ample relation of the garboyles he has raised within, Parmeno, who was left upon the stage, has not above five lines to speak. *C'est bien employé un temps si court*, says the French poet who furnished me with one of the observations: and almost all their tragedies will afford us examples of the like nature.

' 'Tis true, they have kept the continuity or, as you called it, *liaison des scènes*, somewhat better: two do not perpetually come in together, talk, and go out together; and other two succeed them, and do the same throughout the act, which the English call by the name of single scenes; but the reason is, because they have seldom above two or three scenes, properly so called, in every act; for it is to be accounted a new scene, not every time the stage is empty, but every person who enters, though to others, makes it so; because he introduces a new business. Now the plots of their plays being narrow, and the persons few, one of their acts was written in a less compass than one of our well wrought scenes; and yet they are often deficient even in this. To go no further than Terence, you find in the *Eunuch* Antipho entering single in the midst of the third act, after Cremes and Pythias were gone off. In the same play you have likewise Dorias beginning the fourth act alone; and after she has made a relation of what was done at the soldier's entertainment (which by the way was very inartificial[37] to do, because she was presumed to speak directly to the audience, and to acquaint them with what was necessary to be known, but yet should have been so contrived by the poet as to have been told by persons of the drama to one another, and so by them to have come to the knowledge of the people), she quits the stage, and Phaedria enters next, alone likewise: he also gives you an account of himself, and of his returning from the country, in monologue; to which unnatural way of narration Terence is subject in all his plays. In his *Adelphi*, or *Brothers*, Syrus and Demea enter after the scene was broken by the

[36] *Poetices*, VI, iii.
[37] Clumsy.

departure of Sostrata, Geta, and Canthara; and indeed you can scarce look into any of his comedies, where you will not presently discover the same interruption.

'But as they have failed both in laying of their plots, and managing of them, swerving from the rules of their own art by misrepresenting nature to us, in which they have ill satisfied one intention of a play, which was delight; so in the instructive part they have erred worse: instead of punishing vice and rewarding virtue, they have often shown a prosperous wickedness, and an unhappy piety: they have set before us a bloody image of revenge in Medea, and given her dragons to convey her safe from punishment; a Priam and Astyanax murdered, and Cassandra ravished, and the lust and murder ending in the victory of him that acted them. In short, there is no indecorum in any of our modern plays which, if I would excuse, I could not shadow with some authority from the Ancients.

'And one farther note of them let me leave you: tragedies and comedies were not writ then as they are now, promiscuously, by the same person; but he who found his genius bending to the one, never attempted the other way. This is so plain, that I need not instance to you that Aristophanes, Plautus, Terence never any of them writ a tragedy; Aeschylus, Euripides, Sophocles, and Seneca, never meddled with comedy; the sock and buskin were not worn by the same poet. Having then so much care to excel in one kind, very little is to be pardoned them if they miscarried in it; and this would lead me to the consideration of their wit, had not Crites given me sufficient warning not to be too bold in my judgment of it; because the languages being dead, and many of the customs and little accidents on which it depended lost to us, we are not competent judges of it. But though I grant that here and there we may miss the application of a proverb or a custom, yet a thing well said will be wit in all languages; and though it may lose something in the translation, yet to him who reads it in the original, 'tis still the same: he has an idea of its excellency, though it cannot pass from his mind into any other expression or words than those in which he finds it. When Phaedria, in the *Eunuch*, had a command from his mistress to be absent two days, and, encouraging himself to go through with it, said, *tandem ego non illa caream, si opus sit, vel totum triduum?*[38] – Parmeno, to mock the softness of his master, lifting up his hands and eyes, cries out as it were in admiration, *hui! universum triduum!* the elegancy of which *universum*, though it cannot be rendered in our language, yet leaves an impression of the wit upon our souls. But this happens seldom in him; in Plautus oftener, who is infinitely too bold in his metaphors and coining words, out of which

---

[38] *Eunuch*, II, i, 17–18: 'Pray, can't I go without her, if necessary, even for three days running?'

many times his wit is nothing; which questionless was one reason why Horace falls upon him so severely in those verses:

> sed proavi nostri Plautinos et numeros et
> laudavere sales, nimium patienter utrumque,
> ne dicam stolide.[39]

For Horace himself was cautious to obtrude a new word upon his readers, and make custom and common use the best measure of receiving it into our writings:

> multa renascentur quae nunc cecidere, cadentque
> quae nunc sunt in honore vocabula, si volet usus,
> quem penes arbitrium est, et jus, et norma loquendi.[40]

'The not observing this rule is that which the world has blamed in our satirist Cleveland: to express a thing hard and unnaturally, in his new way of elocution. 'Tis true, no poet but may sometimes use a catachresis; Virgil does it:

> mixtaque ridenti colocasia fundet acantho,[41]

in his eclogue of Pollio; and in his 7th Aeneid,

> mirantur et undae,
> miratur nemus insuetum fulgentia longe
> scuta virum fluvio pictasque innare carinas.[42]

And Ovid once so modestly, that he asks leave to do it:

> si verbo audacia detur,
> haud metuam summi dixisse Palatia caeli,[43]

calling the court of Jupiter by the name of Augustus his palace, though in another place he is more bold, where he says *et longas visent Capitolia pompas*.[44] But to do this always, and never be able to write a line without it, though it may be admired by some few pedants, will not pass upon those

---

[39] *Ars Poetica*, ll. 270–2: 'Yet our forefathers, you say, praised both the measures and the wit of Plautus. Too tolerant, not to say foolish.'

[40] Ibid., ll. 70–2: 'Many terms that have fallen out of use shall be born again, and those shall fall that are now in repute, if Usage so will it, in whose hands lies the judgement, the right and the rule of speech.'

[41] *Eclogues*, IV, 20: 'The Egyptian bean blended with the smiling acanthus.'

[42] *Aeneid*, VIII, 91–3: 'In wonder the waves, in wonder the unwonted woods view the far gleaming shields of warriors and the painted hulls floating on the stream.'

[43] *Metamorphoses*, I, 175–6: '[This is the place, which] if I may make bold to say it, I would not fear to call the Palatia of high heaven.'

[44] Ibid., l. 561: 'and long processions climb the Capitol'.

who know that wit is best conveyed to us in the most easy language; and is
most to be admired when a great thought comes dressed in words so
commonly received that it is understood by the meanest apprehensions, as
the best meat is the most easily digested: but we cannot read a verse of
Cleveland's without making a face at it, as if every word were a pill to
swallow: he gives us many times a hard nut to break our teeth, without a
kernel for our pains. So that there is this difference betwixt his satires and
Doctor Donne's, that the one gives us deep thoughts in common language,
though rough cadence; the other gives us common thoughts in abstruse
words. 'Tis true, in some places his wit is independent of his words, as in
that of the *Rebel Scot*:

> Had *Cain* been *Scot*, God would have chang'd his doom;
> Not forc'd him wander, but confin'd him home.[45]

'*Si sic omnia dixisset!*[46] This is wit in all languages: 'tis like mercury, never
to be lost or killed; and so that other:

> For beauty like white-powder makes no noise,
> And yet the silent hypocrite destroys.[47]

You see, the last line is highly metaphorical, but it is so soft and gentle that
it does not shock us as we read it.

'But, to return from whence I have digressed to the consideration of the
Ancients' writing and their wit (of which by this time you will grant us in
some measure to be fit judges), though I see many excellent thoughts in
Seneca, yet he of them who had genius most proper for the stage was Ovid.
He had a way of writing so fit to stir up a pleasing admiration and
concernment, which are the objects of a tragedy, and to show the various
movements of a soul combating betwixt two different passions, that, had he
lived in our age, or in his own could have writ with our advantages, no man
but must have yielded to him; and therefore I am confident the *Medea* is
none of his: for, though I esteem it for the gravity and sententiousness of it,
which he himself concludes to be suitable to a tragedy, *omne genus scripti
gravitate tragaedia vincit*,[48] yet it moves not my soul enough to judge that he
who in the epic way wrote things so near the drama as the story of Myrrha,
of Caunus and Biblis, and the rest, should stir up no more concernment
where he most endeavoured it. The master-piece of Seneca I hold to be that
scene in the *Troades* where Ulysses is seeking for Astyanax to kill him; there

---

[45] Cleveland, 'The Rebel Scot', ll. 63–4.
[46] Juvenal, *Satires*, X, 123–4: 'if he had always spoken thus'.
[47] Cleveland, 'To Prince Rupert', ll. 39–40. White-powder was supposed to explode
without noise.
[48] *Tristia*, II, 381: 'Tragedy surpassed every other kind of writing in gravity.'

you see the tenderness of a mother so represented in Andromache that it raises compassion to a high degree in the reader, and bears the nearest resemblance of anything in their tragedies to the excellent scenes of passion in Shakespeare, or in Fletcher: for love-scenes you will find few among them, their tragic poets dealt not with that soft passion but with lust, cruelty, revenge, ambition, and those bloody actions they produced; which were more capable of raising horror than compassion in an audience: leaving love untouched, whose gentleness would have tempered them, which is the most frequent of all the passions, and which, being the private concernment of every person, is soothed by viewing its own image in a public entertainment.

'Among their comedies, we find a scene or two of tenderness, and that where you would least expect it, in Plautus; but to speak generally, their lovers say little, when they see each other, but *anima mea*, *vita mea*; ζωὴ καὶ ψυχή,[49] as the women in Juvenal's time used to cry out in the fury of their kindness: then indeed to speak sense were an offence. Any sudden gust of passion (as an ecstasy of love in an unexpected meeting) cannot better be expressed than in a word and a sigh, breaking one another. Nature is dumb on such occasions, and to make her speak would be to represent her unlike herself. But there are a thousand other concernments of lovers, as jealousies, complaints, contrivances, and the like, where not to open their minds at large to each other were to be wanting to their own love, and to the expectation of the audience; who watch the movements of their minds, as much as the changes of their fortunes. For the imaging of the first is properly the work of a poet; the latter he borrows of the historian.'

Eugenius was proceeding in that part of his discourse, when Crites interrupted him. 'I see,' said he, 'Eugenius and I are never like to have this question decided betwixt us; for he maintains the Moderns have acquired a new perfection in writing, I can only grant they have altered the mode of it. Homer described his heroes men of great appetites, lovers of beef broiled upon the coals, and good fellows; contrary to the practice of the French romances, whose heroes neither eat, nor drink, nor sleep, for love. Virgil makes Aeneas a bold avower of his own virtues,

sum pius Aeneas, fama super aethera notus;[50]

which in the civility of our poets is the character of a Fanfaron or Hector:[51] for with us the knight takes occasion to walk out, or sleep, to avoid the vanity of telling his own story, which the trusty squire is ever to perform for him. So in their love-scenes, of which Eugenius spoke last, the Ancients

[49] Juvenal, *Satires*, VI, 195: 'my life and my love'.
[50] *Aeneid*, I, 378–9: 'I am Aeneas the good . . . my fame is known in the heavens above.'
[51] Fanfaron or Hector] Swaggerer or blusterer.

were more hearty, we more talkative: they writ love as it was then the mode
to make it; and I will grant thus much to Eugenius, that perhaps one of
their poets, had he lived in our age,

si foret hoc nostrum fato delapsus in aevum[52]

(as Horace says of Lucilius), he had altered many things; not that they were
not as natural before, but that he might accommodate himself to the age he
lived in. Yet in the meantime we are not to conclude anything rashly
against those great men, but preserve to them the dignity of masters, and
give that honour to their memories (*quos Libitina sacravit*)[53] part of which we
expect may be paid to us in future times.'

This moderation of Crites, as it was pleasing to all the company, so it put
an end to that dispute; which Eugenius, who seemed to have the better of
the argument, would urge no farther: but Lisideius, after he had acknowledged himself of Eugenius his opinion concerning the Ancients, yet
told him he had forborne till his discourse were ended to ask him why he
preferred the English plays above those of other nations; and whether we
ought not to submit our stage to the exactness of our next neighbours.

'Though,' said Eugenius, 'I am at all times ready to defend the honour of
my country against the French, and to maintain we are as well able to
vanquish them with our pens as our ancestors have been with their swords;
yet, if you please,' added he, looking upon Neander, 'I will commit this
cause to my friend's management; his opinion of our plays is the same with
mine: and besides, there is no reason that Crites and I, who have now left
the stage, should re-enter so suddenly upon it; which is against the laws of
comedy.'

'If the question had been stated,' replied Lisideius, 'who had writ best,
the French or English, forty years ago, I should have been of your opinion,
and adjudged the honour to our own nation; but since that time', said he
(turning towards Neander) 'we have been so long together bad Englishmen,
that we had not leisure to be good poets. Beaumont, Fletcher, and Jonson
(who were only capable of bringing us to that degree of perfection which we
have) were just then leaving the world,[54] as if, in an age of so much horror,
wit and those milder studies of humanity had no farther business among us.
But the Muses, who ever follow peace, went to plant in another country: it
was then that the great Cardinal of Richelieu began to take them into his
protection;[55] and that, by his encouragement, Corneille and some other

---

[52] Horace, *Satires*, I, x, 68: 'had he fallen by fate upon this our day'.
[53] Horace, *Epistles*, II, i, 49: 'what the goddess of funerals has hallowed'.
[54] Beaumont died in 1616, Fletcher in 1625, and Jonson in 1637.
[55] Referring to the formation of *L'Académie française* in 1635, and Richelieu's supervision of
dramatic writing.

Frenchmen reformed their theatre, which before was as much below ours as it now surpasses it and the rest of Europe. But because Crites in his discourse for the Ancients has prevented me, by touching upon many rules of the stage which the Moderns have borrowed from them, I shall only, in short, demand of you whether you are not convinced that of all nations the French have best observed them? In the unity of time you find them so scrupulous, that it yet remains a dispute among their poets whether the artificial day of twelve hours more or less be not meant by Aristotle, rather than the natural one of twenty-four; and consequently, whether all plays ought not to be reduced into that compass. This I can testify, that in all their dramas writ within these last twenty years and upwards, I have not observed any that have extended the time to thirty hours. In the unity of place they are full as scrupulous; for many of their critics limit it to that very spot of ground where the play is supposed to begin; none of them exceed the compass of the same town or city.

'The unity of action in all plays is yet more conspicuous, for they do not burden them with under-plots, as the English do; which is the reason why many scenes of our tragi-comedies carry on a design that is nothing of kin to the main plot; and that we see two distinct webs in a play, like those in ill wrought stuffs; and two actions, that is, two plays carried on together, to the confounding of the audience; who, before they are warm in their concernments for one part, are diverted to another; and by that means espouse the interest of neither. From hence likewise it arises that the one half of our actors are not known to the other. They keep their distances, as if they were Montagues and Capulets, and seldom begin an acquaintance till the last scene of the fifth act, when they are all to meet upon the stage. There is no theatre in the world has anything so absurd as the English tragi-comedy; 'tis a drama of our own invention, and the fashion of it is enough to proclaim it so; here a course of mirth, there another of sadness and passion, a third of honour, and fourth a duel: thus in two hours and a half we run through all the fits of Bedlam. The French affords you as much variety on the same day, but they do it not so unseasonably, or *mal à propos*, as we: our poets present you the play and the farce together; and our stages still retain somewhat of the original civility of the Red Bull,

atque ursum et pugiles media inter carmina poscunt.[56]

The end of tragedies or serious plays, says Aristotle, is to beget admiration, compassion, or concernment; but are not mirth and compassion things incompatible? and is it not evident that the poet must of necessity destroy the former by intermingling of the latter? that is, he must ruin the sole end

[56] Horace, *Epistles*, II, i, 185–6: 'call in the middle of a play for a bear or for boxers'.

and object of his tragedy to introduce somewhat that is forced in, and is not of the body of it. Would you not think that physician mad who, having prescribed a purge, should immediately order you to take restringents upon it?

'But to leave our plays, and return to theirs, I have noted one great advantage they have had in the plotting of their tragedies: that is, they are always grounded upon some known history; according to that of Horace, *ex noto fictum carmen sequar*;[57] and in that they have so imitated the Ancients that they have surpassed them. For the Ancients, as was observed before, took for the foundation of their plays some poetical fiction such as under that consideration could move but little concernment in the audience, because they already knew the event of it. But the French goes farther:

> atque ita mentitur, sic veris falsa remiscet,
> primo ne medium, medio ne discrepet imum.[58]

He so interweaves truth with probable fiction, that he puts a pleasing fallacy upon us; mends the intrigues of fate, and dispenses with the severity of history, to reward that virtue which has been rendered to us there unfortunate. Sometimes the story has left the success so doubtful, that the writer is free, by the privilege of a poet, to take that which of two or more relations will best suit with his design: as, for example, the death of Cyrus, whom Justin and some others report to have perished in the Scythian war, but Xenophon affirms to have died in his bed of extreme old age. Nay more, when the event is past dispute, even then we are willing to be deceived, and the poet, if he contrives it with appearance of truth, has all the audience of his party; at least during the time his play is acting: so naturally we are kind to virtue, when our own interest is not in question, that we take it up as the general concernment of mankind. On the other side, if you consider the historical plays of Shakespeare, they are rather so many chronicles of kings, or the business many times of thirty or forty years, cramped into a representation of two hours and a half, which is not to imitate or paint nature, but rather to draw her in miniature, to take her in little; to look upon her through the wrong end of a perspective,[59] and receive her images not only much less, but infinitely more imperfect than the life: this, instead of making a play delightful, renders it ridiculous.

> quodcumque ostendis mihi sic, incredulus odi.[60]

---

[57] *Ars Poetica*, l. 240: 'My aim shall be poetry, moulded from the familiar.'
[58] Ibid., ll. 151–2: 'And so skilfully does he invent, so closely does he blend facts and fiction, that the middle is not discordant with the beginning, nor the end with the middle.'
[59] Telescope.
[60] *Ars Poetica*, l. 188: 'Whatever you thus show me, I discredit and abhor.'

For the spirit of man cannot be satisfied but with truth, or at least verisimility; and a poem is to contain, if not τὰ ἔτυμα, yet ἐτύμοιοιν ὁμοία,[61] as one of the Greek poets has expressed it.

'Another thing in which the French differ from us and from the Spaniards is that they do not embarrass or cumber themselves with too much plot; they only represent so much of a story as will constitute one whole and great action sufficient for a play; we, who undertake more, do but multiply adventures; which, not being produced from one another, as effects from causes, but barely following, constitute many actions in the drama, and consequently make it many plays.

'But by pursuing close one argument which is not cloyed with many turns, the French have gained more liberty for verse, in which they write: they have leisure to dwell upon a subject which deserves it; and to represent the passions (which we have acknowledged to be the poet's work), without being hurried from one thing to another, as we are in the plays of Calderon, which we have seen lately upon our theatres under the name of Spanish plots. I have taken notice but of one tragedy of ours, whose plot has that unformity and unity of design in it which I have commended in the French; and that is *Rollo*,[62] or rather, under the name of *Rollo*, the story of Bassianus and Geta in Herodian: there indeed the plot is neither large nor intricate, but just enough to fill the minds of the audience, not to cloy them. Besides, you see it founded upon the truth of history, only the time of the action is not reduceable to the strictness of the rules; and you see in some places a little farce mingled, which is below the dignity of the other parts; and in this all our poets are extremely peccant. Even Ben Jonson himself in *Sejanus* and *Catiline* has given us this oleo[63] of a play, this unnatural mixture of comedy and tragedy, which to me sounds just as ridiculously as the history of David with the merry humours of Golias.[64] In *Sejanus* you may take notice of the scene betwixt Livia and the physician, which is a pleasant satire upon the artificial helps of beauty; in *Catiline* you may see the parliament of women, the little envies of them to one another; and all that passes betwixt Curio and Fulvia: scenes admirable in their kind, but of an ill mingle with the rest.

'But I return again to the French writers who, as I have said, do not burden themselves too much with plot, which has been reproached to them by an ingenious person of our nation as a fault, for he says they commonly make but one person considerable in a play; they dwell upon him, and his

---

[61] 'If not the truth, yet resembling truth'.

[62] *The Bloody Brother, or the Tragedy of Rollo, Duke of Normandy*, a popular tragedy published in 1639.

[63] Mixture.

[64] Golias] A clerical figure of fun in medieval writing.

concernments, while the rest of the persons are only subservient to set him
off. If he intends this by it, that there is one person in the play who is of
greater dignity than the rest, he must tax not only theirs, but those of the
Ancients, and (which he would be loth to do) the best of ours; for 'tis
impossible but that one person must be more conspicuous in it than any
other, and consequently the greatest share in the action must devolve on
him. We see it so in the management of all affairs; even in the most equal
aristocracy, the balance cannot be so justly poised but some one will be
superior to the rest, either in parts, fortune, interest, or the consideration of
some glorious exploit; which will reduce the greatest part of business into
his hands.

'But if he would have us to imagine that in exalting one character the rest
of them are neglected, and that all of them have not some share or other in
the action of the play, I desire him to produce any of Corneille's tragedies,
wherein every person (like so many servants in a well governed family) has
not some employment, and who is not necessary to the carrying on of the
plot, or at least to your understanding it.

'There are indeed some protatic persons[65] in the Ancients whom they
make use of in their plays, either to hear or give the relation: but the French
avoid this with great address, making their narrations only to, or by, such
who are some way interested in the main design. And now I am speaking of
relations, I cannot take a fitter opportunity to add this in favour of the
French, that they often use them with better judgment and more *à propos*
than the English do. Not that I commend narrations in general, but there
are two sorts of them. One, of those things which are antecedent to the play,
and are related to make the conduct of it more clear to us. But 'tis a fault to
choose such subjects for the stage which will inforce us upon that rock,
because we see they are seldom listened to by the audience, and that is many
times the ruin of the play. For, being once let pass without attention, the
audience can never recover themselves to understand the plot; and indeed it
is somewhat unreasonable that they should be put to so much trouble, as
that, to comprehend what passes in their sight, they must have recourse to
what was done, perhaps, ten or twenty years ago.

'But there is another sort of relations, that is, of things happening in the
action of the play, and supposed to be done behind the scenes; and this is
many times both convenient and beautiful; for by it the French avoid the
tumult which we are subject to in England by representing duels, battles,
and the like; which renders our stage too like the theatres where they fight
prizes. For what is more ridiculous than to represent an army with a drum
and five men behind it, all which the hero of the other side is to drive in

---

[65] protatic persons] Characters appearing only in the *protasis*, or first part of a play.

before him; or to see a duel fought, and one slain with two or three thrusts of the foils, which we know are so blunted that we might give a man an hour to kill another in good earnest with them.

'I have observed that, in all our tragedies, the audience cannot forbear laughing when the actors are to die; 'tis the most comic part of the whole play. All *passions* may be lively represented on the stage, if to the well-writing of them the actor supplies a good commanded voice, and limbs that move easily and without stiffness; but there are many *actions* which can never be imitated to a just height: dying especially is a thing which none but a Roman gladiator could naturally perform on the stage, when he did not imitate or represent, but naturally do it; and therefore it is better to omit the representation of it.

'The words of a good writer, which describe it lively, will make a deeper impression of belief in us than all the actor can persuade us to when he seems to fall dead before us: as a poet in the description of a beautiful garden, or a meadow, will please our imagination more than the place itself can please our sight. When we see death represented, we are convinced it is but fiction; but when we hear it related, our eyes (the strongest witnesses) are wanting, which might have undeceived us; and we are all willing to favour the sleight when the poet does not too grossly impose on us. They therefore who imagine these relations would make no concernment in the audience, are deceived by confounding them with the other, which are of things antecedent to the play: those are made often in cold blood (as I may say) to the audience; but these are warmed with our concernments, which are before awakened in the play. What the philosophers say of motion, that when it is once begun it continues of itself, and will do so to eternity without some stop put to it,[66] is clearly true on this occasion: the soul being already moved with the characters and fortunes of those imaginary persons, continues going of its own accord; and we are no more weary to hear what becomes of them when they are not on the stage than we are to listen to the news of an absent mistress. But it is objected, that if one part of the play may be related, then why not all? I answer, some parts of the action are more fit to be represented, some to be related. Corneille says judiciously that the poet is not obliged to expose to view all particular actions which conduce to the principal: he ought to select such of them to be seen which will appear with the greatest beauty, either by the magnificence of the show, or the vehemence of passions which they produce, or some other charm which they have in them, and let the rest arrive to the audience by narration.[67] 'Tis a great mistake in us to believe the French present no part of the action on the

---

[66] Watson cites Descartes, *Principia Philosophiae* (1644).
[67] *Discours des trois unités. Œuvres*, I, 100.

stage: every alteration or crossing of a design, every new-sprung passion, and turn of it, is a part of the action, and much the noblest, except we conceive nothing to be action till they come to blows; as if the painting of the hero's mind were not more properly the poet's work than the strength of his body. Nor does this anything contradict the opinion of Horace, where he tells us,

> segnius irritant animos demissa per aurem,
> quam quae sunt oculis subjecta fidelibus.[68]

For he says immediately after,

>   non tamen intus
> digna geri promes in scenam; multaque tolles
> ex oculis, quae mox narret facundia praesens.[69]

Among which many he recounts some:

> nec pueros coram populo Medea trucidet,
> aut in avem Procne mutetur, Cadmus in anguem, &c.[70]

That is, those actions which by reason of their cruelty will cause aversion in us or, by reason of their impossibility, unbelief, ought either wholly to be avoided by a poet, or only delivered by narration. To which we may have leave to add such as to avoid tumult (as was before hinted), or to reduce the plot into a more reasonable compass of time, or for defect of beauty in them, are rather to be related than presented to the eye. Examples of all these kinds are frequent, not only among all the Ancients, but in the best received of our English poets. We find Ben Jonson using them in his *Magnetic Lady*, where one comes out from dinner, and relates the quarrels and disorders of it to save the undecent appearance of them on the stage, and to abbreviate the story; and this in express imitation of Terence, who had done the same before him in his *Eunuch*, where Pythias makes the like relation of what had happened within at the soldiers' entertainment. The relations likewise of Sejanus's death, and the prodigies before it, are remarkable; the one of which was hid from sight, to avoid the horror and tumult of the representation; the other, to shun the introducing of things impossible to be believed. In that excellent play the *King and No King*, Fletcher goes yet farther; for the

---

[68] *Ars Poetica*, ll. 180–1: 'Less vividly is the mind stirred by what finds entrance through the ears than by what is brought before the trusty eyes.'

[69] Ibid., ll. 182–4: 'Yet you will not bring on the stage what should be performed behind the scenes, and you will keep much from our eyes, which an actor's ready tongue will narrate anon in our presence.'

[70] Ibid., ll. 185 and 187: 'so that Medea is not to butcher her boys before the people . . . nor Procne be turned into a bird, Cadmus into a snake'.

whole unravelling of the plot is done by narration in the fifth act, after the manner of the Ancients; and it moves great concernment in the audience, though it be only a relation of what was done many years before the play. I could multiply other instances, but these are sufficient to prove that there is no error in choosing a subject which requires this sort of narrations; in the ill managing of them, there may.

'But I find I have been too long in this discourse, since the French have many other excellencies not common to us, as that you never see any of their plays end with a conversion, or simple change of will, which is the ordinary way which our poets use to end theirs. It shows little art in the conclusion of a dramatic poem, when they who have hindered the felicity during the four acts, desist from it in the fifth, without some powerful cause to take them off; and though I deny not but such reasons may be found, yet it is a path that is cautiously to be trod, and the poet is to be sure he convinces the audience that the motive is strong enough. As for example, the conversion of the usurer in *The Scornful Lady*[71] seems to me a little forced; for, being an usurer, which implies a lover of money to the highest degree of covetousness (and such the poet has represented him), the account he gives for the sudden change is, that he has been duped by the wild young fellow, which in reason might render him more wary another time, and make him punish himself with harder fare and coarser clothes to get it up again; but that he should look upon it as a judgment, and so repent, we may expect to hear of in a sermon, but I should never endure it in a play.

'I pass by this; neither will I insist on the care they take that no person after his first entrance shall ever appear but the business which brings him upon the stage shall be evident; which, if observed, must needs render all the events in the play more natural; for there you see the probability of every accident, in the cause that produced it; and that which appears chance in the play, will seem so reasonable to you that you will there find it almost necessary; so that in the exits of the actors you have a clear account of their purpose and design in the next entrance (though, if the scene be well wrought, the event will commonly deceive you); for there is nothing so absurd, says Corneille, as for an actor to leave the stage only because he has no more to say.[72]

'I should now speak of the beauty of their rhyme, and the just reason I have to prefer that way of writing in tragedies before ours in blank verse; but because it is partly received by us, and therefore not altogether peculiar to them, I will say no more of it in relation to their plays. For our own, I doubt not but it will exceedingly beautify them, and I can see but one reason why

---

[71] By Beaumont and Fletcher.
[72] *Œuvres*, I, 108.

it should not generally obtain, that is, because our poets write so ill in it. This indeed may prove a more prevailing argument than all others which are used to destroy it, and therefore I am only troubled when great and judicious poets, and those who are acknowledged such, have writ or spoke against it; as for others, they are to be answered by that one sentence of an ancient author: '*sed ut primo ad consequendos eos quos priores ducimus, accendimur, ita ubi aut praeteriri, aut aequari eos posse desperavimus, studium cum spe senescit: quod, scilicet, assequi non potest, sequi desinit; praeteritoque eo in quo eminere non possumus, aliquid in quo nitamur, conquirimus.*' [73]

Lisideius concluded in this manner; and Neander, after a little pause, thus answered him:

'I shall grant Lisideius, without much dispute, a great part of what he has urged against us, for I acknowledge the French contrive their plots more regularly, observe the laws of comedy, and decorum of the stage (to speak generally), with more exactness than the English. Farther, I deny not but he has taxed us justly in some irregularities of ours which he has mentioned; yet, after all, I am of opinion that neither our faults nor their virtues are considerable enough to place them above us.

'For the lively imitation of nature being in the definition of a play, those which best fulfil that law ought to be esteemed superior to the others. 'Tis true, those beauties of the French poesy are such as will raise perfection higher where it is, but are not sufficient to give it where it is not: they are indeed the beauties of a statue, but not of a man, because not animated with the soul of poesy, which is imitation of humour and passions; and this Lisideius himself, or any other, however biased to their party, cannot but acknowledge, if he will either compare the humours of our comedies, or the characters of our serious plays, with theirs. He that will look upon theirs which have been written till these last ten years or thereabouts, will find it an hard matter to pick out two or three passable humours amongst them. Corneille himself, their arch-poet, what has he produced except *The Liar*, and you know how it was cried up in France; but when it came upon the English stage, though well translated, and that part of Dorant acted to so much advantage by Mr Hart as I am confident it never received in its own country, the most favourable to it would not put it in competition with many of Fletcher's or Ben Jonson's. In the rest of Corneille's comedies you have little humour; he tells you himself his way is, first to show two lovers in good intelligence with each other; in the working up of the play

[73] Velleius Paterculus, *History of Rome*, I, xvii: 'And as in the beginning we are fired with the ambition to overtake those whom we regard as leaders, so when we have despaired of being able to surpass or even to equal them, our zeal wanes with our hope; it ceases to follow what it cannot overtake; . . . and passing over that in which we cannot be pre-eminent, we seek for some new object of our effort.'

to embroil them by some mistake, and in the latter end to clear it up.

'But of late years Molière, the younger Corneille,[74] Quinault,[75] and some others, have been imitating afar off the quick turns and graces of the English stage. They have mixed their serious plays with mirth, like our tragi-comedies, since the death of Cardinal Richelieu; which Lisideius and many others not observing, have commended that in them for a virtue which they themselves no longer practise. Most of their new plays are, like some of ours, derived from the Spanish novels. There is scarce one of them without a veil, and a trusty Diego, who drolls much after the rate of the *Adventures*.[76] But their humours, if I may grace them with that name, are so thin sown that never above one of them comes up in any play. I dare take upon me to find more variety of them in some one play of Ben Jonson's than in all theirs together; as he who has seen *The Alchemist*, *The Silent Woman*, or *Bartholomew-Fair*, cannot but acknowledge with me.

'I grant the French have performed what was possible on the ground-work of the Spanish plays; what was pleasant before, they have made regular; but there is not above one good play to be writ upon all those plots; they are too much alike to please often, which we need not the experience of our own stage to justify. As for their new way of mingling mirth with serious plot, I do not with Lisideius condemn the thing, though I cannot approve their manner of doing it. He tells us we cannot so speedily recollect ourselves after a scene of great passion and concernment as to pass to another of mirth and humour, and to enjoy it with any relish: but why should he imagine the soul of man more heavy than this senses? Does not the eye pass from an unpleasant object to a pleasant in a much shorter time than is required to this? and does not the unpleasantness of the first commend the beauty of the latter? The old rule of logic might have convinced him that contraries, when placed near, set off each other. A continued gravity keeps the spirit too much bent; we must refresh it sometimes, as we bait upon a journey, that we may go on with greater ease. A scene of mirth mixed with tragedy has the same effect upon us which our music has betwixt the acts; and that we find a relief to us from the best plots and language of the stage, if the discourses have been long. I must therefore have stronger arguments ere I am convinced that compassion and mirth in the same subject destroy each other; and in the meantime cannot but conclude, to the honour of our nation, that we have invented, increased, and perfected a more pleasant way

---

[74] Thomas Corneille (1625–1709), brother of Pierre.
[75] Philippe Quinault (1635–88).
[76] *The Adventures of Five Hours* (1663) by Sir Samuel Tuke, a very popular rendering of a Spanish play by Coello.

of writing for the stage than was ever known to the ancients or moderns of any nation, which is tragi-comedy.

'And this leads me to wonder why Lisideius and many others should cry up the barrenness of the French plots above the variety and copiousness of the English. Their plots are single, they carry on one design which is pushed forward by all the actors, every scene in the play contributing and moving towards it: ours, besides the main design, have under-plots or by-concernment of less considerable persons and intrigues, which are carried out with the motion of the main plot: just as they say the orb of the fixed stars, and those of the planets, though they have motions of their own, are whirled about by the motion of the *primum mobile*, in which they are contained. That similitude expresses much of the English stage: for if contrary motions may be found in nature to agree, if a planet can go east and west at the same time, one way by virtue of his own motion, the other by the force of the first mover, it will not be difficult to imagine how the under-plot, which is only different, not contrary to the great design, may naturally be conducted along with it.

'Eugenius[77] has already shown us, from the confession of the French poets, that the unity of action is sufficiently preserved if all the imperfect actions of the play are conducing to the main design; but when those petty intrigues of a play are so ill ordered that they have no coherence with the other, I must grant Lisideius has reason to tax that want of due connection; for co-ordination[78] in a play is as dangerous and unnatural as in a state. In the meantime he must acknowledge our variety, if well ordered, will afford a greater pleasure to the audience.

'As for his other argument, that by pursuing one single theme they gain an advantage to express and work up the passions, I wish any example he could bring from them would make it good: for I confess their verses are to me the coldest I have ever read. Neither, indeed, is it possible for them, in the way they take, so to express passion as that the effects of it should appear in the concernment of an audience: their speeches being so many declamations, which tire us with the length; so that instead of persuading us to grieve for their imaginary heroes, we are concerned for our own trouble, as we are in the tedious visits of bad company; we are in pain till they are gone. When the French stage came to be reformed by Cardinal Richelieu, those long harangues were introduced to comply with the gravity of a churchman. Look upon the *Cinna* and the *Pompey*; they are not so properly to be called plays as long discourses of reason of state; and *Polyeucte*[79] in matters of religion is as solemn as the long stops upon our organs. Since that time it is

[77] This should read 'Crites'.
[78] co-ordination] Lack of subordination.
[79] Three plays by Corneille.

grown into a custom, and their actors speak by the hour-glass, as our parsons do; nay, they account it the grace of their parts, and think themselves disparaged by the poet, if they may not twice or thrice in a play entertain the audience with a speech of an hundred or two hundred lines. I deny not but this may suit well enough with the French; for as we, who are a more sullen people, come to be diverted at our plays, so they, who are of an airy and gay temper, come thither to make themselves more serious; and this I conceive to be one reason why comedy is more pleasing to us, and tragedies to them. But to speak generally, it cannot be denied that short speeches and replies are more apt to move the passions and beget concernment in us than the other: for it is unnatural for anyone in a gust of passion to speak long together, or for another in the same condition to suffer him without interruption. Grief and passion are like floods raised in little brooks by a sudden rain; they are quickly up; and if the concernment be poured unexpectedly in upon us, it overflows us: but a long, sober shower gives them leisure to run out as they came in, without troubling the ordinary current. As for comedy, repartee is one of its chiefest graces; the greatest pleasure of the audience is a chase of wit kept up on both sides, and swiftly managed. And this our forefathers, if not we, have had in Fletcher's plays, to a much higher degree of perfection than the French poets can arrive at.

'There is another part of Lisideius his discourse, in which he has rather excused our neighbours than commended them; that is, for aiming only to make one person considerable in their plays. 'Tis very true what he has urged, that one character in all plays, even without the poet's care, will have advantage of all the others; and that the design of the whole drama will chiefly depend on it. But this hinders not that there may be more shining characters in the play: many persons of a second magnitude, nay, some so very near, so almost equal to the first, that greatness may be opposed to greatness, and all the persons be made considerable, not only by their quality but their action. 'Tis evident that the more the persons are, the greater will be the variety of the plot. If then the parts are managed so regularly that the beauty of the whole be kept entire, and that the variety become not a perplexed and confused mass of accidents, you will find it infinitely pleasing to be led in a labyrinth of design, where you see some of your way before you, yet discern not the end till you arrive at it. And that all this is practicable, I can produce for examples many of our English plays: as *The Maid's Tragedy*, [80] *The Alchemist, The Silent Woman*. I was going to have named *The Fox*, but that the unity of design seems not exactly observed in it; for there appear two actions in the play; the first naturally ending with

[80] By Beaumont and Fletcher. The other three plays mentioned are by Ben Jonson.

the fourth act; the second forced from it in the fifth: which yet is the less to be condemned in him, because the disguise of Volpone, though it suited not with his character as a crafty or covetous person, agreed well enough with that of a voluptuary; and by it the poet gained the end he aimed at, the punishment of vice, and the reward of virtue, which that disguise produced. So that to judge equally of it, it was an excellent fifth act, but not so naturally proceeding from the former.

'But to leave this, and pass to the latter part of Lisideius his discourse, which concerns relations, I must acknowledge with him that the French have reason when they hide that part of the action which would occasion too much tumult upon the stage, and choose rather to have it made known by narration to the audience. Farther, I think it very convenient, for the reasons he has given, that all incredible actions were removed; but whether custom has so insinuated itself into our countrymen, or nature has so formed them to fierceness, I know not; but they will scarcely suffer combats and other objects of horror to be taken from them. And indeed, the indecency of tumults is all which can be objected against fighting: for why may not our imagination as well suffer itself to be deluded with the probability of it, as with any other thing in the play? For my part, I can with as great ease persuade myself that the blows which are struck are given in good earnest, as I can that they who strike them are kings or princes, or those persons which they represent. For objects of incredibility, I would be satisfied from Lisideius whether we have any so removed from all appearance of truth as are those of Corneille's *Andromède*,[81] a play which has been frequented the most of any he has writ. If the Perseus, or the son of an heathen god, the Pegasus, and the Monster, were not capable to choke a strong belief, let him blame any representation of ours hereafter. Those indeed were objects of delight; yet the reason is the same as to the probability: for he makes it not a ballet or masque, but a play, which is to resemble truth. But for death, that it ought not to be represented, I have, besides the arguments alleged by Lisideius, the authority of Ben Jonson, who has forborne it in his tragedies; for both the death of Sejanus and Catiline are related; though in the latter I cannot but observe one irregularity of that great poet: he has removed the scene in the same act from Rome to Catiline's army, and from thence again to Rome; and besides, has allowed a very inconsiderable time, after Catiline's speech, for the striking of the battle, and the return of Petreius, who is to relate the event of it to the Senate: which I should not animadvert on him, who was otherwise a painful observer of τὸ πρεπον, or the decorum of the stage, if he had not used extreme severity in his judgment upon the incomparable Shakespeare for

[81] A play in which a great deal of machinery and spectacle were employed.

the same fault. To conclude on this subject of relations, if we are to be blamed for showing too much of the action, the French are as faulty for discovering too little of it: a mean betwixt both should be observed by every judicious writer, so as the audience may neither be left unsatisfied by not seeing what is beautiful, or shocked by beholding what is either incredible or undecent.

'I hope I have already proved in this discourse that though we are not altogether so punctual as the French in observing the laws of comedy, yet our errors are so few and little, and those things wherein we excel them so considerable, that we ought of right to be preferred before them. But what will Lisideius say if they themselves acknowledge they are too strictly tied up by those laws, for breaking which he has blamed the English? I will allege Corneille's words, as I find them in the end of his Discourse of the three Unities: *Il est facile aux spéculatifs d'être sévères, &c.* " 'Tis easy for speculative persons to judge severely; but if they would produce to public view ten or twelve pieces of this nature, they would perhaps give more latitude to the rules than I have done, when by experience they had known how much we are bound up and constrained by them, and how many beauties of the stage they banished from it."[82] To illustrate a little what he has said, by their servile observations of the unities of time and place, and integrity of scenes, they have brought upon themselves that dearth of plot and narrowness of imagination which may be observed in all their plays. How many beautiful accidents might naturally happen in two or three days, which cannot arrive with any probability in the compass of twenty-four hours? There is time to be allowed also for maturity of design, which, amongst great and prudent persons such as are often represented in tragedy, cannot, with any likelihood of truth, be brought to pass at so short a warning. Farther, by tying themselves strictly to the unity of place and unbroken scenes, they are forced many times to omit some beauties which cannot be shown where the act began; but might, if the scene were interrupted, and the stage cleared for the persons to enter in another place; and therefore the French poets are often forced upon absurdities: for if the act begins in a chamber, all the persons in the play must have some business or other to come thither, or else they are not to be shown that act, and sometimes their characters are very unfitting to appear there. As, suppose it were the king's bedchamber, yet the meanest man in the tragedy must come and dispatch his business there rather than in the lobby or court-yard (which is fitter for him), for fear the stage should be cleared and the scenes broken. Many times they fall by it into a greater inconvenience; for they keep their scenes unbroken, and yet change the place; as in one of their

[82] *Œuvres*, I, 122.

newest plays,[83] where the act begins in the street. There a gentleman is to meet his friend; he sees him with his man, coming out from his father's house; they talk together, and the first goes out: the second, who is a lover, has made an appointment with his mistress; she appears at the window, and then we are to imagine the scene lies under it. This gentleman is called away, and leaves his servant with his mistress; presently her father is heard from within; the young lady is afraid the servingman should be discovered, and thrusts him in through a door which is supposed to be her closet. After this, the father enters to the daughter, and now the scene is in a house; for he is seeking from one room to another for this poor Philipin, or French Diego, who is heard from within, drolling and breaking many a miserable conceit upon his sad condition. In this ridiculous manner the play goes on, the stage being never empty all the while: so that the street, the window, the two houses, and the closet, are made to walk about, and the persons to stand still. Now what, I beseech you, is more easy than to write a regular French play, or more difficult than to write an irregular English one, like those of Fletcher or of Shakespeare?

'If they content themselves, as Corneille did, with some flat design which, like an ill riddle, is found out ere it be half proposed, such plots we can make every way regular, as easily as they; but whene'er they endeavour to rise up to any quick turns and counterturns of plot, as some of them have attempted since Corneille's plays have been less in vogue, you see they write as irregularly as we, though they cover it more speciously. Hence the reason is perspicuous why no French plays, when translated, have, or ever can succeed upon the English stage. For if you consider the plots, our own are fuller of variety; if the writing, ours are more quick and fuller of spirit; and therefore 'tis a strange mistake in those who decry the way of writing plays in verse, as if the English therein imitated the French. We have borrowed nothing from them; our plots are weaved in English looms: we endeavour therein to follow the variety and greatness of characters which are derived to us from Shakespeare and Fletcher; the copiousness and well-knitting of the intrigues we have from Jonson; and for the verse itself we have English precedents of elder date than any of Corneille's plays (not to name our old comedies before Shakespeare, which were all[84] writ in verse of six feet, or alexandrines, such as the French now use). I can show in Shakespeare many scenes of rhyme together, and the like in Ben Jonson's tragedies: in *Catiline* and *Sejanus* sometimes thirty or forty lines, I mean besides the Chorus, or the monologues, which, by the way, showed Ben no enemy to this way of writing, especially if you look upon his *Sad Shepherd*, which goes sometimes

---

[83] Thomas Corneille's *L'Amour à la mode* (1651).

[84] Not entirely true; but, again, strict accuracy is not part of Dryden's method in the *Essay*.

upon rhyme, sometimes upon blank verse, like an horse who eases himself upon trot and amble. You find him likewise commending Fletcher's pastoral of *The Faithful Shepherdess*, which is for the most part rhyme, though not refined to that purity to which it hath since been brought. And these examples are enough to clear us from a servile imitation of the French.

'But to return from whence I have digressed, I dare boldly affirm these two things of the English drama: first, that we have many plays of ours as regular as any of theirs, and which, besides, have more variety of plot and characters; and secondly, that in most of the irregular plays of Shakespeare or Fletcher (for Ben Jonson's are for the most part regular) there is a more masculine fancy and greater spirit in the writing than there is in any of the French. I could produce, even in Shakespeare's and Fletcher's works, some plays which are almost exactly formed; as *The Merry Wives of Windsor*, and *The Scornful Lady*; but because (generally speaking) Shakespeare, who writ first, did not perfectly observe the laws of comedy, and Fletcher, who came nearer to perfection, yet through carelessness made many faults, I will take the pattern of a perfect play from Ben Jonson, who was a careful and learned observer of the dramatic laws, and from all his comedies I shall select *The Silent Woman*; of which I will make a short examen,[85] according to those rules which the French observe.'

As Neander was beginning to examine *The Silent Woman*, Eugenius, looking earnestly upon him: 'I beseech you, Neander,' said he, 'gratify the company and me in particular so far, as, before you speak of the play, to give us a character of the author; and tell us frankly your opinion whether you do not think all writers, both French and English, ought to give place to him.'

'I fear,' replied Neander, 'that in obeying your commands I shall draw a little envy upon myself. Besides, in performing them, it will be first necessary to speak somewhat of Shakespeare and Fletcher, his rivals in poesy; and one of them, in my opinion, at least his equal, perhaps his superior.

'To begin, then, with Shakespeare: he was the man who of all modern, and perhaps ancient poets, had the largest and most comprehensive soul. All the images of nature were still present to him, and he drew them not laboriously, but luckily: when he describes anything, you more than see it, you feel it too. Those who accuse him to have wanted learning give him the greater commendation: he was naturally learned; he needed not the spectacles of books to read nature; he looked inwards, and found her there. I cannot say he is everywhere alike; were he so, I should do him injury to compare him with the greatest of mankind. He is many times flat, insipid; his comic wit degenerating into clenches, his serious swelling into bom-

---

[85] Dryden borrows the word from Corneille, who gave 'examens' of his own plays.

bast. But he is always great when some great occasion is presented to him;
no man can say he ever had a fit subject for his wit, and did not then raise
himself as high above the rest of poets,

quantum lenta solent inter viburna cupressi.[86]

The consideration of this made Mr Hales of Eton[87] say that there was no
subject of which any poet ever writ, but he would produce it much better
treated of in Shakespeare; and however others are now generally preferred
before him, yet the age wherein he lived, which had contemporaries with
him Fletcher and Jonson, never equalled them to him in their esteem. And
in the last King's court, when Ben's reputation was at highest, Sir John
Suckling, and with him the greater part of the courtiers, set our Shakespeare far above him.

'Beaumont and Fletcher, of whom I am next to speak, had, with the
advantage of Shakespeare's wit, which was their precedent, great natural
gifts improved by study; Beaumont especially being so accurate a judge of
plays that Ben Jonson, while he lived, submitted all his writing to his
censure, and, 'tis thought, used his judgment in correcting, if not contriving, all his plots. What value he had for him, appears by the verses he writ
to him; and therefore I need speak no farther of it. The first play which
brought Fletcher and him in esteem was their *Philaster*: for before that, they
had written two or three very unsuccessfully; as the like is reported of Ben
Jonson before he writ *Every Man in his Humour*. Their plots were generally
more regular than Shakespeare's, especially those which were made before
Beaumont's death; and they understood and imitated the conversation of
gentlemen much better; whose wild debaucheries, and quickness of wit in
repartees, no poet can ever paint as they have done. This humour of which
Ben Jonson derived from particular persons, they made it not their business
to describe: they represented all the passions very lively, but above all love.
I am apt to believe the English language in them arrived to its highest
perfection: what words have since been taken in, are rather superfluous than
necessary. Their plays are now the most pleasant and frequent entertainments of the stage; two of theirs being acted through the year for one of
Shakespeare's or Jonson's:[88] the reason is because there is a certain gaiety in
their comedies, and pathos in their more serious plays, which suits generally with all men's humours. Shakespeare's language is likewise a little
obsolete, and Ben Jonson's wit comes short of theirs.

---

[86] Virgil, *Eclogues*, 1, 20: 'as cypresses oft do among the bending osiers'.

[87] John Hales (1584–1656). The story of his defence of Shakespeare against the charge of
want of learning is told in Rowe's edition of 1709.

[88] This is quite so. The preference for Beaumont and Fletcher's plays in the Restoration is
very much as Dryden describes.

'As for Jonson, to whose character I am now arrived, if we look upon him while he was himself (for his last plays were but his dotages), I think him the most learned and judicious writer which any theatre ever had. He was a most severe judge of himself as well as others. One cannot say he wanted wit, but rather that he was frugal of it. In his works you find little to retrench or alter. Wit and language, and humour also in some measure, we had before him; but something of art was wanting to the drama till he came. He managed his strength to more advantage than any who preceded him. You seldom find him making love in any of his scenes, or endeavouring to move the passions; his genius was too sullen and saturnine to do it gracefully, especially when he knew he came after those who had performed both to such an height. Humour was his proper sphere, and in that he delighted most to represent mechanic people. He was deeply conversant in the Ancients, both Greek and Latin, and he borrowed boldly from them: there is scarce a poet or historian among the Roman authors of those times whom he has not translated in *Sejanus* and *Catiline*. But he has done his robberies so openly that one may see he fears not to be taxed by any law. He invades authors like a monarch, and what would be theft in other poets is only victory in him. With the spoils of these writers he so represents old Rome to us, in its rites, ceremonies, and customs, that if one of their poets had written either of his tragedies, we had seen less of it than in him. If there was any fault in his language, 'twas that he weaved it too closely and laboriously in his serious plays; perhaps, too, he did a little too much romanize our tongue, leaving the words which he translated almost as much Latin as he found them: wherein, though he learnedly followed the idiom of their language, he did not enough comply with ours. If I would compare him with Shakespeare, I must acknowledge him the more correct poet, but Shakespeare the greater wit. Shakespeare was the Homer, or father of our dramatic poets; Jonson was the Virgil, the pattern of elaborate writing; I admire him, but I love Shakespeare. To conclude of him, as he has given us the most correct plays, so in the precepts which he has laid down in his *Discoveries*, we have as many and profitable rules for perfecting the stage as any wherewith the French can furnish us.

'Having thus spoken of the author, I proceed to the examination of his comedy, *The Silent Woman*.[89]

EXAMEN OF THE SILENT WOMAN

'To begin first with the length of the action, it is so far from exceeding the compass of a natural day that it takes not up an artificial one. 'Tis all

[89] *Epicoene, or The Silent Woman*, first acted in 1609.

included in the limits of three hours and an half, which is no more than is required for the presentment upon the stage. A beauty perhaps not much observed; if it had, we should not have looked on the Spanish translation of *Five Hours* with so much wonder. The scene of it is laid in London; the latitude of place is almost as little as you can imagine: for it lies all within the compass of two houses, and after the first act, in one. The continuity of scenes is observed more than in any of our plays, excepting his own *Fox* and *Alchemist*. They are not broken above twice or thrice at most in the whole comedy; and in the two best of Corneille's plays, the *Cid* and *Cinna*, they are interrupted once apiece. The action of the play is entirely one; the end or aim of which is the settling Morose's estate on Dauphine. The intrigue of it is the greatest and most noble of any pure unmixed comedy in any language; you see in it many persons of various characters and humours, and all delightful. As first, Morose, or an old man, to whom all noise but his own talking is offensive. Some who would be thought critics say this humour of his is forced: but to remove that objection, we may consider him first to be naturally of a delicate hearing, as many are to whom all sharp sounds are unpleasant; and secondly, we may attribute much of it to the peevishness of his age, or the wayward authority of an old man in his own house, where he may make himself obeyed; and this the poet seems to allude to in his name *Morose*. Besides this, I am assured from divers persons that Ben Jonson was actually acquainted with such a man, one altogether as ridiculous as he is here represented. Others say it is not enough to find one man of such an humour; it must be common to more, and the more common the more natural. To prove this, they instance in the best of comical characters, Falstaff: there are many men resembling him; old, fat, merry, cowardly, drunken, amorous, vain, and lying. But to convince these people, I need but tell them that humour is the ridiculous extravagance of conversation, wherein one man differs from all others. If then it be common, or communicated to many, how differs it from other men's? or what indeed causes it to be ridiculous so much as the singularity of it? As for Falstaff, he is not properly one humour, but a miscellany of humours or images, drawn from so many several men. That wherein he is singular is his wit, or those things he says *praeter expectatum*, unexpected by the audience; his quick evasions when you imagine him surprised, which, as they are extremely diverting of themselves, so receive a great addition from his person; for the very sight of such an unwieldy, old, debauched fellow is a comedy alone. And here, having a place so proper for it, I cannot but enlarge somewhat upon this subject of humour into which I am fallen. The Ancients had little of it in their comedies; for the τὸ γελοῖον[90] of the Old Comedy, of which Aris-

---

[90] 'The laughable'.

tophanes was chief, was not so much to imitate a man as to make the people laugh at some odd conceit which had commonly somewhat of unnatural or obscene in it. Thus, when you see Socrates brought upon the stage, you are not to imagine him made ridiculous by the imitation of his actions, but rather by making him perform something very unlike himself: something so childish and absurd as, by comparing it with the gravity of the true Socrates, makes a ridiculous object for the spectators. In their New Comedy, which succeeded, the poets sought indeed to express the $\ddot{\eta}\theta o \varsigma$[91] as in their tragedies the $\pi \acute{a}\theta o \varsigma$[92] of mankind. But this $\ddot{\eta}\theta o \varsigma$ contained only the general characters of men and manners; as old men, lovers, serving-men, courtesans, parasites, and such other persons as we see in their comedies; all which they made alike: that is, one old man or father, one lover, one courtesan, so like another as if the first of them had begot the rest of every sort: *ex homine hunc natum dicas*.[93] The same custom they observed likewise in their tragedies. As for the French, though they have the word *humeur* among them, yet they have small use of it in their comedies or farces; they being but ill imitations of the *ridiculum*, or that which stirred up laughter in the Old Comedy. But among the English 'tis otherwise: where by humour is meant some extravagant habit, passion, or affection, particular (as I said before) to some one person, by the oddness of which he is immediately distinguished from the rest of men; which being lively and naturally represented, most frequently begets that malicious pleasure in the audience which is testified by laughter; as all things which are deviations from common customs are ever the aptest to produce it: though by the way this laughter is only accidental, as the person represented is fantastic or bizarre; but pleasure is essential to it, as the imitation of what is natural. The description of these humours, drawn from the knowledge and observation of particular persons, was the peculiar genius and talent of Ben Jonson; to whose play I now return.

'Besides Morose, there are at least nine or ten different characters and humours in *The Silent Woman*, all which persons have several concernments of their own, yet are all used by the poet to the conducting of the main design to perfection. I shall not waste time in commending the writing of this play, but I will give you my opinion that there is more wit and acuteness of fancy in it than in any of Ben Jonson's. Besides, that he has here described the conversation of gentlemen in the persons of True-Wit and his friends, with more gaiety, air, and freedom, than in the rest of his comedies. For the contrivance of the plot, 'tis extreme elaborate, and yet withal easy; for the $\lambda \acute{v}\sigma\iota\varsigma$, or untying of it, 'tis so admirable that when it is

[91] 'Character'.
[92] 'Passion'.
[93] Terence, *The Eunuch*, l. 400: 'Do you call him a human being?'

done no one of the audience would think the poet could have missed it; and yet it was concealed so much before the last scene that any other way would sooner have entered into your thoughts. But I dare not take upon me to commend the fabric of it, because it is altogether so full of art that I must unravel every scene in it to commend it as I ought. And this excellent contrivance is still the more to be admired because 'tis comedy, where the persons are only of common rank, and their business private, not elevated by passions or high concernments as in serious plays. Here everyone is a proper judge of all he sees; nothing is represented but that with which he daily converses: so that by consequence all faults lie open to discovery, and few are pardonable. 'Tis this which Horace has judiciously observed:

> creditur, ex medio quia res arcessit, habere
> sudoris minimum; sed habet Comedia tanto
> plus oneris, quanto veniae minus.[94]

But our poet, who was not ignorant of these difficulties, had prevailed himself of all advantages; as he who designs a large leap takes his rise from the highest ground. One of these advantages is that which Corneille has laid down as the greatest which can arrive to any poem, and which he himself could never compass above thrice in all his plays; viz. the making choice of some signal and long-expected day, whereon the action of the play is to depend. This day was that designed by Dauphine for the settling of his uncle's estate upon him; which to compass, he contrives to marry him. That the marriage had been plotted by him long beforehand is made evident by what he tells True-Wit in the second act, that in one moment he had destroyed what he had been raising many months.

'There is another artifice of the poet which I cannot here omit, because by the frequent practice of it in his comedies he has left it to us almost as a rule: that is, when he has any character or humour wherein he would show a *coup de maître*, or his highest skill, he recommends it to your observation by a pleasant description of it before the person first appears. Thus, in *Bartholomew Fair* he gives you the pictures of Numps and Cokes, and in this those of Daw, Lafoole, Morose, and the Collegiate Ladies; all which you hear described before you see them. So that before they come upon the stage you have a longing expectation of them, which prepares you to receive them favourably; and when they are there, even from their first appearance you are so far acquainted with them that nothing of their humour is lost to you.

'I will observe yet one thing further of this admirable plot: the business of it rises in every act. The second is greater than the first, the third than the

---

[94] *Epistles*, II, i, 168–70: ' 'Tis thought that Comedy, drawing its themes from daily life, calls for less labour; but in truth it carries a heavier burden, as the indulgence allowed is less.'

second, and so forward to the fifth. There too you see, till the very last scene, new difficulties arise to obstruct the action of the play; and when the audience is brought into despair that the business can naturally be effected, then, and not before, the discovery is made. But that the poet might entertain you with more variety all this while, he reserves some new characters to show you, which he opens not till the second and third act. In the second, Morose, Daw, the Barber, and Otter; in the third, the Collegiate Ladies: all which he moves afterwards in by-walks, or under-plots, as diversions to the main design, lest it should grow tedious, though they are still naturally joined with it, and somewhere or other subservient to it. Thus, like a skilful chess-player, by little and little he draws out his men, and makes his pawns of use to his greater persons.

'If this comedy, and some others of his, were translated into French prose (which would now be no wonder to them, since Molière has lately given them plays out of verse which have not displeased them), I believe the controversy would soon be decided betwixt the two nations, even making them the judges. But we need not call our heroes to our aid; be it spoken to the honour of the English, our nation can never want in any age such who are able to dispute the empire of wit with any people in the universe. And though the fury of a civil war, and power for twenty years together abandoned to a barbarous race of men, enemies of all good learning, had buried the Muses under the ruins of monarchy; yet, with the restoration of our happiness, we see revived poesy lifting up its head, and already shaking off the rubbish which lay so heavy on it. We have seen since his Majesty's return many dramatic poems which yield not to those of any foreign nation, and which deserve all laurels but the English. I will set aside flattery and envy: it cannot be denied but we have had some little blemish either in the plot or writing of all those plays which have been made within these seven years (and perhaps there is no nation in the world so quick to discern them, or so difficult to pardon them, as ours): yet if we can persuade ourselves to use the candour of that poet who (though the most severe of critics) has left us this caution by which to moderate our censures:

> ubi plura nitent in carmine, non ego paucis
> offendar maculis;[95]

if, in consideration of their many and great beauties, we can wink at some slight and little imperfections; if we, I say, can be thus equal to ourselves, I ask no favour from the French. And if I do not venture upon any particular judgment of our late plays, 'tis out of the consideration which an ancient

---

[95] Horace, *Ars Poetica*, ll. 351–2: 'When the beauties in a poem are more in number, I shall not take offence at a few blots.'

writer gives me: *vivorum, ut magna admiratio, ita censura difficilis*:[96] betwixt
the extremes of admiration and malice, 'tis hard to judge uprightly of the
living. Only I think it may be permitted me to say that as it is no lessening
to us to yield to some plays, and those not many, of our nation in the last
age, so can it be no addition to pronounce of our present poets that they have
far surpassed all the Ancients, and the modern writers of other countries.'

This, my Lord, was the substance of what was then spoke on that occasion;
and Lisideius, I think, was going to reply, when he was prevented thus by
Crites: 'I am confident,' said he, 'the most material things that can be said
have been already urged on either side; if they have not, I must beg to
Lisideius that he will defer his answer till another time: for I confess I have a
joint quarrel to you both, because you have concluded, without any reason
given for it, that rhyme is proper for the stage. I will not dispute how
ancient it hath been among us to write this way; perhaps our ancestors knew
no better till Shakespeare's time. I will grant it was not altogether left by
him, and that Fletcher and Ben Jonson used it frequently in their pastorals,
and sometimes in other plays. Farther, I will not argue whether we received
it originally from our own countrymen, or from the French; for that is an
inquiry of as little benefit as theirs who, in the midst of the great plague,
were not so solicitous to provide against it as to know whether we had it
from the malignity of our own air, or by transportation from Holland. I
have therefore only to affirm that it is not allowable in serious plays; for
comedies, I find you already concluding with me. To prove this, I might
satisfy myself to tell you how much in vain it is for you to strive against the
stream of the people's inclination, the greatest part of which are prepossessed
so much with those excellent plays of Shakespeare, Fletcher, and Ben
Jonson (which have been written out of rhyme) that except you could bring
them such as were written better in it, and those too by persons of equal
reputation with them, it will be impossible for you to gain your cause with
them who will still be judges. This it is to which, in fine, all your reasons
must submit. The unanimous consent of an audience is so powerful that
even Julius Caesar (as Macrobius reports of him), when he was perpetual
dictator, was not able to balance it on the other side. But when Laberius, a
Roman knight, at his request contended in the mime with another poet, he
was forced to cry out *etiam favente me victus es, Laberi*.[97] But I will not on this
occasion take the advantage of the greater number, but only urge such
reasons against rhyme as I find in the writings of those who have argued for
the other way. First, then, I am of opinion that rhyme is unnatural in a play,

[96] Paterculus, *History of Rome*, II, 36.
[97] *Saturnalia*, II, 7: 'Even with my support you have been defeated, Laberius.'

because dialogue there is presented as the effect of sudden thought. For a play is the imitation of nature; and since no man without premeditation speaks in rhyme, neither ought he to do it on the stage. This hinders not but the fancy may be there elevated to an higher pitch of thought than it is in ordinary discourse; for there is a probability that men of excellent and quick parts may speak noble things *ex tempore*: but those thoughts are never fettered with the numbers or sound of verse without study, and therefore it cannot be but unnatural to present the most free way of speaking in that which is the most constrained. For this reason, says Aristotle, 'tis best to write tragedy in that kind of verse which is the least such, or which is nearest prose: and this amongst the Ancients was the iambic, and with us is blank verse, or the measure of verse kept exactly without rhyme. These numbers therefore are fittest for a play; the others for a paper of verses or a poem; blank verse being as much below them as rhyme is improper for the drama. And if it be objected that neither are blank verses made *ex tempore*, yet, as nearest nature, they are still to be preferred. But there are two particular exceptions which many besides myself have had to verse; by which it will appear yet more plainly how improper it is in plays. And the first of them is grounded on that very reason for which some have commended rhyme: they say the quickness of repartees in argumentative scenes receives an ornament from verse. Now what is more unreasonable than to imagine that a man should not only light upon the wit, but the rhyme too upon the sudden? This nicking of him who spoke before, both in sound and measure, is so great an happiness that you must at least suppose the persons of your play to be born poets, *Arcades omnes, et cantare pares, et respondere parati*;[98] they must have arrived to the degree of *quicquid conabar dicere*: to make verses almost whether they will or no. If they are anything below this, it will look rather like the design of two than the answer of one: it will appear that your actors hold intelligence together, that they perform their tricks like fortune-tellers, by confederacy. The hand of art will be too visible in it against that maxim of all professions, *ars est celare artem*: that it is the greatest perfection of art to keep itself undiscovered. Nor will it serve you to object that, however you manage it, 'tis still known to be a play; and consequently the dialogue of two persons understood to be the labour of one poet. For a play is still an imitation of nature; we know we are to be deceived, and we desire to be so; but no man ever was deceived but with a probability of truth, for who will suffer a gross lie to be fastened on him? Thus we sufficiently understand that the scenes which represent cities and countries to us are not really such, but only painted on boards and canvas: but shall that excuse the ill painture or designment of them? Nay, rather

[98] Virgil, *Eclogues*, vii, 4–5: 'Arcadians both [omnes = ambo], ready in a match to sing, as well as to make reply.'

ought they not to be laboured with so much the more diligence and exactness to help the imagination? since the mind of man does naturally tend to, and seek after truth; and therefore the nearer anything comes to the imitation of it, the more it pleases.

'Thus, you see, your rhyme is uncapable of expressing the greatest thoughts naturally, and the lowest it cannot with any grace: for what is more unbefitting the majesty of verse than to call a servant, or bid a door be shut, in rhyme? And yet this miserable necessity you are forced upon. But verse, you say, circumscribes a quick and luxuriant fancy, which would extend itself too far on every subject, did not the labour which is required to well turned and polished rhyme set bounds to it. Yet this argument, if granted, would only prove that we may write better in verse, but not more naturally. Neither is it able to evince that; for he who wants judgment to confine his fancy in blank verse, may want it as much in rhyme; and he who has it will avoid errors in both kinds. Latin verse was as great a confinement to the imagination of those poets as rhyme to ours: and yet you find Ovid saying too much on every subject. *Nescivit* (says Seneca) *quod bene cessit relinquere*:[99] of which he gives you one famous instance in his description of the deluge:

> omnia pontus erat, deerant quoque litora ponto.
>
> Now all was sea, nor had that sea a shore.

Thus Ovid's fancy was not limited by verse, and Virgil needed not verse to have bounded his.

'In our own language we see Ben Jonson confining himself to what ought to be said, even in the liberty of blank verse; and yet Corneille, the most judicious of the French poets, is still varying the same sense an hundred ways, and dwelling eternally on the same subject, though confined by rhyme. Some other exceptions I have to verse; but being these I have named are for the most part already public, I conceive it reasonable they should first be answered.'

'It concerns me less than any', said Neander (seeing he had ended), 'to reply to this discourse; because when I should have proved that verse may be natural in plays, yet I should always be ready to confess that those which I have written in this kind come short of that perfection which is required. Yet since you are pleased I should undertake this province, I will do it, though with all imaginable respect and deference both to that person[100]

---

[99] 'He never knew how to give over when he had done well' (Dryden, Preface to *Ovid's Epistles*). As Watson points out, the remark is made by Marcus Seneca, *Controversiae*, ix, 5.

[100] that person] Watson suggests Aristotle. It could, perhaps, be Buckhurst (Eugenius), to whom the *Essay* is dedicated, and who has defended English writers earlier on.

from whom you have borrowed your strongest arguments, and to whose judgment, when I have said all, I finally submit. But before I proceed to answer your objections, I must first remember you that I exclude all comedy from my defence; and next that I deny not but blank verse may be also used, and content myself only to assert that in serious plays, where the subject and characters are great, and the plot unmixed with mirth, which might allay or divert these concernments which are produced, rhyme is there as natural, and more effectual than blank verse.

'And now having laid down this as a foundation, to begin with Crites, I must crave leave to tell him that some of his arguments against rhyme reach no farther than, from the faults or defects of ill rhyme, to conclude against the use of it in general. May not I conclude against blank verse by the same reason? If the words of some poets who write in it are either ill chosen or ill placed (which makes not only rhyme, but all kind of verse in any language unnatural) shall I, for their vicious affectation, condemn those excellent lines of Fletcher which are written in that kind? Is there anything in rhyme more constrained than this line in blank verse?

I heaven invoke, and strong resistance make:

where you see both the clauses are placed unnaturally, that is, contrary to the common way of speaking, and that without the excuse of a rhyme to cause it: yet you would think me very ridiculous if I should accuse the stubbornness of blank verse for this, and not rather the stiffness of the poet. Therefore, Crites, you must either prove that words, though well chosen and duly placed, yet render not rhyme natural in itself; or that, however natural and easy the rhyme may be, yet it is not proper for a play. If you insist upon the former part, I would ask you what other conditions are required to make rhyme natural in itself, besides an election of apt words, and a right disposing of them? For the due choice of your words expresses your sense naturally, and the due placing them adapts the rhyme to it. If you object that one verse may be made for the sake of another, though both the words and rhyme be apt, I answer it cannot possibly so fall out; for either there is a dependence of sense betwixt the first line and the second, or there is none: if there be that connection, then in the natural position of the words the latter line must of necessity flow from the former; if there be no dependence, yet still the due ordering of words makes the last line as natural in itself as the other: so that the necessity of a rhyme never forces any but bad or lazy writers to say what they would not otherwise. 'Tis true, there is both care and art required to write in verse. A good poet never concludes upon the first line till he has sought out such a rhyme as may fit the sense, already prepared to heighten the second: many times the close of the sense falls into the middle of the next verse, or farther off, and he may often prevail himself of the same advantages in English which Virgil had in Latin: he may break off in the hemistich, and begin another line. Indeed, the not observing these two last things makes plays which are writ in verse so tedious: for though, most commonly, the sense is to be confined to the couplet, yet nothing that does *perpetuo tenore fluere*, run in the same channel, can please always. 'Tis like the murmuring of a stream which, not varying in the fall, causes at first attention, at last drowsiness. Variety of cadences is the best rule, the greatest help to the actors, and refreshment to the audience.

'If then verse may be made natural in itself, how becomes it improper to a play? You say the stage is the representation of nature, and no man in ordinary conversation speaks in rhyme. But you foresaw when you said this that it might be answered: neither does any man speak in blank verse, or in measure without rhyme. Therefore you concluded that which is nearest nature is still to be preferred. But you took no notice that rhyme might be made as natural as blank verse by the well placing of the words, &c. All the difference between them, when they are both correct, is the sound in one, which the other wants; and if so, the sweetness of it, and all the advantage resulting from it, which are handled in the preface to *The Rival Ladies*,[101] will yet stand good. As for that place of Aristotle, where he says plays should be writ in that kind of verse which is nearest prose, it makes little for you, blank verse being properly but measured prose. Now measure alone, in any modern language, does not constitute verse; those of the Ancients in Greek and Latin consisted in quantity of words, and a determinate number of feet. But when, by the inundation of the Goths and Vandals into Italy, new languages were brought in, and barbarously mingled with the Latin (of which the Italian, Spanish, French, and ours — made out of them and the Teutonic — are dialects), a new way of poesy was practised; new, I say, in those countries, for in all probability it was that of the conquerors in their own nations.[102] This new way consisted in measure, or number of feet, and rhyme; the sweetness of rhyme, and observation of accent, supplying the place of quantity in words, which could neither exactly be observed by those barbarians, who knew not the rules of it, neither was it suitable to their tongues as it had been to the Greek and Latin. No man is tied in modern poesy to observe any farther rule in the feet of his verse, but that they be dissyllables; whether spondee, trochee, or iambic, it matters not; only he is

---

[101] Before the *Essay*, Dryden had defended the use of rhyme in plays in his Preface to *The Rival Ladies* (1664), and Howard had attacked it in the Preface to *Four New Plays* (1665). The dispute is continued in Howard's Preface to *The Duke of Lerma* (1668) and Dryden's *Defence of An Essay of Dramatic Poesy*, also published in 1668.

[102] 1684 adds: 'at least we are able to prove that the eastern people have used it from all antiquity. *Vid.* Dan. His *Defence of Rhyme.*' The reference is to Samuel Daniel's *Defence* (1603).

obliged to rhyme. Neither do the Spanish, French, Italians, or Germans acknowledge at all, or very rarely, any such kind of poesy as blank verse amongst them. Therefore at most 'tis but a poetic prose, a *sermo pedestris*, and as such most fit for comedies, where I acknowledge rhyme to be improper. Farther, as to that quotation of Aristotle, our couplet verses may be rendered as near prose as blank verse itself, by using those advantages I lately named, as breaks in a hemistich, or running the sense into another line, thereby making art and order appear as loose and free as nature: or not tying ourselves to couplets strictly, we may use the benefit of the Pindaric way practised in *The Siege of Rhodes*;[103] where the numbers vary, and the rhyme is disposed carelessly, and far from often chiming. Neither is that other advantage of the Ancients to be despised, of changing the kind of verse when they please with the change of the scene, or some new entrance: for they confine not themselves always to iambics, but extend their liberty to all lyric numbers, and sometimes even to hexameter. But I need not go so far to prove that rhyme, as it succeeds to all other offices of Greek and Latin verse, so especially to this of plays, since the custom of all nations at this day confirms it: all the French, Italian, and Spanish tragedies are generally writ in it; and sure the universal consent of the most civilized parts of the world ought in this, as it doth in other customs, include the rest.

'But perhaps you may tell me I have proposed such a way to make rhyme natural, and consequently proper to plays, as is unpracticable, and that I shall scarce find six or eight lines together in any play, where the words are so placed and chosen as is required to make it natural. I answer, no poet need constrain himself at all times to it. It is enough he makes it his general rule; for I deny not but sometimes there may be a greatness in placing the words otherwise; and sometimes they may sound better, sometimes also the variety itself is excuse enough. But if, for the most part, the words be placed as they are in the negligence of prose, it is sufficient to denominate the way practicable; for we esteem that to be such, which in the trial oftener succeeds than misses. And thus far you may find the practice made good in many plays: where you do not, remember still that if you cannot find six natural rhymes together, it will be as hard for you to produce as many lines in blank verse, even among the greatest of our poets, against which I cannot make some reasonable exception.

'And this, Sir, calls to my remembrance the beginning of your discourse, where you told us we should never find the audience favourable to this kind of writing till we could produce as good plays in rhyme as Ben Jonson, Fletcher, and Shakespeare had writ out of it. But it is to raise envy to the living, to compare them with the dead. They are honoured, and almost

[103] An operatic work, the first of its kind in England, by Sir William Davenant. It was first performed at Rutland House in 1656.

adored by us, as they deserve; neither do I know any so presumptuous of themselves as to contend with them. Yet give me leave to say thus much, without injury to their ashes, that not only we shall never equal them, but they could never equal themselves, were they to rise and write again. We acknowledge them our fathers in wit, but they have ruined their estates themselves before they came to their children's hands. There is scarce an humour, a character, or any kind of plot which they have not blown upon: all comes sullied or wasted to us: and were they to entertain this age, they could not make so plenteous treatments out of such decayed fortunes. This therefore will be a good argument to us either not to write at all, or to attempt some other way. There is no bays to be expected in their walks; *tentanda via est, qua me quoque possum tollere humo.*[104]

'This way of writing in verse they have only left free to us; our age is arrived to a perfection in it which they never knew; and which (if we may guess by what of theirs we have seen in verse, as *The Faithful Shepherdess*, and *Sad Shepherd*)[105] 'tis probable they never could have reached. For the genius of every age is different; and though ours excel in this, I deny not but that to imitate nature in that perfection which they did in prose, is a greater commendation than to write in verse exactly. As for what you have added, that the people are not generally inclined to like this way; if it were true, it would be no wonder that betwixt the shaking off of an old habit, and the introducing of a new, there should be difficulty. Do we not see them stick to Hopkins' and Sternhold's psalms, and forsake those of David, I mean Sandys his translation of them?[106] If by the people you understand the multitude, the οἱ πολλοί, 'tis no matter what they think; they are sometimes in the right, sometimes in the wrong; their judgment is a mere lottery. *Est ubi plebs recte putat, est ubi peccat.* Horace says it of the vulgar, judging poesy. But if you mean the mixed audience of the populace and the noblesse, I dare confidently affirm that a great part of the latter sort are already favourable to verse; and that no serious plays written since the King's return have been more kindly received by them than *The Siege of Rhodes*, the *Mustapha, The Indian Queen*, and *Indian Emperor*.[107]

'But I come now to the inference of your first argument. You said the dialogue of plays is presented as the effect of sudden thought, but no man speaks suddenly, or *ex tempore*, in rhyme; and you inferred from thence that rhyme, which you acknowledge to be proper to epic poesy, cannot equally

---

[104] Virgil, *Georgics*, III, 8–9: 'I must essay a path where I, too, may rise from earth.'

[105] The first is by Beaumont and Fletcher; the second, an incomplete play by Ben Jonson.

[106] George Sandys (1578–1644) published his *Paraphrase upon the Psalmes* in 1636. Hopkins and Sternhold: cf. *Religio Laici*, l. 456n.

[107] The three latter are heroic plays: *Mustapha* by Roger Boyle, Earl of Orrery (perf. 1665); the other two by Dryden.

be proper to dramatic, unless we could suppose all men born so much more than poets that verses should be made in them, not by them.

'It has been formerly urged by you, and confessed by me, that since no man spoke any kind of verse *ex tempore*, that which was nearest nature was to be preferred. I answer you, therefore, by distinguishing betwixt what is nearest to the nature of comedy, which is the imitation of common persons and ordinary speaking, and what is nearest the nature of a serious play: this last is indeed the representation of nature, but 'tis nature wrought up to an higher pitch. The plot, the characters, the wit, the passions, the descriptions, are all exalted above the level of common converse, as high as the imagination of the poet can carry them with proportion to verisimility. Tragedy, we know, is wont to image to us the minds and fortunes of noble persons, and to portray these exactly, heroic rhyme is nearest nature, as being the noblest kind of modern verse.

> indignatur enim privatis et prope socco
> dignis carminibus narrari coena Thyestae[108]

(says Horace). And in another place,

> effutire leves indigna tragoedia versus.[109]

Blank verse is acknowledged to be too low for a poem, nay more, for a paper of verses; but if too low for an ordinary sonnet,[110] how much more for tragedy, which is by Aristotle, in the dispute betwixt the epic poesy and the dramatic, for many reasons he there alleges, ranked above it?

'But setting this defence aside, your argument is almost as strong against the use of rhyme in poems as in plays; for the epic way is everywhere interlaced with dialogue, or discoursive scenes; and therefore you must either grant rhyme to be improper there, which is contrary to your assertion, or admit it into plays by the same title which you have given it to poems. For though tragedy be justly preferred above the other, yet there is a great affinity between them, as may easily be discovered in that definition of a play which Lisideius gave us. The genus of them is the same, a just and lively image of human nature, in its actions, passions, and traverses of fortune: so is the end, namely for the delight and benefit of mankind. The characters and persons are still the same, viz., the greatest of both sorts; only the manner of acquainting us with those actions, passions, and fortunes, is different. Tragedy performs it *viva voce*, or by action, in dialogue; wherein it excels the epic poem, which does it chiefly by narration, and therefore is not

---

[108] *Ars Poetica*, ll. 90–1: 'The feast of Thyestes scorns to be told in strains of daily life that might well nigh befit the comic sock.'

[109] Ibid., l. 231: 'Tragedy, scorning to babble trivial verses'.

[110] sonnet] Meaning simply a short poem.

so lively an image of human nature. However, the agreement betwixt them is such, that if rhyme be proper for one, it must be for the other. Verse, 'tis true, is not the effect of sudden thought; but this hinders not that sudden thought may be represented in verse, since those thoughts are such as must be higher than nature can raise them without premeditation, especially to a continuance of them, even out of verse; and consequently you cannot imagine them to have been sudden either in the poet or the actors. A play, as I have said, to be like nature, is to be set above it; as statues which are placed on high are made greater than the life, that they may descend to the sight in their just proportion.

'Perhaps I have insisted too long upon this objection; but the clearing of it will make my stay shorter on the rest. You tell us, Crites, that rhyme appears most unnatural in repartees, or short replies: when he who answers (it being presumed he knew not what the other would say, yet) makes up that part of the verse which was left incomplete, and supplies both the sound and measure of it. This, you say, looks rather like the confederacy of two than the answer of one.

'This, I confess, is an objection which is in everyone's mouth who loves not rhyme: but suppose, I beseech you, the repartee were made only in blank verse, might not part of the same argument be turned against you? For the measure is as often supplied there as it is in rhyme; the latter half of the hemistich as commonly made up, or a second line subjoined as a reply to the former; which any one leaf in Jonson's plays will sufficiently clear to you. You will often find in the Greek tragedians, and in Seneca, that when a scene grows up into the warmth of repartees (which is the close fighting of it) the latter part of the trimeter is supplied by him who answers; and yet it was never observed as a fault in them by any of the ancient or modern critics. The case is the same in our verse as it was in theirs; rhyme to us being in lieu of quantity to them. But if no latitude is to be allowed a poet, you take from him not only his licence of *quidlibet audendi*,[111] but you tie him up in a straiter compass than you would a philosopher. This is indeed *Musas colere severiores*.[112] You would have him follow nature, but he must follow her on foot: you have dismounted him from his Pegasus. But you tell us, this supplying the last half of a verse, or adjoining a whole second to the former, looks more like the design of two than the answer of one. Suppose we acknowledge it: how comes this confederacy to be more displeasing to you than in a dance which is well contrived? You see there the united design of many persons to make up one figure: after they have separated themselves in many petty divisions, they rejoin one by one into a gross: the confederacy is

---

[111] 'Attempting anything'.
[112] 'To follow stricter Muses'.

plain amongst them, for chance could never produce anything so beautiful, and yet there is nothing in it that shocks your sight. I acknowledge the hand of art appears in repartee, as of necessity it must in all kind of verse. But there is also the quick and poignant brevity of it (which is an high imitation of nature in those sudden gusts of passion) to mingle with it; and this, joined with the cadency and sweetness of the rhyme, leaves nothing in the soul of the hearer to desire. 'Tis an art which appears; but it appears only like the shadowings of painture, which being to cause the rounding of it, cannot be absent; but while that is considered, they are lost: so while we attend to the other beauties of the matter, the care and labour of the rhyme is carried from us, or at least drowned in its own sweetness, as bees are sometimes buried in their honey. When a poet has found the repartee, the last perfection he can add to it is to put it into verse. However good the thought may be, however apt the words in which 'tis couched, yet he finds himself at a little unrest while rhyme is wanting: he cannot leave it till that comes naturally, and then is at ease, and sits down contented.

'From replies which are the most elevated thoughts of verse, you pass to the most mean ones: those which are common with the lowest of household conversation. In these, you say, the majesty of verse suffers. You instance in the calling of a servant, or commanding a door to be shut in rhyme. This, Crites, is a good observation of yours, but no argument: for it proves no more but that such thoughts should be waived, as often as may be, by the address of the poet. But suppose they are necessary in the places where he uses them, yet there is no need to put them into rhyme. He may place them in the beginning of a verse, and break it off, as unfit, when so debased, for any other use: or granting the worst, that they require more room than the hemistich will allow, yet still there is a choice to be made of the best words, and least vulgar (provided they be apt), to express such thoughts. Many have blamed rhyme in general for this fault, when the poet with a little care might have redressed it. But they do it with no more justice than if English poesy should be made ridiculous for the sake of the Water Poet's[113] rhymes. Our language is noble, full, and significant; and I know not why he who is master of it may not clothe ordinary things in it as decently as the Latin, if he use the same diligence in his choice of words. *Delectus verborum origo est eloquentiae.*[114] It was the saying of Julius Caesar, one so curious in his, that none of them can be changed but for a worse. One would think *unlock the door* was a thing as vulgar as could be spoken; and yet Seneca could make it sound high and lofty in his Latin:

---

[113] John Taylor (1580–1653), a waterman on the Thames, and a prolific writer of doggerel verse.

[114] Cicero, *Brutus*, 72: 'The choice of words is the origin of eloquence.'

reserate clusos regii postes laris.[115]

'But I turn from this exception, both because it happens not above twice
or thrice in any play that those vulgar thoughts are used; and then too (were
there no other apology to be made, yet) the necessity of them (which is alike
in all kind of writing) may excuse them. Besides that the great eagerness
and precipitation with which they are spoken makes us rather mind the
substance than the dress; that for which they are spoken, rather than what is
spoke. For they are always the effect of some hasty concernment, and
something of consequence depends upon them.

'Thus, Critcs, I havc cndcavourcd to answcr your objcctions; it rcmains
only that I should vindicate an argument for verse, which you have gone
about to overthrow. It had formerly been said that the easiness of blank
verse renders the poet too luxuriant, but that the labour of rhyme bounds
and circumscribes an over-fruitful fancy; the sense there being commonly
confined to the couplet, and the words so ordered that the rhyme naturally
follows them, not they the rhyme. To this you answered that it was no
argument to the question in hand; for the dispute was not which way a man
may write best, but which is most proper for the subject on which he writes.

'First, give me leave, Sir, to remember you that the argument against
which you raised this objection was only secondary: it was built upon this
hypothesis, that to write in verse was proper for serious plays. Which
supposition being granted (as it was briefly made out in that discourse, by
showing how verse might be made natural), it asserted that this way of
writing was an help to the poet's judgment, by putting bounds to a wild
overflowing fancy. I think therefore it will not be hard for me to make good
what it was to prove. But you add, that were this let pass, yet he who wants
judgment in the liberty of his fancy, may as well show the defect of it when
he is confined to verse: for he who has judgment will avoid errors, and he
who has it not will commit them in all kinds of writing.

'This argument, as you have taken it from a most acute person,[116] so I
confess it carries much weight in it. But by using the word *judgment* here
indefinitely, you seem to have put a fallacy upon us. I grant, he who has
judgment, that is, so profound, so strong, so infallible a judgment, that he
needs no helps to keep it always poised and upright, will commit no faults
either in rhyme or out of it. And on the other extreme, he who has a
judgment so weak and crazed that no helps can correct or amend it, shall
write scurvily out of rhyme, and worse in it. But the first of these
judgments is nowhere to be found, and the latter is not fit to write at all. To
speak therefore of judgment as it is in the best poets: they who have the

---

[115] *1684* adds a translation: 'Set wide the palace gates'.
[116] Sir Robert Howard, in the preface to *Four New Plays* (1665).

greatest proportion of it want other helps than from it within. As for example, you would be loth to say that he who was endued with a sound judgment had no need of history, geography, or moral philosophy, to write correctly. Judgment is indeed the master-workman in a play; but he requires many subordinate hands, many tools to his assistance. And verse I affirm to be one of these: 'tis a rule and line by which he keeps his building compact and even, which otherwise lawless imagination would raise either irregularly or loosely. At least, if the poet commits errors with this help, he would make greater and more without it: 'tis (in short) a slow and painful, but the surest kind of working. Ovid, whom you accuse for luxuriancy in verse, had perhaps been farther guilty of it, had he writ in prose. And for your instance of Ben Jonson, who you say writ exactly without the help of rhyme; you are to remember, 'tis only an aid to luxuriant fancy, which his was not: as he did not want imagination, so none ever said he had much to spare. Neither was verse then refined so much to be an help to that age as it is to ours. Thus, then, the second thoughts being usually the best, as receiving the maturest digestion from judgment, and the last and most mature product of those thoughts being artful and laboured verse, it may well be inferred that verse is a great help to a luxuriant fancy; and this is what that argument which you opposed was to evince.'

Neander was pursuing this discourse so eagerly, that Eugenius had called to him twice or thrice ere he took notice that the barge stood still, and that they were at the foot of Somerset Stairs[117] where they had appointed it to land. The company were all sorry to separate so soon, though a great part of the evening was already spent; and stood a while looking back upon the water, which the moonbeams played upon, and made it appear like floating quicksilver: at last they went up through a crowd of French people, who were merrily dancing in the open air, and nothing concerned for the noise of guns which had alarmed the town that afternoon. Walking thence together to the Piazze,[118] they parted there; Eugenius and Lisideius to some pleasant appointment they had made, and Crites and Neander to their several lodgings.

FINIS

[117] A landing place near Somerset House.
[118] The Piazza, a fashionable part of Covent Garden.

PREFACE TO *AN EVENING'S LOVE*

An Evening's Love appeared on the stage in 1668, and was printed in 1671. In the Preface, Dryden is conscious of attacks on comedies such as his own which relied on witty conversation and sexual intrigue. Shadwell, especially, in his Preface to *The Royal Shepherdess* (1669), had objected to seeing 'vice encouraged, by bringing the characters of debauched people on the stage, and making them pass for fine gentlemen'. He advocated another sort of comedy, of Jonsonian humours, contending that 'there is more wit and invention required in the finding out good humour, and matter proper for it, than in all their smart repartees' (Preface to *The Sullen Lovers*, 1668). Dryden's defence of libertine comedy is complex in places, for he is describing a complex mode of satire; but it may be noted that he insists firmly on the convention of the concluding marriage.

I had thought, Reader, in this preface to have written somewhat concerning the difference betwixt the plays of our age and those of our predecessors on the English stage: to have shewn in what parts of dramatic poesy we were excelled by Ben Jonson, I mean humour and contrivance of comedy; and in what we may justly claim precedence of Shakespeare and Fletcher, namely in heroic plays. But this design I have waived on second considerations; at least deferred it till I publish the *Conquest of Granada*, where the discourse will be more proper.[1] I had also prepared to treat of the improvement of our language since Fletcher's and Jonson's days, and consequently of our refining the courtship, raillery, and conversation of plays: but as I am willing to decline that envy which I should draw on myself from some old opiniatre[2] judges of the stage; so likewise I am pressed in time so much that I have not leisure, at present, to go through with it. Neither, indeed, do I value a reputation gained from comedy so far as to concern myself about it any more than I needs must in my own defence: for I think it, in its own nature, inferior to all sorts of dramatic writing. Low comedy especially requires, on the writer's part, much of conversation with the vulgar: and much of ill nature in the observation of their follies. But let all men please themselves according to their several tastes: that which is not pleasant to me

---

[1] The essay *Of Heroic Plays*, prefixed to *The Conquest of Granada* (1672).
[2] A French borrowing: stubborn, self-opinionated.

may be to others who judge better; and, to prevent an accusation from my enemies, I am sometimes ready to imagine that my disgust of low comedy proceeds not so much from my judgment as from my temper; which is the reason why I so seldom write it; and that when I succeed in it (I mean so far as to please the audience), yet I am nothing satisfied with what I have done; but am often vexed to hear the people laugh, and clap, as they perpetually do, where I intended 'em no jest; while they let pass the better things without taking notice of them. Yet even this confirms me in my opinion of slighting popular applause, and of contemning that approbation which those very people give, equally with me, to the zany[3] of a mountebank; or to the appearance of an antic on the theatre, without wit on the poet's part, or any occasion of laughter from the actor besides the ridiculousness of his habit and his grimaces.

But I have descended before I was aware from comedy to farce, which consists principally of grimaces. That I admire not any comedy equally with tragedy is, perhaps, from the sullenness of my humour; but that I detest those farces which are now the most frequent entertainments of the stage, I am sure I have reason on my side. Comedy consists, though of low persons, yet of natural actions and characters; I mean such humours, adventures, and designs as are to be found and met with in the world. Farce, on the other side, consists of forced humours and unnatural events. Comedy presents us with the imperfections of human nature: farce entertains us with what is monstrous and chimerical. The one causes laughter in those who can judge of men and manners, by the lively representation of their folly or corruption; the other produces the same effect in those who can judge of neither, and that only by its extravagances. The first works on the judgment and fancy; the latter on the fancy only: there is more of satisfaction in the former kind of laughter, and in the latter more of scorn. But how it happens that an impossible adventure should cause our mirth, I cannot so easily imagine. Something there may be in the oddness of it, because on the stage it is the common effect of things unexpected to surprise us into a delight: and that is to be ascribed to the strange appetite, as I may call it, of the fancy; which, like that of a longing woman, often runs out into the most extravagant desires; and is better satisfied sometimes with loam, or with the rinds of trees, than with the wholesome nourishments of life. In short, there is the same difference betwixt farce and comedy as betwixt an empiric[4] and a true physician: both of them may attain their ends; but what the one performs by hazard, the other does by skill. And as the artist is often unsuccessful while the mountebank succeeds; so farces more commonly take the people than

[3] A buffoon; a comic performer who assisted the mountebank.
[4] Quack.

comedies. For to write unnatural things is the most probable way of pleasing them, who understand not nature. And a true poet often misses of applause because he cannot debase himself to write so ill as to please his audience.

After all, it is to be acknowledged that most of those comedies which have been lately written have been allied too much to farce; and this must of necessity fall out till we forbear the translation of French plays: for their poets, wanting judgment to make or to maintain true characters, strive to cover their defects with ridiculous figures and grimaces. While I say this I accuse myself as well as others: and this very play would rise up in judgment against me, if I would defend all things I have written to be natural: but I confess I have given too much to the people in it, and am ashamed for them as well as for myself, that I have pleased them at so cheap a rate. Not that there is anything here which I would not defend to an ill-natured judge (for I despise their censures, who I am sure would write worse on the same subject): but because I love to deal clearly and plainly, and to speak of my own faults with more criticism than I would of another poet's. Yet I think it no vanity to say that this comedy has as much of entertainment in it as many other which have been lately written: and, if I find my own errors in it, I am able at the same time to arraign all my contemporaries for greater. As I pretend not that I can write humour, so none of them can reasonably pretend to have written it as they ought. Jonson was the only man of all ages and nations who has performed it well, and that but in three or four of his comedies: the rest are but a *crambe bis cocta*;[5] the same humours a little varied and written worse. Neither was it more allowable in him than it is in our present poets to represent the follies of particular persons; of which many have accused him. *Parcere personis, dicere de vitiis*[6] is the rule of plays. And Horace tells you that the Old Comedy amongst the Grecians was silenced for the too great liberties of the poets:

> in vitium libertas excidit et vim
> dignam lege regi: lex est accepta, chorusque
> turpiter obticuit, sublato jure nocendi.[7]

Of which he gives you the reason in another place: where having given the precept,

> neve immunda crepent, ignominiosaque dicta,

---

[5] Literally, twice-cooked cabbage.

[6] Martial, *Epigrams*, x, xxxiii: 'to spare the person, to denounce the vice'.

[7] *Ars Poetica*, ll. 282–4: 'Its freedom sank into excess and a violence deserving to be checked by law. The law was obeyed, and the chorus to its shame became mute, its right to injure being withdrawn.'

he immediately subjoins,

> offenduntur enim quibus est equus, et pater, et res.[8]

But Ben Jonson is to be admired for many excellencies; and can be taxed with fewer failings than any English poet. I know I have been accused as an enemy of his writings; but without any other reason than that I do not admire him blindly, and without looking into his imperfections. For why should he only be exempted from those frailties from which Homer and Virgil are not free? Or why should there be any *ipse dixit* in our poetry, any more than there is in our philosophy? I admire and applaud him where I ought: those who do more do but value themselves in their admiration of him; and, by telling you they extol Ben Jonson's way, would insinuate to you that they can practise it.[9] For my part, I declare that I want judgment to imitate him, and should think it a great impudence in myself to attempt it. To make men appear pleasantly ridiculous on the stage was, as I have said, his talent; and in this he needed not the acumen of wit, but that of judgment. For the characters and representations of folly are only the effects of observation; and observation is an effect of judgment. Some ingenious men, for whom I have a particular esteem, have thought I have much injured Ben Jonson when I have not allowed his wit to be extraordinary: but they confound the notion of what is witty with what is pleasant. That Ben Jonson's plays were pleasant, he must want reason who denies. But that pleasantness was not properly wit, or the sharpness of conceit, but the natural imitation of folly: which I confess to be excellent in its kind, but not to be of that kind which they pretend. Yet if we will believe Quintilian in his chapter *De movendo risu*, he gives his opinion of both in these following words: *stulta reprehendere facillimum est; nam per se sunt ridicula: et a derisu non procul abest risus; sed rem urbanum facit aliqua ex nobis adjectio.*[10]

And some perhaps would be apt to say of Jonson as it was said of Demosthenes: *non displicuisse illi jocos, sed non contigisse.*[11] I will not deny but that I approve most the mixed way of comedy; that which is neither all wit, nor all humour, but the result of both. Neither so little of humour as Fletcher shows, nor so little of love and wit as Jonson; neither all cheat, with which the best plays of the one are filled, nor all adventure, which is the common practice of the other. I would have the characters well chosen, and

---

[8] neve . . . res] Ibid., ll. 247–8: 'They should not crack their bawdy and shameless jokes. For some take offence – knights, freeborn, and men of substance.'

[9] Meaning Shadwell. See headnote.

[10] Combining two passages from the *Institutio Oratoria*: VI, iii, 7 and 71: 'It is easy to make fun of folly, for folly is ridiculous in itself; and laughter is never very far removed from derision; but we may improve such jests by adding something of our own.'

[11] Ibid., VI, iii, 2: 'That he lacked the power of jest, not merely that he disliked to use it.'

kept distant from interfering with each other; which is more than Fletcher
or Shakespeare did: but I would have more of the *urbana, venusta, salsa,
faceta*[12] and the rest which Quintilian reckons up as the ornaments of wit;
and these are extremely wanting in Ben Jonson. As for repartee in particular; as it is the very soul of conversation, so it is the greatest grace of comedy,
where it is proper to the characters. There may be much of acuteness in a
thing well said; but there is more in a quick reply: *sunt enim longe venustiora
omnia in respondendo quam in provocando.*[13] Of one thing I am sure, that no
man ever will decry wit but he who despairs of it himself; and who has no
other quarrel to it but that which the fox had to the grapes. Yet, as Mr
Cowley (who had a greater portion of it than any man I know) tells us in his
character of wit, rather than all wit let there be none.[14] I think there's no
folly so great in any poet of our age as the superfluity and waste of wit was in
some of our predecessors: particularly we may say of Fletcher and of
Shakespeare what was said of Ovid, *in omni eius ingenio, facilius quod rejici,
quam quod adjici potest, invenies.*[15] The contrary of which was true in Virgil
and our incomparable Jonson.

Some enemies of repartee[16] have observed to us that there is a great
latitude in their characters which are made to speak it; and that it is easier to
write wit than humour, because in the characters of humour the poet is
confined to make the person speak what is only proper to it, whereas all
kind of wit is proper in the character of a witty person. But, by their favour,
these are as different characters in wit as in folly. Neither is all kind of wit
proper in the mouth of every ingenious person. A witty coward and a witty
brave must speak differently. Falstaff and the Liar speak not like Don John
in the *Chances*, and Valentine in *Wit Without Money*.[17] And Jonson's Truewit
in the *Silent Woman* is a character different from all of them. Yet it appears
that this one character of wit was more difficult to the author than all his
images of humour in the play: for those he could describe and manage from
his observations of men; this he has taken, at least a part of it, from books:
witness the speeches in the first act, translated *verbatim* out of Ovid *De arte
amandi*; to omit what afterwards he borrowed from the sixth satire of
Juvenal against women.

However, if I should grant that there were a greater latitude in characters

---

[12] In Quintilian's account, the urbanity, grace, sharpness or 'saltiness', and polished
elegance of wit. *Institutio Oratoria*, VI, iii, 17–20.

[13] Ibid., VI, iii, 13: 'For wit always appears to greater advantage in reply than in attack.'

[14] Cowley's 'Ode: Of Wit', l. 36.

[15] Quintilian, VI, iii, 5: 'In all the manifestations of his genius, you will find it easier to
detect superfluities than deficiencies.'

[16] See headnote.

[17] Dryden takes examples from Pierre Corneille's *The Liar* and Beaumont and Fletcher's *The
Chances* and *Wit Without Money*.

of wit than in those of humour, yet that latitude would be of small advantage to such poets who have too narrow an imagination to write it. And to entertain an audience perpetually with humour is to carry them from the conversation of gentlemen, and treat them with the follies and extravagances of Bedlam.

I find I have launched out farther than I intended in the beginning of this preface. And that, in the heat of writing, I have touched at something which I thought to have avoided. 'Tis time now to draw homeward, and to think rather of defending myself than assaulting others. I have already acknowledged that this play is far from perfect: but I do not think myself obliged to discover the imperfections of it to my adversaries, any more than a guilty person is bound to accuse himself before his judges. 'Tis charged upon me that I make debauched persons (such as they say my Astrologer and Gamester are) my protagonists, or the chief persons of the drama; and that I make them happy in the conclusion of my play; against the law of comedy, which is to reward virtue and punish vice. I answer first, that I know no such law to have been constantly observed in comedy, either by the ancient or modern poets. Chaerea is made happy in the *Eunuch*, after having deflowered a virgin; and Terence generally does the same through all his plays, where you perpetually see not only debauched young men enjoy their mistresses, but even the courtesans themselves rewarded and honoured in the catastrophe. The same may be observed in Plautus almost everywhere. Ben Jonson himself, after whom I may be proud to err, has given me more than once the example of it. That in the *Alchemist* is notorious, where Face, after having contrived and carried on the great cozenage of the play, and continued in it without repentance to the last, is not only forgiven by his master, but enriched by his consent with the spoils of those whom he had cheated. And, which is more, his master himself, a grave man and a widower, is introduced taking his man's counsel, debauching the widow first, in hope to marry her afterward. In the *Silent Woman*, Dauphine (who, with the other two gentlemen, is of the same character with my Celadon in the *Maiden Queen*, and with Wildblood in this) professes himself in love with all the Collegiate Ladies: and they likewise are all of the same character with each other, excepting only Madam Otter, who has something singular. Yet this naughty Dauphine is crowned in the end with the possession of his uncle's estate, and with the hopes of enjoying all his mistresses; and his friend Mr Truewit (the best character of a gentleman which Ben Jonson ever made) is not ashamed to pimp for him. As for Beaumont and Fletcher, I need not allege examples out of them; for that were to quote almost all their comedies.

But now it will be objected that I patronize vice by the authority of former poets, and extenuate my own faults by recrimination. I answer that, as I defend myself by their example, so that example I defend by reason, and by the end of all dramatic poesy. In the first place, therefore, give me leave to shew you their mistake who have accused me. They have not distinguished, as they ought, betwixt the rules of tragedy and comedy. In tragedy, where the actions and persons are great, and the crimes horrid, the laws of justice are more strictly to be observed; and examples of punishment to be made to deter mankind from the pursuit of vice. Faults of this kind have been rare amongst the ancient poets: for they have punished in Oedipus, and in his posterity, the sin which he knew not he had committed. Medea is the only example I remember at present who escapes from punishment after murder. Thus tragedy fulfils one great part of its institution, which is, by example, to instruct. But in comedy it is not so; for the chief end of it is divertisement and delight: and that so much, that it is disputed, I think, by Heinsius,[18] before Horace his *Art of Poetry*, whether instruction be any part of its employment. At least I am sure it can be but its secondary end: for the business of the poet is to make you laugh: when he writes humour, he makes folly ridiculous; when wit, he moves you, if not always to laughter, yet to a pleasure that is more noble. And if he works a cure on folly, and the small imperfections in mankind, by exposing them to public view, that cure is not performed by an immediate operation. For it works first on the ill nature of the audience; they are moved to laugh by the representation of deformity; and the shame of that laughter teaches us to amend what is ridiculous in our manners. This being, then, established, that the first end of comedy is delight, and instruction only the second, it may reasonably be inferred that comedy is not so much obliged to the punishment of faults which it represents, as tragedy. For the persons in comedy are of a lower quality, the action is little, and the faults and vices are but the sallies of youth, and the frailties of human nature, and not premeditated crimes: such to which all men are obnoxious, not such as are attempted only by few, and those abandoned to all sense of virtue; such as move pity and commiseration, not detestation and horror; such, in short, as may be forgiven, not such as must of necessity be punished. But, lest any man should think that I write this to make libertinism amiable, or that I cared not to debase the end and institution of comedy so I might thereby maintain my own errors, and those of better poets, I must further declare, both for them and for myself, that we make not vicious persons happy, but only as Heaven makes sinners so: that is, by reclaiming them first from vice. For so 'tis to be supposed they are, when they resolve to marry; for then

---

[18] Daniel Heinsius (1580–1655) whose edition of Horace in 1612 does not in fact support Dryden's argument. The argument that ensues, however, is important, consistent, and should be central in any view of Restoration comedy. See headnote.

enjoying what they desire in one, they cease to pursue the love of many. So Chaerea is made happy by Terence, in marrying her whom he had deflowered: and so are Wildblood and the Astrologer in this play.

There is another crime with which I am charged, at which I am yet much less concerned, because it does not relate to my manners, as the former did, but only to my reputation as a poet: a name of which I assure the reader I am nothing proud; and therefore cannot be very solicitous to defend it. I am taxed with stealing all my plays, and that by some who should be the last men from whom I would steal any part of 'em. There is one answer which I will not make; but it has been made for me by him to whose grace and patronage I owe all things,

et spes et ratio studiorum in Caesare tantum,[19]

and without whose command they should no longer be troubled with anything of mine: that he only desired that they who accused me of theft would always steal him plays like mine. But though I have reason to be proud of this defence, yet I should waive it, because I have a worse opinion of my own comedies than any of my enemies can have. 'Tis true that, wherever I have liked any story in a romance, novel, or foreign play, I have made no difficulty, nor ever shall, to take the foundation of it, to build it up, and to make it proper for the English stage. And I will be so vain to say it has lost nothing in my hands: but it always cost me so much trouble to heighten it for our theatre (which is incomparably more curious in all the ornaments of dramatic poesy than the French or Spanish) that when I had finished my play, it was like the hulk of *Sir Francis Drake*,[20] so strangely altered that there scarcely remained any plank of the timber which first built it. To witness this I need to go no farther than this play: it was first Spanish, and called *El astrologo fingido*; then made French by the younger Corneille; and is now translated into English, and in print, under the name of the *Feigned Astrologer*.[21] What I have performed in this will best appear by comparing it with those: you will see that I have rejected some adventures which I judged were not divertising; that I have heightened those which I have chosen, and that I have added others which were neither in the French nor Spanish. And besides, you will easily discover that the walk[22] of the Astrologer is the least

---

[19] Juvenal, *Satires*, VII, 1: 'On Caesar alone hang all the hopes and prospects of the learned.' Perhaps, as Watson suggests, Dryden is complimenting the Duke of Newcastle, to whom *An Evening's Love* is dedicated.

[20] Sir Francis Drake's ship, *The Golden Hind*, was kept at Deptford, in a poor state of preservation.

[21] Calderon's play was adapted by Thomas Corneille in 1648, and thence translated anonymously into English in 1668.

[22] walk] Course of action assigned to one person in a drama (*OED*).

considerable in my play: for the design of it turns more on the parts of Wildblood and Jacinta, who are the chief persons in it. I have farther to add that I seldom use the wit and language of any romance or play which I undertake to alter: because my own invention (as bad as it is) can furnish me with nothing so dull as what is there. Those who have called Virgil, Terence, and Tasso plagiaries (though they much injured them), had yet a better colour for their accusation; for Virgil has evidently translated Theocritus, Hesiod, and Homer, in many places; besides what he has taken from Ennius in his own language. Terence was not only known to translate Menander (which he avows also in his prologues), but was said also to be helped in those translations by Scipio the African and Laelius. And Tasso, the most excellent of modern poets, and whom I reverence next to Virgil, has taken both from Homer many admirable things which were left untouched by Virgil, and from Virgil himself where Homer could not furnish him. Yet the bodies of Virgil's and Tasso's poems were their own; and so are all the ornaments of language and elocution in them. The same (if there were anything commendable in this play) I could say for it. But I will come nearer to our own countrymen. Most of Shakespeare's plays, I mean the stories of them, are to be found in the *Hecatommithi* or *Hundred Novels* of Cinthio. I have myself read in his Italian that of *Romeo and Juliet*, the *Moor of Venice*, and many others of them.[23] Beaumont and Fletcher had most of theirs from Spanish novels: witness the *Chances*, the *Spanish Curate*, *Rule a Wife and have a Wife*, the *Little French Lawyer*, and so many others of them as compose the greatest part of their volume in folio. Ben Jonson, indeed, has designed his plots himself; but no man has borrowed so much from the Ancients as he has done: and he did well in it, for he has thereby beautified our language.

But these little critics do not well consider what is the work of a poet, and what the graces of a poem. The story is the least part of either: I mean the foundation of it, before it is modelled by the art of him who writes it; who forms it with more care, by exposing only the beautiful parts of it to view, than a skilful lapidary sets a jewel. On this foundation of the story the characters are raised: and, since no story can afford characters enough for the variety of the English stage, it follows that it is to be altered and enlarged with new persons, accidents, and designs, which will almost make it new. When this is done, the forming it into acts and scenes, disposing of actions and passions into their proper places, and beautifying both with descriptions, similitudes, and propriety of language, is the principal employment

---

[23] Geraldi Cinthio's *Hecatommithi* (1565) was the source of *Othello*, though not of *Romeo and Juliet*. Shakespeare used it also for *Measure for Measure*, *Twelfth Night* and *Two Gentlemen of Verona*. As Dryden indicates, Beaumont and Fletcher borrowed extensively from Spanish sources.

of the poet; as being the largest field of fancy, which is the principal quality required in him: for so much the word ποιητής[24] implies. Judgment, indeed, is necessary in him; but 'tis fancy that gives the life-touches, and the secret graces to it; especially in the serious plays, which depend not much on observation. For to write humour in comedy (which is the theft of poets from mankind), little of fancy is required; the poet observes only what is ridiculous and pleasant folly, and by judging exactly what is so, he pleases in the representation of it.

But in general, the employment of a poet is like that of a curious gunsmith or watchmaker: the iron or silver is not his own; but they are the least part of that which gives the value: the price lies wholly in the workmanship. And he who works dully on a story, without moving laughter in a comedy, or raising concernments in a serious play, is no more to be accounted a good poet than a gunsmith of the Minories[25] is to be compared with the best workman of the town.

But I have said more of this than I intended; and more, perhaps, than I needed to have done. I shall but laugh at them hereafter who accuse me with so little reason; and withal contemn their dullness who, if they could ruin that little reputation I have got, and which I value not, yet would want both wit and learning to establish their own; or to be remembered in after ages for anything but only that which makes them ridiculous in this.

[24] 'Maker'.
[25] A street near the Tower of London.

HEADS OF AN ANSWER TO RYMER

The *Heads* are Dryden's notes written in the end-papers of his copy of Thomas Rymer's *The Tragedies of the Last Age Considered* (1677; dated 1678). They were printed first by Tonson in his 1711 edition of Beaumont and Fletcher, and in another version by Johnson after his *Life of Dryden* of 1779. The ordering of the notes differs drastically in the two printings, both taken from the original, which was subsequently destroyed in a fire. Watson gives a satisfying explanation of the differences, and prefers Tonson's version, which is the one given here. Dryden resumes, and expands his arguments concerning plot and the manners of characters, in *The Grounds of Criticism in Tragedy*, prefixed to *Troilus and Cressida* (1679).

He who undertakes to answer this excellent critique of Mr Rymer, in behalf of our English poets against the Greek, ought to do it in this manner.

Either by yielding to him the greatest part of what he contends for, which consists in this, that the μῦθος, i.e. the design and conduct of it, is more conducing in the Greeks to those ends of tragedy which Aristotle and he propose, namely to cause terror and pity; yet the granting this does not set the Greeks above the English poets.

But the answerer ought to prove two things: first, that the fable is not the greatest masterpiece of a tragedy, tho' it be the foundation of it.

Secondly, that other ends as suitable to the nature of tragedy may be found in the English, which were not in the Greek.

Aristotle places the fable first;[1] not *quoad dignitatem, sed quoad fundamentum*;[2] for a fable, never so movingly contrived to those ends of his, pity and terror, will operate nothing on our affections, except the characters, manners, thoughts, and words are suitable.

So that it remains for Mr Rymer to prove that in all those, or the greatest

[1] *Poetics*, ch. vi.
[2] 'Not as pre-eminent, but as fundamental'.

part of them, we are inferior to Sophocles and Euripides; and this he has offered at in some measure, but, I think, a little partially to the Ancients.

To make a true judgment in this competition between the Greek poets and the English in tragedy, consider

> (I) How Aristotle has defined a tragedy.
> (II) What he assigns the end of it to be.
> (III) What he thinks the beauties of it.
> (IV) The means to attain the end proposed.

Compare the Greek and English tragic poets justly and without partiality, according to those rules.

Then, secondly, consider whether Aristotle has made a just definition of tragedy, of its parts, of its ends, of its beauties; and whether he, having not seen any others but those of Sophocles, Euripides, etc., had or truly could determine what all the excellencies of tragedy are, and wherein they consist.

Next show in what ancient tragedy was deficient: for example, in the narrowness of its plots, and fewness of persons, and try whether that be not a fault in the Greek poets; and whether their excellency was so great when the variety was visibly so little; or whether what they did was not very easy to do.

Then make a judgment on what the English have added to their beauties: as, for example, not only more plot, but also new passions; as namely, that of love, scarce touched on by the Ancients, except in this one example of Phaedra, cited by Mr Rymer;[3] and in that how short they were of Fletcher.

Prove also that love, being an heroic passion, is fit for tragedy, which cannot be denied, because of the example alleged of Phaedra; and how far Shakespeare has outdone them in friendship, etc.

To return to the beginning of this enquiry: consider if pity and terror be enough for tragedy to move; and I believe, upon a true definition of tragedy, it will be found that its work extends farther, and that it is to reform manners by delightful representation of human life in great persons, by way of dialogue. If this be true, then not only pity and terror are to be moved as the only means to bring us to virtue, but generally love to virtue and hatred to vice; by shewing the rewards of one, and punishments of the

[3] *Critical Works*, ed. Zimansky, pp. 50–9.

other; at least by rendering virtue always amiable, though it be shown unfortunate; and vice detestable, tho' it be shown triumphant.

If then the encouragement of virtue and discouragement of vice be the proper ends of poetry in tragedy: pity and terror, tho' good means, are not the only. For all the passions in their turns are to be set in a ferment: as joy, anger, love, fear are to be used as the poet's commonplaces; and a general concernment for the principal actors is to be raised by making them appear such in their characters, their words and actions, as will interest the audience in their fortunes.

And if after all, in a larger sense, pity comprehends this concernment for the good, and terror includes destestation for the bad, then let us consider whether the English have not answered this end of tragedy as well as the Ancients, or perhaps better.

And here Mr Rymer's objections against these plays are to be impartially weighed, that we may see whether they are of weight enough to turn the balance against our countrymen.

'Tis evident those plays which he arraigns[4] have moved both those passions in a high degree upon the stage.

To give the glory of this away from the poet, and to place it upon the actors, seems unjust.[5]

One reason is, because whatever actors they have found, the event has been the same, that is, the same passions have been always moved; which shows that there is something of force and merit in the plays themselves, conducing to the design of raising these two passions: and suppose them ever to have been excellently acted, yet action only adds grace, vigour, and more life upon the stage; but cannot give it wholly where it is not first. But secondly, I dare appeal to those who have never seen them acted, if they have not found those two passions moved within them; and if the general voice will carry it, Mr Rymer's prejudice will take off his single testimony.

This, being matter of fact, is reasonably to be established by this appeal:

[4] Rymer examines three plays at length: *The Bloody Brother, or the Tragedy of Rollo, Duke of Normandy* and Beaumont and Fletcher's *A King and No King* and *The Maid's Tragedy*.
[5] Cf. Rymer: 'These say (for instance) *A King and No King* pleases . . . I say that Mr Hart pleases . . . to the most wretched of characters he gives a lustre and a *brillant* which dazzles the sight, that the deformities in the poetry cannot be perceived' (*Critical Works*, p. 19).

as if one man says 'tis night, when the rest of the world conclude it to be day, there needs no further argument against him that it is so.

If he urge that the general taste is depraved, his arguments to prove this can at best but evince that our poets took not the best way to raise those passions; but experience proves against him that those means which they have used have been successful and have produced them.

And one reason of that success is, in my opinion, this, that Shakespeare and Fletcher have written to the genius of the age and nation in which they lived: for tho' nature, as he objects, is the same in all places, and reason too the same,[6] yet the climate, the age, the dispositions of the people to whom a poet writes, may be so different that what pleased the Greeks would not satisfy an English audience.

Whether our English audience have been pleased hitherto with acorns, as he calls it, or with bread,[7] is the next question; that is, whether the means which Shakespeare and Fletcher have used in their plays to raise those passions before named, be better applied to the ends by the Greek poets than by them; and perhaps we shall not grant him this wholly. Let it be yielded that a writer is not to run down with the stream, or to please the people by their own usual methods, but rather to reform their judgments: it still remains to prove that our theatre needs this total reformation.

The faults which he has found in their designs are rather wittily aggravated in many places than reasonably urged; and as much may be returned on the Greeks by one who were as witty as himself.

Secondly, they destroy not, if they are granted, the foundation of the fabric, only take away from the beauty of the symmetry: for example, the faults in the character of the King and No King are not, as he makes them, such as render him detestable, but only imperfections which accompany human nature, and for the most part excused by the violence of his love; so that they destroy not our pity or concernment for him. This answer may be applied to most of his objections of that kind.

[6] Rymer: 'Nature is the same, and man is the same [in Athens and London], he loves, grieves, hates, envies, has the same affections and passions in both places, and the same springs that give them motion. What moved pity there, will here also produce the same effect' (Ibid.).

[7] Rymer: '(Though tragedy is a poem chiefly for men of sense,) yet I cannot be persuaded that the people are so very mad of acorns, but that they could be very well content to eat the bread of civil persons' (Ibid., p. 20).

And Rollo committing many murders, when he is answerable but for one, is too severely arraigned by him; for it adds to our horror and detestation of the criminal; and poetic justice[8] is not neglected neither, for we stab him in our minds for every offence which he commits; and the point which the poet is to gain on the audience is not so much in the death of an offender, as the raising an horror of his crimes.

That the criminal should neither be wholly guilty, nor wholly innocent, but so participating of both as to move both pity and terror, is certainly a good rule, but not perpetually to be observed; for that were to make all tragedies too much alike; which objection he foresaw, but has not fully answered.

To conclude, therefore: if the plays of the Ancients are more correctly plotted, ours are more beautifully written; and if we can raise passions as high on worse foundations, it shows our genius in tragedy is greater, for in all other parts of it the English have manifestly excelled them.

For the fable itself, 'tis in the English more adorned with episodes, and larger than in the Greek poets; consequently more diverting. For, if the action be but one, and that plain, without any counter-turn of design or episode, i.e. under-plot, how can it be so pleasing as the English, which have both under-plot and a turned design, which keeps the audience in expectation of the catastrophe? whereas in the Greek poets we see through the whole design at first.

For the characters, they are neither so many nor so various in Sophocles and Euripides as in Shakespeare and Fletcher; only they are more adapted to those ends of tragedy which Aristotle commends to us: pity and terror.

The manners flow from the characters, and consequently must partake of their advantages and disadvantages.

The thoughts and words, which are the fourth and fifth beauties of tragedy, are certainly more noble and more poetical in the English than in the Greek, which must be proved by comparing them somewhat more equitably than Mr Rymer has done.

After all, we need not yield that the English way is less conducing to

---

[8] The phrase 'poetical justice' is Rymer's invention: 'Then no poetical justice could have touched them [Rollo and Otto]: guilty they were to be, in enjoying their father's crime; but not of committing any new' (Ibid., p. 26).

move pity and terror, because they often shew virtue oppressed and vice punished: where they do not both, or either, they are not to be defended.

That we may the less wonder why pity and terror are not now the only springs on which our tragedies move, and that Shakespeare may be more excused, Rapin confesses that the French tragedies now all run on the *tendre*;[9] and gives the reason, because love is the passion which most predominates in our souls, and that therefore the passions represented become insipid, unless they are conformable to the thoughts of the audience. But it is to be concluded that this passion works not now among the French so strongly as the other two did amongst the Ancients. Amongst us, who have a stronger genius for writing, the operations from the writing are much stronger: for the raising of Shakespeare's passions are more from the excellency of the words and thoughts than the justness of the occasion; and if he has been able to pick single occasions, he has never founded the whole reasonably; yet by the genius of poetry, in writing he has succeeded.

The parts of a poem, tragic or heroic, are:

  (I) The fable itself.
 (II) The order or manner of its contrivance in relation of the parts to the whole.
(III) The manners or decency of the characters in speaking or acting what is proper for them, and proper to be shewn by the poet.
(IV) The thoughts which express the manners.
 (V) The words which express those thoughts.

In the last of these Homer excels Virgil, Virgil all other ancient poets, and Shakespeare all modern poets.

For the second of these, the order: the meaning is that a fable ought to have a beginning, middle, and an end,[10] all just and natural, so that that part which is the middle, could not naturally be the beginning or end, and so of the rest: all are depending one on another, like the links of a curious chain.

If terror and pity are only to be raised, certainly this author follows Aristotle's rules, and Sophocles' and Euripides' example; but joy may be raised too, and that doubly, either by seeing a wicked man punished, or a

---

[9] René Rapin (1621–87), *Réflexions sur la poétique d'Aristote* (1674), 'En particulier', x. Rapin's work was translated into English by Rymer in the same year. A revised edition of the French appeared in 1675.
[10] Aristotle, *Poetics*, ch. vii.

good man at last fortunate; or perhaps indignation, to see wickedness prosperous and goodness depressed: both these may be profitable to the end of tragedy, reformation of manners; but the last improperly, only as it begets pity in the audience: tho' Aristotle, I confess, places tragedies of this kind in the second form.[11]

And, if we should grant that the Greeks performed this better, perhaps it may admit a dispute whether pity and terror are either the prime, or at least the only ends of tragedy.

'Tis not enough that Aristotle has said so, for Aristotle drew his models of tragedy from Sophocles and Euripides; and if he had seen ours, might have changed his mind.

And chiefly we have to say (what I hinted on pity and terror in the last paragraph save one) that the punishment of vice and reward of virtue are the most adequate ends of tragedy, because most conducing to good example of life. Now pity is not so easily raised for a criminal (as the ancient tragedy always represents its chief person such) as it is for an innocent man, and the suffering of innocence and punishment of the offender is of the nature of English tragedy: contrary in the Greek, innocence is unhappy often, and the offender escapes.

Then, we are not touched with the sufferings of any sort of men so much as of lovers; and this was almost unknown to the Ancients; so that they neither administered poetical justice (of which Mr Rymer boasts) so well as we; neither knew they the best commonplace of pity, which is love.

He therefore unjustly blames us for not building upon what the Ancients left us, for it seems, upon consideration of the premisses, that we have wholly finished what they began.

My judgment on this piece is this: that it is extremely learned; but that the author of it is better read in the Greek than in the English poets; that all writers ought to study this critique as the best account I have ever seen of the Ancients; that the model of tragedy he has here given is excellent and extreme correct; but that it is not the only model of all tragedy, because it is too much circumscribed in plot, characters, etc.; and lastly, that we may be taught here justly to admire and imitate the Ancients, without giving them the preference, with this author, in prejudice to our own country.

[11] Ibid., ch. xiii.

Want of method in this excellent treatise makes the thoughts of the author sometimes obscure.

His meaning, that pity and terror are to be moved, is that they are to be moved as the means conducing to the ends of tragedy, which are pleasure and instruction.

And these two ends may be thus distinguished. The chief end of the poet is to please; for his immediate reputation depends on it.

The great end of the poem is to instruct, which is performed by making pleasure the vehicle of that instruction: for poetry is an art, and all arts are made to profit.

The pity which the poet is to labour for is for the criminal, not for those, or him, whom he has murdered, or who have been the occasion of the tragedy. The terror is likewise in the punishment of the same criminal who, if he be represented too great an offender, will not be pitied; if altogether innocent, his punishment will be unjust.[12]

Another obscurity is where he says Sophocles perfected tragedy by introducing the third actor;[13] that is, he meant three kinds of action, one company singing or speaking, another playing on the music, a third dancing.

Rapin attributes more to the *dictio*, that is, to the words and discourses of a tragedy, than Aristotle has done, who places them in the last rank of beauties; perhaps only last in order, because they are the last product of the design, of the disposition or connection of its parts; of the characters, of the manners of those characters, and of the thoughts proceeding from those manners.

Rapin's words are remarkable: ' 'Tis not the admirable intrigue, the surprising events, and extraordinary incidents that make the beauty of a tragedy; 'tis the discourses, when they are natural and passionate.'[14]

So are Shakespeare's.

[12] Ibid.
[13] *Critical Works*, p. 22.
[14] *Réflexions*, 'En général', xxvi.

THE GROUNDS OF CRITICISM IN TRAGEDY

From the PREFACE TO *TROILUS AND CRESSIDA*

Troilus and Cressida, Dryden's adaptation of Shakespeare's play, was printed in 1679. *The Grounds of Criticism in Tragedy* follows the Preface. It amplifies some of the arguments which Dryden had sketched out in *Heads of an Answer to Rymer*, and shows him clearly aware of some of the weaknesses of contemporary drama: 'confused passions' and lack of distinctness between characters.

Tragedy is thus defined by Aristotle[1] (omitting what I thought unnecessary in his definition). 'Tis an imitation of one entire, great, and probable action; not told, but represented; which, by moving in us fear and pity, is conducive to the purging of those two passions in our minds. More largely thus, tragedy describes or paints an action, which action must have all the properties above named. First, it must be one or single, that is, it must not be a history of one man's life: suppose of Alexander the Great, or Julius Caesar, but one single action of theirs. This condemns all Shakespeare's historical plays, which are rather chronicles represented than tragedies, and all double action of plays. As to avoid a satire upon others, I will make bold with my own *Marriage à-la-Mode*, where there are manifestly two actions, not depending on one another: but in *Oedipus* there cannot properly be said to be two actions, because the love of Adrastus and Eurydice has a necessary dependence on the principal design, into which it is woven. The natural reason of this rule is plain, for two different independent actions distract the attention and concernment of the audience, and consequently destroy the intention of the poet: if his business be to move terror and pity, and one of his actions be comical, the other tragical, the former will divert the people, and utterly make void his greater purpose. Therefore, as in perspective, so in tragedy, there must be a point of sight in which all the lines terminate; otherwise the eye wanders, and the work is false. This was the practice of the Grecian stage. But Terence made an innovation in the Roman: all his plays have double actions; for it was his custom to translate two Greek comedies, and to weave them into one of his, yet so that both the actions were comical,

[1] In *Poetics*, ch. vi.

and one was principal, the other but secondary or subservient. And this has obtained on the English stage, to give us the pleasure of variety.

As the action ought to be one, it ought, as such, to have order in it, that is, to have a natural beginning, a middle, and an end. A natural beginning, says Aristotle, is that which could not necessarily have been placed after another thing, and so of the rest.[2] This consideration will arraign all plays after the new model of Spanish plots, where accident is heaped upon accident, and that which is first might as reasonably be last: an inconvenience not to be remedied but by making one accident naturally produce another, otherwise 'tis a farce and not a play. Of this nature is the *Slighted Maid*,[3] where there is no scene in the first act which might not by as good reason be in the fifth. And if the action ought to be one, the tragedy ought likewise to conclude with the action of it. Thus in *Mustapha*,[4] the play should naturally have ended with the death of Zanger, and not have given us the grace cup after dinner of Solyman's divorce from Roxolana.

The following properties of the action are so easy that they need not my explaining. It ought to be great, and to consist of great persons to distinguish it from comedy, where the action is trivial, and the persons of inferior rank. The last quality of the action is that it ought to be probable, as well as admirable and great. 'Tis not necessary that there should be historical truth in it; but always necessary that there should be a likeness of truth, something that is more than barely possible, *probable* being that which succeeds or happens oftener than it misses. To invent therefore a probability, and to make it wonderful, is the most difficult undertaking in the art of poetry; for that which is not wonderful is not great; and that which is not probable will not delight a reasonable audience. This action, thus described, must be represented and not told, to distinguish dramatic poetry from epic: but I hasten to the end or scope of tragedy, which is, to rectify or purge our passions, fear and pity.

To instruct delightfully is the general end of all poetry. Philosophy instructs, but it performs its work by precept: which is not delightful, or not so delightful as example. To purge the passions by example is therefore the particular instruction which belongs to tragedy. Rapin, a judicious critic, has observed from Aristotle that pride and want of commiseration are the most predominant vices in mankind;[5] therefore, to cure us of these two, the inventors of tragedy have chosen to work upon two other passions, which are fear and pity. We are wrought to fear by their setting before our eyes some terrible example of misfortune, which happened to persons of the

[2] *Poetics*, ch. vii.
[3] A comedy of 1663, by Sir Robert Stapylton (d. 1669).
[4] An heroic play by Roger Boyle (1621–79), Earl of Orrery. It was first performed in 1665.
[5] Rapin, *Réflexions*, 'En particulier', xvii.

highest quality; for such an action demonstrates to us that no condition is privileged from the turns of fortune: this must of necessity cause terror in us, and consequently abate our pride. But when we see that the most virtuous, as well as the greatest, are not exempt from such misfortunes, that consideration moves pity in us, and insensibly works us to be helpful to, and tender over, the distressed, which is the noblest and most god-like of moral virtues. Here 'tis observable that it is absolutely necessary to make a man virtuous, if we desire he should be pitied: we lament not, but detest, a wicked man, we are glad when we behold his crimes are punished, and that poetical justice[6] is done upon him. Euripides was censured by the critics of his time for making his chief characters too wicked: for example, Phaedra, though she loved her son-in-law with reluctancy, and that curse upon her family for offending Venus, yet was thought too ill a pattern for the stage. Shall we therefore banish all characters of villainy? I confess I am not of that opinion; but it is necessary that the hero of the play be not a villain: that is, the characters which should move our pity ought to have virtuous inclinations, and degrees of moral goodness in them. As for a perfect character of virtue, it never was in nature, and therefore there can be no imitation of it; but there are allays of frailty to be allowed for the chief persons, yet so that the good which is in them shall outweigh the bad, and consequently leave room for punishment on the one side, and pity on the other.

After all, if anyone will ask me whether a tragedy cannot be made upon any other grounds than those of exciting pity and terror in us, Bossu, the best of modern critics, answers thus in general: that all excellent arts, and particularly that of poetry, have been invented and brought to perfection by men of a transcendent genius; and that therefore they who practise afterwards the same arts are obliged to tread in their footsteps, and to search in their writings the foundation of them; for it is not just that new rules should destroy the authority of the old.[7] But Rapin writes more particularly thus: that no passions in a story are so proper to move our concernment as fear and pity; and that it is from our concernment we receive our pleasure, is undoubted; when the soul becomes agitated with fear for one character, or hope for another, then it is that we are pleased in tragedy by the interest which we take in their adventures.[8]

Here, therefore, the general answer may be given to the first question, how far we ought to imitate Shakespeare and Fletcher in their plots; namely, that we ought to follow them so far only as they have copied the excellencies of those who invented and brought to perfection dramatic poetry: those things only excepted which religion, customs of countries,

---

[6] Cf. p. 550n.
[7] Le Bossu (1631–89), *Du Poème épique* (1675), I, i.
[8] *Réflexions*, 'En particulier', xviii.

idioms of languages, etc., have altered in the superstructures, but not in the foundation of the design.

How defective Shakespeare and Fletcher have been in all their plots, Mr Rymer has discovered in his criticisms: neither can we who follow them be excused from the same or greater errors; which are the more unpardonable in us, because we want their beauties to countervail our faults. The best of their designs, the most approaching to antiquity, and the most conducing to move pity, is the *King and No King*; which, if the farce of Bessus were thrown away, is of that inferior sort of tragedies which end with a prosperous event. 'Tis probably derived from the story of Oedipus, with the character of Alexander the Great, in his extravagancies, given to Arbaces. The taking of this play, amongst many others, I cannot wholly ascribe to the excellency of the action; for I find it moving when it is read: 'tis true, the faults of the plot are so evidently proved that they can no longer be denied. The beauties of it must therefore lie either in the lively touches of the passions: or we must conclude, as I think we may, that even in imperfect plots there are less degrees of nature, by which some faint emotions of pity and terror are raised in us: as a less engine will raise a less proportion of weight, though not so much as one of Archimedes' making; for nothing can move our nature, but by some natural reason, which works upon passions. And since we acknowledge the effect, there must be something in the cause.

The difference between Shakespeare and Fletcher in their plotting seems to be this, that Shakespeare generally moves more terror, and Fletcher more compassion. For the first had a more masculine, a bolder and more fiery genius; the second, a more soft and womanish. In the mechanic beauties of the plot, which are the observation of the three unities, time, place, and action, they are both deficient; but Shakespeare most. Ben Jonson reformed those errors in his comedies, yet one of Shakespeare's was regular before him; which is *The Merry Wives of Windsor*. For what remains concerning the design, you are to be referred to our English critic. That method which he has prescribed to raise it from mistake, or ignorance of the crime, is certainly the best, though 'tis not the only: for amongst all the tragedies of Sophocles, there is but one, *Oedipus*, which is wholly built after that model.

After the plot, which is the foundation of the play, the next thing to which we ought to apply our judgment is the manners, for now the poet comes to work above ground: the ground-work indeed is that which is most necessary, as that upon which depends the firmness of the whole fabric; yet it strikes not the eye so much as the beauties or imperfections of the manners, the thoughts, and the expressions.

The first rule which Bossu prescribes to the writer of an heroic poem, and which holds too by the same reason in all dramatic poetry, is to make the moral of the work; that is, to lay down to yourself what the precept of morality should be, which you would insinuate into the people: as namely Homer's (which I have copied in my *Conquest of Granada*) was that union preserves a commonwealth, and discord destroys it; Sophocles, in his *Oedipus,* that no man is to be accounted happy before his death. 'Tis the moral that directs the whole action of the play to one centre; and that action or fable is the example built upon the moral, which confirms the truth of it to our experience: when the fable is designed, then, and not before, the persons are to be introduced with their manners, characters, and passions.

The manners in a poem are understood to be those inclinations, whether natural or acquired, which move and carry us to actions, good, bad, or indifferent, in a play; or which incline the persons to such or such actions. I have anticipated part of this discourse already, in declaring that a poet ought not to make the manners perfectly good in his best persons; but neither are they to be more wicked in any of his characters than necessity requires. To produce a villain, without other reason than a natural inclination to villainy is, in poetry, to produce an effect without a cause; and to make him more a villain than he has just reason to be, is to make an effect which is stronger than the cause.

The manners arise from many causes; and are either distinguished by complexion, as choleric and phlegmatic, or by the differences of age or sex, of climates, or quality of the persons, or their present condition: they are likewise to be gathered from the several virtues, vices, or passions, and many other commonplaces which a poet must be supposed to have learned from natural philosophy, ethics, and history; of all which whosoever is ignorant, does not deserve the name of poet.

But as the manners are useful in this art, they may be all comprised under these general heads: first, they must be apparent; that is, in every character of the play, some inclinations of the person must appear; and these are shown in the actions and discourse. Secondly, the manners must be suitable, or agreeing to the persons; that is, to the age, sex, dignity, and the other general heads of manners: thus, when a poet has given the dignity of a king to one of his persons, in all his actions and speeches, that person must discover majesty, magnanimity, and jealousy of power, because these are suitable to the general manners of a king. The third property of manners is resemblance; and this is founded upon the particular characters of men, as we have them delivered to us by relation or history: that is, when a poet has the known character of this or that man before him, he is bound to represent him such, at least not contrary to that which fame has reported him to have been. Thus, it is not a poet's choice to make Ulysses choleric, or Achilles patient, because Homer has described 'em quite otherwise. Yet this is a rock on which ignorant writers daily split; and the absurdity is as monstrous as if a painter should draw a coward running from a battle, and tell us it was the picture of Alexander the Great.

The last property of manners is that they be constant and equal, that is, maintained the same through the whole design: thus, when Virgil had once given the name of *pious* to Æneas, he was bound to show him such, in all his words and actions through the whole poem. All these properties Horace has hinted to a judicious observer: 1. *notandi sunt tibi mores*; 2. *aut famam sequere*; 3. *aut sibi convenientia finge*; 4. *servetur ad imum, qualis ab incepto processerat, et sibi constet.*[9]

From the manners, the characters of persons are derived; for indeed the characters are no other than the inclinations, as they appear in the several persons of the poem; a character being thus defined, that which distinguishes one man from another. Not to repeat the same things over again which have been said of the manners, I will only add what is necessary here. A character, or that which distinguishes one man from all others, cannot be supposed to consist of one particular virtue, or vice, or passion only; but 'tis a composition of qualities which are not contrary to one another in the same person: thus the same man may be liberal and valiant, but not liberal and covetous; so in a comical character or humour (which is an inclination to this or that particular folly), Falstaff is a liar, and a coward, a glutton, and a buffoon, because all these qualities may agree in the same man; yet it is still to be observed that one virtue, vice and passion ought to be shown in every man, as predominant over all the rest; as covetousness in Crassus, love of his country in Brutus; and the same in characters which are feigned.

The chief character or hero in a tragedy, as I have already shown, ought in prudence to be such a man who has so much more in him of virtue than of vice, that he may be left amiable to the audience, which otherwise cannot have any concernment for his sufferings; and 'tis on this one character that the pity and terror must be principally, if not wholly, founded. A rule which is extremely necessary, and which none of the critics that I know have fully enough discovered to us. For terror and compassion work but weakly when they are divided into many persons. If Creon had been the chief character in *Oedipus*, there had neither been terror nor compassion moved; but only detestation of the man and joy for his punishment; if Adrastus and Eurydice had been made more appealing characters, then the pity had been divided, and lessened on the part of Oedipus: but making Oedipus the best and bravest person, and even Jocasta but an underpart to him, his virtues and the punishment of his fatal crime drew both the pity and the terror to himself.

[9] *Ars Poetica*, ll. 156, 119, 126–7: 'You must note the manners of each age'; 'either follow tradition, or invent what is self-consistent'; 'have each character kept to the end even as it came forth at first, and have it self-consistent'.

By what has been said of the manners, it will be easy for a reasonable man to judge whether the characters be truly or falsely drawn in a tragedy; for if there be no manners appearing in the characters, no concernment for the persons can be raised; no pity or horror can be moved, but by vice or virtue; therefore, without them, no person can have any business in the play. If the inclinations be obscure, 'tis a sign the poet is in the dark, and knows not what manner of man he presents to you; and consequently you can have no idea, or very imperfect, of that man; nor can judge what resolutions he ought to take; or what words or actions are proper for him. Most comedies made up of accidents or adventures are liable to fall into this error; and tragedies with many turns are subject to it; for the manners never can be evident where the surprises of fortune take up all the business of the stage; and where the poet is more in pain to tell you what happened to such a man than what he was. 'Tis one of the excellencies of Shakespeare that the manners of his persons are generally apparent, and you see their bent and inclinations. Fletcher comes far short of him in this, as indeed he does almost in everything: there are but glimmerings of manners in most of his comedies, which run upon adventures; and in his tragedies, Rollo, Otto,[10] the King and No King, Melantius,[11] and many others of his best, are but pictures shown you in the twilight; you know not whether they resemble vice or virtue, and they are either good, bad, or indifferent, as the present scene requires it. But of all poets, this commendation is to be given to Ben Jonson, that the manners even of the most inconsiderable persons in his plays are everywhere apparent.

By considering the second quality of manners, which is that they be suitable to the age, quality, country, dignity, etc., of the character, we may likewise judge whether a poet has followed nature. In this kind, Sophocles and Euripides have more excelled among the Greeks than Æschylus; and Terence more than Plautus among the Romans. Thus Sophocles gives to Oedipus the true qualities of a king, in both those plays which bear his name; but in the latter, which is the *Oedipus Colonoeus*, he lets fall on purpose his tragic style; his hero speaks not in the arbitrary tone, but remembers, in the softness of his complaints, that he is an unfortunate blind old man; that he is banished from his country, and persecuted by his next relations. The present French poets are generally accused that wheresoever they lay the scene, or in whatsoever age, the manners of their heroes are wholly French. Racine's Bajazet is bred at Constantinople; but his civilities are conveyed to him by some secret passage, from Versailles into the Seraglio. But our Shakespeare, having ascribed to Henry the Fourth the character of a king and of a father, gives him the perfect manners of each relation, when either

[10] The brothers in *Rollo*.
[11] In *The Maid's Tragedy*.

he transacts with his son or with his subjects. Fletcher, on the other side, gives neither to Arbaces, nor to his king in the *Maid's Tragedy*, the qualities which are suitable to a monarch; though he may be excused a little in the latter, for the king there is not uppermost in the character; 'tis the lover of Evadne, who is king only in a second consideration; and though he be unjust, and has other faults which shall be nameless, yet he is not the hero of the play. 'Tis true, we find him a lawful prince (though I never heard of any King that was in Rhodes), and therefore Mr Rymer's criticism stands good; that he should not be shown in so vicious a character. Sophocles has been more judicious in his *Antigona*; for though he represents in Creon a bloody prince, yet he makes him not a lawful king, but an usurper, and Antigona herself is the heroine of the tragedy. But when Philaster wounds Arethusa and the boy, and Perigot his mistress in *The Faithful Shepherdess*, both these are contrary to the character of manhood. Nor is Valentinian managed much better, for though Fletcher has taken his picture truly, and shown him as he was, an effeminate, voluptuous man, yet he has forgotten that he was an emperor, and has given him none of those royal marks which ought to appear in a lawful successor of the throne. If it be inquired what Fletcher should have done on this occasion; ought he not to have represented Valentinian as he was? Bossu shall answer this question for me, by an instance of the like nature: Mauritius, the Greek Emperor, was a prince far surpassing Valentinian, for he was endued with many kingly virtues; he was religious, merciful, and valiant, but withal he was noted of extreme covetousness, a vice which is contrary to the character of a hero, or a prince: therefore, says the critic, that Emperor was no fit person to be represented in a tragedy, unless his good qualities were only to be shown, and his covetousness (which sullied them all) were slurred over by the artifice of the poet.[12] To return once more to Shakespeare: no man ever drew so many characters, or generally distinguished 'em better from one another, excepting only Jonson. I will instance but in one, to show the copiousness of his invention: 'tis that of Caliban, or the Monster in the *Tempest*. He seems there to have created a person which was not in nature, a boldness which at first sight would appear intolerable: for he makes him a species of himself, begotten by an incubus on a witch; but this, as I have elsewhere proved, is not wholly beyond the bounds of credibility, at least the vulgar still believe it. We have the separated notions of a spirit, and of a witch; (and spirits, according to Plato, are vested with a subtle body; according to some of his followers, have different sexes); therefore, as from the distinct apprehensions of a horse, and of a man, imagination has formed a centaur; so from those of an incubus and a sorceress, Shakespeare has produced his monster.

[12] Le Bossu, *Du Poème épique*, IV, vii.

Whether or no his generation can be defended, I leave to philosophy; but of this I am certain, that the poet has most judiciously furnished him with a person, a language, and a character, which will suit him, both by father's and mother's side: he has all the discontents and malice of a witch, and of a devil, besides a convenient proportion of the deadly sins; gluttony, sloth, and lust are manifest; the dejectedness of a slave is likewise given him, and the ignorance of one bred up in a desert island. His person is monstrous, as he is the product of unnatural lust; and his language is as hobgoblin as his person; in all things he is distinguished from other mortals. The characters of Fletcher are poor and narrow, in comparison of Shakespeare's; I remember not one which is not borrowed from him; unless you will except that strange mixture of a man in the *King and No King*: so that in this part Shakespeare is generally worth our imitation; and to imitate Fletcher is but to copy after him who was a copier.

Under this general head of manners, the passions are naturally included as belonging to the characters. I speak not of pity and of terror, which are to be moved in the audience by the plot; but of anger, hatred, love, ambition, jealousy, revenge, etc., as they are shown in this or that person of the play. To describe these naturally, and to move then artfully, is one of the greatest commendations which can be given to a poet: to write pathetically, says Longinus, cannot proceed but for a lofty genius.[13] A poet must be born with this quality; yet, unless he help himself by an acquired knowledge of the passions, what they are in their own nature, and by what springs they are to be moved, he will be subject either to raise them where they ought not to be raised, or not to raise them by the just degrees of nature, or to amplify them beyond the natural bounds, or not to observe the crisis and turns of them, in their cooling and decay: all which errors proceed from want of judgment in the poet, and from being unskilled in the principles of moral philosophy. Nothing is more frequent in a fanciful writer than to foil himself by not managing his strength; therefore, as in a wrestler, there is first required some measure of force, a well-knit body, and active limbs, without which all instruction would be vain; yet, these being granted, if he want the skill which is necessary to a wrestler, he shall make but small advantage of his natural robustuousness: so, in a poet, his inborn vehemence and force of spirit will only run him out of breath the sooner, if it be not supported by the help of art. The roar of passion indeed may please an audience, three parts of which are ignorant enough to think all is moving which is noise, and it may stretch the lungs of an ambitious actor, who will die upon the spot for a thundering clap; but it will move no other passion than indignation and contempt from judicious men. Longinus, whom I have hitherto

[13] Longinus, ch. viii.

followed, continues thus: *If the passions be artfully employed, the discourse becomes vehement and lofty; if otherwise, there is nothing more ridiculous than a great passion out of season*: and to this purpose he animadverts severely upon Æschylus, who writ nothing in cold blood, but was always in a rapture, and in fury with his audience:[14] the inspiration was still upon him, he was ever tearing it upon the tripos; or (to run off as madly as he does, from one similitude to another) he was always at high flood of passion, even in the dead ebb and lowest water-mark of the scene. He who would raise the passion of a judicious audience, says a learned critic,[15] must be sure to take his hearers along with him; if they be in a calm, 'tis in vain for him to be in a huff: he must move them by degrees, and kindle with 'em; otherwise he will be in danger of setting his own heap of stubble on a fire, and of burning out by himself without warming the company that stand about him. They who would justify the madness of poetry from the authority of Aristotle have mistaken the text, and consequently the interpretation: I imagine it to be false read, where he says of poetry that it is εὐφυοῦς ἢ μονικου, that it had always somewhat in it either of a genius, or of a madman.[16] 'Tis more probable that the original ran thus, that poetry was εὐφυοῦς οὐ μανικοῦ, that it belongs to a witty man, but not to a madman. Thus then the passions, as they are considered simply and in themselves, suffer violence when they are perpetually maintained at the same height; for what melody can be made on that instrument all whose strings are screwed up at first to their utmost stretch, and to the same sound? But this is not the worst; for the characters likewise bear a part in the general calamity, if you consider the passions as embodied in them; for it follows of necessity that no man can be distinguished from another by his discourse, when every man is ranting, swaggering, and exclaiming with the same excess: as if it were the only business of all the characters to contend with each other for the prize at Billingsgate; or that the scene of the tragedy lay in Bet'lem.[17] Suppose the poet should intend this man to be choleric, and that man to be patient; yet when they are confounded in the writing you cannot distinguish them from one another: for the man who was called patient and tame is only so before he speaks; but let his clack be set a-going, and he shall tongue it as impetuously, and as loudly, as the errantest hero in the play. By this means, the characters are only distinct in name; but in reality all the men and women in the play are the same person. No man should pretend to write who cannot temper his fancy with his judgment: nothing is more dangerous to a raw horseman than a hot-mouthed jade without a curb.

[14] Ibid., ch. iii.
[15] Le Bossu, III, ix.
[16] *Poetics*, ch. xvii.
[17] I.e. Bedlam.

'Tis necessary therefore for a poet who would concern an audience by describing of a passion, first to prepare it, and not to rush upon it all at once. Ovid has judiciously shown the difference of these two ways, in the speeches of Ajax and Ulysses: Ajax from the very beginning breaks out into his exclamations, and is swearing by his Maker, *agimus, proh Jupiter, inquit*.[18] Ulysses, on the contrary, prepares his audience with all the submissiveness he can practise, and all the calmness of a reasonable man; he found his judges in a tranquillity of spirit, and therefore set out leisurely and softly with 'em, till he had warmed 'em by degrees; and then he began to mend his pace, and to draw them along with his own impetuousness: yet so managing his breath, that it might not fail him at his need, and reserving his utmost proofs of ability even to the last. The success, you see, was answerable; for the crowd only applauded the speech of Ajax:

> vulgique secutum
> ultima murmur erat:[19]

But the judges awarded the prize for which they contended to Ulysses:

> mota manus procerum est; et quid facundia posset
> tum patuit, fortisque viri tulit arma disertus.[20]

The next necessary rule is to put nothing into the discourse which may hinder your moving of the passions. Too many accidents, as I have said, encumber the poet, as much as the arms of Saul did David; for the variety of passions which they produce are ever crossing and jostling each other out of the way. He who treats of joy and grief together is in a fair way of causing neither of those effects. There is yet another obstacle to be removed, which is pointed wit, and sentences affected out of season; these are nothing of kin to the violence of passion: no man is at leisure to make sentences and similes when his soul is in an agony. I the rather name this fault that it may serve to mind me of my former errors; neither will I spare myself, but give an example of this kind from my *Indian Emperor*. Montezuma, pursued by his enemies, and seeking sanctuary, stands parleying without the fort, and describing his danger to Cydaria, in a simile of six lines:

> As on the sands the frighted traveller
> Sees the high seas come rolling from afar, etc.[21]

My Indian potentate was well skilled in the sea for an inland prince, and

---

[18] *Metamorphoses*, XIII, 5.

[19] Ibid., l. 123.

[20] Ibid., ll. 382–3: 'The company of chiefs was moved, and their decision proved the power of eloquence: to the eloquent man were given the brave man's arms.' Dryden omits 'tulit'.

[21] v. ii. 200.

well improved since the first act, when he sent his son to discover it. The image had not been amiss from another man, at another time: *sed nunc non erat hisce locus*:[22] he destroyed the concernment which the audience might otherwise have had for him; for they could not think the danger near when he had the leisure to invent a simile.

If Shakespeare be allowed, as I think he must, to have made his characters distinct, it will easily be inferred that he understood the nature of the passions: because it has been proved already that confused passions make undistinguishable characters: yet I cannot deny that he has his failings; but they are not so much in the passions themselves as in his manner of expression: he often obscures his meaning by his words, and sometimes makes it unintelligible. I will not say of so great a poet that he distinguished not the blown puffy style from true sublimity; but I may venture to maintain that the fury of his fancy often transported him beyond the bounds of judgment, either in coining of new words and phrases, or racking words which were in use into the violence of a catachresis. 'Tis not that I would explode the use of metaphors from passions, for Longinus thinks 'em necessary to raise it; but to use 'em at every word, to say nothing without a metaphor, a simile, an image, or description, is I doubt to smell a little too strongly of the buskin. I must be forced to give an example of expressing passion figuratively; but that I may do it with respect to Shakespeare, it shall not be taken from any thing of his: 'tis an exclamation against Fortune, quoted in his *Hamlet*, but written by some other poet:

> Out, out, thou strumpet Fortune! all you gods,
> In general synod, take away her power,
> Break all the spokes and fellies from her wheel,
> And bowl the round nave down the hill of heaven,
> As low as to the fiends.[23]

And immediately after, speaking of Hecuba, when Priam was killed before her eyes:

> The mobbled queen ran up and down,
> Threatening the flame with bisson rheum; a clout about that head
> Where late the diadem stood; and for a robe,
> About her lank and all o'er-teemed loins,
> A blanket in th' alarm of fear caught up.
> Who this had seen, with tongue in venom steep'd
> 'Gainst Fortune's state would treason have pronounced;
> But if the gods themselves did see her then,

[22] *Ars Poetica*, l. 19: 'For such things there is a place, but not just now.'
[23] *Hamlet*, II. ii. 469–73.

When she saw Pyrrhus make malicious sport
In mincing with his sword her husband's limbs,
The instant burst of clamour that she made
(Unless things mortal move them not at all)
Would have made milch the burning eyes of Heaven,
And passion in the gods.[24]

What a pudder is here kept in raising the expression of trifling thoughts! Would not a man have thought that the poet had been bound prentice to a wheelwright, for his first rant? and had followed a ragman for the clout and blanket, in the second? Fortune is painted on a wheel, and therefore the writer, in a rage, will have poetical justice done upon every member of that engine: after this execution, he bowls the nave down hill, from heaven to the fiends (an unreasonable long mark, a man would think); 'tis well there are no solid orbs to stop it in the way, or no element of fire to consume it: but when it came to the earth, it must be monstrous heavy, to break ground as low as to the centre. His making milch the burning eyes of heaven was a pretty tolerable flight too: and I think no man ever drew milk out of eyes before him: yet, to make the wonder greater, these eyes were burning. Such a sight indeed were enough to have raised passion in the gods; but to excuse the effects of it, he tells you, perhaps they did not see it. Wise men would be glad to find a little sense couched under all those pompous words; for bombast is commonly the delight of that audience which loves poetry, but understands it not: and as commonly has been the practice of those writers who, not being able to infuse a natural passion into the mind, have made it their business to ply the ears and to stun their judges by the noise. But Shakespeare does not often thus; for the passions in his scene between Brutus and Cassius are extremely natural, the thoughts are such as arise from the matter, and the expression of 'em not viciously figurative. I cannot leave this subject before I do justice to that divine poet by giving you one of his passionate descriptions: 'tis of Richard the Second when he was deposed, and led in triumph through the streets of London by Henry of Bullingbrook: the painting of it is so lively, and the words so moving, that I have scarce read anything comparable to it in any other language. Suppose you have seen already the fortunate usurper passing through the crowd, and followed by the shouts and acclamations of the people; and now behold King Richard entering upon the scene: consider the wretchedness of his condition, and his carriage in it; and refrain from pity if you can:

As in a theatre, the eyes of men,
After a well-graced actor leaves the stage,
Are idly bent on him that enters next,

[24] Ibid., ll. 480–94.

Thinking his prattle to be tedious:
Even so, or with much more contempt, men's eyes
Did scowl on Richard: no man cried, God save him:
No joyful tongue gave him his welcome home,
But dust was thrown upon his sacred head,
Which with such gentle sorrow he shook off,
His face still combating with tears and smiles
(The badges of his grief and patience),
That had not God (for some strong purpose) steeled
The hearts of men, they must perforce have melted,
And barbarism itself have pitied him.[25]

To speak justly of this whole matter: 'tis neither height of thought that is discommended, nor pathetic vehemence, nor any nobleness of expression in its proper place; but 'tis a false measure of all these, something which is like 'em, and is not them; 'tis the Bristol-stone,[26] which appears like a diamond; 'tis an extravagant thought, instead of a sublime one; 'tis roaring madness instead of vehemence; and a sound of words instead of sense. If Shakespeare were stripped of all the bombast in his passions, and dressed in the most vulgar words, we should find the beauties of his thoughts remaining; if his embroideries were burnt down, there would still be silver at the bottom of the melting-pot: but I fear (at least let me fear it for myself) that we who ape his sounding words have nothing of his thought, but are all outside; there is not so much as a dwarf within our giant's clothes. Therefore, let not Shakespeare suffer for our sakes; 'tis our fault, who succeed him in an age which is more refined, if we imitate him so ill that we copy his failings only, and make a virtue of that in our writings which in his was an imperfection.

For what remains, the excellency of that poet was, as I have said, in the more manly passions; Fletcher's in the softer: Shakespeare writ better betwixt man and man; Fletcher, betwixt man and woman: consequently, the one described friendship better; the other love: yet Shakespeare taught Fletcher to write love: and Juliet, and Desdemona, are originals. 'Tis true, the scholar had the softer soul; but the master had the kinder. Friendship is both a virtue and a passion essentially; love is a passion only in its nature, and is not a virtue but by accident: good nature makes friendship; but effeminacy love. Shakespeare had an universal mind, which comprehended all characters and passions; Fletcher a more confined and limited: for though he treated love in perfection, yet honour, ambition, revenge, and generally all the stronger passions, he either touched not, or not masterly. To conclude all, he was a limb of Shakespeare.

[25] *Richard II*, v. ii. 23–37.
[26] 'A kind of transparent rockcrystal . . . resembling the diamond in brilliancy' (*OED*).

I had intended to have proceeded to the last property of manners, which is that they must be constant, and the characters maintained the same from the beginning to the end; and from thence to have proceeded to the thoughts and expressions suitable to a tragedy: but I will first see how this will relish with the age. 'Tis, I confess, but cursorily written; yet the judgment which is given here is generally founded upon experience: but because many men are shocked at the name of rules, as if they were a kind of magisterial prescription upon poets, I will conclude with the words of Rapin, in his reflections on Aristotle's work of poetry: 'If the rules be well considered, we shall find them to be made only to reduce nature into method, to trace her step by step, and not to suffer the least mark of her to escape us: 'tis only by these that probability in fiction is maintained, which is the soul of poetry. They are founded upon good sense, and sound reason, rather than on authority; for though Aristotle and Horace are produced, yet no man must argue that what they write is true because they writ it; but 'tis evident, by the ridiculous mistakes and gross absurdities which have been made by those poets who have taken their fancy only for their guide, that if this fancy be not regulated, 'tis a mere caprice, and utterly incapable to produce a reasonable and judicious poem.'[27]

[27] *Réflexions*, 'En général', xii.

From the PREFACE TO OVID'S EPISTLES

Ovid's Epistles, to which, among others, Dryden, Butler, Otway, and Tate contributed, appeared in 1680, with a Preface by Dryden. Dryden thus began a long and productive career in translation, and the Preface is important for a statement of his views on it. Johnson (in the *Life of Dryden*) considered that Dryden was responsible for 'breaking the shackles of verbal interpretation': 'It was reserved for Dryden', he says, 'to fix the limits of poetical liberty, and give us just rules and examples of translation.'

. . . Thus much concerning the poet, whom you find translated by divers hands, that you may at least have that variety in the English which the subject denied to the author of the Latin. It remains that I should say somewhat of poetical translations in general, and give my opinion (with submission to better judgments) which way of version seems to me the most proper.

All translations, I suppose, may be reduced to these three heads.

First, that of metaphrase, or turning an author word by word, and line by line, from one language into another. Thus, or near this manner, was Horace his Art of Poetry translated by Ben Jonson. The second way is that of paraphrase, or translation with latitude, where the author is kept in view by the translator, so as never to be lost, but his words are not so strictly followed as his sense, and that too is admitted to be amplified, but not altered. Such is Mr Waller's translation of Virgil's Fourth Aeneid. The third way is that of imitation, where the translator (if now he has not lost that name) assumes the liberty not only to vary from the words and sense, but to forsake them both as he sees occasion; and taking only some general hints from the original, to run division[1] on the ground-work, as he pleases. Such is Mr Cowley's practice in turning two Odes of Pindar, and one of Horace, into English.

Concerning the first of these methods, our master Horace has given us this caution:

[1] A musical term: to produce an accompaniment to, or a variation on, a theme.

nec verbum verbo curabis reddere, fidus
interpres.[2]
Nor word for word too faithfully translate;

as the Earl of Roscommon[3] has excellently rendered it. Too faithfully is
indeed pedantically: 'tis a faith like that which proceeds from superstition,
blind and zealous. Take it in the expression of Sir John Denham to Sir
Richard Fanshawe, on his version of the *Pastor Fido*:

> That servile path thou nobly dost decline,
> Of tracing word by word, and line by line:
> A new and nobler way thou dost pursue,
> To make translations and translators too:
> They but preserve the ashes, thou the flame,
> True to his sense, but truer to his fame.[4]

'Tis almost impossible to translate verbally, and well, at the same time;
for the Latin (a most severe and compendious language) often expresses that
in one word which either the barbarity or the narrowness of modern tongues
cannot supply in more. 'Tis frequent also that the conceit is couched in
some expression which will be lost in English:

> atque idem venti vela fidemque ferent.[5]

What poet of our nation is so happy as to express this thought literally in
English, and to strike wit, or almost sense, out of it?

In short, the verbal copier is encumbered with so many difficulties at
once that he can never disentangle himself from all. He is to consider at the
same time the thought of his author, and his words, and to find out the
counterpart to each in another language; and, besides this, he is to confine
himself to the compass of numbers, and the slavery of rhyme. 'Tis much like
dancing on ropes with fettered legs: a man may shun a fall by using caution,
but the gracefulness of motion is not to be expected: and when we have said
the best of it, 'tis but a foolish task; for no sober man would put himself into
a danger for the applause of scaping without breaking his neck. We see Ben
Jonson could not avoid obscurity in his literal translation of Horace,
attempted in the same compass of lines: nay, Horace himself could scarce
have done it to a Greek poet:

---

[2] *Ars Poetica*, ll. 133–4.
[3] Roscommon published a translation of the *Ars Poetica* in 1680.
[4] Denham's verses to Fanshawe's translation of 1647. Dryden's quotation omits four lines
from the original.
[5] Ovid, *Heroides*, VII, 8: 'And shall the same winds bear away from me at once your sails and
your promises?'

brevis esse laboro, obscurus fio:[6]

either perspicuity or gracefulness will frequently be wanting. Horace has indeed avoided both these rocks in his translation of the three first lines of Homer's Odysses, which he has contracted into two:

> dic mihi, Musa, virum captae post tempora Trojae,
> qui mores hominum multorum vidit, et urbes.[7]

> Muse, speak the man who, since the siege of Troy,
> So many towns, such change of manners saw.
>
> *Earl of Rosc.*

But then the sufferings of Ulysses, which are a considerable part of that sentence, are omitted:

$$\text{Ὃς μάλα πολλὰ πλάγχθη}$$

The consideration of these difficulties, in a servile, literal translation, not long since made two of our famous wits, Sir John Denham and Mr Cowley, to contrive another way of turning authors into our tongue, called by the latter of them, *imitation*. As they were friends, I suppose they communicated their thoughts on this subject to each other,[8] and therefore their reasons for it are little different; though the practice of one is much more moderate. I take imitation of an author, in their sense, to be an endeavour of a later poet to write like one who has written before him on the same subject; that is, not to translate his words, or to be confined to his sense, but only to set him as a pattern, and to write as he supposes that author would have done, had he lived in our age, and in our country. Yet I dare not say that either of them have carried this libertine way of rendering authors (as Mr Cowley calls it) so far as my definition reaches; for in the *Pindaric Odes* the customs and ceremonies of ancient Greece are still preserved. But I know not what mischief may arise hereafter from the example of such an innovation, when writers of unequal parts to him shall imitate so bold an undertaking. To add and to diminish what we please, which is the way avowed by him, ought only to be granted to Mr Cowley, and that too only in his translation of Pindar, because he alone was able to make him amends, by giving him better of his own whenever he refused his author's thoughts. Pindar is generally known to be a dark writer, to want connection (I mean as to our understanding), to soar out of sight, and leave his reader at a gaze. So wild and ungovernable a poet cannot be translated literally, his genius is too

---

[6] *Ars Poetica*, ll. 25–6: 'Striving to be brief, I become obscure.'
[7] Ibid., ll. 141–2.
[8] Denham's rendering of the second book of Virgil's *Aeneid* (The *Destruction of Troy*) and Cowley's imitations of Pindar both appeared in 1656.

strong to bear a chain, and Samson-like he shakes it off. A genius so elevated and unconfined as Mr Cowley's was but necessary to make Pindar speak English, and that was to be performed by no other way than imitation. But if Virgil, or Ovid, or any regular, intelligible authors be thus used, 'tis no longer to be called their work, when neither the thoughts nor words are drawn from the original; but instead of them there is something new produced, which is almost the creation of another hand. By this way, 'tis true, somewhat that is excellent may be invented, perhaps more excellent than the first design; though Virgil must be still excepted, when that perhaps takes place. Yet he who is inquisitive to know an author's thoughts will be disappointed in his expectation. And 'tis not always that a man will be contented to have a present made him, when he expects the payment of a debt. To state it fairly, imitation of an author is the most advantageous way for a translator to shew himself, but the greatest wrong which can be done to the memory and reputation of the dead. Sir John Denham (who advised more liberty than he took himself), gives this reason for his innovation, in his admirable preface before the translation of the Second Aeneid: 'Poetry is of so subtle a spirit that, in pouring out of one language into another, it will all evaporate; and if a new spirit be not added in the transfusion, there will remain nothing but a *caput mortuum*.' I confess this argument holds good against a literal translation; but who defends it? Imitation and verbal version are in my opinion the two extremes which ought to be avoided; and therefore, when I have proposed the mean betwixt them, it will be seen how far his argument will reach.

No man is capable of translating poetry who, besides a genius to that art, is not a master both of his author's language and of his own. Nor must we understand the language only of the poet, but his particular turn of thoughts and of expression, which are the characters that distinguish and, as it were, individuate him from all other writers. When we are come thus far, 'tis time to look into ourselves, to conform our genius to his, to give his thought either the same turn, if our tongue will bear it, or if not, to vary but the dress, not to alter or destroy the substance. The like care must be taken of the more outward ornaments, the words. When they appear (which is but seldom) literally graceful, it were an injury to the author that they should be changed. But since every language is so full of its own proprieties, that what is beautiful in one is often barbarous, nay sometimes nonsense, in another, it would be unreasonable to limit a translator to the narrow compass of his author's words: 'tis enough if he choose out some expression which does not vitiate the sense. I suppose he may stretch his chain to such a latitude; but by innovation of thoughts, methinks he breaks it. By this means the spirit of an author may be transfused, and yet not lost: and thus 'tis plain that the reason alleged by Sir John Denham has no farther force than to expression;

for thought, if it be translated truly, cannot be lost in another language; but the words that convey it to our apprehension (which are the image and ornament of that thought) may be so ill chosen as to make it appear in an unhandsome dress, and rob it of its native lustre. There is therefore a liberty to be allowed for the expression, neither is it necessary that words and lines should be confined to the measure of their original. The sense of an author, generally speaking, is to be sacred and inviolable. If the fancy of Ovid be luxuriant, 'tis his character to be so, and if I retrench it, he is no longer Ovid. It will be replied that he receives advantage by this lopping of his superfluous branches, but I rejoin that a translator has no such right. When a painter copies from the life, I suppose he has no privilege to alter features and lineaments, under pretence that his picture will look better: perhaps the face which he has drawn would be more exact if the eyes or nose were altered, but 'tis his business to make it resemble the original. In two cases only there may a seeming difficulty arise, that is, if the thought be notoriously trivial or dishonest. But the same answer will serve for both, that then they ought not to be translated.

et quae
desperes tractata nitescere posse, relinquas.[9]

Thus I have ventured to give my opinion on this subject against the authority of two great men, but I hope without offence to either of their memories, for I both loved them living, and reverence them now they are dead. But if, after what I have urged, it be thought by better judges that the praise of a translation consists in adding new beauties to the piece, thereby to recompense the loss which it sustains by change of language, I shall be willing to be taught better, and to recant. In the meantime, it seems to me that the true reason why we have so few versions which are tolerable is not from the too close pursuing of the author's sense, but because there are so few who have all the talents which are requisite for translation; and that there is so little praise and so small encouragement for so considerable a part of learning.

To apply, in short, what has been said, to this present work, the reader will here find most of the translations with some little latitude or variation from the author's sense: that of Oenone to Paris is in Mr Cowley's way of imitation only. I was desired to say that the author,[10] who is of the fair sex, understood not Latin. But if she does not, I am afraid she has given us occasion to be ashamed who do.

---

[9] Horace, *Ars Poetica*, ll. 149–50: 'and what he fears [desperat] he cannot make attractive with his touch he abandons'.

[10] Aphra Behn (1640–89).

For my own part, I am ready to acknowledge that I have transgressed the rules which I have given and taken more liberty than a just translation will allow. But so many gentlemen whose wit and learning are well known being joined in it, I doubt not but that their excellencies will make you ample satisfaction for my errors.

From the DISCOURSE CONCERNING SATIRE

The Satires of Decimus Junius Juvenalis, Translated into English Verse by Mr Dryden and Several Other Eminent Hands, Together with the Satires of Aulus Persius Flaccus was published in 1692. Dryden translated all of Persius and the first, third, tenth, and sixteenth satires of Juvenal. The *Discourse Concerning the Original and Progress of Satire* is both a dedication (to Charles, Earl of Dorset) and a critical preface: a circumstance which Dryden uses to achieve some of his finest modulations in prose. The transition from the comparison of Horace and Juvenal to a personal apologia, and back again, is, to the editor's mind, quite surpassing. The latter half of the *Discourse* is given here, omitting the skilful, derivative history of satire of the first part.

. . . This is what I have to say in general of satire: only, as Dacier[1] has observed before me, we may take notice that the word *satire* is of a more general signification in Latin than in French or English. For amongst the Romans it was not only used for those discourses which decried vice, or exposed folly, but for others also, where virtue was recommended. But in our modern languages we apply it only to invective poems, where the very name of satire is formidable to those persons who would appear to the world what they are not in themselves. For in English, to say satire is to mean reflection,[2] as we use that word in the worst sense; or as the French call it, more properly, *médisance*. In the criticism of spelling, it ought to be with *i* and not with *y*, to distinguish its true derivation from *satura* not from *satyrus*. And if this be so, then 'tis false spelled throughout this book: for here 'tis written *satyr*. Which having not considered at the first, I thought it not worth correction afterwards. But the French are more nice, and never spell it any other ways than *satire*.

I am now arrived at the most difficult part of my undertaking, which is to compare Horace with Juvenal and Persius. 'Tis observed by Rigaltius, in his preface before Juvenal written to Thuanus,[3] that these three poets have all their particular partisans and favourers. Every commentator, as he has taken pains with any of them, thinks himself obliged to prefer his author to

---

[1] In *Remarques critiques sur les œuvres d'Horace, avec une nouvelle traduction* (Paris, 1681–89).
[2] Imputation, censure.
[3] An edition published in 1616.

the other two; to find out their failings, and decry them, that he may make room for his own darling. Such is the partiality of mankind, to set up that interest which they have once espoused, though it be to the prejudice of truth, morality, and common justice; and especially in the productions of the brain. As authors generally think themselves the best poets, because they cannot go out of themselves to judge sincerely of their betters; so it is with critics, who having first taken a liking to one of these poets, proceed to comment on him, and to illustrate him; after which they fall in love with their own labours, to that degree of blind fondness that at length they defend and exalt their author, not so much for his sake as for their own. 'Tis a folly of the same nature with that of the Romans themselves, in their games of the Circus: the spectators were divided in their factions betwixt the Veneti and the Prasini; some were for the charioteer in blue, and some for him in green. The colours themselves were but a fancy; but when once a man had taken pains to set out those of his party, and had been at the trouble of procuring voices for them, the case was altered: he was concerned for his own labour, and that so earnestly, that disputes and quarrels, animosities, commotions, and bloodshed, often happened; and in the declension of the Grecian Empire, the very sovereigns themselves engaged in it, even when the barbarians were at their doors; and stickled for the preference of colours, when the safety of their people was in question. I am now myself on the brink of the same precipice; I have spent some time on the translation of Juvenal and Persius; and it behoves me to be wary lest, for that reason, I should be partial to them, or take a prejudice against Horace. Yet, on the other side, I would not be like some of our judges, who would give the cause for a poor man, right or wrong; for though that be an error on the better hand, yet it is still a partiality: and a rich man, unheard, cannot be concluded an oppressor. I remember a saying of K. Charles the Second on Sir Matthew Hales[4] (who was doubtless an uncorrupt and upright man) that his servants were sure to be cast on any trial which was heard before him: not that he thought the judge was possibly to be bribed, but that his integrity might be too scrupulous; and that the causes of the crown were always suspicious when the privileges of subjects were concerned.

It had been much fairer, if the modern critics who have embarked in the quarrels of their favourite authors had rather given to each his proper due; without taking from another's heap to raise their own. There is praise enough for each of them in particular, without encroaching on his fellows, and detracting from them, or enriching themselves with the spoils of others. But to come to particulars: Heinsius and Dacier are the most principal of those who raise Horace above Juvenal and Persius. Scaliger the

---

[4] Sir Matthew Hale (1609–76), a lawyer famed for his honesty. He was Lord Chief Justice from 1671 to 1676.

father, Rigaltius, and many others, debase Horace that they may set up Juvenal. And Casaubon,[5] who is almost single, throws dirt on Juvenal and Horace, that he may exalt Persius, whom he understood particularly well, and better than any of his former commentators: even Stelluti,[6] who succeeded him. I will begin with him who, in my opinion, defends the weakest cause, which is that of Persius; and labouring, as Tacitus professes of his own writing, to divest myself of partiality or prejudice, consider Persius, not as a poet whom I have wholly translated, and who has cost me more labour and time than Juvenal, but according to what I judge to be his own merit; which I think not equal, in the main, to that of Juvenal or Horace, and yet in some things to be preferred to both of them.

First, then, for the verse; neither Casaubon himself, nor any for him, can defend either his numbers, or the purity of his Latin. Casaubon gives this point for lost, and pretends not to justify either the measures or the words of Persius: he is evidently beneath Horace and Juvenal in both.

Then, as his verse is scabrous and hobbling, and his words not everywhere well chosen, the purity of Latin being more corrupted than in the time of Juvenal, and consequently of Horace, who writ when the language was in the height of its perfection; so his diction is hard, his figures are generally too bold and daring, and his tropes, particularly his metaphors, insufferably strained.

In the third place, notwithstanding all the diligence of Casaubon, Stelluti, and a Scotch gentleman[7] (whom I have heard extremely commended for his illustrations of him), yet he is still obscure. Whether he affected not to be understood, but with difficulty; or whether the fear of his safety under Nero compelled him to this darkness in some places; or that it was occasioned by his close way of thinking, and the brevity of his style, and crowding of his figures; or lastly, whether after so long a time many of his words have been corrupted, and many customs, and stories relating to them, lost to us; whether some of these reasons, or all, concurred to render him so cloudy; we may be bold to affirm that the best of commentators can but guess at his meaning, in many passages; and none can be certain that he has divined rightly.

After all, he was a young man, like his friend and contemporary Lucan; both of them men of extraordinary parts and great acquired knowledge, considering their youth. But neither of them had arrived to that maturity of

---

[5] Isaac Casaubon (1559–1614), French scholar, upon whose works Dryden draws extensively. His De satyrica Graecorum poesi et Romanorum satira was published in 1605, his edition of Persius in the same year.

[6] Stelluti's edition of Persius, with an Italian translation, appeared in 1630.

[7] David Wedderburn (1580–1646) of Aberdeen. His edition of Persius was published in Amsterdam in 1664.

judgment which is necessary to the accomplishing of a formed poet. And this consideration, as on the one hand it lays some imperfections to their charge, so on the other side 'tis a candid excuse for those failings which are incident to youth and inexperience; and we have more reason to wonder how they, who died before the thirtieth year of their age, could write so well, and think so strongly, than to accuse them of those faults from which human nature, and more especially in youth, can never possibly be exempted.

To consider Persius yet more closely: he rather insulted over vice and folly, than exposed them like Juvenal and Horace. And as chaste and modest as he is esteemed, it cannot be denied but that in some places he is broad and fulsome, as the latter verses of the fourth satire, and of the sixth, sufficiently witness. And 'tis to be believed that he who commits the same crime often, and without necessity, cannot but do it with some kind of pleasure.

To come to a conclusion: he is manifestly below Horace, because he borrows most of his greatest beauties from him; and Casaubon is so far from denying this that he has written a treatise purposely concerning it, wherein he shews a multitude of his translations from Horace, and his imitations of him, for the credit of his author; which he calls *Imitatio Horatiana*.

To these defects, which I casually observed while I was translating this author, Scaliger has added others. He calls him, in plain terms, a silly writer, and a trifler; full of ostentation of his learning; and after all, unworthy to come into competition with Juvenal and Horace.

After such terrible accusations, 'tis time to hear what his patron Casaubon can allege in his defence. Instead of answering, he excuses for the most part; and when he cannot, accuses others of the same crimes. He deals with Scaliger as a modest scholar with a master. He compliments him with so much reverence that one would swear he feared him as much at least as he respected him. Scaliger will not allow Persius to have any wit: Casaubon interprets this in the mildest sense, and confesses his author was not good at turning things into a pleasant ridicule; or, in other words, that he was not a laughable writer. That he was *ineptus*, indeed, but that was *non aptissimus jocandum*. But that he was ostentatious of his learning, that, by Scaliger's good favour, he denies. Persius shewed his learning, but was no boaster of it; he did *ostendere*, but not *ostentare*; and so, he says, did Scaliger: where, methinks, Casaubon turns it handsomely upon that supercilious critic, and silently insinuates that he himself was sufficiently vainglorious, and a boaster of his own knowledge. All the writing of this venerable censor, continues Casaubon, which are χρυσοῦ χρυσότερα, more golden than gold itself, are everywhere smelling of that thyme which, like a bee, he has gathered from ancient authors; but far be ostentation and vainglory from a gentleman so well born, and so nobly educated as Scaliger. But, says Scaliger, he is so obscure, that he has got himself the name of Scotinus, a dark writer. Now, says Casaubon, 'tis a wonder to me that anything could be obscure to the divine wit of Scaliger, from which nothing could be hidden. This is indeed a strong compliment, but no defence. And Casaubon, who could not but be sensible of his author's blind side, thinks it time to abandon a post that was untenable. He acknowledges that Persius is obscure in some places; but so is Plato, so is Thucydides; so are Pindar, Theocritus, and Aristophanes, amongst the Greek poets; and even Horace and Juvenal, he might have added, amongst the Romans. The truth is, Persius is not sometimes, but generally, obscure; and therefore Casaubon, at last, is forced to excuse him by alleging that it was *se defendendo*, for fear of Nero; and that he was commanded to write so cloudily by Cornutus,[8] in virtue of holy obedience to his master. I cannot help my own opinion; I think Cornutus needed not to have read many lectures on him on that subject. Persius was an apt scholar; and when he was bidden to be obscure in some places, where his life and safety were in question, took the same counsel for all his book; and never afterwards wrote ten lines together clearly. Casaubon, being upon this chapter, has not failed, we may be sure, of making a compliment to his own dear comment. If Persius, says he, be in himself obscure, yet my interpretation has made him intelligible. There is no question but he deserves that praise which he has given to himself; but the nature of the thing, as Lucretius says, will not admit of a perfect explanation. Besides many examples which I could urge, the very last verse of his last satire, upon which he particularly values himself in his preface, is not yet sufficiently explicated. 'Tis true, Holyday[9] has endeavoured to justify his construction; but Stelluti is against it; and, for my part, I can have but a very dark notion of it. As for the chastity of his thoughts, Casaubon denies not but that one particular passage, in the fourth satire, *at si unctus cesses*, etc., is not only the most obscure, but the most obscene of all his works. I understood it; but for that reason turned it over. In defence of his boisterous metaphors, he quotes Longinus, who accounts them as instruments of the sublime: fit to move and stir up the affections, particularly in narration. To which it may be replied that where the trope is far-fetched and hard, 'tis fit for nothing but to puzzle the understanding; and may be reckoned amongst those things of Demosthenes which Aeschines called θαύματα and ῥήματα, that is, prodigies, not words. It must be granted to Casaubon that the knowledge of many things is lost in our modern ages which were of familiar notice to the Ancients; and that satire is

---

[8] Persius' tutor.
[9] Barten Holyday (1593–1661). His translation of Persius appeared in 1616, his Juvenal not until 1673.

a poem of a difficult nature in itself, and is not written to vulgar readers. And through the relation which it has to comedy, the frequent change of persons makes the sense perplexed, when we can but divine who it is that speaks; whether Persius himself, or his friend and monitor; or, in some places, a third person. But Casaubon comes back always to himself, and concludes that if Persius had not been obscure there had been no need of him for an interpreter. Yet when he had once enjoined himself so hard a task, he then considered the Greek proverb, that he must χελώνης φαγεῖν ἢ μὴ φαγεῖν, either eat the whole snail, or let it quite alone; and so he went through with his laborious task, as I have done with my difficult translation.

Thus far, my Lord, you see it has gone very hard with Persius: I think he cannot be allowed to stand in competition either with Juvenal or Horace. Yet, for once, I will venture to be so vain as to affirm that none of his hard metaphors, or forced expressions, are in my translation. But more of this in its proper place, where I shall say somewhat in particular of our general performance, in making these two authors English. In the meantime, I think myself obliged to give Persius his undoubted due, and to acquaint the world, with Casaubon, in what he has equalled, and in what excelled, his two competitors.

A man who has resolved to praise an author, with any appearance of justice, must be sure to take him on the strongest side, and where he is least liable to exceptions. He is therefore obliged to choose his mediums accordingly. Casaubon, who saw that Persius could not laugh with a becoming grace, that he was not made for jesting, and that a merry conceit was not his talent, turned his feather, like an Indian, to another light, that he might give it the better gloss. Moral doctrine, says he, and urbanity, or well-mannered wit, are the two things which constitute the Roman satire. But of the two, that which is most essential to this poem, and is, as it were, the very soul which animates it, is the scourging of vice and exhortation to virtue. Thus wit, for a good reason, is already almost out of doors; and allowed only for an instrument, a kind of tool, or a weapon, as he calls it, of which the satirist makes use in the compassing of his design. The end and aim of our three rivals is consequently the same. But by what methods they have prosecuted their intention is farther to be considered. Satire is of the nature of moral philosophy, as being instructive: he, therefore, who instructs most usefully, will carry the palm from his two antagonists. The philosophy in which Persius was educated, and which he professes through his whole book, is the Stoic: the most noble, most generous, most beneficial to human kind, amongst all the sects, who have given us the rules of ethics, thereby to form a severe virtue in the soul; to raise in us an undaunted courage against the assaults of fortune; to esteem as nothing the things that are without us, because they are not in our power; not to value riches, beauty, honours, fame, or health, any farther than as conveniences, and so many helps to living as we ought, and doing good in our generation. In short, to be always happy, while we possess our minds with a good conscience, are free from the slavery of vices, and conform our actions and conversation to the rules of right reason. See here, my Lord, an epitome of Epictetus; the doctrine of Zeno, and the education of our Persius. And this he expressed, not only in all his satires, but in the manner of his life. I will not lessen this commendation of the Stoic philosophy by giving you an account of some absurdities in their doctrine, and some perhaps impieties, if we consider them by the standard of Christian faith: Persius has fallen into none of them; and therefore is free from those imputations. What he teaches might be taught from pulpits, with more profit to the audience than all the nice speculations of divinity, and controversies concerning faith, which are more for the profit of the shepherd than for the edification of the flock. Passion, interest, ambition, and all their bloody consequences of discord and of war, are banished from this doctrine. Here is nothing proposed but the quiet and tranquillity of mind; virtue lodged at home, and afterwards diffused in her general effects, to the improvement and good of human kind. And therefore I wonder not that the present Bishop of Salisbury[10] has recommended this our author, and the tenth satire of Juvenal, in his Pastoral Letter, to the serious perusal and practice of the divines in his diocese, as the best commonplaces for their sermons, as the store-houses and magazines of moral virtues, from whence they may draw out, as they have occasion, all manner of assistance for the accomplishment of a virtuous life, which the Stoics have assigned for the great end and perfection of mankind. Herein then it is that Persius has excelled both Juvenal and Horace. He sticks to his one philosophy; he shifts not sides, like Horace, who is sometimes an Epicurean, sometimes a Stoic, sometimes an Eclectic, as his present humour leads him; nor declaims like Juvenal against vices, more like an orator than a philosopher. Persius is everywhere the same: true to the dogmas of his master. What he has learnt, he teaches vehemently; and what he teaches, that he practises himself. There is a spirit of sincerity in all he says: you may easily discern that he is in earnest and is persuaded of that truth which he inculcates. In this I am of opinion that he excels Horace, who is commonly in jest, and laughs while he instructs; and is equal to Juvenal, who was as honest and serious as Persius, and more he could not be.

Hitherto I have followed Casaubon, and enlarged upon him; because I

---

[10] Gilbert Burnet (1643–1715), in A *Discourse of the Pastoral Care* (1692), p. 162: 'The satirical poets Horace, Juvenal and Persius may contribute wonderfully to give a man a detestation of vice, and a contempt of the common methods of mankind.'

am satisfied that he says no more than truth; the rest is almost all frivolous. For he says that Horace, being the son of a tax-gatherer, or a collector, as we call it, smells everywhere of the meanness of his birth and education: his conceits are vulgar like the subjects of his satires; that he does *plebeium sapere*,[11] and writes not with that elevation which becomes a satirist: that Persius, being nobly born, and of an opulent family, had likewise the advantage of a better master; Cornutus being the most learned of his time, a man of a most holy life, the chief of the Stoic sect at Rome, and not only a great philosopher, but a poet himself, and in probability a coadjutor of Persius; that, as for Juvenal, he was long a declaimer, came late to poetry, and had not been much conversant in philosophy.

'Tis granted that the father of Horace was *libertinus*, that is, one degree removed from his grandfather, who had been once a slave. But Horace, speaking of him, gives him the best character of a father which I ever read in history;[12] and I wish a witty friend of mine[13] now living had such another. He bred him in the best school, and with the best company of young noblemen. And Horace, by his gratitude to his memory, gives a certain testimony that his education was ingenuous. After this, he formed himself abroad, by the conversation of great men. Brutus found him at Athens, and was so pleased with him that he took him thence into the army, and made him *tribunus militum*, a colonel in a legion, which was the preferment of an old soldier. All this was before his acquaintance with Maecenas, and his introduction into the court of Augustus, and the familiarity of that great Emperor; which, had he not been well-bred before, had been enough to civilize his conversation, and render him accomplished and knowing in all the arts of complacency and good behaviour, and, in short, an agreeable companion for the retired hours and privacies of a favourite, who was first minister. So that, upon the whole matter, Persius may be acknowledged to be equal with him in those respects, tho' better born, and Juvenal inferior to both. If the advantage be anywhere, 'tis on the side of Horace; as much as the court of Augustus Caesar was superior to that of Nero. As for the subjects which they treated, it will appear hereafter that Horace writ not vulgarly on vulgar subjects, nor always chose them. His style is constantly accommodated to his subject, either high or low. If his fault be too much lowness, that of Persius is the fault of the hardness of his metaphors, and obscurity: and so they are equal in the failings of their style; where Juvenal manifestly triumphs over both of them.

The comparison betwixt Horace and Juvenal is more difficult, because their forces were more equal. A dispute has always been, and ever will

---

[11] 'Smacks of commonness'.
[12] In *Satires*, I, vi.
[13] William Wycherley, whose father refused to pay his debts.

continue, betwixt the favourers of the two poets. *Non nostrum est tantas componere lites*.[14] I shall only venture to give my own opinion, and leave it for better judges to determine. If it be only argued in general which of them was the better poet, the victory is already gained on the side of Horace. Virgil himself must yield to him in the delicacy of his turns, his choice of words, and perhaps the purity of his Latin. He who says that Pindar is inimitable, is himself inimitable in his Odes. But the contention betwixt these two great masters is for the prize of satire; in which controversy all the Odes and Epodes of Horace are to stand excluded. I say this, because Horace has written many of them satirically, against his private enemies; yet these, if justly considered, are somewhat of the nature of the Greek *silli*, which were invectives against particular sects and persons. But Horace had purged himself of this choler before he entered on those discourses which are more properly called the Roman satire. He has not now to do with a Lyce, a Canidia, a Cassius Severus, or a Menas; but is to correct the vices and follies of his time, and to give the rules of a happy and virtuous life. In a word, that former sort of satire, which is known in England by the name of lampoon, is a dangerous sort of weapon, and for the most part unlawful. We have no moral right on the reputation of other men. 'Tis taking from them what we cannot restore to them. There are only two reasons for which we may be permitted to write lampoons; and I will not promise that they can always justify us. The first is revenge, when we have been affronted in the same nature, or have been any ways notoriously abused, and can make ourselves no other reparation. And yet we know that, in Christian charity, all offences are to be forgiven; as we expect the like pardon for those which we daily commit against Almighty God. And this consideration has often made me tremble when I was saying our Saviour's prayer; for the plain condition of the forgiveness which we beg is the pardoning of others the offences which they have done to us: for which reason I have many times avoided the commission of that fault, even when I have been notoriously provoked. Let not this, my Lord, pass for vanity in me; for 'tis truth. More libels have been written against me than almost any man now living; and I had reason on my side to have defended my own innocence. I speak not of my poetry, which I have wholly given up to the critics: let them use it as they please: posterity, perhaps, may be more favourable to me; for interest and passion will lie buried in another age, and partiality and prejudice be forgotten. I speak of my morals, which have been sufficiently aspersed: that only sort of reputation ought to be dear to every honest man, and is to me. But let the world witness for me that I have been often wanting to myself in that particular; I have seldom answered any scurrilous lampoon, when it was in my power to

---

[14] Virgil, *Eclogues*, III, 108: 'It is not for me to settle so high a contest between you.'

have exposed my enemies: and being naturally vindicative, have suffered in silence, and possessed my soul in quiet.

Anything, tho' never so little, which a man speaks of himself, in my opinion, is still too much, and therefore I will waive this subject; and proceed to give the second reason which may justify a poet when he writes against a particular person; and that is, when he is become a public nuisance. All those whom Horace in his Satires, and Persius and Juvenal have mentioned in theirs with a brand of infamy, are wholly such. 'Tis an action of virtue to make examples of vicious men. They may and ought to be upbraided with their crimes and follies: both for their own amendment, if they are not yet incorrigible, and for the terror of others, to hinder them from falling into those enormities which they see are so severely punished in the persons of others. The first reason was only an excuse for revenge; but this second is absolutely of a poet's office to perform. But how few lampooners are there now living who are capable of this duty! When they come in my way, 'tis impossible sometimes to avoid reading them. But, good God, how remote they are, in common justice, from the choice of such persons as are the proper subject of satire! And how little wit they bring for the support of their injustice! The weaker sex is their most ordinary theme; and the best and fairest are sure to be the most severely handled. Amongst men, those who are prosperously unjust are entitled to a panegyric. But afflicted virtue is insolently stabbed with all manner of reproaches. No decency is considered, no fulsomeness omitted; no venom is wanting, as far as dullness can supply it. For there is a perpetual dearth of wit; a barrenness of good sense and entertainment. The neglect of the readers will soon put an end to this sort of scribbling. There can be no pleasantry where there is no wit; no impression can be made where there is no truth for the foundation. To conclude, they are like the fruits of the earth in this unnatural season: the corn which held up its head is spoiled with rankness; but the greater part of the harvest is laid along, and little of good income and wholesome nourishment is received into the barns. This is almost a digression, I confess to your Lordship; but a just indignation forced it from me. Now I have removed this rubbish, I will return to the comparison of Juvenal and Horace.

I would willingly divide the palm betwixt them, upon the two heads of profit and delight, which are the two ends of poetry in general. It must be granted by the favourers of Juvenal that Horace is the more copious and profitable in his instructions of human life. But in my particular opinion, which I set not up for a standard to better judgments, Juvenal is the more delightful author. I am profited by both, I am pleased with both; but I owe more to Horace for my instruction, and more to Juvenal for my pleasure. This, as I said, is my particular taste of these two authors: they who will have either of them to excel the other in both qualities can scarce give better reasons for their opinion than I for mine. But all unbiased readers will conclude that my moderation is not to be condemned. To such impartial men I must appeal; for they who have already formed their judgment may justly stand suspected of prejudice; and tho' all who are my readers will set up to be my judges, I enter my *caveat* against them, that they ought not so much as to be of my jury. Or, if they be admitted, 'tis but reason that they should first hear what I have to urge in the defence of my opinion.

That Horace is somewhat the better instructor of the two is proved from hence, that his instructions are more general, Juvenal's more limited. So that, granting that the counsels which they give are equally good for moral use, Horace, who gives the most various advice, and most applicable to all occasions which can occur to us in the course of our lives, as including in his discourse not only all the rules of morality, but also of civil conversation, is undoubtedly to be preferred to him who is more circumscribed in his instructions, makes them to fewer people, and on fewer occasions than the other. I may be pardoned for using an old saying, since 'tis true and to the purpose: *bonum quo communius, eo melius*.[15] Juvenal, excepting only his first satire, is in all the rest confined to the exposing of some particular vice; that he lashes, and there he sticks. His sentences are truly shining and instructive; but they are sprinkled here and there. Horace is teaching us in every line, and is perpetually moral; he had found out the skill of Virgil, to hide his sentences: to give you the virtue of them, without shewing them in their full extent; which is the ostentation of a poet, and not his art. And this Petronius charges on the authors of his time, as a vice of writing which was then growing on the age: *ne sententiae extra corpus orationis emineant*:[16] he would have them weaved into the body of the work, and not appear embossed upon it, and striking directly on the reader's view. Folly was the proper quarry of Horace, and not vice; and as there are but few notoriously wicked men, in comparison with a shoal of fools and fops, so 'tis a harder thing to make a man wise than to make him honest; for the will is only to be reclaimed in the one, but the understanding is to be informed in the other. There are blind sides and follies, even in the professors of moral philosophy; and there is not any one sect of them that Horace has not exposed: which, as it was not the design of Juvenal, who was wholly employed in lashing vices, some of them the most enormous than can be imagined; so, perhaps, it was not so much his talent.

> omne vafer vitium ridenti Flaccus amico
> tangit, et admissus circum praecordia ludit.[17]

---

[15] 'The more general, the better'.

[16] *Satyricon*, 118: 'Let not the epigrams stand out from the body of the speech.'

[17] Persius, *Satires*, I, 116–17: 'Horace, the rogue, manages to probe every fault while

This was the commendation which Persius gave him: where by *vitium* he means those little vices which we call follies, the defects of human understanding, or at most the peccadillos of life, rather than the tragical vices, to which men are hurried by their unruly passions and exorbitant desires. But in the word *omne*, which is *universal*, he concludes with me that the divine wit of Horace left nothing untouched; that he entered into the inmost recesses of nature; found out the imperfections even of the most wise and grave, as well as of the common people; discovering, even in the great Trebatius, to whom he addresses the first satire, his hunting after business, and following the court, as well as in the persecutor Crispinus,[18] his impertinence and importunity. 'Tis true, he exposes Crispinus openly, as a common nuisance; but he rallies the other as a friend, more finely. The exhortations of Persius are confined to noblemen, and the Stoic philosophy is that alone which he recommends to them; Juvenal exhorts to particular virtues, as they are opposed to those vices against which he declaims; but Horace laughs to shame all follies, and insinuates virtue rather by familiar examples than by the severity of precepts.

This last consideration seems to incline the balance on the side of Horace, and to give him the preference to Juvenal, not only in profit, but in pleasure. But, after all, I must confess that the delight which Horace gives me is but languishing. Be pleased still to understand that I speak of my own taste only: he may ravish other men; but I am too stupid and insensible to be tickled. Where he barely grins himself and, as Scaliger says, only shews his white teeth, he cannot provoke me to any laughter. His urbanity, that is, his good manners, are to be commended, but his wit is faint; and his salt, if I may dare to say so, almost insipid. Juvenal is of a more vigorous and masculine wit, he gives me as much pleasure as I can bear; he fully satisfies my expectation; he treats his subject home; his spleen is raised, and he raises mine; I have the pleasure of concernment in all he says; he drives his reader along with him; and when he is at the end of his way, I willingly stop with him. If he went another stage, it would be too far; it would make a journey of a progress, and turn delight into fatigue. When he gives over, 'tis a sign the subject is exhausted, and the wit of man can carry it no farther. If a fault can be justly found in him, 'tis that he is sometimes too luxuriant, too redundant; says more than he needs, like my friend the Plain Dealer,[19] but never more than pleases. Add to this that his thoughts are as just as those of Horace, and much more elevated. His expressions are sonorous and more noble; his verse more numerous, and his words are suitable to his thoughts,

---

making his friend laugh; he gains his entrance, and plays about the innermost feelings'
(Conington trans.).

[18] *Satires*, I, iv.

[19] In Wycherley's comedy of 1676.

sublime and lofty. All these contribute to the pleasure of the reader, and the greater the soul of him who reads, his transports are the greater. Horace is always on the amble, Juvenal on the gallop: but his way is perpetually on carpet ground. He goes with more impetuosity than Horace; but as securely; and the swiftness adds a more lively agitation to the spirits. The low style of Horace is according to his subject, that is, generally grovelling. I question not but he could have raised it. For the first epistle of the Second Book, which he writes to Augustus (a most instructive satire concerning poetry) is of so much dignity in the words, and of so much elegancy in the numbers, that the author plainly shews the *sermo pedestris*[20] in his other satires was rather his choice than his necessity. He was a rival to Lucilius, his predecessor, and was resolved to surpass him in his own manner. Lucilius, as we see by his remaining fragments, minded neither his style nor his numbers, nor his purity of words, nor his run of verse. Horace therefore copes with him in that humble way of satire, writes under his own force, and carries a dead weight, that he may match his competitor in the race. This, I imagine, was the chief reason why he minded only the clearness of his satire, and the cleanness of expression, without ascending to those heights to which his own vigour might have carried him. But limiting his desires only to the conquest of Lucilius, he had his ends of his rival who lived before him; but made way for a new conquest over himself by Juvenal, his successor. He could not give an equal pleasure to his reader, because he used not equal instruments. The fault was in the tools, and not in the workman. But versification and numbers are the greatest pleasures of poetry: Virgil knew it, and practised both so happily that, for aught I know, his greatest excellency is in his diction. In all other parts of poetry, he is faultless; but in this he placed his chief perfection. And give me leave, my Lord, since I have here an apt occasion, to say that Virgil could have written sharper satires than either Horace or Juvenal, if he would have employed his talent that way. I will produce a verse and half of his, in one of his Eclogues, to justify my opinion; and with commas after every word, to shew that he has given almost as many lashes as he has written syllables. 'Tis against a bad poet, whose ill verses he describes:

> non tu, in triviis, indocte, solebas,
> stridenti, miserum, stipula, disperdere carmen?[21]

But to return to my purpose: when there is anything deficient in numbers and sound, the reader is uneasy and unsatisfied; he wants something of his complement, desires somewhat which he finds not: and this being the

---

[20] Horace, *Ars Poetica*, l. 95: 'pedestrian style'.
[21] *Eclogues*, III, 26–7: 'Was it not you, Master Dunce, who at the crossroads used to murder a sorry tune on a scrannel straw.'

manifest defect of Horace, 'tis no wonder that, finding it supplied in Juvenal, we are more delighted with him. And besides this, the sauce of Juvenal is more poignant, to create in us an appetite of reading him. The meat of Horace is more nourishing; but the cookery of Juvenal more exquisite; so that, granting Horace to be the more general philosopher, we cannot deny that Juvenal was the greater poet, I mean in satire. His thoughts are sharper, his indignation against vice is more vehement; his spirit has more of the commonwealth genius; he treats tyranny, and all the vices attending it, as they deserve, with the utmost rigour: and consequently, a noble soul is better pleased with a zealous vindicator of Roman liberty than with a temporizing poet, a well-mannered court slave, and a man who is often afraid of laughing in the right place; who is ever decent, because he is naturally servile. After all, Horace had the disadvantage of the times in which he lived; they were better for the man, but worse for the satirist. 'Tis generally said that those enormous vices which were practised under the reign of Domitian were unknown in the time of Augustus Caesar; that therefore Juvenal had a larger field than Horace. Little follies were out of doors when oppression was to be scourged instead of avarice: it was no longer time to turn into ridicule the false opinions of philosophers, when the Roman liberty was to be asserted. There was more need of a Brutus in Domitian's days, to redeem or mend, than of a Horace, if he had then been living, to laugh at a fly-catcher. This reflection at the same time excuses Horace, but exalts Juvenal. I have ended, before I was aware, the comparison of Horace and Juvenal, upon the topics of instruction and delight; and, indeed, I may safely here conclude that commonplace; for, if we make Horace our minister of state in satire, and Juvenal of our private pleasures, I think the latter has no ill bargain of it. Let profit have the pre-eminence of honour, in the end of poetry. Pleasure, though but the second in degree, is the first in favour. And who would not choose to be loved better, rather than to be more esteemed? But I am entered already upon another topic, which concerns the particular merits of these two satirists. However, I will pursue my business where I left it, and carry it farther than that common observation of the several ages in which these authors flourished.

When Horace writ his satires, the monarchy of his Caesar was in its newness, and the government but just made easy to the conquered people. They could not possibly have forgotten the usurpation of that prince upon their freedom, nor the violent methods which he had used in the compassing of that vast design. They yet remembered his proscriptions, and the slaughter of so many noble Romans, their defenders: amongst the rest, that horrible action of his, when he forced Livia from the arms of her husband, who was constrained to see her married, as Dion relates the story, and, big with child as she was, conveyed to the bed of his insulting rival. The same

Dion Cassius gives us another instance of the crime before mentioned: that Cornelius Sisenna, being reproached in full Senate with the licentious conduct of his wife, returned this answer, that he had married her by the counsel of Augustus; intimating, says my author, that Augustus had obliged him to that marriage that he might, under that covert, have the more free access to her. His adulteries were still before their eyes, but they must be patient where they had not power. In other things that Emperor was moderate enough: propriety was generally secured; and the people entertained with public shows and donatives, to make them more easily digest their lost liberty. But Augustus, who was conscious to himself of so many crimes which he had committed, thought in the first place to provide for his own reputation by making an edict against lampoons and satires, and the authors of those defamatory writings which my author Tacitus, from the law-term, calls *famosos libellos*.

In the first book of his *Annals*, he gives the following account of it, in these words: *primus Augustus cognitionem de famosis libellis, specie legis ejus, tractavit; commotus Cassii Severi libidine, qua viros fœminasque inlustris procacibus scriptis diffamaverat*. Thus in English: August was the first who under the colour of that law took cognisance of lampoons; being provoked to it by the petulancy of Cassius Severus, who had defamed many illustrious persons of both sexes in his writings. The law to which Tacitus refers was *Lex laesae majestatis*; commonly called, for the sake of brevity, *majestas*; or, as we say, high treason. He means not that this law had not been enacted formerly: for it had been made by the Decemviri, and was inscribed amongst the rest in the Twelve Tables: to prevent the aspersion of the Roman Majesty, either of the people themselves, or their religion, or their magistrates: and the infringement of it was capital; that is, the offender was whipped to death with the *fasces*, which were borne before their chief officers of Rome. But Augustus was the first who restored that intermitted law. By the words *under colour of that law*, he insinuates that Augustus caused it to be executed on pretence of those libels which were written by Cassius Severus against the nobility; but, in truth, to save himself from such defamatory verses. Suetonius likewise makes mention of it thus: *sparsos de se in curia famosos libellos, nec expavit, et magna cura redarguit: ac ne requisitis quidem auctoribus, id modo censuit, cognoscendum posthac de iis qui libellos aut carmina ad infamiam cuiuspiam sub alieno nomine edant.*[22] Augustus was not afraid of libels, says that author; yet he took all care imaginable to have them answered; and then decreed that for the time to come the authors of them should be punished. But Aurelius[23] makes it yet more clear, according to my sense, that this Emperor for his own sake durst not permit them: *fecit id Augustus in*

[22] Seutonius, *Lives of the Caesars*, II, lv.

[23] Identified by Noyes as a French commentator, not a Roman historian.

speciem, ut quasi gratificaretur populo romano, et primoribus urbis; sed revera ut sibi consuleret: nam habuit in animo, comprimere nimiam quorundam procacitatem in loquendo, a qua nec ipse exemptus fuit, nam suo nomine compescere erat invidiosum, sub alieno facile et utile. Ergo speci legis tractavit, quasi populi romani majestas infamaretur. This, I think, is a sufficient comment on that passage of Tacitus. I will add only by the way that the whole family of the Caesars, and all their relations, were included in the law; because the majesty of the Romans in the time of the empire was wholly in that house. *Omnia Caesar erat*: they were all accounted sacred who belonged to him. As for Cassius Severus, he was contemporary with Horace; and was the same poet against whom hc writes in his Epodes under this title, *In Cassium Severum maledicum poetam*; perhaps intending to kill two crows, according to our proverb, with one stone, and revenge both himself and his Emperor together.

From hence I may reasonably conclude that Augustus, who was not altogether so good as he was wise, had some by-respect in the enacting of this law: for to do anything for nothing was not his maxim. Horace, as he was a courtier, complied with the interest of his master; and, avoiding the lashing of greater crimes, confined himself to the ridiculing of petty vices, and common follies; excepting only some reserved cases, in his Odes and Epodes, of his own particular quarrels, which either with permission of the magistrate or without it, every man will revenge, tho' I say not that he should; for *prior laesit* is a good excuse in the civil law, if Christianity had not taught us to forgive. However, he was not the proper man to arraign great vices, at least if the stories which we hear of him are true, that he practised some which I will not here mention, out of honour to him. It was not for a Clodius to accuse adulterers, especially when Augustus was of that number; so that though his age was not exempted from the worst of villanies, there was no freedom left to reprehend them, by reason of the edict. And our poet was not fit to represent them in an odious character, because himself was dipped in the same actions. Upon this account, without farther insisting on the different tempers of Juvenal and Horace, I conclude that the subjects which Horace chose for satire are of a lower nature than those of which Juvenal has written.

Thus I have treated, in a new method, the comparison betwixt Horace, Juvenal, and Persius; somewhat of their particular manner belonging to all of them is yet remaining to be considered. Persius was grave, and particularly opposed his gravity to lewdness, which was the predominant vice in Nero's court at the time when he published his satires, which was before that Emperor fell into the excess of cruelty. Horace was a mild admonisher, a court satirist, fit for the gentle times of Augustus, and more fit, for the reasons which I have already given. Juvenal was as proper for his times as they for theirs. His was an age that deserved a more severe chastisement.

Vices were more gross and open, more flagitious, more encouraged by the example of a tyrant, and more protected by his authority. Therefore, wheresoever Juvenal mentions Nero, he means Domitian, whom he dares not attack in his own person, but scourges him by proxy. Heinsius[24] urges in praise of Horace that, according to the ancient art and law of satire, it should be nearer to comedy than to tragedy; not declaiming against vice, but only laughing at it. Neither Persius nor Juvenal were ignorant of this, for they had both studied Horace. And the thing itself is plainly true. But as they had read Horace, they had likewise read Lucilius, of whom Persius says *secuit urbem; et genuinum fregit in illis*;[25] meaning Mutius and Lupus. And Juvenal also mentions him in these words: *ense velut stricto, quoties Lucilius ardens infremuit*,[26] etc. So that they thought the imitation of Lucilius was more proper to their purpose than that of Horace. They changed satire, says Holyday, but they changed it for the better; for the business being to reform great vices, chastisement goes farther than admonition; whereas a perpetual grin, like that of Horace, does rather anger than amend a man.

Thus far that learned critic, Barten Holyday, whose interpretation and illustrations of Juvenal are as excellent as the verse of his translation and his English are lame and pitiful. For 'tis not enough to give us the meaning of a poet, which I acknowledge him to have performed most faithfully, but he must also imitate his genius and his numbers, as far as the English will come up to the elegance of the original. In few words, 'tis only for a poet to translate a poet. Holyday and Stapylton had not enough considered this when they attempted Juvenal. But I forbear reflections; only I beg leave to take notice of this sentence, where Holyday says, 'a perpetual grin, like that of Horace, rather angers than amends a man.' I cannot give him up the manner of Horace in low satire so easily. Let the chastisements of Juvenal be never so necessary for his new kind of satire; let him declaim as wittily and sharply as he pleases; yet still the nicest and most delicate touches of satire consist in fine raillery. This, my Lord, is your particular talent, to which even Juvenal would not arrive. 'Tis not reading, 'tis not imitation of an author, which can produce this fineness: it must be inborn; it must proceed from a genius, and particular way of thinking, which is not to be taught; and therefore not to be imitated by him who has it not from nature. How easy it is to call rogue and villain, and that wittily! But how hard to make a man appear a fool, a blockhead, or a knave, without using any of those opprobrious terms! To spare the grossness of the names, and to do the thing yet more severely, is to draw a full face, and to make the nose and cheeks stand out, and yet not to employ any depth of shadowing. This is the

[24] Heinsius' edition of Horace was published in 1612.
[25] Persius, *Satires*, I, 114–15: 'Lucilius flayed our city, and broke his jaw over them'.
[26] Juvenal, I, 165–6: 'when Lucilius roars and rages, as if with sword in hand'.

mystery of that noble trade, which yet no master can teach to his apprentice: he may give the rules, but the scholar is never the nearer in his practice. Neither is it true that this fineness of raillery is offensive. A witty man is tickled while he is hurt in this manner, and a fool feels it not. The occasion of an offence may possibly be given, but he cannot take it. If it be granted that in effect this way does more mischief; that a man is secretly wounded, and though he be not sensible himself, yet the malicious world will find it for him: yet there is still a vast difference betwixt the slovenly butchering of a man, and the fineness of a stroke that separates the head from the body, and leaves it standing in its place. A man may be capable, as Jack Ketch's[27] wife said of his servant, of a plain piece of work, a bare hanging; but to make a malefactor die sweetly was only belonging to her husband. I wish I could apply it to myself, if the reader would be kind enough to think it belongs to me. The character of Zimri[28] in my *Absalom* is, in my opinion, worth the whole poem: 'tis not bloody, but 'tis ridiculous enough. And he for whom it was intended was too witty to resent it as an injury. If I had railed, I might have suffered for it justly: but I managed my own work more happily, perhaps more dexterously. I avoided the mention of great crimes, and applied myself to the representing of blindsides, and little extravagancies; to which, the wittier a man is, he is generally the more obnoxious. It succeeded as I wished; the jest went round, and he was laughed at in his turn who began the frolic.

And thus, my Lord, you see I have preferred the manner of Horace, and of your Lordship, in this kind of satire, to that of Juvenal; and, I think, reasonably. Holyday ought not to have arraigned so great an author for that which was his excellency and his merit: of if he did, on such a palpable mistake, he might expect that someone might possibly arise, either in his own time or after him, to rectify his error, and restore to Horace that commendation of which he has so unjustly robbed him. And let the Manes of Juvenal forgive me if I say that this way of Horace was the best for amending manners, as it is the most difficult. His was an *ense rescindendum*;[29] but that of Horace was a pleasant cure, with all the limbs preserved entire; and as our mountebanks tell us in their bills, without keeping the patient within doors for a day. What they promise only, Horace has effectually performed. Yet I contradict not the proposition which I formerly advanced: Juvenal's times required a more painful kind of operation; but if he had lived in the age of Horace, I must needs affirm that he had it not about him. He took the method which was prescribed him by his own genius, which was sharp and eager; he could not rally, but he could declaim; and as his

---

[27] John Ketch (d. 1686), a public hangman notorious for his cruelty at executions.
[28] *Absalom and Achitophel*, ll. 544–64.
[29] Ovid, *Metamorphoses*, I, 191: 'cutting away with the knife'.

provocations were great, he has revenged them tragically. This notwith-standing, I am to say another word which, as true as it is, will yet displease the partial admirers of our Horace. I have hinted it before; but 'tis time for me now to speak more plainly.

This manner of Horace is indeed the best; but Horace has not executed it altogether so happily, at least not often. The manner of Juvenal is confessed to be inferior to the former; but Juvenal has excelled him in his perfor-mance. Juvenal has railed more wittily than Horace has rallied. Horace means to make his reader laugh, but he is not sure of his experiment. Juvenal always intends to move your indignation; and he always brings about his purpose. Horace, for aught I know, might have tickled the people of his age; but amongst the Moderns he is not so successful. They who say he entertains so pleasantly may perhaps value themselves on the quickness of their own understandings, that they can see a jest farther off than other men. They may find occasion of laughter in the wit-battle of the two buffoons, Sarmentus and Cicerrus;[30] and hold their sides for fear of burst-ing, when Rupilius and Persius are scolding.[31] For my own part, I can only like the characters of all four, which are judiciously given: but for my heart I cannot so much as smile at their insipid raillery. I see not why Persius should call upon Brutus to revenge him on his adversary; and that because he had killed Julius Caesar, for endeavouring to be a king, therefore he should be desired to murther Rupilius, only because his name was Mr King. A miserable clench, in my opinion, for Horace to record: I have heard honest Mr Swan[32] make many a better, and yet have had the grace to hold my countenance. But it may be puns were then in fashion, as they were wit in the sermons of the last age, and in the court of King Charles the Second. I am sorry to say it, for the sake of Horace; but certain it is, he has no fine palate who can feed so heartily on garbage.

But I have already wearied myself, and doubt not but I have tired your Lordship's patience, with this long, rambling, and, I fear, trivial discourse. Upon the one half of the merits, that is, pleasure, I cannot but conclude that Juvenal was the better satirist. They who will descend into his particular praises, may find them at large in the dissertation of the learned Rigaltius to Thuanus. As for Persius, I have given the reasons why I think him inferior to both of them. Yet I have one thing to add on that subject.

Barten Holyday, who translated both Juvenal and Persius, has made this distinction betwixt them, which is no less true than witty; that in Persius the difficulty is to find a meaning, in Juvenal to choose a meaning; so crabbed is Persius, and so copious is Juvenal; so much the understanding is

---

[30] Horace, *Satires*, I, v, 51f.
[31] Ibid., I, vii.
[32] Richard Swan, a well-known punster.

employed in one, and so much the judgment in the other; so difficult it is to find any sense in the former, and the best sense of the latter.

If, on the other side, anyone suppose I have commended Horace below his merit, when I have allowed him but the second place, I desire him to consider if Juvenal, a man of excellent natural endowments, besides the advantages of diligence and study, and coming after him, and building upon his foundations, might not probably, with all these helps, surpass him? And whether it be any dishonour to Horace to be thus surpassed, since no art or science is at once begun and perfected, but that it must pass first through many hands, and even through several ages? If Lucilius could add to Ennius, and Horace to Lucilius, why, without any diminution to the fame of Horace, might not Juvenal give the last perfection to that work? Or rather, what disreputation is it to Horace that Juvenal excels in the tragical satire, as Horace does in the comical? I have read over attentively both Heinsius and Dacier, in their commendations of Horace; but I can find no more in either of them for the preference of him to Juvenal, than the instructive part: the part of wisdom, and not that of pleasure; which therefore is here allowed him, notwithstanding what Scaliger and Rigaltius have pleaded to the contrary for Juvenal. And to shew I am impartial, I will here translate what Dacier has said on that subject.

I cannot give a more just idea of the two books of satires made by Horace than by comparing them to the statues of the Sileni, to which Alcibiades compares Socrates in the *Symposium*.[33] They were figures which had nothing of agreeable, nothing of beauty, on their outside; but when anyone took the pains to open them, and search into them, he there found the figures of all the deities. So, in the shape that Horace presents himself to us in his satires, we see nothing at the first view which deserves our attention. It seems that he is rather an amusement for children than for the serious consideration of men. But when we take away his crust, and that which hides him from our sight, when we discover him to the bottom, then we find all the divinities in a full assembly: that is to say, all the virtues which ought to be the continual exercise of those who seriously endeavour to correct their vices.

'Tis easy to observe that Dacier, in this noble similitude, has confined the praise of his author wholly to the instructive part: the commendation turns on this, and so does that which follows.

In these two books of satire, 'tis the business of Horace to instruct us how to combat our vices, to regulate our passions, to follow nature, to give bounds to our desires, to distinguish betwixt truth and falsehood, and betwixt our conceptions of things, and things themselves; to come back from our prejudicate opinions, to understand exactly the principles and

[33] Plato, *Symposium*, 215A.

motives of all our actions; and to avoid the ridicule into which all men necessarily fall who are intoxicated with those notions, which they have received from their masters, and which they obstinately retain, without examining whether or no they are founded on right reason.

In a word, he labours to render us happy in relation to ourselves; agreeable and faithful to our friends; and discreet, serviceable, and well bred in relation to those with whom we are obliged to live and to converse. To make his figures intelligible, to conduct his readers through the labyrinth of some perplexed sentence, or obscure parenthesis, is no great matter. And as Epictetus says, there is nothing of beauty in all this, or what is worthy of a prudent man. The principal business, and which is of most importance to us, is to shew the use, the reason, and the proof of his precepts.

They who endeavour not to correct themselves according to so exact a model, are just like the patients who have open before them a book of admirable receipts for their diseases, and please themselves with reading it, without comprehending the nature of the remedies, or how to apply them to their cure.

Let Horace go off with these encomiums, which he has so well deserved.

To conclude the contention betwixt our three poets, I will use the words of Virgil, in his fifth Aeneid, where Aeneas proposes the rewards of the footrace to the three first who should reach the goal:

> tres praemia primi
> accipient, flavaque caput nectentur oliva.

Let these three Ancients be preferred to all the Moderns, as first arriving at the goal; let them all be crowned as victors, with the wreath that properly belongs to satire. But after that, with this distinction amongst themselves:

> primus equum phaleris insignem victor habeto.

Let Juvenal ride first in triumph:

> alter Amazoniam pharetram, plenamque sagittis
> Threiciis, lato quam circumplectitur auro
> balteus, et tereti subnectit fibula gemma.[34]

Let Horace, who is the second, and but just the second, carry off the quivers and the arrows, as the badges of his satire, and the golden belt and the diamond button:

---

[34] *Aeneid*, v, 308–13: 'The three first shall receive prizes, and have pale-green olive crown their heads. Let the first take as winner a horse gay with trappings; the second an Amazonian quiver, filled with Thracian arrows, girt about by a broad belt of gold and clasped by a buckle with polished gem.'

tertius Argolico hoc clypeo contentus abito.[35]

And let Persius, the last of the first three worthies, be contented with this Grecian shield, and with victory not only over all the Grecians, who were ignorant of the Roman satire, but over all the Moderns in succeeding ages; excepting Boileau and your Lordship.

And thus I have given the history of satire, and derived it as far as from Ennius to your Lordship; that is, from its first rudiments of barbarity to its last polishing and perfection; which is, with Virgil, in his address to Augustus:

> nomen fama tot ferre per annos,
> Tithoni prima quot abest ab origine Caesar.[36]

I said, only from Ennius; but I may safely carry it higher, as far as Livius Andronicus; who, as I have said formerly, taught the first play at Rome, in the year *ab urbe condita* 514. I have since desired my learned friend, Mr Maidwell,[37] to compute the difference of times betwixt Aristophanes and Livius Andronicus; and he assures me, from the best chronologers, that *Plutus*, the last of Aristophanes his plays, was represented at Athens in the year of the 97th Olympiad; which agrees with the year *urbis conditae* 364: so that the difference of years betwixt Aristophanes and Andronicus is 150; from whence I have probably deduced that Livius Andronicus, who was a Grecian, had read the plays of the Old Comedy, which were satirical, and also of the New; for Menander was fifty years before him, which must needs be a great light to him in his own plays, that were of the satirical nature. That the Romans had farces before this, 'tis true; but then they had no communication with Greece; so that Andronicus was the first who wrote after the manner of the Old Comedy in his plays: he was imitated by Ennius, about thirty years afterwards. Though the former writ fables, the latter, speaking properly, began the Roman satire; according to that description which Juvenal gives of it in his first:

> quicquid agunt homines, votum, timor, ira, voluptas,
> gaudia, discursus, nostri est farrago libelli.[38]

This is that in which I have made bold to differ from Casaubon, Rigaltius, Dacier, and indeed from all the modern critics, that not Ennius, but Andronicus was the first who, by the *Archaea Comedia* of the Greeks, added

[35] Ibid., l. 314: 'With this Argive helmet let the third depart content.'
[36] *Georgics*, III, 47–8: 'to bear his name in story through as many years as Caesar is distant from the far-off birth of Tithonus'.
[37] Lewis Maidwell, author of works on education and mathematics.
[38] *Satires*, I, 85–6: 'All the doings of mankind, their vows, their fears, their angers and their pleasures, their joys and goings to and fro, shall form the motley subject of my page.'

many beauties to the first rude and barbarous Roman satire: which sort of poem, tho' we had not derived from Rome, yet nature teaches it mankind in all ages, and in every country.

'Tis but necessary that after so much has been said of satire, some definition of it should be given. Heinsius, in his dissertations on Horace, makes it for me in these words: 'Satire is a kind of poetry, without a series of action, invented for the purging of our minds; in which human vices, ignorance, and errors, and all things besides, which are produced from them in every man, are severely reprehended; partly dramatically, partly simply, and sometimes in both kinds of speaking; but for the most part figuratively, and occultly; consisting in a low familiar way, chiefly in a sharp and pungent manner of speech; but partly, also, in a facetious and civil way of jesting; by which either hatred, or laughter, or indignation, is moved.' – Where I cannot but observe that this obscure and perplexed definition, or rather description, of satire, is wholly accommodated to the Horatian way; and excluding the works of Juvenal and Persius as foreign from that kind of poem. The clause in the beginning of it (*without a series of action*) distinguishes satire properly from stage-plays, which are all of one action, and one continued series of action. The end or scope of satire is to purge the passions; so far it is common to the satires of Juvenal and Persius. The rest which follows is also generally belonging to all three; till he comes upon us with the excluding clause (*consisting in a low familiar way of speech*), which is the proper character of Horace; and from which the other two, for their honour be it spoken, are far distant. But how come lowness of style, and the familiarity of words, to be so much the propriety of satire, that without them a poet can be no more a satirist than without risibility he can be a man? Is the fault of Horace to be made the virtue and standing rule of this poem? Is the *grande sophos*[39] of Persius, and the sublimity of Juvenal, to be circumscribed with the meanness of words and vulgarity of expression? If Horace refused the pains of numbers, and the loftiness of figures, are they bound to follow so ill a precedent? Let him walk afoot with his pad[40] in his hand, for his own pleasure; but let not them be accounted no poets who choose to mount, and shew their horsemanship. Holyday is not afraid to say that there was never such a fall as from his Odes to his Satires, and that he, injuriously to himself, untuned his harp. The majestic way of Persius and Juvenal was new when they began it, but 'tis old to us; and what poems have not, with time, received an alteration in their fashion? Which alteration, says Holyday, is to aftertimes as good a warrant as the first. Has not Virgil changed the manners of Homer's heroes in his *Aeneis*? Certainly he has, and for the better. For Virgil's age was more civilized, and better bred; and he

39 'The high wisdom' (Watson).
40 Saddle.

writ according to the politeness of Rome, under the reign of Augustus
Caesar; not to the rudeness of Agamemnon's age, or the times of Homer.
Why should we offer to confine free spirits to one form, when we cannot so
much as confine our bodies to one fashion of apparel? Would not Donne's
satires, which abound with so much wit, appear more charming if he had
taken care of his words, and of his numbers? But he followed Horace so very
close that of necessity he must fall with him. And I may safely say it of this
present age, that if we are not so great wits as Donne, yet certainly we are
better poets.

But I have said enough, and it may be too much, on this subject. Will
your Lordship be pleased to prolong my audience only so far till I tell you my
own trivial thoughts how a modern satire should be made? I will not deviate
in the least from the precepts and examples of the Ancients, who were
always our best masters. I will only illustrate them, and discover some of
the hidden beauties in their designs, that we thereby may form our own in
imitation of them. Will you please but to observe that Persius, the least in
dignity of all the three, has notwithstanding been the first who has
discovered to us this important secret in the designing of a perfect satire:
that it ought only to treat of one subject; to be confined to one particular
theme; or at least, to one principally. If other vices occur in the management of the chief, they should only be transiently lashed, and not be
insisted on so as to make the design double. As in a play of the English
fashion, which we call a tragi-comedy, there is to be but one main design;
and tho' there be an under-plot, or second walk of comical characters and
adventures, yet they are subservient to the chief fable, carried along under
it, and helping to it; so that the drama may not seem a monster with two
heads. Thus the Copernican system of the planets makes the moon to be
moved by the motion of the earth, and carried about her orb, as a dependent
of hers. Mascardi, in his discourse of the *doppia favola*,[41] or double tale in
plays, gives an instance of it in the famous pastoral of Guarini called *Il
Pastor Fido*; where Corisca and the Satyr are the under-parts: yet we may
observe that Corisca is brought into the body of the plot, and made
subservient to it. 'Tis certain that the divine wit of Horace was not ignorant
of this rule, that a play, though it consists of many parts, must yet be one in
the action, and must drive on the accomplishment of one design; for he
gives this very precept, *sit quodvis simplex duntaxat et unum*;[42] yet he seems
not much to mind it in his Satires, many of them consisting of more
arguments than one; and the second without dependence on the first.
Casaubon has observed this before me, in his preference of Persius to

[41] Ker traces the reference to Agostino Mascardi's *Prose Volgari* (1630), 'Discorso settimo:
dell' unità della favola drammatica'.
[42] *Ars Poetica*, l. 23: 'Be the work what you will, let it be simple and one.'

Horace; and will have his own beloved author to be the first who found out and introduced this method of confining himself to one subject. I know it may be urged in defence of Horace that this unity is not necessary; because the very word *satura* signifies a dish plentifully stored with all variety of fruits and grains. Yet Juvenal, who calls his poems a *farrago*, which is a word of the same signification with *satura*, has chosen to follow the same method of Persius, and not of Horace. And Boileau, whose example alone is a sufficient authority, has wholly confined himself, in all his satires, to this unity of design. That variety which is not to be found in any one satire is, at least, in many written on several occasions. And if variety be of absolute necessity in every one of them, according to the etymology of the word, yet it may arise naturally from one subject, as it is diversely treated in the several subordinate branches of it, all relating to the chief. It may be illustrated accordingly with variety of examples in the subdivisions of it, and with as many precepts as there are members of it; which altogether may complete that *olla*, or hotchpotch, which is properly a satire.

Under this unity of theme, or subject, is comprehended another rule for perfecting the design of true satire. The poet is bound, and that *ex officio*, to give his reader some one precept of moral virtue, and to caution him against some one particular vice or folly. Other virtues, subordinate to the first, may be recommended under that chief head; and other vices or follies may be scourged besides that which he principally intends. But he is chiefly to inculcate one virtue, and insist on that. Thus Juvenal, in every satire excepting the first, ties himself to one principal instructive point, or to the shunning of moral evil. Even in the sixth, which seems only an arraignment of the whole sex of womankind, there is a latent admonition to avoid ill women, by shewing how very few who are virtuous and good are to be found amongst them. But this, tho' the wittiest of all his satires, has yet the least of truth or instruction in it. He has run himself into his old declamatory way, and almost forgotten that he was now setting up for a moral poet.

Persius is never wanting to us in some profitable doctrine, and in exposing the opposite vices to it. His kind of philosophy is one, which is the Stoic; and every satire is a comment on one particular dogma of that sect; unless we will except the first, which is against bad writers; and yet even there he forgets not the precepts of the Porch. In general, all virtues are everywhere to be praised and recommended to practice; and all vices to be reprehended, and made either odious or ridiculous; or else there is a fundamental error in the whole design.

I have already declared who are the only persons that are the adequate object of private satire, and who they are that may properly be exposed by name for public examples of vices and follies; and therefore I will trouble your Lordship no farther with them. Of the best and finest manner of satire,

I have said enough in the comparison betwixt Juvenal and Horace: 'tis that sharp, well-mannered way of laughing a folly out of countenance, of which your Lordship is the best master in this age. I will proceed to the versification which is most proper for it, and add somewhat to what I have said already on that subject. The sort of verse which is called *burlesque*, consisting of eight syllables, or four feet, is that which our excellent *Hudibras* has chosen.[43] I ought to have mentioned him before, when I spoke of Donne; but by a slip of an old man's memory he was forgotten. The worth of his poem is too well known to need my commendation, and he is above my censure. His satire is of the Varronian kind, though unmixed with prose. The choice of his numbers is suitable enough to his design, as he has managed it; but in any other hand, the shortness of his verse, and the quick returns of rhyme, had debased the dignity of style. And besides, the double rhyme (a necessary companion of burlesque writing) is not so proper for manly satire; for it turns earnest too much to jest, and gives us a boyish kind of pleasure. It tickles awkwardly with a kind of pain, to the best sort of readers: we are pleased ungratefully and, if I may say so, against our liking. We thank him not for giving us that unseasonable delight, when we know he could have given us a better, and more solid. He might have left that task to others who, not being able to put in thought, can only make us grin with the excrescence of a word of two or three syllables in the close. 'Tis, indeed, below so great a master to make use of such a little instrument. But his good sense is perpetually shining through all he writes; it affords us not the time of finding faults. We pass through the levity of his rhyme, and are immediately carried into some admirable, useful thought. After all, he has chosen this kind of verse, and has written the best in it: and had he taken another, he would always have excelled; as we say of a court favourite that whatsoever his office be, he still makes it uppermost, and most beneficial to himself.

The quickness of your imagination, my Lord, has already prevented me; and you know beforehand that I would prefer the verse of ten syllables, which we call the English heroic, to that of eight. This is truly my opinion. For this sort of number is more roomy. The thought can turn itself with greater ease in a larger compass. When the rhyme comes too thick upon us, it straitens the expression; we are thinking of the close, when we should be employed in adorning the thought. It makes a poet giddy with turning in a space too narrow for his imagination. He loses many beauties without gaining one advantage. For a burlesque rhyme[44] I have already concluded to be none; or if it were, 'tis more easily purchased in ten syllables than in eight. In both occasions 'tis as in a tennis-court, when the strokes of greater

[43] Samuel Butler (1612–80), author of *Hudibras* (1663–78).
[44] That is, a rhyme of more than one syllable.

force are given when we strike out and play at length. Tassone and Boileau have left us the best examples of this way, in the *Secchia rapita* and the *Lutrin*; and next them Merlin Coccaius in his *Baldus*.[45] I will speak only of the two former, because the last is written in Latin verse. The *Secchia rapita* is an Italian poem, a satire of the Varronian kind. 'Tis written in the stanza of eight, which is their measure for heroic verse. The words are stately, the numbers smooth, the turn both of thoughts and words is happy. The first six lines of the stanza seem majestical and severe: but the two last turn them all into a pleasant ridicule. Boileau, if I am not much deceived, has modelled from hence his famous *Lutrin*. He had read the burlesque poetry of Scarron[46] with some kind of indignation, as witty as it was, and found nothing in France that was worthy of his imitation. But he copied the Italian so well that his own may pass for an original. He writes it in the French heroic verse, and calls it an heroic poem; his subject is trivial, but his verse is noble. I doubt not but he had Virgil in his eye, for we find many admirable imitations of him, and some parodies; as particularly this passage in the fourth of the *Aeneids*:

> nec tibi diva parens, generis nec Dardanus auctor,
> perfide; sed duris genuit te cautibus horrens
> Caucasus; Hyrcanaeque admorunt ubera tigres.[47]

Which he thus translates, keeping to the words, but altering the sense:

> Non, ton père à Paris ne fut point boulanger:
> Et tu n'es point du sang de Gervais l'horloger;
> Ta mère ne fut point la maîtresse d'un coche:
> Caucase dans ses flancs te forma d'une roche:
> Une tigresse affreuse, en quelque antre écarté,
> Te fit, avec son lait, sucer sa cruauté.

And, as Virgil in his fourth Georgic of the bees, perpetually raises the lowness of his subject by the loftiness of his words, and ennobles it by comparisons drawn from empires, and from monarchs:

> admiranda tibi levium spectacula rerum,
> magnanimosque duces, totiusque ordine gentis
> mores et studia, et populos, et proelia dicam;

[45] Alessandro Tassoni (1565–1635) published his *La Secchia rapita* in 1622; Boileau his *Lutrin* in 1674, and two further cantos in 1683; and Merlin Coccaius (the assumed name of Teofilo Folengo, 1491–1544) his *Baldus* in 1517.
[46] Paul Scarron (1610–60), author of *Virgile travesti* (1648).
[47] *Aeneid*, IV, 365–7: 'False one! no goddess was thy mother, nor was Dardanus founder of thy line, but rugged Caucasus on his flinty rocks begat thee, and Hyrcanian tigresses gave thee suck.'

and again:

> sed genus immortale manet; multosque per annos
> stat fortuna domus, et avi numerantur avorum;[48]

we see Boileau pursuing him in the same flights; and scarcely yielding to his
master. This, I think, my Lord, to be the most beautiful and most noble
kind of satire. Here is the majesty of the heroic, finely mixed with the
venom of the other; and raising the delight which otherwise would be flat
and vulgar, by the sublimity of the expression. I could say somewhat more
of the delicacy of this and some other of his satires; but it might turn to his
prejudice if 'twere carried back to France.

I have given your Lordship but this bare hint, in what verse and in what
manner this sort of satire may be best managed. Had I time, I could enlarge
on the beautiful turns of words and thoughts; which are as requisite in this,
as in heroic poetry itself, of which this satire is undoubtedly a species. With
these beautiful turns I confess myself to have been unacquainted, till about
twenty years ago, in a conversation which I had with that noble wit of
Scotland, Sir George Mackenzie.[49] He asked me why I did not imitate in
my verses the turns of Mr Waller and Sir John Denham, of which he
repeated many to me. I had often read with pleasure, and with some profit,
those two fathers of our English poetry; but had not seriously enough
considered those beauties which give the last perfection to their works.
Some sprinklings of this kind I had also formerly in my plays; but they were
casual, and not designed. But this hint, thus seasonably given me, first
made me sensible of my own wants, and brought me afterwards to seek for
the supply of them in other English authors. I looked over the darling of my
youth, the famous Cowley; there I found, instead of them, the points of wit,
and quirks of epigram, even in the *Davideis*, an heroic poem, which is of an
opposite nature to those puerilities; but no elegant turns either on the word
or on the thought. Then I consulted a greater genius (without offence to the
Manes of that noble author), I mean Milton. But as he endeavours everywhere to express Homer, whose age had not arrived to that fineness, I found
in him a true sublimity, lofty thoughts, which were clothed with admirable
Grecisms, and ancient words which he had been digging from the mines of
Chaucer and of Spenser, and which, with all their rusticity, had somewhat
of venerable in them. But I found not there neither that for which I looked.
At last I had recourse to his master Spenser, the author of that immortal

---

[48] *Georgics*, IV, 3–5, 208–9: 'The wondrous pageant of a tiny world – chiefs great-hearted, a
whole nation's character and tastes and tribes and battles – I will in due order unfold to
thee . . . yet the race abides immortal, for many a year stands firm the fortune of the
house, and grandsire's grandsires are numbered on the roll.'

[49] Mackenzie (1636–91), Lord Advocate for Scotland and a voluminous writer.

poem called the *Fairy Queen*; and there I met with that which I had been looking for so long in vain. Spenser had studied Virgil to as much advantage as Milton had done Homer; and amongst the rest of his excellencies had copied that. Looking farther into the Italian, I found Tasso had done the same; nay more, that all the sonnets in that language are on the turn of the first thought; which Mr Walsh,[50] in his late ingenious preface to his poems, has observed. In short, Virgil and Ovid are the two principal fountains of them in Latin poetry. And the French at this day are so fond of them that they judge them to be the first beauties. *Délicat, et bien tourné* are the highest commendations which they bestow on somewhat which they think a masterpiece.

An example of the turn on words, amongst a thousand others, is that in the last book of Ovid's *Metamorphoses*:

> heu! quantum scelus est, in viscera, viscera condi!
> congestoque avidum pinguescere corpore corpus;
> alteriusque animantem animantis vivere leto.[51]

An example of the turn both on thoughts and words is to be found in Catullus, in the complaint of Ariadne, when she was left by Theseus:

> tum jam nulla viro juranti faemina credat;
> nulla viri speret sermones esse fideles;
> qui, dum aliquid cupiens animus praegestit apisci,
> nil metuunt jurare, nihil promittere parcunt:
> sed simul ac cupidae mentis satiata libido est,
> dicta nihil metuere, nihil perjuria curant.[52]

An extraordinary turn upon the words is that in Ovid's *Epistolae Heroidum*, of Sappho to Phaon:

> si, nisi quae forma poterit te digna videri,
> nulla futura tua est, nulla futura tua est.[53]

Lastly, a turn, which I cannot say is absolutely on words, for the thought

---

[50] William Walsh (1663–1708). The observation which Dryden attributes to him has not been traced.

[51] xv, 88–90: 'Oh, how criminal it is for flesh to be stored away in flesh, for one greedy body to grow fat with food gained from another, for one live creature to go on living through the destruction of another living thing.'

[52] Catullus, LXIV, 143–8: 'Let no woman believe a man's oath, let none believe that a man's speeches can be trustworthy. They, while their mind desires something and longs eagerly to gain it, nothing fear to swear, nothing spare to promise; but as soon as the lust of their greedy mind is satisfied, they fear not then their words, they heed not their perjuries.'

[53] *Heroides*, xv, 39–40: 'If none shall be yours unless deemed worthy of you for her beauty's sake, then none shall be yours at all.'

turns with them, is in the fourth Georgic of Virgil; where Orpheus is to
receive his wife from Hell, on express condition not to look on her till she
was come on earth:

> cum subita incautum dementia cepit amantem;
> ignoscenda quidem, scirent si ignoscere Manes.[54]

I will not burthen your Lordship with more of them; for I write to a
master who understands them better than myself. But I may safely conclude
them to be great beauties. I might descend also to the mechanic beauties of
heroic verse; but we have yet no English *prosodia*, not so much as a tolerable
dictionary, or a grammar; so that our language is in a manner barbarous;
and what government will encourage any one, or more, who are capable of
refining it, I know not: but nothing under a public expense can go through
with it. And I rather fear a declination of the language than hope an
advancement of it in the present age.

I am still speaking to you, my Lord, though in all probability you are
already out of hearing. Nothing which my meanness can produce is worthy
of this long attention. But I am come to the last petition of Abraham: if
there be ten righteous lines in this vast preface, spare it for their sake; and
also spare the next city, because it is but a little one.

I would excuse the performance of this translation, if it were all my own;
but the better, tho' not the greater part, being the work of some gentlemen
who have succeeded very happily in their undertaking, let their excellencies
atone for my imperfections, and those of my sons.[55] I have perused some of
the satires which are done by other hands; and they seem to me as perfect in
their kind as anything I have seen in English verse. The common way which
we have taken is not a literal translation, but a kind of paraphrase; or
somewhat which is yet more loose, betwixt a paraphrase and imitation. It
was not possible for us, or any men, to have made it pleasant any other way.
If rendering the exact sense of these authors, almost line for line, had been
our business, Barten Holyday had done it already to our hands: and by the
help of his learned notes and illustrations, not only of Juvenal and Persius
but, what yet is more obscure, his own verses, might be understood.

But he wrote for fame, and wrote to scholars: we write only for the
pleasure and entertainment of those gentlemen and ladies who, tho' they are
not scholars, are not ignorant: persons of understanding and good sense
who, not having been conversant in the original, or at least not having made
Latin verse so much their business as to be critics in it, would be glad to find
if the wit of our two great authors be answerable to their fame and

---

[54] *Georgics*, IV, 488–9: 'When a sudden frenzy seized the unwary lover, frenzy meet for
pardon, did Hell know how to pardon.'
[55] Dryden's son Charles translated Juvenal's seventh, and John the fourteenth satire.

reputation in the world. We have therefore endeavoured to give the public all the satisfaction we are able in this kind.

And if we are not altogether so faithful to our author as our predecessors Holyday and Stapylton, yet we may challenge to ourselves this praise, that we shall be far more pleasing to our readers. We have followed our authors at greater distance, tho' not step by step, as they have done. For oftentimes they have gone so close that they have trod on the heels of Juvenal and Persius, and hurt them by their too near approach. A noble author would not be pursued too close by a translator. We lose his spirit, when we think to take his body. The grosser part remains with us, but the soul is flown away in some noble expression, or some delicate turn of words or thought. Thus Holyday, who made this way his choice, seized the meaning of Juvenal; but the poetry has always escaped him.

They who will not grant me that pleasure is one of the ends of poetry, but that it is only a means of compassing the only end, which is instruction, must yet allow that, without the means of pleasure, the instruction is but a bare and dry philosophy: a crude preparation of morals, which we may have from Aristotle and Epictetus, with more profit than from any poet. Neither Holyday nor Stapylton have imitated Juvenal in the poetical part of him, his diction and his elocution. Nor had they been poets, as neither of them were, yet, in the way they took, it was impossible for them to have succeeded in the poetic part.

The English verse, which we call heroic, consists of no more than ten syllables; the Latin hexameter sometimes rises to seventeen; as, for example, this verse in Virgil:

> pulverulenta putrem sonitu quatit ungula campum.[56]

Here is the difference of no less than seven syllables in a line, betwixt the English and the Latin. Now the medium of these is about fourteen syllables; because the dactyl is a more frequent foot in hexameters than the spondee.

But Holyday, without considering that he writ with the disadvantage of four syllables less in every verse, endeavours to make one of his lines to comprehend the sense of one of Juvenal's. According to the falsity of the proposition was the success. He was forced to crowd his verse with ill-sounding monosyllables, of which our barbarous language affords him a wild plenty: and by that means he arrived at his pedantic end, which was to make a literal translation. His verses have nothing of verse in them, but only the worst part of it, the rhyme: and that, into the bargain, is far from good. But, which is more intolerable, by cramming his ill chosen and worse sounding monosyllables so close together, the very sense which he

[56] *Aeneid*, VIII, 596: 'With galloping tramp the horsehoof shakes the crumbling plain.' Dryden replaces 'quadrupedante' with 'pulverulenta' ('dust-raising').

606 Dryden: A Selection

endeavours to explain is become more obscure than that of his author. So that Holyday himself cannot be understood without as large a commentary as that which he makes on his two authors. For my own part, I can make a shift to find the meaning of Juvenal without his notes: but his translation is more difficult than his author. And I find beauties in the Latin to recompense my pains; but in Holyday and Stapylton, my ears, in the first place, are mortally offended; and then their sense is so perplexed that I return to the original as the more pleasing task, as well as the more easy.

This must be said for our translation, that if we give not the whole sense of Juvenal, yet we give the most considerable part of it. We give it, in general, so clearly that few notes are sufficient to make us intelligible. We make our author at least appear in a poetic dress. We have actually made him more sounding, and more elegant, than he was before in English; and have endeavoured to make him speak that kind of English which he would have spoken had he lived in England, and had written to this age. If sometimes any of us (and 'tis but seldom) make him express the customs and manners of our native country rather than of Rome, 'tis either when there was some kind of analogy betwixt their customs and ours, or when, to make him more easy to vulgar understandings, we give him those manners which are familiar to us. But I defend not this innovation, 'tis enough if I can excuse it. For to speak sincerely, the manners of nations and ages are not to be confounded: we should either make them English, or leave them Roman. If this can neither be defended nor excused, let it be pardoned at least, because it is acknowledged; and so much the more easily, as being a fault which is never committed without some pleasure to the reader.

Thus, my Lord, having troubled you with a tedious visit, the best manners will be shewn in the least ceremony. I will slip away while your back is turned, and while you are otherwise employed; with great confusion for having entertained you so long with this discourse; and for having no other recompense to make you than the worthy labours of my fellow-undertakers in this work, and the thankful acknowledgments, prayers, and perpetual good wishes, of

MY LORD,

    Your Lordship's

        Most obliged, most humble,

            and most obedient servant,

                    JOHN DRYDEN.

Aug. 18, 1692.

PREFACE TO THE FABLES

In February 1699 Dryden wrote to Mrs Elizabeth Steward describing his labours on the Fables: 'In the meantime, betwixt my intervals of physic and other remedies which I am using for my gravel, I am still drudging on: always a poet, and never a good one. I pass my time sometimes with Ovid, and sometimes with our old English poet, Chaucer; translating such stories as best please my fancy; and intend besides them to add somewhat of my own: so that it is not impossible but ere the summer be passed, I may come down to you with a volume in my hand, like a dog out of the water, with a duck in his mouth' (Ward, ed., *Letters*, p. 109). *Fables Ancient and Modern, translated into verse from Homer, Ovid, Boccace and Chaucer; with original poems* was published as a folio volume in March 1700, about two months before Dryden's death. The Preface is acknowledged to be one of Dryden's finest prose pieces, in his later style, varied, allusive, and vigorous.

'Tis with a poet as with a man who designs to build, and is very exact, as he supposes, in casting up the cost beforehand; but, generally speaking, he is mistaken in his account, and reckons short of the expense he first intended: he alters his mind as the work proceeds, and will have this or that convenience more of which he had not thought when he began. So has it happened to me; I have built a house where I intended but a lodge; yet with better success than a certain nobleman,[1] who, beginning with a dogkennel, never lived to finish the palace he had contrived.

From translating the first of Homer's *Iliads* (which I intended as an essay to the whole work), I proceeded to the translation of the twelfth book of Ovid's *Metamorphoses*, because it contains, among other things, the causes, the beginning, and ending, of the Trojan War. Here I ought in reason to have stopped; but the speeches of Ajax and Ulysses[2] lying next in my way, I could not balk 'em. When I had compassed them, I was so taken with the former part of the fifteenth book[3] (which is the masterpiece of the whole *Metamorphoses*), that I enjoined myself the pleasing task of rendering it into English. And now I found, by the number of my verses, that they began to

---

[1] Probably referring to George Villiers, second Duke of Buckingham, and his extravagant buildings at Cliveden.
[2] From *Metamorphoses*, XIII.
[3] 'Of the Pythagorean Philosophy'.

swell into a little volume; which gave me an occasion of looking backward on some beauties of my author, in his former books: there occurred to me the Hunting of the Boar, Cinyras and Myrrha, the good-natured story of Baucis and Philemon,[4] with the rest, which I hope I have translated closely enough, and given them the same turn of verse which they had in the original; and this, I may say without vanity, is not the talent of every poet. He who has arrived the nearest to it, is the ingenious and learned Sandys,[5] the best versifier of the former age; if I may properly call it by that name, which was the former part of this concluding century. For Spenser and Fairfax both flourished in the reign of Queen Elizabeth; great masters in our language, and who saw much farther into the beauties of our numbers than those who immediately followed them. Milton was the poetical son of Spenser, and Mr Waller of Fairfax; for we have our lineal descents and clans as well as other families: Spenser more than once insinuates that the soul of Chaucer was transfused into his body; and that he was begotten by him two hundred years after his decease.[6] Milton has acknowledged to me that Spenser was his original; and many besides myself have heard our famous Waller own that he derived the harmony of his numbers from *Godfrey of Bulloign*, which was turned into English by Mr Fairfax.[7]

But to return: having done with Ovid for this time, it came into my mind that our old English poet Chaucer in many things resembled him, and that with no disadvantage on the side of the modern author, as I shall endeavour to prove when I compare them; and as I am, and always have been, studious to promote the honour of my native country, so I soon resolved to put their merits to the trial, by turning some of the *Canterbury Tales* into our language, as it is now refined; for by this means, both the poets being set in the same light and dressed in the same English habit, story to be compared with story, a certain judgment must be made betwixt them by the reader, without obtruding my opinion on him: or, if I seem partial to my countryman and predecessor in the laurel, the friends of antiquity are not few; and besides many of the learned, Ovid has almost all the beaux, and the whole fair sex, his declared patrons. Perhaps I have assumed somewhat more to myself than they allow me, because I have adventured to sum up the evidence; but the readers are the jury, and their privilege remains entire to decide according to the merits of the cause: or, if they please, to bring it to another hearing before some other court. In the meantime, to follow the thread of my discourse (as thoughts, according to

---

[4] *Metamorphoses*, VIII; X; VIII.

[5] George Sandys published his *Ovid's Metamorphosis Englished* in 1626.

[6] *Fairie Queen*, IV, ii, 34.

[7] Edward Fairfax's translation of Tasso: *Godfrey of Bulloigne; or, The Recovery of Jerusalem* (1600).

Mr Hobbes, have always some connection), so from Chaucer I was led to think on Boccace, who was not only his contemporary, but also pursued the same studies; wrote novels in prose, and many works in verse; particularly is said to have invented the octave rhyme,[8] or stanza of eight lines, which ever since has been maintained by the practice of all Italian writers who are, or at least assume the title of, heroic poets. He and Chaucer, among other things, had this in common, that they refined their mother-tongues; but with this difference, that Dante had begun to file their language, at least in verse, before the time of Boccace, who likewise received no little help from his master Petrarch; but the reformation of their prose was wholly owing to Boccace himself, who is yet the standard of purity in the Italian tongue; though many of his phrases are become obsolete, as in process of time it must needs happen. Chaucer (as you have formerly been told by our learned Mr Rymer[9]) first adorned and amplified our barren tongue from the Provençal, which was then the most polished of all the modern languages; but this subject has been copiously treated by that great critic, who deserves no little commendation from us his countrymen.

For these reasons of time, and resemblance of genius, in Chaucer and Boccace, I resolved to join them in my present work; to which I have added some original papers of my own, which whether they are equal or inferior to my other poems, an author is the most improper judge; and therefore I leave them wholly to the mercy of the reader. I will hope the best, that they will not be condemned; but if they should, I have the excuse of an old gentleman who, mounting on horseback before some ladies, when I was present, got up somewhat heavily, but desired of the fair spectators that they would count fourscore and eight before they judged him. By the mercy of God, I am already come within twenty years of his number; a cripple in my limbs, but what decays are in my mind the reader must determine. I think myself as vigorous as ever in the faculties of my soul, excepting only my memory, which is not impaired to any great degree; and if I lose not more of it, I have no great reason to complain. What judgment I had, increases rather than diminishes; and thoughts, such as they are, come crowding in so fast upon me that my only difficulty is to choose or to reject, to run them into verse or to give them the other harmony of prose: I have so long studied and practised both that they are grown into a habit, and become familiar to me. In short, though I may lawfully plead some part of the old gentleman's excuse, yet I will reserve it till I think I have greater

---

[8] Ker indicates that Boccaccio did not invent *ottava rima*, but that he was responsible for establishing this metre in Italian heroic and romantic verse.

[9] In *A Short View of Tragedy* (1693), pp. 126–7 of Zimansky's edition. Rymer is 'the source of Dryden's misinformation in this passage as to Chaucer, who was strongly affected by French and Italian literature, but not at all by Provençal' (Noyes).

need, and ask no grains of allowance for the faults of this my present work, but those which are given of course to human frailty. I will not trouble my reader with the shortness of time in which I writ it, or the several intervals of sickness. They who think too well of their own performances are apt to boast in their prefaces how little time their works have cost them, and what other business of more importance interfered; but the reader will be as apt to ask the question, why they allowed not a longer time to make their works more perfect? and why they had so despicable an opinion of their judges as to thrust their indigested stuff upon them, as if they deserved no better?

With this account of my present undertaking, I conclude the first part of this discourse: in the second part, as at a second sitting, though I alter not the draught, I must touch the same features over again, and change the dead-colouring[10] of the whole. In general, I will only say that I have written nothing which savours of immorality or profaneness; at least, I am not conscious to myself of any such intention. If there happen to be found an irreverent expression, or a thought too wanton, they are crept into my verses through my inadvertency: if the searchers find any in the cargo, let them be staved[11] or forfeited, like counterbanded goods; at least, let their authors be answerable for them, as being but imported merchandise, and not of my own manufacture. On the other side, I have endeavoured to choose such fables, both ancient and modern, as contain in each of them some instructive moral; which I could prove by induction, but the way is tedious, and they leap foremost into sight without the reader's trouble of looking after them. I wish I could affirm with a safe conscience that I had taken the same care in all my former writings; for it must be owned that, supposing verses are never so beautiful or pleasing, yet, if they contain anything which shocks religion or good manners, they are at best what Horace says of good numbers without good sense, *versus inopes rerum*, *nugaeque canorae*.[12] Thus far, I hope, I am right in court, without renouncing to my other right of self-defence, where I have been wrongfully accused, and my sense wire-drawn into blasphemy or bawdry, as it has often been by a religious lawyer,[13] in a late pleading against the stage; in which he mixes truth with falsehood, and has not forgotten the old rule of calumniating strongly, that something may remain.

I resume the thread of my discourse with the first of my translations, which was the first Iliad of Homer. If it shall please God to give me longer life, and moderate health, my intentions are to translate the whole *Ilias*; provided still that I meet with those encouragements from the public which

[10] 'The first or preparatory layer of colour in a painting' (*OED*).
[11] I.e. destroyed, as contraband wine by breaking the cask into staves.
[12] *Ars Poetica*, l. 322: 'verses void of thought and sonorous trifles'.
[13] Jeremy Collier, in his *Short View of the Immorality and Profaneness of the English Stage* (1698).

may enable me to proceed in my undertaking with some cheerfulness. And
this I dare assure the world beforehand, that I have found, by trial, Homer a
more pleasing task than Virgil (though I say not the translation will be less
laborious). For the Grecian is more according to my genius than the Latin
poet. In the works of the two authors we may read their manners and natural
inclinations, which are wholly different. Virgil was of a quiet, sedate
temper: Homer was violent, impetuous, and full of fire. The chief talent of
Virgil was propriety of thoughts, and ornament of words: Homer was rapid
in his thoughts, and took all the liberties, both of numbers and of expressions, which his language and the age in which he lived allowed him.
Homer's invention was more copious, Virgil's more confined: so that if
Homer had not led the way, it was not in Virgil to have begun heroic
poetry. For nothing can be more evident than that the Roman poem is but
the second part of the *Ilias*; a continuation of the same story, and the persons
already formed. The manners of Aeneas are those of Hector, superadded to
those which Homer gave him. The adventures of Ulysses in the *Odysseis* are
imitated in the first six books of Virgil's *Aeneis*; and though the accidents
are not the same (which would have argued him of a servile copying, and
total barrenness of invention), yet the seas were the same in which both the
heroes wandered; and Dido cannot be denied to be the poetical daughter of
Calypso. The six latter books of Virgil's poem are the four-and-twenty
Iliads contracted: a quarrel occasioned by a lady, a single combat, battles
fought, and a town besieged. I say not this in derogation to Virgil, neither
do I contradict anything which I have formerly said in his just praise: for his
episodes are almost wholly of his own invention, and the form which he has
given to the telling makes the tale his own, even though the original story
had been the same. But this proves, however, that Homer taught Virgil to
design; and if invention be the first virtue of an epic poet, then the Latin
poem can only be allowed the second place. Mr Hobbes, in the preface to his
own bald translation of the *Ilias*[14] (studying poetry as he did mathematics,
when it was too late), Mr Hobbes, I say, begins the praise of Homer where
he should have ended it. He tells us that the first beauty of an epic poem
consists in diction, that is, in the choice of words, and harmony of numbers.
Now the words are the colouring of the work, which in the order of nature is
last to be considered. The design, the disposition, the manners, and the
thoughts, are all before it: where any of those are wanting or imperfect, so
much wants or is imperfect in the imitation of human life, which is in the
very definition of a poem. Words, indeed, like glaring colours, are the first
beauties that arise and strike the sight; but if the draught be false or lame,
the figures ill disposed, the manners obscure or inconsistent, or the

[14] *The Iliads and Odysses of Homer* (1677).

thoughts unnatural, then the finest colours are but daubing, and the piece is a beautiful monster at the best. Neither Virgil nor Homer were deficient in any of the former beauties; but in this last, which is expression, the Roman poet is at least equal to the Grecian, as I have said elsewhere; supplying the poverty of his language by his musical ear, and by his diligence.

But to return: our two great poets, being so different in their tempers, one choleric and sanguine, the other phlegmatic and melancholic; that which makes them excel in their several ways is that each of them has followed his own natural inclination, as well in forming the design as in the execution of it. The very heroes shew their authors: Achilles is hot, impatient, revengeful,

impiger, iracundus, inexorabilis, acer, etc.[15]

Aeneas patient, considerate, careful of his people, and merciful to his enemies; ever submissive to the will of heaven,

quo fata trahunt retrahuntque, sequamur.[16]

I could please myself with enlarging on this subject, but am forced to defer it to a fitter time. From all I have said, I will only draw this inference, that the action of Homer, being more full of vigour than that of Virgil, according to the temper of the writer, is of consequence more pleasing to the reader. One warms you by degrees; the other sets you on fire all at once, and never intermits his heat. 'Tis the same difference which Longinus makes betwixt the effects of eloquence in Demosthenes and Tully; one persuades, the other commands.[17] You never cool while you read Homer, even not in the second book (a graceful flattery to his countrymen); but he hastens from the ships, and concludes not that book till he has made you an amends by the violent playing of a new machine.[18] From thence he hurries on his action with variety of events, and ends it in less compass than two months. This vehemence of his, I confess, is more suitable to my temper; and therefore I have translated his first book with greater pleasure than any part of Virgil. But it was not a pleasure without pains: the continual agitations of the spirits must needs be a weakening of any constitution, especially in age; and many pauses are required for refreshment betwixt the heats; the *Iliad* of itself being a third part longer than all Virgil's works together.

This is what I thought needful in this place to say of Homer. I proceed to

[15] *Ars Poetica*, l. 121: 'impatient, passionate, ruthless, fierce'.
[16] *Aeneid*, v, 709: 'Whither the Fates, in their ebb and flow, draw us, let us follow.'
[17] *On the Sublime*, ch. xii.
[18] Zeus' message brought by Iris impersonating Polites: *Iliad*, II, 786–806.

Ovid and Chaucer; considering the former only in relation to the latter. With Ovid ended the golden age of the Roman tongue: from Chaucer the purity of the English tongue began. The manners of the poets were not unlike: both of them were well-bred, well-natured, amorous, and libertine, at least in their writings, it may be also in their lives. Their studies were the same, philosophy and philology.[19] Both of them were knowing in astronomy, of which Ovid's books of the *Roman Feasts* and Chaucer's *Treatise of the Astrolabe* are sufficient witnesses. But Chaucer was likewise an astrologer, as were Virgil, Horace, Persius, and Manilius. Both writ with wonderful facility and clearness; neither were great inventors: for Ovid only copied from Grecian fables, and most of Chaucer's stories were taken from his Italian contemporaries, or their predecessors.[20] Boccace his *Decameron* was first published, and from thence our Englishman has borrowed many of his *Canterbury Tales*: yet that of *Palamon and Arcite* was written in all probability by some Italian wit in a former age, as I shall prove hereafter. The tale of Grizild was the invention of Petrarch; by him sent to Boccace, from whom it came to Chaucer. *Troilus and Cressida* was also written by a Lombard author, but much amplified by our English translator, as well as beautified; the genius of our countrymen in general being rather to improve an invention than to invent themselves; as is evident not only in our poetry, but in many of our manufactures. I find I have anticipated already, and taken up from Boccace before I come to him: but there is so much less behind; and I am of the temper of most kings, who love to be in debt, are all for present money, no matter how they pay it afterwards. Besides, the nature of a preface is rambling, never wholly out of the way, nor in it. This I have learned from the practice of honest Montaigne, and return at my pleasure to Ovid and Chaucer, of whom I have little more to say.

Both of them built on the inventions of other men; yet since Chaucer had something of his own, as *The Wife of Bath's Tale, The Cock and the Fox*, which I have translated, and some others, I may justly give our countryman the precedence in that part; since I can remember nothing of Ovid which was wholly his. Both of them understood the manners; under which name I comprehend the passions and, in a larger sense, the descriptions of persons, and their very habits. For an example, I see Baucis and Philemon as perfectly before me as if some ancient painter had drawn them; and all the Pilgrims in the *Canterbury Tales*, their humours, their features, and the very dress, as distinctly as if I had supped with them at the Tabard in Southwark.

[19] The study of literature.
[20] Dryden's knowledge of Chaucer's sources is faulty. It is not certain that Chaucer knew the *Decameron*. He derived his Knight's Tale ('Palamon and Arcite') from Boccaccio's *Teseida*; the Clerk's tale of Griselda was drawn from Petrarch's Latin translation of the final story of the Decameron; and the source for *Troilus and Cressida* was Boccaccio's *Filostrato*.

Yet even there, too, the figures of Chaucer are much more lively, and set in a better light; which though I have not time to prove, yet I appeal to the reader, and am sure he will clear me from partiality.

The thoughts and words remain to be considered in the comparison of the two poets, and I have saved myself one half of that labour by owning that Ovid lived when the Roman tongue was in its meridian, Chaucer in the dawning of our language: therefore that part of the comparison stands not on an equal foot, any more than the diction of Ennius and Ovid, or of Chaucer and our present English. The words are given up as a post not to be defended in our poet, because he wanted the modern art of fortifying. The thoughts remain to be considered; and they are to be measured only by their propriety; that is, as they flow more or less naturally from the persons described, on such and such occasions. The vulgar judges, which are nine parts in ten of all nations, who call conceits and jingles wit, who see Ovid full of them, and Chaucer altogether without them, will think me little less than mad for preferring the Englishman to the Roman. Yet, with their leave, I must presume to say that the things they admire are only glittering trifles, and so far from being witty that in a serious poem they are nauseous, because they are unnatural. Would any man who is ready to die for love describe his passion like Narcissus? Would he think of *inopem me copia fecit*,[21] and a dozen more of such expressions, poured on the neck of one another, and signifying all the same thing? If this were wit, was this a time to be witty, when the poor wretch was in the agony of death? This is just John Littlewit in *Bartholomew Fair*, who had a conceit (as he tells you) left him in his misery; a miserable conceit.[22] On these occasions the poet should endeavour to raise pity: but instead of this, Ovid is tickling you to laugh. Virgil never made use of such machines when he was moving you to commiserate the death of Dido: he would not destroy what he was building. Chaucer makes Arcite violent in his love, and unjust in the pursuit of it; yet when he came to die, he made him think more reasonably: he repents not of his love, for that had altered his character; but acknowledges the injustice of his proceedings, and resigns Emilia to Palamon. What would Ovid have done on this occasion? He would certainly have made Arcite witty on his deathbed: he had complained he was farther off from possession, by being so near, and a thousand such boyisms,[23] which Chaucer rejected as below the dignity of the subject. They who think otherwise would by the same reason prefer Lucan and Ovid to Homer and Virgil, and Martial to all four of them. As for the turn of words, in which Ovid particularly excels all poets, they

---

[21] Ovid, *Metamorphoses*, III, 466: 'the very abundance of my riches beggars me'.

[22] Ben Jonson's play opens with Littlewit: 'A pretty conceit, and worth the finding! I ha' such luck to spin out these fine things still, and like a silkworm, out of myself.'

[23] An uncommon word: puerilities.

are sometimes a fault, and sometimes a beauty, as they are used properly or improperly; but in strong passions always to be shunned, because passions are serious, and will admit no playing. The French have a high value for them; and, I confess, they are often what they call delicate, when they are introduced with judgment; but Chaucer writ with more simplicity, and followed nature more closely than to use them. I have thus far, to the best of my knowledge, been an upright judge betwixt the parties in competition, not meddling with the design nor the disposition of it; because the design was not their own, and in the disposing of it they were equal. It remains that I say somewhat of Chaucer in particular.

In the first place, as he is the father of English poetry, so I hold him in the same degree of veneration as the Grecians held Homer, or the Romans Virgil. He is a perpetual fountain of good sense; learned in all sciences; and therefore speaks properly on all subjects. As he knew what to say, so he knows also when to leave off; a continence which is practised by few writers, and scarcely by any of the Ancients, excepting Virgil and Horace. One of our late great poets[24] is sunk in his reputation, because he could never forgive any conceit which came in his way; but swept like a drag-net, great and small. There was plenty enough, but the dishes were ill sorted; whole pyramids of sweetmeats for boys and women, but little of solid meat for men. All this proceeded not from any want of knowledge, but of judgment; neither did he want that in discerning the beauties and faults of other poets; but only indulged himself in the luxury of writing; and perhaps knew it was a fault, but hoped the reader would not find it. For this reason, though he must always be thought a great poet, he is no longer esteemed a good writer; and for ten impressions which his works have had in so many successive years, yet at present a hundred books are scarcely purchased once a twelve-month;[25] for, as my last Lord Rochester said, though somewhat profanely, *Not being of God, he could not stand.*

Chaucer followed nature everywhere, but was never so bold to go beyond her; and there is a great difference of being *poeta* and *nimis poeta*,[26] if we may believe Catullus, as much as betwixt a modest behaviour and affectation. The verse of Chaucer, I confess, is not harmonious to us; but 'tis like the

---

[24] Abraham Cowley. Cf. *A Discourse Concerning Satire*, p. 602.

[25] Cowley's *Works* of 1668 was reprinted with approximately the frequency that Dryden claims in the ten years following, and at short intervals for some forty years thereafter. His rapid decline from favour is summed up by Pope:

> Who now reads Cowley? if he pleases yet,
> His moral pleases, not his pointed wit.
>
> (*Imitations of Horace*, Ep. II, i, 75–6).

[26] 'Too much of a poet'. Taken from Martial, III, 44, not from Catullus.

eloquence of one whom Tacitus commends, it was *auribus istius temporis accommodata*.[27] They who lived with him, and some time after him, thought it musical; and it continues so, even in our judgment, if compared with the numbers of Lydgate and Gower, his contemporaries: there is the rude sweetness of a Scotch tune in it, which is natural and pleasing, though not perfect. 'Tis true, I cannot go so far as he who published the last edition of him;[28] for he would make us believe the fault is in our ears, and that there were really ten syllables in a verse where we find but nine. But this opinion is not worth confuting; 'tis so gross and obvious an error that common sense (which is a rule in everything but matters of faith and revelation) must convince the reader that equality of numbers, in every verse which we call *heroic*, was either not known or not always practised in Chaucer's age. It were an easy matter to produce some thousands of his verses which are lame for want of half a foot, and sometimes a whole one, and which no pronunciation can make otherwise. We can only say that he lived in the infancy of our poetry, and that nothing is brought to perfection at the first. We must be children before we grow men. There was an Ennius, and in process of time a Lucilius, and a Lucretius, before Virgil and Horace; even after Chaucer there was a Spenser, a Harington, a Fairfax, before Waller and Denham were in being; and our numbers were in their nonage till these last appeared. I need say little of his parentage, life, and fortunes; they are to be found at large in all the editions of his works. He was employed abroad, and favoured by Edward the Third, Richard the Second, and Henry the Fourth, and was poet, as I suppose, to all three of them. In Richard's time, I doubt, he was a little dipped in the rebellion of the Commons; and being brother-in-law to John of Gaunt, it was no wonder if he followed the fortunes of that family; and was well with Henry the Fourth when he had deposed his predecessor. Neither is it to be admired that Henry, who was a wise as well as a valiant prince, who claimed by succession, and was sensible that his title was not sound, but was rightfully in Mortimer, who had married the heir of York; it was not to be admired, I say, if that great politician should be pleased to have the greatest wit of those times in his interests, and to be the trumpet of his praises. Augustus had given him the example, by the advice of Maecenas, who recommended Virgil and Horace to him; whose praises helped to make him popular while he was alive, and after his death have made him precious to posterity. As for the religion of our poet, he seems to have some little bias towards the opinions of Wickliff, after John of

---

[27] 'Suited to the ears of that time'. After Tacitus, *De Oratoribus*, xxi (*auribus iudicum accommodata*).

[28] Thomas Speght's edition was published in 1597 and 1602, and reprinted in 1687. He expressed the view, correctly, that Chaucer's verse could be made to scan.

Gaunt his patron; somewhat of which appears in the *Tale of Piers Plowman*.[29]
Yet I cannot blame him for inveighing so sharply against the vices of the
clergy in his age: their pride, their ambition, their pomp, their avarice,
their worldly interest, deserved the lashes which he gave them, both in
that, and in most of his *Canterbury Tales*. Neither has his contemporary
Boccace spared them. Yet both those poets lived in much esteem with good
and holy men in orders; for the scandal which is given by particular priests
reflects not on the sacred function. Chaucer's Monk, his Canon, and his
Friar, took not from the character of his Good Parson. A satirical poet is the
check of the laymen on bad priests. We are only to take care that we involve
not the innocent with the guilty in the same condemnation. The good
cannot be too much honoured, nor the bad too coarsely used; for the
corruption of the best becomes the worst. When a clergyman is whipped,
his gown is first taken off, by which the dignity of his order is secured. If he
is wrongfully accused, he has his action of slander; and 'tis at the poet's peril
if he transgress the law. But they will tell us that all kinds of satire, though
never so well deserved by particular priests, yet brings the whole order into
contempt. Is then the peerage of England anything dishonoured when a
peer suffers for his treason? If he be libelled, or any way defamed, he has his
scandalum magnatum to punish the offender. They who use this kind of
argument seem to be conscious to themselves of somewhat which has
deserved the poet's lash, and are less concerned for their public capacity
than for their private; at least, there is pride at the bottom of their
reasoning. If the faults of men in orders are only to be judged among
themselves, they are all in some sort parties; for, since they say the honour of
their order is concerned in every member of it, how can we be sure that they
will be impartial judges? How far I may be allowed to speak my opinion in
this case, I know not; but I am sure a dispute of this nature caused mischief
in abundance betwixt a King of England and an Archbishop of Canterbury;[30] one standing up for the laws of his land, and the other for the honour
(as he called it) of God's Church; which ended in the murther of the prelate,
and in the whipping of his Majesty from post to pillar for his penance. The
learned and ingenious Dr Drake[31] has saved me the labour of inquiring into
the esteem and reverence which the priests have had of old; and I would
rather extend than diminish any part of it: yet I must needs say that when a
priest provokes me without any occasion given him, I have no reason, unless
it be the charity of a Christian, to forgive him: *prior laesit* is justification

---

[29] Referring to *The Plowman's Tale*, a spurious poem included among Chaucer's works in
Thynne's edition of 1542 and retained by Speght.

[30] Henry II and Thomas à Becket.

[31] James Drake (1667–1707), political writer, who wrote a reply to Collier entitled *The
Ancient and Modern Stages Surveyed* (1699).

sufficient in the civil law. If I answer him in his own language, self-defence, I am sure, must be allowed me; and if I carry it farther, even to a sharp recrimination, somewhat may be indulged to human frailty. Yet my resentment has not wrought so far, but that I have followed Chaucer in his character of a holy man, and I have enlarged on that subject with some pleasure, reserving to myself the right, if I shall think fit hereafter, to describe another sort of priests, such as are more easily to be found than the Good Parson; such as have given the last blow to Christianity in this age, by a practice so contrary to their doctrine. But this will keep cold till another time.

In the meanwhile, I take up Chaucer where I left him. He must have been a man of a most wonderful comprehensive nature, because, as it has been truly observed of him, he has taken into the compass of his *Canterbury Tales* the various manners and humours (as we now call them) of the whole English nation in his age. Not a single character has escaped him. All his pilgrims are severally distinguished from each other; and not only in their inclinations, but in their very physiognomies and persons. Baptista Porta[32] could not have described their natures better than by the marks which the poet gives them. The matter and manner of their tales, and of their telling, are so suited to their different educations, humours, and callings, that each of them would be improper in any other mouth. Even the grave and serious characters are distinguished by their several sorts of gravity: their discourses are such as belong to their age, their calling, and their breeding; such as are becoming of them, and of them only. Some of his persons are vicious, and some virtuous; some are unlearned, or (as Chaucer calls them) *lewd*, and some are learned. Even the ribaldry of the low characters is different: the Reeve, the Miller, and the Cook, are several men, and distinguished from each other as much as the mincing Lady Prioress and the broad-speaking, gap-toothed Wife of Bath. But enough of this: there is such a variety of game springing up before me that I am distracted in my choice, and know not which to follow. 'Tis sufficient to say, according to the proverb, that here is God's plenty. We have our forefathers and great-grand-dames all before us, as they were in Chaucer's days; their general characters are still remaining in mankind, and even in England, though they are called by other names than those of Monks, and Friars, and Canons, and Lady Abbesses, and Nuns: for mankind is ever the same, and nothing lost out of nature, though everything is altered. May I have leave to do myself the justice (since my enemies will do me none, and are so far from granting me to be a good poet that they will not allow me so much as to be a Christian, or a moral man), may I have leave, I say, to inform my reader that I have

---

[32] Giambattista della Porta (1535?–1615), Italian scientist and physiognomist.

confined my choice to such tales of Chaucer as savour nothing of immodesty. If I had desired more to please than to instruct, the Reeve, the Miller, the Shipman, the Merchant, the Sumner, and above all, the Wife of Bath, in the Prologue to her Tale, would have procured me as many friends and readers as there are beaux and ladies of pleasure in the town. But I will no more offend against good manners: I am sensible as I ought to be of the scandal I have given by my loose writings; and make what reparation I am able, by this public acknowledgment. If anything of this nature, or of profaneness, be crept into these poems, I am so far from defending it that I disown it. *Totum hoc indictum volo.*[33] Chaucer makes another manner of apology for his broad speaking, and Boccace makes the like; but I will follow neither of them. Our countryman, in the end of his characters before the *Canterbury Tales*, thus excuses the ribaldry, which is very gross in many of his novels:

> But first, I pray you, of your courtesy,
> That ye ne arrete it nought my villany,
> Though that I plainly speak in this mattere
> To tellen you her words, and eke her chere:
> Ne though I speak her words properly,
> For this ye knowen as well as I,
> Who shall tellen a tale after a man,
> He mote rehearse as nye as ever he can:
> Everich word of it ben in his charge,
> *All speke he, never so rudely, ne large.*
> Or else he mote tellen his tale untrue,
> Or feine things, or find words new:
> He may not spare, altho he were his brother,
> He mote as wel say o word as another.
> *Christ* spake himself full broad in holy writ,
> And well I wote no villany is it.
> Eke *Plato* saith, who so can him rede,
> The words mote been cousin to the dede.[34]

Yet if a man should have enquired of Boccace or of Chaucer what need they had of introducing such characters, where obscene words were proper in their mouths, but very undecent to be heard, I know not what answer they could have made: for that reason, such tales shall be left untold by me. You have here a specimen of Chaucer's language which is so obsolete that his sense is scarce to be understood; and you have likewise more than one example of his unequal numbers, which were mentioned before. Yet many

[33] 'I wish all this unsaid.'
[34] Prologue, A. ll. 725–42.

of his verses consist of ten syllables, and the words not much behind our present English: as for example, these two lines in the description of the Carpenter's young wife:

> Wincing she was, as is a jolly colt,
> Long as a mast, and upright as a bolt.[35]

I have almost done with Chaucer, when I have answered some objections relating to my present work. I find some people are offended that I have turned these tales into modern English, because they think them unworthy of my pains, and look on Chaucer as a dry, old-fashioned wit, not worth receiving. I have often heard the late Earl of Leicester[36] say that Mr Cowley himself was of that opinion; who, having read him over at my Lord's request, declared he had no taste of him. I dare not advance my opinion against the judgment of so great an author: but I think it fair, however, to leave the decision to the public. Mr Cowley was too modest to set up for a dictator; and being shocked perhaps with his old style, never examined into the depth of his good sense. Chaucer, I confess, is a rough diamond, and must first be polished ere he shines. I deny not likewise that, living in our early days of poetry, he writes not always of a piece, but sometimes mingles trivial things with those of greater moment. Sometimes also, though not often, he runs riot, like Ovid, and knows not when he has said enough. But there are more great wits beside Chaucer whose fault is their excess of conceits, and those ill sorted. An author is not to write all he can, but only all he ought. Having observed this redundancy in Chaucer (as it is an easy matter for a man of ordinary parts to find a fault in one of greater) I have not tied myself to a literal translation, but have often omitted what I judged unnecessary, or not of dignity enough to appear in the company of better thoughts. I have presumed farther in some places, and added somewhat of my own where I thought my author was deficient, and had not given his thoughts their true lustre, for want of words in the beginning of our language. And to this I was the more emboldened because (if I may be permitted to say it of myself) I found I had a soul congenial to his, and that I had been conversant in the same studies. Another poet, in another age, may take the same liberty with my writings; if at least they live long enough to deserve correction. It was also necessary sometimes to restore the sense of Chaucer, which was lost or mangled in the errors of the press. Let this example suffice at present: in the story of Palamon and Arcite, where the Temple of Diana is described, you find these verses in all the editions of our author:

[35] Miller's Tale, A. ll. 3263–4.
[36] Philip Sidney (1619–98), third Earl of Leicester, to whom Dryden had dedicated *Don Sebastian* in 1690.

> There saw I *Danè* turned unto a tree.
> I mean not the goddess *Diane*,
> But *Venus* daughter, which that hight *Danè*.[37]

Which, after a little consideration, I knew was to be reformed into this sense, that *Daphne*, the daughter of Peneus, was turned into a tree. I durst not make thus bold with Ovid, lest some future Milbourne[38] should arise, and say I varied from my author because I understood him not.

But there are other judges who think I ought not to have translated Chaucer into English, out of a quite contrary notion: they suppose there is a certain veneration due to his old language, and that it is little less than profanation and sacrilege to alter it. They are farther of opinion that somewhat of his good sense will suffer in this transfusion, and much of the beauty of his thoughts will infallibly be lost, which appear with more grace in their old habit. Of this opinion was that excellent person whom I mentioned, the late Earl of Leicester, who valued Chaucer as much as Mr Cowley despised him. My Lord dissuaded me from this attempt (for I was thinking of it some years before his death), and his authority prevailed so far with me as to defer my undertaking while he lived, in defence to him. Yet my reason was not convinced with what he urged against it. If the first end of a writer be to be understood, then as his language grows obsolete, his thoughts must grow obscure:

> multa renascentur, quae nunc cecidere; cadentque
> quae nunc sunt in honore vocabula, si volet usus,
> quem penes arbitrium est et jus et norma loquendi.[39]

When an ancient word for its sound and significancy deserves to be revived, I have that reasonable veneration for antiquity to restore it. All beyond this is superstition. Words are not like landmarks, so sacred as never to be removed: customs are changed, and even statutes are silently repealed, when the reason ceases for which they were enacted. As for the other part of the argument, that his thoughts will lose of their original beauty by the innovation of words: in the first place, not only their beauty but their being is lost, where they are no longer understood, which is the present case. I grant that something must be lost in all transfusion, that is, in all translations; but the sense will remain, which would otherwise be lost, or at least be maimed, when it is scarce intelligible, and that but to a few. How few are there who can read Chaucer so as to understand him perfectly? And if imperfectly, then with less profit, and no pleasure. 'Tis not for the use of

---

[37] A. ll. 2062–4.
[38] Luke Milbourne (1649–1720), poet and clergyman, author of the censorious *Notes on Dryden's Virgil* (1698).
[39] See p. 499n.

some old Saxon friends[40] that I have taken these pains with him; let them neglect my version, because they have no need of it. I made it for their sakes who understand sense and poetry as well as they, when that poetry and sense is put into words which they understand. I will go farther, and dare to add that what beauties I lose in some places, I give to others which had them not originally: but in this I may be partial to myself; let the reader judge, and I submit to his decision. Yet I think I have just occasion to complain of them who, because they understand Chaucer, would deprive the greater part of their countrymen of the same advantage, and hoard him up, as misers do their grandam gold, only to look on it themselves, and hinder others from making use of it. In sum, I seriously protest that no man ever had, or can have, a greater veneration for Chaucer than myself. I have translated some part of his works only that I might perpetuate his memory, or at least refresh it, amongst my countrymen. If I have altered him anywhere for the better, I must at the same time acknowledge that I could have done nothing without him: *facile est inventis addere*[41] is no great commendation; and I am not so vain to think I have deserved a greater. I will conclude what I have to say of him singly, with this one remark: a lady of my acquaintance, who keeps a kind of correspondence with some authors of the fair sex in France, has been informed by them that Mademoiselle de Scudery,[42] who is as old as Sibyl, and inspired like her by the same god of poetry, is at this time translating Chaucer into modern French. From which I gather that he has been formerly translated into the old Provençal (for how she should come to understand old English, I know not). But the matter of fact being true, it makes me think that there is something in it like fatality; that, after certain periods of time, the fame and memory of great wits should be renewed, as Chaucer is both in France and England. If this be wholly chance, 'tis extraordinary; and I dare not call it more, for fear of being taxed with superstition.

Boccace comes last to be considered who, living in the same age with Chaucer, had the same genius, and followed the same studies. Both writ novels, and each of them cultivated his mother tongue. But the greatest resemblance of our two modern authors being in their familiar style, and pleasing way of relating comical adventures, I may pass it over, because I have translated nothing from Boccace of that nature. In the serious part of poetry, the advantage is wholly on Chaucer's side; for though the Englishman has borrowed many tales from the Italian, yet it appears that those of Boccace were not generally of his own making, but taken from authors of former ages, and by him only modelled; so that what there was of invention

[40] Meaning Anglo-Saxon scholars.
[41] 'It is easy to add to what has already been invented.'
[42] Madeleine de Scudéry (1607–1701), poet and novelist.

in either of them may be judged equal. But Chaucer has refined on Boccace and has mended the stories which he has borrowed in his way of telling; though prose allows more liberty of thought, and the expression is more easy when unconfined by numbers. Our countryman carries weight, and yet wins the race at disadvantage. I desire not the reader should take my word; and therefore I will set two of their discourses on the same subject in the same light, for every man to judge betwixt them. I translated Chaucer first, and amongst the rest pitched on *The Wife of Bath's Tale*; not daring, as I have said, to adventure on her Prologue, because 'tis too licentious. There Chaucer introduces an old woman of mean parentage, whom a youthful knight of noble blood was forced to marry, and consequently loathed her. The crone being in bed with him on the wedding-night, and finding his aversion, endeavours to win his affection by reason, and speaks a good word for herself (as who could blame her?) in hope to mollify the sullen bride-groom. She takes her topics from the benefits of poverty, the advantages of old age and ugliness, the vanity of youth, and the silly pride of ancestry and titles without inherent virtue, which is the true nobility. When I had closed Chaucer, I returned to Ovid, and translated some more of his fables; and by this time had so far forgotten *The Wife of Bath's Tale* that when I took up Boccace, unawares I fell on the same argument of preferring virtue to nobility of blood and titles, in the story of Sigismonda; which I had certainly avoided for the resemblance of the two discourses, if my memory had not failed me. Let the reader weigh them both; and if he thinks me partial to Chaucer, 'tis in him to right Boccace.

I prefer in our countryman, far above all his other stories, the noble poem of *Palamon and Arcite*, which is of the epic kind, and perhaps not much inferior to the *Ilias* or the *Aeneis*: the story is more pleasing than either of them, the manners as perfect, the diction as poetical, the learning as deep and various, and the disposition full as artful: only it includes a greater length of time, as taking up seven years at least; but Aristotle has left undecided the duration of the action; which yet is easily reduced into the compass of a year, by a narration of what preceded the return of Palamon to Athens. I had thought, for the honour of our nation, and more particularly for his, whose laurel, tho' unworthy, I have worn after him, that this story was of English growth, and Chaucer's own: but I was undeceived by Boccace; for, casually looking on the end of his seventh *Giornata*, I found Dioneo (under which name he shadows himself) and Fiametta (who represents his mistress, the natural daughter of Robert, King of Naples), of whom these words are spoken: *Dioneo e Fiametta gran pezza cantarono insieme d'Arcita, e di Palemone;*[43] by which it appears that this story was written

[43] *Decameron*, VII, x: 'For a long while Dioneo and Fiametto sang in concert of Arcite and Palamon.'

before the time of Boccace; but the name of its author being wholly lost, Chaucer is now become an original; and I question not but the poem has received many beauties by passing through his noble hands. Besides this tale, there is another of his own invention, after the manner of the Provençals, called *The Flower and the Leaf*;[44] with which I was so particularly pleased, both for the invention and the moral, that I cannot hinder myself from recommending it to the reader.

As a corollary to this preface, in which I have done justice to others, I owe somewhat to myself: not that I think it worth my time to enter the lists with one M———, or one B———,[45] but barely to take notice that such men there are who have written scurrilously against me without any provocation. M———, who is in orders, pretends amongst the rest this quarrel to me, that I have fallen foul on priesthood. If I have, I am only to ask pardon of good priests, and am afraid his part of the reparation will come to little. Let him be satisfied that he shall not be able to force himself upon me for an adversary. I contemn him too much to enter into competition with him. His own translations of Virgil have answered his criticisms on mine. If (as they say he has declared in print) he prefers the version of Ogilby[46] to mine, the world has made him the same compliment: for 'tis agreed on all hands that he writes even below Ogilby. That, you will say, is not easily to be done; but what cannot M——— bring about? I am satisfied, however, that, while he and I live together, I shall not be thought the worst poet of the age. It looks as if I had desired him underhand to write so ill against me; but upon my honest word I have not bribed him to do me this service, and am wholly guiltless of his pamphlet. 'Tis true I should be glad if I could persuade him to continue his good offices, and write such another critique on anything of mine; for I find by experience he has a great stroke with the reader, when he condemns any of my poems to make the world have a better opinion of them. He has taken some pains with my poetry; but nobody will be persuaded to take the same with his. If I had taken to the Church (as he affirms, but which was never in my thoughts), I should have had more sense, if not more grace, than to have turned myself out of my benefice by writing libels on my parishioners. But his account of my manners and my principles are of a piece with his cavils and his poetry: and so I have done with him for ever.

As for the City Bard, or Knight Physician,[47] I hear his quarrel to me is

---

[44] Now considered not to be by Chaucer.
[45] Luke Milbourne, and Sir Richard Blackmore (d. 1729).
[46] Ogilby's translation of Virgil was published in 1649.
[47] In 1697 Blackmore was appointed physician in ordinary to William III and received a knighthood.

that I was the author of *Absalom and Achitophel*, which he thinks is a little hard on his fanatic patrons in London.

But I will deal the more civilly with his two poems, because nothing ill is to be spoken of the dead: and therefore peace be to the Manes of his *Arthurs*.[48] I will only say that it was not for this noble Knight that I drew the plan of an epic poem on King Arthur in my preface to the translation of Juvenal. The Guardian Angels of kingdoms were machines too ponderous for him to manage; and therefore he rejected them as Dares did the whirl-bats of Eryx when they were thrown before him by Entellus.[49] Yet from the preface he plainly took his hint; for he began immediately upon the story, though he had the baseness not to acknowledge his benefactor, but instead of it to traduce me in a libel.

I shall say the less of Mr Collier, because in many things he has taxed me justly; and I have pleaded guilty to all thoughts and expressions of mine which can be truly argued of obscenity, profaneness, or immorality, and retract them. If he be my enemy, let him triumph; if he be my friend, as I have given him no personal occasion to be otherwise, he will be glad of my repentance. It becomes me not to draw my pen in the defence of a bad cause, when I have so often drawn it for a good one. Yet it were not difficult to prove that in many places he has perverted my meaning by his glosses, and interpreted my words into blasphemy and bawdry of which they were not guilty. Besides that, he is too much given to horse-play in his raillery, and comes to battle like a dictator from the plough. I will not say, *The zeal of God's house has eaten him up*; but I am sure it has devoured some part of his good manners and civility. It might also be doubted whether it were altogether zeal which prompted him to this rough manner of proceeding; perhaps it became not one of his function to rake into the rubbish of ancient and modern plays; a divine might have employed his pains to better purpose than in the nastiness of Plautus and Aristophanes, whose examples, as they excuse not me, so it might be possibly supposed that he read them not without some pleasure. They who have written commentaries on those poets, or on Horace, Juvenal, and Martial, have explained some vices which, without their interpretation, had been unknown to modern times. Neither has he judged impartially betwixt the former age and us.

There is more bawdry in one play of Fletcher's, called *The Custom of the Country*, than in all ours together. Yet this has been often acted on the stage in my remembrance. Are the times so much more reformed now than they were five-and-twenty years ago? If they are, I congratulate the amendment of our morals. But I am not to prejudice the cause of my fellow-poets,

---

[48] Blackmore's heroic poems, *Prince Arthur* (1695) and *King Arthur* (1697).
[49] *Aeneid*, V, 400.

though I abandon my own defence: they have some of them answered for themselves; and neither they nor I can think Mr Collier so formidable an enemy that we should shun him. He has lost ground at the latter end of the day by pursuing his point too far, like the Prince of Conde at the battle of Senneph:[50] from immoral plays to no plays, *ab abusu ad usum, non valet consequentia*. But, being a party, I am not to erect myself into a judge. As for the rest of those who have written against me, they are such scoundrels that they deserve not the least notice to be taken of them. B——and M——are only distinguished from the crowd by being remembered to their infamy:

> Demetri, teque, Tigelli,
> discipularum inter jubeo plorare cathedras.[51]

[50] Senef in Flanders, where, on 11 August 1674, the Prince of Condé suffered heavy losses in pursuing the forces of the Prince of Orange.

[51] Horace, *Satires*, I, x, 90–1: 'But you, Demetrius, and you, Tigellius, I bid you go whine amidst the easy chairs of your female pupils.'

BIBLIOGRAPHY

This list is intended only as a guide, and is not comprehensive in any way. Articles are not listed, as Dryden is well provided with checklists, selected bibliographies, and collections of studies.

I EDITIONS OF DRYDEN'S WORKS

The Works of John Dryden, ed. Sir Walter Scott, revised and corrected by George Saintsbury. 18 vols. Edinburgh, 1882–93.

The Works of John Dryden, an edition planned in 20 volumes, in progress. From the University of California Press, 1956–   . Volumes so far published are:

- I: *Poems, 1649–1680*, ed. E. N. Hooker, H. T. Swedenberg, Jr., and Vinton A. Dearing. 1956.
- II: *Poems, 1681–1684*, H. T. Swedenberg, Jr., and Vinton A. Dearing. 1972.
- III: *Poems, 1685–1692*, ed. Earl Miner and Vinton A. Dearing. 1969.
- IV: *Poems, 1693–1696*, ed. A. B. Chambers and William Frost. 1974.
- VIII: *Plays, The Wild Gallant, The Rival Ladies, The Indian Queen*, ed. J. H. Smith, Dougald MacMillan, and Vinton A. Dearing. 1962.
- IX: *Plays, The Indian Emperour, Secret-Love, Sir Martin Mar-all*, ed. John Loftis and Vinton A. Dearing. 1966.
- X: *Plays, The Tempest, Tyrannick Love, An Evening's Love*, ed. Maximillian E. Novak and George R. Guffey. 1970.
- XVII: *Prose, 1668–1691*, ed. Samuel H. Monk, A. E. Wallace Maurer, and Vinton A. Dearing. 1971.
- XVIII: *Prose: The History of the League, 1684*, ed. Alan Roper. 1974.

The Poems of John Dryden, ed. James Kinsley. 4 vols. (Oxford English Texts.) Oxford: The Clarendon Press, 1958.

The Poetical Works of John Dryden, ed. George R. Noyes. Boston: Houghton Mifflin Co., 1909. Revised and enlarged 1950.

Essays of John Dryden, ed. W. P. Ker. 2 vols. Oxford: Clarendon Press, 1900.

Of Dramatic Poesy and Other Critical Essays, ed. George Watson. 2 vols. Everyman's Library. London and New York, 1962.

John Dryden: Four Comedies and *John Dryden: Four Tragedies*, ed. L. A. Beaurline and Fredson Bowers. (Curtain Playwrights.) Chicago and London: The University of Chicago Press, 1967.

Dryden, The Dramatic Works, ed. Montague Summers. 6 vols. London: Nonesuch Press, 1931–2.

The Letters of John Dryden, with Letters Addressed to Him, ed. Charles E. Ward. Durham: Duke University Press, 1942.

The Prologues and Epilogues of John Dryden: A Critical Edition, ed. W. B. Gardner. New York: Columbia University Press, 1951.

The Songs of John Dryden, ed. Cyrus L. Day. Cambridge, Mass.: Harvard University Press, 1932.

II OTHER EDITIONS

Critical Essays of the Seventeenth Century, ed. J. E. Spingarn. 3 vols. Oxford: Clarendon Press, 1908.

Poems on Affairs of State: Augustan Satirical Verse, 1660–1714. In seven volumes: *1: 1660–78*, ed. G. De F. Lord; *2: 1678–81*, ed. E. F. Mengel; *3: 1682–85*, ed. H. H. Schless; *4: 1685–88*, ed. G. M. Crump; *5: 1688–97*, ed. W. J. Cameron; *6: 1697–1704* and *7: 1704–14*, ed. F. H. Ellis. New Haven and London: Yale University Press, 1963–76.

Œuvres de P. Corneille, ed. Ch. Marty-Laveaux. 12 vols. Paris, 1862.

Dryden and Howard, 1664–1668: the text of An Essay of Dramatic Poesy, The Indian Emperor, and The Duke of Lerma, with other controversial matter, ed. D. D. Arundell. Cambridge: Cambridge University Press, 1929.

The Dramatic Works of Sir George Etherege, ed. H. F. B. Brett-Smith. (Percy Reprints, no. 6.) 2 vols. Oxford: Basil Blackwell, 1927.

The Poems of Sir George Etherege, ed. J. Thorpe. Princeton: Princeton University Press, 1963.

The Works of Nathaniel Lee, ed. Thomas B. Strong and Arthur L. Cooke. 2 vols. New Brunswick, N.J.: The Scarecrow Press, 1954.

The Diary of Samuel Pepys, ed. R. Latham and W. Matthews. 9 vols. London: G. Bell and Sons, 1970–6.

The Critical Works of Thomas Rymer, ed. Curt A. Zimansky. New Haven: Yale University Press, 1956.

The Complete Works of Thomas Shadwell, ed. Montague Summers. 5 vols. London: Fortune Press, 1927.

III BIBLIOGRAPHIES

BOND, DONALD F. *The Age of Dryden*. (Goldentree Bibliographies in Language and Literature.) New York: Appleton-Century Crofts, 1970.

MACDONALD, HUGH. *John Dryden: A Bibliography of Early Editions and of Drydeniana*. Oxford: Clarendon Press, 1939.

MONK, SAMUEL H. *John Dryden: A List of Critical Studies Published from 1895 to 1948*. Minneapolis: University of Minnesota Press, 1950.

STRATMAN, CARL J., DAVID G. SPENCER, and MARY ELIZABETH DEVINE, eds. *Restoration and Eighteenth Century Theatre Research: A Bibliographical Guide, 1900–1968*. Carbondale: Southern Illinois University Press, 1971.

ZAMONSKI, JOHN A. *An Annotated Bibliography of John Dryden: Texts and Studies, 1949–73*. Dawson: Garland Publishing, 1975.

IV FOR REFERENCE

ADEN, JOHN M., ed. *The Critical Opinions of John Dryden: A Dictionary*. Nashville: Vanderbilt University Press, 1963.

JENSEN, H. J. *A Glossary of John Dryden's Critical Terms*. Minneapolis: University of Minnesota Press, 1969.

MONTGOMERY, GUY, et al. *Concordance to the Poetical Works of John Dryden*. Berkeley: University of California Press, 1967.

VAN LENNEP, WILLIAM, ed. *The London Stage, 1660–1800, Part I: 1600–1700*. Introduction by E. L. Avery and A. H. Scouten. Carbondale: Southern Illinois University Press, 1965.

V STUDIES

A Books

ALLEN, N. B. *The Sources of John Dryden's Comedies*. (University of Michigan Publications in Language and Literature, Vol. XVI.) Ann Arbor: University of Michigan Press, 1935.

AMARASINGHE, UPALI. *Dryden and Pope in the Early Nineteenth Century: a Study of Changing Literary Taste*. Cambridge: Cambridge University Press, 1962.

BORGMAN, ALBERT S. *Thomas Shadwell: His Life and Comedies*. New York: New York University Press, 1928.

BREDVOLD, LOUIS I. *The Intellectual Milieu of John Dryden: Studies in Aspects of Seventeenth-Century Thought*. (University of Michigan Publications in Language and Literature, Vol. XII.) Ann Arbor: University of Michigan Press, 1934.

BUDICK, S. *Dryden and the Abyss of Light: A Study of Religio Laici and The Hind and the Panther*. New Haven and London: Yale University Press, 1970.

DOBRÉE, BONAMY. *Restoration Comedy, 1660–1720*. Oxford: Clarendon Press, 1924.

ELIOT, T. S. *John Dryden: The Poet, the Dramatist, the Critic*. New York: T. and Elsa Holiday, 1932.

——. *Homage to John Dryden*. London: L. and Virginia Woolf, 1924.

FROST, W. *Dryden and the Art of Translation*. (Yale Studies in English, 128.) New Haven: Yale University Press, 1955.

FUJIMURA, THOMAS H. *The Restoration Comedy of Wit*. Princeton: Princeton University Press, 1952.

GARRISON, JAMES D. *Dryden and the Tradition of Panegyric*. Berkeley: University of California Press, 1975.

HAGSTRUM, JEAN. *The Sister Arts*. Chicago: University of Chicago Press, 1958.

HAMILTON, K. G. *The Two Harmonies: Poetry and Prose in the Seventeenth Century*. Oxford: Clarendon Press, 1963.

HARTH, PHILLIP. *Contexts of Dryden's Thought*. Chicago and London: The University of Chicago Press, 1968.

HUME, R. D. *Dryden's Criticism*. Ithaca and London: Cornell University Press, 1970.

JOHNSON, SAMUEL. *Lives of the English Poets,* ed. G. B. Hill. 3 vols. Oxford: Clarendon Press, 1905.

KING, BRUCE. *Dryden's Major Plays*. Edinburgh and London: Oliver and Boyd, 1966.

KIRSCH, A. C. *Dryden's Heroic Drama*. Princeton: Princeton University Press, 1965; New York: Gordian Press, 1972.

MINER, EARL. *Dryden's Poetry*. Bloomington and London: Indiana University Press, 1967.

——. *The Restoration Mode from Milton to Dryden*. Princeton: Princeton University Press, 1974.

MOORE, FRANK HARPER. *The Nobler Pleasure: Dryden's Comedy in Theory and Practice*. Chapel Hill: University of North Carolina Press, 1963.

NEVO, RUTH. *The Dial of Virtue: A Study of Poems on Affairs of State in the Seventeenth Century*. Princeton: Princeton University Press, 1963.

NICOLL, ALLARDYCE. *A History of English Drama 1660–1900. Vol. I: Restoration Drama, 1660–1700*. 4th edition. Cambridge: Cambridge University Press, 1952.

OGG, DAVID. *England in the Reign of Charles II*. 2 vols. Oxford: Clarendon Press, 1955.
——. *England in the Reigns of James II and William III*. Oxford: Clarendon Press, 1955.
OSBORN, JAMES M. *John Dryden: Some Biographical Facts and Problems*. New York: Columbia University Press, 1940. Revised edition: Gainsville: University of Florida Press, 1965.
PECHTER, EDWARD. *Dryden's Classical Theory of Literature*. Cambridge: Cambridge University Press, 1975.
PROUDFOOT, L. *Dryden's Aeneid and its Seventeenth Century Predecessors*. Manchester: Manchester University Press, 1960.
ROPER, A. *Dryden's Poetic Kingdoms*. London: Routledge and Kegan Paul, 1965.
SCHILLING, BERNARD N. *Dryden and the Conservative Myth: a Reading of Absalom and Achitophel*. New Haven: Yale University Press, 1961.
SINGH, S. *The Theory of Drama in the Restoration Period*. New Delhi: Orient Longmans, 1963.
SMITH, DAVID NICHOL. *John Dryden*. Cambridge: Cambridge University Press, 1950.
SUTHERLAND, JAMES R. *English Literature of the Late Seventeenth Century*. New York and Oxford: Oxford University Press, 1969.
SWEDENBERG, H. T., JR. *The Theory of the Epic in England, 1650–1800*. Berkeley and Los Angeles: University of California Press, 1944.
VAN DOREN, MARK. *John Dryden. A Study of his Poetry*. Bloomington: Indiana University Press, 1960. Originally published as *The Poetry of John Dryden*, New York, 1920.
WALLERSTEIN, RUTH. *Studies in Seventeenth Century Poetic*. Madison: University of Wisconsin Press, 1950.
WARD, CHARLES E. *The Life of John Dryden*. Chapel Hill: University of North Carolina Press, 1961.
WILLEY, BASIL. *The Seventeenth Century Background*. Oxford: Clarendon Press, 1934.
WILLIAMSON, GEORGE. *The Senecan Amble*. London: Faber and Faber, 1951.
WILSON, J. H. *The Court Wits of the Restoration*. Princeton: Princeton University Press, 1948.

B *Collections*

KING, BRUCE, ed. *Dryden's Mind and Art*. Edinburgh: Oliver and Boyd, 1969; New York: Barnes and Noble Inc., 1970.

KING, BRUCE, *Twentieth Century Interpretations of All for Love.* (Twentieth Century Interpretations.) Englewood Cliffs: Prentice-Hall Inc., 1968.

KINSLEY, JAMES and HELEN, eds. *Dryden: the Critical Heritage.* (The Critical Heritage Series.) New York: Barnes and Noble Inc.; London: Routledge and Kegan Paul Ltd, 1971.

McHENRY, R., and DAVID G. LOUGEE, eds. *Critics on Dryden.* (Readings in Literary Criticism.) London: George Allen and Unwin Ltd, 1973.

MINER, EARL, ed. *John Dryden.* (Writers and Their Background.) Athens: Ohio University Press; London: G. Bell and Sons Ltd, 1972.

SCHILLING, BERNARD, ed. *Dryden: A Collection of Critical Essays.* (Twentieth Century Views.) Englewood Cliffs: Prentice-Hall Inc., 1963.

SWEDENBERG, H. T., JR., ed. *Essential Articles for the Study of John Dryden.* (The Essential Articles Series.) London: Frank Cass and Co Ltd; Hamden, Conn.: Archon Books, 1966.

KING ALFRED'S COLLEGE
LIBRARY